THE BRITISH HOUSEWIFE

Frontispiece from William Augustus Henderson, The Housekeeper's Instructor, *6th edition, c.1800. This same picture appeared in the very first edition of c.1791 and it shows the mistress presenting the cookery book to her servant, while a young man is instructed in the art of carving with the aid of another book. For the full text accompanying the image, see Appendix III.*

THE
BRITISH HOUSEWIFE

COOKERY BOOKS, COOKING AND
SOCIETY IN EIGHTEENTH-CENTURY BRITAIN

GILLY LEHMANN

PROSPECT BOOKS

2003

First published in Great Britain by Prospect Books in 2003 at Allaleigh House, Blackawton, Totnes, Devon TQ9 7DL.

BRITISH LIBRARY CATALOGUING IN PUBLICATION DATA:
A catalogue entry for this book is available from the British Library.

ISBN 1-903018-04-8

Typeset and designed by Tom Jaine.

Printed and bound in Great Britain by the Cromwell Press, Trowbridge, Wiltshire.

Contents

Illustrations

Acknowledgements

I N THE COURSE OF THE MANY YEARS WHICH HAVE INTERVENED SINCE
I first thought of turning idle curiosity into serious research, and then of
turning a doctoral thesis in French into a book in English, I have accumulated debts to substantial numbers of people: other researchers, whether
academic or not, librarians and archivists, friends and family who have offered
moral (and sometimes gastronomic) support, and, of course, the army of
previous authors on domestic history whose work provides a wealth of stimulating material and unexpected nuggets of information.

Most of my research has been done in the British Library, and I must thank
the staff of the various reading-rooms for their help in dealing with my problems of document supply and occasional obscure questions. More recently, I
have had the opportunity to test the Library's online services, and have found
all the electronic developments wonderfully efficient. Other libraries and
archives where I have worked and whose staff have always been helpful are the
Brotherton Library of the University of Leeds, the Public Record Office in
London, the Kent Archives Office, Maidstone, and the Norfolk Record Office,
Norwich. Many librarians supplied me with valuable bibliographical information in the early stages of my research, most notably the Fawcett Library in
London, Glasgow University Library and, more recently, Newcastle City
Library. My thanks go also to all the administrators of National Trust houses
who have answered questions on books in their libraries and on the locations
of manuscripts, and to the archivists of several other record offices and
repositories who have answered requests for information with all the speed the
impatient researcher has come to expect in the electronic age.

I am grateful to the British Library for permission to reproduce Patrick
Lamb's bill of fare illustrated on page 280. I am also grateful to Liz Seeber for
the image of Patrick Lamb's title-page illustrated on page 60, and to the Keeper

of Special Collections at the Brotherton Library of the University of Leeds for supplying the images of frontispieces illustrated on pages 2, 128 and 292.

In the French academic world, my greatest debts are to Michel Baridon, who agreed to take on someone whose research area was unusual to the point of eccentricity and who, as my thesis supervisor, encouraged the work with unfailing enthusiasm; and to Jacques Carré, who gave me the first push towards academic research and who has been a constant source of support and stimulating criticism ever since. Although my own commitments did not allow me to attend them very often, the late Jean-Louis Flandrin's seminars at the Ecole des Hautes Etudes in Paris always provided fresh impetus and his comments set me right on the use of statistics in the analysis of receipts. Also in Paris, Philip and Mary Hyman have always been generous donors of facts and food, the former generally in response to a panic-stricken, last-minute appeal. My own University of Franche-Comté in Besançon contributed materially to this book by giving me two periods of sabbatical leave to pursue research in England, in 1986 and again in 1998, without which my work would have been poorer and even later. Another material contribution came from the American Institute of Wine and Food in Paris, which gave me a grant towards my research on connections between English and French food in 1996.

On the other side of the Channel, Alan Davidson helped in many ways, giving me access to his collection of cookery books, and providing suggestions, encouragement, and even alcoholic refreshment at strategic moments. Tom Jaine has been a stalwart prop and support to the business of turning research into print, ever since he asked me to write the introduction to the reprint of Martha Bradley's weighty tomes. The participants in the Oxford Symposium on Food and Cookery (not to mention the organizers) always widen one's horizons: I thank them all. I must also record the great generosity of Chris Lewin, who has shared with me so much information on manuscript cookery books and who has responded to all my requests for further information concerning problems of dating. Others who have passed on information include Anne Wilson, Ivan Day, Fiona Lucraft, Elizabeth Gabbay, and Robin Weir and, from places further afield, Beatrice Fink and Rachel Laudan.

Some of the comments on the influence of politics on eighteenth-century perceptions of food have already appeared in my article, "Politics in the Kitchen" (*Eighteenth-Century Life* 23 (2), May 1999), and I am grateful to the Johns Hopkins University Press for permission to re-publish copyright material here.

Finally, a heartfelt thank-you to the sufferers from this enterprise: to my sister in London, for giving me a base for my work and producing restoring food and drink at the ungodly hours I adopt when the passion for research keeps me at my desk in the library until closing-time; and of course to my husband and computer-guru who saves me from disaster and accepts ungastronomic meals and improbable meal-times with equanimity.

GILLY LEHMANN
Bonnevaux-le-Prieuré, 2003

Note on the text

Original spelling, punctuation and capitalization have been retained throughout, although I have silently amended early typographical peculiarities, such as 'v' to 'u', and 'i' to 'j', where necessary. Quotations from foreign sources are given in English in the text with the original, where used, supplied in the notes. Unless otherwise stated, all translations are by the author.

This book is based more on research among primary printed sources, principally cookery books, than on manuscripts or secondary works. The bibliography contains details of the books I have used and which contain relevant information whether cited in the text or not, but I have eliminated many of the increasingly numerous secondary sources of dubious value. In the notes, only abbreviated references are given, using author name, title and date for a work's first appearance in each chapter, and author name and date thereafter.

Introduction

THIS BOOK BEGAN LIFE AS A DISSERTATION, WRITTEN IN FRENCH FOR a doctorate at the university of Burgundy in Dijon and defended successfully in June 1989. At the time, the jury recommended publication, either in English or in French; I personally believed that there would be a wider audience for its subject if it came out in English, and my ambition was to continue the work I had already done on the eighteenth century by going backwards in time to examine the history of cookery books and culinary styles in the period from the late Middle Ages to 1700. Since then my own research has proceeded at a rather slow pace, and thus when Tom Jaine suggested that he publish the thesis in some form or other I welcomed the suggestion and set to work. This book is the result.

Obviously, some ten years after completion of the original thesis, my ideas have moved on; I have been able to do further research on some points, and this has modified the conclusions I came to earlier. New research, and new conclusions, have been incorporated into this version of my original text, but some sections of what I originally wrote, especially on the development of culinary styles in the course of the eighteenth century, remain largely unchanged. The first text devoted a substantial section to cookery books, culinary styles and the table before 1700; this part has been severely reduced, in order to focus on eighteenth-century developments.

It is essential at this stage to give the reader an idea of the research design of my work, and thus of what he will and will not find here. My aim was to place the cookery books, by far our best source for any examination of the history of cookery, at the centre of the research. Too many histories of cookery give no picture of what dishes (as opposed to foodstuffs) people were actually eating at a given period; even such a complete and well-researched work as Anne Wilson's pioneering *Food and Drink in Britain* (1973) fails to give such

a view, as its chapters are organized by category of food rather than chrono-
logically. Other serious books on food history (and there are many less serious
ones, whose authors appear hardly to have consulted a cookery book at all, with
ludicrously inept results) such as the collective work edited by Maggie Black,
A Taste of History (1993), or Sara Paston-Williams' *The Art of Dining* (1993), try
to cover so much territory, including kitchen technology, food supply, dining-
rooms and table-settings, table manners and suchlike, that the analysis of how
the food on the table changed does not receive adequate attention. My aim,
then, has been to examine more thoroughly than before the cookery books
themselves. While I cannot pretend to have studied every book listed in
Virginia Maclean's bibliography, I have scrutinized the cookery books and their
successive editions listed in my own bibliography, and I do not believe that a
more exhaustive study would produce significantly different conclusions from
those set out here.

Thus the focus of this study is firmly on the cookery books, with three main
parts: firstly, the books themselves, their authors and readers, and how the
cookery book reached an ever-widening market in the course of the eighteenth
century; secondly, the changing culinary styles which are revealed in the books;
finally, the eighteenth century at table – when and how it ate, what was really
on the table, and how people reacted to the dishes set before them. The
purpose of the last section, which sometimes takes us away from the cookery
books, is twofold: to see how far the prescriptions of the cookery books were
being followed, and at what levels of society; and to try to demonstrate the
links between the culinary styles analysed in the second part and wider social
and cultural trends. This book does not examine foodstuffs and their distribution, or the links between diet and health, whether in contemporary opinion
or from today's standpoint, nor does it devote space to changes in the house,
whether upstairs in the dining-room or downstairs in the kitchen. Readers
wishing for information on these points are referred to the classic study by
Drummond and Wilbraham, *The Englishman's Food* (1939) for diet and health,
to Pamela Sambrook and Peter Brears' *The Country House Kitchen* (1996) for
the 'downstairs' side of food provisioning, and to Mark Girouard's *Life in the
English Country House* (1978) for changing patterns in the architecture and use
of 'upstairs'. Those seeking a general overview should consult the books by
Black and Paston-Williams mentioned above. Less complete, but with expert
comments on significant moments in British food history and superb illus-

trations of re-created meals, is the book edited by Ivan Day, *Eat, Drink and Be Merry* (2000).

One important aspect of the cookery books remains largely untouched in this study. In the first decades of the eighteenth century, and again at the end, many devoted a substantial portion of their text to remedies. I felt that it would be prudent for me to abstain from comment on these sections. The one striking feature that does stand out, and that I have tried to bring out in the chapters on the authors and their readers, is the shift from home-made remedies, drawn from manuscript sources (and thus often of considerable antiquity by the time of publication) which appear in the first period, and the prescriptions of eminent physicians which take over at the end of the century. This phenomenon is clearly part of the profession's increasing stranglehold on the practice of medicine, but it can also be seen as a further aspect of the commercialization of goods and services which has led some historians to situate the birth of the consumer society at this period.

Finally, another omission: I must point out that I examine the discourse of the cookery books only for the purpose of identifying the authors and readers, in order to show the ever-increasing spread of such manuals down the social scale. But this leaves a rich vein of material for future researchers. The title-pages and the prefaces of the cookery books contain images of cookery which range over the fundamental polarities of eighteenth-century ideas: art versus nature, high culture versus popular culture, the city versus the country, the ancients versus the moderns. The metaphorical and the imaginary are areas which merit serious attention, and of course any exploration of this side of culinary literature would lead the researcher on to other representations of food, such as those found in fiction or in painting. Indeed, one of the pleasurably frustrating aspects of my research has been the realization that the subject could be extended far beyond the limited scope of my thesis and of this book.

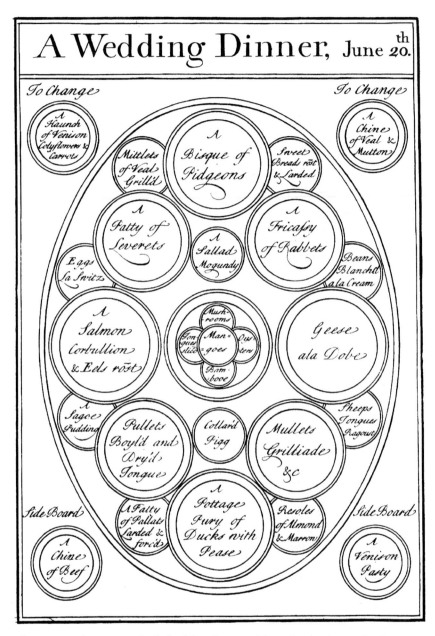

A Wedding Dinner, June 20th.

To Change

To Change

A Haunch of Venison Colyflowers & Carrots

A Chine of Veal & Mutton

Mittlets of Veal Grill'd

A Bisque of Pidgeons

Sweet Breads rost & Larded

A Fatty of Leverets

A Sallad Mogundy

A Fricasy of Rabbets

Eggs La Switz

Beans Blanch'd ala Cream

A Salmon Cotbullion & Eels rost

Mush-rooms
Con gues stick Man= goes Oys ten
Bam boue

Geese ala Dobe

A Sagoe Pudding

Sheeps Tongues Ragoust

Pullets Boyl'd and Dry'd Tongue

Collar'd Pigg

Mullets Grilliade &c

Side Board

A Fatty of Pallats Larded & forc'd

A Pottage Fury of Ducks with Pease

Resoles of Almond & Marrow

Side Board

A Chine of Beef

A Venison Pasty

This page and opposite: the bill of fare for a wedding dinner from Charles Carter,
The Complete Practical Cook, *1730. It represents the final phase of court-style
dining, with two removes for the garnished soups and the good English roast beef
and venison pasty relegated to the sideboard.*

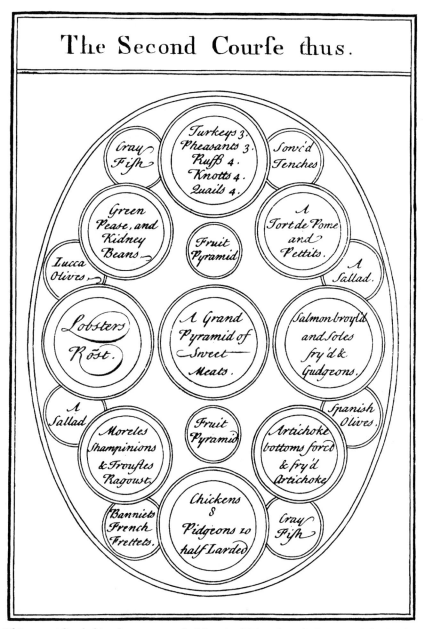

The Second Courſe thus.

- Cray Fiſh
- Turkeys 3.
  Pheasants 3.
  Ruß 4.
  Knotts 4.
  Quails 4.
- Soric'd Tenches
- Green Pease, and Kidney Beans
- Fruit Pyramid
- A Tort de Pome and Pettits.
- Lucca Olives
- A Sallad.
- Lobsters Rōst.
- A Grand Pyramid of Sweet Meats.
- Salmon broyld and Soles fry'd & Gudgeons.
- A Sallad
- Fruit Pyramid
- Spanish Olives.
- Moreles Shampinions & Troufles Ragoust.
- Artichoke bottoms forc'd & fry'd Artichoke.
- Banniets French Frettets.
- Chickens 8 Pidgeons 10 half Larded
- Cray Fiſh

This was ridiculed in the account of a 'disguised' French-style dinner in The Tatler.
*Carter follows French menu-planning in having the same number of dishes at each
course. In the second, the pyramid presentation of the sweetmeats and fruit is typical
of the fashion inspired by Massialot.*

15

Part I

*Cookery Books and Cookery before
1700*

B EFORE EMBARKING ON THE STUDY OF EIGHTEENTH-CENTURY
cookery books and their contents, a brief account of what had gone
before is necessary. It may seem superfluous to begin with the Middle
Ages, but many aspects of Georgian cookery and dining trace their roots back
this far. Flavour combinations – most notably the sweet and savoury mix – the
way menus were planned, the hierarchical distribution of food, the rituals of
the table: all display features which had been present in the fourteenth and
fifteenth centuries.

MEDIEVAL AND EARLY TUDOR: FROM MANUSCRIPT TO PRINT

Until today's researchers began to examine and publish reliable versions of early
English cookery manuscripts, the general impression of the culinary scene in
the medieval period was gleaned from the very limited number of sources
which had received the attention of Samuel Pegge and Richard Warner in the
eighteenth century, the most notable of these being *The Forme of Cury*. The
1888 edition of two fifteenth-century cookery books by Thomas Austin added
to the literature, but comments still tended to be based more on Warner, who
viewed the cookery of *The Forme of Cury* as French-inspired and thus disguised
and metamorphosed into 'complex and non-descript gallimaufries',[1] an attitude which tells us more about the eighteenth-century approach to French
cuisine than about medieval practice, but which influenced historians' judgements on medieval cookery until recently.[2] The situation today is very
different. In 1992 Constance Hieatt suggested that there were well over fifty

[1] Warner, *Antiquitates Culinariæ* (1791), p. xxxii.
[2] See, for instance, Bridget Henisch's comments on indiscriminate spicing and disguised food in *Fast and Feast* (1976), pp. 101–2.

medieval manuscripts containing culinary receipts still in existence. This figure did not take into account the many medical collections which might also include culinary items. The number of culinary receipts varied from one or two, where the main focus of the manuscript lay elsewhere, to anything from twenty to over two hundred in what were essentially cookery books. Hieatt's preliminary catalogue of extant manuscripts listed seven 'families' of receipts, each represented by between two and six copies, plus partial versions in other texts. She contended that virtually any other manuscript with more than a few receipts was related to one or other of these basic families.[3] Even among these, later manuscripts borrowed from their predecessors: *The Forme of Cury* from the earlier *Diversa Servicia*; the earliest printed cookery book, the *Boke of Cokery* produced by Pynson in 1500, from a version of the late fifteenth-century manuscript *A Noble Boke off Cookry*, itself a compilation based largely on the mid-fifteenth-century MS Beinecke 163 (printed by Hieatt as *An Ordinance of Pottage*, 1988) and *A Boke of Kokery* (BL Harleian 4016), a text also from the middle of the fifteenth century.[4]

These sources enable us to go back as far as fourteenth-century cookery, although the culinary traditions represented by the receipts reach back to the twelfth, and continued well into the sixteenth.[5] Continuity rather than change is the characteristic, although later manuscripts do offer variations on the same dish and changes in the use of ingredients did occur.[6] A notable feature of these early receipts is their lack of precision. Even though the tendency is for successive versions to become more detailed, what we would consider workable instructions are not supplied. Quantities of ingredients are not always indicated, cooking times are seldom given; although a feature of English MSS is that they offer more such details than their French counterparts.[7] Nobody could learn to cook from these receipts and interpreting them today is problematic. Modern

---

[3] Hieatt, 'Listing and Analysing the medieval English culinary recipe collections' in Lambert (1992), pp. 15–21. While there are 6 complete or nearly complete versions of *The Forme of Cury*, receipts from it appear in 4 other MSS, as is clear from the catalogue by Hieatt, Lambert, Laurioux and Prentki in the same volume, pp. 314–362.

[4] For a discussion of the borrowings between the English culinary MSS, see Laurioux, *Le Règne de Taillevent* (1997), pp. 201–5.

[5] See Hieatt & Butler (eds), *Curye on Inglysch* (1985), p. 1; also Hieatt (1992), p. 17.

[6] For examples of how receipts for the same dish changed in the course of the fourteenth and fifteenth centuries, see Hieatt & Butler (1985), pp. 8–10.

[7] See Hieatt & Butler (1985), p. 8.

researchers are still debating such contentious points as the precise quantities of spices used in the medieval kitchen. If the receipts did not teach how to prepare the dishes, who used them?

The diversity of the MSS points to an equally diverse readership. As Bruno Laurioux points out, each copy was different, often made for a specific buyer or reader, and varied from the utilitarian to the luxurious.[8] The nature of the manuscript also indicates many different intentions: the luxurious versions might well be designed principally to record the splendour of court feasts, enhancing the prestige of the royal host. More rough-and-ready copies were for use by an individual owner and his servants. English MSS are sometimes devoted exclusively to cookery, others more to medical matters with the addition of some culinary items. This observation, combined with the rudimentary nature of the receipts, gives a fair indication of possible uses. Manuscripts devoted exclusively to cookery and related topics, such as service at table, might have been for the staff of a great household. Two of the MS versions of *The Forme of Cury* which attribute the receipts to Richard II's master-cooks (BL Add. MS 5016 and Manchester, John Rylands Library Eng. 7) were designed to give the aristocracy's cooks useful reminders of the basis of royal cookery. They did not need full receipts, as they were already trained. Other household officers, responsible for overseeing supplies and ensuring there was no waste, had to know what ingredients were required for a particular dish in order to dole out to the cook what he needed and no more. On the other hand, there are MSS in which cookery is associated with medical matters, used by practising doctors (such as BL Sloane 374) and apothecaries (such as BL Royal 8.B.iv) or patients themselves (such as BL Arundel 334) and, at the other end of the spectrum of association, those in which cookery forms part of a vast range of domestic lore, used as a practical guide to estate management by householders (as, for instance, BL Add. MS 5467).[9]

But no matter how the environment of the cookery sections of these manuscripts changed to suit various users, the receipts themselves originated in courtly kitchens. The same was true for most Continental cookery treatises and, as Terence Scully puts it, 'rather than being national and creative, aristocratic cookery in the Middle Ages tended to be international in its scope and

---

[8] See Laurioux (1997), pp. 276–94.

[9] Ibid., pp. 311–30.

evolutionary in its development'.[10] While the basic nature of fourteenth- and fifteenth-century cuisine in (for instance) France and England was largely similar, characterized by the use of spices, acid and often slightly bitter sauces, and a very limited use of fats compared to later periods, there were regional differences which offer pointers to how distinct national culinary styles would develop. A comparison of French and English receipts shows that there were considerable variations in the use of spices and acid or sweet elements. A study by Jean-Louis Flandrin in 1984 reveals the extent of these national differences. He based his work on (among others) the Bibliothèque Nationale version of Taillevent's *Viandier* (dating from the second half of the fourteenth century but before 1392) and the later Vatican version with extra receipts (dating from the 1450s), compared to the Warner version of *The Forme of Cury*, BL Add. MS 5016 (*c.*1400–25) and *A Boke of Kokery*, BL Harleian MS 4016 (*c.*1440), as reproduced by Thomas Austin in 1888.[11] In both countries, the most frequently-used spices were saffron and ginger, but their use was greatest in England. The figures are that saffron is found in 20 per cent of the receipts in the first version of the *Viandier* and 22 per cent of those in the second – the French – and in 40 per cent of those in *The Forme of Cury* and 36 per cent of those included in *A Boke of Kokery* – the English. Ginger figured in 18 and 27 per cent of the French receipts respectively and in 28 and 46 per cent of the English. The use of cinnamon rose more over the same period in England than in France: from 12 to 29 per cent as opposed to 14 and 17 per cent. Cloves followed the same path in each country: 12 and 16 per cent in France, 7 and 16 per cent in England. Grains of paradise, which appear in 9 and 16 per cent of the French receipts, figure in only one per cent of the earlier English receipts and then disappear. Nutmeg in the French receipts (3 and 2 per cent) is replaced in the English ones by mace (3 and 14 per cent). Pepper, now the cheapest and commonest of the spices, appears in only 9 and 5 per cent of French receipts, but in 10 and 35 per cent of the English. It seems that in France grains of paradise, with their exotic name and connotations, had replaced the less prestigious pepper, while in

---

[10] Scully, *The Art of Cookery in the Middle Ages* (1995), p. 197. But Scully does tend to over-emphasize the 'international' aspect of late-medieval cookery as opposed to national specificities, in a book which treats the culinary scene in Europe as a whole.

[11] See Flandrin, 'Internationalisme, nationalisme et régionalisme dans la cuisine des XIVe et XVe siècles: le témoignage des livres de cuisine' (1984), especially the tables pp. 85–6. The dates for the MSS are those given in the catalogue by Hieatt, Lambert, Laurioux and Prentki in Lambert (1992), pp. 317–362.

England, no such shift had taken place.[12] Another ingredient used more often in English medieval cookery was almonds, in 9 and 15 per cent of the receipts, while in France the percentage remained stable at 8 per cent. A more important difference is that sugar or another sweet element such as honey or dried fruit was used more frequently in England than in France. The French receipts show 8 and 13 per cent, the English ones 49 and 38 per cent. The acid element – from vinegar, verjuice, wine or sour fruit – appears most regularly in France (72 and 69 per cent, as opposed to the English 44 and 61 per cent). It is clear from these statistics that there were significant national variations in the use of spices, and that the English preferred sweeter, perhaps blander flavours, while the French were more attached to sharpness.[13]

My own count of these ingredients in the mid-fifteenth century Beinecke MS 163 confirms Flandrin's findings. Ginger appears in 47 per cent of the 189 receipts, saffron in 35 per cent; cloves come next, at 25 per cent, followed by cinnamon (24 per cent), pepper (21 per cent), and mace (18 per cent). Nutmeg is never mentioned, 'grains' appear once, cubebs six times. But in 24 per cent of the receipts a mixed spice powder (and there were various mixes: mild, strong, Lombard) is found, suggesting the use of spices was becoming less specific. Herbs have little place, mentioned in only 16 per cent of the receipts; spice in one form or another appeared in 77 per cent. In one-fifth of these prescriptions the spice or some other agent was used specifically to give colour. The most often found are yellow from saffron, brown from cinnamon, and red from sanders; green was obtained from parsley, blue from turnsole. That this aspect is mentioned so often underlines the importance of appearance. The emphasis on colour is another aspect of English cookery which lingered long after the Middle Ages.

In this Beinecke MS, the balance of sweet and sour is virtually equal: 51 per cent of the receipts contain one or more sweet elements, in the form of sugar, honey, dried fruit or sweet wine; 52 per cent a sour element, in the form of vinegar, verjuice or wine (there can be no doubt that the wine did bring in an acid element, as a receipt occasionally suggests using vinegar or wine). On the whole, the flavourings of the sweet dishes are fairly bland. In 26 per cent of the

---

[12] This suggestion about the importance of the name and connotation of the spice is from Laurioux, *Le Moyen Age à table* (1989), p. 44.

[13] For a brief discussion of exchanges, similarities and differences between French and English medieval cookery books, see Wilson, 'The French Connection: Part 1' (1979).

receipts, the sweet and sour are combined to give the flavour the English called 'egerdouce'. The texture of medieval dishes was frequently that of a purée, usually quite thick, and with some pieces in it: often, it is not clear whether one should consider the result to be a stew with small pieces of meat or fish in sauce, or closer to a purée. In the Beinecke MS, 48 per cent of the receipts would produce a result somewhere along the stew-purée continuum. Otherwise, there are thinner pottages, roasted game birds (often served simply with salt or with ginger sauce), cold jellies, pies, fritters, and a few hot drinks of the posset type. What is noticeable in this collection (and in other versions of it) is that the way the receipts are grouped gives an idea of the order in which they were consumed: the everyday dishes come first and the more 'curious' dishes later.[14]

Beyond the statistics, receipts and menus give a better idea of what was actually cooked and eaten, but it is important to remember that receipts in cookery books are often for dishes which would appear only at the high table, while the lesser guests at a feast would be given more basic fare. One illustration of this is the virtual absence of receipts for beef in medieval cookery books (beef was considered a 'gross' meat, fit for the lower orders), while game and all sorts of birds were highly esteemed, with large numbers of receipts either to cook them or for sauces to serve with them.[15] Yet the 'gross' meats were what appeared most frequently at table. This becomes very obvious when one examines household accounts. In the relatively modest gentry household of Alice de Bryene between 1418 and 1419, beef represented 48 per cent of the total meat consumption, mutton 14 per cent, pork 28 per cent, poultry 9 per cent and game of all kinds a mere 1 per cent. In the grander establishment of John de Vere, Earl of Oxford, beef represented 56 per cent of the total, mutton 14 per cent, pork 17 per cent, poultry 6 per cent and game 7 per cent, with venison as the main game item.[16] Seasonal patterns of consumption show that, contrary

---

[14] See Hieatt's comments on one of the MSS of *The Forme of Cury* (BL Add. MS 5016) and on two versions of *An Ordinance of Pottage* (Beinecke MS 163, Oxford Bodleian MS Rawlinson D 1222), in Hieatt (ed.), *An Ordinance of Pottage* (1988), pp. 16–17.

[15] See Flandrin, *Chronique de Platine* (1992), pp. 181–188; the same was true in England – for instance, Hieatt notes that there is no receipt for roast beef in the mid fifteenth-century Yale University Beinecke MS 163, and that only the commoners at the coronation of Richard III in 1483 were served this dish. See Hieatt (1988), p. 18. The only receipt for beef in the Beinecke MS is for 'Alosed beef', which are what later centuries would call 'beef olives', in fact *paupiettes*. Otherwise beef appears only as an ingredient for forcemeat or broth.

[16] See the tables in Dyer, *Standards of living in the later Middle Ages* (1989), p. 59.

to a persistent myth, not all domestic food animals were slaughtered in the autumn. At least for the upper classes, fresh meat was available all the year round. The peripatetic lifestyle of the great magnate was dictated in part by the need to move to a new supply of fresh meat. The fact that fresh meat was readily available counters the argument that spices were used to disguise the flavour of tainted or salted meat. In reality, the use of spices was culturally induced, with the prestige of the expensive and the exotic as its main motor. Although historians are still divided over the amount of spice used in medieval dishes, it seems plausible to suggest that most of what appeared in financial accounts for a particular occasion was consumed by a minority of the people present. Thus those who did consume spices probably ate spicier dishes than today.[17]

Three receipts from the Beinecke MS will give an idea of the associations of flavours in late medieval English cooking. As was noted earlier, the basics were dishes dominated by the acid, by the sweet, or by the sweet and sour mix. An example of the first type is the receipt for 'Conynggez in cyve':

> Chop conyngys in pecys; do hem in a pott. Take onyons and good herbes ychopyd togedyr, boyle hem up in swete brothe; do therto poudyr of pepyr. Make a lyour of paryngys of crustys if whyte bredde drawyn with wyn and a lytylle blode; aley hit up but a lytyll. Do therto poudyr of canell, a grete dele, sesyn hit up with poudyr of gynger, wenigger, & salt.[18]

This would produce a fairly thin sauce for the pieces of meat: here we are at the stew end of the spectrum. Characteristic of medieval cookery is the use of bread to thicken the sauce, and the wine, spice and vinegar base to the sauce. The other 'cyve' receipts in this collection have similar sauces.

The sweet-sour combination is represented by 'Blaunch bruet':

---

[17] Hieatt represents the 'less spice' view: see, for instance, Hieatt (1988), p. 19. Bruno Laurioux stands at the other extreme, taking the view that the Middle Ages used far more spice than we do today: see Laurioux, 'Spices in the Medieval Diet: A New Approach' (1985). For an example of the earlier view that indiscriminate spicing was the norm, see Henisch (1976), p. 101.

[18] Receipt 33 from Hieatt (1988), p. 46. The other 'cyve' receipts are nos. 29 and 36.

Take hennys of porke, rostyd & chopyd; do hit in a pott. Do almonde mylke therto. Aley hit up with floure of rys. Do theryn a lytyll broth & a quantyte of wyne, clovys & macys, & sesyn hit up with venyger & pouderes & a lytyll sygure, steynyd with alkenet.[19]

Most (seven out of nine) of the 'bruet' receipts contain the sweet-sour mix, and in seven the colour is specified, varying from red to yellow, with one green sauce. These sauces were also quite thin, while the stews which are interspersed with the bruets have even thinner sauces, often not thickened at all.

One of the sweet meat (or fish) dishes was 'mortruys', here in its meat version, 'Mortruys of flesch':

Take brawn of capons & porke, sodyn & groundyn; tempyr hit up with milke of almondes drawn with the broth. Set hit on the fyre; put to sigure & safron. When hit boyleth, tak som of thy mylke, boylyng, fro the fyre & aley hit up with yolkes of eyron that hit be ryght chargeaunt; styre hit wel for quelling. Put therto that othyr, & ster hem togedyr, & serve hem forth as mortruys; and strew on poudyr of gynger.[20]

This is a very thick purée, bright yellow from egg yolks and saffron, sweet, and with a final flavouring and decoration of powdered ginger sprinkled over the mound on the dish. All the 'mortruys' receipts indicate a purée of this nature, often white and decorated with a scattering of 'blaunch poudyr', a pale spice mix. If, as Hieatt suggests, the order in which these receipts follow each other in the manuscript corresponds even loosely to the order of consumption, the implication is that the dishes with sweet-and-sour or simply sweet flavours were thought more prestigious than those with an acid-spice component. This hypothesis is strengthened by the directions for 'Mawmene ryall' (an elaborate stew of small pieces of meat from several different birds with a rich, sweet, spiced, dried-fruit-based sauce) which tell the cook to 'florysch hit with sygure plate stikyd uppon'.[21] The exotic and expensive flavours of the dish are signalled visually by the sugar decoration. Another point about the order of

---

[19] Receipt 55 in Hieatt (1988), p. 53. The other receipts for 'bruet' are nos. 45–49 and 52–54.
[20] Receipt 79 in Hieatt (1988), p. 61. The other receipts for 'mortruys' are nos. 78–81.
[21] Receipt 99 in Hieatt (1988), p. 74.

receipts is that the general tendency is for dishes with thin sauces to precede thick purées, pies and fritters: the dishes become progressively less 'liquid', a feature of modern British meals noted by the structuralist Mary Douglas.[22]

Medieval dinners followed the rhythm of meat days and fish days imposed by the religious calendar and it is often possible to see a kind of 'fast' equivalent of the meat dishes: for instance, the porpoise which replaced venison on fish days.[23] Surviving bills of fare show that the number of courses varied according to the status of the diners: for instance, at Richard III's coronation in 1483, the King's table had three courses, while the lords and ladies were given two, and the commoners one. The number of dishes was greater for the higher ranks too, of course, and the most spectacular dishes, such as the peacock, were served only to the King's table. Roast crane and heron was a fairly ordinary dish for the King, served at the first course, but was presented as more of a delicacy, served at the second course, for the lords and ladies; the commoners, not surprisingly, were not offered anything of the kind. Not all the reputed 3,000 guests tasted the exotic spiced dishes, and the total quantities of spice provided, such as the 11 lb of saffron (8 for the kitchen, 3 for the saucery), 26 lb of ginger (18 for the kitchen, 8 for the saucery), and 39 lb of cinnamon (28 for the kitchen, 11 for the saucery), cannot simply be divided by the number of guests in order to reach a conclusion on how spicy food was at this date. It is clear from the bill of fare that the more elaborate dishes (which were also the most heavily spiced) were served to the King and, to a lesser extent, to the nobility.[24] This hierarchical distribution of food is occasionally noted in the cookery books: a receipt for pike and eel in broth tells the reader to 'serve hole pykys for lordys & quarters for othir men', while another for conger, turbot and halibut suggests that one should 'serve congure ii or iii pecys on a chargeor for thy soveraynys, … & serve the remnaunt for othir men'.[25] The theory was that the lord needed larger portions in order to be able to distribute titbits to those close to him at the board as a mark of favour.[26] But of course, the ostentatious display of plenty for the lord was part of the spectacle.

---

[22] See Douglas & Nicod, 'Taking the Biscuit' (1974).

[23] For examples of fish-day substitutions, see Henisch (1976), p. 44.

[24] The bill of fare and the accounts are reproduced in Sutton & Hammond (eds), *The Coronation of Richard III* (1983), pp. 294–99.

[25] See Hieatt (1988), pp. 40, 103.

[26] This idea is set out in the rules written *c.* 1241 by Robert Grosseteste for the widowed Countess of Lincoln; see Lamond (ed.), *Walter of Henley's Husbandry* (1890), p. 137.

Where there were two or three courses, the 'gross' dishes were served at the first course, and the more refined dishes came later; another feature was that the number of dishes at each course increased as the feast went on. These same features of menu-planning can be observed in bills of fare for other occasions and in the specimen menus offered by some cookery books.[27] These differed from those obtaining in France, and Jean-Louis Flandrin's comments on the dynamic and circular nature of English menus (each course organized in the same way, with a pottage in some form followed by roasts, followed by *entremets*)[28] need to be tempered by the basic rule of everyday dishes first and dainties later, still a feature of English bills of fare in the eighteenth century.

This brief tour of the medieval scene leaves too much unexplored, most notably the relationship between medical theory and flavour combinations, and the feast as spectacle, with its symbolic programme involving elaborate ceremonial in the serving of the meal and in the subtleties which provided a vehicle for political messages at the end of each course.[29] Both these aspects would survive and develop in the sixteenth and seventeenth centuries, before

---

[27] See, for instance, the menus from the late fourteenth-century Durham University Library MS Cosin v.iii. 11, reproduced in Hieatt & Butler (1985), pp. 39–41; the fifteenth-century BL MS Sloane 442, reproduced in Hieatt (1988), p. 110; the feast menus reproduced in Napier (ed.), *A Noble Boke off Cookry* (1882), pp. 3–12.

[28] Flandrin, 'Structure des menus français et anglais aux XIVe et XVe siècles' in Lambert (1992), pp. 173–192. He analyses the position of various types of dish in the enumeration of the courses of dinner: in France, there were more numerous courses, and different types of foods were associated with each course; the roasts ('rost') always appeared at the centre of the meal and were preceded by one or two courses, the 'assiette', then the 'potages'; the roasts were followed by a variable number of courses, the 'entremès', the 'desserte' and the 'issue', before the final course, the 'boutehors', composed of wine and spices to aid digestion. An analysis of the contents of each course shows that the rigid order of the eighteenth-century French menu plan was already present in embryonic form, with what we would call 'hors d'œuvre' first, and the 'gross' meats next; later in the meal, the 'entremets' had not yet reached any fixed position, appearing with or after the roast. Thus the apparent disorder of French medieval menus is only an illusion produced largely by the variable number of courses. In England, by contrast, the courses were far less numerous, and each course followed the same pattern, leading Flandrin to the conclusion that dishes were handed round in a fixed order, with no freedom left to the diners. But a comparison of the grand feasts for royalty and the general suggestions for less grandiose occasions in Hieatt & Butler (1985), pp. 39–41, shows that the repetitive structure noted by Flandrin is not always present at the lesser meals.

[29] These aspects of medieval food culture are referred to by Scully (1995), especially pp. 41–53, on the links between medical theory and medieval cookery; Henisch (1976), especially pp. 228–36 on the use of subtleties; and more generally by Laurioux (1989).

gradually declining or taking other forms in the eighteenth, but some characteristics of the fifteenth century survived much longer: the English addiction
to sugar and to sweet and savoury mixes; the love of coloured food; the basic
rule of menu-planning which placed ordinary dishes first and delicacies later.

As noted, the first printed cookery book, the *Boke of Cokery* produced by
Pynson in 1500, was based on fifteenth-century texts. There was no immediate
rush to print; what did appear were books of advice on diet and health, and on
household and estate management, two areas often associated with receipts in
medieval manuscripts. The best-known of the first type are Sir Thomas Elyot's
Castel of Helth (1539), and Andrew Boorde's *Dyetary of Helth* (c.1542). The two
books are remarkably similar, giving advice based on Galen about a healthy lifestyle, though both authors offer comments on what is suitable for Englishmen,
adapting Galenic theory to their readers.[30] A rival, Thomas Cogan, based his
Haven of Health (1584) on Elyot, but changed the order of his book to follow
Hippocrates rather than Galen, and supplied a much more extensive commentary on a wider variety of herbs than the earlier writer. In these texts one can begin
to discern signs of change at the dinner-table, with Elyot's remarks on the whole-
someness of beef for the healthy Englishman, and Cogan's on salads, eaten at the
beginning of the meal, and on apple tarts, eaten at the end.[31] The second type
of publication is best represented by Thomas Tusser's doggerel *A Hundreth good
pointes of husbandrie* (1557), expanded to *Five hundreth points* in 1573. The
expanded version gives advice to housewives, stressing their role as providers of
care and medicines for the sick, as well as managers of the daily routine of the
household.[32] Soon books would cater to women's needs in both these areas.

---

[30] See, for instance, Elyot's comments on beef and mutton, (1539), f. 29v; Boorde's comments on beer,
in *A Compendyous Regyment*, ed. Furnivall (1852), p. 256.

[31] See Elyot (1539), f. 29v; Cogan (1584), pp. 75, 89–90.

[32] See Tusser (1573), part 2, f. 13.

Elizabethan and Jacobean:
Expansion and New Developments

Only towards the end of the sixteenth century did publication of cookery books begin in earnest. Anticipating the rush, there were two earlier works: *A Proper Newe Booke of Cokerye* (undated, possibly as early as 1545) and the first book on confectionery, *The Secretes of the Reverende Maister Alexis of Piemont* (1558), a translation via French of a work by Girolamo Ruscelli, an Italian alchemist and apothecary. By the 1590s there were several on the market, including at least two by John Partridge, *The Treasurie of Commodious Conceites* (1573, plus six reprints) and *The Good Hous-wives Handmaide* (1594). Two other important works were A.W.'s *Book of Cookrye* (1591), and Thomas Dawson's *Good Huswife's Jewell* (two parts, 1585, plus reprints in 1596/97). By the end of the century, 12 new titles had appeared, and 29 editions placed on the market. If the print-run of each was 500, this means that 14,500 copies were in circulation. The titles point to two new strands of development. Firstly there were books of 'secrets', concerned mainly with remedies and confectionery. The two topics were usually combined because at the outset they were both the province of the apothecary. Secondly, the idea had taken hold that cookery books were written with women in mind. The early seventeenth century saw continuing production of these two types, their titles marking a difference in the social level of their readers. New books devoted entirely or mainly to confectionery carried such titles as *Delightes for Ladies* (1600) by Sir Hugh Plat, or *A Daily Exercise for Ladies and Gentlewomen* (1617) by John Murrell;[1] both these were elegant productions, the text surrounded by a decorative border. Cookery books or books combining cookery and household management, by contrast, were less ambitious about their readers, and the best-seller of the period, by Gervase Markham, was called simply *The English Hus-wife* (1615).

It is difficult to ascertain who acquired these books. Occasionally one finds one of the books of 'secrets' in the library of a nobleman. For instance, in 1584 the second Earl of Bedford had two medical works out of a total of 221, of which 161 were religious and devotional, and a later list shows that he also had

---

[1] Plat's book is devoted mostly to confectionery and the products of the still-room: out of 175 receipts, 73 are for confectionery, 25 for distilling, 36 for sweet powders and ointments, and only 41 for cookery and housewifery. Murrell's book is for nothing but confectionery.

the 1598 edition of Ruscelli's book.[2] Most inventories, however, fail to give details of all but religious works.[3] If cookery books and books of 'secrets' were used principally by women, they would probably have been kept in the lady's closet, along with her stock of various waters. Frustratingly, even seventeenth- and eighteenth-century inventories mention books without specifying their titles.[4] What is clear is that the authors or, rather, compilers of these books believed their audience was essentially female even though the historian David Cressy estimates that in the middle of the sixteenth century only 5 per cent of women were literate. He puts it at 10 per cent by c.1640 but points out that literacy and illiteracy were part of a spectrum and many girls were taught to read but not to write.[5] However, the fact of low literacy levels, combined with the need for money not only to purchase a book but to obtain the ingredients required to use the receipts, does not suggest that readership went very far down the social scale. This is an area which requires much more investigation, as the comment that Elizabethan cookery books were bought by 'the middling sort'[6] is vague and unsatisfactory. Cressy suggests that the whole book produc- tion of the early seventeenth century, assuming a print-run of 1,500 copies per edition, could be absorbed by a market composed of the gentry, the clergy, and the professions.[7] The internal evidence from cookery books themselves appears to confirm this judgement.

In theory the authors of these books were men, but open Markham's *The English Hus-wife* and it is clear that the receipts were not by him at all. The reverse of the title-page states:

Thou mayst say (gentle Reader) what hath this man to doe with Hus- wifery.... I shall desire thee therefore to understand, that this is no collection of his whose name is prefixed to this worke, but an approved

---

[2] See Byrne & Thomson, 'My Lord's Books' (undated reprint of 1931 article), pp. 2, 6, 11.

[3] See, for instance, Wanklyn, *Inventories of Worcestershire Landed Gentry, 1537–1786* (1998), passim; Emmison, 'Jacobean Household Inventories' (1938), pp. 34–5. See also the comment in Cressy, *Literacy and the Social Order* (1980), p. 49.

[4] For instance Wanklyn (1998), p. 343; the 1711 inventory made by Elizabeth Freke before a journey to London shows that she possessed several medical works, and 'severall other small Books' kept in her closet along with a large stock of cordial waters. See BL Add. MS 45718, ff. 173–181.

[5] See Cressy, 'Literacy in context' in Brewer & Porter (1993), pp. 313–4.

[6] Wilson, 'The French Connection: Part I' (1979), p. 14.

[7] Cressy (1980), p. 47.

Manuscript which he happily light on, belonging sometime to an honorable Personage of this kingdome, who was singular amongst those of her ranke for many of the qualities here set forth.

Later editions say that the 'honorable Personage' was 'an Honourable Countesse'.[8] The use of the past tense to describe this lady suggests that she was dead by 1615, and therefore that her manuscript receipts date back to the Elizabethan period, if not earlier. Markham was not the only author to pillage ladies' receipt books: as Karen Hess points out, internal evidence suggests very strongly that Dawson did the same.[9] This period marks a very important development in English cookery literature: from now on, authors saw their readers as essentially female, and women were also often the real authors of the receipts, though at first they were hidden behind the men who presented the books. This is so different from France, where the first overt reference to the woman cook in a title comes with *La Cuisinière bourgeoise* (1746), that it needs to be further examined.

How did women come to be readers and authors? Several factors were at work. Standard accounts of female involvement in domestic work point out that the medieval household was almost entirely made up of men: the only women were the ladies of the family, nursemaids and laundresses. This did not change until the seventeenth century.[10] The lady of the house might have a managerial role in her husband's absence, and she might produce some remedies, but she was certainly not active in producing food of any kind. In fact, such accounts are valid only for the aristocracy; below this level, things had altered much earlier. Among the gentry, housekeepers were being employed by the 1550s and this suggests a shift to female supervision of everyday household tasks.[11] Mistress and upper servants shared in the preparation of remedies, and of the confectionery that went with remedies (sugar itself being considered beneficial to health and often used as a remedy in its own right).[12] Both of these were made

---

[8] Markham, *A Way to get Wealth*, ed. 11 (1660), which includes *The English Hous-Wife*, in the dedication.

[9] See Hess (ed.), *Martha Washington's Booke of Cookery* (1981), p. 454.

[10] For this view, Girouard, *Life in the English Country House* (1980), pp. 27–8, 142. Other writers suggest a more nuanced approach: Marshall, *The English Domestic Servant in History* (1949), pp. 6–8.

[11] E.g. Sir William Petre's wage lists for 1550, in Emmison, *Tudor Secretary* (1961), pp. 151–3.

[12] One example was Lady Grace Mildmay (1552–1620), renowned for her skill in medicine and confectionery, who prepared such items as 'balm' with her housekeeper, Bess. See Pollock, *With Faith and Physic* (1993), pp. 2, 35, 140–41; also Spurling, *Elinor Fettiplace's Receipt Book* (1986), p. 165.

in the still-room, not the kitchen, but soon women were involving themselves in cookery as well. Sugar seems to have been the ingredient which drew all three strands of household receipts together.

Ladies' manuscript books containing all three types of receipt were probably being kept by the middle of the sixteenth century, at first by the aristocracy and the wealthy gentry. One surviving example is Elinor Fettiplace's, dated 1604: it contains more than 300 remedies (plus perfumes), followed by confectioneries, and a limited number of cookery receipts.[13] Anne Wilson suggests the latter were more 'modern' than the others, which had been collected over several generations.[14] Although the manuscript was copied out by a secretary, Lady Fettiplace continued to add comments to the text until her death in 1647. Her additions show that she took an active part in the kitchen as well as the still-room.[15] The proportions of the three types of receipt in this collection indicate a hierarchy of prestige: remedies were foremost, followed by confectionery, with cookery at the bottom of the pile. Elite ladies were more likely to be interested in the first two than the third, and there is a considerable body of evidence to show that even aristocrats took part in the gathering and preserving of fruit for confectioneries.[16] Ladies collected receipts, either copying down family prescriptions from earlier generations or obtaining new items from friends, but this did not stop them from acquiring printed books as well. Lady Fettiplace owned *The Countrey Farme* (1600), the English translation of Charles Estienne's *La Maison rustique*. Karen Hess' suggestion that the upper classes had their prestigious family receipt books and that only those socially beneath them were constrained to collect receipts from their friends or purchase a printed book is an over-simplification.[17]

The cookery which one discovers from the books of the period stands in a direct line of development from the fifteenth century. The earliest, not surprisingly, are closest to the medieval tradition. Bills of fare for Henry VIII

---

[13] See Spurling (1986), pp. 15, 20.

[14] See Wilson, 'A Cookery book and its Context' (1987), pp. 8–11, 17–18.

[15] See Spurling (1986), pp. 20–22, 29, 35.

[16] See Bourcier, thesis (1977), pp. 208–9, 224; Mendelson, 'Stuart women's diaries and occasional memoirs' in Prior (1985), p. 190. One example is Lady Anne Clifford (1590–1676): her Knole diary for 1616–1619 shows her making rosemary cakes, gathering cherries, and even making pancakes with her women; at the end of her life, her waiting-gentlewoman, Frances Pate, made preserves of apples and lemons for her. See Clifford (ed.), *The Diaries of Lady Anne Clifford* (1990), pp. 52, 57, 68, 255, 261.

[17] See Hess (1981), p. 451.

are very similar to those for fifteenth-century kings.[18] By the 1590s, the emphasis had changed. In the area of cookery proper, the main preoccupation was now a balance between sweet and sour elements, and often, the sauce was tempered by the addition of butter, an ingredient which was to become increasingly present in seventeenth-century receipts. Herbs were beginning to replace spices, although spices were still well to the fore. A.W.'s *Book of Cookrye* (1591) gives 37 receipts for stews and sauces for meat. In these, sugar and/or dried fruit figure in 76 per cent, verjuice or vinegar in 78 per cent, wine in 43 per cent, and butter in 41 per cent; spices appear in 62 per cent, and herbs, mostly thyme, in 35 per cent.[19] A piece of general advice from Markham gives an idea of the desired result:

> When a broth is too sweet, to sharpen it with verjuice, when too tart to sweet it with sugar, when flat and wallowish to quicken it with orenge and lemmons, and when too bitter to make it pleasant with hearbes and spices.[20]

It is significant that herbs precede spices in this enumeration, and one notices the use of orange and lemon, never mentioned in the Beinecke manuscript, to liven up a sauce. In Markham's book, 75 per cent of the receipts for meat in sauce contain the sweet-sour combination, which is also found in sauces for roasts and in meat pies. In the receipts without a sweet-sour flavour, more subtle tastes and new textures are appearing, as in this receipt for chickens:

---

[18] See the menu for the Garter feast in 1619, reproduced in Ashmole, *The Institute, Laws and Ceremonies of the most Noble Order of the Garter* (1672), pp. 603–4; the supper menu for Henry and his Queen on 3 June 1532 shows the first sign of change, in that an appetizer course of raw and boiled salads was served before a typically medieval three-course meal, and that after this came a fourth course which is more than the medieval 'void', but less than the sixteenth-century 'banquet'; this menu is reproduced in Murray & Bosanquet (eds), *The Manuscript of William Dunche* (1914), p. 59.

[19] A.W., *A Book of Cookrye* (1591; facs. repr. 1976), ff. 3–14v. The book borrowed extensively from the earlier *A Proper Newe Booke of Cokerye*, but it contains far more receipts – 164 as opposed to 49 in the 1575 edition of the earlier work. For the rest of this part of the book, our statistical analysis of flavours needs to be confined to receipts for stews and sauces for meat in order to avoid the distortion which the inclusion of purely sweet tarts and preserves, to which A.W., for instance, devotes several pages, would create.

[20] Markham (1615), p. 53.

If you will boile Chickens … daintily, you shal … fill their bellies as full
of Parsley as they can hold, then boile them with salt and water only till
they be enough: then take a dish and put into it verjuice and butter and
salt and when the butter is melted, take the Parsley out of the Chickens
bellies and mince it very small, and put it to the verjuice and butter and
stirre it well together, then lay in the Chickens and trimme the dish with
sippets, and so serve it foorth.[21]

Elinor Fettiplace's book gives another version of boiled chickens, with a sauce
of gooseberries and sugar, the flavour and texture again tempered with butter.[22]

The enthusiasm for sugar was not confined to such receipts. A dinner now
ended with a new course, the 'banquet', where all sorts of confectionery, from
preserves of fruit to marchpanes, sweet biscuits, comfits, and moulded sugar
shaped like birds, snails or other creatures, provided a glamorous show. Even the
plates and cups on the table might be made from sugar.[23] The banquet had
grown out of the medieval 'void', which consisted of sweet wine and spices in
the form of comfits served at the end of dinner to aid digestion. But the Elizabethan and Jacobean version, with lavish provision of sugar in every conceivable
form and of ingenuity in its use of shapes and colours, was a vehicle for display
of wealth. Ladies vied to produce the brightest, clearest fruit preserves and the
most elaborate imitations in sugar or marchpane of animals, playing-cards, slices
of bacon and suchlike. This sugar-work was the most important innovation of
the Renaissance table: one modern commentator describes it as the only one.[24]

In England, at least, there are signs of other changes, for example in the
order of service. Markham divides his receipts into five categories: salads and
fricassees, boiled meats and broths, roast meats and carbonadoes (broiled
meat), baked meats and pies, and finally banqueting stuff and made dishes.[25]
Later editions give greatly expanded directions for setting out a meal: the first
course was to consist of salads, fricassees, roast and boiled meats, hot and cold
baked meats and carbonadoes; the second of game and tame birds, hot and

---

[21] Markham (1615), p. 52.

[22] Spurling (1986), p. 124.

[23] For an idea of the appearance of a 'banquet', see the illustration in Day, *Eat, Drink and Be Merry*
(2000), p. 46.

[24] Revel, *Un Festin en paroles* (1979), p. 172.

[25] Markham (1615), p. 39.

cold baked meats, and made dishes.[26] Although the order of the receipts is a trifle confused, it does indeed correspond to the order of serving. Some of these types of dish are new and Markham points out that carbonadoes and 'compound Fricases' are not English but foreign (the first is French, the second comes from France, Spain and Italy).[279] Clearly there was a perception that English cookery was now different from Continental cuisine. The Scottish traveller Fynes Moryson set out the differences between English and French food in 1617:

> The French are commended and said to excell others in boyled meats, sawces, and made dishes.... And the cookes are most esteemed, who have best invention in new made and compounded meats.
>
> In generall, the Art of Cookery is much esteemed in England; ... yet the English Cookes, in comparison with other Nations, are most commended for roasted meates.[28]

Moryson's remarks suggest that French cookery was already developing its own area of excellence, one which would be revealed as a completely new style with the publication of La Varenne's *Cuisinier françois* in 1651. Meanwhile, the English were becoming renowned for roast meat, implying that roast beef, the national dish *par excellence* in the eighteenth century, was beginning to shed its medieval image as 'gross' meat.

Unfortunately, the complete absence of any new French cookery books between 1560 and 1650 leaves a gap in our knowledge of the pre-La Varenne phase of development. One English cookery book does offer an insight into what was going on across the Channel. John Murrell's *New Booke of Cookerie* (1615) contains a section in which most of the receipts are described as French (there are a few others scattered elsewhere), and another entitled 'London Cookerie'. In the next edition (1617), the latter is described as 'English Cookerie', and the title-page indicates that the directions are set out in the 'now, new, English and French fashion'. A comparison of the two groups shows that the French were beginning to discard the sugar and dried fruit, still much

---

[26] Markham (1664), pp. 98–101.

[27] Markham (1615), pp. 43, 63.

[28] Moryson, *An Itinerary* (1617), part 3, pp. 134, 150.

more present in the English receipts (there is sugar in 47 per cent, dried fruit in 21 per cent of the French receipts, as against 57 and 53 per cent respectively of the English); verjuice or vinegar, with pepper to season, plus butter added to the sauce, are typical of the French receipts (in 89, 84, and 74 per cent respectively, compared to 43, 30, and 43 per cent of the English receipts).[29] These are the flavours which Sarah Peterson ascribes to the new French cuisine which was to usher in modern cooking in the seventeenth century.[30]

---

[29] Murrell, *A New Booke of Cookerie* (1615; facs. repr., 1972), pp. 1–13, 48–9, 70–72 (French receipts), pp. 53–78 (English or 'London' receipts). For these statistics, I have excluded from both groups the receipts for sousing, which automatically contain acid and would thus give a false impression.
[30] See Peterson, *Acquired Taste* (1994), pp. 183–86. But of course, acid had been an important component of sauces, especially in France, in the Middle Ages.

The production of new cookery books ground virtually to a halt under Charles I. The period of the Civil War was not propitious, of course, but there were hardly any new books after 1625. This changed when the Commonwealth brought renewed stability. Between 1650 and 1659, eight new titles appeared, several going into many editions. Clearly, the demand was there, and the enthusiasm with which these books were bought, read and copied demonstrates that Puritanism did not have the deadening effect on English cookery some-times attributed to it by popular historians.[1] There were two main sources for this wave of publications: ladies' manuscript collections, and translations from the French. The two most successful were from the first category. In 1653 W.J. presented two books in one, *A Choice Manual* (remedies) and *A True Gentle-womans Delight* (cookery and confectionery); the first was attributed to the Countess of Kent, who was famous for her medical skills, but the association of the two books led many to believe the cookery was hers too.[2] By 1699, there had been at least twelve reprints (the 1687 edition was numbered the nineteenth, which suggests even more than listed by Oxford). Aristocratic origin of the receipts was a selling-point and books began to emphasize their upper-class sources. One which appeared in 1654 announced on the title-page that the receipts were 'By Persons of quality whose names are mentioned', as indeed they were.[3] The other best-seller was *The Queens Closet Opened* (1655), which went into ten editions by 1700 and, like the Countess of Kent's receipts, was further reprinted in the eighteenth century. It was in three parts, 'The Pearl of Practise' (remedies), 'A Queens Delight' (confectionery), and 'The Compleat Cook' (cookery). The presenter, W.M., informed readers that these were Henrietta Maria's own receipts:

---

[1] For the negative view of the impact of Puritanism, see Pullar, *Consuming Passions* (1970), pp. 125–31. The 'Pullar hypothesis' has already been comprehensively demolished in Mennell, *All Manners of Food* (1985), pp. 104–108.

[2] On the true authorship of the two books, see David, 'A True Gentlewomans Delight' (1979).

[3] See Oxford, *English Cookery Books to the Year 1850* (1979), pp. 25–26.

As they were presented to the Queen by the most Experienced Persons of our Times, many whereof were honoured with her own practice, when she pleased to descend to these more private Recreations. Never before published. Transcribed from the true Copies of her Majesties own Receipt Books.

Here too, there are named receipts, most numerous in the first volume, which confirm the hierarchy of prestige of the three types of domestic activity. The title of the book is also significant, evoking the status of these 'secret' receipts kept in the closet, a private space denoting intimacy and social success for those admitted into the inner sanctum.[4]

The snob value of these 'secrets' is also set out by Jos. Cooper, the author of *The Art of Cookery* (1654), who presented himself as 'chiefe Cook to the Late King', although his name does not appear in the royal warrants. In his address to the reader, he says:

> Ladies, forgive my confidence if I tell you, that I know this piece will prove your favourite; and if any thing displeases you, it will be to see so many uncommon, and undeflour'd *Receipts* prostituted to the publique view, which perchance you will think might have been plac'd better among the paper-secrets in a few of your Cabinets; but 'tis easie to pardon that offence, which is only committed in favour of the Common good.

The fascination with the culinary secrets of the aristocracy and of royalty provides an interesting comment on the public mood during the Commonwealth. Nostalgia for the old order is obvious, and would become even more so at the Restoration, when Robert May, commenting on his own (much-quoted) instructions for producing a set-piece for the banquet, concludes:

> These were formerly the delights of the Nobility, before good House-keeping had left *England*, and the Sword really acted that which was only counterfeited in such honest and laudable Exercises as these.[5]

---

[4] For a discussion of the prestige of the closet in the formal houses of the seventeenth century, see Girouard (1980), pp. 128–35, 144–46.

[5] May, *The Accomplisht Cook* (1660), in the unnumbered pages at the beginning.

May's book was not published until 1660, when the author was 72; the cookery he describes dates from before the Restoration.

The other source of new receipts was France. *The French Cook*, a translation of La Varenne's *Cuisinier françois* (1651) came out in 1653, and in 1656 'Mounsieur Marnettè' brought out his translation of *Le Pastissier françois* (1653), entitled *The Perfect Cook* (the book also contains other material). These were highly influential: some of the receipts from the first found their way into 'The Compleat Cook',[6] and the second was one of May's sources, from which he borrowed 35 receipts (although he also borrowed from the ladies' manuscript books).[7] The French culinary revolution set out by La Varenne marked the beginning of the end of the cuisine of 'mixtures', giving way to a cuisine of 'impregnation and essences' which was to find its final expression in the eighteenth and nineteenth centuries.[8] But, as Jean-François Revel points out, there was still much to do. Although French cookery writers praised simple, clean, natural flavours, their receipts did not produce such 'modern' results: the impulse to classical simplicity was there in the discourse but not in culinary practice.[9] La Varenne's book sets out some of the basics: his sauce bases, stews and fricassees, his use of the *bouquet garni*, and of a *roux* to thicken sauces, are all part of the repertoire of French cooking today. But he also gives spiced mixtures with sweet and sour flavours, and purée textures which look back to previous centuries.[10] However, La Varenne was soon denounced as old-fashioned and lacking in refinement by L.S.R., the author of *L'Art de bien traiter* (1674), for his revolting mixtures of meat with sweet sauces, his use of saffron, and his butterless *potages*, amongst other horrors.[11] (Not that L.S.R.'s receipts are always a model of refined simplicity.) Of the French cooks who followed La Varenne, the most innovative was probably Pierre de Lune, author of *Le Cuisinier* (1656), but the most influential, especially in England, was

[6] See Wilson, 'The French Connection: Part II' (1980), p. 11.

[7] See Marcus Bell's introduction to May (1994), p. 19. The fact that May did not borrow from *The French Cook* suggests rejection of La Varenne's culinary revolution, and indeed, May's dishes use far more of the older flavour combinations than La Varenne's.

[8] These terms are those used by Revel (1979), p. 206.

[9] Revel (1979), pp. 183–5.

[10] For an appreciation of La Varenne's culinary style, see Wheaton, *Savouring the Past* (1983), pp. 114–19; Willan, *Great Cooks and their Recipes* (1977), pp. 47–54.

[11] See L.S.R. (1674), reproduced in Laurendon & Laurendon (eds), *L'Art de la cuisine française au XVIIe siècle* (1995), pp. 22–23.

Massialot, whose *Cuisinier roïal et bourgeois* came out in 1691.[12] Massialot showed the full-blown French 'court' style of cookery: his book is much more royal than bourgeois (the author's disdain for more modest readers appears clearly in his preface). The key dishes of the court style were the fricassee, the *bisque* (a soup-stew hybrid, lavishly garnished) and the *poupeton* (a rich braised mixture baked inside a forcemeat crust, known as a 'pupton' in English), which had already been presented by La Varenne. To these Massialot added the *oille* (another soup-stew hybrid, known in English as an olio), and the *coulis* (what the English called cullis, a rich sauce base and an essential ingredient in eighteenth-century cooking). The aim of these authors, from La Varenne to Massialot, was to produce rich, intensely-flavoured sauces, what the French today call *relevées*, and what was then called *de haut goût*. In La Varenne's receipts, capers and citrus juice are often used to achieve this effect; in Massialot, the result is achieved by using cullis, meat juices and a touch of lemon. *Le Cuisinier roïal et bourgeois* was not translated into English until 1702 and its impact was felt in the first third of the eighteenth century, so we shall return later to this important work.

Meanwhile, what had been happening to English cookery, and how did the English react to the new style imported from across the Channel? Ladies' manuscript receipts, the principal source for English cookery books of the 1650s, reveal the cookery of the gentry (the aristocracy employed men-cooks), and of the aristocracy and gentry in the areas of remedies and confectionery. The instructions for confectionery in *A True Gentlewomans Delight* and 'A Queens Delight' show the same care about texture, colour and clarity in the fruit preserves which can already be observed in Lady Fettiplace's receipts. For instance, by varying the cooking method, one could control the colour of a preserve, making it white, amber, or red. Instructions for this appear in all these receipts.[13] This was an area of considerable expertise among ladies, but it was not the only one. According to Marnette, English ladies were 'so well vers'd in the Pastry Art, as that they may out-vie the best Forreign Pastry Cooks'.[14]

---

[12] For a discussion of the contribution of La Varenne and his successors to the development of the new French style, see the chapter on 'Naissance de la cuisine moderne' in Michel, *Vatel et la naissance de la gastronomie* (1999), pp. 151–93.

[13] See Spurling (1986), pp. 184–85; Markham (1615), p. 71; *A True Gentlewomans Delight* (1653), pp. 25–26, 29; W.M. (1655, repr. 1984), 'A Queens Delight' pp. 1–2, 3, 8.

[14] Marnette (1656), dedication.

Baking was another area which was an English speciality: one where, as we shall see, eighteenth-century English women cooks developed their own style which owed nothing to France. In the seventeenth century, pastry, pies and tarts were another vehicle for display, and while the ladies' efforts at decoration were quite modest, the men-cooks' pies and tarts were elaborate in the extreme. *A True Gentlewomans Delight* suggests cutting the pastry round the edge of a dish containing a florentine 'round about like Virginal keys, then turn up one, and let the other lie'; the men offer instructions and illustrations for geometric and floral shapes, not to mention pies whose shapes reflect their contents.[15] The fillings for the pies, however, often look back to earlier spiced mixtures of meat, dried fruit, sugar, spice and verjuice. Baking also produced regional specialities, such as the 'Banbury Cake' or the 'Devonshire Whitepot' noticed by Fynes Moryson in the 1590s. There are receipts for both in 'The Compleat Cook', and the second (a rich bread-and-butter pudding) is very similar to Lady Fettiplace's 'The Lord of Devonshire his Pudding'.[16] These receipts had been circulating in manuscript long before they reached the printed cookery books.

The receipts for meat in sauce show varying degrees of adaptation to new fashions. In *A True Gentlewomans Delight*, sugar or dried fruit are present in 47 per cent of them, as are vinegar or verjuice. Spices figure in 56 per cent, while 31 per cent call for citrus juice, 6 per cent for wine, and 12 per cent for anchovy.[17] These last three are the new flavours, not yet ubiquitous, which would come to dominate English made dishes after the Restoration. In books more influenced by French cuisine, the new flavours are more obvious. In Cooper's book, 36 per cent of the receipts contain sugar or dried fruit, 45 per cent vinegar or verjuice, 52 per cent citrus juice, and 12 per cent anchovy. In 'The Compleat Cook' these proportions are respectively 16, 44, 44, and 34 per cent.[18] The second book is more 'modern', with its reduced use of sugar and

---

[15] See *A True Gentlewomans Delight* (1653), p. 77; Cooper (1654), pp. 99–108; May (1660), pp. 196–202, 224–25, 274, 284, 303–4, 360, 378; Rabisha, *The Whole Body of Cookery dissected* (1661), pp. 140, 152–53, 162, 167–68. The 'virginal key' decoration lived on, to be re-discovered by Dorothy Hartley in the 1950s in the North of England, known now as the 'gable' pattern. See Hartley, *Food in England* (1985), pp. 607–10.

[16] See Moryson (1617), part 3, p. 54; W.M. (1984) 'The Compleat Cook' p. 12; Spurling (1986), pp. 213–14.

[17] See *A True Gentlewomans Delight* (1653), pp. 67–73, 93–96 (32 receipts).

[18] See Cooper (1654), pp. 1–37, 48–77, 83–87 (67 receipts, for meat, fish and vegetables in sauce); 'The Compleat Cook' (1984), passim (44 receipts).

its increased use of anchovy, than the first. It is perhaps easier to follow these shifts in flavouring by looking at different versions of a receipt for roasted shoulder of mutton stuffed with oysters. In 1615, Markham adds a sauce of dried fruit, sugar and verjuice. In 1653, *A True Gentlewomans Delight* adds dried fruit to the oysters in the stuffing, but the sauce is made from white wine, butter and oysters. In 1654, Cooper eliminates the sweet ingredients and makes a sauce of the meat juices, oysters and their liquor, white wine, vinegar and citrus juice.[19]

But even where the sugar-acid component is still present, the impression is that sauces were becoming less aggressive than in the past, although the unsweetened sauces seem more acid than we might like. Two examples of receipts, one of the older style and one of the new, will illustrate this. The first is for a 'Frigasie of Chickens':

> Kill your Chickens, pull skin and feathers off together, cut them in thin slices, season them with Thyme and Lemon minced, Nutmeg and Salt, a handful of Sorrel minced, and then fry it well with six spoonfuls of water, and some fresh Butter, when its tender take three spoonfuls of Verjuice, one spoonfull of Sugar, beat it together, so dish it with sippets about.[20]

This is quite close to Markham's receipt, quoted above; what it does make clear is that the sugar is used to temper the acidity of the sauce rather than to produce a sweet and sour flavour. The second, a 'Frikese of a loyne of Veale' shows the new flavour combinations:

> Cut your loyne of Veale into thin steakes, … then beat it … as thin as you can, then prepare greene toppes of Thyme, a handfull of Capers, two or three Anchoves, an Onion; mince these together very small, and put to it a sliced Nutmeg, a little beaten Pepper and Salt; then hack a handfull of Sorrell and Parsley together, but do not mince it small; fry your Veale in butter, … put to the Veale about a quart of strong Broth or Wine, with the Ingredients which you minced small, and fry it in the

---

[19] See Markham (1615), pp. 55–56; *A True Gentlewomans Delight* (1653), p. 11; Cooper (1654), pp. 48–49.
[20] *A True Gentlewomans Delight* (1653), pp. 93–94.

pan till half consumed; then put in your Sorrel and Vinegar, frying it a
little longer; when you think it is well, put into it a minced Lemmon or
two, with halfe a pound of Butter: …[T]his being ready, … garnish it
with Lemmon, Barberries, and tostes in the dish, … sippit it and serve
it up hot to the Table.[21]

The association of flavours is similar to that in La Varenne, but certain differences stand out: the larger number of ingredients, the use of anchovy and the
final garnish of lemon, barberries and sippets (slices of toasted bread) are part
of English habits throughout the sixteenth and seventeenth centuries.[22]

One change which was taking place is hardly visible in cookery books.
Household accounts show that consumption of fruit and vegetables was rising
by the middle of the seventeenth century. In the kitchen and pantry books of
the Savile household, the references to these items are rare before 1630, but in
the 1630s and 1640s there was a widening of purchases to include more fruit.
After the Restoration there was a still greater variety of both fruit and vegetables.[23] A similar picture is obtained from the account books of the Bedford
family at Woburn and in London in the 1650s and 1660s when large quantities
of fruit and vegetables were bought from outside the estate. For example, in
one week in June 1663, these included pippins, cherries, gooseberries, strawberries, white and red currants, raspberries, oranges and lemons. The list of
vegetables and herbs mentions peas, artichokes, cucumbers, carrots, turnips,
asparagus, lettuce, sorrel, parsley, onions and potherbs.[24] Yet there are still very
few receipts for vegetables as such in cookery books. In 1654, Cooper gives
suggestions for stewed artichokes and potatoes (which would be sweet potatoes
at this date), and for fried artichokes, skirrets, mushrooms and beans; of these,
only the mushrooms are not sweet.[25] The 1665 edition of Robert May includes
a few vegetables in the chapter on 'Pottages for Fish-Days', and here the buttered peas, asparagus, cauliflower, cucumbers, and beans are dressed with salt
and pepper rather than turned into sweet dishes.[26] Although these receipts are

---

[21] Cooper (1654), pp. 67–68.

[22] For the use of barberries, see Wilson, *Food and Drink in Britain* (1976), pp. 306, 320.

[23] Phillips, 'The Diet of the Savile Household in the Seventeenth Century' (1959), pp. 64–5, 67–70.

[24] See Thomson, *Life in a Noble Household* (1937), pp. 138, 145.

[25] Cooper (1654), pp. 35–37, 74–78.

[26] May (1994), pp. 421, 427–29.

not very numerous, their changing nature indicates that another aspect of the culinary revolution was taking hold.

While the books mentioned show the beginnings of French influence, France was not yet the dominant model. 'The Compleat Cook' gives receipts for Spanish, Portuguese, Italian, Turkish and Persian dishes,[27] and Robert May states in his preface that he has included the best receipts from France, Spain and Italy. This international outlook is what distinguishes May's book, the work of a professional cook, from those drawn from ladies' manuscript collections. In many ways, however, it merely offers a more developed and elaborate version of the ladies' style, and this is particularly obvious in the sections on baking. May was conscious of belonging to a European tradition, but he was worried by the rising prestige of French cuisine, and his preface attacks the influence of French cooks on the English aristocracy:

> The *French by their Insinuations*, … have bewitcht some of the *Gallants of our Nation* with Epigram Dishes, smoak't rather then drest, so strangely to captivate the *Gusto*, their *Mushroom'd Experiences* for Sauce rather then Diet, for the *generality* howsoever called *A la mode*, not being worthy of taken notice on.

He was right to be worried. French influence was rampant. A sign of the times was when the newly-ennobled Earl of Sandwich told Pepys that he intended to adopt the aristocratic lifestyle and employ a French cook; Pepys' comment was that he had become a 'perfect courtier'.[28] French cuisine was *de rigueur*, and one of the posthumous reproaches aimed at Cromwell was that he had not served French dishes at his table; the Lord Protector had not known how to play the prince.[29]

It seems from the books by Cooper and May that English cooks were well aware of what was going on across the Channel, and were quite capable of

---

[27] 'The Compleat Cook', pp. 30, 56, 58, 77, 87.

[28] Pepys, *Diary*, vol. 1, p. 269 (20 October 1660).

[29] This accusation appears in the Royalist satirical cookery book, *The Court and Kitchin of Elizabeth, Commonly called Joan Cromwel* (1664), pp. 30-32. Contrary to what some historians apparently believe, these receipts are not by Elizabeth Cromwell at all; the book contains gaps and repetitions in the pagination, and is cobbled up from bits of other cookery books, including, ironically, 'The Compleat Cook'. Its *raison d'être* is its disobliging comments on the Protector and his wife.

incorporating the new combinations of flavours into their own repertoire, without abandoning the older style. Exactly when the new fashion took over and ousted the old is difficult to determine, since the cookery books by professional cooks or by those close to court circles such as Sir Kenelm Digby represent the earliest phase of French influence. To see the newest developments at work one must look beyond the printed book. One significant moment comes in 1674, when Charles II signed a warrant to appoint 'a Pottagier or a french Cooke for the making of Pottages for Our Dyet' over and above the normal complement of servants in the King's privy kitchen; the new man, 'John Tattau alias La Brie', was duly appointed on 9 December.[30] The term 'pottages' included the grand court dishes, the bisks, olios and terrines, which were the key elements of the court style of cookery currently being created in France. The fact that it was felt necessary to recruit a Frenchman suggests that English cooks (the King's master cook at this date was John Sayers) had not kept up with the latest tendencies. It is also eloquent of how far the prestige of Versailles contributed to impose French cuisine on all the courts of Europe. The French fashions that arrived with the Restoration were not yet those of the 1670s and later, when the culinary revolution initiated by La Varenne had finally ousted the older style.

There can be no doubt about the domination of French fashions, whether in food, dress or deportment. Restoration comedies show the gallants of the period adopting French modes, as well as spirited heroines who enjoy the pleasures of London society and witty conversation: not for them a life in the country, sewing and preserving and keeping up the family receipt book. Of course, one should not take such literary representations as reality, but the changing image of the fashionable lady, which was to have an important influence on the development of the cookery book in the eighteenth century, begins here.

In the 1660s and 1670s cookery book production continued unabated, with eight new titles per decade; thereafter, however, the number of new works declined, dropping to five in the 1680s and three in the 1690s. The main period of revelations from aristocratic kitchens was from 1650 to 1670; after this, there are signs that the sources were drying up. One of the last such books was by Sir Kenelm Digby, whose manuscript receipt collection was published after his death, in 1669. The book was calculated to appeal to the socially ambitious,

---

[30] PRO LS 13/253, f. 55.

since it is larded with French terms, and Digby's intimacy with the great of the time enabled him to add such throwaway remarks as 'My Lady of Portland told me since, that she finds Neats-tongues to be the best flesh for Pies', and to supply the reader with receipts to make 'Hydromel as I made it weak for the Queen Mother', or 'The Queens Hotchpot from her Escuyer de Cuisine, Mr. La Montague'.[31] The demand for such receipts was still strong: not only was there Digby, but reprints of the Countess of Kent's and Henrietta Maria's books continued to sell, and were very popular. The evidence for this lies not simply in the number of editions, but in the fact that ladies copied out receipts from these books into their own manuscript collections. Examples are found in the collection by Rebecca Price (1660–1740), the daughter of an upwardly-mobile family which had made a fortune in London and moved out to join the country gentry. She began her work in 1681 with material from relatives and friends. Although she kept adding to the manuscript until at least 1710, many of the receipts were given by people of her parents' generation, and were thus probably first copied out before the starting-date of the manuscript. Several of Rebecca's donors (449 receipts out of 556 give the name of the donor) took items from *The Queens Closet Opened*: Lady Sheldon (wife of the Lord Mayor of London in 1675) took two receipts for fish and one for goose, and adapted a receipt for a cream; Rebecca's two Clerke cousins adapted several of its receipts; as did two unidentified ladies, Mrs Lord and Mrs Whitehead.[32] This copying shows how receipts circulated from manuscript to print and back to manuscript; in other words, printed cookery books simply reproduced on a larger scale the established mode of transmission of new receipts. Exchanges between manuscript and print were not entirely in one direction, and each enriched the other.[33]

---

[31] Digby, *The Closet Of the Eminently Learned Sir Kenelme Digbie Kt. Opened* (1669; repr. 1997), pp. 129, 26, 125.

[32] Compare Masson (ed.), *The Compleat Cook* (1974), pp; 69, 62, 79, 162–63, and W.M. (1984), 'The Compleat Cook' pp. 7, 46, 102–3, 65, 73–4 (Lady Sheldon's borrowings); Masson, pp. 86–7, 146, 155, 165, and W.M., 'The Compleat Cook' pp. 45, 71–2, 13, 32–3 (the Clerkes' adaptations); Masson, pp. 264–5, 255, and W.M., 'The Compleat Cook' pp. 116–7, 'A Queens Delight' p. 69 (Mrs Lord and Mrs Whitehead's adaptations).

[33] For a more extensive discussion of these exchanges between manuscript and print, see Lehmann, 'Echanges entre livres de cuisine imprimés et recueils de recettes manuscrits en Angleterre, 1660–1730' (1996).

The most prolific author of the period 1660–1675 is Hannah Woolley, the first woman writer to proclaim herself as such on the title-page of her books. Woolley produced four books, beginning with *The Ladies Directory*, dealing with confectionery and remedies, in 1661; this was followed by a book of cookery, *The Cooks Guide*, in 1664. The way the receipts are arranged in this, in small groups of related preparations but otherwise at random, suggests that Woolley simply transcribed a manuscript collection, perhaps her own, perhaps belonging to one of her employers. After a gap of six years, Woolley produced two more titles in quick succession: *The Queen-like Closet* (1670) and *The Ladies Delight* (1672), which is in fact a reprint of her first two books as one volume. Finally, *The Gentlewomans Companion*, a book which combines cookery and conduct advice, appeared in 1673, bearing Woolley's name but apparently the result of a fraudulent transformation of her manuscript by the publisher, Dorman Newman. She is important as the first woman to try to make money, if not a living, from writing cookery books.

She was not, however, the only woman author to put her name forward on the title-page. In 1678 Mary Tillinghast produced a small book of pastry-work 'for the Use of her Scholars'.[34] The owners of cookery schools (which often specialized in baking) produced several small cookery books in London between this date and 1750, but the tradition lasted much longer in the north of England and in Scotland, where one finds such works until the end of the eighteenth century. Another anonymous book, 'for my Scholars', this time dealing with confectionery, appeared in 1681,[35] and M.H.'s *The Young Cooks Monitor*, a more general work, again 'for the Use and Benefit of my Scholars', appeared in 1683. Otherwise, a few new titles appeared, one of them another translation from French, of *L'Escole parfaite des officiers de bouche* (1662), rendered somewhat ineptly as *A perfect School of Instructions for the Officers of the Mouth* (1682). The translation was signed by Giles Rose, who describes himself as 'one of the Master Cooks in His Majesties Kitchen', but who was in fact at this date one of the yeomen in the household kitchen.[36] One of the last books to evoke 'secret' aristocratic receipts was *The Accomplished Ladies Rich Closet of Rarities*, which probably came out in the early 1680s, since the second edition dates from 1687. Although the preface is signed by John Shirley, at least

---

[34] Tillinghast, *Rare and Excellent Receipts* (1690), title-page.

[35] See Oxford (1979), p. 40.

[36] PRO LS 13/254, f. 35v.

part of it was lifted from Hannah Woolley.[37] Several other books plagiarized Woolley, amongst them *The Accomplish'd Lady's Delight* (1675), which was signed by T.P., and the anonymous *Compleat Servant Maid* (1677).

These plagiarisms confirm Woolley's position as the dominant figure amongst cookery authors. What is known of her comes from the brief autobiography in *The Gentlewomans Companion* and the slightly different version given in the supplement to later editions of *The Queen-like Closet*.[38] Since the first of these works was transformed by the publisher, the version contained in the supplement must be preferred. According to this, Woolley learned household skills from her mother and elder sisters; then, at the age of seventeen, she was taken up by a noble lady who recognized her talent and bought her ingredients and books. She stayed with this lady for seven years, and then, aged twenty-four, left to marry Woolley, who was the master of a free school at Newport Pond in Essex; after seven years they moved to Hackney, where they kept a school and had over 60 boarders. No more details are given, although the alternative version does say that her husband and children died, and she herself became ill and impoverished. The information she gives may be supplemented by the dates of her two marriages, the first to Woolley in 1647, which ended in widowhood with four sons to support; the second to Francis Challinor in 1666.[39] If, as she says, she was married at the age of 24, she was born in 1623, and learned her skills at home and then honed them in the 1640s while she was employed by the noble lady. In the early 1660s, during her widowhood, she may have worked in the household of Lady Anne Wroth and her daughter Mary, to whom *The Cooks Guide* is dedicated. What does seem certain is that her books were part of an attempt to make money; she complained bitterly about the underhand practices of the publisher of *The Gentlewomans Companion*, Dorman Newman, whose transformed version of her text would, she claimed, endanger her reputation;[40] and she used her books

---

[37] See Oxford (1979), pp. 43–4.

[38] See Woolley, *The Gentlewomans Companion* (1673), pp. 10–14; *The Queen-like Closet* (1684), supplement, pp. 8–12.

[39] See Parry (ed.), *Chambers Biographical Dictionary of Women* (1996).

[40] Woolley (1684), supplement, pp. 60–1, 93–4. She accuses Newman of employing another author to transform her book, *The Ladies Guide*, which she had written and was selling for 12d. and which he brought out and sold for 2s. 6d. Her complaint is that with her name to the book, her reputation as an author will be ruined by the changed text. But in spite of her rejection of the changes made by Newman, when the second edition of *The Gentlewomans Companion* came out in 1675, published by Edward Thomas and bearing her name as author, the text was identical to that of the first.

to advertise her services as a teacher of embroidery and preserving. Woolley herself was educated in the skills of a gentlewoman but was forced to trade these skills to make a living.

The advice in *The Gentlewomans Companion* (which may be based on Woolley's original manuscript, by virtue of many similarities to *The Queen-like Closet*) provides a glimpse of the changes at work in women's lives. Directed at gentlewomen – either impoverished and sliding down the social scale, or only just scrambling up to join the ranks of the gentry – there are directions to mistresses, advising them how to behave and how to direct servants, as well as to servants, telling them what is expected of them in different positions. These latter are presumed gentlewomen who 'though well born are notwithstanding by indigency necessitated to serve some person of Quality'.[41] In an earlier book, Woolley had attributed this problem of impoverished gentlewomen to 'the late Calamities, viz. the Late Wars, Plague, and Fire'.[42] (Modern historians might be more inclined to attribute the problem of unprovided-for girls to demographic factors: more upper-class girls were remaining unmarried by the end of the seventeenth century than at the beginning.[43]) It is clear from the directions to waiting-gentlewomen and housekeepers that the tasks of preserving and distilling, once shared by the mistress and her servants, were now being undertaken by servants alone, and that these upper servants prepared the dishes for the banquet course. Even ministering to the local poor was now becoming a job for the servant, since 'all good and charitable Ladies do make this part of their House-keepers business.'[44]

Woolley's own career, and the advice in her books, shows that the assumption that cookery book readers were drawn from the ranks of the country gentry was no longer entirely valid. And although *The Gentlewomans Companion* gives advice to those who hope to serve the aristocracy, the author also mentions the more arduous duties of servants working for 'Gentle-women in City and Country'.[45] Another sign of the cookery book reaching a new audience is the way in which writers such as Woolley adapted aristocratic fashions to the means of an aspiring middle class striving for gentility.

---

[41] Woolley (1673), p. 204.

[42] Woolley, *The Queen-like Closet* (1670), p. 379.

[43] See Stone, *The Family, Sex and Marriage* (1977), pp. 43–47.

[44] Woolley (1673), p. 207; for other directions see pp. 205–6.

[45] Woolley (1673), p. 207.

Occasionally there are signs that such readers might reject aristocratic cookery: the adaptor of *The Gentlewomans Companion* lifted all the cookery receipts from Robert May (here Woolley's own hand is totally absent), but one receipt, for a complicated bisque, concludes by denigrating the whole thing:

> Gentlewomen, I must crave your pardon, since I know I have tired your patience in the description of a Dish, which though it be frequently used in Noblemens houses, and with all this cost and trouble put together by some rare whimsical *French* cook, yet I cannot approve of it, but must call it a Miscellaneous hodg-podg of studied vanity; and I have here inserted it not for your imitation, but admiration.[46]

On the whole, however, the tendency is to adapt the complex receipts of aristocratic cookery to make them more accessible. Perhaps because Woolley recognized that her books would be read by fairly modest readers, she gives receipts which would enable the reader to be in fashion by imitating French dishes (the title-page of *The Cooks Guide* promises to give the reader 'the best Directions for all manner of Kickshaws, and the most Ho good Sawces'); and in *The Queen-like Closet*, she offers simplified versions of court dishes: for instance, an olio is composed of various meats and birds, cooked separately and assembled for service, whereas French receipts and English ones by authors like May tell the cook to stew all the ingredients together.[47] The flavours of Woolley's dishes are a mix of the old and the new: in the 87 receipts for meat, fish and vegetables in sauce in *The Queen-like Closet*, sugar or dried fruit are used in 30 per cent, verjuice and vinegar in 30 per cent, but the dominant flavours are wine (53 per cent) and anchovy (34 per cent).[48] A typical receipt representing the new flavours is the following for soles:

> Take one pair of your largest Soals, and flay them on both sides, then fry them, ... then lay them into a Dish, and put into them some Butter, Claret Wine and two Anchovies, cover them with another Dish, and set them over a Chafingdish of Coals, and let them stew a while, then serve

---

[46] Woolley (1673), p. 121.

[47] See Woolley (1670), p. 197.

[48] Ibid., pp. 183–344.

them to the Table, garnish your Dish with Orange or Limon, and squeeze some over them.[49]

The anchovy-wine combination and the simple garnish of slices of fruit gives an example of the way in which the ladies' receipts adapted the French style to modest kitchens. Thus the 'domestic' version of the new cookery adopted the new flavours while rejecting the extravagant complexity being developed by the men-cooks.

Woolley's receipts show a mix of old and new, but manuscript cookery books demonstrate that the pace of elimination of the old was speeding up. Rebecca Price's manuscript is remarkably modern, even though some of the receipts date back to before the Restoration. The difference between savoury and sweet is established, and the dominant flavour in the savoury dishes is the anchovy-wine combination. In the 90 receipts for savoury dishes and sauces, 42 per cent contain wine, 56 per cent anchovy; sugar or dried fruit are present in only 6 per cent. Another novelty is the five cream sauces, a great rarity in printed cookery books before 1700. Price's manuscript includes a receipt for an olio: like Woolley's, it is an assembly, since the vast quantities of different meats could not possibly be cooked together in a mere gentry kitchen.[50] Even so, the dish is impressive, and others also imitate the lavishly-garnished court style which was emerging and which would appear in printed cookery books at the beginning of the eighteenth century. A typical example of the more modest dishes in this collection is the following for 'Scotch-collops', a dish found in every eighteenth-century cookery book, although the flavours here belong to the Restoration:

> Take some leane of the veal and cutt it in thyne slices, and beat them with the back of your knife, then lay them all night in claret-wine, then frye them browne in butter, and some great pickled oysters with them, then frye some slices of bacon also browne, then take it out of the pan and stew it altogether in the claret it was steeped in, with some sliced nutmeg, two anchovies, and mushrooms (if you have them) and so serve it.[51]

---

[49] Ibid., p. 212.

[50] See Masson (1974), p. 90.

[51] Masson (1974), p. 97. The receipt came from 'Aunt Rye'.

Another manuscript which is more 'modern' than the printed books is that of Ann Blencowe, dated 1694. Here too, flavours are new-style, and the garnished soups, 'Beef à la mode' and 'Dobe' all show that French court-cookery was being widely imitated.[52] In spite of exchanges with printed cookery books, some manuscript collections were well ahead of published works in adopting new fashions.

Changing culinary fashions went hand in hand with changes in the way meals were served and eaten. The bill of fare now mixed meat and fish, fast-days and Lent having disappeared from the English calendar: even Robert May, a Catholic, gives just one bill of fare 'formerly used in Fasting days', and William Rabisha tells the reader that he may mix fish and flesh as he pleases.[53] These cooks' bills of fare tend to be lavish, but May gives some more modest suggestions after his feasts for the end of the year. A feature of all his recommendations is that the two courses have the same number of dishes, but with extras often tacked on to the end of the second course. The old rule of 'gross' meats first prevails; salads, where present, appear only at the first course; dishes classified as pottages, including olios, hashes, and fricassees, also appear only at the first course; pies appear at both courses. The bills of fare in Hannah Woolley's various books follow similar rules but the number of dishes at each course is sometimes the same, sometimes variable. An important difference is that whereas May's bills show venison, whether roast or as a pasty, as always a first-course dish, Woolley's place it in the first course for dinners designed for the nobility, but at the second for lesser mortals; for these humbler diners, where both pasty and roast are proposed, the pasty comes in at the first course, the roast at the second. The logic of this is that of prestige: the haunch was a status symbol, and was thus a delicacy to be kept for the second course amongst the gentry – the venison in a pasty might well be beef.[54] Although these bills of fare are closer to French ones than in the past, the 'food hierarchy' was different in England, and pies and puddings fell outside the rules of French menu-planning.

---

[52] See *The Receipt Book of Mrs. Ann Blencowe, A.D. 1694* (1925), pp. 8, 19, 24, 25–6, 26–7, 30–1.

[53] May (1660), in the bills of fare; Rabisha, *The whole Body of Cookery dissected* (1661), in the bills of fare.

[54] Woolley gives bills of fare in *The Queen-like Closet* (1670) and in *The Ladies Delight* (1672). For more on venison as a 'social meat', and the case of the fraudulent venison pasty, see Lehmann & Perez Siscar, 'Food and Drink at the Restoration' (1998), pp. 16–17.

Important changes had taken place in the serving of meals. The feast as spectacle still continued, and the banquet had made some form of display accessible to more people, but the grand feasts at court were now a show of baroque profusion, such as the ambigue of 99 cold dishes and 46 hot (with a further 30 hot dishes for the second course) for the coronation of James II in 1685, or the more modest feast for the Garter ceremonies in 1671, where the King's table was served with two courses of 20 dishes each, followed by a banquet which included ice-cream.[55] A more significant change for most people at the Restoration was in table-manners, as the fork began to win acceptance. Books of advice on correct behaviour show that the fork was by no means universally used, but in polite society it was becoming obligatory for carving and serving others. This laid a particular burden on the lady of the house, who was now the carver: she had to manipulate a fork with dexterity instead of using her hands and sucking them during the process, which might disgust other diners, according to *The Gentlewomans Companion*; this was not just exaggeration, since Pepys records his disgust at his aunt's 'greasy manner of carving'.[56] The mistress also had to understand the rules of precedence, in order to distribute the best pieces first to the most important guests. There is no evidence whatsoever to suggest that dishes were handed round in succession by servants: all the advice in the conduct-books shows that the mistress presided and carved, but where the food required no carving, the guests were expected to help themselves and their neighbours from the dish, while still respecting the rules of precedence.[57] Although some conduct-books told the reader to eat from his own plate with a fork, they also told him to wipe his spoon before putting it into the communal dish in order not to offend the 'delicate', and to wipe his hands on his napkin rather than on the tablecloth.[58] Our form of 'civilized' behaviour, with its invisible barriers between individuals, was only in its infancy.

---

[55] See Sandford, *A History of the Coronation* (1687), pp. 108–11; Ashmole, *The Institution, Laws and Ceremonies of the most Noble Order of the Garter* (1672), pp. 608–612, and the more accessible account of the feast in Day (2000), pp. 33–37. The 'ambigue' was a meal where hot and cold, savoury and sweet dishes were all served simultaneously.

[56] Woolley (1673), pp. 65–6; Pepys, *Diary*, vol. 4, pp. 107–8.

[57] See, for instance, Woolley (1673), p. 65; *The Rules of Civility* (1671), pp. 91, 97, 100; *The Ladies Dictionary* (1694), pp. 412–20.

[58] See *The Rules of Civility* (1671), pp. 97–104. The book is a translation of *Nouveau Traité de la civilité* (1671) by Antoine de Courtin.

By the end of the seventeenth century the market for cookery books had widened to include the middle class, at least in London. Just how far down the social scale the cookery book had penetrated is difficult to determine. Gregory King's estimates of income and expenditure in the 1690s show that what may be considered as 'middling' families, spending between £122 and £294 a year, would have between £5 and a little over £16 per head left after food and clothing, the two necessary items which together accounted for the highest proportion of outlay (between 72 and 63 per cent).[1] Although King's figures are probably too low, it does suggest that only the more prosperous shopkeepers and tradesmen would have income sufficient to enable their wives to buy a cookery book, the price of which at this period was between 2s. and 3s., the most common being 2s.[2] Although cookery books were being written with upper servants as well as their mistresses in mind, illiteracy limited the number of potential readers. In the country, only those upper servants drawn from the impoverished gentry were likely to be literate. At Woburn between 1660 and 1700, only two or three of the women servants could write their names. Though one housekeeper, Ann Upton, could write well, her predecessor had been illiterate.[3] In London, servant literacy was probably much higher. Evidence from inventories of cookery book ownership is scanty, although manuscript receipt collections enable us to confirm the popularity of such books as *The Queens Closet Opened*. However, whether the ladies who copied or adapted receipts from this source owned the book itself is impossible to tell. One attested owner of Sir Kenelm Digby's book is Katherine Windham of Felbrigg Hall in Norfolk: her 'note of my Books', dated 24 June 1689, includes 'Mr Kenelm Digby closet'.[4]

The style of the books themselves is perhaps the best guide to readership. An ambitious work like Robert May's, representing the cookery practised in the wealthiest houses, cannot have been of interest to those below the level of the upper gentry or the richest merchants. Men-cook authors assumed they were addressing fellow professionals. William Rabisha stated that he was publishing

---

[1] For King's figures and a discussion of their reliability, see Earle, *The Making of the English Middle Class* (1989), pp. 269–72.

[2] See Arber, *The Term Catalogues, 1668–1709* (1903–6), passim.

[3] See Thomson, *Life in a Noble Household, 1641–1700* (1937), p. 120.

[4] In her memorandum book, Norfolk RO, WKC 6/12.

his receipts for the benefit of 'young Practitioners in this Art'; Giles Rose pointed out that his book contained not only 'imployment for Men' but things of interest to women too: 'ordering of Linnen', and 'the use of the Preserving Pan'.[5] The 'Ladies and Gentlewomen' of Rose's title-page were not expected to be interested in cookery. It was the books by women, which adapted expensive, complicated dishes for more modest kitchens, which attracted a wider readership. The nature of the encyclopaedic books which go beyond cookery also offers an indication of the changing market. In 1615, Markham's *English Hus-wife* offered a homily on the housewife's duties but was essentially a practical guide to running a country household living off its own production. In 1673, *The Gentlewomans Companion* gave its readers an initiation into gentility, with manners and other social advice occupying a large proportion of the text. This is not to say that one type of book replaced the other: Markham was reprinted until 1683, *The Gentlewomans Companion* until 1711, so there was a continuing demand for both types. But the cookery-and-conduct genre aimed at women was new in the 1670s. Thus the men's and the women's books catered to different audiences, and the gap between the two groups would widen in the eighteenth century.

The fashion for collecting receipts which originated in aristocratic houses and which advertised the names of their owners, whether via manuscript or print, was already dying out by the last quarter of the century. This may be a sign of the market expanding downwards, to people less interested in learning how to reproduce aristocratic style, but it also points to a change in fashion. The flood of books offering receipts with names attached had devalued them: by the 1670s, what had once been 'secret' and prestigious was secret no longer, with corresponding loss of cachet. This process of diffusion followed by distortion and devaluation has been analysed by Norbert Elias, and it can be seen at work not just in the area of food, but in every aspect of people's behaviour and consumption at this period. According to Elias, the élite developed its own distinctive style, and then this style was imitated by those below the élite; the more widely the style was imitated, the faster it lost its value as a sign of distinction. Soon the élite adopted a new style, which for a while retained its prestige, and then the cycle of diffusion and devaluation began again. The older style, now rejected by the élite, continued its progress downwards, becoming ever more distorted.[6]

---

[5] Rabisha (1661), address to the reader; Rose (1682), dedication.
[6] See Elias, *The Civilising Process*, vol. 1: *The History of Manners* (1978), pp. 100-101.

In seventeenth-century cookery, this model can be seen at work in the rise and fall of the banquet course. At the beginning of the century, it was still a luxury and, for the lady of the house, a good show conferred prestige, as is seen by the admiring comment on that prepared by Lady Mildmay in honour of James I.[7] But the massive diffusion of confectionery receipts in the 1650s initiated the devaluation of this elegant pastime. By the Restoration a new code of distinction at table was felt to be necessary. This was to be provided by the importation of the new French style, which had co-existed in English cookery books with other foreign imports in the 1650s but which triumphed after 1660. We have already seen that a French cook was part of the lifestyle of the 'perfect courtier' after the Restoration. Since the most important aspect of the French culinary revolution was the separation of sweet and savoury, the adoption of the new style reinforced the loss of prestige of sugar, whether in savoury dishes or as the essential ingredient of the banquet. By the 1680s, the favoured term for the final course of dinner was the French word 'dessert',[8] and fruit was beginning to take over from sugar as the key constituent. Such changes did not take place overnight. Cookery books continued to give instructions for the banquet (Woolley gives detailed instructions for setting it out[9]), and 'banqueting houses' continued to be built in country-house gardens for much time to come.

The phenomenon of a new style of cookery gradually becoming visible while at the same time the old style is still well represented in cookery books will be seen again in the eighteenth century. This is why it is important to look at the authors and readers of the books, because of the time-lag between the introduction of a new fashion amongst the élite and its diffusion down the social scale. Indeed, as the cookery book enlarged its audience downwards, a new style might well become distorted almost beyond recognition before it reached readers at many removes from the upper echelons of society. The cookery books of the later seventeenth century reflect a wide diversity of readers, and the books and the receipts are designed to cater to different groups. It is not surprising that the picture of cookery one obtains should be so heterogeneous and often difficult to interpret. It will be no less complex in the future.

---

[7] Quoted in Mildmay, *A Brief Memoir of the Mildmay Family* (1913), p. 64.

[8] This is the term (spelt 'deseart') used by Rose (1682), p. 125.

[9] Woolley (1670), pp. 379–83.

Part II

Cookery Books,
Authors and Readers
in the Eighteenth Century

ROYAL-COOKERY:

OR, THE

Compleat Court-Cook.

CONTAINING THE

Choiceſt Receipts in all the ſeveral
Branches of Cookery, *viz.* for making of
Soops, Biſques, Olio's, Terrines, Surtouts,
Puptons, Ragoos, Forc'd-Meats, Sauces,
Pattys, Pies, Tarts, Tanſies, Cakes,
Puddings, Jellies, *&c.*

As likewiſe

Forty Plates, curiouſly engraven on Copper,
of the Magnificent Entertainments at Coronations and Inſtalments ; of Balls, Weddings,
&c. at Court ; as likewiſe of City-Feaſts.

To which are added,

Bills of Fare for every Month in the Year.

By PATRICK LAMB, *Eſq;*

Near Fitty Years Maſter-Cook to their late
Majeſties King *Charles* II. King *James* II. King *William* and
Queen *Mary,* and Queen *Anne.*

The Second Edition, with the Addition of ſeveral new
Cuts, and above five Hundred new Receipts, all diſpoſed
Alphabetically.

LONDON:

Printed for *J. Nutt,* and *A. Roper* ; and to be ſold by *B. Nutt*
at the *Middle-Temple-Gate* in *Fleetſtreet,* 1716. Price 6 s.

Title-page of Patrick Lamb, Royal Cookery, *2nd edition, 1716. This exploits the
royal connection to the hilt.*

THE HISTORY OF COOKERY BOOKS IN THE EIGHTEENTH CENTURY IS of a gradual descent down the social scale: aimed largely at the gentry class at the beginning, at the middle classes and a growing readership amongst servants by its end. Perhaps the most striking aspect, comparing England to other countries, notably France, is that authors and readers were very often women. In France, cookery books were usually by professional male cooks who thought they were addressing other men, mostly *maîtres d'hôtel*. Even in the eighteenth century, the best-selling *Cuisinière bourgeoise* by Menon, published in 1746, is the exception rather than the rule, although the fact that it is so overtly aimed at a female readership may be one reason for its success. In England, the feminization of the cookery book was hardly new; as we have already seen, the names of male authors often concealed the fact that the receipts were by women, as far back as the late Elizabethan period, while the first woman author to advertise herself to the public was Hannah Woolley, who produced four, perhaps five books between 1661 and 1673. The women writers of the first half of the eighteenth century were usually discreet about their authorship – E. Smith's *Compleat Housewife* appeared in 1727 with the author's initials on the title-page, her surname appearing only after her death; Hannah Glasse's *Art of Cookery* was announced as 'By a Lady' on the title-page of the first edition in 1747, and her identity was revealed by the insertion of her trade card, and her signature on the title-page, in the fourth edition of 1751. By the 1750s women were putting their names to their works and boasting of their long experience as cooks and housekeepers. Such authors, working as servants, had less to lose in terms of social status by advertising their authorship than their more genteel predecessors; indeed, there was the hope that authorship might bring sufficient rewards to enable a woman to retire from her career as a servant.

The downward trend observable in the status of authors is paralleled by that amongst readers. We have already noted that ownership of cookery books is hard to identify: that wills and inventories seldom give an itemized list of books, rather lumping them together as a single valuation.[1] Although one does find books marked with the owner's name (typical examples are the British Library's copy of the second (1725) edition of Richard Smith's *Court Cookery*, inscribed 'Alicia Snape her book given her by her Grandpapa Joseph : Hayes Feb 16 : 1724', or Elizabeth Pennell's copy of Robert Abbot's *Housekeeper's Valuable Present*, which has the inscription, 'Anne Jones, Dec. 18, 1791' inside the cover[2]), such inscriptions are of little use as the owners are usually unknown to us. Estimates of literacy and the market for books provide some general basis for defining potential readers. Early seventeenth-century book production was small and could be absorbed by a market composed of the gentry, clergy and the professions. By the 1720s production had risen considerably and literacy was more common, particularly among women. The percentage of London women unable to sign their names (making a mark instead) drops from 78 per cent in the 1670s to 44 per cent in the 1720s. In East Anglia, the reduction was slighter, from 87 to 74 per cent.[3] In London at least, literacy was the rule rather than the exception among servants in the eighteenth century.[4] Peter Earle suggests that by the end of the seventeenth century, the middle-class (made up of the professions and the commercial classes) was 'almost universally literate', and that books were being produced to cater to their thirst for self-improvement; amongst these were, of course, manuals of cookery.[5] In the north of England, female literacy was also

---

[1] Researchers who have made a systematic study of such documents state that titles of books are hardly ever given. This is the case in the 3,000 probate inventories for the period 1675–1725, and in 300 inventories of the Court of Orphans for the same years, both used by Lorna Weatherill in her *Consumer Behaviour and Material Culture in Britain 1660–1760* (1996); see pp. 7–13, 207. See also the comment on the lack of information in inventories in Cressy, *Literacy and the Social Order* (1980), p. 49.

[2] Pennell, *My Cookery Books* (1903), p. 165.

[3] See Cressy (1980), pp. 47, 144–149.

[4] Cressy (1980), p. 129; see also Hecht, *The Domestic Servant Class in Eighteenth-Century England* (1956), pp. 216–7. As an example, nearly all of the 4th Duke of Bedford's female servants could write in 1753; the four who could not occupied inferior posts. See Thomson, *The Russells in Bloomsbury 1669–1771* (1940), p. 238. Cressy has also pointed out that literacy and illiteracy were not simply alternatives, but were part of a spectrum; for many girls in charity schools, for instance, reading was taught but not writing, and many people could read print but not handwriting. See Cressy, 'Literacy in context', in Brewer & Porter (1993), pp. 312–13.

[5] Earle, *The Making of the English Middle Class* (1991), p. 10.

rising, particularly in the larger towns: by the period 1720–49, over just 40 per
cent of city women were literate, while in market towns the figure was 31 per cent
and in villages 21 per cent; amongst servants, only 12 per cent were literate over
the period 1640–1750, and all these literate servants worked for the gentry or
upper-middle class.[6]

Another guide to potential readership is price of purchase relative to wages.
During the first third of the century, the cost of a reasonably comprehensive
cookery book ranged from 2s. 6d. to 6s. – although a few cost more, the
highest (exceptionally) being 16s. for Charles Carter's *Complete Practical Cook*
(1730).[7] In the middle of the century, the range was widening, from the 15s.
required to buy the three-volume second edition of Vincent La Chapelle's
Modern Cook in 1736, to the 1s. for Penelope Bradshaw's *Valuable Family Jewel*
in 1748. Such best-sellers as Hannah Glasse's *Art of Cookery* (1747) cost 5s.
bound or 3s. unbound. By the end of the century, the price of more up-market
books – for example Elizabeth Raffald (1769), John Farley (1783) and Mary
Cole (1788) – was 6s., while more modest titles could be bought for 1s., for
instance Elizabeth Price's *New Book of Cookery* (*c*.1780), or even 6d. for
Charlotte Cartwright's *Lady's best Companion* (1789). To make cookery books
more accessible, some were published in monthly parts, such as John Thacker's
Art of Cookery, which came out in monthly sheets in 1746 before being
published as a whole in 1758; or weekly, such as Sarah Jackson's *The Director*
(1754), or Martha Bradley's monumental *British Housewife* (1756) which cost
3d. for each instalment. In comparison, London labourers' and artisans' weekly
wages, which remained fairly stable from 1700 to about 1765, ranged from
approximately £4 for the most skilled trades to 10s. among textile workers, the
lowest-paid of all. From the 1770s, wages rose rapidly, especially in the 1790s.[8]
Estimates of middle-class incomes go from the annual £45–£400 from Gregory
King in 1688 (generally thought too low by modern historians), to the £150–
£1350, with an expenditure of £100–£900, calculated by Joseph Massie in
1760.[9] The upper strata of the middle-classes had more than enough disposable
cash to afford cookery books.

---

[6] See Houston, 'The Development of Literacy: Northern England, 1640–1750' (1982), pp. 208, 210.
[7] Prices for cookery books are known either from the title-pages or from advertisements announcing
new books; these prices are given in Virginia Maclean's bibliography.
[8] See George, *London Life in the Eighteenth Century* (1976), pp. 166–168.
[9] Earle (1991), pp. 269–270.

One occupational group, however, was certainly among the purchasers, despite what seem to us low incomes. Servants' wages, claimed Defoe in 1725, had risen from £2 or less to £6–£8 a year during his lifetime.[10] J.J. Hecht's study shows that a housemaid could earn anything from £4 at the beginning of the century to £11 in the 1790s, whereas a cook's salary ranged from £3 (this is exceptionally low) to £21, and that of a cook-housekeeper from £10 to £25.[11] Since the servant was housed and fed, and usually saved her wages, she might consider it a good investment to buy a cookery book in the hope of working her way up the domestic hierarchy. The records of sales between 1746 and 1784 by the Clays, booksellers in Warwickshire, show that 50 servants bought a total of 70 books during the period. 'How-to' manuals accounted for 29 per cent of these, amongst them several cookery books.[12] Philippa Hayes, housekeeper at Charlecote Park near Stratford-on-Avon, bought Susannah Carter's *Frugal Housewife* for 1s. in 1771 (by this date Mrs Hayes, who had been housekeeper since 1744, had given up her job, although she still lived at Charlecote, where she died in 1772[13]); a draper's maid bought the same book for the same price in 1774; and 'Mr Clarke's servant' (a man) bought two unspecified cookery books for 4s. in 1766. Other servants – an attorney's maid and a widow's man-servant – also bought books aimed at servants: the maid bought Anne Barker's *Complete Servant Maid* for 1s. in 1771, and the manservant 'Johnson's every young woman's companion', which is in fact the first edition of Mary Johnson's *Young Woman's Companion* (1753). The first of these books is a guide to the tasks of different servants, the second contains all sorts of practical information including cookery. Two of the five buyers were men, but they may have been buying on behalf of another (female) servant. It is also possible that Mrs Hayes bought the book for another servant rather than for herself, since she had already retired from her post.

A further indication that cookery books were bought and used by a wide range of social groups is the sheer scale of production. It is now impossible to discover the size of a single edition: modern historians' estimates vary from 1,000

---

[10] Earle (1991), p. 219.

[11] See Hecht (1956), pp. 146–147.

[12] See Fergus, 'Provincial servants' reading in the late eighteenth century' in Raven, Small & Tadmor (1996), pp. 202–225. The table showing purchases is p. 218.

[13] These details about Philippa Hayes are found in Fairfax-Lucy, *Charlecote and the Lucys* (1990), pp. 192, 218.

(or less) to 2,000 copies, but always advert to the lack of reliable information.[14] By taking a fairly arbitrary (but not implausible) figure of 1,250 copies per edition, and multiplying this by the 425 new books plus reprints (excluding editions whose existence is dubious and those printed in Dublin) which appeared between 1700 and 1799, one obtains a total production of 531,250 cookery books.[15] This is enormous: in France, there were an estimated 273,600 volumes between 1700 and 1789, and if one takes the number of titles rather than volumes, the figure is reduced to 186,000.[16] These figures are no more than approximate but they do give an idea of scale. The table by decade in Appendix I shows also how production, both of new titles and of reprints, jumped first in the 1730s and again in the 1750s. The most prolific decade was the 1780s, with a total of over 70 editions published. From 1750 onwards, however, production was consistently high, never falling below 50 editions, against an average of 26 every ten years in the first half of the century.

Such general indications are of some help, but for more detail one must turn to the internal evidence of the books themselves. Authors or booksellers usually included an address to the reader, and these show whom they thought their audience. Further and more telling evidence derives from changes made to later editions in order to adapt to the requirements of the buyers. These, combined with a tally of the relative success of various types of book (gauged by the number of editions), supplies precious information about what really sold well and what did not. Finally, the contents of the books and the tone of the

---

[14] In 1939, Marjorie Plant suggested the figure of 2,000 copies for most eighteenth-century print-runs; see Plant, *The English Book Trade* (1939), p. 94. John Feather agreed with this suggestion in 1985 (Feather, *The Provincial Book Trade in Eighteenth-Century England*, p. 44), but later revised his estimate downwards to 1,000 copies or fewer ('The Seventeenth-century Book Trade', 1993, p. 14). C. J. Mitchell says, 'Most eighteenth-century works were probably printed in editions of 2,000 copies, and usually much smaller, although a few were very much larger. Today it is simply not possible to calculate the size of most editions of most works.' ('Provincial Printing in Eighteenth-Century Britain', 1987, p. 6.) This is hedging one's bets, which is probably all one can do.

[15] These figures are based on the titles and editions in Maclean's bibliography, with the addition of a few unrecorded items I have uncovered. Any editions whose existence is dubious have been excluded. I have included books of cookery and confectionery, and domestic manuals which include a substantial number of receipts, but excluded those which contain only a few receipts, such as H. Kirkpatrick's pamphlet on the potato published in 1796. Given the uncertainty surrounding some books (the number of editions of Penelope Bradshaw's books is difficult to gauge, to say the least), these figures should be seen as estimates.

[16] The figures for France are based on the work of Alain Girard, 'Le Triomphe de la *Cuisinière bourgeoise*' (1977), p. 501.

receipts themselves show that there was not a single type of cookery book, but a multitude of variants designed to appeal to different social and occupational groups.

But before proceeding to an examination of the books, their authors and their readers, period by period, one important point needs to be made. With the greater prosperity of the middle ranks of society, an increasing number of women aspired to become ladies of leisure. Here was a phenomenon often deplored by contemporary commentators, which was not just confined to the gentry class, but spread down to citizens' wives.[17] Certainly, by the end of the century, contemporaries were convinced the model of gentility which excluded housewifery had reached as far down the social scale as tradesmen's wives and daughters. Francis Grose, contrasting past and present tradesmen, commented that once the daughters of such men were taught 'all kinds of needle-work, and at a certain age were initiated into all the culinary secrets of the family, preserved in a manuscript handed down from their great grandmother'. But now, the 'young ladies' learned accomplishments at boarding-school, and 'as to housewifery, they could as soon make a smoke-jack as a pudding.'[18] As the century progressed, more and more women aspired to join the leisured class, and the standard model of femininity became one which no longer included practical involvement in day-to-day cookery. It was seen as more important for a young girl to learn 'accomplishments', such as needlework, music, drawing and painting, and French, than the practicalities of domestic management. This gap in genteel girls' education is seen in cookery books of the 1770s onwards, which often give advice on all sorts of household matters as well as on cookery proper. The ladies' move away from the kitchen and still-room towards the drawing-room is another factor in the cookery book's move down the social scale. This ideological shift which redefined the image of the good housewife is so important that a brief examination of the theory, and how far it became practice, is needed.

This draws us inevitably into the current debate on the theory of 'separate spheres' which proposes that at some point between the late seventeenth and late eighteenth centuries women lost their position as valued members of the world of work, and became confined to the home, the 'private sphere', while

---

[17] Earle (1991), pp. 163–166.
[18] Grose, *The Olio* (1792), pp. 26–28.

men took over entirely the 'public sphere' of business and government. By the nineteenth, the genteel woman's rôle was that of the 'angel in the house'; in fact, she became a prisoner of the image of purely domestic virtue. As Amanda Vickery has recently pointed out, this conveniently ignores the increased opportunities for women's active participation in public forms of social life in the eighteenth century (provided not merely in London but also in the provinces, in the form of assembly-rooms, circulating libraries, pleasure gardens and, of course, shops), and it places too much emphasis on the positive aspects of hard physical work.[19] The brief study which follows is not aimed primarily at taking up a stance in this debate, since it is concerned with the degree to which ladies took an active rôle in the kitchen, but the conclusions do not support the notion of 'separate spheres'. If women did become confined to a purely domestic rôle, one might expect advice literature and cookery books to emphasize the importance of culinary knowledge for the mistress of a family. This is far from being the case. All the evidence points to the ladies' desire to play a managerial rôle from a distance: conduct-books warned against active participation in the kitchen, and by the middle of the century cookery books made a selling-point of the fact that a book could relieve the mistress of the need to teach her servants to cook. Whether such an ideal could be attained in real life was another matter.

As we have seen, the assumption in the seventeenth century was that the lady of the house would be interested in receipts for remedies, confectionery and cookery, in that order. The hierarchy of prestige was very obvious, but even grand ladies, whose gentlewomen did the actual work of preparing waters and preserves, were expected to be able to direct the activities of their servants, and even to join in making some of the sweetmeats and cordials. At upper-gentry level, the mistresses of households did their own preserving, one reason being that sugar was still too expensive an ingredient to be entrusted to a servant.[20] Cookery books were dedicated to ladies, the most spectacular example being, of course, *The Queens Closet Opened* which purported to contain receipts presented to and used by Queen Henrietta Maria. Whether the Queen actually took part in any culinary activities is almost beside the point: the cookery book

---

[19] Vickery (*The Gentleman's Daughter*, 1998) discusses the theory of separate spheres in her introduction, pp. 1–12; on the points above, see particularly pp. 2, 9.

[20] This explanation is advanced in Wilson, 'The Evolution of the Banquet Course', Wilson (1991), p. 31.

was the emblem of the good housewife, and this particular instance offered an example of domestic virtue at the very highest level. But the publication of such collections (and *The Queens Closet Opened* was enormously popular, being reprinted until 1713) ensured such widespread diffusion of the receipts that their prestige was diminished. Cookery was the first item to go: when John Dunton published a miscellany of entertainment and instruction, *The Ladies Dictionary*, in 1694, cookery was deliberately omitted:

> As for the methods and manner of Cookery, we think them no ways convenient to be inserted in this Book, as not so suitable to our purpose; … Ladies very rarely meddling in that affair, or if they do, we are very well assured, it is not very pleasing to their Maids, whose proper Province it is.[21]

Medicine and confectionery, however, were still recommended by this book, and the reader was directed to 'The Queens Closet' and 'The Countess of Kents Secrets', amongst others.[22]

By the early years of the eighteenth century, moralists were already complaining that ladies had abandoned their culinary activities for more frivolous pursuits.[23] At the same time, women were also being offered an image of the ideal wife which made much of her rôle as rational companion to her husband. Defoe proposed setting up an academy for women, in order to 'cultivate the Understandings of the Sex' to equip them for this, and in doing so he implicitly rejected the skills of housewifery:

> I cannot think that God Almighty ever made them so delicate, so glorious Creatures, … with Souls capable of the same Accomplishments with Men, and all to be only Stewards of our Houses, *Cooks and Slaves.*
>
> Not that I am for exalting the Female Government in the least: But, in short, *I wou'd have Men take Women for Companions, and Educate them to be fit for it.*[24]

---

[21] N.H., *The Ladies Dictionary* (1694), p. 420.

[22] N.H. (1694), pp. 90, 106.

[23] See, for instance, the conduct-book by John Essex quoted below (n. 27).

[24] Defoe, *An Essay upon Projects* (1698), pp. 293, 302–303.

Similar ideas were given much wider publicity in such periodicals as the *Tatler* and the *Spectator*, which gave the new and growing middle-class audience a model of fashionable lifestyle. In the well-known number of the *Spectator* where he computes the number of readers of the magazine, Addison points out its relevance to female readers:

> There are none to whom this Paper will be more useful, than to the Female World. I have often thought there has not been sufficient Pains taken in finding out proper Employments and Diversions for the Fair ones. Their Amusements seem contrived for them rather as they are Women, than as they are reasonable Creatures; and are more adapted to the Sex than to the Species. ... Their more serious Occupations are Sowing and Embroidery, and their greatest Drudgery the Preparation of Jellies and Sweet-meats. This, I say, is the State of ordinary Women; tho' I know there are Multitudes of those of a more elevated Life and Conversation, that move in an exalted Sphere of Knowledge and Virtue, that join all the Beauties of the Mind to the Ornaments of Dress, and inspire a kind of Awe and Respect, as well as Love, into their Male-Beholders. I hope to encrease the Number of these by Publishing this daily Paper, which I shall always endeavour to make an innocent if not an improving Entertainment.[25]

The linking of embroidery and confectionery reminds us that both were expensive pastimes open only to the moneyed classes; more importantly, the writer places intellectual and moral attainments above such practical matters. Later essays point to a rejection of cookery, for instance in the request of 'Coquetilla' that the magazine's catalogue of books suitable for a lady's library should contain neither manuals of devotion nor books of housewifery, or in the complaint of an old-fashioned aunt whose nieces devote their time to dress, tea and visits rather than to 'writing out Receipts, or working Beds, Chairs and Hangings' – which leads 'Mr Spectator' ironically to recommend tapestry as a way of keeping women away from such unsuitable subjects of conversation as scandal and politics.[26] There is no question of recommending a return to the family receipt book.

---

[25] *The Spectator*, number 10 (1711).
[26] *The Spectator*, number 92 (1711), number 606 (1714).

Commentators were convinced that upper-class ladies had already abandoned their traditional domestic pursuits; in 1722 one conduct-book for young
girls stigmatizes such behaviour, attributing it to a combination of snobbery
and laziness:

> The great Fatigue, or rather Slavery, of House-keeping … of late Years
> is but too much neglected by Ladies of Fashion, as an Imployment …
> too mean and insignificant for Persons of their Quality; and rather fit
> for Women of inferior Rank and Condition, as Farmers Wives, &c. or,
> at best, is most proper for their House-keepers; when at the same time
> this is only an Excuse for their Laziness.[27]

But even so vigorous an author as this does not suggest that girls should return
to the kitchen: they should merely acquire enough knowledge to be able to
direct their servants.[28] To be a 'lady' was incompatible with taking an active part
in food preparation, a point made forcefully by Eliza Haywood in the 1740s:

> In my opinion, a lady of condition should learn just as much of cookery
> and of work, as to know when she is imposed upon by those she
> employs, in both these necessary occasions, but no more: – to pass too
> much of her time in them, may acquire her the reputation of a *notable
> housewife*, but not of a woman of *fine taste*, or any way qualify her for
> polite conversation, or of entertaining herself agreeably when alone.[29]

By the middle of the eighteenth century, a lady was not expected to join in
such domestic activities, and fiction of all kinds kept this firmly in readers'
minds. Pamela, the eponymous heroine of Richardson's novel, promises before
her marriage to Mr B. that she will continue to assist the housekeeper in preparing cordials and preserves, but afterwards she does no such thing, devoting
her time to more exalted good works, teaching bourgeois virtue to her husband
and children.[30] Dr Johnson devotes a number of the *Rambler* to the fictitious

---

[27] Essex, *The Young Ladies Conduct* (1722), pp. xxxiv–xxxv.   [28] Ibid., p. 88.
[29] [Haywood], *The Female Spectator* (2nd ed., 1748), vol. 3, p. 154. Another author of advice to ladies
tells them to cultivate their minds and not to spend too much time on needlework or cookery; see
Wilkes, *A Letter of Genteel and Moral Advice to a Young Lady* (1740), pp. 96–97, 121–122.
[30] Richardson, *Pamela* (1740–41), Everyman ed., vol. 1, p. 234, vol. 2, passim.

letter from a young girl spending the summer in the country with 'Lady Bustle', an old-fashioned housewife whose proudest possession is her book of receipts; the young girl anxiously asks if she should follow the old lady's example. The tone of the piece makes the answer obvious to every reader.[31] By the 1770s the country lady fussing over her preserves or her dairy had become a stock figure of fun, exploited by Smollett in his creation of Tabitha Bramble in *Humphry Clinker* (1771), and in such periodicals as *The Lady's Magazine*, number 7 (1776), which uses the device of the letter from a young girl spending the summer with her aunt in the country to laugh at old-fashioned domestic activities.

Even the writers of moralizing homilies ceased to exhort women to learn practical housewifely skills: at most, a lady should be capable of directing her servants. Whereas in 1740 Wetenhall Wilkes had invited girls to spend some (explicitly limited) time on cookery and pastry as well as on needlework, drawing, music, singing, gardening and foreign languages, in later decades John Gregory referred vaguely to 'domestic economy', with needlework advised as a way to pass the time, and as a skill to be learned in order to direct others.[32] In 1797, Thomas Gisborne recommended 'virtuous activity' in the domestic sphere, but this did not include cookery, considered as belonging to 'the last age': now, a lady was to devote herself to soothing the fevered brow of her husband, exhausted by his efforts in the public sphere, to educating her children, and to exercising charity towards the neighbouring poor (her own contribution to the 'public sphere', of course).[33] It must be remembered, however, that in all these manuals, 'domestic management' was seen as the 'indispensable duty of a married woman'.[34] What had changed was the nature of her involvement in the domestic economy: her rôle was now purely supervisory, and she needed just enough theoretical knowledge to be able to direct her servants.

The message was clear: a woman who aspired to be a lady should not demean herself by displaying familiarity with kitchen or still-room, now the servants' domain. An example of this image of gentility translated into real life appears in Mrs Thrale's comment on her own obsession with books and children during the early years of her marriage, from 1763 to 1773:

---

[31] Johnson, *The Rambler*, number 51 (1750).

[32] See Wilkes (1740), pp. 121–2; Gregory, *A Father's Letters to his Daughters* (1774), pp. 51–2.

[33] See Gisborne, *An Enquiry into the Duties of the Female Sex* (1797), pp. 10–13, 18–22, 221.

[34] Ibid., p. 271.

We kept the finest table possible at Streatham Park, but ... his wife was
not to think of the kitchen. So I never knew what was for dinner till I
saw it. ... From a gay life my mother held me fast. Those pleasures Mr
Thrale enjoyed alone. ... Driven thus on literature as my sole resource,
no wonder if I loved my books and my children.[35]

It is unlikely that Mrs Thrale would really have enjoyed thinking of the
kitchen, but her social status (or rather, her husband's notions of what was due
to his station) excluded any such idea. Conspicuous leisure was the hallmark
of gentility, and those ladies who did play an important managerial rôle strove
to conceal their industry, since one sign of a well-run household was that it
operated as if by magic.[36]

A few examples of what happened to ladies' manuscript receipt books
suggest that often such collections were no longer being maintained by upper-
class families. By the Restoration, the vogue for collecting receipts from one's
friends and writing their illustrious names against the titles of the receipts had
passed amongst the aristocracy, as these named receipts had now flooded the
market in printed books. Collecting receipts moved lower down the social
scale, just as the printed works enabled those below the aristocracy to share
their secrets. Two volumes which were examined earlier show how interest in
such things was falling off. In 1647 Elinor Fettiplace left her book to her niece,
Anne Horner, and several more receipts were added during the last years of the
century. After these additions, the book ceased to be used, although it was
retained by the family.[37] The Fairfax family book was overtaken by a different
fate. On the death of Rev. Henry Fairfax in 1665, it was handed down the
generations, but not added to until a descendant of Ann Fairfax (Henry's
grand-daughter) gave it to a neighbour, Robert Green, around 1730. He added
much over about forty years.[38] As we shall see in the study of the cookery
books, the impression is that many of the aristocratic receipt collections of the
seventeenth century were passed on to servants – the cooks and housekeepers
who then published them. At gentry level, one still finds manuscript collections
dating from the first half of the eighteenth century, such as Diana Astry's book

[35] Quoted in Stone, *The Family, Sex and Marriage* (1977), p. 459.
[36] See Vickery (1998), p. 131.
[37] See Spurling, *Elinor Fettiplace's Receipt Book* (1986), p. 35.
[38] See Weddell (ed.), *Arcana Fairfaxiana* (1890), pp. xvi–xviii.

which she compiled before her marriage in 1708, then continued to augment.[39] Another belonged to Margaretta Buckeridge (1727/8–1794), the daughter of a gentry family who married Abraham Acworth in 1745. The first 128 receipts were probably written out for her by her mother, but she added to them, exchanging receipts with friends and relatives, until she had about 350 in all.[40]

A more unusual case is that of Katherine Ashe (1652–1729), who married William Windham of Felbrigg in 1669, was widowed in 1689, but did not start her book of receipts until 1707, adding to it until at least 1726; the book covers all aspects of running a country house, from cookery and confectionery to managing poultry and doctoring horses.[41] It is a distillation of her experience, accumulated over forty years and more, and was perhaps compiled for her son Ashe. Later in the century, there is a shift of focus in such manuscript books amongst the prosperous gentry. Caroline Lybbe Powys' book, begun in 1762 and added to until the 1790s, devotes as much space to household hints and hobbies such as japanning and shellwork as to cookery and confectionery.[42] Collections devoted entirely to cookery tend to belong to women lower down the social scale, such as Elizabeth Raper, the daughter of an East India Company merchant, who kept a notebook of receipts in the 1760s, and whose diary comments somewhat ironically on her culinary activities; or Martha Lloyd, the impoverished friend of Jane Austen.[43]

Today, it is hard to gauge what was happening here. The abandoning of earlier receipt collections may well indicate that ladies who had once kept these

---

[39] See Stitt (ed.), 'Diana Astry's Recipe Book' (1957), pp. 83–87.

[40] See the introduction to a selection from this manuscript by Frank and Alice Prochaska, *Margaretta Acworth's Georgian Cookery Book* (1987), pp. 10–15. The manuscript is now PRO C107/108. Unfortunately the editors have chosen to give only about a quarter of the receipts, eliminating all receipts which are 'alien to modern tastes', which is singularly unhelpful to the researcher.

[41] Katherine Windham's collection is now in Norfolk RO, WKC 6/457.

[42] BL Add. MS 42,173. Of the 143 receipts, 40 are for cookery, 13 for preserves, pickles and drinks, 37 for medicines and cosmetics, and 53 for household hints and hobbies.

[43] Elizabeth Raper's receipts and parts of her diary were published in Grant (ed.), *The Receipt Book of Elizabeth Raper* (1924). On 10 June 1757 she noted that she went 'into the kitchen, made a custard and tarts, was very notable' (p. 14). The use of the word 'notable' is clearly ironic, and recalls Eliza Haywood's use of the term. Martha Lloyd's receipts have been published in Hickman (ed.), *A Jane Austen Household Book* (1977), and extracts from her collection appear also in Black & Le Faye (eds), *The Jane Austen Cookbook* (1995). Unfortunately Hickman's transcription is incomplete; she admits to finding some items impossible to decipher, and there are numerous examples of incorrect transcriptions in the receipts she does give.

collections with enthusiasm had now given up such activities; equally, this could be due to changes in culinary fashions, as the older styles became hopelessly out of date. My own researches into this question have been too limited to reach any serious conclusions, but the manuscripts I have examined do point to a move down the social scale of these collections after the early eighteenth century – although it would be unwise to conclude that there were no aristocratic receipt collections by this period. Ladies had plenty of more agreeable ways to spend their time, especially when the circulating library brought vast numbers of novels within their reach. How far such an ideal of leisure could be attained in real life is another matter.

One major obstacle to any lady's desire to abandon culinary activities was the servant problem. Hecht shows the extraordinary mobility of servants,[44] and scattered case-histories reveal how often the mistress had to find a new cook and perhaps teach her the job. Lady Grisell Baillie's household accounts show that in 1717 the new cook arrived on 1 February and stayed for a fortnight; the next candidate spent precisely one night in the house; her replacement lasted ten weeks. It was not until July that Lady Grisell found a cook who endured.[45] She, Ann Griffeth, was paid £7 a year, 'and 8 if she dos well', perhaps signalling her employer's relief. My Lady was well equipped to teach the more elaborate dishes: in 1696 she spent £15 on cookery lessons, and bought cookery books on two occasions, in 1715 and 1731–2.[46]

At a less exalted level, a gentry family in Buckinghamshire in the 1740s experienced similar difficulties. In September 1744 Mrs Purefoy of Shalstone wrote to a friend asking her to help find a cook, which she duly did. The servant was engaged, but before she could take up her post, she returned her half-crown earnest, informing Mrs Purefoy that she was getting married.[47] Working for Mrs Purefoy was no sinecure, as the following letter to the mother of a prospective employee shows:

> I had notice that your Daughter desired to come & live with mee. She must milk 3 or 4 cows & understand how to manage that Dairy, & know how to boyll & roast ffowlls & butcher's meatt. Wee wash once

---

[44] See Hecht (1956), pp. 78–91.

[45] See Scott-Moncrieff, *The Household Book of Lady Grisell Baillie* (1911), pp. 160–161.

[46] Ibid., pp. 37, xlv.

[47] Eland (ed.), *Purefoy Letters 1735–1753* (1931), vol. I, pp. 146–7.

a month, she & the washerwoman wash all but the small linnen …. She helps the other maid wash the rooms, … she makes the Garrett beds & cleans them, & cleans ye great stairs & scours all the Irons & scours the Pewter in use, & wee have an woman to help when 't is all done. There is very good time to do all this, … & when she has done her worke she sits down to spin.[48]

The same problem recurred in 1746, and Mrs Purefoy's letter to Betty Hows suggests that she was resigned to demanding rather less of the new cook:

If you can roast & boyll & help clean an House, & make up Butter, & milk 2 or 3 cows, but you go into the cowhouse to milk, which is near the house, and ye Boy fetches up the Cows. Wee wash once a month, … & you help iron & get up ye Cloaths. If you can do these things wee will endeavour to teach you ye rest of the Cookery.[49]

It is clear that Elizabeth Purefoy played an active part in her kitchen, not only because of the dearth of suitable cook-maids. A letter of 1736 shows her sending '5 dozen of black hog puddings wch I made myself' to the wife of her London agent.[50] Here we have a country housewife of the old school, un-touched by London fashions. Not surprisingly, the only cookery books known to have been in the household's possession are not the most up-to-date: a 'Compleat ffamily Peice' and a 'Compleat Servant Maid' were noted by Elizabeth Purefoy's son Henry in his catalogue of his books made in April 1728[51] – the second can probably be identified as an anonymous work first published in 1677 and reprinted until 1729,[52] but the first (which cannot be the 1736 *Complete Family-Piece*) is impossible to identify, since no such title is known before 1728.

In the late 1770s, after moving to a new house, Susanna Whatman, the wife of a wealthy Kentish papermaker (James Whatman had an annual income of over £6,000), wrote out a manual detailing the duties of her various servants,

---

[48] Eland (1931), vol. 1, p. 147.

[49] Ibid., vol. 1, p. 153.

[50] Ibid., vol. 2, p. 348.

[51] Ibid., vol. 2, p. 273.

[52] See Oxford, *English Cookery Books to the Year 1850* (1979), pp. 39–40.

the object being that her housekeeper should use these instructions to supervise new staff. Although there were six or seven men-servants, the cook was a woman, and there was a total of six female servants. Of the six employed in 1778, four had left by the end of 1779, and at least two of their replacements stayed for less than a year.[53] The instructions concerning the cook show the precise rules laid down by the mistress:

> When a new Cook comes, much attention is necessary till she is got into all the common rules and observances: ... filling the hog pails: washing up butter dish, sallad bowl, etc.: giving an eye to the scowering of saucepans by the Dairy-maid: preserving the water in which the meat is boiled for broth: keeping all her places clean: managing her fire and her kitchen linen: making good bread etc.[54]

In fact, Mrs Whatman depended on the housekeeper to ensure that these rules were obeyed, since the mistress of a household 'can neither afford the time, nor even have it in her power, to see what her servants are about'.[55] By the last decades of the eighteenth century, in an ideally-run home with a full comp-lement of servants, the housekeeper had assumed the rôle of the housewife of the early years of the century; as we shall see, this shift of responsibilities is reflected in the cookery books. Amongst the lesser gentry and the professional class, where one servant combined the functions of cook and housekeeper, the mistress had of necessity to undertake at least part of the supervision of lower servants which was normally done by the housekeeper, and sometimes even had to do some of the work herself. This was the situation of the genteel Lancashire mistresses analysed by Amanda Vickery. Her prime example, Elizabeth Shackleton, experienced exactly the same problems of unreliable servants in the 1770s as did Mrs Purefoy in the 1740s.[56]

The problem of servant mobility was compounded by the ignorance of the servants who were recruited. In 1746 Elizabeth Purefoy recognized that she would have to teach cookery beyond roasting and boiling to her new maid, but

---

[53] Hardyment (ed.), *The Housekeeping Book of Susanna Whatman* (1987), p. 4.
[54] Ibid., p. 44.
[55] Ibid., p. 52.
[56] See Vickery (1998), pp. 129–160; for Elizabeth Shackleton's difficulties, see particularly pp. 136–37.

even such basic knowledge could not be counted on later in the century, as the new model of female education spread down the social scale. A writer in the *London Chronicle* in 1759 complained that the daughters of 'low tradesmen and mechanics' were being sent to boarding-school to learn accomplishments rather than useful skills; the writer, assuming that the natural destiny of such girls was to enter domestic service, recommended an alternative plan:

> I would propose that schools for the education of such girls should be kept by discreet women; those who have been housekeepers in large families would be the properest persons for this purpose; that the young people should be taught submission and humility to their superiors. ... That they should be very well instructed in all kinds of plain work, reading, writing, accounts, pastry, pickling, preserving and other branches of cookery; be taught to weave and wash lace and other linen. Thus instructed, ... they may have a right to expect the kindest treatment from their mistresses; ... whereas young ladies are the most useless of God's creatures.[57]

This was in the city. In the country the situation was no better. The farmer's daughter sitting at her piano in the parlour was a favourite target for moralists and caricaturists, who would have preferred to see her in the kitchen or the dairy.[58] While one should not take such complaints from potential employers too literally, cookery books themselves provide corroborative evidence of the increasing ignorance of servants, and of their mistresses. By the last decades of the century, many mistresses lacked the experience to take on the managerial rôle which was still universally seen as their duty.

The hard realities of difficulties with servants, then, often conspired to force the genteel mistress back to the kitchen despite her preference for the drawing-room, particularly in the countryside, where the household could not rely on buying ready-made dishes. In London, finished dishes could be bought from the cook-shops, and the pastry-cooks and confectioners provided all that was needed for the last course of a smart dinner. By the middle of the century, such

---

[57] *The London Chronicle*, 1759, quoted in Jarrett, *England in the Age of Hogarth* (1976), p. 73.

[58] See Jarrett (1976), p. 73, on Arthur Young's rage at finding a piano in a farmer's parlour; and Stone, *The Family, Sex and Marriage* (1977), pl. 17, which shows 'Farmer Giles and his daughter' grouped around the piano.

services were also available in many provincial towns.[59] On country estates, pickling and preserving, and making home-made wines, were still an important part of the domestic economy; in the 1770s Elizabeth Shackleton recorded many such seasonal activities,[60] which meant more supervision of servants. For the lady who could not delegate to a trusted housekeeper, it was a weary round. There can be little doubt of many women's desire to escape from the drudgery of cooking and teaching new servants. From the 1740s, cookery writers were eager to help. This trend goes hand in hand with the disappearance of some categories of receipt. Family medical prescriptions fell from favour, and there was far less emphasis on sweetmeats by the middle of the century. Each was the result of the increased provision of goods and services by way of trade. The cookery book itself was part of this, enabling women who could not yet aspire to lives of leisure at least to imitate the diet of their betters.

The producers of cookery books, both authors and printers, sought to respond to the changing needs of the reading public, and their efforts supply much information about their readers. The books are also the most important source on the authors, most of whom are obscure. In recent years, after much research, a fuller biography of a small number is possible, for instance Patrick Lamb, Hannah Glasse, William Verral and Elizabeth Raffald. But the most that can be said about the majority is what can be deduced from their title-pages. However, even this must be taken cautiously. Mary Eales, for example, announced that she was 'Confectioner to her late Majesty Queen Anne', but there is no trace of her in the royal household accounts, and the presumption must be that she was an outside supplier to whom the salaried royal confectioners turned for extra items.[61] Similarly, Lydia Fisher was described in the text accompanying the frontispiece to the 24th edition of her *Prudent Housewife* as 'Late Cook & House-keeper to the Duke of Newcastle, Marquis of Rockingham, &c. – upward of 50 Years', but I have been unable to find any sign of her in the household accounts of either the first or the second Duke of Newcastle-under-Lyme; and the complete list of Rockingham's servants, drawn up at his death in 1782, contains no such person.[62] The claims of authors to

---

[59] See Borsay, *The Eighteenth Century Town* (1990), pp. 159–87.

[60] See Vickery (1998), p. 153.

[61] See the introduction to Prospect Books' facsimile reprint of Mary Eales (1985).

[62] The first Duke of Newcastle's household accounts are scattered in various volumes of the Newcastle papers deposited in the British Library, most notably Add. MSS 33,321 (James Waller's

have worked for illustrious patrons were not necessarily spurious, but cannot be taken simply at face-value. Of course, some authors had no hand at all in writing the books which bear their names: the most flagrant example of this is John Farley, who put his name to *The London Art of Cookery* in 1783 although the printer and hack writer Richard Johnson noted that on 1 November 1782 he 'began writing Farley's London Art of Cookery', for which he was paid £21.[63] Nor was Farley the only false author of the day.

Given the nature of the evidence, it would be unthinkable to separate discussion of authors from that of readers. Although the relationship between one sort of author and a certain type of reader is by no means constant, the dominance of a particular group of authors at a given period is a feature of the history of eighteenth-century cookery books. The study which follows is thus organized into three periods, the same as will be used when we examine shifts in culinary styles. The first, from 1700 to 1730, is dominated by the presence of two rival groups, male chefs cooking for the aristocracy or even royalty, and women housewives or cooks working for the gentry. The two groups clearly thought they were addressing different types of reader, but the evidence suggests that this was not true. Between 1730 and 1760, male authors diminished in number while women were in the majority (with an increasing tally publishing from the north of England). From 1760 to 1800 there are once more two distinct groups: male chefs, now working in well-known taverns rather than for the aristocracy, and – the dominant force – professional women, cooks and housekeepers or, in the north of England, owners of cookery schools. These changing patterns correspond to phases in development of the readership.

---

accounts, 1737–54), 33,158 (Sam Burt's accounts, 1742–52), 33,137 (various lists of servants, 1734–5); the second Duke's papers are deposited in Nottingham University Library's MS department; the second Marquis of Rockingham's papers are now in the Sheffield Archives, as the Watson-Wentworth MSS (the list of servants mentioned is MS A1202): I owe the information from the last two repositories to the archivists concerned.

[63] See Targett, 'Richard Johnson or John Farley?' (1998), pp. 31–33. Given that Fiona Lucraft had already shown that Farley's book was plagiarized from a variety of sources ('The London Art of Plagiarism' (1992), pp. 7–24, and 43 (1993), pp. 34–46), there seems little reason to doubt that the real 'author' was indeed Johnson.

The COMPLETE

Practical COOK:

Or, A NEW

SYSTEM

Of the Whole ART and MYSTERY of

COOKERY.

Being a SELECT COLLECTION of

Above Five Hundred RECIPES for Dreffing, after
the moft Curious and Elegant Manner (as well FOREIGN as
ENGLISH) all Kinds of FLESH, FISH, FOWL, &c.

As alfo DIRECTIONS to make all Sorts of excellent *Pottages* and *Soups*,
fine *Paftry*, both fweet and favoury, delicate *Puddings*, exquifite *Sauces*, and rich
Jellies. With the beft RULES for PRESERVING, POTTING, PICKLING, &c.

FITTED FOR ALL OCCASIONS:

But more efpecially for the moft *Grand* and *Sumptuous* ENTERTAINMENTS.

Adorned with Sixty Curious COPPER PLATES;
Exhibiting the full SEASONS of the YEAR, and *Tables* proper for *Every
Month*; As alfo Variety of *large Ovals* and *Rounds*, and *Ambogues*
and *Square Tables* for CORONATION-FEASTS, INSTALMENTS, &c.

The WHOLE intirely NEW;
And none of the RECIPES ever publifhed in any Treatife of this Kind.

Approved by divers of the Prime NOBILITY;
And by feveral MASTERS of the ART and MYSTERY of COOKERY.

By CHARLES CARTER,
Lately Cook to his Grace the Duke of *Argyll*, the Earl of *Pontefract*,
the Lord *Cornwallis*, &c.

LONDON
Printed for W. MEADOWS, in *Cornhill*; C. RIVINGTON, in St. *Paul's
Church-Yard*; and R. HETT, in the *Poultry*. M.DCC.XXX.

Title-page of Charles Carter, The Complete Practical Cook, *1730. Elegant though
it is, it remains overloaded with self-advertisement.*

By the beginning of the eighteenth century, although some books published fifty years earlier were still being reprinted (the last edition of the best-selling *Queens Closet Opened* appeared in 1713, and the Countess of Kent's *Choice Manuall* in 1708), many had disappeared. They had had a remarkably long life: Sir Hugh Plat's *Delightes for Ladies* and Markham's *English Hus-wife* were in print until 1683. The 1680s were a turning-point, with the last reprintings of many authors, such as Robert May and Hannah Woolley. The most popular books from this period seem to have been those purporting to reveal aristocratic ladies' own receipts, rather than those produced by professional cooks such as May and Rabisha, or more humble authors such as Hannah Woolley. The grandiose dishes suggested by May and imitated (somewhat reluctantly) by Hannah Woolley were beginning to seem out of date because of their old-fashioned flavourings. The evidence of manuscript receipt collections points to the adoption of new flavours by the 1680s, at least in gentry circles.

Thus by 1700 there was potential demand for new books. A new generation responded to this, while improving on the poorly organized and presented collections once typical. Although there were exceptions, such as Markham and May, with receipts grouped into sections of like dishes, most earlier works simply reproduced the haphazard arrangement of the manuscripts on which they were based. *The Queens Closet Opened* and Hannah Woolley's first books, for example, show no attempt at re-ordering. One reason for this improvement in arrangement was that cookery books were now being 'manufactured' by the author with a view to publication; not always the case in the past. The presenters of the books derived from ladies' receipts had simply sent a manuscript to the printers without further preparation. Another stimulus was the enormous influence of the first alphabetically-organized manual, the English translation of Massialot's *Cuisinier roïal et bourgeois* (1691), which came out in 1702. Several English books followed its example. Although alphabetical organization was only a passing fashion in English cookery books, the habit did gradually develop of grouping receipts by category, so that by the end of our period this had become a fairly standard feature.

During the years 1700–1730, two groups of authors rivalled each other: male chefs working for the aristocracy or for royalty, and women authors who were either housewives or cooks and housekeepers working in gentry households.

Some books, however, fitted neither category. Two – *The Whole Duty of a Woman* (1701) and *The Accomplish'd Female Instructor* (1704) – offered the same mix of conduct- and cookery-book which characterized *The Gentlewomans Companion* (1673). In both, the still-room is more important than the kitchen, with more remedies, cosmetics and confectionery than cookery. The presenter of the second, R.G., has this to say: 'The curious Art of Preserving, is not only a Recreation, but very commendable in Ladies and Gentlewomen, and highly commends them for their Dexterity.'[1] A similar recommendation introduces the pastry receipts.[2] For this author at least, books concentrating on the still-room were expected to appeal to the ladies of the gentry class, but these early eighteenth-century versions of the traditional compilation were now aimed at less fashionable sectors of the upper classes. *The Pastry-Cook's Vade-Mecum* (1705) suggests such books were useful especially to country ladies: the small number of cookery receipts, explains the preface, are for women hoping to find a place as a cook-maid; the confectionery receipts are for mistresses and servants; and the medical receipts are for those who live too far from a town to have recourse to a doctor, or are unable to afford his fee.[3] The seventeenth-century hierarchy of receipts survives, but the emphasis on utility to the country gentry is new: there is none such in Hannah Woolley. It is also significant that although Mary Eales announced to readers that she was 'Confectioner to her late Majesty Queen Anne,' there was no attempt to suggest that the Queen took any personal interest in the receipts – unlike what W.G. had said of Henrietta Maria in 1655.[4] Nobody expected a grand lady to busy herself in the still-room.

The women who did continue to work in the kitchen and still-room were either cooks and housekeepers or mistresses from lower down the social scale, though still part of the gentry class. Mary Kettilby's cookery book was made up of receipts contributed by 'several hands', as is stated on the title-page. The preface adds more information about potential readers:

---

[1] [R. G.], *The Accomplish'd Female Instructor* (1704), p. 63.

[2] Ibid., p. 104.

[3] *The Pastry-Cook's Vade-Mecum* (1705), preface. Cookery occupies 18 pages out of a total of 100, confectionery 34, and distilling (mostly for medicinal purposes) and remedies 48.

[4] Eales, *Mrs Mary Eales's Receipts* (1718), title-page.

I can assure you, that a Number of very Curious and Delicate Housewives Clubb'd to furnish out this Collection, for the Service of Young and
Unexperienc'd Dames, who may from hence be Instructed in the Polite
Management of their Kitchins, and the Art of Adorning their Tables with
a Splendid Frugality. Nor do I despair but the Use of it may descend into
a Lower Form, and teach Cook-maids at Country Inns to serve us up a
very agreeable Meal, from such Provisions as are Plainest, and always at
hand; instead of Spoiling those which are most Rare and Costly.[5]

The source of the culinary receipts, as so often in the past, was ladies' manuscripts but they are described simply as 'housewives', with no suggestion of
aristocratic connections. The emphasis on frugality also implies a move down
the social scale. Mary Kettilby states that her medical receipts come from 'the
most Eminent Hands in that Profession', presumably via their publications. This
marks the start of a turning-away from family receipt books which had been the
main source of remedies until this date. When a second edition appeared in
1719, it had acquired a new part with additional receipts. Its introductory preface
thanks all the ladies who have taken an interest in the book and contributed new
receipts. It also refers, perhaps somewhat nostalgically, to:

> those Ladies who have so true a Judgment, as to Esteem the Character
> of a good Œconomist, not only consistent with, but becoming and
> ornamental, to the Education and Title of a Gentlewoman.[6]

It also shows that these same ladies continued to make sweetmeats for the
banquet course, since readers had complained of the lack of confectionery
receipts in the first edition:

> What has been represented to me as chiefly deficient in the First *Part*,
> is the want of a sufficient Number of *RECEIPTS*, in the Art of *Preserving
> and Conserving of Sweetmeats*, which is for that Reason more largely
> supply'd in this Second, with such as are admirable in their Kind, and

---

[5] Kettilby, *A Collection of above Three Hundred Receipts in Cookery, Physick and Surgery* (1714), title-
page and preface.
[6] Kettilby, *A Collection of above Three Hundred Receipts* (1719), preface to Part 2.

curious in their Variety, and used by the best and most expert Mistresses in that nice Affair.[7]

In spite of this reassurance to the reader, the second part contains only fourteen receipts for fruit preserves, most of the new section being devoted to cookery.

Another woman aiming at much the same type of reader, whose receipts also came from manuscript sources, was E. Smith. When her *Compleat House-wife* first came out in 1727, it was signed only by the initials E– S–. The surname did not appear until the posthumous 5th edition. She was a profes-sional cook or housekeeper (it is not clear which) working for the aristocracy and gentry:

> What I here present the World with, is the Product of my own Experience, and that for the Space of thirty Years and upwards, during which time, I have been constantly employed in fashionable and noble Families, in which the Provisions ordered according to the following Directions, have had the general Approbation of such as have been at many noble Entertainments.[8]

While presenting the culinary receipts as her own, her remedies came from traditional sources:

> As for the Receipts for Medicines, ... &c. which amount to near two hundred, they are generally Family Receipts, that have never been made publlick; excellent in their Kind, and approved Remedies, which have not been obtained by me but with much Difficulty; and of such Efficacy ... that they have cured when all other Means have failed.[9]

Some of them date back to the middle of the seventeenth century: there are receipts for waters by Lady Allen and Lady Hewet, two ladies also associated in Martha Bradley's *British Housewife*, which contains a large number of receipts

---

[7] Ibid.

[8] E– S–, *The Compleat Housewife* (1728), preface.

[9] Ibid.

from Lady Hewet's manuscript collection, amongst them one attributed to Sir Theodore Mayerne. Lady Allen's water also appears in two Kentish MS collections from the seventeenth and early eighteenth centuries.[10] Smith's medical receipts also contain items by 'Lady Onslow' and 'Denzil Onslow';[11] these are readily identified as Denzil Onslow of Pyrford (1641?–1721), whose table was admired by John Evelyn,[12] and his sister-in-law, Mary Foote (1630–1706), the second wife of Sir Arthur Onslow. Looking back to the tradition of the family receipt book, E. Smith's medical section is one of the last upholders of the old ways. The terms of the preface imply that the author had to prise the receipts away from their owners, suggesting that they were not yet ready to abandon them to a servant. It also informs the reader that the medical part will prove useful to gentlewomen who wish to help their poor country neighbours. In other words, such remedies were no longer used on the family (who would call in the doctor), but on the poor.

The rôle of helpmeet to the poor was moving downwards socially. We have already seen that one author thought ladies would delegate this rôle to their housekeepers, and although some maintained the tradition, such as Lady Anne Wynne whose charitable activities were described after her death in 1748 as 'a rare Example in this extravagant and luxurious Age',[13] it was increasingly the wives of the clergy and other lesser country-dwellers who were ministering to their inferiors. In 1736 James Fretwell of Yorkshire (who is described as a yeoman in his will) wrote a memorial of his mother who had recently died. Amongst her virtues he noted how she helped the sick:

> She was very serviceable to many, by her advice and assistance in times of sickness; and for surgery, she had, for many years, much time imployed that way, in which (by God's blessing) she was very successful.…The poor have a great loss of her, upon this account.[14]

---

[10] E– S– (1728), pp. 219, 221. See also M. Bradley, *The British Housewife* (1756), vol. 1, p. 369, and vol. 2, pp. 605-8, 618. The two manuscripts are by Mary Watts (Kent Archives U49 F15), receipt number 56, and a loose leaf in an early eighteenth-century hand which is part of 'My Lady Rachells booke', attributed to Lady Rachel Fane (Kent Archives U269 F38/2); one of the receipts in this almost exclusively medical collection bears the date 26 November 1650. The two MS receipts are virtually identical.

[11] E– S– (1728), pp. 233, 244.

[12] See Driver (ed.), *John Evelyn, Cook* (1997), p. 18.

[13] See Lewis & Williams, *Private Charity in England, 1747–1757* (1938), p. 41.

[14] Jackson (ed.), 'A Family History begun by James Fretwell' (1877), p. 217.

Such a eulogy shows how the medical sections might be of interest to readers below the level of the gentry; it also helps explain the emphasis on country-dwellers which is a feature of early eighteenth-century books.

Confirmation of this new readership is supplied by Richard Bradley's *Country Housewife and Lady's Director* (1727). This was in fact the third volume of a series. His ambition was to provide a complete guide to domestic economy, writing *The Country Gentleman and Farmer's Monthly Director* (1726), then *The Science of Good Husbandry* (1727). In the first, he solicited contributions from readers in addition to those he had already received from various country ladies.[15] The result was 64 receipts from his readers and 56 from his own collection amassed in the course of travels in England and abroad.[16] Bradley explained at the outset that he was writing for lesser gentry and farmers with an annual income between £300 and £400 – yet who aspired to live as well as those with an income twice as great. Incomes for this level of society are usually put from £200 to £5,000.[17] His cookery book was reasonably priced at 2s. 6d., as was Mary Kettilby's. E. Smith's cost 5s. 6d., placing it among the more expensive produced during the 1720s, when the median price was 4s. 3d.[18]

The preface to the *Country Housewife* explains how Bradley hoped to show his readers how to improve their day-to-day standard of living: he invites them to make greater use of vegetables, and he gives advice on food to take on journeys since the food provided at English inns is so abominable. In 1732 he published a second part, incorporating further suggestions from his readers.[19] (One notices the remarkable similarities between Bradley's and Kettilby's books.) Caroline Davidson's analysis of the social status of the contributors to the two parts shows that of the eighty-two correspondents, five had titles (four of them women), five men emphasized their genteel status by adding 'Esquire' after their names, but most were just plain 'Mr' or 'Mrs' (men outnumbered women, although of course, some husbands may have supplied their wives'

---

[15] See the introduction by Caroline Davidson to the Prospect Books reprint of the 6th (1736) edition (1980), pp. 16–18.

[16] See R. Bradley (1727), pp. viii–ix.

[17] See Burnett, *A History of the Cost of Living* (1969), p. 149.

[18] The prices mentioned here and later are given either on the title-pages of the books themselves, or in advertisements. Known prices are to be found in Maclean's bibliography.

[19] See Bradley (1732), p. 1.

receipts).[20] What is clear is that neither Bradley's nor Kettilby's readers had abandoned all interest in cookery. Quite the contrary: the moralists' complaints were certainly not justified amongst the modest country gentry.

But while these people were not following fashionable lifestyles, they were interested in dishes *à la mode*. Women authors offered them adapted versions of grand court-style dishes, as well as their new savoury flavours, which were the height of fashion at the beginning of the century. They brought a whiff of aristocratic manners to readers at several removes from court circles, while at the same time retaining the traditional mix of cookery, confectionery, cosmetics and remedies which had been a feature of the manuscripts on which their books were still based.

Those who had higher ambitions turned to books which offered a glimpse of aristocratic and royal cuisine. These no longer came from the manuscripts of illustrious personages, but from their servants, the court-cooks. These male chefs form the largest group of authors at this period, and their books are deliberately very different from those of their female rivals. The men's books tend to concentrate on cookery, perhaps adding confectionery, but excluding cosmetics and remedies. As one author puts it:

> I have not indeed filled my Book with Washes and Beautifiers for Ladies, or making of Ale for Country 'Squires, all which is foreign to my Purpose; and a Person that's well acquainted with *Cookery*, cannot be also acquainted in clearing the Skin and the fining of Ale: What I have inserted is noble, handsome, necessary, and plain ....[21]

'Country squires' – the intended readers of Richard Bradley's volumes – are rudely rejected here: the author was aiming higher.

---

[20] See Davidson's introduction (1980), pp. 19–20.

[21] R. Smith, *Court Cookery* (1723), address to the reader. The standard bibliographies give the author's name as Robert; there is, however, no justification for this in any edition of his book. Smith states that he had worked under Patrick Lamb in the royal kitchens for eight years during the reign of William III; a Richard Smith was employed as a turnspit in the household kitchen for about that length of time after his appointment on 30 March 1689: by October 1699 he was receiving a pension as one of the royal servants who were no longer employed (see PRO LS 13/10 f. 14v, LS 13/40, f. 26). If this is the author of the book, he was being creative with the truth: he never worked under Lamb, who was in the King's kitchen, while Richard Smith was a humble turnspit in the household kitchen, under the orders of the master cook there, Henry Smith.

The most eminent, and certainly the most famous, of the court-cooks was Patrick Lamb, whose *Royal Cookery* appeared in 1710, a year after his death. Lamb had been employed in the royal kitchens for many years, as the presenter of his posthumous work did not fail to point out:

> As for the Author of these Sheets, his Name and Character are so well known and establish'd in all the Courts of *Christendom*, that I need observe no more of him, that that he liv'd and dy'd a very great Rarity, having maintain'd his Station at Court, and the Favour of his Prince, for about Fifty Years together ....[22]

In fact, Lamb had joined the royal service on 26 March 1662, as the 'youngest child of the pastry' (with a yearly wage of £2 and board-wages of £10), following in the footsteps of his father, also Patrick Lamb, who was a yeoman of the pastry and who died in 1667, and of his grandfather, James Lamb.[23] By 1672 he had progressed to become a 'child of the Queen's kitchen'; by June 1674 he had moved up to become a groom of the Queen's kitchen; in November 1676 he graduated to the post of sergeant of the pastry, and on 2 August 1677 the warrant making him master cook in the Queen's kitchen was signed.[24] In February 1683 he became first master cook in the King's kitchen on the death of the previous incumbent, John Sayers.[25] When Charles II died and James II came to the throne, new warrants were signed and a new Establishment Book made, and from these we learn that Lamb lost his position as first master cook, since he was

---

[22] Lamb, *Royal Cookery* (1710), preface.

[23] The warrants concerning Patrick Lamb, his father and grandfather are now in the Public Record Office (PRO). A useful, albeit occasionally inaccurate, summary of Lamb's career is given in Aylett & Ordish, *First Catch Your Hare* (1965), pp. 93–106; the remarks on Lamb's book and on court dining are, however, less reliable. The warrant for Lamb's first appointment in 1662 is PRO LS 13/252, f. 238v. A warrant dated 19 January 1683 authorizing our Patrick Lamb to sell liquor and tobacco at the royal palaces mentions that similar warrants were given by James I and by Charles I to his father, Patrick Lamb, and to his grandfather, James Lamb: PRO LS 13/253, f. 94.

[24] See the warrants of Charles II, 1666–1683, for swearing him in on 3 April 1672 (PRO LS 13/252, f. 181) and for authorizing extra boardwages to Lamb in 1672, and for swearing him in again in 1676 and 1677 (PRO LS 13/253, ff. 30, 62, 67). The Establishment Book for June 1674 shows that he was a groom in the Queen's kitchen and a child of the pastry at that date (PRO T 48/10, pp. 196, 197; this book is paginated).

[25] PRO LS/253, f. 94v.

now simultaneously second master cook of the King's privy kitchen at £80 a year (the first master cook was Claude Fourment who earned £150), and sole yeoman of the pastry at £50.[26] After the Glorious Revolution, Lamb regained his position as first master cook of the King's kitchen and first yeoman of the pastry at £150 and £50 a year.[27] In the 1690s Lamb received various passes for travel to France, and was the contractor for victualling the hospitals in Flanders during the 1695 campaign.[28] The arrival of Queen Anne in 1702 did not lead to any changes, and Lamb continued in his two posts until his death in February 1709. At the beginning of March two warrants swore in John Faverall to replace him as first master cook to the Queen and as first yeoman of the pastry.[29]

It is uncertain how well-known Lamb was before the publication of his book, but his name was still famous many years later, as shown by an anecdote in the *Universal Spectator* in 1736, a time when the battle between traditional English food and French '*nouvelle cuisine*' was raging. Lamb, presented as the Duke of Marlborough's cook during his campaigns, invites the cook of one of the marshals of France to a dinner of beef and pudding, which astounds the Frenchman, but Lamb informs him that this is the fare which 'has carried my Countrymen twice through France already' and will do so again, a prophecy vindicated by subsequent English victories.[30] (It is paradoxical to see Lamb presented here as an upholder of good patriotic English fare, since he was one of the leading practioners of French court-style cuisine. The nostalgia-ridden political comparison between the good old days when England went to war and triumphed over France, and the 1730s when Walpole's preoccupation was to steer clear of such conflicts, wasted no time on such inconvenient facts. Eighteenth-century commentators on food invariably looked back to a golden age of beef and pudding, the two patriotic dishes *par excellence*, whenever they wished to contrast English food with insubstantial French raggoos.)

---

[26] For the warrants, see the Cheque Roll of warrants, PRO LS 13/10, ff. 7, 10; for the salaries, see the Establishment Book of James II, from 1 July 1685, PRO T 48/10, pp. 167, 168.

[27] See the warrants of William and Mary, 1689–1701, PRO LS 13/257, p. 3; for the salaries, see the Establishment Book of William and Mary, from 1 April 1689, PRO T 48/10, pp. 220, 221; also LS 13/39, ff. 20, 22.

[28] See CSP Dom. for these details.

[29] For the 1702 warrants re-appointing Lamb on the accession of Queen Anne, see PRO LS 13/258, f. 7. For the warrants appointing Faverall, see LS 13/258, f. 74v, LS 13/259, f. 41.

[30] This piece, entitled 'Essay on Eating', was reproduced in the *Gentleman's Magazine* 6 (1736), pp. 455–456.

The presenter of *Royal Cookery* also strikes a patriotic note, while at the same time emphasizing the grand occasions for which the receipts are destined:

> His [Lamb's] chief Aim was to represent the *Grandeur* of the *English* Court and Nation, by an Instance which lay most within his View and Province: the Magnificence, I mean, of those publick *Regales* made on the more solemn Occasions of admitting Princes to their *Thrones*, Peers to their *Honours*, Ambassadors to their *Audiences*, and Persons of Figure to the Nuptial-Bed. Now, these are Solemnities which call for good Looks and better *Chear* than ordinary; what in other Cases might be justly term'd *Profuseness*, does, in this, change its Name, and become a Debt, both to Custom and Decency: And, in Truth, no Kingdom in the World either deserves, or has acquir'd a better Name, on the score of a frank and hospitable Genius, than this of Great-Britain.[31]

The book does indeed offer a glimpse of court-cookery, with receipts for the most prestigious dishes placed at the outset, some up to six pages long, with instruction on the latest ways of serving. The presenter implies this is a manual for the grandest entertainments, of interest to aristocratic hosts and their clerks of the kitchen (who would have found the 35 copper-plates particularly valuable); the receipts themselves are clearly intended for professionals.[32] One notable owner was Sir Robert Walpole, whose library contained a copy. Whether it ever served a practical purpose is another matter, since he employed a French cook, Solomon Sollis, from 1714 onwards.[33]

The purchaser of Lamb's book was looking for élite cuisine, but the contents might well have been a disappointment. The original contains no more than 87 receipts, for cookery only, and while the beginning is elaborate and fashionable, the book tails off into short prescriptions for ordinary English dishes. When a second edition appeared in 1716, it had been vastly expanded with 'above five Hundred new Receipts'. The aim was to widen the market:

---

[31] Lamb (1710), preface.

[32] See the comments aimed at the cook, such as this, at the end of a receipt for braised lettuce: 'You may stew Sallary or Endive the same way, if the Place where you are can afford it.' Lamb (1710), p. 86.

[33] See Plumb, 'Sir Robert Walpole's Food' (1952), p. 67, and Plumb, *Sir Robert Walpole,* vol. 1 (1956), pp. 272, 273n.

We have endeavour'd to make it of a more general Use than it was before, when it was calculated only for the Kitchens of Princes and Great Men, by adding above five Hundred new Receipts, which not being so expensive as the others, may be useful in those of private Gentlemen likewise.[34]

What the preface did not say is that the new material, and its alphabetical presentation, was borrowed with some adaptation from Massialot's *Court and Country Cook*. A third edition, with more new receipts, allegedly supplied by another royal cook, came out in 1726 and was reprinted in 1731, and this last reprinting may have kept Lamb's name sufficiently in public view to justify the story about him in 1736.

Another book which apparently sold on the strength of the author's name was Henry Howard's *England's Newest Way*, which first appeared in 1703. When the bookseller produced a second edition 'with Additions' in 1708, he informed readers that the first printing had sold in less than a year, and in 1710, for the third edition, he announced yet more additions, to appeal to women:

I have made it my particular Care and Study to find out such other Receipts excellent in their Kind, as may tend to the further Improvement of those that are curious in the necessary and commendable Art of Cookery.... Besides these, I have here added for the sake of that beter [sic] Part of Mankind, the Fair Sex, several choice Receipts for making Beautifying Waters, Oils, Ointments, and Powders. ...

The Receipts you find added in this Edition are singularly good in their Respective Kinds, extracted out of Choice Manuscripts of several Ladies who were particularly Excellent in Cookery and beautifying the Face. As for those in the former Edition, I need not say much, the Name of the Author, Mr. *Howard*, is a sufficient Character for them, besides the speedy Vent of two Impressions.[35]

This is eloquent of changes since the seventeenth century: although the pillaging of ladies' manuscript receipt books continues (and note the use of the

---

[34] Lamb, *Royal-Cookery* (1716), preface.
[35] Howard, *England's Newest Way*, (1710), bookseller's address.

past tense, suggesting that the 'new' receipts were in fact quite old), none of the new receipts carries an attribution to a particular lady; prestige now lies in the name of the cook who, according to the title-page, had worked for such patrons as the Duke of Ormonde. The inclusion of cosmetics, specifically appealing to ladies, implies that female readers were not expected to take much interest in the culinary sections, unlike their earlier counterparts who 'were particularly Excellent in Cookery'. Amongst the purchasers of Howard's book was Lady Grisell Baillie, who bought a copy in 1715 for 2s. At the same time she bought *The Court and Country Cook*, which was much more expensive at 5s., and an unidentified 'book of choise recepts' which cost 2s. 6d.[36] These may have been bought for Lady Grisell's daughter Rachel, who married in 1715, but since Lady Grisell bought more cookery books in the 1730s, they may equally well have been for her own use.

The receipts in Howard are somewhat old-fashioned when compared to the English version of Massialot. The court-cooks' books can be split between those which look back to the seventeenth century and those which follow Massialot's lead. Among the former is T. Hall's *The Queen's Royal Cookery* (1709) whose preface emphasizes that the receipts are new and up-to-date:

> It is not stuff'd with superfluous Trifles, as most of its Nature are; or *with old and antiquated* Receipts; but with Things wholly new and useful, which are daily the Practice of every Nobleman's and Gentleman's Kitchen.[37]

This is hugely misleading, as nearly 40 receipts are lifted from Sir Kenelm Digby, either directly or via the book by his steward, George Hartman. This is the most old-fashioned of all the court-cooks' books, but in spite of this, it went into three editions, being reprinted in 1713 and 1729. Amongst the second group is John Nott's *Cook's and Confectioner's Dictionary* (1723), which was inspired by Massialot, although Nott's source was probably the second edition of Lamb rather than *The Court and Country Cook* itself. One interesting feature is that it is addressed 'To all Good Housewives',[38] whereas his fellow-cooks

---

[36] Scott-Moncrieff (ed.), *The Household Book of Lady Grisell Baillie* (1911), p. 37.

[37] Hall, *The Queen's Royal Cookery*, (1713), preface.

[38] Nott (1723), introduction.

usually addressed the nobility and gentry. Richard Smith was one such, refusing to give cosmetics for ladies or brewing for country squires. His prefatory address is dedicated firmly to 'the Nobility and Gentry of Great Britain'. However, he also took care not to make his book too expensive by adding copper-plates:

> I design'd to have set some Rules for the Ordering of Courses, … but then there must have been Engrav'd Draughts, and that woud [sic] have enhanc'd the Price considerably: Besides, the Generality of Noblemen, and Gentlemens Cooks, will be govern'd by their own Fancies and Judgments; and the inferior People have no Occasion for such Directions, and therefore I laid that Thought aside.[39]

Smith's book cost 3s. 6d., which places it towards the bottom of the price-range for this period. As so often, there is contradiction in his addressing the upper classes while at the same time emphasizing his own efforts to limit the cost of his book. (The style of his receipts places him somewhere between grand court-cookery and its domestic version developed by women authors, and this makes his book very appealing to the modern reader.) Such contradictions will become more marked as the century progresses.

Another court-cook is equally firm in addressing the élite: Charles Carter dedicated *The Complete Practical Cook* (1730) to a well-known gastronome, the Earl of Albemarle. His address to the reader makes clear it is aimed at both the noble employer – who will find the copper-plates useful when it comes to choosing a bill of fare and giving instructions – and at his cook who, armed with the receipts, will be able to give of his best. Naturally, the whole is designed for grand occasions rather than every day:

> The following Rules are chiefly calculated for the more *Grand* and *Sumptuous* Manner of Entertainments; for 'twill be very easy for an *ordinary Cook*, when he is well instructed in the *most Elegant* Parts of his Profession, to *lower his Hand* at any time; and he that can excellently perform in a *Courtly* and *Grand Manner*, will never be at a loss in *any other*.[40]

---

[39] R. Smith, (1723), address to the reader.
[40] Carter, *The Complete Practical Cook* (1730), address to the reader.

He emphasizes the advantage of having employers capable of appreciating the superior talents of a good cook, and his discourse is aimed at raising the status of the cook to that of artist:

> If Gentlemen were made a little acquainted with some of the Sovereign Rules of this Noble Art, they would the less depend upon the *unartful* Management of a dark-proceeding, and often ignorant *Juggler*, who, under the Cloak of Reserving to himself the Secrets of his Profession, is only affecting a sullen, and, perhaps, sawcy *Pre-eminence* in his way, to conceal his Ignorance; which, were it once discover'd, his Noble Master would not, for the Sake of saving a few Pounds *per Annum*, reject a *thorough-pac'd* Artist, and suffer a *Raw*, and perhaps *Tavern-bred Dabbler* in the Science, to waste and destroy the most *costly Ingredients* to no manner of Purpose; and so, of Consequence, a *due Value* would be put upon the *thorough-bred* Artist.[41]

While Carter is making a claim for better pay and consideration, he also implies that an aristocrat's appreciation of the table was part of his connoisseur-ship of the arts, an aspect of the cult of connoisseurship totally neglected by modern historians.[42] There is, however, considerable evidence that keeping a good table was an important aspect of the social and cultural prestige of the great Whig magnates, especially in the period 1730–1760.[43]

Another interesting feature of both Carter's and Smith's presentations is their denunciation of other cookery books. With the large number of titles allegedly by chefs working for the aristocracy or even royalty (seven such authors published between 1700 and 1730) there was inevitably a good deal of borrowing but, according to Smith, shady practice went much further:

---

[41] Ibid.

[42] While it is not surprising that there is no mention of the table in such discussions of English eighteenth-century culture as John Brewer's *The Pleasures of the Imagination* (1997), the lack of more than passing references to food in J. H. Plumb's *Georgian Delights* (1980) is regrettable; even studies which focus on consumption and material culture do not address the question of the table as cultural vehicle: see, for instance, Simon Varey's essay in Porter & Roberts (eds), *Pleasure in the Eighteenth Century* (1996), pp. 36–47.

[43] This point will be discussed at more length in the study of authors and readers in the middle of the century.

It's true, there are several Books of Cookery already extant, but most of 'em very defective and erroneous, and others fill'd with old Receipts, that are impracticable at this Time. I was near eight Years with Mr. *Lamb*, … and therefore knew most of his Receipts and Methods of Dressing; yet several of those Receipts, as they are now printed in His Royal Cookery, were never made or practis'd by him; and others are extreme defective and imperfect, and made up of Ingredients unknown to him; … it's impossible for a Cook to serve up a Dish, if they were only to follow the Receipts now in Being: I was the more inclin'd to print this Book … by finding that several of my Receipts, which I had given to satisfy the Importunity of Friends had been publish'd to the World, as the Labours of other People; and besides that, the material Ingredients, proper to some of them, had been left out. All which Defects I have in the ensuing Receipts supply'd.[44]

Of course, it is hardly surprising that Lamb should never have used many of the receipts in the later editions of his book, given the massive additions and the removal of much of the original text which had transformed *Royal Cookery*. A few years later, Smith's accusations were repeated by Carter in a piece of delicious eighteenth-century prose:

This is almost the only Book that has of late Years been publish'd, the *Recipe*'s whereof are the Result of the Author's *Practice*, and to which the Name of the Writer has been put without any other Consideration than the Publick Service: And the little low Arts used by Persons who have wanted to vamp up *Old Books*, and pass them upon the World for *New*, with the Name of a *Modern Artist* prefix'd, who has had no other hand in the whole, than the extending of it to receive Five or Ten Guineas for the Credit of his Name, are so well known, that I need not descend to Particulars on this Head; nor would I be thought to recommend my own Performances by depreciating those of others.[45]

---

[44] R. Smith (1723), address to the reader.
[45] Carter (1730), address to the reader.

There is evidence his accusations were justified – T. Hall pretended to novelty whilst lifting receipts from Digby – suggesting that unscrupulous booksellers, eager to cash in on the demand for books by well-known chefs, were prepared to cobble up books from whatever materials came to hand, and as many cooks were prepared to put their names to these productions.

But how popular were such titles? When one compares the fate of books by the court-cooks with those of their female rivals, the women win hands down. Lamb's remodelled *Royal Cookery* was reprinted three times until 1731; John Nott went through four editions until 1733; Smith's *Court Cookery* had a second edition in 1725; Henry Howard's *England's Newest Way* went through five editions until 1726. Paradoxically, the most influential of them all, Massialot's *Court and Country Cook*, is known only in its original 1702 edition but, of course, variations on Massialot's receipts were disseminated by Lamb and Nott. By contrast, Mary Kettilby's book had seven editions and was still being reprinted in 1759; E. Smith, the best seller of the early eighteenth century, remained in print until 1773, the date of the 18th London edition, with several American editions between 1742 and 1764; Richard Bradley's *Country House-wife*, closer in style to the women's books than to the court-cooks', was also more successful, the sixth edition being reprinted in 1762.

It seems clear the market preferred the traditional mix of culinary receipts and remedies to the grandiose dishes of ambitious court-cooks. Charles Carter's book, published at the end of the period, underwent a series of changes which confirm this. Court-cookery was falling out of favour by the 1730s, and Carter was not a great success. In 1732 he produced a second work, *The Compleat City and Country Cook: or, Accomplish'd Housewife*. The title indicates a different audience, while both the preface and receipts are simplified versions of material from his first book. In fact, Carter's own receipts occupy only 144 pages out of 280, the remainder being an appendix of receipts of interest to the 'Mistress of a House or House-keeper',[46] that is, for the products of the still-room: preserves, pickles, drinks, cosmetics and remedies (although there are also culinary receipts, some at least borrowed from Edward Kidder). The medical part is described on the title-page as being 'The Collection of a Noble Lady Deceased' – in other words, an aristocratic family receipt book. This version was reprinted 'with large additions' in 1736; finally, in 1749, another version, now entitled *The*

---

[46] Carter, *The Compleat City and Country Cook* (1732), p. viii.

London and Country Cook, appeared, 'Revised and much improved by a Gentlewoman; Many Years Housekeeper to an eminent Merchant in the City of
London', though Carter's name was still present on the title-page. Thus the
court-cook's book had been completely transformed: the addition of receipts
from a manuscript collection, the simplification of the original receipts, and the
attack on the chefs' books in the 1749 preface,[47] in terms remarkably similar to
those used by Mary Kettilby in 1714, all combine to make this a woman's book.

Women authors were conscious that their books were different from those
of their male rivals, and the terms in which they attacked them implied the
men ridiculed their old-fashioned cooking. Mary Kettilby presented her own
receipts in the following way:

> The Directions relating to *Cookery* are Palatable, Useful, and Intelligible,
> which is more than can be said of any now Publick in that kind; some
> great Masters having given us Rules in that Art so strangely odd and
> fantastical, that 'tis hard to say, Whether the Reading has given more
> Sport and Diversion, or the Practice more Vexation and Chagrin, in
> spoiling us many a good Dish, by following their Directions. But so it
> is, that a Poor Woman must be Laugh'd at, for only Sugaring a Mess of
> Beans; whilst a Great Name must be had in Admiration, for Contriving
> Relishes a thousand times more Distastful to the Palate, provided they
> are but at the same time more Expensive to the Purse.[48]

We shall return later to the conflict of culinary styles which lies behind this
comment. Here, the most pertinent criticism is that the chefs' receipts are
impractical and extravagant. (Given the date of this diatribe, it seems probable
that the 'Great Name' refers to Patrick Lamb.) E. Smith complained in a
similar vein:

> There are indeed already in the World various Books that treat on this
> Subject, and which bear great Names, as Cooks to Kings, Princes, and
> Noblemen, and from which one might justly expect something more than
> many, if not most of these I have read, perform, but found my self

---

[47] See Carter, *The London and Country Cook* (1749), pp. v–vi.
[48] Kettilby (1714), preface.

deceived in my Expectations; for many of them to us are impracticable, others whimsical, others unpalatable, unless to depraved Palates, some unwholsome, many things copied from old Authors, and recommended without (as I am persuaded) the Copiers ever having had any Experience of the Palatableness, or had any regard to the Wholsomeness of them: ... And I cannot but believe, that those celebrated Performers, notwithstanding all their Professions of having ingenuously communicated their Art, industriously concealed their best Receipts from the Publick.[49]

Mrs Smith was certainly familiar with John Nott's book (she lifted parts of her preface from him), but whether he is the particular target is impossible to say. One can detect here the woman cook's resentment of the secrecy of the all-male profession: women were excluded from apprenticeship, and several male chefs who published their own receipts took care to defend themselves against possible accusations of betraying trade secrets.[50] While the women resented the superior attitude of the chefs, they in turn were trying to improve their own professional status by emphasizing the degree of knowledge required and pointing out that a competent cook could not also be brewer and apothecary. The woman servant was in a very different position: working in a less exalted household, often expected to combine the functions of cook and housekeeper or, lower down the social scale, cook and housemaid. The mutual hostility of the two groups was the result of problems of status, of conflict at a time when court-style cookery was establishing itself as the dominant fashion, and of competition in the developing market for cookery books amongst the lesser gentry and the prosperous middle classes.

By the end of our period, the court-cooks' books were disappearing. In the 1730s a new culinary style was coming into fashion, and cooks working for the élite learned about it not from books (and the court-cookery books all describe the style of the turn of the century), but from practical experience in the kitchen. As these older works disappear, their kind of title, the last to evoke royalty or the court, disappears too. By the 1730s the court no longer offered the model of fashionable cuisine; now it was the Whig aristocracy who vied with one another for the reputation of keeping the best table and employing the most

---

[49] E– S– (1728), preface.
[50] See, for instance, Carter (1730), address to the reader.

fashionable cook – invariably a Frenchman. Court-cookery books no longer had a market.

By contrast, the women's books continued to be successful without requiring the wholesale alteration made to later editions of their male counterparts. Although new receipts were added to Kettilby and E. Smith, these do not transform the content by adding whole new categories. The success of Smith is easy to understand: it offered the traditional mix of cookery, confectionery, pickles, drinks, and a section on medicines, as well as adapted versions of grand court dishes, and was the only woman's book to include bills of fare (lifted from Lamb) and copper-plates indicating the placing of dishes on the table. It thus managed to combine reassuring female traditions with some features of up-market books, and its price (5s. 6d.) placed it firmly amongst them. People did not buy *The Compleat Housewife* because it was cheap, but because it offered the features they were looking for. In this first period, the evidence of cookery books is of plenty of interest in domestic activities among the gentry, contrary to claims of moralists of the time. However, the assumption on the part of the sellers of court-cookery books that only cosmetics would be of interest to female readers suggests that at the apex of society the traditions of the seventeenth century were dying if not dead.

An example of the continuing tradition of receipt collecting amongst the lesser gentry is the manuscript which belonged to Margaretta Acworth. Born in 1727 or 1728, she was the daughter of a Hertfordshire gentleman. In April 1745 she married Abraham Acworth, also from a prosperous gentry family. Her husband had a post as clerk of the Exchequer, and they lived in London. He died in 1781, and Margaretta lived until 1794.[51] The manuscript contains two series of receipts, one for cookery and confectionery, the second for remedies. Both show evidence of collection over a long period: each begins with a neatly written and numbered group, with discrete tables of contents. There is then a series of accretions. Culinary receipts were added on four different occasions, squeezed into every available space, with a large number left on odd scraps of paper. Among these scraps are some dating from the 1720s and 1730s, including material from printed sources such as the *London Journal*. The modern editors suggest that the first parts of each series were written out by Margaretta's

---

[51] The biographical details are taken from Alice and Frank Prochaska's introduction to a sample of the receipts: see Prochaska, *Margaretta Acworth's Georgian Cookery Book* (1987), pp. 10–15.

mother, Anne Ball, and the rest by Margaretta herself, but the dates of at least some of the loose receipts means that Margaretta cannot have collected all of them. Furthermore, the first part of the medical series contains items from the sixteenth and seventeenth centuries, such as 'Doctor Stevens's water' (number 17), and 'The lady allens water' (number 33), but these are entered after a receipt by Dr Lower (number 4), who died in 1691 and whose receipt for a 'tincture' was published in 1700; this means that this section was a fair copy of an arrangement of receipts collected over a very long period. The culinary sections suggest a smaller time-range, although the emphasis on preserving and banqueting dishes in the very first section suggests the seventeenth rather than the eighteenth century. The later additions contain more cookery, and while the earlier ones still give several savoury pies with sugar, suggesting a late seventeenth-century date, the last set includes a receipt for 'English Turtle', a dish which did not enter the repertoire before the middle of the eighteenth century.[52] Margaretta Acworth was thus keeping up a collection which had been begun at least a hundred years before.

The gap between the chefs' books and those by women was considerable and would grow even greater by the 1750s. Those describing the latest trends in *haute cuisine* – by male chefs who worked for the aristocracy and saw changing fashions at first hand – would become very thin on the ground, while the more modest works by women who learned of what was going on in the culinary stratosphere through books whose receipts they then adapted to the needs of less lavish households would dominate the market.

---

[52] Margaretta Acworth's manuscript is now in the PRO, C 107/108. While the first sections of culinary and medical receipts are numbered (1–128 and 1–72), the remaining receipts are not numbered, and neither are the pages. But the order of copying of the culinary series is clear: after the 128 numbered receipts, a new scribe turned over and copied 42 receipts, under the heading 'Mr Lillys Receipts'; then come 46 receipts, mostly attributed to various donors; finally the last additions follow on, and when the scribe ran out of space, she added more receipts squeezed on to the last pages of the first section, then on to the first leaf at the very beginning of the book, and finally she used some of the space between the table of culinary receipts (which follows the receipts) and the table of medical receipts (which precedes the receipts). The normal practice of turning the book upside down and starting from both ends, so that the two series would meet in the middle, was not followed here, because the book had originally been used for another purpose, and at the back a leaf had already been written on.

The 1730s saw the end of books written by court-cooks: the last editions of the earlier works by Lamb and others, and the last new title, John Middleton's *Five Hundred New Receipts* (1734), date from these years. By contrast, those by women continued to sell, and women wrote the most successful books of the middle of the century. Their number grew too: Virginia Maclean gives 19 new works printed between 1720 and 1739 (excluding books devoted exclusively to medicine or to drinks), of which 6 can be attributed with certainty to women. Between 1740 and 1759, out of 44 new titles, 19 are certainly by women.

The gap between the two groups – chefs writing for noble patrons and their cooks, and women writing for housewives – is exemplified in two works published in 1733. The chef was a Frenchman, Vincent La Chapelle, who brought out *The Modern Cook* in London, in English. (The first edition in French was published in The Hague in 1735.) He was working in London as cook to Lord Chesterfield, who had probably recruited him in Paris through the good offices of the Duke of Richmond in 1728, before going to The Hague as British ambassador.[1] After illness and leave of absence in 1731, Chesterfield was formally relieved of his post in February 1732, returning to London. La Chapelle was still employed by him in 1733, but by 1735 had left to join the service of the Prince of Orange. At this date, the prestige of French cooks in London was very high, and *The Modern Cook*, dedicated to La Chapelle's employer, was designed as a comprehensive description of cookery, considered as one of the fine arts. Its title-page distinguishes it from the competition: its elegant sobriety omits the self-advertisement which characterizes English cookery books of the time.

In his preface, La Chapelle claims the advances made in culinary art over the previous twenty years have made a new manual absolutely necessary, to replace the *Cuisinier roïal et bourgeois*.[2] While denigrating Massialot's work as

---

[1] A letter from Chesterfield in The Hague, dating from October 1728, asks Richmond to find him a cook in Paris who is 'at the top of his profession'. See Lennox, *A Duke and his Friends* (1911), vol. 1, p. 157; also Dobrée (ed.), *The Letters of Philip Dormer Stanhope, 4th Earl of Chesterfield* (1932), vol. 6, pp. 2948–9. The connection is reinforced by the fact that Richmond and La Chapelle were Freemasons: La Chapelle's name appears in the 1730 list of members, and Richmond was grand master in 1724–25. See Songhurst, 'The Minutes of the Grand Lodge of Freemasons of England, 1723–39' (1913), pp. 183, 193, 197. I owe this nugget of information to Beatrice Fink.

[2] La Chapelle, *The Modern Cook* (1733), vol. 1, pp. i–ii.

old-fashioned, La Chapelle actually borrowed about one-third of his own receipts from that source,[3] so that he represents a transitional stage between the old court-cookery and the new style. As one might expect, the three volumes are devoted almost exclusively to cookery (confectionery is given a few pages at the end of the third volume), and the dishes described are for royal and aristocratic tables. The book is designed to be used by the author's colleagues: most of the preface is devoted to advice to the *maître d'hôtel*, whereas English cooks usually addressed the upper-classes. Here, the noble patron to whom the book is dedicated is not expected to look further than the sycophantic dedication itself, contrary to the implication of Charles Carter's remarks on educating employers to appreciate true artists in the kitchen.

In the same year, 1733, Sarah Harrison brought out her book, *The House-keeper's Pocket-book*. It is dedicated 'To the House-Wives, in Great-Britain', and this dedication, and the preface, explain how useful it will be. The work is comprehensive. Despite being cheap (it cost 2s. 6d.), it gives receipts which are easy to follow, where all superfluous expense has been eliminated.[4] The author emphasizes that the dishes are not too rich, in a way calculated to flatter the reader whose purse would not rise to the more luxurious ingredients:

> The Receipts are excellent in their Kind, tho' at the same time all possible care has been taken in general, to single out the least Expensive and the least Embarassed; *a few good Ingredients make the best Dishes, and a crowd of rich Things, are apter to satiate than to please the Palates of those who have the nicest Taste.*[5]

This may suggest taste was turning away from the complex dishes of the court-cooks but, in spite of this, the receipts are still 'domestic' versions of court dishes, as we shall see in the study of culinary styles. Mrs Harrison also informs the reader that she may rely on the receipts, since they are the author's own, 'wholly furnish'd from my own Experience'.[6] She directs it explicitly at those of modest income:

---

[3] Hyman & Hyman, 'La Chapelle and Massialot: an 18th Century Feud' (1979), pp. 44–54.
[4] Harrison, *The House-keeper's Pocket-book* (1733), pp. v–xii.
[5] Ibid., p. xi (numbered ix in the book).
[6] Ibid., p. vi.

As I have been persuaded to print my Book of Receipts, I think it necessary to acquaint the Reader of the design of the Undertaking, which is to inform such House-keepers as are not in the higher rank of Fortune, how to Eat or Entertain Company, in the most elegant Manner at a small Expence.[7]

The preface states that 'the Country is the Place where generally Works of this Nature are best Received',[8] thus confirming that Mrs Harrison was aiming at the same type of reader as Richard Bradley six years earlier. The contents show how carefully it was written with such an audience in mind. Medical receipts are included expressly for the benefit of country people who have no easy access to a doctor (although there are only thirteen pages of remedies, whereas Mary Kettilby devoted nearly half her space to them); there is advice on buying good-quality spices and dried herbs at a moderate price; there are indications on substitutions when a particular ingredient is not available; and when an expensive dish is given, the reader is warned of the fact.[9] When the second edition was published, in 1739, it had 400 additional receipts, 'sent to the Author by several worthy Persons'.[10] Thus it seems that Sarah Harrison's book produced the same response from readers as Mary Kettilby and Richard Bradley, although Bradley was the only one to have publicly solicited such contributions.

The contrast between La Chapelle and Harrison is very striking, and the subsequent career of the two works demonstrates once again the greater success of the woman author. La Chapelle was reprinted in English until 1751, with no changes to the text except that by the fourth (1751) edition the receipt titles had been translated into English, and the title had been changed to *The Modern Cook's, and Complete Housewife's Companion*. This relatively short life is perhaps not surprising, given that it described the early stages of a new culinary style. But in spite of the obvious need for a replacement, no English work described the new French cookery until William Verral brought out his *Complete System of Cookery* in 1759. Sarah Harrison's book was reprinted, with vast additions, until 1777. Her emphasis on economy, contained in the dedication and the

---

[7] Harrison (1733), pp. 1–2.

[8] Ibid., p. xii.

[9] Ibid., pp. xii, 2, 7–8, 10, 20, 22.

[10] Ibid., title-page.

preface of the first edition, now appeared on the title-page: the second edition
stresses that the book will help the reader to provide 'an Agreeable Variety of
Dishes, at a Moderate Expence', and the title also points out that the instructions are 'Plain and Easy' – words which would shortly inspire Hannah
Glasse's best-seller. Once again, the woman's product was much better adapted
to the requirements of the cookery-book-buying public than the chef's
magnum opus.

During the 1730s there were relatively few new cookery books printed, but
the subject occupies a substantial amount of space in two important compilations. The other material included in these works gives further clues to the
identity of buyers. *The Complete Family-Piece* came out in 1736, aimed at
country families just like the 'domestic' cookery books of the 1720s. It contained remedies for the use of charitable ladies, all sorts of receipts for cookery,
confectionery, preserves and drinks – the latter category included to help
families to economize by preparing such items at home – as well as instructions
for hunting, fishing, gardening and estate management. While clearly aimed
at the gentry, the presentation of the chapter on hunting states that the instructions are:

> For the Benefit and Advantage … of such Gentlemen who retire from
> Business to live in the Country, … the First Chapter of the Second Part
> … gives you full Instructions to be observed in Hunting and Coursing.[11]

Thus a manual for the rising middle-class who were hoping to join the ranks
of county society. The various chapters offer advice to husband and wife, bringing together several books in one volume, a point stressed in the preface.[12]
Indeed, this was an economical way of obtaining E. Smith's receipts, since
virtually all the receipts for cookery and confectionery are borrowed directly
from *The Compleat Housewife* (though the remedies come from another source).
This domestic encyclopaedia cost only 3s. 6d., whereas E. Smith was 5s. 6d.

Another compilation, this time addressed exclusively to female readers, mixed
moralizing advice and receipts. This massive volume began life as *The Whole Duty
of a Woman* (1737) but from the second edition in 1740 it dropped this

---

[11] *The Complete Family-Piece* (1737), p. vii. The title-page and the first pages (preface and table of
contents) are missing from the BL copy of the first edition (1736).
[12] *The Complete Family-Piece* (1737), p. iv.

obnoxiously old-fashioned title to become *The Lady's Companion*. By the time it reached its sixth edition in 1754, all moralizing content had disappeared, leaving only receipts, which now numbered over three thousand. Books which equated cookery with female duty had been popular at the end of the seventeenth century, but were now much less acceptable to the mistress: the mix of homily and house-wifery was deemed fit for servants, but not for their betters. The first version of the text took its receipts from a variety of sources: E. Smith again, but also Richard Bradley, Charles Carter and La Chapelle.[13] It was by such borrowings, rather than through the expensive original editions, that the receipts of French cooks, first Massialot, then La Chapelle, circulated more widely.

While the ladies were rejecting books which gave receipts and long homilies on their duties, they were thought appropriate for servants. In the 1740s, the genre was not new: in the 1670s *The Gentlewomans Companion* was addressed to the gentlewoman-turned-servant, and books aimed at less well-born domestics, such as the *Compleat Servant Maid* in Henry Purefoy's library in the 1720s, were already in existence. This decade and the next saw the appearance of several works that the mistress was expected to buy to give to her servants, obvious from such titles as *A Present for a Servant-Maid* (1743), and *Madam Johnson's Present* (1754). They were a response to the vociferous complaints about laziness and lack of subservience which characterized contemporary comment. The first of these books, by Eliza Haywood, tried to persuade the servant that obedience and hard work were in her own interest:

> It is not to be wondered at, that in an Age abounding with Luxury, and overrun with Pride, Servants should be in general so bad, ... and it is high Time to endeavour a Cure of so growing an Evil. ... A due Obser-vance of the Rules contained in this little Treatise, cannot fail of making every *Mistress* of a Family perfectly contented, and every *Servant-Maid* both happy and beloved; and I hope whoever of the latter shall read what I have set down, will find it so much her Interest, as well as her Duty, to behave in a contrary Manner from what too many for some Years have done; that she will make it her whole Study to avoid the Errors she may see in others, and reform such as she has been guilty of herself.[14]

---

[13] See Stead, 'Quizzing Glasse or Hannah Scrutinized, Part II' (1983), pp. 27–30.

[14] [Haywood], *A Present for a Servant-Maid* (1743), preface.

Mrs Haywood endeavoured to make the servant realize how much better off she was than her employer, an uphill task:

> A good Mistress will doubtless allow her Servants a Taste of every thing in Season; but then you are not to expect it as often, or in as full Proportion as she has it herself; that were to destroy all Disparity, and put you too much on a Level with those you serve.
>
> This, perhaps, you think a hard Lesson; but yet were you to know the real Pinches some endure who keep you, you would find the Balance of Happiness wholly on your Side.[15]

Although the book is presented as an exhaustive guide, the emphasis is on moral instruction: receipts occupy only one-fifth of the book.

The second book was more practical. It had started life in 1753 as *The Young Woman's Companion; or the Servant-Maid's Assistant* – a title whose substitution of the word 'woman' for 'lady' is significant. The author was Mary Johnson, who had been a housekeeper in York: she offered guidance on English grammar and spelling, on arithmetic, on cookery and confectionery, and on the duty of a servant towards her employer and God. The first sections make it clear that the servant was expected to be able to read but not to write, since models of hand-writing are offered for copying. The book was reprinted in 1754 and 1755 with the new title, *Madam Johnson's Present*, and a small amount of additional material (see Appendix III for details). The new title made it clear the buyer would be the mistress, whereas the original would not have attracted her attention. Both Mrs Haywood and Mrs Johnson emphasized the low price of their books: the title-page of the first stated that although a single copy cost 1s., 25 copies could be had for 1 guinea if the books were to be given away; that of the second announced:

> The Compiler, Madam Johnson, in order to make this Book come as cheap as possible to the Purchasers, has, out of her Benevolence, fixed the Price at 1s. 6d. bound, tho' it contains double the Quantity that is usually sold for that Sum.[16]

---

[15] Haywood (1743) p. 30.
[16] Johnson (1755), title.

Note that Mary Johnson is described not as the author, but as the compiler. Mistresses were encouraged by such offers to buy these books as presents, in a gesture of charitable self-interest.

Cookery receipts were thus found in different types of work, a sign that booksellers were catering to the needs of a variety of buyers. Another indication of the increasing market for cookery books (and for consumer goods in general) is the sudden development of provincial printings from the 1740s. There had been a limited number of titles published outside London before that date, such as the first in Scotland, *Mrs. McLintock's Receipts* (printed in Glasgow in 1736), or John Emmett's *A Choice Collection of Excellent Receipts in Confectionary*, printed in York in 1737, but the appearance in 1741 of Elizabeth Moxon's *English House-wifry* was the first in a series of best-selling cookery books published in the north of England. It was printed in Leeds by John Lister, owner of the local newspaper, the *Leeds Mercury. English Housewifry* was one of his first non-theological publications. After his death in 1753, the newspaper was bought by Griffith Wright. He continued to publish Moxon: it went through thirteen editions and was still in print in the 1790s.

These provincial printers recognized a buoyant market. Griffith Wright also printed Ann Peckham's *Complete English Cook* in 1767. Another newspaper owner, Thomas Slack of Newcastle, brought out Mary Smith's *Complete House-keeper* in 1772.[17] Earlier Newcastle publications include C. Douglass' *The Summer's Amusements* (1746), and Ann Cook's *Professed Cookery* (1754). Other titles were published in Liverpool in 1742, and in Manchester and Berwick upon Tweed in 1769. The most prolific centres were, however, Leeds and Newcastle. This development is eloquent of growing sales amongst the middle classes, but they were not the only buyers. It has often been argued that sales were restricted to that class alone, on the grounds that the gentry already possessed family manuscript receipt books and had no need for printed versions.[18] But the gentry *did* buy cookery books (one has only to remember Lady Grisell Baillie or Sir Robert Walpole), and provincial publications should be seen as an extension of the market rather than as a radical shift.

When Elizabeth Moxon published her *English Housewifry* in 1741, she announced that it was aimed at both mistress and servant:

---

[17] For a discussion of provincial production of cookery books, see Hunter, 'Printing in the Pennines', in Wilson (1991), pp. 9–37.

[18] See, particularly, Hess, *Martha Washington's Booke of Cookery* (1981), p. 451; Hunter (1991), p. 10.

> A Book necessary for Mistresses of Families, higher and lower Women
> Servants, and confined to Things Useful, Substantial and Splendid, and
> calculated … upon the Measures of Frugality.[19]

At this date, mistress and servants, who are defined as women – one notes that
men wrote for other men, women for women – are associated, with no suggestion that each group would be interested in discrete parts. The book contained
cookery receipts and bills of fare, some of them illustrated, but no remedies,
which marked a change from the usual pattern of the 1720s and 1730s. Although
some of the receipts were certainly adapted from E. Smith, Moxon's alterations
made the receipts her own and, as far as I have been able to ascertain, there was
no wholesale copying from other works. The book was very successful, and was
further diffused by Sarah Jackson's *The Director* (1754) which took all but two of
its culinary receipts from the fourth edition of Moxon.

The most successful cookery writer of the eighteenth century also provides
a link with northern England: Hannah Glasse came from Hexham, although
her book was published in London. *The Art of Cookery, Made Plain and Easy*
appeared in 1747 and was an instant success. A second edition came out in the
same year, and by 1755 it was into its fifth. It continued to be printed until 1843.
Before examining the nature of the book and the reasons for its extraordinary
impact, it is worth having a look at the career of the author, since Hannah
Glasse is one of the few whose history is known to us. When first issued in 1747,
it was described as 'By a Lady'. Glasse's name was not revealed until the fourth
edition of 1751, when her trade card was inserted into the book and her signature
appeared on the title-page. In spite of this, eighteenth-century pundits believed
the book to be by Dr John Hill (Boswell's *Life of Johnson* recounts a dinner-table
conversation in which the publisher Dilly affirmed that the book was by Hill,
although Johnson himself doubted the attribution[20]). Nineteenth- and early
twentieth-century historians of the table continued to attribute the book to Hill
or to an unknown hand.[21] The truth was finally revealed thanks to the research

---

[19] Moxon (1741), title-page.

[20] Boswell, *Life of Johnson* (1960), pp. 942–943.

[21] See, for instance, Jeaffreson, *A Book about the Table* (1875), vol. 2, pp. 125–129; Ellwanger, *The Pleasures of the Table* (1903), p. 108; Cooper, *The English Table in History and Literature* (1929), pp. 140–148.

of Madeleine Hope Dodds in the 1930s and others since, most notably Dr A.H.T. Robb-Smith, whose work unfortunately remains unpublished.[22]

Hannah Glasse was the illegitimate daughter of Isaac Allgood of Hexham and an Irish widow, Hannah Reynolds; she was baptized on 24 March 1708 at St Andrew's, Holborn. Her father was the son of the vicar of Simonburn in Northumberland, and he was educated at Cambridge; in 1707 he married Hannah Clark, the daughter of a London vintner. He had one legitimate child, his son and heir, Lancelot Allgood, who was born in 1711, and two other children, born in 1709 and 1712, by his mistress. Although this liaison seems to have come to an end by 1714, Hannah was taken into her father's family and brought up with her half-brother. By 1724 Isaac Allgood's wife had died, and he himself was in poor health and in financial difficulties. Hannah was sent to London to stay with her grandmother, and from there she contracted a secret marriage with a subaltern on half-pay, John Glasse, by special licence in August 1724. The marriage was not discovered until September, when she left her grandmother's house and moved with her husband into rooms in the Haymarket. The marriage caused a flurry of correspondence between London and Northumberland. Although Hannah's relations had to accept the fact of the marriage, they were not pleased with her choice of husband. When Isaac Allgood died in 1725, his will settled £30 a year on his daughter, on terms designed to ensure that her husband could have no access to the money.

In 1728 Hannah was expecting her first child, and she resumed her correspondence with her aunt Margaret in the north country. By now the Glasses were living in Broomfield in Essex, in the service of the fourth Earl of Donegall. Hannah Glasse gave birth to three daughters, in 1728, 1729 and 1732. Some time after the death of the Countess of Donegall in 1732, they left the Earl's service and moved back to London. In 1734 Hannah gave birth to a fourth daughter, in Westminster, and the family later moved to Greville Street near Hatton Garden – to the very house where Hannah had been born and where they lived for nine years, from 1738 to 1747. Meanwhile, a long-drawn-out lawsuit brought by Hannah's mother to enforce the settlement in favour of her and her children made by Isaac Allgood in 1714 was concluded in 1740, and Hannah received a further annuity, which she gradually compounded for lump

---

[22] For the early research, see Dodds, 'The Rival Cooks: Hannah Glasse and Ann Cook' (1938), pp. 43–68. A useful summary of the known facts about Glasse's life is given in the introduction to Prospect's facsimile reprint of *The Art of Cookery* (1995), pp. vii–xiv.

sums. This was a stroke of fortune inasmuch as John Glasse seems to have been involved in a variety of unsuccessful business ventures, and it fell to his wife to try to rescue the family fortunes.

First, in 1744, she toyed with the idea of setting up a business to sell 'Dr Lower's Tincture', a patent medicine which had been 'invented' as 'Daffy's Elixir' around 1660, and published as Dr Lower's receipt in 1700 (the scheme came to nothing). By November 1745 Hannah told her aunt that she had begun her book and was 'going on with subscriptions'; in January 1746 she announced that the book was going on very well and was in the press – rapid progress indeed. The book was entered in the Register of Stationers' Hall on 16 August 1746, but did not finally come out (if the date on the first edition is to be believed) until 1747. Meanwhile, Hannah was pursuing another project, setting up as a dressmaker with her second daughter Margaret. This is revealed in John Glasse's last letter to his half-brother-in-law before his death in June 1747. For this new business venture, she moved to Tavistock Street, and at first was very successful, numbering the Princess of Wales amongst her customers. Despite commercial success, however, Hannah Glasse was in financial difficulties, and she began raising loans in 1749. She was finally declared bankrupt in May 1754, with debts of over £10,000. After bankruptcy, little is known of her career: she disappears from the Allgood papers entirely. She wrote two more books, *The Servant's Directory* (1760), and *The Compleat Confectioner* (*c.*1760, an edition published in Dublin being dated 1762). Finally, her death in London on 1 September 1770 was announced in the *London Magazine*, and in the *Newcastle Courant* of 8 September.

These details of Hannah Glasse's life show that she was a housewife rather than a professional cook, and that she wrote her book with the aim of making money. Even allowing for her erratic habits of correspondence, which might account for the apparently brief time-lapse between beginning and finishing her manuscript, it appears that the text was composed at high speed. This becomes more plausible in the light of how it was written. Jennifer Stead and Priscilla Bain have shown that she lifted 342 of her 972 receipts from other books, most notably from the 1743 edition of *The Lady's Companion* (which had begun life as *The Whole Duty of a Woman* in 1737).[23] Amongst these borrowings, she tended to take the receipts for sweet dishes verbatim, whereas savoury

---

[23] Stead (1983), p. 25; Bain, 'Recounting the Chickens: Hannah Further Scrutinized' (1986), p. 38.

dishes underwent a process of testing and adaptation.[24] This is a sign of Glasse's modernity: prestige no longer attached to the sweet (as it had in the seventeenth century), but to the French-influenced savoury. She clearly had practical experience in the kitchen, directing her servants even if she did not herself do the cooking. Her borrowings show that she must have possessed a copy of *The Lady's Companion* (she could not possibly have adopted so much without it to hand), and she was familiar with the books by E. Smith, Henry Howard and, possibly, John Nott. It seems likely too that she had seen Sarah Harrison's book, with its use of the phrase 'Plain and Easy', and its author's efforts to adapt her text to the needs of her readers. Hannah Glasse is generally thought of as an author, but her work also offers an image of her as a reader.

Glasse's book was such a resounding success because it appealed to both buyers and readers. One must make a distinction between the two: at 5s. bound, the book was not cheap, although it could be purchased simply stitched for 3s. The title-page, the address to the reader and the nature of the contents are designed with the mistress in mind; the receipts are explained in simple enough language to be accessible to the servant; and the instructions include the most basic techniques, such as roasting and boiling. The title-page manages to be elegant while at the same time giving a complete list of the chapters in the book; it is 'By a Lady', thus vouching for the social status of the author, who is no vulgar domestic and who knows what a lady requires. And the address to the reader sets out in no uncertain terms what that is. Hannah Glasse wanted to help relieve ladies of the burden of teaching their cook-maids. This is explained at some length:

> I believe I have attempted a Branch of Cookery which Nobody has yet thought worth their while to write upon: But as I have both seen, and found by Experience that the Generality of Servants are greatly wanting in that Point, therefore I have taken upon me to instruct them in the best Manner I am capable; and I dare say, that every Servant who can but read will be capable of making a tollerable good Cook, and those who have the least Notion of Cookery can't miss of being very good ones.
>
> If I have not wrote in the high, polite Stile, I hope I shall be forgiven; for my Intention is to instruct the lower Sort, and therefore must treat

---

[24] See Stead, 'Quizzing Glasse … Part II', p. 26.

them in their own Way. For Example; when I bid them lard a Fowl, if I should bid them lard it with large Lardoons, they would not know what I meant: But when I say they must lard with little Pieces of Bacon, they know what I mean. So in many other Things in Cookery, the great Cooks have such a high Way of expressing themselves that the poor Girls are a Loss to know what they mean.[25]

She concludes:

I shall say no more, only hope my Book will answer the Ends I intend it for; which is to improve the Servants, and save the Ladies a great deal of Trouble.[26]

Jennifer Stead has shown that Glasse's reformulation of her predecessors' receipts produced clearer texts, with indications of quantities and methods as well as replacement of technical terms used by her sources.[27] She performed what she promised, at least where she adapted receipts, which is not always the case.

Glasse was also innovative (especially in a book written by a woman) in being no more than a cookery book. Compare this to Kettilby or E. Smith, or such compendiums as *The Lady's Companion*:

I shall not take upon me to meddle in the physical Way farther than two Receipts which will be of use to the Publick in general: One is for the Bite of a Mad Dog; and the other, if a Man should be near where the Plague is, he shall be in no Danger; which, if made Use of, would be found of very great Service to those who go Abroad.

Nor shall I take upon me to direct a Lady in the Oeconomy of her Family, for every Mistress does, or at least ought to know what is most proper to be done there; therefore I shall not fill my Book with a deal of Nonsense of that Kind, which I am very well assur'd none will have Regard to. …

Nor shall I take upon me to direct a Lady how to set out her Table; for that would be impertinent, and lessening her Judgment in the

---

[25] [Glasse], *The Art of Cookery, Made Plain and Easy* (1747), p. i.

[26] Ibid., p. ii.

[27] Stead, 'Quizzing Glasse: or Hannah Scrutinized, Part I' (1983), pp. 11–17.

Oeconomy of her Family. I hope she will here find every Thing necessary for her Cook, and her own Judgment will tell her how they are to be placed. Nor indeed do I think it would be pretty, to see a Lady's Table set out after the Directions of a Book.[28]

As for the cookery itself, she boasts that she will show how to make rich sauces without the expense entailed by following a French cook's receipts:

In all Receipt Books yet printed there are such an odd Jumble of Things as would quite spoil a good Dish; and indeed some Things so extravagant, that it would be almost a Shame to make Use of them, when a Dish can be made full as good, or better without them. For Example; when you entertain ten or twelve People you shall use for a Cullis a Leg of Veal and a Ham; which, with the other Ingredients, makes it very expensive, and all this only to mix with other Sauce. And again, the Essence of a Ham for Sauce to one Dish; when I will prove it for about three Shillings I will make as rich and high a Sauce as all that will be, when done. ... So that really one might have a genteel Entertainment for the Price the Sauce of one Dish comes to. But if Gentlemen will have *French* Cooks, they must pay for *French* Tricks.[29]

The xenophobic note was the finishing touch to preliminaries designed to appeal to the middle-class mistress. It reassured the buyer about her own status: she was a lady, who knew how to manage her household, but who hoped to delegate the work of cookery to her servants without having to supervise them too much; she wanted elegant dishes, but without the extravagant expenditure which was associated with French cooks. The rejection of French fashions was something of a problem: in matters of food especially, French cuisine was the height of fashion amongst the Whig political élite, and those who aspired to modishness were obliged to produce French dishes on their tables. At the same time hostility to France and to the aristocratic ethos of conspicuous consumption was rife lower down the social scale among those who did not share the élite's cosmopolitan outlook. Hannah Glasse solves this contradiction by giving French

---

[28] Glasse (1747), p. ii.
[29] Ibid., pp. i–ii.

dishes in her book (she borrows receipts from Vincent La Chapelle via *The Lady's Companion*), while heaping abuse on French cooks in her presentation.

The Art of Cookery appealed because it was thoroughly up-to-date in two ways. Firstly, it was a specialized book of cookery which gave receipts for fashionable dishes without excessive expense, and it made very obvious the fact that it was different from earlier best-sellers. Secondly, it recognized that part of a woman's social ambition was to become a lady of leisure who no longer spent hours in the kitchen instructing her servants. The influence of the new model of femininity is plain to see. The first edition was financed by subscription: there were 202 subscribers, many of them connected to the Allgood family.[30] Most were women, of whom only five bore titles ('Lady' or 'Hon.'). The book was printed 'for the Author' and was sold not through booksellers but at a china-shop. This was probably another reason for its success: ladies might frequent the one but not usually set foot in the other.

Hannah Glasse's popularity did not please everybody. In 1754 Ann Cook published a book called *Professed Cookery* which contained receipts and an 'Essay upon the Lady's Art of Cookery'. The second and third editions of 1755 and *c*.1760 also contained a 'Plan of House-keeping'. The 'Essay' is a detailed attack on Glasse's receipts. The 'Plan' begins by giving advice on housewifery and the care of poultry, then goes on to tell how the author taught her friend to look after poultry too. From here, the text converts to biography, with the friend telling her story first, then Ann Cook accounting for her own married life and hardships. This is a tale of the persecution she and her husband endured at the hands of 'Esquire Flash', whom the historian Madeleine Hope Dodds convincingly identified as Hannah Glasse's half-brother, Lancelot Allgood, when she reconstructed the story of Ann Cook's career and her feud with the Allgoods.[31]

To summarize briefly, Ann Cook was probably born in the 1690s, and entered service as a cook; in about 1725 she married John Cook, the tenant of the Black Bull Inn at Hexham. From Ann Cook's own narrative, it appears that their eldest daughter was born in 1728 and that she had a large family, although the damaged parish register gives no information other than the date of baptism of a son, Robert, in August 1737. By 1740 Lancelot Allgood had become an important man in the area: he had inherited his father's estate in 1725, and

---

[30] See Dodds (1938), p. 47.
[31] Ibid., pp. 49–63.

acquired further wealth and property by his marriage in 1739 to his cousin Jane after his return from the grand tour (1736–8). He was high sheriff for the county in 1745, MP from 1748 to 1752, and was knighted in 1760. Hexham was an assize town, and when the judge on the Lent circuit arrived in 1740, he, the chancellor and his attendants were lodged at the Black Bull. Allgood sent a message to John Cook to tell him that the judge and his party might have French wine from his own cellar. Cook accordingly sent to borrow six bottles of French wine, which he paid for and charged on the lawyers' bill. But when the party reached Carlisle, the chancellor was asked how he liked the wine Allgood had sent as a gift, and the party concluded that Cook had cheated them and resolved never to patronize the Black Bull again. News of this reached Allgood, who summoned Cook and publicly accused him of theft, swearing to ruin him. The upshot was a violent quarrel. The feud continued for several years, until the Cooks left Hexham in 1745 to take the lease of the Queen's Head Inn at Morpeth to escape the vindictiveness of Allgood. Unfortunately this house was owned by Thomas Pye, a relation of the Allgoods, so the persecution continued, unsuccessfully, according to Ann Cook's account. However, they had entered into a bond for £369 on entering the Queen's Head and, although they managed to discharge £320, Pye insisted on full payment. Finally, they sold their possessions in Morpeth and moved to Newcastle, where Ann Cook hoped to set up a pastry-cook's shop, but their creditors would not allow them any breathing-space, and Cook was sent to a debtors' prison. Ann Cook's narrative ends at this juncture, and all that is known of her subsequent career is that by *c.*1760 she was living in lodgings in Holborn from where she was selling the third edition of her book.

Ann Cook's feud with Lancelot Allgood explains the virulence of her attack on Hannah Glasse in the 'Essay'. This consists of summaries of Glasse's receipts, subjected to a critique sometimes verging on the hysterical. For example, this on 'A Farce Meagre Cabbage':

> The white Cabbage is the poorest of all Cabbages, and the real value cannot be above a Half-penny; to which there is … two Shillings and a Penny, to farce and sauce this Half-penny Cabbage; and when it is done, if Man, Woman or Child, Hog, Sow or Dog eat it, my Judgment deceives me.[32]

---

[32] Cook, *Professed Cookery* (1754), p. 65; for the original receipt, see Glasse (1747), p. 104.

The rest of the essay, all 68 pages, is in the same vein. Not content, she wrote an address to the reader in the form of a poem. Her appalling doggerel pursues the theme of her own woes and Hannah Glasse's iniquity. She ridicules both the idea of a 'lady' writing a cookery book, and Hannah Glasse's claim to the title; and she (correctly) accuses Glasse of plagiarism:

> A Lady claims such Skill in dressing Meat,
> Prescribes to Lords and Ladies what to eat;
> From what she does collect makes up a Book,
> Assumes the Author and the sov'reign Cook.
> [...]
> She steals from ev'ry Author to her Book,
> Infamously branding the pillag'd Cook,
> With Trick, Booby, Juggler, Legerdemain,
> Right Pages to bear up vain Glory's Train.
> Can this be Honour to the *British* Nation,
> To gild her Book with Defamation?
> [...]
> If Genealogy was understood,
> It's all a Farce, her Title is not good;
> Can Seed of noble Blood, or renown'd 'Squires,
> Teach Drudges to clean Spits, and build up Fires?
> [...]
> Look at the Lady in her Title Page,
> How fast it sells the Book, and gulls the Age.
> [...]
> A profess'd Cook, born in a homely Cottage,
> Beholds the Surfeits of her Meat and Pottage;
> Muses upon the Purport of the Book,
> With God sends Meat, but who could send the Cook.[33]

These accusations demonstrate Ann Cook's familiarity with both Glasse and Vincent La Chapelle, since he is the indirect source of many of Glasse's French receipts, and Glasse uses the epithets here reproduced by Ann Cook in her

---

[33] Cook (1754), pp. iii–vii.

diatribe against French cooks. It appears from the reference to genealogy that Ann Cook knew of Glasse's illegitimate birth; this is confirmed later in the poem, when she refutes potential criticism of her own lack of respect towards her social superior, the lady, by asking the rhetorical question, 'What Title can be due to broken Glass'?[34]

The most interesting point made by this feeble verse, however, is its ridicule of the idea of a lady being capable of teaching cookery. (Ann Cook herself is an example of a cookery book author and reader who was certainly not a lady: after an eighteen-year career as a cook, she married and helped run an inn before turning to authorship, like her rival, to make money.) The implication is that a real lady was no longer expected to have any practical knowledge of cookery, whereas earlier, the opposite was true. The sub-title of E. Smith's book was, after all, the 'Accomplished Gentlewoman's Companion'. From the 1750s, the vast majority of women authors were professional cooks or housekeepers, and others kept cookery-schools, especially in the north of England. Such women could not pretend to the title of 'lady'. From The Art of Cookery onwards, authors would stress how their receipts were adapted for use by servants, although at first the discourse of presentation would still be aimed at the mistress, the presumed purchaser. They reinforced the argument by pointing to ease of comprehension for the ill-educated cook and by emphasizing their own professional status and experience, upon which the mistress could depend.

This was central to Glasse's appeal: the words 'plain and easy' in her title were immediately picked up by others. In 1750 Elizabeth Clifton entitled her book The Cookmaid's Assistant, or Art of Cookery, Made Plain and Easy; in 1753 Arabella Fairfax used the expression for her Family's Best Friend: or the whole Art of Cookery, made Plain and Easy; in 1754 one of the later editions of Penelope Bradshaw's Family Jewel bears exactly the same sub-title. None of these mentions the word 'lady', even less the now old-fashioned word 'gentlewoman'. Both Fairfax and Bradshaw advertise their practical experience, the first with 'above thirty Years Practice and Experience', the second 'Housekeeper Forty Years to a Noble Family of Great Taste, but Proper Oeconomy'.[35]

---

[34] Cook (1754), p. viii.

[35] The text of Fairfax's title-page is taken from Oxford (1913), p. 85. Maclean (p. 48) suggests, on the basis of similarities between the title-pages, that Fairfax's book is a pirated version of Bradshaw's, but I think this unlikely; I am more struck by the similarity of Bradshaw's 1754 title-page to Moxon's.

Twenty years after Hannah Glasse's first publication, it is possible to see how far her influence reached. Ann Peckham's *Complete English Cook* appeared in Leeds in 1767: the author announced proudly on her title-page that she had been famous as one of the best cooks in the county of York for forty years, a point she underlined in her preface. The title-page also pointed out that the book was 'made easy to the meanest Capacity',[36] a material point given the design of the undertaking:

> Such mistresses as think it a burden to be continually dangling after their maids in the kitchen, may be exempted in a great measure from that trouble, by putting these rules into the hands of their servants; for special care is taken to make every thing easy and intelligible to the meanest understanding. And it is certain, that the directions which may be read with coolness and deliberation at a leisure hour, will more easily be retained in the memory, than those that are given in the hurry of business from the mouth of the most respectable mistress.[37]

Few authors are so explicit about their intention of relieving the mistress, and since the earlier parts of the preface advertise the fact that the book is designed not only for the 'wealthy and hospitable' but also for the 'middling and lower ranks', this suggests that the need to supervise the servants was seen as a burden even by those below gentry status. Peckham also follows Glasse in an outburst of xenophobia, although such attacks were becoming less frequent, as the perceived threat from French cooks and cookery receded with the cookery book's step down the ladder of society:

> The following collection of receipts ... is not stuff'd with a nauseous hodge-podge of French kickshaws; and yet the real delicacies of the most sumptuous entertainments are by no means neglected.[38]

---

[36] Most of the title-page, as Maclean points out, is identical to that by Catharine Brooks; the second edition of Brooks' *Complete English Cook* came out in about 1762. The books, however, are not the same.

[37] Peckham (1767), p. iv.

[38] Ibid., p. iii.

Glasse had identified her buyers and her readers and had inspired the women authors who followed her to emphasize the same selling-points which had brought her success.

The titles and presentations of these women's books of the 1750s and 1760s show how the genre was moving down the social scale. Soon, authors would be addressing servants as buyers, as well as readers. But what was happening at the top end of the market? As was noted earlier, Vincent La Chapelle's *Modern Cook* was reprinted until 1751, by which time French cuisine had moved on, and there was no book in English representing the best and latest French manner. Few male cooks produced new titles between 1740 and 1760. The exceptions were by Edward Lambert, a professional confectioner in Pall Mall, which came out in around 1744, and two by a cook who called himself 'Jassintour Rozea' (undoubtedly a pseudonym), the first, apparently incomplete, published in Edinburgh in 1753, the second in London in 1756.[39] Two fairly ambitious books appeared in the late 1750s. The first was by John Thacker, who had in fact put out his *Art of Cookery* as early as 1746 as a part-work, although it was not printed as a single volume until 1758. The receipts are organized into chapters corresponding to the months of the year, but the later volume-form includes bills of fare for the 'Residence in the College of Durham' in 1753. (Thacker was at this time employed as cook to the dean and chapter of Durham cathedral.) As the title-page makes clear, however, the receipts were not original, since they were 'the most approv'd Receipts heretofore published'. Thacker also attacks French cooks, saying that a great many 'French' dishes are in fact of English origin, and that they have been given French names 'to excite Curiosity'. French cooks' ways of dressing are simply 'profess'd Hotch-Potch'.[40] He also remarks that good manners prevent him from making invidious comparisons with 'any particular Book, or Books on this Subject, intitled *Practical* Cookery' – an allusion to Rozea, whose title for his first work (issued in parts, of which only two of the intended twelve ever saw the light) was *The Gift of Comus; or, Practical Cookery*. Thacker's hostility to French cuisine, even though he gives his receipt titles in

---

[39] Only the first two out of the intended twelve parts of Rozea's first work, *The Gift of Comus; or, Practical Cookery*, were published. The title is clearly inspired by Marin's *Les Dons de Comus* (1739). Rozea's second book, *The Compleat Cook, Market Woman, and Dairy Maid*, described him as 'Principal Cook to the late Charles Seymour, Duke of Somerset'. For further details, see Maclean, pp. 125–6.

[40] Thacker (1758), preface.

both English and French (but the French is often very approximate), makes him a poor guide to what was happening in the kitchens of the élite.

A better companion is William Verral, whose *Complete System of Cookery* appeared in 1759. The book was based upon his experience under Pierre Clouet, the Duke of Newcastle's cook, in the late 1730s. In other words, there is a twenty-year gap between the practice and the description of the cookery. Since both Verral's life and the Duke of Newcastle's kitchens are relatively well documented, we shall pause at this point to examine both. Verral offers a rare view of the career of a male cookery author who, we can be sure, actually wrote the book which bears his name. The ducal kitchens show the Whig political élite's appreciation of fine French food. The association between this tiny minority and French cuisine helped to fuel hostility to the latter, with the resulting anti-French discourse in books aimed at the middle classes like Glasse.

The extent to which French cooks and cuisine were fashionable and desirable in eighteenth-century England is a matter of some uncertainty among historians. Earlier accounts took it for granted that the influence of French fashions followed a simple progression, in matters of food as in other areas. Hecht's study of servants, published in 1956, stated baldly that 'the upper classes and their imitators grew increasingly devoted to Parisian diet as the century advanced'.[41] More recently, the emphasis has gone in the opposite direction, concentrating on satires on French cookery and negative comments in diaries and letters, so that in 1982 Roy Porter wrote that even among the rich, 'French cooks were rare and rather despised'.[42] The relevance of this to cookery book production may seem limited, but the image of French cuisine and of French cooks was central to the nature and contents of cookery books. Quantitative research on who employed French cooks is obviously difficult, since it involves a detailed examination of large numbers of household accounts. The most exhaustive study of servants so far, by Hecht, does not attempt such an analysis, but his summary, presented as lists of wages, gives nine examples of a man-cook, at annual salaries of £20 to 90 guineas (these figures do not represent chronological progression), whereas he was able to find 94 female cooks and 8 cook-housekeepers, at salaries which ranged from £4 to £25.[43] Since the lower level of male salary would certainly have been insufficient to attract a French

---

[41] Hecht, *The Domestic Servant Class in Eighteenth-Century England* (1956), p. 43.

[42] Porter, *English Society in the Eighteenth Century* (1982), p. 234.

[43] Hecht (1956), pp. 142, 146–147.

cook, it seems probable that no more than half Hecht's sample of men were French: only 4 earned more than £50 a year.

My own limited researches into the question have always found a link between French cook and Whig employer, and Newcastle offers an excellent example of this, with much interesting information to be gleaned from his household accounts and correspondence. Newcastle's cook, Pierre Clouet, was the most famous, or rather notorious, French cook working in London in the 1730s and 1740s. He appears in the letters of Lady Mary Wortley Montagu – who, like many of the English, calls him 'Chloe' – of Lord Chesterfield, and of Horace Walpole. It is clear from their remarks that a dinner prepared by Clouet was the *ne plus ultra* in *haute cuisine*.[44] Clouet was probably recruited in 1737: lists of servants and wages for 1734 and 1735 show that at these dates, Newcastle was employing a French cook called Hubert Bonote, at a salary of £50 per annum; Bonote was assisted by an English under-cook, John Morris, at a salary of £20 in 1734 and £25 in 1735. There was also a French confectioner, Daniel Tiphaine, at £60, and his assistant, a man called Bone, at £20. This staff, which also included kitchen-maids, was supervised by Thomas Northcote, the 'Clerk of the Kitchen', at £50.[45] The first payment to Clouet, of £31 10s., appears in November 1737, and more or less regular payments, of £52 10s. for half a year's wages, appear from 1738 to 1741; alongside Clouet's name is that of Jean Jorre, whose half-yearly salary was £15 15s.[46] The partial payment in 1737 suggests that Clouet joined the staff at Newcastle House in that year. There were clearly some negotiations about the terms of his employment, for a letter from him setting out his conditions has survived: he demanded sole control of the kitchens.[47] Clouet was certainly still with Newcastle in December 1745,[48] but by 1753 he was in Paris, working as *maître d'hôtel* to the Earl of Albemarle, British ambassador from 1749 until his

[44] See Halsband (ed.), *The Complete Letters of Lady Mary Wortley Montagu*, vol. 2 (1966), pp. 120, 261; Dobrée (1932), vol. 2, p. 580; *Walpole Correspondence*, vol. 17, p. 485, vol. 30, p. 91.

[45] BL Add. MS 33137, ff. 397–8, 396, 447.

[46] BL Add. MS 33321, passim.   [47] BL Add. MS 33072, f. 529.

[48] Chesterfield asked Newcastle to invite a Dutch visitor to London to a Clouet dinner in March that year ('I beg that you will let Chloe stuff him once or twice', Dobrée (1932), vol. 2, p. 580), and a political print showing Newcastle and Clouet appeared late in 1745. This means that Walpole's story that Clouet was dismissed at the instance of the Duke of Grafton, for whom he had refused to dress a dinner for Maréchal Belle-Isle, saying 'he had tired himself with playing at bowls' is apocryphal, since Grafton's dinner for Belle-Isle took place on 30 July 1745, and the marshal left England on 13 August. See *Walpole Correspondence*, vol. 17, p. 485n. For the date of the print, which cannot be before December 1745, see Atherton, *Political Prints in the Age of Hogarth* (1974), p. 235.

death in December 1754. After Clouet's departure, and following some sort of fracas with Jorre, who was still being paid in 1751 and 1752 – apparently receiving an even higher salary than Clouet – Newcastle found himself without a cook in September 1752.[49]

A year later he wrote to Albemarle soliciting help in finding a replacement. As many details of this correspondence were published by Romney Sedgwick in 1955,[50] only a summary will be given here. The first selection, a young man called Hervé, arrived soon after Newcastle's plea for assistance – he was already working at the beginning of October 1753 – but his cooking did not please, and Newcastle wrote in December to Albemarle to express his disappointment. In February the next year, reluctant to trouble Albemarle again, Newcastle wrote to Clouet to ask his opinion. Clouet's reply defended Hervé, and implicitly censured Newcastle and his friends for failing to understand the latest French cookery. For a while nothing happened, but in June 1754 Newcastle, having dismissed Hervé, appealed once more to Albemarle. The Earl and his *maître d'hôtel* hunted for a suitable candidate. The first they found, called Quoindare, changed his mind at the last minute and refused to cross the Channel; others also had no wish to leave France. Finally, in September, Albemarle sent a cook called Fontenelle and, after a fortnight's trial, Newcastle declared himself satisfied. The Ambassador himself died in December, leaving Clouet responsible for the massive debts due on supplies to his kitchens over a period of seven months; Clouet asked Newcastle's help to persuade King George II to honour Albemarle's debts and thus relieve his *maître d'hôtel*.[51] Meanwhile Jorre, having left Newcastle, was working for Lord Montfort. When Montfort committed suicide on 1 January 1755, Lord Lincoln, Newcastle's nephew and heir, hoped to get Jorre for himself, only to discover that he had already been engaged by Lord Ashburnham. A violent quarrel ensued, in which Newcastle was obliged to intervene to restore peace.[52]

---

[49] Sam Burt's accounts show payments to Jorre of £107 14s. on 4 July 1751, 'for Wages', and of £126 on 9 March 1752; BL Add. MS 33158, ff. 60, 62. In his letter of 14 February 1754 to Clouet, Newcastle says that 'Joire' has behaved in such a way to him that he no longer employs him: 'Il s'est comporté envers moi d'une telle façon, que Je ne l'employe plus'; BL Add. MS 32734, f. 139.

[50] See Sedgwick, 'The Duke of Newcastle's Cook' (1955), pp. 308–316.

[51] For the last letter, see BL Add. MS 33,853, f. 236–239.

[52] An account of this quarrel, see *Walpole Correspondence*, vol. 35, p. 246; Walpole gives the cook's name as 'Joras'. Walpole's account is confirmed by a similar one from the pen of Audrey Townshend. The two letters concerned are dated 28 and 27 August 1755.

This episode shows the fierce competition amongst the political élite for the services of the most fashionable French cooks, who earned enormous salaries. Newcastle always employed one or more, and did not even consider recruiting an Englishman. Indeed, in great Whig circles, anyone other than a Frenchman was unthinkable. The second Duke of Richmond employed a man called Thomas Jacquemar as his head cook, occupying sufficiently privileged a position in the household to bandy obscene jokes with his employer.[53] When the Duke's daughter Emily married the Earl of Kildare and went to live in Ireland, she was horrified to discover that the locals had their confectionery made by their housekeepers: she would have no truck with this, and asked her father to find her a confectioner in Paris.[54] Similarly, the fourth Duke of Bedford always employed a French cook from the 1730s until his death in 1771: for most of this period, the cook was a man called L'Allemande, who earned £60 a year. The English cook earned only half this sum, and the housekeeper a mere £12.[55] Such differentials in salary help to explain the hostility of English cooks to their French rivals, particularly when the English were turning out French dishes. French cooks were expensive, and so was French cuisine. No wonder the average cookery book buyer preferred the discourse and the apparently more modest receipts offered by Hannah Glasse and her imitators.

When William Verral published his defence of Clouet and Clouet's receipts in 1759, he was adopting a high-risk strategy which did not pay off. Beyond the limited circles where French cuisine was part of a cosmopolitan lifestyle, the Duke of Newcastle and others like him were the target of virulent satire. The general hostility towards French cooks meant that a book which defended them was unlikely to meet with a rapturous reception. In spite of this, William Verral took up the cudgels on behalf of Clouet, whose methods he had observed while working in the ducal kitchens.

Verral's own career gives us another glimpse of the cook turned author. As was so often the case, he apparently took up the pen to recoup his finances. He was born in Lewes (Sussex) on 10 April 1715, the fifth son of Richard and Sarah Verrall (there were nine children in all). In about 1724 his father became the

---

[53] In July 1749 Richmond reported to Newcastle that his cook had invented a lewd nickname for the Modenese minister in London. See McCann (ed.), *The Correspondence of the Dukes of Richmond and Newcastle 1724–1750* (1984), p. 286.

[54] See Lennox, *A Duke and his Friends* (1911), vol. 2, p. 682.

[55] See Thomson, *The Russells in Bloomsbury* (1940), pp. 226–230.

master of the White Hart Inn, a house which had formerly been the Pelham (Newcastle) family mansion.[56] The Verralls depended very much on the patronage of the Duke of Newcastle, with Richard Verrall running the inn, and his eldest son Richard junior and (after his death in 1742) his fourth son Henry, managing a coffee-house which catered for the Duke's political supporters. Other members of the family solicited the Duke's help in obtaining lucrative places. When Verrall senior died in May 1737, William was chosen to take over the inn, which he did after leaving the Duke's employment at the end of July 1738. Although Verral's book states that he had 'several Years Experience' under Clouet, Newcastle's household accounts mention only one payment to him, 'William Verrall Wages in full from Lady Day 1738 to 31 July 1738 ... £7', although a further payment was made by Newcastle's trustees, suggesting that Verral was employed for a total of about two and a half years.[57] By August 1738 Verral was supplying ball suppers when the Duke visited Lewes. Further such payments followed in 1742 and 1744.[58] At first Verral did well, and was a prosperous and respected member of the community. In 1742 he contributed 3 guineas to the subscription for building a new hospital in the town, and in January 1745 his name headed the list of tradesmen who protested to Sir Francis Poole about the protracted quartering in Lewes of a company of soldiers.[59] He served as a headborough in 1748–9, was High Constable in 1753–4, and was again a town official in 1756.[60] In 1757 his wife Ann died, and from this point a decline in his fortunes seems to have set in. The publication of *A Complete System of Cookery* in 1759 did not improve the situation, and may indeed have been one of the sources of his troubles, since it must have offended his local gentry patrons, who are ridiculed in the preface as rustics with no appreciation of fine cuisine. In 1761 Verral solicited the Duke of Newcastle for a place, and

---

[56] The most complete account of Verral is found in Perceval Lucas' article, 'The Verrall Family of Lewes', *Sussex Archæological Collections* 58 (1916), pp. 91–131. Unless otherwise stated, the biographical information which follows is from this source. The spelling of the family name varied from one member to another: Edward Verral the bookseller and William, at the end of his life, spelled it with one 'l', but other family members preferred the spelling with two. I have followed William Verral's spelling of his name in his book.

[57] See the title-page of Verral's *Complete System of Cookery* (1759), and BL Add. MS 33321, f. 49. For the trustees' payment, see BL Add. MS 33322, f. 24.

[58] BL Add. MSS 33137 f. 529; 33158, ff. 27, 45.

[59] See V. Smith (ed.), *The Town Book of Lewes 1702–1837* (1973), pp. 37–38; BL Add. MS 32704 f. 22.

[60] See V. Smith (1973), pp. 42, 46–48.

was recommended to the JPs of Middlesex as Keeper of the House of Correction, but by 12 March he had been declared bankrupt, which made him unfit for the post. On 2 March 1761 he married Hannah Turner, but he died that same month, and was buried on 26 March.

Verral did his best to defend Clouet against the more ludicrous of the stories which circulated against him:

> Much has been said of his extravagance, but I beg pardon for saying it, he was not that at all. … The story of his *assiette* of popes-eyes, the quintessence of a ham for sauce, and the gravy of twenty-two partridges for sauce for a brace, was always beyond the credit of any sensible person; so shall leave that untouch'd.[61]

When he comes to the receipts, Verral frequently points out how Clouet would produce several neat little dishes from odd pieces of meat which the English cook would reject as useless. The discourse of the preface is of great interest. It ridicules Sussex squires who want fashionable food yet refuse to equip their kitchens with more than a single stew-pan and who do not even understand the meaning of the term 'remove' or the need for symmetry in the presentation of the dishes at each course of a respectable dinner. Although these anecdotes are a pretext for Verral to write at length upon the proper equipment for a kitchen, they cannot have recommended the book to its potential buyers. A book which actively promoted French cookery and defended a French cook at the height of the Seven Years' War was almost certain to provoke a hostile reaction, and the notice in the *Critical Review* (October 1759) accused Verral of writing 'A Complete System of Politics' with the book's preface as a vast political allegory and the receipts an attempt to poison the nation.[62] The result was that Verral, unlike so many of his contemporaries, was never reprinted, even though it offered a glimpse of high-class cuisine for the modest price of 4s.

One which suffered the same fate was the other important pro-French cookery book of the period, by Martha Bradley. Mrs Bradley was a professional

---

[61] Verral (1759), pp. xxx–xxxi.

[62] *The Critical Review* 8 (1759), pp. 284–289.

cook working in Bath in the 1740s.[63] In 1756 her *British Housewife* was issued as a part-work, in weekly instalments which cost 3d. each. This monumental book, which deals not only with cookery and still-room but also with remedies for man and beast, and gardening, plus advice on how to present food and how to be a perfect hostess, finally ran to two volumes and over 1200 pages. Publication was probably complete by October (there are 42 weekly parts), and the whole book cost 10s. 6d. Its contents show that it was aimed at as wide a readership as possible: the master and mistress of a household, and their servants, from the housekeeper and cook down to the farrier and the gardener. The lowliest servant-maid was not forgotten: the densely-printed title-page states that by the copper-plates 'even *those who cannot read* will be able to instruct themselves', although the text of the receipts themselves is aimed at Mrs Bradley's fellow cooks. Mrs Bradley was clearly familiar with Hannah Glasse, Patrick Lamb and Vincent La Chapelle: she took many receipts from these authors, but adapted and improved on the originals. The comments she adds to explain a method or to offer variants are all her own.[64] Like Verral, Mrs Bradley offers a balanced discussion of the merits of French cuisine, although unlike him she does inject a few xenophobic remarks into her discourse to pander to current prejudice.[65] Despite this prudent measure, her book apparently failed to sell, since its publication in finished book form in 1758 almost certainly re-used the remaining copies of the 1756 printing.

The most successful authors of the middle of the century were the less ambitious ones who confined themselves to cookery: Hannah Glasse, whose book went through more than twenty editions in the eighteenth century and was reprinted until 1843, and Elizabeth Moxon, whose *English Housewifry* was frequently reprinted after its first appearance in 1741, the 13th edition dating from 1789 and being reprinted in the 1790s. Both launched their books by subscription, covering the initial costs of printing. Hannah Glasse had 202 subscribers, the vast majority (157) being women; as was noted earlier, only 5 of these ladies had titles (either 'Lady' or 'Hon.'); of the men, 3 affirmed their

---

[63] See her comment on a dish which she made popular in Bath in 1749; *The British Housewife* (1756), vol. 1, p. 433.

[64] For a full discussion of Mrs Bradley's book and her culinary style, see my introduction to the Prospect facsimile reprint of the book (1996–8), vol. 1, pp. 7–49.

[65] See, for instance, her comment on French cooks having 'beggared many great Families', vol. 1, p. 327.

gentlemanly status with the suffix 'Esq.' When one compares this list to that of contributors to Richard Bradley's two parts of *The Country Housewife* in 1727 and 1732, one notices the increased proportion of women (men had out-numbered women as contributors to Bradley) and the diminished number of those of gentry status (12 per cent of Bradley's contributors against 4 per cent of Glasse's subscribers). Admittedly, contributors and subscribers are not quite the same, but the trend is too marked to be ignored. The cookery book was moving steadily down the social scale, and the authors and booksellers were correct in believing that the buyer was usually a woman. Whereas the court-cooks of earlier decades had aimed their books at male aristocratic patrons, from the mid-century onwards, even the male authors would address the female reader.

The Fair, *who's* Wise *and oft consults our* BOOK,
And thence directions gives her Prudent Cook;
With CHOICEST VIANDS, *bids her Table Crownd,*
And Health, *with Frugal Ellegance is found.*

Frontispiece from Hannah Glasse, The Art of Cookery, *new edition, c.1775. The mistress has copied a receipt for her cook, preserving the printed text from the ravages of the kitchen itself.*

By the 1750s, cookery books had diversified. There were encyclopaedic volumes such as Martha Bradley's designed to appeal to all involved in running a country estate; cookery manuals aimed at the middle-class mistress and her servants; and cheaper books which mixed cookery and homily, aimed directly at the servant as reader, if not buyer. The last forty years of the century see new patterns emerging in both content and authorship to reflect the now dominant middle-class ethos among readers, even if some of them may still belong to the gentry.

The emphasis on economy which had first appeared in the presentation of cookery books in the 1730s was by now standard, and the dearth of books on *haute cuisine* is another sign of shifting readership. Whereas the luxury books of earlier decades had been by cooks working for the aristocracy, towards the end of the century their counterparts were cooks working in celebrated taverns in London. The aspirational model of cookery was no longer presented by a cook with a string of noble employers' names to impress the potential buyer, but by the tavern cook whose food could be sampled by all who had enough money to pay for a meal. The pleasures of polite society were open to all who could afford them, not simply to those who had been born into them.

These tavern cooks, however, though forming an important group of authors, were not the principal force in cookery writing. That honour remains with the women, and especially to one whose book served as a model and a source for all the major writers who followed her. Elizabeth Raffald, the author of *The Experienced English House-keeper*, which came out in 1769, was also a successful businesswoman; her life has been extensively researched by Roy Shipperbottom, and an accurate picture of her career is now possible.[1]

She was born Elizabeth Whitaker in 1733 in Doncaster, and after an early education which included a little French, she went into service around 1748, working for several Yorkshire families. In December 1760 she moved to Cheshire, to Arley Hall, the residence of Sir Peter and Lady Elizabeth Warburton. As housekeeper, she was responsible for making preserves and pickles, jellies and cakes, and wines, and she also bought provisions from itinerant traders; her salary was £16 a year. She remained at Arley Hall until,

---

[1] The following account of Raffald is based on two complementary publications by Roy Shipperbottom: 'Elizabeth Raffald (1733–1781)' (1996); and his introduction to the reprint of Raffald's book, ed. Bagnall (1997), pp. vii–xvi.

on 3 March 1763, she married the head gardener, John Raffald. On 23 April she left to set up a business in Manchester. Her brother-in-law had a nursery and a stall at the market, so her husband was assured work; the couple rented a property in Fennell Street where Elizabeth sold fine food and confectionery from her shop and set up a register office which supplied servants for a fee. Helped by her regular use of advertisements in the *Manchester Mercury* and, later, *Prescott's Journal*, the business went well, and soon she added cookery classes to her activities. In 1766 the Raffalds moved to the Market Place near the Exchange, and in 1769 Elizabeth advertised her book, which was supported by over 800 subscriptions from the North-West, Yorkshire and London. Subscribers were offered the book for 5s., whereas those who bought through booksellers had to pay 6s. The book was printed by her neighbour, Joseph Harrop, who also printed and published the weekly *Manchester Mercury*.

The book was an immediate success; a second edition appeared in 1771, and included about 100 additional receipts which had been contributed by various ladies, as Raffald herself admitted. She also compiled and published a *Manchester Directory* in 1772, and a second directory in 1773. Between 1764 and 1772 she gave birth to six daughters (not the sixteen she is usually credited with), as is recorded in the parish registers. In 1772 the Raffalds moved again, this time to take over the King's Head in Salford, where they organized Florists' Feasts, with competitions for the best carnations, and card assemblies on Thursdays during the winter season. But business at the inn did not flourish as the shops had done, probably because of John Raffald's drinking. In 1776 Elizabeth's sister Mary Whitaker opened a shop opposite the inn, plying the same trade as her sister, selling confectionery and reinstating the register office for servants. The Raffalds' creditors began to press them, and they were forced to leave the King's Head. Elizabeth herself started a refreshment business at the race-course on Kersal Moor 'during the strawberry season', selling beverages and, of course, strawberries and cream. John Raffald became master of the Exchange Coffee House in Manchester, and his wife took over the catering. She compiled and issued a third *Manchester Directory*, but on 19 April 1781 she died 'of a spasm', and was buried at Stockport. By the time of her death her book had already gone through seven editions, and the eighth was in preparation.

It is clear, even without the enormous family she has traditionally been credited, that Elizabeth Raffald was a woman of extraordinary industry and vision, thoroughly attuned to the needs of the expanding provincial society around her. Her own activities as a caterer provided her with both a showcase for her wares and advance advertising for her book; one of the most important parts of the book is the series of receipts for dessert dishes, creams, jellies and so on, which she sold at her shop. So it is not surprising that her book should have been such a success: it went into over 33 editions and remained in print until 1834; and, as Roy Shipperbottom and others have pointed out, receipts from it were copied into many manuscript collections.[2] It was also one of the most widely plagiarized works of the whole eighteenth century: the books by the tavern cooks drew heavily on her, as we shall see.

Elizabeth Raffald was thus the second most popular author after Hannah Glasse, and a comparison shows that Raffald followed Glasse's lead but went even further in adapting to the needs of polite society. Raffald dedicated her book to her former employer, Lady Elizabeth Warburton, but the dedication makes clear that upper-class ladies were not really expected to read the text:

> I … hope these Receipts (wrote purely from Practice) may be of use to young Persons who are willing to improve themselves.
>
> I rely on your Ladyship's Candour, and whatever Ladies favour this Book with reading it, to excuse the plainness of the Style, as in Compliance with the desire of my Friends, I have studied to express myself so as to be understood by the meanest Capacity.[3]

The 'young Persons' are clearly inexperienced servants. What has changed is that whereas Glasse presented her own plain style as a novelty, twenty years later Raffald takes it for granted that the book will be given to the servant rather than read by the mistress. As one might expect, Raffald also mentions the economical nature of her receipts, adopting at the same time a rather defensive attitude to French dishes:

---

[2] Shipperbottom mentions particularly the receipts copied out by Princess Victoria herself (1997, p. xvi); Florence White notes that Raffald's receipt for 'Bride Cake' was copied into contemporary manuscript collections by housewives in Leicestershire, Somerset and Berkshire (*Good Things in England* (1932), p. 331); I have myself found receipts from Raffald copied into the manuscript containing receipts collected between 1747 and 1824, attributed to Elizabeth Serrell of Wells (Baines & Imray (eds), *Elizabeth Serrell of Wells: Her Recipes & Remedies* (1986), pp. 5, 6–7.

[3] Raffald, *The Experienced English House-keeper* (1769), dedication.

Though I have given some of my Dishes French Names, as they are only known by those Names, yet they will not be found very Expensive, nor add Compositions but as plain as the Nature of the Dish will admit of.[4]

This looks more like hostility to French cookery among her readers than an attack on French cooks; once again, the emphasis has shifted. Hannah Glasse denounced the extravagance of French cooks, but gave plenty of French receipts; Raffald selects only the simpler French dishes, and offers substitutes for those pet English hates, cullis and rich sauces. In fact, virulently anti-French discourse was on the wane, and even Raffald's remarks have something of the ritual about them, lacking conviction. Soon such comments would disappear from cookery books altogether.

Like Glasse, Raffald rejects medical receipts on the grounds that she does not wish to tread on doctors' territory:

The Number of Receipts in this Book, are not so numerous as in some others, but they are what will be found useful and sufficient for any Gentleman's Family, – neither have I meddled with Physical Receipts, leaving them to the Physicians superior judgment, whose proper Province they are.[5]

Medicine is an area best left to the specialist. The home remedies so prominent in E. Smith and Mary Kettilby in the 1720s are implicitly rejected. Just as the kitchen was the proper province of the servant not the mistress, so the care of the sick was no longer part of her duties either. The discourse of this book reinforces the image of the lady of leisure, a consumer of others' services. Aspirations to a fashionable lifestyle are also apparent in the content: while French dishes, reassuringly simplified, are given, the main area of display is in the important sections on the dessert. Decorative jellies, flummeries and whips moulded into temples or ponds with fish swimming in them, and other conceits, enabled the housekeeper to set out a landscape garden on the table.[6] Such dishes were by no means entirely new (Martha Bradley had offered a few in

---

[4] Raffald (1769), address to the reader, p. ii.
[5] Ibid., p. iii.
[6] Ibid., pp. 162–180.

1756),[7] but the emphasis placed on them by Raffald, in both the text and on the title-page, shows how this new style had supplanted the display of wet and dry sweetmeats harking back to the banquet course of the seventeenth century. Raffald's receipts were widely copied in later printed cookery books.[8]

Since part of Raffald's reputation was due to these instructions in sweet dishes and confectionery, it may be opportune to look at what else was available. Before 1750, there had been few specialized titles: Mary Eales' little book in 1718, John Emmett's *Choice Collection of Excellent Receipts in Confectionary*, published at York in 1737, and Edward Lambert's *Art of Confectionary* (*c*.1744) were the only ones. All these authors were professional confectioners: Mary Eales styled herself 'Confectioner to her late Majesty Queen Anne', Emmett had worked for the Duke of Grafton, and Lambert had a shop in Pall Mall.[9] Their books were almost exclusively devoted to sugar-work and preserves, although Eales gave the first English receipt for ice-cream. Of course, some of the more compendious productions of the early part of the century also included confectionery, like John Nott's *Cook's and Confectioner's Dictionary* of 1723. The emphasis was still on the old-style 'wet and dry sweetmeats', though Nott does offer a charming suggestion for the presentation of these – in little baskets so that the diner could eat the confections on top at once and carry the rest home for later.[10] But fashion was moving on; in grand houses, a French confectioner was as essential as a French cook. We have already seen how the Duke of Newcastle employed Daniel Tiphaine, and read of the dilemma of the Countess of Kildare when she discovered that in Ireland 'there is nobody… upon the footing of Robinson in London, and every Bodys Housekeeper is their Confectioner'. She was accustomed to better things, though she did not want to pay her confectioner more than £30 a year, as she did not need the 'very Tip Top sort'.[11] Soon there

---

[7] See M. Bradley, *The British Housewife* (1756), vol. 1, pp. 362–365.

[8] See, for instance, *The Bath Cookery Book* (*c*.1790), pp. 182–5; Briggs, *The English Art of Cookery* (1788), pp. 467–8, 473–4; Cole, *The Lady's Complete Guide* (1788), pp. 449–455; Collingwood & Woollams, *The Universal Cook* (1792), pp. 262, 267, 269; Farley, *The London Art of Cookery* (1783), pp. 331, 333, 336–7; M. Smith, *The Complete House-keeper, and Professed Cook* (1772), pp. 287–291.

[9] The information on all these authors comes from their title-pages, with further details on Lambert in David, *Harvest of the Cold Months* (1996), p. 315.

[10] See Nott (1723), in the instructions for dessert; this detail is lifted from Massialot (1702).

[11] See above p. 123. Richard Robinson was a well-known confectioner with premises in New Bond Street; he appears frequently in the Bedford household accounts. See Scott Thomson, *The Russells in Bloomsbury 1669–1771* (1940), p. 252.

would be a need for books to reveal to a wider audience what was being produced for such aristocrats.

After 1750, another specialized work was Hannah Glasse's *Compleat Confectioner* of *c.*1760. It covered not only sugar work and preserves, but various cakes, creams, jellies and cordials. As was her wont, she borrowed a large proportion of her receipts: the whole text of Lambert's book (81 receipts), and others from E. Smith's *Compleat Housewife* (18th edition, 1758), *The Family Magazine* (1741), and from her own earlier book of 1747. Over half the receipts were copied.[12] Glasse added bills of fare for desserts (whereas she had deemed these for the main courses of a dinner unnecessary in her earlier work on cookery), explaining that she realized such instructions were needed by the 'young and unexperienc'd'.[13] She pointed out that most people who gave 'grand deserts' either employed a confectioner, or bought their dessert ready-made from a shop; but, away from London, this was difficult, hence Glasse's emphasis on 'country ladies' who might amuse themselves by making the dishes and setting out a dessert:

> Giving directions for a grand desert would be needless, for those persons who give such grand deserts, either keep a proper person, or have them of a confectioner; ... though every young lady ought to know both how to make all kind of confectionary, and dress out a desert; in former days, it was look'd on as a great perfection in a young lady to understand all these things, if it was only to give directions to her servants; and our dames of old, did not think it any disgrace to understand cookery and confectionary.
>
> But for country ladies it is a pretty amusement, both to make the sweet-meats and dress out a desert, as it depends wholly on fancy and but little expence.[14]

The emphasis is similar to the discourse of the cookery books of the first third of the century; once again, the countryside was where old skills lingered

---

[12] For further information on Glasse's sources, see Gillies, 'Seeing Through Glasse' (1986), p. 32, and Lucraft, 'A Study of *The Compleat Confectioner* by Hannah Glasse', *PPC* 56 (1997), pp. 23–35, and *PPC* 57 (1997), pp. 13–24.

[13] Glasse, *The Compleat Confectioner* (*c.* 1760), p. 252.

[14] Glasse (*c.*1760), pp. 252–3; see also the address to the reader, p. iii.

longest, although Glasse clearly believed that confectionery was no longer a standard part of a young girl's education.

In spite of its borrowings, the contents of Glasse's book are a step towards Raffald's dessert ideas, though her decorative dishes are neither as numerous nor as elaborate. It represents a transitional stage from the older style of banqueting dishes to the new dessert. Soon after this, London confectioners began to reveal their secrets to the public: the first was a man called Borella, who worked for the Spanish ambassador. His *The Court and Country Confectioner* appeared in 1770. Although it was dedicated 'To the Ladies of Great Britain', its contents were directed at housekeepers who might replace the professional confectioner employed in great houses. The author sought to defend himself against accusations of revealing trade secrets, as the court-cooks had done earlier:

> Many master confectioners … will be a good deal irritated; for … their whole art may be said to consist in being known to none but its professors; and while it must be owned, that, in noblemen's families the assistance of a confectioner on many occasions, cannot be avoided; yet … there are few or no receipts in confectionary and distilling but what may be easily and successfully practised by the English house-keeper.[15]

This offers an interesting sidelight on changing culinary styles, since the fury of the cooks and, later, of the confectioners appears at a time when a new style is beginning to replace older traditions. In the 1740s Edward Lambert had felt no such need to defend himself. The real novelty of Borella lay in the many receipts for ices, both ice-creams and water-ices. Although some had appeared in earlier works, they were not particularly satisfactory. Mary Eales concentrated on the freezing process rather than on the mixture, and Glasse (in her *Compleat Confectioner*, which derived the receipt from the 5th edition of her own *Art of Cookery*) is also vague about the raspberry and cream mixture.[16] Borella, however, gives a great variety, with such unusual flavours as tea, white coffee and brown bread. Some of the receipts are from Menon's *Soupers de la Cour* (of which more later), others from Emy's *L'Art de Bien Faire les Glaces* (1768).[17]

---

[15] [Borella], *The Court and Country Confectioner* (1770), pp. 2–3.

[16] See Eales (1718), pp. 92–3; Glasse (*c.* 1760), p. 161.

[17] For the chapter on ices, see Borella (1770), pp. 75–96; for his sources, see Day, 'Which *Compleat Confectioner?*' (1998), p. 51.

Borella was followed by others: in 1789 Frederick Nutt produced his *Complete Confectioner*, based on experience as an apprentice with the celebrated firm of Negri and Witten.[18] Domenico Negri had been trading from the 'Pot and Pineapple' in Berkeley Square since at least 1765,[19] first on his own account, then with Gunter, who left to set up his own business, then (from 1780) with Witten.[20] Nutt's preface also makes discreet reference to professional secrets, and suggests a knowledge of confectionery would be helpful to women obliged to earn a living:

> Whilst we consider the manifest advantage that would undoubtedly accrue to numbers by unfolding a knowledge of Confectionary, it appears rather extraordinary that the contracted ideas of self-interest have as yet so uniformly taken place as to prohibit a publication on the subject: the vast expence attending the instructions given by those even poorly qualified, has in a great measure kept it concealed from the observation of many, whose prospects in life might turn upon a situation where it would infinitely serve: those unprovided females in particular, who wish to improve, and perhaps excel, however narrow their abilities, will find in the following sheets wherewith to satisfy their desires with regard to every information in the business.[21]

Although the author mentions the expense of lessons, his own book was hardly cheap: at 10s. 6d. it was one of the dearest of the period, comparable to those by the court-cooks of the first decades of the century.

Shortly after, another apprentice who had been with the same firm – when it was Negri and Gunter – produced a cheaper book (it cost 2s. sewn or 2s. 6d. bound),[22] containing much the same type of information. Robert Abbot also addressed women servants, as is seen in the title, *The Housekeeper's Valuable Present*. It appeared in or before 1791. His preface makes clear that lessons of a sort were given in Negri and Gunter's workshops:

---

[18] See Nutt (1789), title-page.

[19] See Day (1998), p. 47 and n.

[20] See David, *Harvest of the Cold Months* (1996), pp. 311–312. But on p. 317 David contradicts herself by saying that Gunter became Negri's partner 'in the 1780s'.

[21] Nutt (1789), pp. v–vii.

[22] Abbot, *The Housekeeper's Valuable Present* [*c.* 1790], title-page.

> During the course of my apprenticeship … many housekeepers to
> noblemen and gentlemen, on special occasions, were frequently present,
> in order to observe our *peculiar method* of preparing confects.
>
> Since I left Messrs. Negri and Gunter, I have had frequent appli-
> cations from those persons, as well as others, for receipts and
> information respecting improvements and additions to this art. But
> being engaged in the service of several noblemen, … I determined to
> form the following Treatise.[23]

Clearly, famous London confectioners were not afraid that opening their workshops would cause any loss of trade; in fact, it seems that this was useful
advertising. Furthermore, Abbot's comments on the demand for up-to-date
receipts suggest that fashions were still changing and that housekeepers, well
aware of this, were determined to keep up. They knew their position at the top
of the female domestic hierarchy depended on their ability to satisfy their
employers' desire for modish desserts.

The professionalism of these women, housekeepers and cooks, stands out in
the cookery books, and this offers an interesting glimpse of the shift in attitude
towards culinary activities. Elizabeth Raffald recognized that she was going to
be read by her fellow-servants rather than by mistresses. By 1769, this was no
longer something new, and the women authors who followed her were usually
themselves either professional cooks working for the aristocracy and gentry, or
semi-professionals making a living by running a cookery-school. The most
important names amongst the first group are Mary Smith (*The Complete Housekeeper*, 1772), Charlotte Mason (*The Lady's Assistant*, 1773), Mary Cole (*The
Lady's Complete Guide*, 1788), and Sarah Martin (*The New Experienced English
Housekeeper*, 1795); amongst the second, Susanna Maciver (*Cookery, and Pastry*,
1773), Elizabeth Marshall (*The Young Ladies' Guide in the Art of Cookery*, 1777),
the three Kellets (*A Complete Collection of Cookery Receipts*, 1780), and Mrs
Frazer (*The Practice of Cookery*, 1791). All those in the second group published
their books in either Newcastle-upon-Tyne or Edinburgh.

It is significant that these authors' names and, where appropriate, the names
of their employers, were proclaimed on their title-pages, whereas E. Smith and
Mary Kettilby had preferred anonymity. By the 1740s, women authors' names

---

[23] Abbot [*c*.1790], p. iii.

were beginning to appear, but it was not until the 1770s that they furnished the identities of their employers as well, following the earlier example of the court-cooks. For instance, in 1772 Mary Smith set out her credentials:

> By Mary Smith, late House-keeper to Sir Walter Blackett, Bart. and formerly in the Service of the Right Hon. Lord Anson, Sir Tho. Sebright, Bart. and other Families of Distinction, as House-keeper and Cook.[24]

Mary Smith names a member of the aristocracy, Lord Anson (she may have been the Anson housekeeper in London, since the family's accounts for the period 1763–68, kept at Shugborough, contain the weekly note, 'Paid Mary's account'[25]), and a wealthy industrialist, Sir Walter Blackett, the 'King of Newcastle', whose family had made a fortune by investing in the Durham coal-fields.[26] Money was as much of a reference as title. Increasingly, women authors stressed their own status as a 'professed cook' or a 'professed housekeeper'; Ann Cook was the first to do so, but later Isabella Moore, Charlotte Mason, Mary Cole, Sarah Martin and Mary Holland all mention either one of these terms or their service to respectable (if not noble) employers. Even quite obscure names were pressed into service. Sarah Martin announced that she had been 'Many Years Housekeeper to the late Freeman Bower Esq. of Bawtry'.[27]

There is a new sense of pride here, due to the fact that these women were at the top of the domestic hierarchy, but without being degraded members of the gentry class. For them, their position and, even more, their authorship, marked a step up rather than down in the social hierarchy. Whereas it had been an accepted route to advancement for a gentlewoman to serve in an aristocratic household in the sixteenth and early seventeenth centuries, in the eighteenth century service was seen as ignoble, and the gulf between polite society above stairs and the servants in the basement became ever more marked.[28] By the end of the century, the gentlewoman who served her wealthier relations as a house-

[24] M. Smith, *The Complete Housekeeper* (1772), title-page.

[25] Private communication from the curator at Shugborough to the author, 27 November 1981.

[26] See Holderness, *Pre-Industrial England* (1976), p. 152; also Horsley, *Eighteenth-Century Newcastle*, 1971, pp. 13, 184, 210.

[27] Martin, *The New Experienced English-Housekeeper* (1795), title-page.

[28] See Girouard, *Life in the English Country House* (1980), pp. 184–9.

keeper (as Fleetwood Butler had done for her distant cousin Sir Thomas
Haggerston between 1691 and 1709[29]) was a thing of the past, a fact which
elicited the following comment from Francis Grose:

> When I was a young man there existed in the families of … the rank of
> gentlemen, a certain antiquated female, either maiden or widow, com-
> monly an aunt or cousin. …
>
>   By the side of this good old lady gingled a bunch of keys, securing,
> in different closets and corner-cupboards, all sorts of cordial waters, …
> washes for the complexion, … a rich seed cake, a number of pots of
> currant jelly and rasberry jam, with a range of gallipots and phials, con-
> taining salves … and purges, for the use of the poor neighbours. … Alas!
> this being is no more seen, and the race is … totally extinct.[30]

A gentlewoman in financial straits now had no choice but to earn her living
in service with strangers or in some kind of trade. At the end of the century,
there was another factor which increased the female presence amongst the
servants even in grand houses: the tax imposed on male servants in 1777 led
many employers to place a woman in charge of the kitchens, and men-servants
tended to be employed in 'visible' positions, such as those of butler or footman,
where they would contribute more to the prestige of their master.[31]

   These women learned their skills while in service and from books. It is clear
from the contents of their cookery books that they were familiar with the work
of their predecessors: Mary Smith had used and adapted receipts from the translation (1767) of Menon's *Soupers de la Cour* (1755), and Mary Cole had read vast
numbers of cookery books and had probably also worked under a man-cook.
When she presented her own volume, *The Lady's Complete Guide*, in 1788, she
described it on the title-page as 'the most complete System of Cookery ever yet
exhibited'. The reference to a 'system' implies familiarity with the French
modular method of organizing the work in a well-staffed kitchen when such
references are quite rare amongst other English authors. When she presents her
receipts and her methods in the preface, Mrs Cole emphasizes her many years'

[29] See Forster (ed.), *Selections from the Disbursement Book (1691–1709) of Sir Thomas Haggerston, Bart*
(1965), pp. x, 13, 22, 26, 61.
[30] See Grose, *The Olio* (1792), pp. 40–41.
[31] See C. Davidson, *A Woman's Work is Never Done* (1982), p. 180.

experience, and her critical reading of other cookery books:

> Being determined to arrive as near perfection as possible in the line of my
> profession, I purchased, with avidity, every new publication on the subject
> of Cookery, which appeared in either the French or English languages. I
> soon perceived that every subsequent writer had borrowed very largely
> from those who had preceded. *Mrs. Glasse*'s book contains the best receipts
> which she could discover in the four esteemed works of this kind then
> extant. *Mrs. Mason*, *Mrs. Raffald*, and *Mr. Farley*, have pursued similar
> steps; but have not, like myself, candidly acknowledged their
> obligations.[32]

Mrs Cole announced that she gives the original author's name each time the
receipt is not her own;[33] but despite this resounding declaration, and an
impressive array of attributions in the text, not all the borrowings are acknowledged. Mrs Cole's honesty is not perfect.

In the quotation above, she cited the best-known names among contemporary cookery writers, but she had in fact perused other works:

> Besides my Original Receipts, the result of many years experience and
> assiduity in my profession, the best of my judgment has been exercised
> in selecting whatever is valuable from the works of others, which, after
> proving their excellence, I regularly entered in my common-place book.
> The following pages are enriched with every article that merits preser-
> vation in the productions of *Clermont, Glasse, Mason, Dalrymple,*
> *Dupont, Commc, Desang, Verno, Troas, Delatour, Valois, Verral, Raffald,*
> *Farley,* &c.'[34]

While the English authors at the beginning and end of this list are readily identi-
fiable, the French are not. Are these real authors of whom no trace now exists
(an unlikely hypothesis)? Or did Mrs Cole invent the names in order to impress
her readers? Or, as Alan Davidson suggests,[35] was it to laugh at those English

---

[32] Cole (1788), preface.
[33] Ibid.   [34] Ibid.
[35] See Davidson, 'The Natural History of British Cookery Books' (1982), in *A Kipper with my Tea*
(1990), p. 104.

writers who 'made a great to-do about following French authors'? This last idea also seems unlikely, given that Mrs Cole herself took receipts from Clermont, the translator of *Les Soupers de la Cour*, and from Verral, who, as we have seen, defended the celebrated Clouet against xenophobic abuse. Whatever the truth of the matter, Mrs Cole's preface seems to show that the high-class books were a form of self-instruction for the ambitious servant. However, despite her avid reading, she seems to have failed to notice that Dalrymple's book is almost entirely plagiarized from Clermont, since she attributes receipts sometimes to one, and sometimes to the other. This casts reasonable doubt on the very fact of her existence: it is indeed probable that the book is simply a compilation, and that Mrs Cole (if she existed) merely lent her name to the work of a hack writer.

Before pursuing the question of the readership of the more up-market books by women authors such as Mary Cole (the second edition of the book in 1789 cost 6s. in boards, or 7s. bound), it is worth pausing to look at the sources available to women cooks and housekeepers who wanted to keep abreast of fashionable developments. Clearly, Raffald was a useful guide to the new form of the dessert, but for recent trends in French cookery since '*nouvelle cuisine*' these readers had to look elsewhere. Between 1760 and 1780, only four English men-cooks published cookery books. Two had worked for the aristocracy: William Gelleroy, author of *The London Cook* (1762), for the Duchess of Argyll, and John Townshend, author of *The Universal Cook* (1773) for the Duke of Manchester before becoming master of a Greenwich tavern. The other two, James Jenks and J. Skeat, simply present themselves as professional cooks. These works offer no information that was not already available: Gelleroy is largely copied from Hannah Glasse; Townshend is openly a compilation with some additions by the author; the others describe the cookery of the middle of the century.

Those who wanted to follow the progress of French cuisine since La Chapelle and Clouet had to turn to the translation of Menon's *Les Soupers de la Cour* (1755), which was published in 1767 with the title *The Art of Modern Cookery Displayed*. The English version was the work of a man named B. Clermont, who had worked as clerk of the kitchen to 'some of the first Families in this Kingdom'.[36] He informed readers that the translation was augmented by

[36] The translator-adapter's name does not appear until the third edition (1776); see Maclean, p. 99. The quotations are from the title-page of the second edition, which appeared with a new title, *The Professed Cook*, in 1769. The text of this edition is identical to that of the first, with only the title-page changed, according to Maclean.

'the best Receipts which have ever appear'd in the French Language'. A second edition appeared in 1769, with a different title, *The Professed Cook*, but identical contents. This incorporated as its sub-title Hannah Glasse's phrase, somewhat adapted, 'Or the Modern Art of Cookery, Pastry, and Confectionary, Made Plain and Easy' – another indication that Glasse continued to dominate the market. The book was aimed at professionals, and Clermont diplomatically explains that English cooks were often uncertain of French terminology:

> As Bills of Fare are mostly made in French, I … thought it very necessary and of particular great Use, to retain all the French Names and Appellations, giving at the same time a literal Translation.… It is more particularly useful to English Cooks, House-keepers, and every one employed in providing and making Bills of Fare, who have not had Opportunity of being acquainted with French *Cookery*.… I have myself … been Witness of the Diffidence of English Cooks, in looking at Bills of Fare, of which they had probably executed the whole several Times, only under different Denominations. This has been my greatest Inducement, to retain all French Names as in the Original.[37]

Thus the book is a cookery manual and a glossary, aimed at cooks familiar with the dishes but not their names. If this was indeed the situation, it explains some of the English hostility to French cooks who, they believed, were 'stealing' dishes and calling them French; it also casts light on Elizabeth Raffald's comment on giving French names to some of her dishes. While the cookery receipts were aimed at cooks, the confectionery section was for the benefit of house-keepers, and perhaps even their mistresses:

> To the Complete *Cookery*, the Author has also added Confectionary; in which I have been more particularly exact, as knowing it to be very much wanted amongst English Servants. Ladies who delight in the *profitable* Amusement of making their own Sweet-meats, and House-keepers, whose Business it is to do in most Families in England, will find it of very great Utility.[38]

---

[37] [Clermont], *The Professed Cook* (1769), pp. iii–v.
[38] Ibid. pp. v–vi.

This confirms Hannah Glasse's comments on confectionery as an amusement for ladies, even though it was now mostly work for the housekeeper. What also stands out is the need for instruction, since the old seventeenth-century skills were no longer part of a girl's education. Whereas the very early eighteenth-century manuals presumed an interest in such matters among gentlewomen, the books of this third period had to adopt a more persuasive tone.

The Professed Cook went into several editions,[39] and was given further exposure in the work of a British cook, George Dalrymple, who published *The Practice of Modern Cookery* in Edinburgh in 1781. He took nearly all his material from Clermont, adding only his own receipts for puddings (omitting some of Clermont to make room). Dalrymple was unusual in that he saw his readers as fellow men-cooks, addressing them in terms reminiscent of Charles Carter in 1730:

> I am persuaded that this Work will excite the attention of many, especially Cooks; it is their approbation I have endeavoured to gain. As to the little artists of that profession, who have too often a self-sufficient knowledge, their applause or censure is alike to me. There are many of these half-bred gentry that affect to despise the knowledge received through such a channel; although people, eminent in other professions, seek with avidity any new publications that treat of their respective subjects. Cookery, like most arts, has its theory, which is of essential use to a workman who knows how to work by rules laid down to him. …
>
> There are several excellent Treatises published, wherein you see the Ancient Cookery in a very perfect Degree: but I trust that this Work will show the Modern Manner, with its improvements, in no despicable light.[40]

Dalrymple does not mention women, which is very unusual at this period since most authors, even amongst the men, knew that female servants were the

---

[39] Maclean (p. 99) cites only three editions (1767, 1769, 1776); but Oxford (p. 101) mentions the 10th edition of 1812, as well as the other three, although he incorrectly gives the date of the first edition as 1766, failing to realize that it is the same work as *The Professed Cook*; Bitting (p. 92) also cites the 10th edition of 1812 as part of her collection. Whether there were 6 editions published between 1776 and 1812 is uncertain.

[40] Dalrymple (1781), pp. v–vi.

readers of such works. Either they extolled their own receipts and the cheapness of their book, as did Townshend in 1773 (unfortunately, there is no indication of what the price was), or, like Jenks in 1768, they stated quite baldly that the book was 'for the assistance of the Cook-maid'.[41]

For those who wanted to study French cuisine, Clermont was virtually the only source. None of the other great French books of the second half of the century was translated, and the French best-seller, *La Cuisinière bourgeoise* (1746), which might have been expected to appeal to a largely female English readership, did not appear in English until 1793, with the title *The French Family Cook*. By contrast, descriptions of luxury cuisine such as *Le Cuisinier roïal et bourgeois* and *Les Soupers de la Cour* had appeared quite rapidly, within eleven and twelve years respectively. For the English, French cooking was by its very nature princely, and a book presenting homely French fare – 'Adapted to the Tables ... of Persons of moderate Fortune and Condition'[42] – was self-contradictory. *The French Family Cook*'s success is difficult to gauge: a fourth edition of 1796 is recorded, with the word 'French' deleted from the title,[43] but whether there were really four editions in the space of as many years must remain uncertain.

While the audience for these books was mainly, but not exclusively, women servants, some parts were aimed explicitly at their mistresses. Confectionery was often seen as their 'amusement'; and they would also be interested in the bills of fare, especially if they were new to housekeeping. As Charlotte Mason pointed out in 1773:

> The great inconvenience I myself experienced, on commencing mistress of a family, from the want of such assistance, has since prompted me to attempt a set of bills of fare, which I flatter myself will be of great use to ladies in general, but particularly to the younger part of my sex, who ... are greatly at a loss how to conduct their table with that decency and propriety which are so much to be desired, not only in making dinners for company, but also in a family way.
>
> It is certain that a woman never appears to greater advantage than at the head of a well-regulated table.... Though a dinner be small and

---

[41] See Townshend, *The Universal Cook* (1773), preface; Jenks, *The Complete Cook* (1768), p. ix.

[42] [Menon], *The French Family Cook* (1793), title-page.

[43] Maclean, p. 101.

simple, the manner of serving it will make it appear to great advantage; and I think I may venture to say, that with the assistance of these bills of fare, … a table may be so conducted as to do credit both to the taste and management of the mistress.[44]

More than a third of her work was devoted to bills of fare, enabling the novice mistress to devise dinners and suppers in the 'correct' manner. These were not intended to be fashionable, but rather conforming to standards of respectability, suggesting a middle-class rather than upper-class readership. There are already overtones of the 'Victorian prelude' here, with the development of the idea of 'separate spheres', which relegated women to a purely domestic rôle.[45] After her lengthy presentation of bills of fare, Mason passed on to receipts, 'Besides which, I have given whatever instructions are necessary for a servant in a plain way; so that…she may…be made capable of any cook's place, where a man is not required.'[46] The receipts, however, were secondary to the advice on organizing meals according to the rules of polite society.

Such rules were often presented as necessary for the servant rather than the mistress. Mary Smith gave receipts, bills of fare, and lists of foods in season, stating that, 'A Servant, by giving due Attention thereto, may be capable of sending a genteel Dinner to Table with the greatest Ease.'[47] All the mistress had to do was approve the bill of fare presented to her. One encyclopaedic work of 1790 describes the duties of the housekeeper: she should be knowledgeable in cookery and confectionery (in order to supervise other servants); she should deal with tradesmen and organize household supplies; she should 'provide good servants for the kitchen'; she should draw up bills of fare and plan entertainments in such a way as to make serving easier; she must arrange the dessert and make sure that nothing went to waste, locking up those leftovers which would reappear later and distributing the rest to the servants.[48] This corresponds exactly to what Susanna Whatman expected of her housekeeper, Hester Davis.

---

[44] [Mason], *The Lady's Assistant* (1773), pp. iii–iv.

[45] The expression 'Victorian prelude' comes from the title of Maurice Quinlan's 1941 study of English manners in the period 1700–1830. Quinlan suggests that by the beginning of the nineteenth century, women's activities had become limited to the home and to charitable visiting (pp. 139–159).

[46] Mason (1773), p. iv.

[47] M. Smith (1772), p. iv.

[48] *The Ladies' Library* (1790), vol. 2, pp. 61–4.

Other chapters in cookery books might, however, interest a mistress of the house. From about 1775, one type of receipt which had disappeared began to creep back. We saw earlier that both Hannah Glasse and Elizabeth Raffald had refused to give medical advice, considering it the business of neither cook nor even housekeeper. The remedies which had appeared so frequently in early eighteenth-century books were the home-made waters, cordials and salves derived from the family manuscripts of the seventeenth. But when remedies reappeared in a few books of cookery, they were prescriptions from physicians. Everyone now deferred to their 'superior judgment', as Raffald put it. Why did they reappear? The discourse concerning them suggests two reasons, both linked to the ideology of female virtue. The lady of the house was enabled to exercise her charity towards the poor, and at the same time was able to preserve her modesty which forbade her from communicating her ailments even to a doctor. One example of prescriptions by doctors offered for charitable purposes is found in Mary Cole's book, which contains advice on health and receipts for remedies under the title 'The Family Physician'. The main source for this was William Buchan's *Domestic Medicine* (1769), the medical best-seller which was in its seventeenth edition by 1800.[49] But Mrs Cole also had recourse to other celebrated physicians such as Mead, Sydenham, Tissot, Fothergill and Elliot, whose names all appeared on her title-page, guaranteeing the quality of this part of the text. The sub-title to the medical section is 'The Country Lady's Benevolent Employment',[50] a reminder of the emphasis on 'country gentle-women' in the cookery books of the early years of the century. She adopts a moralizing tone:

> I have always found peculiar pleasure in acquiring useful information; without it, we can do little good in society. Medicine, and the appli-cation of it to the most general complaints, have occupied a part of my leisure hours,... and enabled me sometimes to relieve those whose circumstances would not permit them to call in the aid of a physician.[51]

---

[49] Cole states that most of her medical lore was taken from Buchan; see Cole (1788), preface. See also Maclean, pp. 18–20.

[50] Cole (1788), p. 514.

[51] Cole (1788), preface.

If Mrs Cole herself had offered medical assistance to the local poor, we have yet another example of what had once been the responsibility of the mistress descending to the servant, since Mrs Cole announced she was cook to the Earl of Drogheda.[52]

Female delicacy was invoked by the presenter of *The Ladies' Library* (1790):

The LADIES … are often prevented from receiving the benefit of medical advice by an unwillingness, the offspring of delicacy, to apply for it. This, however, is here fully obviated; every indisposition, to which *they* are more peculiarly subject, is fully treated of; … and they will happily find the means of restoring themselves to health, without injuring their delicacy by a communication of their feelings to any person, or revealing the nature or cause of their indisposition.[53]

Such remarks are a further reminder that the stifling conventions of the Victorian period originated in the eighteenth century. The emphasis here on modesty offers a foretaste of Thomas Gisborne's harping on female purity in 1798.[54] As in Mary Cole, much of the medical advice came from Buchan; the cookery was compiled from 'almost Thirty different authors', with additions from the manuscript of a practising cook, John Perkins.[55] These instances notwithstanding, most medical prescriptions were confined to the encyclopaedic works of advice and instruction for both mistress and servant. Buchan's *Domestic Medicine* was more popular than chapters in cookery books, at least for those who could afford to purchase two discrete works of reference.

That group of works by men who followed the trade of tavern cook took advantage of the reputation of certain London eating-places, most notably the London Tavern. Of the six titles in question, three were by men who worked there. It was indeed renowned: Francis Grose tells the story of a gourmet so fastidious that he was 'in danger of starving in the larder of the London Tavern'.[56] But, to judge from Catherine Hutton's remarks, it was not frequented by the upper classes:

---

[52] Cole (1788), title-page.

[53] *The Ladies' Library* (1790), vol. i, p. viii.

[54] See Gisborne, *An Enquiry into the Duties of the Female Sex* (1797), passim.

[55] For details of the culinary sources, see *The Ladies' Library* (1790), vol. i, pp. iv–v.

[56] Grose (1792), p. 65.

Did I ever tell you of the London Assembly? I think not. It is at the London Tavern, in the finest room that my eyes ever beheld. ... The subscription is five guineas for eight nights, and the requisites for appearing are a dress coat or a laced frock. After all, it is much less genteel than the City Assembly, to become a member of which requires as great interest as to become a member of the House of Commons. Ladies who are in the habit of frequenting the City generally make it a point to go to the 'London' once in the season.[57]

The assemblies contributed to the reputation of an establishment which was splendid enough to impress but not so magnificent as to be intimidating. Other well-known London taverns, such as the Crown and Anchor or the Globe, appear on the cooks' title-pages. Clearly, the centre of gravity had shifted: whereas in earlier decades, the prestigious reference had been service to the nobility or royalty, with the implication that the cookery book revealed a cuisine inaccessible to most readers, now, the sources of good food were open to all-comers. It is partly the result of the spread of the cookery book down the social scale, but also sign of the displacement of court society by the bourgeois world.

But these books did not in fact reveal the secrets of what was eaten at taverns. Though signed by John Farley, Francis Collingwood and John Woollams, and T. Williams and his friends, they were simply compilations by a hack writer, Richard Johnson, who recorded being paid by the publishers for 'writing' Farley's *London Art of Cookery* (1783) and for 'compiling' Collingwood and Woollams' *Universal Cook* (1792), in 1782–3 and in 1792. Johnson also 'compiled' Williams' *Accomplished Housekeeper* in 1792,[58] although the book did not come out until 1797. *The Accomplished Housekeeper* was nothing more than an abridged edition of *The Universal Cook*, so it must have made sense to compile them at the same time. These productions derive very largely from Glasse and Raffald, to the extent of offering virtually identical receipts. The tavern cooks' names and the roll-call of places where they worked were simply devices to appeal to buyers. These were expected to be women servants. John Farley's title-page stated, 'Made Plain and Easy to the Understanding of every Housekeeper, Cook, and Servant in the Kingdom.' His preface also empha-sized how the receipts covered a wide range of dishes and culinary abilities:

As this Work is intended for the Use of all Ranks in general, not only for those who have attained a tolerable Knowledge of Cookery, but also for those who are but young in Experience, we have occasionally given the most simple with the most sumptuous Dishes, and thereby directed them how properly to decorate the Table of either the Peer or the Mechanic.[59]

In fact, the tavern cooks imitated the women's presentation as well as their receipts. Richard Briggs stressed his simple style in terms reminiscent of Hannah Glasse:

I presume to offer the following Sheets to the Public, in hopes that they will find the Directions and Receipts more intelligible than in most Books of the Kind. I have bestowed every Pains to render them easily practicable, and adapted to the Capacities of those who may be ordered to use them. To waste Language and high Terms on such Subjects, appears to me to render the Art of Cookery embarrassing, and to throw Difficulties in the Way of the Learner.[60]

Finally, another male author (but not one of the tavern cooks), placed as his frontispiece an engraving which sums up the situation at the end of the century: a kitchen scene shows a man showing a younger servant how to carve, while a lady presents a woman servant with a cookery book. The caption reads, 'A Lady presenting her Servant with the *Universal Family Cook* who diffident of her own knowledge has recourse to that Work for Information.'[61] This was now the total of the mistress' involvement in culinary matters.

Everything we have examined so far, whether by women cooks and house-keepers, teachers, tavern cooks or confectioners, belong to the upper end of the market. They were expensive. Clermont's version of *Les Soupers de la Cour* cost 6s.; Raffald, Cole and Farley the same. Briggs was slightly more expensive, at 7s., and Nutt's book on confectionery was 10s.6d. When T. Williams' *Accomplished Housekeeper* came out in 1797, it was clearly stated that the abridgement was a

---

[59] Farley (1783), title-page, p. v.
[60] Briggs (1788) p. iii.
[61] Henderson, *The Housekeeper's Instructor; or, Universal Family Cook* [c. 1795], frontispiece.

cheap version for the benefit of those who could not afford *The Universal Cook*.[62] The books by women who ran cookery schools were somewhat cheaper: in 1773 Mrs Maciver cost 2s. 6d., and her successor Mrs Frazer charged 3s. in the 1790s.

Between 1770 and 1780, many works appeared which offered the same types of information as their bigger, more luxurious counterparts but which were priced more competitively, appealing to a market that was unable to afford more than a few pence. They were aimed at both mistress and servant, and the discourse presenting them is remarkably similar to that of the books by women in the middle of the century. At this level of society, the mistress, as well as the servant, was quite possibly a reader. Elizabeth Price's *The New Book of Cookery*, published around 1780, offered a variety of receipts for English and French dishes, and for traditional still-room activities, but it also gave instructions for marketing, bills of fare, advice on laundering, and receipts for cosmetics and remedies. All this cost a mere 1s.[63] The address to the reader emphasizes the attempt to unite elegance and economy in the receipts, and concludes:

> I … humbly hope that it will meet with a favourable reception, as it treats of an art which deservedly claims the attention of the Ladies in general, and of Maid-Servants in particular, who, by a careful perusal of the following sheets, will soon become perfectly accomplished in the whole Art of Cookery.[64]

Even here, the idea is clearly that the cookery sections are more for the servant, while the remaining sections are for the mistress.

Elizabeth Price offered the same wide-ranging content as the domestic manuals of the 1720s and as Mary Cole's voluminous work of 1788. Her medical section supplies, like Cole, receipts from trained physicians. But Price's book was cheap because it offered all this in reduced form: 114 pages instead of the 564 of Cole. In fact, Price was a compilation relying heavily on Glasse.

---

[62] See the preface to Williams (1797), p. iii. The book cost 3s.

[63] The price of *The New Book of Cookery* is given on the title-page of an edition of Mrs Price's other work, *The New, Universal, and Complete Confectioner*. Clearly the two books were published at around the same time; the bookseller's advertisement at the back of the first work includes a book by George Alexander Gordon, *The Complete English Physician*, which appeared in 1779.

[64] Price, *The New Book of Cookery* [c.1780], p. iv.

At about the same time, the printer Alexander Hogg brought out another book by Mrs Price, *The New, Universal, and Complete Confectioner*. As Ivan Day recently pointed out, the first edition was a compilation made up largely of receipts from Glasse's *Compleat Confectioner* and Borella, Lambert and Eales.[65] But for all subsequent issues of this book Hogg substituted another text, which was nothing more than a pirate edition of Glasse's *Compleat Confectioner*. (Hogg dated none of the editions of either title by Elizabeth Price, but the 1780s seem more plausible than the 1760s suggested by Maclean, given that he is known to have worked from 16 Paternoster Row, the address given on the title-page of both, from 1778 until 1805.[66])

Price's books were not the only ones to offer cheap imitations. In 1781 a former housekeeper, A. Smith of Stafford, brought out *A New Book of Cookery* (one notices the title is almost identical to Price's). Here too, the reader found receipts for cookery, cosmetics and remedies, the last being openly taken 'from the works of several eminent Physicians'. This was another small book, 219 pages, offering contents similar to Mary Cole's. The title-page shows it was aimed at the ladies:

> The whole calculated to assist the *prudent Housewife* in furnishing the *cheapest* and *most elegant* Set of Dishes in the various Departments of Cookery, and to instruct the Ladies in many other Particulars of great Importance.

This discourse is repeated in the address to the public, and the medical section is headed, 'The good Wife's daily Companion'.[67] Thus as the cookery book goes down the social scale, the potential reader may well be the mistress rather than the servant, whereas the more expensive works are absolutely certain that the reader of the receipts must belong to the servant class. Another title, undated but probably *c*.1785, gave more precise indication of its readership. *The Ladies Best Companion* by Amelia Chambers contained cookery, cosmetics, remedies and instructions for all sorts of household jobs; the whole took up 196 pages, priced at 2s. unbound. The preface announced:

---

[65] See Day (1998), p. 47.
[66] See Maxted (1977), p. 112.
[67] A. Smith, *A New Book of Cookery* (1781), title-page, pp. 3–4, 155.

It is well known, that the woman who is ignorant of cookery is neither qualified to be a mistress or a servant; for the dressing of victuals, either in a plain or a more polite manner is so essential a part of female education, that those who neglect to acquire some knowledge of it, labour under many difficulties in their advanced years, and many have lost very valuables places for the want of such necessary qualifications. …

With respect to cookery, every thing has been inserted according to the practice of the present age, and nothing left out that could be useful, so that either the mistress, housekeeper, cook, or servant may at all times find directions for the dressing of victuals in any manner whatever.

By this assistance, the mistress of a family will be enabled to give proper directions for preparing every necessary entertainment, and those under them will be directed how to act in a proper manner.[68]

Oddly enough, the book does not give any bills of fare, in spite of the emphasis in the preface on preparing entertainments.

In 1789 an even cheaper version of Chambers' book appeared, with the author named as Charlotte Cartwright but with a virtually identical title and sub-title. This abridged version was a mere 48 pages and sold for 6d. There was no space for a preface, but the title-page (which advertised the price) gave an idea of the variety of subjects treated:

Containing the whole Arts of *Cookery, Pastery, Confectionary, Potting, Pickling, Preserving, Candying, Collaring, Brewing, &c.* With plain Instructions for making English Wines.… *To which is added,* The approved Family Physician.[69]

In such a small book, only a few receipts are given under each heading, and these are very simple: plain roasting and boiling predominate, and there are only eight for made dishes, even though the chapter devoted to them begins by saying, 'made dishes are esteemed by the politest companies'.[70]

The lowest price for a cookery book was by now 6d. The catalogue of books printed for Alexander Hogg which appears at the end of Elizabeth Price's *The*

---

[68] Chambers, *The Ladies Best Companion* [*c.* 1785], pp. iii–iv.

[69] Cartwright, *The Lady's best Companion* (1789), title-page.

[70] Ibid., p. 26.

New Book of Cookery includes an advertisement for Ann Partridge's *The Universal Cook*, costing 6d., presumably sold for the benefit of servants who were looking for something less elegant than Price:

> Mrs. Ann Partride [sic] begs Leave to inform young Women in general, that the following, which is the cheapest Book of Cookery according to the present Taste ever before Printed, is now published solely for their Benefit and Advantage. It would make a most valuable, though cheap Present, from every Mistress to her Maid Servant.[71]

By this date, the idea of putting a book into the hands of the servant had reached a much wider section of society than when Hannah Glasse had set out to make her text accessible to ignorant maids. The contents described by the advertisement are purely practical; there is none of the moralizing which had been such a feature of books explicitly designed as presents for servants in the 1740s and 1750s. This is probably a sign that there was now a middle-class moral code common to mistress and servant. It was no longer necessary to persuade the servant of her good fortune, as it had been when she was daily a witness to the inaccessible luxury of upper-class masters. The great emphasis on the cheapness of the book also demonstrates how far down the social scale the model of the lady of leisure had come. Moralists' complaints about the pretensions of tradesmen's wives and daughters begin to look more plausible. Another sign of the diffusion of such notions is that some books offered a mixture of cookery and entertainment, for the benefit of women who needed an initiation into both the duties and the pleasures of life in respectable society. As its title-page indicates, Isabella Moore's *Useful and Entertaining Family Miscellany* combines receipts in cookery and medicine, advice on menus and placing dishes on the table, directions for marketing, and songs suitable for ladies ('The Fair One's Pleasing Songster').

At an even humbler level, the chapbook cookery books published in the 1780s reached small farmers and the poorer urban classes. Often, the printers of such works simply used whatever text they had to hand, with the result that the receipts were very old-fashioned. *A Choice Collection of Cookery Receipts*, printed in Newcastle, contains material which looked back to the beginning

---

[71] See Price, *The New Book of Cookery*, p. 24 of the catalogue at the end.

of the century (they are similar to those in John Nott's *Cooks and Confectioners Dictionary*, 1723). *The Accomplished Lady's Delight*, with its seventeenth-century title, contains receipts which belong to that century: the frequent use of spices and verjuice suggests an early-seventeenth-century provenance, and indeed, the receipt 'To stew a Rack of Veal' is almost identical to the one given by John Murrell in 1615.[72]

From the 1770s onwards, the cookery book was a very variable creature appealing to a wide range of buyers. At the top of the social scale, among the gentry and wealthy urban classes, luxury books sold to mistresses who enjoyed lives of leisure, who might read the bills of fare and the medical sections before handing over the receipts to the cook and the housekeeper. Or they were bought by ambitious servants, eager to gain a better position in the domestic hierarchy by honing their skills. At a less elevated level, books such as those by Price and Chambers were aimed at mistresses who still took an active part in supervising their servants, and at servants hoping to improve their position. Yet here there was also a diversity of target, revealed by the very titles: Powell's *Guide to Preferment* is clearly aimed at the servant (even though the full text of the title-page suggests that it will be useful to masters and servants alike); whereas *The British Jewel, or Complete Housewife's Best Companion* (1776), or Sarah Saunders' *Fountain of Knowledge; or, Complete Family Guide* (*c*.1781) imply household manuals for middle-class mistresses. Printers and booksellers produced compilations designed for specific groups. The enterprising Alexander Hogg offered one entitled *The Farmer's Wife*, containing advice on raising barnyard fowl and pigs, and receipts to deal with the produce of the farm (butter and cheese, cider, fruit wines, honey, bacon, sausages, and so on), plus some very limited cookery. For the most part, however, books devoted mainly to cookery were aimed at women readers, mistresses and/or servants in towns. One noticeable feature of the title-pages after 1770 is the disappearance of the phrase 'country housewife' which had been a standard component of titles in the first half of the century.

But cookery books as a whole do not offer a simple, homogeneous image of the downward progression of the feminine model which had been adopted early in the century by the aristocracy and its imitators. As was noted earlier, the second half of the century saw several books published by women who ran

---

[72] Compare *The Accomplished Lady's Delight in Cookery* [*c.* 1780], p. 4; Murrell, *A Newe Booke of Cookerie* (1615), p. 50.

cookery schools, all in the north of England or Scotland. A few such works had appeared in London, but much earlier. In about 1720 Edward Kidder had produced a very elegant little book, each page engraved in flowing script on copper-plates, devoted largely to pastry. Kidder was a pastry-cook who had opened a school, and his book indicated that ladies could be taught in their own houses, a sign that the pupils did not belong to the servant class.[73] In 1734, the address to the reader in *The Young Lady's Companion in Cookery and Pastry* announced that the book was the work of a gentlewoman who had been the owner of a school for young ladies. But by the middle of the century the curriculum for young ladies offered accomplishments other than housewifery, and such books ceased to appear in London. In the north, however, books by mistresses of schools were a phenomenon of the second half of the century. The first to appear was Elizabeth Cleland's *New and Easy Method of Cookery* in Edinburgh in 1755, 'Chiefly intended for the Benefit of the Young Ladies who attend Her School'.[74] Further Edinburgh publications were those of Susanna Maciver in 1773 and Mrs Frazer in 1791. These two women kept a school which was advertised in Maciver's name in the *Caledonian Mercury* in 1768 and 1786,[75] and in Frazer's name in 1788 and 1789, and again, in the *Edinburgh Directory*, during the period 1794–96.[76] Frazer's book is clearly a follow-up to Maciver's: many of the receipts came from the first. Originally, the receipts were published for the pupils at the school. Maciver's address to the reader says:

> The Author's situation in life hath led her to be much conversant in Cookery, Pastry, &c. and afforded her ample opportunity of knowing the most approved methods practised by others, and also of making experiments of her own. Some years ago she opened a school in this city for instructing young Ladies in this necessary branch of female education, and she hath the satisfaction to find that success hath

---

[73] The title-pages of both editions (*c.*1720 and *c.*1725) of *E. Kidder's Receipts of Pastry and Cookery* say, 'Ladies may be taught at their own Houses.' Kidder was born in 1666 and died in 1739.

[74] See Cleland, *A New and Easy Method of Cookery* (1755), title-page.

[75] See Law, 'Teachers in Edinburgh in the Eighteenth Century', in *The Book of the Old Edinburgh Club*, number 32 (1966), p. 140.

[76] Law (1966), p. 127. Other advertisements show cookery schools run by Mr Hautbois, who stated that he had been cook to the Earl of Albemarle, in 1747–8 (p. 132), by Mrs Wilkie in 1749 and 1758 (p. 155), and by Mrs Johnstone in 1749 and 1752 (p. 135).

accompanied her labours. And many of her scholars, and others, having
repeatedly solicited her to make her receipts public; these solicitations,
joined to an hearty desire of doing every thing that it was thought could
be useful in the way of her business, have at length determined her to
this publication.[77]

This is typical of such books, for instance two produced in Newcastle. Both
Elizabeth Marshall in 1777 and the women of the Kellet family in 1780 stated
that their work was a response to the solicitations of their scholars.[78]

The older model of female education lingered much longer in the north of
England and in Scotland than in London. In Edinburgh and Glasgow young
girls of the gentry class were still attending cookery schools at the end of the
century. In 1795, during a visit to Edinburgh, Mary Fairfax went every day for
a lesson with a pastry-cook, where she learned to make creams and jellies for
supper.[79] In Scotland, young ladies were still expected to be able to prepare the
light, decorative dishes which were the eighteenth-century equivalent of the still-
room products which had occupied so much of the seventeenth-century
gentlewoman's time. This was obviously the case in the north of England too;
clearly there were schools teaching cookery in Newcastle, and the great Elizabeth
Raffald had opened a school in Manchester in the 1760s. But even in the distant
provinces, one can find signs of change. A comparison of the presentations of
Maciver's and Frazer's books reveals that the tone has shifted between 1773 and
1791. Whereas Maciver had said that her school (and thus her book) was for
'young Ladies', Frazer no longer refers to her 'scholars', emphasizing instead
general utility:

As this work … is intended for the benefit of all ranks and conditions,
as well for those who have attained a tolerable knowledge of these arts,
as those who have had little opportunity of forming any proper notion
of them, we have occasionally given examples of the most plain and
simple, and of the most sumptuous and elegant dishes, presently in

[77] Maciver, *Cookery, and Pastry … The Third Edition* (1782), pp. iii–iv. The advertisement is dated
'November 1773' and is presumably identical to that in the first edition of 1773.
[78] See Marshall, *The Young Ladies' Guide in the Art of Cookery* (1777), p. iii; S., E. and M. Kellet, *A
Complete Collection of Cookery Receipts* (1780), dedication.
[79] See Plant, *The Domestic Life of Scotland in the Eighteenth Century* (1952), pp. 16–18.

vogue; and … have used such familiarity of expression and regularity of method, as that any person, with the slightest attention, may comprehend them.[80]

The preface is in fact inspired by that of John Farley; the author seems uncertain of her readers, unlike her predecessor nearly twenty years before.

At the end of the eighteenth century, there were several books offering receipts for cheap dishes to feed the poor in response to the economic crisis and bad harvests which had pushed up the price of meat and bread in the course of the 1790s. Letters and diaries show the upper classes were aware of the distress among those below them. In March 1793 Maria Holroyd, the daughter of Lord Sheffield, wrote to a friend:

> It seemeth to my youth and inexperience as if we eat a Monstrous deal of Meat. The Butcher's Bill comes to 4*l.* a week. I do not like to see and know what the necessaries of life cost, because it makes me uncomfortable to think how it is possible the poor people can buy meat now it is so high.[81]

A few years later, the situation had deteriorated. The Reverend William Holland, seeing the never-ending rain, exclaimed in his diary in November 1799:

> Still more rain, where will it end? The Poor, the Poor, how are they to live this winter? we must do all we can to assist and Providence will do the rest.[82]

These preoccupations surfaced in books. In 1798 Eliza Melroe produced a book of receipts and moralizing advice with the title *An Economical, and New Method of Cookery*. At 2s. 6d. it was not particularly cheap, but it could be purchased for less by and for the poor: 'Price 2s. 6d. or six for 10. 6d. if purchased by Clubs of the labouring Poor, or intended for their Use.'[83] Most of

---

[80] See Frazer (1791), pp. iii–iv.

[81] Adeane (ed.), *The Girlhood of Maria Josepha Holroyd* (1896), pp. 212–213.

[82] Ayres (ed.), *Paupers and Pig Killers* (1984), p. 17.

[83] Melroe, *An Economical, and New Method of Cookery* (1798), title-page.

the receipts are for 'nourishing soups', which was what the medical theories of the period advised,[84] and foreign cuisine is praised for being based on soups, unlike English cookery that was founded on boiled and roasted meat:

> It unfortunately happens in England, that a pound of butcher's meat is but a meal for one man, whilst in other countries, by making it into soup, is a meal for six men.[85]

This is an echo of ideas about the 'democratic' nature of soups which had been developed in France by the authors of the *Encyclopédie*.[86] Receipts for such soups were not new: they had appeared in periodicals in mid-century, again in response to the distress of the poor. In 1757 Dr James Stonhouse published six receipts in the *Northampton Mercury*, and they were reprinted in the *Universal Magazine*. The author's aim was to provide receipts for the poor and those who wanted to help them, but others seeking economical dishes also made use of them. In January 1758 Thomas Turner, the Sussex shopkeeper, read the receipt for soup and had it made for himself. He liked it so much that he repeated the experience a month later.[87]

Another response to crises of subsistence was to promote the potato. It was already being grown and sold in Lancashire in the 1680s, probably because of the influence of Irish immigrants, whence it spread outwards to the north of England. In the south, potatoes were still regarded with suspicion. In Lewes (Sussex) one electoral slogan in the 1760s was 'No Popery, no Potatoes'.[88] In 1796 a pamphlet advocating use of the potato appeared, with advice on growing and a few receipts. It was not aimed at the poor (the receipts call for eggs and beef-steaks as well as potatoes), but at prosperous southerners, to try to persuade them to eat potatoes and thus reduce their consumption of grain, flour and bread. In the north, says the author, potatoes are a staple food for the poor, and they 'are also in great estimation amongst persons of higher rank'.[89]

---

[84] See Drummond and Wilbraham (1939), pp. 306–307; also *Directions and Observations relative to Food Exercise and Sleep* (1772), pp. i–ii, 14.

[85] Melroe (1798), p. 88.

[86] See Lévi-Strauss, *Mythologiques*, vol. 3: *L'Origine des manières de table*, (1968), p. 402.

[87] See Vaisey (1985), pp. 131–132, 137.

[88] See Salaman, *The History and Social Influence of the Potato* (1949), pp. 120, 451–3.

[89] Kirkpatrick, *An Account of the Manner in which Potatoes are cultivated* (1796), p. 2; the advantages of the consumption of the potato are described p. 41.

This is a rare example of a food going up the social scale rather than down; the more orthodox cookery books of the period suggest that 'scollopped potatoes' (mashed, mixed with butter and cream, then browned in scallop shells under a salamander or in a Dutch oven) might appear as a side dish, or at supper.[90] Patriotic efforts to persuade people to accept substitutes for pure wheaten bread were also made: in July 1795 *The Times* reported that the King's bread was made either of mixed wheat and rye flour, or of mixed wheat and potato flour; it exhorted its readers to follow the royal example.[91] Two months later, Maria Holroyd remarked:

> I think people are pretty well disposed to make use of substitutes. Potatoes come in aid extremely well; our bread is one third made of them, and there cannot be better bread when pains is taken about it.[92]

At the beginning of the following year, Maria noted that her father was selling his wheat to 'all the Poor who he puts upon his list', and that the Sheffield family had obtained receipts for making 'Pottage of Bones and the coarsest pieces of Meat', the resulting broth being 'very nourishing and excellent'.[93] The efforts of the ruling classes, however, did not impinge much on their own comfort or on their finances.

By the end of the century, distributing soup to the poor had become fashionable, thanks to the Evangelical movement and to propaganda produced by Hannah More in her series of *Cheap Repository Tracts* and later in her novel, *Cœlebs in Search of a Wife* (1808).[94] The tracts appeared between 1795 and 1798. Several were devoted to an account of Mrs Jones, the widow of a wealthy tradesman, who recovered from her melancholy state after the death of her husband by channelling her energies into charitable activities. Number 45 tells how she undertook to reform the sharp practices of the village bakers and grocers, how she had a communal oven built, and how, with the help of the vicar's housekeeper, she taught the local girls to sew and to prepare cheap food. The story ends with exhortations to follow the heroine's example, with hints and a few

---

[90] See, for instance, Raffald (1769), p. 263.

[91] See Ashton, *The History of Bread from Pre-historic to Modern Times* (1904), p. 163.

[92] Adeane (1896), p. 335.

[93] Adeane (1896), p. 361.

[94] See Quinlan (1941), pp. 155–9.

receipts given as encouragement.[95] These pamphlets were accessible to all at 1d. each, or more cheaply still in quantity (4s. 6d. for 100), and there was a cheaper edition for hawkers.[96] But they were designed as much for the gentry as for the poor: the simple stories might appeal to the one, but the call for charity was to the other, particularly as it hardly questioned the established social order.[97] Their principle was to show the poor how to live better on what they had, rather than to suggest any redistribution of wealth. Nor were generous benefactors expected to open their purses too much. As Eliza Melroe put it:

> It highly interests all conversant with the poor, who ought to be literally all, … to consult and co-operate with them in the practice of œconomy; it is far more useful to teach them to spend less, or to save a little, than to give them more.[98]

The message was that one had a duty to help the poor, but there was no question of radical reform. The conservative ideology of good works corresponds exactly to the discourse of Thomas Gisborne's book, which advised ladies to practise piety and purity in the home and charity outside. The books of economical receipts were not addressed directly to the working classes; to find such books, one must wait until the middle of the nineteenth century and the appearance of Francatelli's *Plain Cookery Book for the Working Classes* (1852), and Soyer's *Shilling Cookery for the People* (1854).

---

[95] See [More], *The Cottage Cook, or, Mrs. Jones's Cheap Dishes* [1796], pp. 2–16.
[96] This information is given on the title-page.
[97] See Quinlan (1941), pp. 83–5.
[98] Melroe (1798), p. 93.

This study of the authors and readers of the eighteenth-century cookery book has shown how it changed as it reached an ever-widening audience. We have noticed the dearth of information to be derived from those we know to have owned the books: although a number of copies now in libraries contain inscriptions, often dated, these are not of much interest unless the owner can be identified, a very rare case. An exception is the poet Thomas Gray who possessed a copy of Verral's *Complete System of Cookery* to which he added his own receipts and notes;[1] other records of ownership, such as those relating to Sir Robert Walpole, Katherine Windham and Lady Grisell Baillie, we have touched upon. However, the titles, dedications, advertisements, addresses, prefaces and the contents themselves supply valuable information about who was targeted by authors and booksellers.

The evidence marks the shift from an aristocratic to a bourgeois model. The first three decades of the century saw two dominant types of book and author. There was first the male chef working for the nobility or for royalty, producing a book which revealed the latest developments of 'court-cookery' (all more or less inspired by Massialot) to their fellow-professionals. The second group consisted of women authors who often chose to hide their identity. Their books continued to be based on domestic manuscript receipt collections and their culinary style was more modest. Both groups were successful at the outset, but gradually there come signs that the women were more in tune with the requirements of readers. The leading women, Mary Kettilby, E. Smith and Sarah Harrison, remained in print long after the chefs' books had disappeared. The fate of Charles Carter, progressively adapted until a book of 'court-cookery' had become, by the time of the second re-working (by a woman rather than the original author), a 'domestic' manual close to those of the women authors, also points to a shift in readership around the beginning of the 1730s. Demand among the ruling class had virtually disappeared: the highest echelons hired a man-cook, who was French if the employer could afford such a luxury, or a French-trained Englishman, or simply an English 'professed cook' who knew something of the niceties of French dishes. While such men might consult one of the court-cooks in search of new ideas or methods, their training meant that they had picked up

---

[1] See the reprint entitled *The Cook's Paradise* (1948), introduced by Mégroz. Gray's copy is now in the British Library, shelfmark C. 28. f. 13.

the essentials on the job and books were unnecessary.[2] Besides, culinary fashion was moving on and the court-cooks' ideas were beginning to look out of date. Something describing the ultra-fashionable style of the moment (even if that moment had already passed) would date much more quickly than one which followed fashion at some distance.

Although the court-cooks clearly addressed their receipts to people who had to please demanding employers, and cunningly suggested that the discerning gentleman himself should be knowledgeable enough to judge his servants, it seems likely that their work was as often read by women as by men. The women servants employed as cooks and housekeepers used books to supply the information which men obtained from apprenticeship. The comments by Kettilby and Smith on the 'fantastical' or 'whimsical' receipts given by the 'great Masters' of cookery show that they had certainly read some of the court-cooks.[3] But they did not reproduce their receipts, they adapted them, making them simpler, less lavish and less expensive, while retaining their essential flavour combinations. This ensured longevity for the female authors and reassured an audience which wanted to follow fashion but avoid its excesses. Their discourse, ridiculing the court-cooks' receipts, marks the beginning of a gap between the food of the élite and the food of the lesser gentry and its imitators, just as a gap begins to open up between the aspirations of these social groups.

The new women authors clearly thought the market for their books lay among the lesser gentry and families who, as Richard Bradley said in the presentation of his *Country Gentleman and Farmer's Monthly Director*, had incomes of

---

[2] Exactly how many households employed a man-cook is uncertain. After the tax on male servants was imposed in 1777, the 1780 tax returns for England and Wales (PRO T 47/8) show that 14,959 people employed one servant, 4,661 two, 2,134 three, and 1,048 four. Thereafter the numbers drop sharply, with 620 employers of five servants, and 90 of ten. Employers of 10 or more men were mostly titled, and the servants were generally employed in London rather than in the country. For instance, the Duke of Northumberland had only 3 men-servants at his seat at Alnwick, but 18 in Westminster; similarly, the Duchess of Bedford had 4 men at Woburn but 18 in Great Russell Street (ff. 384, 389v, 22). Since men were employed primarily to deal with horses, and as butlers, footmen and valets, only households with at least five (and probably more) men-servants were likely to employ a man in the kitchen. This leaves fewer than 2,000 households (or under 8 per cent) as potential employers of men-cooks out of a total of about 24,750 employers of men. A case in point from the early eighteenth century is that of Sir Thomas Haggerston, who on an income of about £1,200 p.a. employed six men and five women in 1706; the cook and the under-cook were both women (see Forster, *Selections from the Disbursements Book* (1965), pp. x, 72).

[3] See Kettilby (1714), preface, and E–S– (1728), preface.

£300–400 a year and aspired to live as well as the gentlemen who had more than twice that amount. Hence the emphasis from the 1730s on uniting elegance and economy, a theme first introduced by Sarah Harrison, and developed by virtually every cookery book thereafter. Another feature of this period is the frequent mention of the country: several authors presume 'country gentlewomen' to be their principal readers.[4] In general, however, this class was expected to confine its interest to medical and cosmetic receipts and the more decorative side of cookery (confectionery and pastry), leaving the rest to servants. Thus it is not surprising to find the first texts that stress their suitability for use by servants were published in the 1730s. Their employers might still read the appropriate section, but only to give directions. Manuals of confectionery, by contrast, were invariably addressed to the ladies, as evidenced by John Emmett's *Choice Collection* (1737), whose preface is addressed to his lady subscribers, or R.G.'s compendium, *The Accomplish'd Female Instructor* (1704), which combines conduct-book with confectionery, pastry and other household hints. These show the limits to how far the aspirational lady should play an active part in the kitchen. The female paradigm was moving from the good housewife towards the lady of leisure, and this ideal was moving rapidly down the social scale.

The real development in the market for cookery books, however, would take place among the urban middle classes. It is no accident that total production leapt from just over 20 editions in the 1720s to over 35 in the 1730s. At the same time, more prosperous tradesmen in London were acquiring the trappings of an affluent lifestyle, were more likely to own china and almost as likely to own knives and forks and silverware as were the gentry. There was a rapid increase in the use of tableware after 1720, largely the result of the spread of tea-drinking, but also linked to increased sociability involving food and drink in the home.[5] Lorna Weatherill's survey of 300 inventories from the London Court of Orphans for the period 1675–1725 shows that ownership of saucepans rose from 32 per cent of the sample in 1675 to 84 per cent in 1725; of pewter plates from 4 per cent to 76 per cent; of china from 4 per cent to 80 per cent; and of knives and forks from 8 per cent to 64 per cent.[6] Her conclusion is that the expectations of the tradesmen led them to be more interested in new things

---

[4] See R. Bradley (1727 and 1732), titles; E– S– (1728), preface; Harrison (1733), preface.

[5] See Shammas, *The Pre-industrial Consumer* (1990), p. 186.

[6] See Weatherill, *Consumer Behaviour and Material Culture* (1996), pp. 26–27. Other relevant tables are found pp. 76, 168.

and in more varied domestic goods than the gentry class: the 'consumption hierarchy' was not the same as the social hierarchy.[7] These consumers did not necessarily want to emulate the aristocracy and gentry, and the changing discourse of the cookery writers is a response to their aspirations.

Hannah Glasse's book appealed particularly to city-dwellers. She made no reference to 'country gentlewomen', and there was none of the old-fashioned lore which went with traditions of gentry hospitality. Another feature, and of virtually all those who followed her, was the greater emphasis on receipts adapted to the capacities of the servant – always presumed a woman. Glasse's famous phrase 'Made Plain and Easy' became a standard expression in titles after 1747, and many subsequent books stressed that their texts were designed to be given by the mistress to her servants.

Glasse was followed by a spate of new (or supposedly new) titles: the number jumps from 13 in the 1740s to 23 in the 1750s. The number of reprints went up too, from 25 to 35, pointing to an increased market rather than mere desire to replace old with new. After the 1750s, the number of editions (new titles and reprints) per decade never fell below 50. The market was expanding rapidly, not only in London but far beyond, most notably in the north of Britain. Sales of provincial works were equal to those published in London. One of the earliest, Elizabeth Moxon's *English Housewifry* (Leeds, 1741) was reprinted until 1798; Elizabeth Cleland's *New and Easy Method of Cookery* (Edinburgh, 1755) went through four impressions until 1770; and Ann Peckham's *Complete English Cook* (Leeds, 1767) six until about 1790. These were not regional works containing local specialities (with certain Scottish exceptions), but had national application. The emergence of a national market, helped by simultaneous improvements in transportation, meant that the few recognizably regional foodstuffs were offered for sale far beyond their area of origin. An example was the Yorkshire Christmas pie for which Glasse supplied a receipt in 1747.[8] Today, the Euroterroirs inventory of traditional foods of Britain states, 'Not much of our food is regional', although there are many foods peculiar to Britain.[9] The success of Raffald's book in London (though first published in Manchester) shows that this was already true by the middle of the eighteenth century.

---

[7] Ibid., pp. 20–21, 185–96.

[8] Glasse (1747), p. 73. Glasse comments that these pies are often sent to London.

[9] Mason & Brown, *Traditional Foods of Britain* (1999), p. 13.

The women authors' triumph during the middle decades demonstrates their understanding of what the readership required: ladies (or would-be ladies) hoped to escape the task of teaching their servants by putting the book in cook's hands, while the aspiring servant was eager to read a manual which, as Martha Bradley promised, would give living proof that 'an English Girl, properly instructed,… can equal the best French Gentleman in every thing but Expence'.[10] The women authors – once cooks and housekeepers themselves – had also studied: Martha Bradley had read, tested and adapted many receipts by Vincent La Chapelle, as well as Lamb and Glasse. Such instances show us the reader as well as the author: not all borrowings can be dismissed as mere plagiarism.

By the 1770s, the fact that cookery receipts were to be read by servants was so well established that many authors took it for granted. But as the cookery book reached an ever-increasing audience, new types of information gained prominence. Glasse and Raffald had refused to give either medical receipts or bills of fare, leaving the first to doctors and the second to the imagination of the mistress or housekeeper who was presumed to know what was proper. Novice housewives aspiring to gentility, however, now needed the information which an education in accomplishments failed to supply. Charlotte Mason devoted over one-third of her book to bills of fare, ranging from 'family dinners' of five dishes to grand entertainments and cold suppers, on the grounds that young ladies 'are greatly at a loss how to conduct their table with … decency and pro-priety', a sign of lack of basic instruction as well as a growing readership among new recruits to the middle classes. Medical chapters reappear in cookery books as a consequence of two ideological developments, the rise of the Evangelical movement, with its emphasis on charity, and exaggerated notions of female delicacy. Most such sections took their prescriptions from the works of leading physicians, most notably the popular William Buchan; the old tradition of the family receipt-book, although it survived in manuscript collections, was no longer an adequate reference.

Thus the most important phenomenon of the last thirty years of the century is the diversification of cookery books, which offered various 'mixes' of ingre-dients to please different groups of buyers. Cookery is found associated with bills of fare, medical lore and receipts, household management, hints on helping the poor, advice on estate management, gardening, or farming, and a whole

---

[10] M. Bradley (1756), vol. 1, p. 314.

variety of sections designed to instruct and entertain the female sex. This diversity goes even further than the encyclopaedic manuals (such as *The Complete Family-Piece*, 1736) of the first half of the century. And there were cookery books to suit every pocket, from the six-shilling productions of the tavern cooks and the more ambitious women authors, to the sixpenny manuals offering initiation into the cultural norms of respectable society, with chapters ranging from food and remedies, to being a successful hostess and entertaining the company with genteel songs.

The one constant throughout the second half of the century was the intended female readership, evidenced in the titles of books, the discourse of their presentations, and in frontispieces. There were, of course, exceptions. One was Peregrine Montague's *Family Pocket-Book*, *c*.1760 which contained a very short section on cookery among miscellaneous information on horses, poultry, household hints and hobbies, horticulture and other things, designed to appeal to master and mistress alike. In cookery books, the kitchen scenes in frontispieces nearly always show women at work (for instance, in the sixth edition of *The Lady's Companion*, 1753, in Martha Bradley's *British Housewife*, 1756, or in Elizabeth Price's *New Book of Cookery*, *c*.1780). Even where men are present, as for instance in Henderson's *Housekeeper's Instructor*, *c*.1790, or in Mary Holland's *Complete British Cook*, 1800, it is the woman who is shown using the cookery book. This contrasts with the frontispiece to the second edition of T. Hall's *Queen's Royal Cookery* (1713), which shows a kitchen scene with two men and one woman, and two other scenes of women preparing pastry and distilling. The court-cooks had assumed that the cook was a man but, with the downward spread of cookery books, this was no longer warranted.

The shifting social status of the buyers and readers was obviously at the heart of the changes in content as well as in presentation. The social status of the reading public was also an important factor in the way culinary styles evolved over the century. The aristocratic model was eagerly followed in the first decades, but rejected later by an audience which had no desire to imitate the extravagances of an élite which continued to take the lead from France. The result, as we shall see in the next part, was a period of ambivalent attitudes to French cuisine in mid-century, followed by the development of an English manner which mixed purely English dishes with a bastardized version of the earlier French court style. Once again, the aristocratic gave way to the bourgeois.

Part III

Culinary Styles
in the Eighteenth Century

A

COLLECTION

Of above Three Hundred

RECEIPTS

I N

Cookery,

Physick *and* Surgery;

For the Ufe of all
Good Wives, Tender Mothers,
and Careful Nurfes.

By feveral Hands.

L O N D O N,
Printed for RICHARD WILKIN, at the
King's Head in St. Paul's Church-yard.
MDCCXIV.

Title-page of Mary Kettilby, A Collection of above Three Hundred Receipts,
*1714. Her anonymous collection of receipts from 'notable housewives' emphasizes
cookery at the expense of its medical content. Yet, remedies occupy nearly half the
book's extent.*

THE MODERN READER WHO DELVES FOR THE FIRST TIME INTO THE receipts of the eighteenth century emerges feeling confused: those from the early years appear very similar to those at the end. This impression that there were few significant changes belies a considerable shift in culinary styles. The illusion of continuity comes from the fact that the new never replaces the old in one fell swoop; they coexist. Furthermore, authors of cookery books have, from the very beginning, borrowed and adapted from their predecessors. The eighteenth-century was no exception. Quite the contrary: we have already seen examples of borrowing from author to author as well as from manuscript collection to printed text. Receipts from such sources are often much older than first appears: many household manuscripts contained matter written out by several generations of young girls, each of whom may have copied from her mother and even her grandmother before passing it on to her own daughter. Thus one finds receipts dating back to the sixteenth century in books printed in the eighteenth. Another cause of this apparent continuity is that authors and printers did not hesitate to re-use material from other printed works in order to produce a 'new' book or to complete a new edition of a volume which seemed to lack some type of receipt. Sometimes, these additions go so far as a complete revision, the second edition bearing no resemblance to the first.

Advantages gained from study of these changes include a profile of the sort of reader authors and publishers were aiming to attract as well as indication of shifts in taste and fashion. However, there are countervailing problems. With a few exceptions, only the first edition of any title represents the style (often tinged with others' ideas) of the author: later editions tend to be compilations from various sources, printed or manuscript. Even a first edition offers no guarantee of originality, since plagiarism was as frequent amongst authors as it was among printers. Short of consulting every edition of every cookery book published during the century, it is not possible to state with certainty when, or by whom, such and such a dish was 'invented'. One can sometimes discover the first appearance of a dish in print, but generally receipts for that same dish had been circulating in manuscripts for some years before. Second and subsequent editions of a book are useful only when they can be compared to the original version. This is a personal view: other culinary historians would not agree.[1]

Cookery books played a twofold and contradictory rôle: they contributed to the diffusion of new dishes, while at the same time perpetuating older ones. Thus works by court-cooks published at the beginning of the century presented French-inspired aristocratic cookery to the gentry; later, this was adapted by, most notably, women authors who spread the new style in ever-widening circles. But printed receipts, by their very nature, also have a stultifying effect on culinary practice. As Alain Girard has pointed out, once written down, especially in print, a receipt is 'fixed' in definitive form.[2] The normative effect of the printed word means the potential for innovation and adaptation diminishes, and continues to lessen as receipts become ever more detailed and precise. Thus cookery books, by offering a model to which to conform, exert a conservative influence on those who use them. Such pressures can be seen mainly in the books by women, where it is possible to trace the origins of many receipts back as far as manuscript collections dating from the seventeenth, and even the sixteenth, centuries. This is particularly noticeable in the medical sections. To give just one example, receipts for 'Dr Stephens' Water' are found in several early manuscripts as well as in printed works two hundred years later.[3] The contradictory tendency of cookery books both to

---

[1] See David, 'Hunt the Ice Cream' (1979), p. 8.

[2] See Girard, 'Du manuscrit à l'imprimé: le livre de cuisine en Europe aux 15ᵉ et 16ᵉ siècles', in Margolin & Sauzet (1982), pp. 108–109; Mennell, *All Manners of Food* (1985), p. 67.

[3] Spurling, *Elinor Fettiplace's Receipt Book* (1986), p. 18; Hess (ed.), *Martha Washington's Booke of Cookery* (1981), pp. 402–405; Weddell (ed.), *Arcana Fairfaxiana* (1890), p. 132; Markham, *The English Hus-wife* (1615), p. 29; W.M., *The Queens Closet Opened* (1655), pp. 21, 87–88; E– S–, *The Compleat Housewife* (1728), p. 222. It is interesting to note that the receipt copied out by the Rev. Henry Fairfax was taken from the collection belonging to his brother-in-law, Henry Cholmely, and that the comment added to the receipt, stating that it was communicated to the Archbishop of Canterbury by Dr Stephens shortly before his death, also appears in the printed version of the receipt given by Markham; it looks as though Henry Cholmely copied out his receipt from the printed work.

encourage and inhibit change contributes to the confusing impression given by them where new and old are so often juxtaposed.

With these remarks in mind, the reader should not be surprised to find that the following chapters cannot follow a neatly linear progression: it will often be necessary to look backwards to the seventeenth century or even earlier. The same receipts reappear, but with different names; or the same name hides considerable variations, so much so that the results must be treated as another dish. Change and continuity go hand in hand.

The EXPERIENCED

Englifh Houfe-keeper,

For the Ufe and Eafe of

Ladies, Houfe-keepers, Cooks, &c.

Wrote purely from PRACTICE,

And dedicated to the

Hon. Lady ELIZABETH WARBURTON,

Whom the Author lately ferved as Houfe-keeper.

Confifting of near 800 Original Receipts, moft of which never
appeared in Print.

PART FIRST, Lemon Pickle, Browning for all Sorts of Made
Difhes, Soups, Fifh, plain Meat, Game, Made Difhes both hot
and cold, Pyes, Puddings, &c,

PART SECOND, All Kind of Confeftionary, particularly the
Gold and Silver Web for covering of Sweetmeats, and a Defert
of Spun Sugar, with Direftions to fet out a Table in the moft
elegant Manner and in the modern Tafte, Floating Iflands, Fifh
Ponds, Tranfparent Puddings, Trifles, Whips, &c.

PART THIRD, Pickling, Potting, and Collaring, Wines, Vinegars, Catchups, Diftilling, with two moft valuable Receipts,
one for refining Malt Liquors, the other for curing Acid Wines,
and a correft Lift of every Thing in Seafon in every Month of
the Year.

By ELIZABETH RAFFALD.

MANCHESTER:

Printed by *J. Harrop*, for the Author, and fold by Meffrs. *Fletcher*
and *Anderfon*, in *St. Paul's* Church-yard, *London;* and by
Eliz. Raffald, Confeftioner, near the *Exchange, Manchefter*, 1769.

The Book to be figned by the Author's own Hand-writing, and
entered at Stationers Hall.

Title-page of Elizabeth Raffald, The Experienced English House-keeper, *1769.
The most important book of the second half of the century; its title-page lays due
emphasis on dishes for the dessert course which contributed greatly to Raffald's
success.*

Earlier chapters have demonstrated the importance of the court-cooks: how their books offered a glimpse of an *haute cuisine* that was the final stage of development of a style with roots in the French culinary revolution of the mid-seventeenth century typified by La Varenne and his successors. While they owed much to the French, especially to Massialot, they also inherited more specifically English notions from Robert May and his contemporaries. But women writers of the time viewed their male rivals with suspicion, while the men, conscious of their status, tended to look down on the women. So it is hardly surprising that their respective culinary styles should be rather different. The women authors belong to a much more traditional register deriving in large part from household manuscript collections. However, their receipts were not immune to the influence of the court style. Indeed, it is at this period that there seems to have been the greatest desire among the gentry as a whole to follow élite culinary fashions. It is therefore logical that we should begin with the receipts of the court-cooks, in order to discover what would later colour the work of more modest women authors.

In 1730, Charles Carter drew the reader's attention to the excellence of some particular receipts in his book which, he said, were the choicest and richest and would bring the greatest credit to the cook.[1] Among those mentioned are 'olios', 'terrines' and 'bisques', as well as different sorts of hams and multi-coloured decorative jellies. After emphasizing the prestige of such receipts in his address to the reader, Carter begins by giving receipts for broth and 'gravy' (at this date, an even stronger form of stock than the broth upon which it was based and used as a foundation for sauces) as introduction to the 'made dishes', amongst which appear the olios, terrines and bisques – the most prestigious of the group, duly placed towards the beginning of the section. The presentation takes up once more the theme of the festive nature of such dishes:

> The First Part of the most rare and noble Art and Mystery of Cookery, is the Boiling Part, from which is compos'd all Sorts of boil'd Meats and Made dishes, proper for all Feasts and Entertainments, such as, Olio's, Terrenes and Bisques, Pottages, Soops, Corbullions, Bullions, Puries, Coolio's, Royals, Dobes, Poveroys, Castroles, Alamodes, Sattoots,

---

[1] See Carter, *The Complete Practical Cook*, (1730), address to the reader.

Marrianates, Ragousts, Fricassies, and Hashes, and many others. The chief Source of this Part of Cookery is the Strong Broth Pot; for … strong Broth well made, and good Gravies well drawn off, are very principal Ingredients in the composing of all Made dishes;… and a curious Cook, that has a good Fancy, shall find out many Novelties, hitherto unknown, and Add much to Cookery; so that future Ages will be ever finding out of new Rarities.[2]

Here, Carter shows that he understands the way in which the French had developed a modular system by which the cook, working from basic ingredients such as broths and sauce bases, could produce a great variety of dishes, and keep inventing 'new rarities'. Most English writers simply give a series of individual receipts, without stressing the basic system which lies behind. Another striking aspect of this text is that all the names of dishes are French, albeit in an occasionally garbled form. Here we see the triumph of French *haute cuisine*.

Before examining the receipts of English cooks, it is therefore important to look at what had happened in France since La Varenne, whose *Le Cuisinier françois* (1651) revealed the early stages of the process which swept away flavours inherited from medieval cookery. La Varenne gives receipts for the basic preparations which enable the cook to make a whole range of sauces. Even though one still finds old-style prescriptions in his book, there are also new flavours, where the taste of meat heightened by the use of herbs or by a sharp note provided by capers or citrus juice has begun to replace the spices and sugar of the sixteenth century. In the next fifty years, other cooks followed in his footsteps. Pierre de Lune, L.S.R. and Massialot all helped to develop the new style and, with it, a culinary system. The most important of these authors, from the point of view of subsequent English developments, was Massialot, whose *Cuisinier roïal et bourgeois* appeared in 1691 and was translated into English with the title *The Court and Country Cook*, in 1702 – the translation also includes his book on confectionery, *Nouvelle Instruction pour les Confitures* of 1692.

Massialot's book was aimed at the professional cook or clerk of the kitchen and, to facilitate its use, was organized as an alphabetical dictionary of ingredients and types of dish. An index enables the reader to find each receipt and its variations for fast days. It contains such basic preparations as the *coulis*, a

---

[2] Carter (1730), p. 1.

sauce base made from meat roasted then pounded in a mortar, simmered slowly with broth and breadcrumbs, the whole then passed through a sieve. A second is the *essence* (especially essence of ham), a sauce base made with ham and onions, this time thickened with a brown roux rather than bread, again strained through a fine sieve.[3] These foundations permitted the cook to create a great variety of dishes by using standardized ingredients: as Barbara Wheaton points out, this kind of culinary system was developed in large kitchens where the cooks worked as a team rather than alone or in small groups.[4]

Le Cuisinier roïal et bourgeois shows the large-scale set-pieces so characteristic of French *haute cuisine* at the end of the seventeenth century. Barbara Wheaton notices that in the first edition the *grandes entrées* are the dominant feature of the bills of fare set out in the book, whereas in the re-worked editions of 1712 and later, smaller dishes, *entremets* and *hors d'œuvres*, become increasingly important.[5] It was the big dishes of the earlier editions which formed the key elements of the court style in England. The most important of these were the *oille* (which the English called the olio), the *terrine*, the *bisque* and the *poupeton* (Anglicized to pupton). The last two had already appeared in La Varenne,[6] but the first pair were absent.

The olio was, of course, a version of the Spanish *olla podrida*, thought a peasant dish today but seen then as fit for the best tables. Pepys tasted it at the Spanish ambassador's on 5 May 1669 and was less than enthusiastic; he preferred the version he had been given a month earlier, prepared by a cook who had been with Lord Sandwich in Spain.[7] Massialot's receipt is a classic example of one of these monumental dishes where several meats cook together before being served with the cooking liquid as an accompanying soup. Massialot's receipts will be given in their English version (which is a translation, not an adaptation, based on the 1698 edition, references to which are also given in the notes) in order to make comparisons with the English cooks' receipts easier:

---

[3] See Massialot, *Le Cuisinier roïal et bourgeois* (1698), pp. 209–215, 278, 232; *The Court and Country Cook*, (1702), part 1, pp. 101–104, 129, 270.

[4] For an analysis of the French culinary system, and Massialot's contribution to it, see Wheaton, *Savouring the Past*, (1983), pp. 151–156.

[5] *Ibid.*, p. 155.

[6] See La Varenne, *Le Cuisinier françois* (1652), pp. 4–5, 66; *The French Cook* (1653), pp. 4, 52–53.

[7] Pepys' comment on 5 April 1669 was 'the *Oleo* was endeed a very noble dish, such as I never saw better, or any more of.' See *Diary*, vol. 9, pp. 509, 544.

An Oil for Flesh-days.

Take all sorts of good Meats, *viz.* Part of a Buttock of Beef, a Fillet of Veal, a piece of a Leg of Mutton, Ducks, Partridges, Pigeons, Chickens, Quails, a piece of raw Gammon, Sausages and a Cervelas, all roasted or fried brown: Let them be put into a Pot, every Thing according to the time that is requisite for boiling it, and let a thickening Liquor be made of the brown Sauce to be mingled together. As soon as the scum is taken off, season your Meats, with Pepper, Salt, Cloves, Nutmeg, Coriander-seed and Ginger, all well pounded, with Thyme and sweet Basil, and wrapt up in a Linnen-cloth. Afterwards add all sorts of Roots and Herbs well scalded, accordingly as you shall think fit .... In the mean while, you are to provide *Cuvets*, Silver-pots and other Vessels proper for that Purpose, and when your Potage is sufficiently boil'd, let some Crusts be broken into pieces, and laid a soaking in the same Broth, after it has been clear'd from the Fat, and well season'd. Before it is serv'd up, pour in a great deal more Broth, ... dress your Fowls and other Meats, ... putting the *Cuvets* on a Silver-dish with a Silver-ladle in it, with which every one of the Guests may take out some Soop, when the *Oil* is set on the Table.[8]

He follows this with a receipt for an olio for fasting days. To modern eyes, this *pot-au-feu* does not appear particularly aristocratic, but these pottages, which combined a soup with various meats and vegetables, were indeed the height of fashion. The *bisque* (or bisk as the English usually called it) was closer to our stews, with a somewhat thicker sauce:

To make a Bisk of Pigeons.
Take Pigeons newly kill'd; scald, pick and parboil them, and let them be stew'd, in clear Broth, with several *Bards* or thin Slices of Bacon, and Onion stuck with Cloves, and two Slices of Lemmon, all well scumm'd. ... In order to make a proper Ragoo for them, 'tis requisite to take some Veal-Sweet-breads cut into two parts, Mushrooms cut into small pieces, *Truffles* in Slices, Artichoke-bottoms cut into four quarters, and one whole, to be put into the middle of the Potage. You must carefully fry

---

[8] *The Court and Country Cook* (1702), part I, pp. 166–167. See also *Le Cuisinier roïal et bourgeois* (1698), pp. 336–337.

this Ragoo, with a little Lard, fine Flower, … and stew it, with a Slice of Lemmon. In the mean while, cause to be boiled a-part in a little Pot, some Cocks-combs well scalded and pickt, with thin Slices of Bacon, Veal-sewet, some clear Broth, a Slice of Lemmon and an Onion stuck with three Cloves; but care must be more especially taken, that the whole Mixture be well parboil'd:… Your Pigeons, Cocks-combs and Ragoo being ready, make Sippets, with Crusts of Bread toasted at the Fire, and lay the Potage a soaking with good Broth: Then dress the Pigeons therein, and the Artichoke-bottom in the middle; the Ragoo being put between the Pigeons, and the Cocks-combs upon their Stomacks: When the Fat is thoroughly taken away, pour in the rest of the Ragoo. At the same time you are to provide a piece of Beef or Veal half roasted, which is to be cut, in a Stew-pan or on a Dish, and to be squeez'd hard, to get all the Gravy: It ought to be set at a distance from the Fire, to the end that it may become white; and when the Potage is dress'd, sprinkle it with this Gravy, that it may be well marbled. It must be garnish'd with Lemmon, one half of which may be squeez'd there-upon, and serv'd up hot to Table.[9]

One notices the multifarious garnish (the words ragoo or raggoo in the seventeenth and eighteenth centuries could mean either a garnish simmered in sauce or a whole dish), the marbling of the sauce with meat juice (very frequent in Massialot's receipts), and the final squeeze of lemon juice to add a sharp note to the sauce.

Massialot's *terrine* is very similar to his bisk (here again, the terms have very different meanings from the modern ones), since it too was a dish of birds and other meats in sauce:

A *Terrine* is a very considerable Side-dish, and may be thus prepar'd: Take six Quails, four young Pigeons, two Chickens, and a Breast of Mutton cut into Pieces; and let all be bak'd or stew'd in an earthen Pan, call'd *Terrine* in French, between two gentle Fires, with Bacon-*Bards* at the bottom to keep them from burning, or young streaked Bacon cut into pieces: Then let the Fat be drain'd off, and some good

---

[9] *The Court and Country Cook*, part 1, pp. 67–68. See also *Le Cuisinier roïal et bourgeois*, pp. 131–133.

Veal-gravy put in its place, with boil'd Lettice, a little green Pease-soop, and green Pease or Asparagus-tops: Let all be stew'd again together for some time, and thoroughly clear'd from the Fat, before they are serv'd up to Table.[10]

The explanation of the nature of the dish at the beginning of the receipt, which also appears in the original French text, leads one to suspect that the *terrine* was unfamiliar to contemporary cooks. But its components were perfectly recognizable: several meats are stewed together, and the cook is expected to have ready to hand the meat juice and the choice vegetables to finish the dish at the end.

The last of the key dishes at this period is the pupton or *poupeton*, a kind of cake made with pigeons and a garnish, all these ingredients being placed inside a crust of veal forcemeat, seasoned and bound with egg. The pupton was cooked very gently, in the embers, and then reversed on to the serving dish.[11] It was of variable size: when it was small, it appeared as one of the *hors d'œuvres* (meaning one of the little dishes placed at the sides of the table, the more important dishes being placed in the centre and at the top and bottom); when it was made as a bigger dish, it was served as an *entrée*, one of the central dishes. The other small dishes which surrounded the *grandes entrées* were miniature versions of the bisks and the terrines: one last example, of a fricassee, shows that such dishes used the same type of ingredients, and the same methods of preparation, as the bigger ones:

Let the ... Chickens be ... fry'd with Lard. Then stew them in a little Butter, Broth or Water, and a Glass of white Wine, season'd with Pepper, Salt, Nutmeg, Chervil chopt very small and whole *Ciboulets*. Make a thick'ning Liquor, with some of the same in which the Chickens were dress'd, with a little Flower; putting into it some Veal-sweet-breads, Mushrooms, Artichoke-bottoms and other Ingredients. Let them be garnish'd with *Fricandoes* and roasted Poupiets, or Slices of Lemmon, and served up with Mutton-gravy and Lemmon-juice.[12]

---

[10] *The Court and Country Cook*, part 1, pp. 251–252. See also *Le Cuisinier roïal et bourgeois*, p. 470.

[11] See *The Court and Country Cook*, part 1, pp. 225–226. See also *Le Cuisinier roïal et bourgeois*, pp. 267–268.

[12] *The Court and Country Cook*, part 1, p. 85. *Le Cuisinier roïal et bourgeois*, pp. 436–437.

As in the receipt for a bisk, the flavour is heightened by the use of meat juice, here of mutton, and given a sharp note by lemon juice. One notices also that even a relatively simple dish is given a lavish garnish of a raggoo of veal sweet-breads, mushrooms and artichoke bottoms, with fricandeaux and paupiettes added too. This receipt is followed by others which offer variations on the theme: Massialot gives two more chicken fricassees, one *au blanc* with a liaison of egg yolks and lemon juice, the other with a cream sauce. The author gives a detailed description in his first receipt, then proposes other versions of the same dish. What is on offer is a modular system of cookery.

Most of Massialot's receipts are devoted to dishes of meat in a sauce, whether these be *potages*, which, like the olio, contain large pieces of meat and birds as well as the liquid (these take up about fifty pages),[13] or the smaller dishes with rather less sauce such as the fricassee above. In all these, one notices the characteristics of the court style: lavish garnishes, a tendency to put several whole birds into the bigger dishes and, in the flavouring, a reduction in the number of spices, now limited mostly to cloves and nutmeg, and the total absence of sugar. This fully-fledged culinary manner made its appearance in print in England with the publication of the translation of Massialot in 1702. *The Court and Country Cook* is an unadapted translation, but the receipts are presented in a different order, since the book is organized alphabetically and a glossary of technical terms is supplied. This latter gives definitions of fashion-able dishes: the olio, the pupton and the bisk appear but the fricassee does not, and the raggoo is given only a brief description: '*Ragoo*, a high season'd Dish, after the *French* Way.'[14] The word was applied to the garnish and its sauce, but the expression '*en ragoût*', which became 'in a Ragoo' in English, meant that the word rapidly came to mean the whole dish as well as the sauce.

Some of these dishes made their first appearance in English here, but this does not mean *The Court and Country Cook* revealed a mode of cookery hitherto unknown. The 'aristocratic' works of the Restoration had included a number of them, though at a less advanced stage of development. Robert May, for instance, has a section on 'Boyled Meates' which contains olios and bisks, and elsewhere in his book are other French confections such as hashes and fricassees;

---

[13] See *The Court and Country Cook*, part I, pp. 197–225, passim; *Le Cuisinier roïal et bourgeois*, pp. 375–425, passim.

[14] See *The Court and Country Cook*, in the unnumbered pages at the beginning of the book.

William Rabisha also describes bisks and fricassees.[15] Sir Kenelm Digby's collection offers a few fricassees, several pottages, and one olio,[16] although the meat garnish which goes into Massialot's *potages* is only rarely present and is indicated as optional. There are no receipts for puptons or terrines in these books; these did not appear until later. Already, however, some of the grandiose dishes from the Restoration version of court-cookery were filtering down from the aristocracy to the gentry. We have seen that in 1673 *The Gentlewomans Companion* gave a receipt for a bisk in order to ridicule the strange mixtures invented by the court-cooks.

Since the most characteristic dishes of the latest version of court-cookery do not appear in printed books until after the appearance of Massialot in English in 1702, it is necessary to turn back to manuscript receipt collections to see how far the style had spread at the end of the seventeenth century. Although the names of the dishes do not go beyond those found in May and his contemporaries, the flavours are very different from the mixed savoury and sweet-and-savoury in the printed books. Rebecca Price's receipts, copied out for the most part in 1681, show that sugar as a flavouring for meat dishes was on its way out, indicating the influence of the new style. A sweet element, in the form of sugar or dried fruit, is present in only 6 per cent of the savoury receipts. This same influence is also visible in the type of receipts she recorded: there are several for fricassees, and one for an olio supplied by a friend, Mrs Whitehead.[17] This is very similar to that given by Hannah Woolley in her *Queen-like Closet* in 1670.[18] Both are based on a fricassee of calf's head, with braised pigeons added. To this, Mrs Woolley adds a goose, Mrs Whitehead a leg of mutton. The garnish is more copious in the manuscript version. It is significant that both rely on a last-minute assembly of ingredients which have been separately cooked. Here is the adaptation to a smaller kitchen of the grand style, since the court-cooks' receipts cook all the different meats together. However, the adjustment to make it feasible in gentry kitchens is an eloquent sign of a desire to emulate court-cookery.

---

[15] See May, *The Accomplisht Cook* (1660), pp. 1–8, 39–80; Rabisha, *The whole Body of Cookery dissected* (1661), pp. 45–46, 110, 81–86, 92, 123–124, 133.

[16] See Digby, *The Closet ... Opened* (1669), pp. 187, 217, 141–155, 195–196.

[17] See Masson (ed.), *The Compleat Cook* (1974), p. 90.

[18] See Woolley, *The Queen-like Closet*, 1670, p. 197.

But such large-scale dishes are rare in manuscript collections. Much more typical is the following from Rebecca Price. It is for something which figures often in the eighteenth century. Here, modest scale combines with the new savoury flavours:

Scotch-collops: my Aunt Rye's Receipt
Take some leane of the veal and cutt it in thyne slices, and beat them with the back of your knife, then lay them all night in claret-wine, then frye them browne in butter, and some great pickled oysters with them, then frye some slices of baccon also browne, then take it out of the pan and stew it altogether in the claret it was steeped in, with some sliced nutmeg, two anchovies, and mushrooms (if you have them) and so serve it.[19]

The receipt is characteristic of this particular collection, in which anchovy and wine are the dominant ingredients in sauces for dishes of meat and fish. One also notices the simplicity, and the absence of any added garnish.

Further instances of the same association of flavours are to be found in a second manuscript collection written out in 1683 in Yorkshire. This collection contains a receipt for 'Scotch Collopps' which is very similar to Rebecca Price's, except that mutton replaces the veal. A receipt for stewed pigeons gives another example of the flavours which will be so much in evidence in the cookery books of the eighteenth century, but which had already entered the repertoire of the gentry kitchen by the end of the seventeenth:

To stew Pigeons.
First stuffe your bellies & crops with forc'd meat, then sett them … as close as you can into a skillett & fill them up with water & a good piece of butter, also some balls of forced meat, & a bundle of sweet herbs, … a nutmegge, some mace, a little whole pepper, a little cloves, & Ginger, two Onyons, when they are almost enough, putt in two or three Anchovees, … then take halfe a pint of white wine, & the Yolks of three or four egges, & so thicken the liquor … and serve them upp in sippetts of bread; you may squeez in the juice of a Lemon, if you please.[20]

---

[19] Masson (1974), p. 97.
[20] A receipt from the Savile MS, quoted in Brears, *The Gentlewoman's Kitchen* (1984), p. 40. For the receipt for 'Scotch Collopps', see p. 30.

This uses the anchovy-wine combination, just as in Rebecca Price. The sweet herbs and nutmeg, together with the lemon juice at the end, are similar to Massialot's flavourings for his fricassees.

A third manuscript collection – that of Diana Astry, the eldest daughter of a wealthy gentry family in Gloucestershire, who copied out her receipts at the beginning of the eighteenth century – contains several examples of the same association of flavours. In this collection, however, preserving and other still-room activities are more important than dishes from the kitchen.[21] Here, too, sugar is notably absent. In this last notebook, of somewhat later date than the other two, there is a receipt for a French dish where the influence of the court style, with its lavish garnishes, is obvious. The spelling of this manuscript is particularly exotic:

> 163. To regoa a breast of veal. (S. Gr.)
> Take a breast of veal, bone it & lard it with bacon & season it with peper & nutmeg & salt, & take the yolkes of eggs & some melted butter & beat it together & wash it over; take ½ pt. strong broth, som thinn slices of fat bacon & lay it in a botam of a dish, cut the veal into peices & stuff the skinn in with forst meat & put it in the oven to bake.
>
> The sawce for itt: Take sum gravy & butter, set the swee bread of the veal & a pear or 2 of lambs' tones then cut them in piceses a little biger than dice, & fry them & sum cowcumbers fryed, & forcest meat balls, & aspragraus boyled & cut in peices, & simper it up together & pouer it on the veal.[22]

The dish has been adapted to bring it within the reach of ordinary kitchens: the 'regoa', borrowed from court-cookery, is poured over the baked meat at the last minute. Thus the stuffed breast of veal is given a modish air by the final garnish.

These manuscripts demonstrate that in gentry kitchens, cookery had moved on since the Restoration. The separation of savoury and sweet dishes is already much in evidence in collections of the last twenty years of the seventeenth century, and there are signs of adapted versions of the grand dishes of

---

[21] See Stitt (ed.), 'Diana Astry's Recipe Book' (1957), pp. 93, 115–116, 117, 131, 138, 140, 146, 148.
[22] Ibid., p. 120.

the court-cooks which would appear in print only after 1700. This raises the question of how far the flavour revolution is due to French influence, and how far it should be seen as a separate but parallel development. The fact that these manuscripts so often show the distinctive flavour combination of anchovy and wine which is not found in French books, suggests that this was, at least in part, a purely English phenomenon. On the other hand, it is the 'made dishes', of meat or fish in sauce, which show such combinations; in areas of more 'English' cookery, such as pies and puddings, the sweet-savoury mixtures survived much longer. It looks then as if the movement to separate sweet and savoury, while not purely French in origin, was greatly assisted by the adoption of the French version of the fashionable court style. The appearance in our manuscripts of key elements of this French style, albeit in a limited number of receipts, suggests that dishes in this manner were already a familiar feature of aristocratic tables by the 1670s, if not earlier, even though receipts for the 'noble' versions of the dishes do not appear in print before 1700.

This in turn raises the question of the time-lag between cookery in practice and cookery in print. Elizabeth David suggested that this gap may be anything from thirty to forty years.[23] One can state with certainty that some receipts, such as that for 'pocket soup' (a meat stock reduced to a very firm jelly, which could be carried around to make a broth by adding boiling water), for instance, were circulating in manuscript form at least thirty years before they appeared in print.[24] So there is every reason to believe that the cookery found in books by court-cooks published in the first decades of the eighteenth century represents the practice of the end of the seventeenth, rather than what was actually being cooked in the mansions of the aristocracy at the date of publication. However, the cooks do sometimes add details to the preparation or the presentation of their dishes which are supposed to give the latest fashionable touch, bringing something old-hat fully up-to-date.

Massialot's book, organized as a dictionary, offers a systematic presentation of the receipts with the basic method set out first, often followed by variations at the end. With the exception of Charles Carter, who begins with broth and

---

[23] Quoted in Mennell, *All Manners of Food* (1985), p. 65.

[24] This receipt appears in the manuscript collection of Mrs Ann Blencowe, which dates from 1695, with the title 'Veal Glew'; it reaches printed cookery books in 1723. See *The Receipt Book of Mrs. Ann Blencowe* (1925), p. 23; R. Smith, *Court Cookery* (1723), part 1, pp. 80–81; R. Bradley, *The Country Housewife and Lady's Director* (1727), pp. 58–59.

gravy before going on to dishes requiring the use of these essentials, books by
English cooks are not presented so programmatically. Rather, they tend to give
a series of unconnected receipts and often presume their readers – professional
cooks – will be familiar with basic preparations. Such is the case for Patrick
Lamb's book (at least, in its first edition – later editions were remodelled in
dictionary form): all the ingredients of Massialot-style court-cookery are
present, but, while there are receipts for 'Bisque', 'Olio', 'Terreyné' and
'Pupton',[25] there are only references to *coulis* (or cullis, as the English usually
termed it), called for several times but never explained. Lamb's instructions for
these prestigious dishes (which appear at the beginning, as they do in Charles
Carter) are extremely long. A few extracts from his receipt for a terrine give
some idea of the importance of presentation:

> *To make a* Terreyné.
> Take a small Quantity of all the Ingredients above-mentioned in the *Olio*
> [i.e. beef, mutton, veal and pork, as well as birds and several different
> vegetables], and stew them down after the same manner; then place them
> into your Dish that you intend to serve it in, or in a *Terreyné*-Dish, if you
> have one. A *Terreyné*-Dish, at Court, is made of Silver, round and upright,
> … with two Handles, such as a small Cistern has. … you must stew it in
> it an Hour;… whereas you put your soak'd Bread under your *Olio*, you
> must soak it in some of the same Broth, and put it on the Top of your
> *Terreyné*, … then it will look like the Upper part of a Brown Loaf; … do
> not let your *Terreyné*-Pan be fill'd quite up to the Top, because your
> Cowley ought to swim as high as your Bread. … You may dish it up after
> the same Manner, if you have no *Terreyné*-Dish, with a good Rim to hold
> the Liquor in: Let not your Meat be much higher than your Rim, because
> it will look too much like an *Olio*, only the Bread being on the Top makes
> it another thing. To make an Alteration, you may bake it in an Oven …
> till your Bread and Cowley comes to a Crust on the Top of it. We do not
> use to bake it at Court now, but only pour our Cowley hot over the Top
> of it when you serve it; but baking is the good old way, therefore I leave
> either of them to your Discretion.[26]

---

[25] See Lamb, *Royal Cookery* (1710), pp. 27–28, 30–35, 36–38, 43–45.

[26] Ibid., pp. 36–38. One finds the same suggestions in the receipt given by John Nott, who took his
receipt from Lamb. See Nott, *The Cook's and Confectioner's Dictionary* (1723), T 25.

Lamb's 'Cowley' is of course the cullis, which serves to thicken the sauce. Lamb does not tell the cook exactly how to make the dish, only how to compose it. This gives a modish air to the 'new' version of something which was beginning to look old-fashioned.

Lamb also enables the reader to see a fugitive fashion at court, that for Dutch dishes prepared in honour of William III. There is a receipt for 'Pike-Cabilow', with the latest vogueish details as for the terrine. In Holland, says Lamb, the sauce is simply melted butter but for the Queen (Queen Anne by the date of publication) the English cooks make a thick butter sauce emulsified with water and lemon juice:

> For the Queen, we draw our Butter up. A Pound of Butter, with a Spoonful of Water, drawn up, is as thick as a Cream, squeeze a Lemon, *and so serve it hot.*[27]

The flavours of Lamb's dishes are close to those of Massialot: sugar has disappeared from savoury dishes with the exception of two sauces to be served with game,[28] and vegetables and herbs have replaced the older spices – except in the olio, where saffron is used to season the broth, as it was in Digby's receipt in 1669.[29] Contrary to what has been stated by Jean-Louis Flandrin, garlic had not yet disappeared from English cookery: Lamb uses it in his olio, and we shall see other examples of its employment by court-cooks.[30]

These grand dishes, and the 'soups' which are similar to the bisk, are placed at the beginning of Lamb's book. After the first fifty pages, the receipts become much more succinct as he moves on to more English things such as puddings, cakes and sweet dishes. In fact, there are very few of the last category, the emphasis being on made dishes. Out of a total of 87 receipts, 41 have French titles in the index – in the text itself, the 'Patties' (i.e. *Pâtés*) tend to turn into 'Pies'. The order of presentation and the frequent use of French confirm the high status of the French-inspired court-cookery at this date.

---

[27] Lamb (1710), p. 55.

[28] Ibid., pp. 94, 102.

[29] Ibid., p. 33; Digby (1669), p. 196. In the 26 receipts for made dishes in Lamb's book, cloves appear 8 times, and nutmeg 6 times. Apart from the saffron in the olio, these are the only spices he uses. See Lamb (1710), pp. 1–50.

[30] See Flandrin, 'Différence et différenciation des goûts' (1981), p. 104.

The emphasis on presentation in Lamb's works is echoed by the large number of plates (35) illustrating the placing of dishes. The menu of a dinner served to Queen Anne in 1705 shows French influence dominating the royal table, despite the presence of some English items. At the first course, there was an olio, a dish of chine of mutton and veal cutlets, beef 'alà Royalé', a 'Hamb Pie with Chickens', a 'Supe Lorrain' and a 'Turky Spaniola'; the second course was made up of four dishes of roast birds (geese, snipe, partridges and woodcocks) surrounding a centrepiece of a lamb's head, veal olives, pies (called 'Petit Pattys' in the list), a pupton of lobster, and 'Carps Civet'. The third was composed of small dishes of oyster loaves, asparagus, 'Butter'd Chickens', various kinds of mushrooms, smelts in cream, tansy, cockscombs, and sweetbreads and marrow, with a central dish of 'Plates of cold things and Jeillys of all sorts'.[31] Lamb's copper-plates give fashionable menus; the bills of fare at the end of the book, presented as unadorned lists, contain fewer grand dishes, and are closer to the domestic style found in books by women authors. Again, the presentation of the menus confirms the hierarchy of prestige implied by the order of the receipts.

Books by other court-cooks do not offer such clear indications of relative status, but contain the same dishes as Patrick Lamb. John Nott's substantial work is presented in dictionary form, like Massialot. There are several basic preparations, and the grand productions of the court style are present too, but the book also gives far more English domestic dishes than Lamb. One example of the court style contains many of the elements that we have seen in Massialot:

> 249. To make a Bisk of Pullets.
> Truss your Pullets neatly, fry them brown, then put them into a Pot with good Broth, several slices of fat Bacon, a slice or two of lean, and a slice or two of Beef beaten, green Citron, Cloves, a Bunch of sweet Herbs, and other Seasoning; set these over a gentle Fire to stew: Garnish your Bisk with Cocks-combs, Veal Sweet-breads, Mushrooms, Truffles, and Artichoke Bottoms: Make a Ring round about the Potage with Lemon-juice, and a Veal Cullis just when you are serving it up.[32]

---

[31] See Lamb (1710), pl. 22, between pages 4 and 5.
[32] Nott (1723), P 249.

One finds here the same type of garnish, the same marbling of the sauce, the same lemon juice at the end. The receipt is not taken from *The Court and Country Cook*; it is adapted directly from the French version of a bisk of quails in the *Cuisinier roïal et bourgeois*,[33] with a defective translation of 'citron verd' which becomes 'green Citron' ('Citron', in English, usually referred to the candied rind). While some of Nott's receipts are clearly inspired by Massialot, the borrowings are not systematic, and it seems that his book is compiled from a variety of sources, perhaps the most important being the second (1716) edition of Lamb which contains far more receipts than the 87 of the original. Unlike Lamb, John Nott (or the compiler hidden behind his name) gives instructions for cullis, showing how the author had followed the latest developments in French cuisine. Whereas Massialot's coulis were based on roast meat, puréed in a mortar, Nott's is closer to those found in Vincent La Chapelle's *Modern Cook*: meat and vegetables are browned in a pan together, and the thickening agent is flour, browned with the other ingredients before gravy and broth are added; the addition of bread crusts gives a further liaison.[34] The '*haut-goût*' of French dishes depended on these sauce bases, richly flavoured with meat, vegetables, and herbs.

Not all the court-cooks were so forward-looking. Henry Howard's book seems rather old-hat compared to Lamb and Nott. Howard gives an olio which harks back to La Varenne: the use of claret and capers is typical of the style which had been introduced into England before the Restoration:

78. *The Olea.*
Take twelve Pigeons, six Chickens; pull the Pigeons, dry them, and put them in whole; scald the Chickens, cut them in halves; then half roast a Rabbit, and cut it into pieces as long as ones Finger; boil a Neats-tongue very tender, cut it in thin pieces as big as half Crowns, with Sweet-breads pulled in little pieces: Put to all this Meat one Quart of Claret, and three Pints of strong Gravy, let it stew softly with the Meat; put to it a little whole Pepper, four whole Onions, Time, Savory, and

---

[33] See *Le Cuisinier roïal et bourgeois* (1698), pp. 133–134.

[34] See Nott (1723), C 236. At the end of the receipt, Nott gives variations, for a game cullis, of the older type. There is a similar receipt in R. Smith's book (1723); as in Nott's work, there are also receipts for cullises similar to Massialot's. See R. Smith (1723), pp. 32, 8, 20, 29–30. The last receipt, for duck cullis, contains garlic, as does the essence of ham, pp. 35–36.

Majoram tied up in a bunch; let all these stew together 'till the Meat is
almost enough; then put in a good many Capers shred small, twenty
pickled Oysters with three spoonfuls of their Liquor, four blades of large
Mace, the Peel of a Limon shred, and a Limon and half cut into pieces
as big as Dice; mingle all these well together; then beat twelve Eggs into
the Liquor, let them scald in it to thicken it; rub the Dish you intend
to serve them in with Garlick; then build the Meat up in an heap and
pour the Liquor all over it; then lay upon the Meat Marrow, being first
boiled, Oysters fried, Limon sliced, Mace, Sausages crispt, Bacon and
Balls … with blanched Beans, and French-beans: serve it.[35]

The pyramid of meats belongs to the early eighteenth-century court manner
(and we shall see further examples of this presentation when we turn to the
dessert) but the flavours are more seventeenth-century. The receipts for made
dishes in this rather old-fashioned book contain the same flavours as those
found in Rebecca Price's manuscript: out of a total of 48 receipts, none contains
sugar or dried fruit; 56 per cent contain anchovy, 71 per cent contain wine.[36]
A comparison of Howard's receipt for an olio and earlier versions will serve to
summarize the major shifts in culinary style since the beginning of the seventeenth century. In 1615 Markham gave a receipt which called for sugar and
dried fruit; by the time of the Restoration, these had disappeared, but saffron
was essential, present among ingredients listed by May and Digby (and the dish
was clearly seen as Spanish – remember Pepys). By about 1700, the dish appears
amongst other pottages inspired by French cookery, even though the word
'Spanish' still occurs from time to time, and the saffron was on its way out.
Lamb adds it, but Howard and Smith do not, and Nott uses it in only one of
his two receipts.[37]

It is time to return to Charles Carter's list of top dishes. We have seen
examples of terrines, bisks and olios, but he also mentions pottages and soups,
'Royals', daubes, 'Poveroys', 'Castroles', 'Alamodes', 'Sattoots' and 'Marrianates', as well as smaller affairs like raggoos, fricassees and hashes. At first sight,

---

[35] Howard, *England's Newest Way* (1708), pp. 38–39.
[36] Ibid., pp. 26–62.
[37] See Markham, *The English Hus-wife* (1615), pp. 49–50; May (1660), pp. 1–5; Digby (1669), p. 195;
Pepys, *Diary*, vol. 9, pp. 509, 544; Lamb (1710), p. 33; R. Smith (1723), pp. 87–88; Nott (1723), O 31,
O 32.

it is surprising to find pottages and soups, but these humble names conceal important items: the olio, terrine and bisk are all classified among the pottages. Carter gives a receipt for 'POTTAGE LA REINE', in which are found many aspects characteristic of Massialot. Besides the basic gravy and herb-flavoured broth, a cullis for the pottage is prepared, using a sieved mixture of broth, partridge flesh, veal sweetbreads and ground almonds. When it is time to serve, the dish is filled first with a layer of slices of bread soaked in broth, then with partridges, stuffed and baked, and blanched lettuce and celery-root to fill up the interstices. Next, partridge breasts stuck with almonds are added, and lastly the cullis (which is called 'Coolio' here) is poured over in rings, to give a marbled effect, before a final garnish of celery, slices of forcemeat and lemon.[38] The other pottages in Carter's book are just as elaborately garnished: even the vegetable ones are accorded a loaf hollowed out and filled with an appropriate mixture.[39] Soups and pottages were almost invariably given such a solid element at this date. Lady Grisell Baillie, dining at Lord Sunderland's, wrote in her notebook that one of the dishes on the menu was a 'Soup without anything init [sic]',[40] clearly because this struck her as incongruous.

The other dishes in Carter's list were less 'liquid': these are meat and fish in sauce, always garnished with a raggoo, in the eighteenth-century meaning of the term. The only exception to this is the 'Sattoot' (the English translation of the French *en surtout*), which is remarkably similar to the pupton.[41] The constant of every item in this list is an elaborate garnish. With very few exceptions, none of Carter's receipts contains sugar. The only ones where it is present are capon pottage and 'plumb pottage', a traditional Christmas dish, and in a group of meatless pottages made with milk, almonds, and peas (and these are explicitly presented to the reader as '*Sweet* POTTAGES').[42] There is never a sweet ingredient in the dishes garnished with a raggoo.

This court version of *haute cuisine* in England had two important characteristics: the enormous quantities of meat it used, as a main ingredient or as a

---

[38] See Carter (1730), pp. 9–10.

[39] Ibid., pp. 8–36.

[40] Scott-Moncrieff (ed.), *The Household Book of Lady Grisell Baillie* (1911), p. 287.

[41] See Carter (1730): the 'Royals' and the 'Dobes' will be found on pp. 36–37, 51–52, 55–56; the 'Poveroy' pp. 60–61; the 'Castroles' pp. 39–40, 58, 68–69; the 'Alamodes' pp. 37, 39; the 'Sattoots' pp. 40, 58–59; the 'Marrianate' p. 91.

[42] Ibid., pp. 20–21, 34–36.

garnish – the sheer amounts being expressed in the heaped-up presentation as well as by their mere presence – and the separation of sweet and savoury, at least in the made dishes. Books by male cooks show this style at more or less advanced stages: Carter, Lamb, Nott and Smith are among the moderns, Howard is less so, and another professional cook, T. Hall, is thoroughly old-fashioned. But even the most modern are offering something already well-established – indeed, soon to be abandoned – among the élite. If we turn now to the more 'domestic' cookery found in books by women authors, this less grand cookery had adopted the new flavours, but only rarely had it borrowed the elaborate dishes of the true court manner. The gap between culinary practice in aristocratic houses and its reflection in print is even greater than among the master-cooks.

The separation of sweet and savoury which was, as we have already seen, well developed in manuscript collections of receipts at the end of the seventeenth century, is a feature of printed books by women in the first decades of the next. Mary Kettilby is a useful source on this aspect of changing tastes. In her first edition, sugar is conspicuously absent, just as in Carter above: no made dish contains either sugar or dried fruit.[43] In the second edition of 1719, however, in which new receipts supplied by the compiler's correspondents form the second part of the book, sugar reappears. But each time, Mrs Kettilby warns her readers that these sweet sauces are old-fashioned:

A Sweet Sauce for Boil'd Mutton, very Good.
Take a quarter of a pint of the Broth,… put to it four Spoonfuls of the Pickle of Capers or Samphire, set it on the Fire to boil; then shred a Carrot, which has been first boil'd tender, and four spoonfuls of Capers or Samphire shred, put this into the Liquor; when it boils stir in four Ounces of Butter, and shake a very little Flower, sweeten it, and pour it over the Meat: 'Tis a grateful, tho' old fashion'd Sauce.[44]

This brings to mind Mrs Kettilby's words in her preface, where she says that people laugh at the cook-maid for sugaring a dish of beans. It is not difficult

---

[43] See Kettilby, *A Collection of above Three Hundred Receipts* (1714), pp. 1–122 (pages devoted to cookery).
[44] Ibid., part 2, pp. 13–14. See also part 2, pp. 8–9.

to guess at the underlying conflict between the traditional style, with its sweet and sour combinations inherited from the cookery of the beginning of the seventeenth century and even earlier, and the *haut-goût* of 'modern' cookery which had already ousted the older style in élite circles and was in the process of doing so amongst the gentry. The presence of this receipt in the second part of the book suggests that the elimination of the old style was meeting some resistance from more conservative palates. Mary Kettilby is not the only author to mention the old-fashioned nature of such sauces. T. Hall in *The Queen's Royal Cookery* gives a receipt for a sweet-sour sauce to serve with mutton, and concludes it by saying: 'If you please, you may eat it without Sugar, which is most in fashion now.'[45] By the end of our period, such remarks are found in more modest works. In 1733, Sarah Harrison proposes a list of dishes suitable for each season and notices that the traditional sweet sauce served with roast pork is no longer a fashionable tracklement:

> Pig roasted, to be serv'd with Gravy in the Dish, or white Wine, Water and Salt warm'd for the Sauce .... Curran Sauce is not in Fashion.[46]

This change in taste had reached both the irredeemably conservative *and* the less expensive. (Mrs Harrison's book was the first to mention economy, first in its preface, later on the title-page.)

The dominant flavour for made dishes in Mary Kettilby is that combination of wine and anchovy seen in Rebecca Price, implying a time-lag of over thirty years between manuscript and print. Kettilby's receipt for hare stew exemplifies its use:

> *To stew a* Hare.
> Pull your Hare to pieces, and bruise the Bones, and put it into a Stew-pan, with three pints of strong Broth, and at the same time put in an Onion, and a faggot of Sweet-herbs; let it stew leisurely for four hours, then put in a pint of Claret; let it stew two or three hours longer, 'till 'tis tender; take out what Bones you can find, with the Herbs and Onion, if not dissolv'd; put in an Anchovy or two with the Claret: Stewing so

---

[45] Hall, *The Queen's Royal Cookery* (1713), p. 105.
[46] Harrison, *The House-keeper's Pocket-Book* (1733), p. 13.

long, it will be thick enough; you need only shake it up with half a
pound of Butter, when ready for the Table.[47]

As well as the anchovy and claret, the use of herbs and a large quantity of
butter are equally reminiscent of Rebecca Price, further evidence of culinary
hangover: her 'correspondents', after all, were probably raiding their own
manuscript receipt books for their contributions.

But while all this reflected modernizing trends, the grand dishes of the court
style are not represented in Kettilby. There are a few, however, in E. Smith's work
of 1727, even if here, too, one is struck by the same anchovy-wine combination.
Smith offers the reader some large-scale set-pieces and uses elaborate raggoos to
garnish those smaller dishes which were, of course, more accessible to her readers
than the monumental productions proposed by the likes of Patrick Lamb. A
receipt for a fricassee shows this woman imitating the court-cooks:

A brown Fricasy.
Take Lamb or Rabbet cut in small pieces; grate on it a little Nutmeg, or
Lemon-Peel; fry it quick and brown with Butter; then have some strong
Broth, in which put your Morels and Mushrooms, a few Coxcombs
boil'd tender, and Artichoke-Bottoms; a little Walnut-liquor, and a Bay-
leaf; then roll a bit of Butter in Flour, shake it well, and serve it up. You
may squeeze an Orange or Lemon over it.[48]

The mushrooms, cockscombs and artichoke-bottoms are typical of the court-
style garnish, but this receipt does not add the rich flavour of a cullis which the
men would have used to produce the *haut-goût* of French cuisine. It has been
adapted to make it easier for the single-handed cook. A few years later, Sarah
Harrison gives a receipt for a chicken fricassee which combines Rebecca Price's
flavourings with a rather more down-market sort of garnish:

A Brown Fricassee of Chickens.
Take Chickens fresh kill'd and Skin them; cut them in pieces and fry
them in Butter or Lard, when they are fry'd take them out and let them

---

[47] Kettilby (1714), p. 20.
[48] E– S–, *The Compleat Housewife* (1728), p. 45.

drein, then make some Balls of force-Meat, and fry them, then take some strong Gravy, a Shallot or two, some Spice, a Bunch of sweet Herbs, a little Anchovy Liquor, a Glass of Claret, some thin lean Tripe cut with a jagging Iron to imitate Cocks Combs, thicken your Sauce with burnt Butter, then put in your Chickens and toss them up together; garnish it with fry'd Mushrooms dip'd in Butter, or Lemon slic'd, or Parsley fry'd.[49]

The forcemeat balls, the mushrooms (or the two alternatives which are suggested) and, most importantly, the imitation cockscombs, show the desire to imitate the aristocratic style without the expense. These two receipts give a striking example of the way in which a dish could be gradually transformed as it went down the social scale.

The same signs of adaptation are present in the receipts for set-pieces in E. Smith. For instance, she gives a pupton (entitled 'Pulpatoon of Pigeons')[50] and a bisk, also made with pigeons, which calls for twelve birds, simmered with the garnish ingredients (veal sweetbreads, palates, and lamb's stones), then dished up on top of slices of bread soaked in broth, with slices of broiled bacon and forcemeat balls. At the end, the author suggests a cheaper way: 'You may leave out the Sweet-breads, and Palates, and Lamb-stones, and put in scalded Herbs, as for a Soop, … and but six Pigeons.'[51] Prepared with neither garnish nor the cullis to enrich the sauce, the dish bears little resemblance to the court-style original.

A second example of a rather different kind of transformation shows an aristocratic dish changing its nature at the hand of a woman cook. This is E. Smith's receipt for a terrine:

To make a Tureiner.
Take a China Pot or Bowl, and fill it as follows: At the bottom lay some fresh Butter; then put in three or four Beef-steaks larded with Bacon; then cut some Veal Steaks from the Leg; hack them, and … lay it all over with Forc'd Meat, and roll it up, and lay it in with young Chickens, Pigeons, and Rabbits, … Sweet-breads, Lamb-stones, Coxcombs,

---

[49] Harrison (1733), p. 83.
[50] E– S– (1728), p. 41.
[51] Ibid., p. 36.

Palates,… Tongues,… whole yolks of hard Eggs, Pistachia Nuts peeled, forced Balls, … Lemon sliced, … Barberries and Oysters; season all these with Pepper, Salt, Nutmeg, and Sweet-herbs mix'd together after they are cut very small, and strew it on every Thing as you put it in your Pot: Then put in a quart of Gravy, and some Butter on the top, and cover it close with a Lid of Puff-paste, pretty thick. Eight hours will bake it.[52]

The lavish ingredients bring us closer to the aristocratic model but, covered with pastry and baked, it is more a pie than a terrine. Although Patrick Lamb gave a variation where the terrine was topped with bread and baked, he stated this was old-fashioned. Mrs Smith is at once conservative and, moreover, assimilating the dish into an English repertoire.

By the middle of the seventeenth century, pies had become a peculiarly English speciality; even the French were prepared to concede superiority. By the time Smith was writing, they had a long and honourable past, and were thus less susceptible to foreign influences than the made dishes at which the French were held to excel. If it is true that there was a parallel trend in both countries towards separating savoury from sweet, it is not surprising that the English pies should have followed the general movement, but it is noticeable that they did so very much more slowly than made dishes. English books of the eighteenth-century contain many receipts for meat pies with sweet and sour elements, whereas in France sugar was banished from the list of ingredients much more rapidly. It is still there in Massialot, but had disappeared by 1733 when La Chapelle was first published.[53] What is perhaps the best-known English mixture of meat and sugar, the mince-pie, retained this combination until well into the nineteenth century, and survives, without the lean meat but with beef suet, to our own day.[54] But even in the area of pies, the distinction between sweet and savoury was beginning to operate and was visible in English texts before 1700. A sweet element, either sugar or dried fruit, was almost always present in Markham's receipts (in all his pies, except those made with game, in fact), in Jos. Cooper only 14 receipts out of a total of 23 contain some

---

[52] E– S– (1728), p. 101.

[53] See *Le Cuisinier roïal et bourgeois* (1698), pp. 472–494; La Chapelle, *The Modern Cook* (1733), vol. 2, pp. 30–38, 61–91.

[54] See Wilson, *Food and Drink in Britain* (1976), p. 245.

sweetness, and in Rebecca Price's manuscript, the proportion is 16 out of 22.[55] One of Price's receipts suggests how tastes were changing, with some people still attached to the older flavours, since the addition of sugar is given as optional:

> Oyster pye: my Lady Howe's Receipt
>
> Take great oysters … perboyle them in their own liquor, season them with a little peper, nutmeg whole mace, shred some time, persly, sorill, sweet-marjerome, with a great deale of buter: and if you love it sweet strew some suger one it, lay one ye top slices of Lemon, and when it comes out of ye oven put in a caudle of whitewine [sic] and eggs, it must not be over baked, neither must you put a caudle in except you make it a sweete pye.[56]

By the earliest years of the eighteenth century, there are great differences between individual texts. Out of the 14 receipts for pies in *The Accomplish'd Female Instructor* (1704), 10 contain sugar or dried fruit, whereas out of 9 receipts in *The Whole Duty of a Woman* (1701), only 2 combine meat and sugar.[57] The distinction between savoury and sweet pies did not become really obvious in the cookery books until around 1720. The cooks closest to French culinary practice had either removed sugar entirely: Patrick Lamb, for instance, never included it in his savoury pie instructions.[58] Or they emphasized the distinction between the two categories: Charles Carter separated his totally savoury pies from his sweet-and-savoury ones.[59] Even the women authors were beginning to mark the difference: E. Smith gave pies with chicken and with lamb in both savoury and sweet versions, but allowed the confusion of flavours to persist in her vegetable and mince pies – in other words, those where the sweet-savoury association lingered the longest.[60]

---

[55] See Markham (1615), pp. 66–68; Cooper, *The Art of Cookery* (1654), pp. 90–113; Masson (1974), pp. 137–150.

[56] Masson (1974), p. 140.

[57] See R. G., *The Accomplish'd Female Instructor* (1704), pp. 107–114; *The Whole Duty of a Woman* (1701), pp. 152–158.

[58] See Lamb (1710), pp. 67–77.

[59] See Carter (1730), pp. 134–162.

[60] See E– S– (1728), pp. 102–120.

This was at a time when sauces with sugar were already unfashionable. Diners who had begun to reject that sort of sauce were starting to reject sugar in other savoury preparations although some were much more attached to old traditions than others. When Mary Kettilby presents a receipt for a beef or mutton pasty, she is careful to explain to the reader who might be shocked by her use of sugar (the meat is marinaded in sugar for twenty-four hours before the sugar is wiped off and the meat baked in a crust) that the result is delicious:

> Let no one dislike the laying it in Sugar, till they have try'd it, for how preposterous an Ingredient soever it may seem in a savory Pye, I must beg leave to assure the Reader, that nothing gives so certain a shortness and tenderness to the Meat as Sugar; and if carefully wash'd or wip'd off, it leaves a Delicacy that is equal to Venison.[61]

The comment confirms the distinction between savoury and sweet. Kettilby's final remark also offers a glimpse of a hierarchy of prestige which is somewhat different to that obtaining in court-cookery. Whereas for the élite, the most prestigious dishes were the *grosses entrées* of French cuisine, for the gentry venison played just as important a rôle in impressing one's friends. Game was the preserve of the landowning classes, and to dine on venison was to affirm one's place amongst the upper classes.[62] One sent venison as a gift to friends, and it was a compliment to neighbours to invite them to partake of a choice piece, as did Henry Purefoy in 1749:

> I shall have an haunch of young fat Venison for dinner on Tuesday next & desire the favour of yours or Mr. Wallbank's and Miss Barrett's good company to eat some of it. Mr. & Mrs. Haws will be with us.[63]

Hardly surprisingly, cookery books were full of receipts for 'mock' venison pasties. Nor were they confined to those works aimed at least partly at readers, such as Mary Kettilby's, without access to game; Charles Carter, for instance,

---

[61] Kettilby (1719), part. 2, p. 14.

[62] See E.P. Thompson, *Whigs and Hunters* (1975), p. 158.

[63] Eland (ed.), *Purefoy Letters 1735–1753* (1931), vol. 2, p. 387. See also Thomson, *Life in a Noble Household* (1937), p. 235.

gives one for a mutton pasty to imitate venison.[64] Mrs Kettilby's marinade of sugar and Carter's of saltpetre were not the only methods. E. Smith suggests marinading the meat in blood.[65] Nor were these stratagems new at the beginning of the eighteenth century: *The Compleat Cook* had one in 1655.[66]

So the separation of savoury from sweet pies had begun but the disappearance of sugar in pies was still a long way off. All authors, male or female, give receipts for both types. Here at least, the flavours of the master-cooks are similar to those of the ladies. In this area of traditional English excellence, the mingling of flavours was slow to disappear, confirming the importance of French influence in made dishes and sauces where the combination of sweet and savoury disappeared more quickly. But, while the same mixtures are still found in receipts by both master-cooks and women writers, the men's contain a feature absent from those of their female rivals. Several gave copper-plates or other illustrations showing the shape and decoration of each kind of pie.[67] The shape was a good indication of its contents. These often elaborate designs were, of course, the prolongation of the 'decorative' cookery of Restoration cooks such as Robert May who gave several pages of plates depicting a host of different pie shapes. Court-cookery in England had taken up its indigenous inheritance as well as borrowing from the French. It can thus be seen as a combined process in which continuity played as great a part as innovation.

Thoroughly English dishes are, however, more visible in the books by women authors. Generally, their receipts are less complicated and call for fewer ingredients. The areas where the lady of the house had taken an active rôle in the past, sweet dishes and preserves of all kinds, are well to the fore. Among the preserves are pickles and collared meats, like this breast of veal given by E. Smith:

To collar a Breast of Veal.
Take a Breast of Veal, and bone it, and wash it, and dry it in a clean Cloth; then shred Thyme, Winter-savory, and Parsley, very small, and

---

[64] See Carter (1730), pp. 143–144. At the end of the receipt, Carter states: 'It has, and may deceive many, who will take it for Venison.'

[65] See E– S– (1728), pp. 24–25.

[66] See W. M., *The Compleat Cook* (1655), p. 120.

[67] See, for instance, Howard (1708), 2 pl. between pages 146 and 147; Hall (1713), pl. facing page 132; a later example is to be found in Thacker, *The Art of Cookery* (1758), p. 292. A more humble book gives written instructions; see R.G. (1704), p. 107.

mix it with Salt, Pepper, Cloves, Mace, and Nutmeg; then strew it on the inside of your Meat, and roll it up hard, beginning at the Neck end; tye it up with Tape, and put it in a Pot fit to boil it in, standing upright: You must boil it in Water and Salt, and a bunch of Sweet-herbs; when 'tis boiled enough, take it off the Fire, and put it in an earthen Pot, and when the Liquor is cold pour it over it:... When you serve it to the Table, cut it in round slices.[68]

The receipt mixes old, by its use of spices, and new, by the sweet herbs which had begun to replace spices during the seventeenth century. One finds similar instructions until the end of the eighteenth century, and meat prepared in this fashion is a feature of many bills of fare, especially for suppers.

But the women's most important contribution to the continuing development of English cookery was in sweet dishes – puddings, tarts, pancakes and cakes – and, of course, in the creams and sweetmeats of the banquet course which had been so important an aspect of a seventeenth-century lady's culinary activity. One indication of women's continuing interest in sweet dishes is the complaint by readers (as we have already seen) about the lack of receipts for preserving in the first edition of Mary Kettilby's collection. Among the wide variety of such dishes in these authors' books, we shall concentrate on four types – three served at dinner, the fourth, a cake, presented to guests in the afternoon (which, at this date, means after dinner).

The first is for one of the basic dishes of the English table in gentry and middle-class circles. The pudding, as Henri Misson pointed out (in a remark so often quoted in its relentlessly quaint English translation of 1719 that many modern commentators have missed its irony), was a many-splendoured thing, varying greatly in its ingredients and in the way it was cooked.[69] At the first course of a dinner, it tended to appear in its boiled form, which was generally the least sweet. Mary Kettilby gives four receipts for boiled puddings, including this:

An excellent Plumb-Pudding.
Take one pound of Suet, shred very small and sifted, one pound of Raisons ston'd, four spoonfuls of Flower, and four spoonfuls of Sugar,

---

[68] E– S– (1728), p. 23.
[69] See Misson, *Mémoires et Observations* (1698), pp. 394–395.

five Eggs, but three Whites; beat the Eggs with a little Salt: Tie it up
close, and boil it four Hours at least.[70]

The 'plumbs' of the title refer, of course, to the dried fruit. As will be shown
in the study of bills of fare below, plum pudding was virtually obligatory at
country dinners, especially when feasting one's social inferiors.

But in the books by E. Smith and Mary Kettilby, puddings baked in the
oven, and thus very similar to tarts, are as important as those which were
boiled. Here is an example of a baked pudding from Kettilby, with her own
comment:

> *The best* Orange-Pudding *that ever was tasted.*
> Pare the Yellow Rind of two fair *Sevil*-Oranges, so very thin that no part
> of the White comes with it; shred and beat it extremely small in a large
> Stone-mortar; add to it, when very fine, half a pound of Butter, half a
> pound of Sugar, and the yolks of sixteen Eggs; beat all together in the
> Mortar 'till 'tis all of a Colour; then pour it into your Dish in which you
> have laid a Sheet of Puff-paste. I think Grating the Peel saves Trouble, and
> does it finer and thinner than you can shred or beat it: But you must beat
> up the Butter and Sugar with it, and the Eggs with all, to mix them well.[71]

This is clearly what we would call a tart with a puff-pastry base. The eighteenth
century tended to use puff-pastry where we would use short-crust or sweet
pastry. Kettilby's comment suggests that she had tried this before including it
in her book (it was presumably contributed by one of her 'notable housewives').
One notices the pragmatic attitude which characterizes the women authors; the
easier method proposed does nothing to detract from an excellent receipt.

Kettilby also gives one of the earliest receipts for especially thin and delicate
pancakes. This is found, with minor variations, in many other eighteenth-
century cookery books:

---

[70] Kettilby (1714), p. 89. See also the similar receipt in E– S– (1728), p. 84.

[71] Kettilby (1714), pp. 52–53. Other examples of puddings, both boiled and baked, are to be found
in E– S– (1728), pp. 79–100; Nott (1723), P 231 – P 248; Lamb (1710), pp. 103–105; Howard (1708),
pp. 1–12. It is interesting to see how little space Lamb, the grandest of the cooks, devotes to puddings.

Thin Cream Pan-cakes, *call'd* a Quire of Paper.
Take to a pint of Cream, eight Eggs, leaving out two Whites, three
spoonfuls of fine Flower, three spoonfuls of Sack, and one spoonful of
Orange-flower-Water, a little Sugar, a grated Nutmeg, and a quarter of
a pound of Butter, melted in the Cream; mingle all well together …
that it may be smooth: Butter your Pan for the first Pancake, and let
them run as thin as you can possibly to be whole, when one side is
colour'd 'tis enough; take them carefully out of the Pan, and strew some
fine sifted Sugar between each; lay them as even on each other as you
can: This quantity will make Twenty.[72]

Like the instructions for the orange pudding, this also gives plenty of detailed
advice on method as well as indicating quantities. This is far more frequent in
women's receipts, as these authors knew they were not addressing a fellow-cook
who was already familiar with basic kitchen skills.

The last receipt, for a cake, shows important changes occurring. The big
cakes which appear in the cookery books of the middle of the seventeenth
century were all raised with yeast.[73] Here, eggs do the job, and the reader who
knows only the yeast-raised type is warned not to follow the same method:

Another Seed-Cake.
Take a pound of Flour, dry it by the Fire, add to it a pound of fine Sugar
beaten and sifted; then take a pound and a quarter of Butter and work it
in your Hand till 'tis like Cream; beat the Yolks of ten Eggs, the Whites
of six; mix all these together with an ounce and a half of Carrawy-seeds,
and a quarter of a pint of Brandy; it must not stand to rise.[74]

The use of eggs alone to lighten a cake was a recent 'invention'; both types of
cake are to be found in cookery books of the first half of the eighteenth century
but, by the end, yeast was kept for bread.[75]

---

[72] Kettilby (1714), pp. 57–58. See also, for instance, Glasse, *The Art of Cookery* (1747), p. 83; Peckham,
The Complete English Cook (1767), p. 121.
[73] See, for instance, the cake receipts in W. M., *The Compleat Cook* (1655), pp. 12, 13–14, 17–18, 38–
39, 109–111, 114–115.
[74] E– S– (1728), p. 138.
[75] See Wilson (1976), pp. 241–243.

We have already seen that in the seventeenth century the banquet was an area where ladies could display their skills. The 'banqueting' receipts of the eighteenth are those which show the greatest debt to the past. One still finds many fruit preserves – whether pastes, clear cakes, marmalades or jellies – in different colours, with the same emphasis on appearance as before, as for instance in the following from the book on confectionery by Mary Eales:

> *To make* CURRANT CLEAR-CAKES.
> Strip the Currants, wash 'em, and to a Gallon of Currants put about a Quart of Water; boil it very well, run it thro' an Hair Sieve; set your Jelly on the Fire, let it just boil; then shake in the Sugar, stir it well, and set it on the Fire, and make it scalding hot; then put it thro' a Strainer in a broad Pan, to take of the Scum, and fill it in Pots: When it is candy'd, turn it on Glass 'till that Side be dry; then turn it again, to dry on the other Side.
>
>   Red and white Currants are done the same Way; but as soon as the Jelly of the White is made, you must put it to the Sugar, or it will change Colour.[76]

It would be easy to give further examples of the care with which these preserves were made in order to control their colour and brilliance. *The Pastry-Cook's Vade-Mecum* gives receipts for green and amber-coloured apple preserves, and for white quince preserve and for a red quince marmalade; E. Smith shows how to make red and white quince marmalades, and plum preserves coloured green and black.[77] Amongst the limited number of conserves which appear in the second, added, part of Mary Kettilby's book in 1719 (the readers had complained of the lack of receipts for confectionery in the first edition) is a receipt for red quince marmalade which gives very precise instructions, concluding with the following advice:

> You must carefully watch the Colour, because it turns muddy and black in a Moment, and the Colour is as Delicate as the Taste in this and all Sweet-Meats.[78]

[76] Eales, *Mrs Mary Eales's Receipts* (1718), p. 12.
[77] See *The Pastry-Cook's Vade-Mecum* (1705), pp. 7–9, 28–29; E– S– (1728), pp. 160–161, 190.
[78] Kettilby (1719), part 2, pp. 35–36.

There is an echo in these detailed instructions of the prestige attached to a fine display of confectionery in the seventeenth century. By the beginning of the eighteenth, the price of sugar had fallen and its consumption no longer conferred quite the same air of distinction as it had in the past. Nor was the banquet course composed almost exclusively of sweetmeats displayed on dishes moulded out of sugar-paste. After the Restoration, cookery books contain ever more numerous receipts for creams and syllabubs and, as we shall see later, these delicacies were becoming increasingly important in menus for the banquet. Another sign of changing tastes was that the final stage of a grand dinner was losing its old name, 'banquet', and was becoming known as 'desert': another sign of French influence. The new word is one of the terms explained in the glossary included in *The Court and Country Cook* in 1702: '*Desert*, a Banquet of Sweet-meats'.[79]

Creams and syllabubs were a very English speciality, and our cookery books devote far more space to this type of dish than does Massialot. *The Court and Country Cook* gives only 11 receipts, whereas Mary Eales gives 23, John Nott 19, and E. Smith 21.[80] By the eighteenth-century, syllabub was usually made by whisking the cream, wine and other ingredients together to obtain a light, whipped cream confection and instructions to make it 'under the cow' disappear. Mary Kettilby gives a receipt typical of the period:

> *A Whipt* Sillibub, *Extraordinary*.
> Take a quart of Cream, and boil it, let it stand 'till 'tis cold; then take a pint of White-wine; pare a Lemon thin, and steep the Peel in the Wine two Hours before you use it; to this add the Juice of a Lemon, and as much Sugar as will make it very sweet: Put all this together into a Bason, and whisk it all one way 'till 'tis pretty thick: Fill your Glasses, and keep it a Day before you use it; 'twill keep good three or four Days. … If you like it Perfum'd, put in a grain or two of Ambergreese.[81]

The fact that ambergris is optional marks its gradual disappearance from such

---

[79] See the glossary which precedes the index to the second part of the work, in the unnumbered pages at the front of the book.
[80] See *The Court and Country Cook*, part. 1, pp. 93–97; Eales (1718), pp. 80–94; Nott (1723), C 209 – C 226, C 228; E– S– (1728), pp. 139–153.
[81] Kettilby (1714), p. 76.

receipts, though greatly in fashion in the mid-seventeenth century. Its presence here suggests the receipt may come from a manuscript source dating back to that time. E. Smith's more 'modern' instructions do not mention ambergris.[82]

The creams for the banquet were usually cooked and thickened with egg yolks, as this lemon cream from Rebecca Price's manuscript:

To make Lemon Cream. My Lady How's Receipt
Take a quart of cream and boyle it; then put to it a spoonfull of grated lemon pill very fine and small; the yolks of six eggs well beaten, and let it boyle a little, always stiring it; then, take it off and stir it till it be almost cold, then squeeze in the juice of 2 lemons and sweeten it; stir it till it is cold that it may not skin on ye top.[83]

The manuscript and printed cookery books of the beginning of the eighteenth century give the same kind of receipts, but one also begins to find a great novelty, chocolate cream, a luxury dish at the time:

To make CHOCOLATE-CREAM.
Take a Quarter of a Pound of Chocolate, breaking it into a Quarter of a Pint of boiling Water; mill it and boil it, 'till all the Chocolate is dissolv'd; then put to it a Pint of Cream and two Eggs well-beaten; let it boil, milling it all the while; when it is cold, mill it again, that it may go up with a Froth.[84]

Diana Astry's manuscript contains a receipt for chocolate cream in which almonds are put to infuse in the cream with the chocolate.[85] There can be no doubt that this was a dish of very recent invention: Rebecca Price has nothing like it, in a book written out mostly in 1681 and added to until the early years of the eighteenth century. Another way of using chocolate was to use the cream as a filling for a tart, but then the dish would appear at the second course of a dinner rather than at the third.[86]

---

[82] See E– S– (1728),pp. 144, 149, 153.

[83] Masson (1974), p. 157.

[84] Eales (1718), p. 91.

[85] See Stitt (1957), p. 105.

[86] For instance, the receipt given in Middleton, *Five Hundred New Receipts* (1734), p. 24.

The greatest novelty of all in the dessert at the beginning of the eighteenth century was ice-cream. The English as a whole had begun to discover the pleasures of ice after the Restoration. The first ice-houses were built in royal parks as early as the 1620s and in the grounds of private houses from 1680.[87] The first printed English receipt for ice-cream is found in Mary Eales in 1714:

To ice CREAM.
Take Tin Ice-Pots, fill 'em with any Sort of Cream you like, either plain or sweeten'd, or Fruit in it; shut your Pots very close; to six Pots you must allow eighteen to twenty Pound of Ice, breaking the Ice very small; there will be some great Pieces, which lay at the Bottom and Top: You must have a Pail, and lay some Straw at the Bottom; then lay in your Ice, and put in amongst it a Pound of Bay-Salt; set in your Pots of Cream, and lay Ice and Salt between every Pot, that they may not touch; but the Ice must lye round 'em on every Side; lay a good deal of Ice on the Top, cover the Pail with Straw, set it in a Cellar where no Sun or Light comes, it will be froze in four Hours, but it may stand longer; then take it out just as you use it; hold it in your Hand and it will slip out.[88]

The extremely detailed instructions concerning the freezing process, while the remarks about the cream itself are very brief, demonstrate how much of a novelty this was. It is odd that this receipt should not have been seized on straight away by other authors. Receipts for ice-cream remain rare until the middle of the century. It is also uncommon to find the dish on bills of fare, even for grand entertainments: Lady Grisell Baillie, for instance, never

---

[87] See David, *Harvest of the Cold Months* (1996), p. 287; Girouard, *Life in the English Country House* (1980), p. 262.

[88] Eales (1718), pp. 92–93. Research by W.S. Stallings Jr. confirms that this is the earliest printed receipt; see the note by the editors of *Petits Propos Culinaires* 2, 'Waist-deep in Ice Cream', (1979), p. 36. Massialot's book of confectionery, translated into English in 1702, gives instructions for making 'eaux glacées' (a kind of sorbet), but offers no receipts for 'fromage glacé' (alias ice-cream); the latter type of receipt is not found until later, in French cookery books of the eighteenth century. See *The Court and Country Cook* (1702), part 3, p. 4. In her book on the subject, however, Elizabeth David states that there is a receipt for ice-cream, called, interestingly, 'Fromage à l'Angloise', in the French version of Massialot's work, stashed away amongst the creams, junkets and fresh cream cheeses – see *Harvest of the Cold Months*, p. 107. The earliest manuscript receipt for ice-cream is probably that in Grace Granville's notebook; see David, 'Fromages Glacés and Ice Creams' (1979), pp. 26–27.

mentions it. Despite this early receipt, it would seem that only the great houses, where a confectioner was employed, could aspire to serve this luxury dish.

In books by men-cooks, the receipts for sweet dishes and creams resemble those by women authors.[89] But their instructions concerning the presentation of the dessert show that this third course of a dinner was as much an opportunity for display as were the grand dishes of the court style which we have already examined. Decorative dishes were well to the fore, as they had been in Robert May's day. John Middleton tells how to make a miniature orchard to decorate the table using almond paste and preserved and candied fruit and flowers:

> *To dish up a Dish of Fruit with preserved Flowers.*
> Take a very large Dish, and cover it with a Dish of the same Sort or Size; cover the uppermost with Paste of Almonds inlaid with several Colours, as red, green and yellow Marmalade, in the Form of Flowers and green Banks; then take the Branches of preserved Flowers, and candied Flowers, and fix them upright on little Bushes erected with Paste, and green Leaves hanging on the Branches; fix your candied and preserved Cherries, Plumbs, Gooseberries, Currants and Apples each in their respective Places. This is very proper in Winter.[90]

This carries on the tradition of the bright colours and decorative shapes of the Elizabethan and early Stuart banquet. But to create a fashionable dessert it was not enough to produce the multicoloured array of the earlier period. *The Court and Country Cook* tells the confectioner to place the fruit and sweetmeats on the table in a symmetric display, then proceeds to illustrate this by means of an elevation rather than plan of the table. The plate gives a perspective view with several dishes placed symmetrically, each with sweetmeats piled up to form a pyramid. A similar presentation is described by John Nott:

> A Desert is … dispos'd in China Dishes:… That in the Middle being rais'd higher than the others, upon which several small Pyramids are to be erected of an exact Proportion: So that the same Sort of Comfits, the

---

[89] See, for instance the receipts in Howard (1708), pp. 107–128.

[90] Middleton (1734), p. 164. There is a similar receipt in Howard (1708), p. 124.

same Colours may appear on every Side, at the opposite Angles. Lastly,
a Row or Border of raw Fruits, may be made round about the Dishes;…
and the whole Desert is to be set out with Flowers, Greens, and other
Ornaments, according to the Season.[91]

The emphasis here is on exact symmetry of colour and shape; the way in which
the dishes are set out recalls the formal French garden style. It is the presentation of the dessert rather than its contents which adds the fashionable note.

This particular fashion was not destined to last much beyond 1730, at least
in those circles which followed the French mode. In 1750 Menon's *Science de
Maître d'Hôtel, Confiseur* ridicules the fashion of twenty years before:

> What has become of those pyramids erected with more labour and effort
> than taste and elegance, which used to be seen on our tables? What has
> become of that confused piling-up of fruit which was more a display of
> profusion than of intelligence and refinement?[92]

The use of the word 'profusion' summarizes exactly the key aspect of the court
style adopted by the élite at the beginning of the century. The dessert, like the
other courses of a grand dinner, was expected to create an impression of
abundance and luxury. The pyramid presentation of meats or of sweet things
expressed the idea of superabundance as did the great dishes of meat, with their
enormous quantity and variety and vast garnishes. The pyramid was part of a
baroque aesthetic of the table which sat well with the monumentalism of
English architecture by such practitioners as Vanbrugh and Hawksmoor. The
formality of presentation contributed to the image of courtly luxury and reflected a rigidly hierarchical code of manners. This same formality links the culinary
style irrevocably to its period. As England shifted (albeit gradually) away from
the 'court' model of society in the years following the Glorious Revolution,
giving way to a more 'open', more sociable structure, so the aristocratic manner
of cookery was replaced.

---

[91] Nott (1723), at the end of the book, before the index.

[92] 'Que sont devenues ces pyramides érigées avec plus de travail & d'industrie que de goût &
d'élegance qu'on voyait sur nos tables? Qu'est devenu cet amas confus de fruits où il éclatoit plus
de profusion que d'intelligence et de délicatesse?' [Menon], *La Science du Maître d'Hôtel, Confiseur*
(1750), p. iii.

Before the middle of the century, the élite in both England and France rejected the elaborate constructs of their parents' generation in favour of smaller, simpler, but equally luxurious dishes. The new paradigm makes its apparent debut in a book by Vincent La Chapelle first published in English in London in 1733 – two years before the earliest edition, printed in The Hague, in the author's mother-tongue. However, it is difficult to establish precisely the origins of this style since no new cookery books had been issued in France during the first thirty years of the century and the gap may well conceal the first signs of its emergence. La Chapelle was only too keen to dismiss the writings of Massialot, dating from the 1690s, as ridiculously old-fashioned, just as the latter had been eager to rubbish *his* predecessor, La Varenne. Despite this, La Chapelle borrowed substantially from Massialot. His debt has been studied by the historians Philip and Mary Hyman who conclude that none the less, *The Modern Cook* does demonstrate a more 'modern' style, most notably in the area of sauce bases.[1]

By 1700, French cookery had developed a system adapted to cooks working as a team rather than as individuals. Each worker made his own contribution, but did not follow any one dish through from start to finish. What happened next was a refinement of these principles, using a series of basic preparations to create an infinite variety of dishes. The fully-fledged version of this new style does not appear in literature until some years after *The Modern Cook*. In La Chapelle, the new co-exists with the old, but succeeding authors vigorously eliminated relics of past custom and afford us a better chance to grasp the essentials. In 1739, two important new books appeared in France: the *Nouveau Traité de la Cuisine* by Menon and the *Dons de Comus* by Marin. The second of these was not, strictly speaking, a cookery book – I speak here of its first edition; in 1742, the author would add three volumes of receipts – rather, it was a manual for the *maître d'hôtel*, showing how to compose a fashionable menu. Marin gave only one detailed receipt, for a 'quintessence': a rich, concentrated essence from a bouillon base, used in the preparation of sauces.[2] The nature

---

[1] See Hyman & Hyman, 'La Chapelle and Massialot: an Eighteenth-Century Feud', *PPC* 2 (1979), pp. 44–45, and 8 (1981), pp. 35–40.

[2] See Mennell, *All Manners of Food* (1985), pp. 77–80; Wheaton, *Savouring the Past* (1983), pp. 204–205.

of this single receipt is significant: in French cuisine, dishes of meat in sauce
were far more important than roasts, and a cuisine which depended on sauces
marks the end of the era of a cuisine based on 'mixing', which gives way to a
cuisine of 'impregnation', to use the terms applied by Jean-François Revel.[3] In
Marin's suggested menus, one finds a large number of such dishes in sauce.
Another striking aspect is the small number of dishes at each course. A menu
for a meal 'in the modern taste'[4] (*selon le goût moderne*) has nine courses, but
each contains only two or three dishes, which brings us closer to later *à la russe*
dinners, where dishes were handed round in succession by servants. Contemporary service *à la française*, by contrast, consisted of placing on the table all
the dishes at one course, some of which would have removes.

The address to the reader in the *Dons de Comus*, which Vicaire attributes
to two Jesuits, Fathers Brunoy and Bouvant,[5] presents the new cuisine in the
following terms:[6]

> Nowadays a distinction is made, among professionals and among those
> who pride themselves on keeping a good table, between old and new
> cuisines. The old cuisine is that which the French made fashionable all
> over Europe, and which was still being followed until less than twenty
> years ago. The modern style of cuisine, based upon the old, but with less
> complication, less pomp, and as much variety, is simpler, neater, and
> perhaps even more recherché. The old style was very complicated and

---

[3] See Revel, *Un Festin en paroles* (1979), p. 206. But contrary to what Revel suggests, this was not a
sudden transformation which took place in the eighteenth century, but a long drawn-out process
which began with La Varenne.

[4] Reproduced in Mennell (1985), pp. 78–79.

[5] See Vicaire, *Bibliographie gastronomique* (1890), p. 285.

[6] 'On distingue aujourd'hui chez les gens du métier & chez les personnes qui se piquent d'avoir une
bonne table, la Cuisine ancienne & la Cuisine moderne. La Cuisine ancienne est celle que les
François ont mise en vogue par toute l'Europe, & qu'on suivoit generalement il n'y a pas encore vingt
ans. La Cuisine moderne établie sur les fondemens de l'ancienne, avec moins d'embarras, moins
d'appareil, & avec autant de varieté, est plus simple, plus propre, & peut-être encore plus sçavante.
L'ancienne Cuisine étoit fort compliquée, & d'un détail extraordinaire. La Cuisine moderne est une
espece de Chymie. La science du Cuisinier consiste aujourd'hui à décomposer, à faire digérer & à
quintessencier des viandes, à tirer des sucs nourrissans & legers, à les mêler & les confondre ensemble,
de façon de rien domine & que tout se fasse sentir; enfin à leur donner … une harmonie de tous
les goûts, réunis ensemble.' Reproduced in Mennell (ed.), *Lettre d'un Pâtissier Anglois, et autres
contributions à une polémique gastronomique du XVIIIème siècle* (1981), p. 6.

extraordinarily meticulous. Modern cuisine is a form of chemistry. Today, the cook's skill consists in breaking down meats, making them digestible and turning them into essences, drawing light, nourishing juices from them, and creating such subtle mixtures that no single ingredient dominates and yet each is present; in fact … all the flavours come together in perfect harmony.

Harmony and simplicity are the key words, and it is interesting to see the cook elevated to the status of a scientist, since this is a claim which would be made in England by some of the men-cooks of the second half of the century.

The address to the reader in the *Dons de Comus* provoked a satirical response, the 'Lettre d'un Pâtissier anglois', from the pen of an otherwise unknown author, Desalleurs. He ridicules both the intellectual pretensions of the address and the behaviour of gastronomes of the period who gave food more than its due share of attention:

> Our meals have become academies of civilities and compliments, which would last for the whole duration of supper, if they were not interrupted by learned analyses of every dish and every sauce, which being very numerous, necessarily require a great length of time for such discussion.[7]

Food had become a subject worthy of dinner-table conversation. Desalleurs' discussions have a modern echo. He also attacked cooks who were masters at reducing each ingredient to a 'quintessence' in order to produce a 'delicately refined' result,[8] and it was he who used the term *'nouvelle cuisine'*. Notice also that the meal mentioned was not dinner but supper, which seemed more representative of the new style in France. It was lighter – one of the characteristics most often emphasized in *nouvelle cuisine* – and the dishes on offer were smaller and more refined than the soups and *grosses entrées* of old. Of course, refinement and delicacy were precisely what its detractors complained of.

---

[7] 'Nos repas sont devenus une Ecole de civilité & de complimens, qui dureroient tout le tems du souper, s'ils n'étoient coupés par des Analises sçavantes de tous les plats & de toutes des sauces, qui étant en grand nombre, emportent nécessairement beaucoup de tems à les discuter.' Mennell (1981), p. 17.

[8] Ibid., p. 16.

In fact, eighteenth-century *nouvelle cuisine* marks a shift away from the conspicuous consumption of profusion, expressed in the way food was presented,
to one where the dominant image was of elegance. This fundamental difference
was identified by Louis-Sébastien Mercier:

> In the previous century great piles of meat were served, and they were
> served in pyramids. These small dishes, which cost ten times more than
> one big one, were as yet unknown. Refined eating has been known for
> no more than half a century. The delicious cuisine of Louis XV's reign
> was unheard of even by Louis XIV.[9]

(The *nouvelle cuisine* of the eighteenth century produced 'petits plats'; its
twentieth-century version had a weakness for *petits légumes*. A parallel may be
drawn. Small is beautiful.) As had been the case in the previous culinary transformation, the new style depended as much on how the dish was presented as
on how it was cooked. The address in the *Dons de Comus* emphasizes that the
new manner was based firmly on its predecessor; its novelty lay in the gradual
elimination of the composite dishes of the court style such as the olio, bisque
and terrine and their replacement by the classical simplicity of such items as
the 'filet de 3 lapereaux aux morilles' and the 'filet mignon, sauce à la bonne
femme' which formed the third course of Marin's menu 'in the modern taste'.

The culinary style revealed by La Chapelle's book is not the mature version
described by these later French commentators, but it is easy to see in its pages
the changes in the wind. For instance, he gives receipts for olios, as had
Massialot, but the presentation has altered. Whereas Massialot told the cook to
pile up the meats on top of bread soaked in cooking juices before pouring the
rest of the bouillon over the finished dish, La Chapelle suggests this in only one
receipt, an olio '*à l'espagnole*'; his other olios are much closer to soups, since the
pile of various meats is no longer mentioned.[10] This alteration corresponds with
the note by Mercier.

---

[9] 'Dans le dernier siècle, on servait des masses considérables de viande, et on les servait en pyramide.
Ces petits plats, qui coûtent dix fois plus qu'un gros, n'étaient pas encore connus. On ne sait manger
délicatement que depuis un demi-siècle. La délicieuse cuisine du règne de Louis XV fut inconnue
même à Louis XIV'. Mercier, *Tableau de Paris* (1994), vol. 1, p. 1059.

[10] See Massialot, *Le Cuisinier roïal et bourgeois*, 1698, pp. 336–338; *The Court and Country Cook*, 1702,
part 1, p. 166; La Chapelle, *The Modern Cook*, 1733, vol. 1, pp. 2–5.

There had been a similarly important change in the manner of preparing a *coulis*. The mid-eighteenth-century *coulis* was one of the basic preparations. It could be used on its own as a sauce or as a component of the raggoo, which in turn was often not a dish in its own right but a sauce-and-garnish to be poured over other meats. Cullis was one of the essentials of *nouvelle cuisine*, related to the modern *sauce espagnole*. It was a brown sauce, based on veal or ham, with a brown roux liaison. It was gently simmered for a long time before being de-greased and passed through a hair-sieve.[11] The fast-day version was very similar but built on fish and vegetables instead of meat.[12] Massialot's cullis was founded on cooked meat, pounded to a purée in a mortar, with crusts of bread often added to help thicken the sauce. La Chapelle's uses flour-based roux as the thickener. Cullis was enormously useful to the cook, especially when combined with the ingredients of a garnish. With this to hand, it was easy to create a number of variations, for example by adding to a basic braised chicken different raggoos – of crayfish, cucumbers, mushrooms, asparagus or oysters, to mention only some of La Chapelle's suggestions.[13] From the 1730s, French cooks acquired the reputation of being capable of producing all sorts of small dishes from a single type of meat.

Two instances will give an idea of the *petits plats* which Mercier so admired. The first of these is for a raggoo of asparagus tips, to be used with different kinds of meat:

A Ragout with the Heads of Asparagus.
Cut the Heads of some Asparagus, and whiten them. When they are blanched enough, put them in a Stewing-pan with some Cullis and a little Essence of Ham; and let the whole stew on a slow Fire. When it is stewed enough, throw therein a bit of Butter no bigger than a Nut, dip'd in some fine Flower, and stir your Ragoût now and then. Take care, that it be relishing, pour in a little Vinegar, and serve it hot. You may make use of this Ragoût for all sorts of Fowls or other Meat.[14]

---

[11] See La Chapelle (1733), vol. 1, pp. 82–87.

[12] Ibid., vol. 3, pp. 25–33.

[13] Ibid., vol. 1, pp. 274–276, 281–282, 306; vol. 2, pp. 296–307.

[14] Ibid., vol. 2, p. 299.

These are the methods of the assembly-line: the receipt assumes that the cook
has cullis and essence of ham to hand but, with these essentials ready, the
raggoo is very simple to create. The sauce is further thickened with *beurre
manié*, another 'modern' touch.

The second receipt is for a dish of chicken with crayfish. Here, too, cullis
is used as the basis for the sauce:

> Chickens with Cray-fish, another way.
> Take Chickens, ... put the Livers on the Table with a little rasped Bacon,
> Parsley, young Onions, Salt, Pepper, Sweet-herbs, fine Spices,
> Champinions and Truffles, if you have any, and a piece of Butter: hash
> the whole, put it in the body of your Chickens, and blanch them in a
> Stew-pan, with Butter, Parsley, young Onions, Salt, Pepper and Sweet-
> herbs. When they are well blanch'd, put them on the Spit, cover them
> with Bards of Bacon, and Sheets of Paper. When they are enough, lay
> them in their Dish, and add to 'em a Ragoût ... or a Cullis of Cray-
> fish;... and serve them hot for a first Course.[15]

It is interesting to compare La Chapelle's receipt with the one given by
Massialot, who adds a raggoo of sweetbreads, truffles, asparagus tips and
artichoke bottoms to his roast chickens before pouring a crayfish cullis over the
whole.[16] The difference is typical of the changes which had taken place during
the forty years which separate the two books: Massialot has an elaborately
multifarious garnish, whereas the later author suggests chickens and their sauce,
with no further additions. La Chapelle shows the first stage of a process of
simplification: the cullis or the raggoo which is poured over the meat has one
single dominant flavour, instead of the mixture favoured by the earlier style.

La Chapelle was the pioneer. After him, *nouvelle cuisine* was developed by
others such as Marin, Menon and, of course, cooks who did not publish their
receipts. Menon was author of what was perhaps the most ambitious cookery
book of the middle of the century, *Les Soupers de la Cour*, which came out in
Paris in 1755. Twelve years later, the book was translated into English with the
title *The Professed Cook*. It is one of those rare books which give an idea of what

---

[15] La Chapelle (1733), vol. 2, p. 95.
[16] See Massialot, *Le Cuisinier roïal et bourgeois*, pp. 432–433.

French cookery for the élite had become – at least, that small fraction of the upper-classes, particularly Whig aristocrats, who followed closely French culinary fashion. Even in this next phase of development, terrines and olios are still present,[17] but the terrines have become meat stews without any excessive garnishes, and the olios are now vegetable soups, except for a single *pot-au-feu* which still shows its kinship with the olios of the court style. Whereas authors of the first thirty years of the century had emphasized the differences in presentation between the olio and the terrine, Menon's translator B. Clermont often refers to an 'Olio, or Turine'.[18] The particularities of the two dishes had become confused, sure sign of their loss of prestige. Small elegant dishes were now the vogue, replacing the *grosses entrées* at the summit of the culinary hierarchy. Clermont, like La Chapelle, includes a chapter devoted to sauces, but this is more substantial than in the earlier work. In *The Modern Cook*, 32 sauces are grouped with cullisses,[19] whereas in *The Professed Cook*, 71 sauces are given a chapter to themselves.[20] A comment at the outset underlines their importance:

> This is where true Taste shows itself, and must meet with Approbation or Condemnation; as all boiled Meat stewed or brazed are to be made relishing, with the Addition of a well-timed good Sauce.[21]

Before examining the English version of the new style, it is worth glancing briefly at subsequent developments in France. From the middle of the century culinary fashions followed one another at an increasingly rapid pace without, however, rejecting the essentials put forward during the 1730s. It was invariably a matter of detail, not a radical shift. Something was the rage for a moment, then was superseded.[22] An engraving of a woman cook, published in 1759, bore this accompanying verse:

---

[17] See Clermont, *The Professed Cook* (1769), pp. 13–14, 24–25, 28, 29, 176–182.

[18] Ibid., pp. 13, 29.

[19] See La Chapelle (1733), vol. 1, pp. 94–104.

[20] See Clermont (1769), pp. 31–51.

[21] Ibid., p. 30.

[22] See Wheaton (1983), pp. 220, 228–229, 232.

Every year a new cuisine,
For every year brings in new wishes;
And every day requires new dishes:
So be a chemist now, Justine.[23]

To gain some idea of *nouvelle cuisine* as practised in England in the 1730s and 1740s, we must turn to English authors. Male writers were thin on the ground and those there were offer receipts little different from their female rivals: hardly encapsulating the influence of France. One, however, is exceptional: William Verral, who had worked in the kitchens of the Duke of Newcastle under the famous chef Clouet in the late 1730s. The correspondence between Newcastle, Albemarle and Clouet (who had left Newcastle's service to work as Albemarle's *maître d'hôtel* in the embassy in Paris) concerning the difficulty of finding a French cook who might please the Duke, confirms the importance of *nouvelle cuisine*. The first sent by Albemarle, Hervé (Hervey to the English), failed to give satisfaction. In December 1753, Newcastle wrote to Albemarle to explain:

> I own I like the man extremely, his temper and disposition. But I can't say that his qualities as a cook are quite what I wish.... His *plats* don't seem to please here; and are not just what I like. They are generally composed of a variety of things, and are not the light dishes and clear sauces which Cloé excell'd in.[24]

Two months later, Newcastle had made up his mind to dismiss Hervé, and he unburdened himself to his former cook, Clouet, in a letter written in French:

> It may be that the new cuisine does not please us here, but I cannot believe that he has mastered the art. His soups are usually too strong, and his entrées and entremets are so disguised and so mixed-up that nobody can tell what they are made of. He never serves small hors

---

[23] 'Tous les ans nouvelle cuisine,
   Car tous les ans changent les goûts;
   Et tous les jours nouveaux ragoûts:
   Soyez donc chimiste, Justine.' Reproduced in Wheaton (1983), p. 198.
[24] Quoted in Sedgwick, 'The Duke of Newcastle's Cook' (1955), p. 311.

d'oeuvres or light entrées, and he has no idea of the simple, unified dishes that you used to make for me and which are so much in fashion here, such as veal tendons, rabbit fillets, pigs' and calves' ears, and several other little dishes of the same kind. … In a word, he has no resemblance to your ways and your cuisine, and to what I require.[25]

The description of the 'simple, unified' dishes prepared by Clouet demonstrates that the process of simplification begun by Vincent La Chapelle had been taken further between 1730 and 1750. This letter might lead one to think that Hervé was a cook of the old school who produced dishes similar to the complicated dishes of court-cookery. But Clouet sent a reply vigorously defending Hervé. The reply is interesting for the self-assured tone of the professional cook, confident of his own status, and because we see that each cook had his own personal style. Incidentally, Clouet's own letter is written in a form of French that is purely phonetic, with sentences in which groups of words are not divided into meaningful units – Clouet, in spite of his assurance, was barely literate. The letter quoted is a fair copy made by a secretary:[26]

As regards his mixed-up entrées and entremets, French cuisine has never been anything but mixtures. This is what gives it that great variety which places it above all the other cuisines of Europe. Masters who do not like these mixtures should be so good as to inform the cook of this, and to let

---

[25] 'Il se peut que la nouvelle cuisine ne plait pas ici; mais je ne puis croire qu'il en est maître. Ses soupes sont ordinairement trop forts; et les entrées et les entreméts sont si deguisés et tellement compotés qu'on ne peut deviner de quoi ils sont faits. Il ne donne jamais les petits hors d'oeuvres et les entrées legeres; et n'a aucune idée des plats unis et simples que vous étiez accoutumé de me faire et qui sont tant en vogue ici; savoir, les tendrons de veau, les filets de lapreaux, les oreilles de veau et de cochon, et plusieurs autres petits plats de cette sorte. … En un mot, il ne ressemble en aucune façon à vos maniéres et à votre cuisine, et à ce qu'il me faut.' Sedgwick (1955), p. 312. Sedgwick's transcription of this letter is inaccurate: the MS says 'fortes', not 'forts', and 'composés', not 'compotés'. See BL Add. MS 32734, f. 138.

[26] 'A l'égard de ses entrées et de ses entremêts composés, la cuisine Française n'a jamais été que composition. C'est ce qui lui donne cette grande variété qu'elle a sur toutes les cuisines de l'Europe. Les maîtres, à qui ses compositions ne plaisent pas, il faut qu'ils ayent la bonté de dire, où de faire dire, leur intention, et la façon dont ils veulent etre servis; en conséquence le cuisinier montre son abilité en si conformant. Il est aussi bien malheureux pour un cuisinier que son maître ne puisse point juger de lui lui-même, et que tres souvent il soit jugé par des censeurs qui n'y connoissent rien.' Sedgwick, p. 312. Again, the transcription is not entirely accurate; see BL Add. MS 32734, f. 152.

him know how they wish to be served, so that the cook can show his skill
by conforming to their desires. It is also most unfortunate for a cook that
his master should be incapable of judging his performance for himself, so
that he is very often judged by critics who are totally ignorant.

What emerges from this exchange of correspondence is that culinary fashions
were changing much faster than before: the *nouvelle cuisine* practised by Hervé,
to which Newcastle alludes, is the very latest fashion in Paris, and is clearly not
the same as that of the 1730s and 1740s when Clouet was in the ducal kitchens.
England, as far as cookery was concerned, was some way behind French
developments, even among the political élite.

Thanks to Verral, we have a precise idea of the dishes prepared by Clouet
at the end of the 1730s. The first is for bouillon,[27] the basis of soups and sauces.
It is immediately obvious that Verral, like Charles Carter before him, had
adopted the French system – an idea expressed in the very title, *A Complete
System of Cookery*. Then come soups: although they are less abundantly garnished than Massialot's, they still contain pieces of meat or a bird of some
kind.[28] But with the '*gros entrées*' [sic],[29] the difference between Clouet's cuisine
and that of his predecessors becomes more apparent. After cullis, Verral offers
a receipt for veal with a brown sauce:

> *Longe de veau marinée, sauce brune.*
> Loin of veal marinaded, with a brown sauce.
> Your loin of veal should be put into the marinade the day before; take
> about two quarts of new milk, and put to it some green onions, a shallot
> or two, parsley, a little spice, whole pepper, salt, two or three bay leaves,
> and some coriander seed; put your veal in, and keep it well turned so as
> to soak it well, till it should be spitted next day, cover it with paper with
> butter rubb'd on it, and roast it gently till it is well done. I have known
> a cook baste with this marinade, but Mr. Clouet never, nor with any-
> thing else. For your sauce, mix about a pint of your cullis thinned with
> a little gravy, mince two or three mushrooms and capers, a little parsley,

---

[27] See Verral, *A Complete System of Cookery* (1759), pp. 1–6.
[28] Ibid., pp. 7–22.
[29] Ibid., pp. 41–67.

and a shallot or two, pour it into your dish, adding the juice of a lemon.[30]

The other entrées are similar: dishes of meat served with a sauce, without any other form of garnish.

This is already a considerable simplification compared to the court style, but it is with the '*petits entrées*'[31] and the '*hors d'ouvres* [sic]'[32] that we discover the *nouvelle cuisine*, those small dishes so appreciated by Newcastle and his friends. As one might expect, Verral emphasizes their fashionable nature. At the end of the first series of receipts, he adds: 'I must beg leave to add four more of these *petits entrées*, because they are dishes in high fashion, and very much admired.'[33]

The following examples illustrate the principles of the system, the first with a sauce he describes as 'now in high vogue'[34]:

Poitrine des poulardes a la Benjamele.
Breast of fowls a la Benjamele.
Two fowls make two dishes, but in different ways; cut off the legs …, and the next shall give directions how to manage them. But the breasts you must roast, but without the pinions, they may serve for something else; when roasted, take off the skin, and cut off the white flesh, slice it in thickish pieces, put it into a stewpan, and provide your sauce as follows; take about half a pint of cream, a bit of butter mixt with flour, put in a green onion or two whole, a little parsley, pepper and salt, stir it over a slowish fire till it boils to its thickness, and pass it through an etamine, put it to your fowl in a stewpan, and then boil it till it is hot through; add nothing more than the juice of an orange, and send it up.

This sauce may serve for any sort of white meat, and is now very much in fashion.[35]

---

[30] Verral (1759), pp. 42–43.
[31] Ibid., pp. 68–110.
[32] Ibid., pp. 111–157.
[33] Ibid., p. 103.
[34] Ibid., p. 81.
[35] Ibid., pp. 135–136.

Note that the cook is warned against adding anything but orange juice. The last-minute squeeze of citrus was nigh-on invariable in Verral. Massialot also frequently added lemon but tended to use whole slices of fruit. This is typical of the changes which had overtaken cookery in the intervening years. The first receipt was simple but delicious and it left the legs of the birds for the next:

> *Des petits balons aux cuisses des poulardes.*
> Balons of legs of fowls.
> This is to be done with the four legs; take out the thigh and leg-bone;…
> lay them a little while in a marinade of white wine and vinegar, &c.
> prepare a forcemeat, such as is for several things before, and spread over
> the insides; draw them up nice and round, and stew them in a little
> braize for an hour, or a little more; make a neat sauce of a ladle of cullis
> and gravy, a dash of white wine, a bit of shallot and parsley minced; take
> your balons … clean from fat; … boil your sauce a minute, and squeeze
> in the juice of an orange or lemon, and send it up.[36]

Far from extravagant or expensive, this is extremely pared-down, leaving clean flavours and not requiring vast quantities of additional ingredients. It would be tempting to reproduce many other receipts from Verral, showing the simple but refined dishes he had learned under Clouet, which offer such a striking contrast to the complexities of court-cookery.

All the dishes described by Verral up to this point were destined to appear at the first course; the second consisting of roasts and '*entremets*'. Verral gave about forty receipts for the latter,[37] which he described as being 'the most fashionable'.[38] These, even smaller and lighter than anything served earlier, included shellfish and vegetables, eggs and a few sweet dishes, mostly creams and fritters. One instance will suffice:

> *Des ecrevisses de mer farcéz dans les coquilles.*
> Forcemeat of lobsters in the shells.
> Two middle-sized lobsters will do for this dish; take the tails with the

---

[36] Verral (1759), pp. 137–138.

[37] Ibid., pp. 157–223.

[38] Ibid., p. 157.

soft part of the insides, and chop very small, put to it the flesh of a plaice, and pound all together, but only to mix it well, grate in a little nutmeg, pepper, a spoonful of oil and vinegar, minced parsley, the soft of a bit of bread soak'd in broth or cream, a couple of eggs, stir all well together, cut the body shells in two pieces longways, trim them neatly, and fill them with your forcemeat, brush them over with a little butter and egg, strew a few bread crumbs over, and bake them in a slow oven about half an hour, squeeze on the juice of an orange or lemon, and serve them up hot.[39]

Several times, the comments added by Verral show that he had compared the methods used in France and England to prepare a given dish.[40] He almost invariably prefers the French method for dishes with sauce but for roasts he admits Gallic inferiority:

> I propose … to shew the manner of the French in getting up their roast for second course; but shall say but little, because the old English way, in my opinion, is much to be preferred before it, both for goodness and beauty.…
> [T]hey lard almost all, as if bacon should be equally good sauce for a quail or a snipe as it is for a fowl or a chicken: … they use no flour, or basting of any sort to give colour.… In short, let the French send ever so many pretty *entremets* to table, their roast is apt to darken it all.[41]

(English cooks sprinkled flour or breadcrumbs over their roasts on the spit, in order to create a crust on the meat.) The traditional strengths of the two national cuisines had not changed very much. Verral gives a glimpse of what was particularly appreciated, even if his comments were somewhat out of date by the time he published in 1759. He tells the reader what is in fashion and sometimes how one dish or another may be received in the dining-room. For instance, he remarks at the end of a receipt for anchovies with Parmesan that, though not apparently exciting, it never returns to the kitchens untouched.[42]

---

[39] Verral (1759), pp. 183–184.
[40] Ibid., pp. 44–45, 94–96, 101–103, 110, 157, 158, 176, 184–185, 187, 192–193, 209, 224, 231.
[41] Ibid., pp. 231–232.
[42] Ibid., pp. 219–220.

This reveals both the cook's anxiety as he awaits the verdict of consumers, and that the impressive bills of fare of the period are not signs of gluttony, for the diners did not eat everything on the table; in fact, they did not even partake of every dish, some of which returned intact to the kitchens.

How great was the impact of this new culinary style in England? As we have seen, the élite followed French fashions with enthusiasm, and competed for the services of the best chefs. The comings and goings of Clouet, Hervé, La Grange and his pupil Joire (alias Joras or Jorre)[43] and others like them involved the cream of English society: the Dukes of Newcastle, Bedford and Richmond, Lords Montfort, Lincoln and Ashburnham.[44] All these nobles were attached, more or less, to the Whig interest. It was not entirely coincidence or political opportunism that satirists lampooned the culinary excesses of the Whig oligarchy, from Sir Robert Walpole to Newcastle. Keeping a good table and being up with the latest gastronomic fashions was one way of displaying one's credentials as a connoisseur and as a member of the inner circle of the powerful. But beyond these circles, the benefits of culinary one-upmanship were dubious.

The political élite competed for the reputation of having the best cook and the best table, and guests were aware of the important place of eating during a country-house visit. In a letter to the Duke of Richmond declining an invitation to Goodwood, William Pulteney explains that his delicate state of health precludes acceptance:

> I should be extreamly happy if I dorst venture to accept of Your Graces most obliging invitation, but indeed I am not yet well enough established in my health to do it. Temperance and Regularity are still necessary for me to observe, and at Goodwood I believe no one ever heard of either of them, for my part I am determined not to come within a house that has a French Cooke in it for six months.... Not but I ... flatter myself that I shall have the honour of eating many a good dish with you

---

[43] See Sedgwick (1955), pp. 309, 312, 315–316. Sedgwick gives the name of the cook as Joire, but the Yale edition of Horace Walpole's correspondence, which contains references to this quarrel, calls him Joras. Newcastle's accounts show payments in the 1730s to a 'Jean Jorre', who is certainly the same person. See Lewis (ed.), *Walpole Correspondence* (1937–83), vol. 35, p. 246 and n.; BL Add. MS 33321, ff. 30, 48, 50.

[44] See Thomson, *The Russells in Bloomsbury 1669–1771* (1940), pp. 225–230.

again, & swallowing many a bottle of popping Champaigne, but for the present a little discretion is absolutely necessary.[45]

But not everyone could afford to pay for the services of a such an artist, Newcastle's peevish complaint that even the lowliest country gentleman had his French cook notwithstanding.[46] Those who had the problem of champagne tastes on a beer income endeavoured to procure the services of a competent cook by other means. In 1738 Sir Thomas Prendergast, a cousin of the Duchess of Richmond and an MP, wrote to ask if the Duke's cook would agree to take an 'apprentice' under his wing:

> Lady Prendergast … has … desired me to ask your Grace whether Monsr. Jaquemar would condescend to let a young potatoe-roaster see him *chaw his meat* and *fricasee his frogs* for a year or too; in plain English, whether it would be inconvenient to have a tolerably clean boy serve in your Grace's kitchen as scullion, etc., untill he might pick up a little knowledge.[47]

The other possibility for the impecunious was, of course, to purchase a book like Verral's to catch up (slightly late in the day) with the latest fashion. Verral's own comments on the superiority of French cuisine and his anecdotes concerning meals he had served up to Sussex squires (of which more later) show that he believed he was addressing people not hostile to French cookery. He saw his audience as fellow-cooks keen to learn about *nouvelle cuisine* or employers hoping to keep abreast of the times. But his book was a flop and his tales of rustic ignorance of the niceties of the table may well have offended rather than flattered potential readers.

Martha Bradley's enormous and ambitious book also gives a favourable verdict on French cookery while offering a glimpse of how the aristocratic style was being imitated in the houses of the rich gentry. It contains an impressive number of receipts, many of which represent the practice of the author, a professional cook in Bath in the 1740s.[48] Bath was, of course, a great centre for

---

[45] Lennox, *A Duke and his Friends* (1911), vol. 1, p. 195.
[46] See Sedgwick (1955), p. 314.
[47] Lennox (1911), vol. 1, p. 330.
[48] See M. Bradley, *The British Housewife* (1756), title-page, and vol. 1, p. 433.

fashion, where the aristocracy and the gentry mixed in the ritualized social life
which Beau Nash had imposed on the city. Mrs Bradley's book contained
receipts borrowed from various sources. While a substantial number were taken
from Hannah Glasse with little adaptation, many more come from the third,
vastly expanded, edition of Patrick Lamb, or from Vincent La Chapelle. These
had clearly been re-worked. Her culinary style is thus a mix of the older court
style (the receipts added to Patrick Lamb's book after the first edition are all
Massialot-inspired), with some of the more recent from La Chapelle. A striking
aspect of the book is its emphasis on made dishes rather than on baking and
confectionery, the traditional female domains. Martha Bradley's borrowings
and her careful explanations of all the preliminary preparations before a dish
is finally assembled, show that she was thoroughly familiar with the modular
French system of cookery, and that that was where her interest lay. Another
valuable aspect of her receipts is her frequent personal comments, indicating
why such a method is to be preferred, suggesting variations, or telling the
reader that a dish is particularly popular. These remarks are invariably Mrs
Bradley's own and owe nothing to her original sources. *The British Housewife*
is one of the few books which inspire confidence. Mrs Bradley had clearly
practised high-class cookery and had evolved her own personal style, to judge
by some of the changes she makes to her sources' receipts, and which are
peculiar to her. She stresses the reliability of the receipts, based on personal
experience:

> We shall deliver nothing in it … but what the Mistress and the Cook
> may equally depend upon; nothing being set down but what have been
> frequently done for my Company, and the Receipts printed from the
> exact Copies of my own.[49]

The receipts often give the impression that the author was perfectly aware of
fashionable trends but that her employers and their guests still preferred the
older style.

Though mixing the old and the new, Bradley herself clearly prefers the latter,
with its rejection of heavy garnishing, but some receipts still contain the
ubiquitous raggoo added to a dish at the last minute, bringing to mind

---

[49] M. Bradley (1756), vol. I, p. 336.

Newcastle's recriminations about Hervé's 'composed' dishes. For the old-fashioned, the book continues to offer receipts for olios, puptons and bisks, but the essence of ham, cullisses, raggoos and fricassees of *nouvelle cuisine* are well represented.[50] The *grandes entrées* are still described as particularly prestigious, for instance in the comment on a pigeon bisk ('This is a great and very elegant Dish, fit for the greatest Table'[51]) – which recalls the words of Charles Carter – and another sign of the lingering of old fashions is seen in the remark concerning a 'Spanish Olio': 'Remember it is not a Soup, but an Olio, the Things are to be eaten in Preference of the Liquor.'[52] As we have seen, in ultra-fashionable circles the olio was beginning to be considered as a soup by this date.

Other things show that change was coming. She gives a receipt for soup 'à la Reine': a standard item in books by professional cooks, to wit a white chicken soup garnished with a hollowed-out loaf stuffed with minced chicken. Mrs Bradley, however, gives an ungarnished version, but at the end of offers the following comment:

> This is the Way in which the French at present most commonly eat Soup Lorrain; but as some add to it a Loaf, and other Ingredients, we shall not leave the Cook uninstructed.... [The receipt follows.]
>
>   The Loaf was the old Way of eating it, and for People that love very rich Dishes it is the best.[53]

Not everyone was prepared to follow the French fashion for simpler dishes, it seems. Bradley also preferred the plain version of a capon roasted with herbs, but at the end of the receipt she stated that the addition of a raggoo (meaning a sauce with a garnish) will make the dish more fashionable, although she herself does not approve:

> The French, who never know when to stop, serve up a Capon done in this Manner with a rich Raggoo about it, but this is Confusion, and the Taste of one Thing destroys that of another.

---

[50] M. Bradley (1756), vol. 1, pp. 238, 331–336, 342–345, 377–378, 433.

[51] Ibid., vol. 1, p. 433.

[52] Ibid., vol. 1, p. 345.

[53] Ibid., vol. 1, p. 241.

They who would be at the Top of the French Taste may serve it in this Manner, but with Gravy it is a very delicate and fine Dish, and no Way extravagant in the Expence.[54]

The authentic French 1750s version of the dish which appears in *The Professed Cook*[55] contains no suggestion of the raggoo Bradley proposes, and hers evokes the habits of the court-cooks rather than the elegance of *nouvelle cuisine*. A few pages further on, she again criticizes excessive use of raggoos:

> When these Roasts and Raggoos are kept separate they make a Variety, but in this new Way of putting one to another, all their Dishes are alike.
>
> This I have observed for the two last Years here at Bath is growing very common, and the Quality begin to find it out. Mr. Le Strange doubtless was a very good Cook, but I heard one who understands delicate Eating, no Body better, say at one of the Entertainments of his dressing, that all the Dishes were alike.[56]

These comments make fascinating reading, but are difficult to interpret. Was the addition of a raggoo a new fashion, or a relic of the older court style? Were the diners of Bath rejecting the very latest whim, or were they somewhat belatedly rejecting the earliest phase of *nouvelle cuisine* as practised by La Chapelle, where raggoo-garnishes, albeit in a less elaborate form than those of Massialot, were still present? Recalling that many of Bradley's receipts had originally come from the school of court-cookery and from La Chapelle himself, the latter may be correct, but in the light of Newcastle's complaints about Hervé, it is equally plausible that, after a phase of simplification in the 1730s and 1740s, there was a brief return to the use of lavish raggoos in the 1750s, before a reassertion of the unadorned.

It is tempting to reproduce many of Martha Bradley's receipts and comments, but a few will suffice to give the flavour. Like Verral, she has a discriminating attitude, preferring sometimes the French, sometimes the English, method, despite some xenophobic remarks about French cooks.[57] She

---

[54] M. Bradley (1756), vol. 1, p. 398.
[55] See Clermont (1769), pp. 214–215.
[56] M. Bradley (1756), vol. 1, pp. 402–403.
[57] Ibid., vol. 1, pp. 314, 327.

is particularly enthusiastic about vegetable-based sauces (sorrel, celery, onion, lettuce), because they are more refined than anything in the English repertoire:

> Our English Sauces in general are too plain and gross. These which we
> have here mentioned are what our People admire so greatly in France
> and Italy;… the Charge of them is little or nothing, and they will give
> a great Grace to the plainest Dishes.[58]

Occasionally, a comment shows which dish was in fashion at a particular moment: for instance, a beef dish (*Beef a la Vinaegrotte*) to be eaten cold – the beef is braised in wine with cloves and herbs, then served with a sprinkling of vinegar and lemon juice:

> In my small way I have serv'd it often, and have been asked for more
> Receipts for the making it, than for any one Dish that I remember. I
> made it in a manner Universal at Bath, in the Year 1749.[59]

Other comments show the extent to which she understood the basic principles of French cuisine. She emphasizes the importance of standard bases such as cullis or essence of ham, and the excellence of French sauces.[60] She explains why so many ingredients are required for a sauce (the receipt calls for truffles, morels, mushrooms and artichoke bottoms, plus two very English ingredients, pickled mushrooms and mushroom ketchup):

> This is a troublesome Dish, and some, who are no Judges of the Prin-
> ciples of Cookery, may think it wrong for having so many Ingredients,
> several of which they may think useless; but it is from this Mixture of
> Tastes, properly suited and proportioned, that we have the true high
> Flavour of the French Cookery. When this is done properly, no one
> Ingredient is tasted, but a fine mellow Mixture of all.[61]

---

[58] M. Bradley (1756), vol. 1, p. 654. Receipts pp. 652–654.

[59] Ibid., vol. 1, pp. 432–433.

[60] Ibid., vol. 1, pp. 238, 327, 331.

[61] Ibid., vol. 1, pp. 54–55.

The great Clouet himself pronounced that French cuisine had never been anything but composition, and Martha Bradley was perfectly aware of the fact. Here is one of the rare woman cooks who does not try to produce 'economical' French dishes, but she did work in Bath, where there were enough wealthy people to patronize such a lavish approach. In books aimed at a more middle-class readership, things were very different.

The ambiguous attitude which prevailed amongst authors who were less involved with *haute cuisine* has already been noticed. Hannah Glasse offers an excellent example of this ambivalence since she denounces French cooks in her address to the reader but includes much of French origin in her text. One of the chapters is headed, '*Read this* CHAPTER, *and you will find how expensive a* French *Cook's Sauce is*',[62] then proceeds to detail eight French sauces, with comments on their expense, all taken, directly or indirectly, from works by professional cooks.[63] Here is an example of her remarks, found at the end of a receipt entitled '*The* French *Way of Dressing* Partridges':

> This Dish I do not recommend; for I think it an odd Jumble of Trash, by that time the Cullis, the Essence of Ham, and all other Ingredients are reckoned, the Partridges will come to a fine Penny; but such Receipts as this, is what you have in most Books of Cookery yet printed.[64]

As Jennifer Stead points out, and as Ann Cook noticed at the time, Mrs Glasse gave receipts which were quite as expensive as those she ridiculed;[65] even one for essence of ham almost identical to that in her chapter denouncing such preparations.[66] The less expensive alternatives to cullis and essence of ham which she proposed in her address to the reader as instances of low-cost, rich sauces bear close resemblance to the men-cooks' suggestions:

---

[62] See Glasse, *The Art of Cookery* (1747), pp. 53–54.

[63] See Stead, 'Quizzing Glasse: or Hannah Scrutinized, Part II' (1983), pp. 17–20, 28. Jennifer Stead believes that Hannah Glasse consulted several sources when she wrote this chapter, but all the borrowed receipts are probably taken either from Vincent La Chapelle, via *The Whole Duty of a Woman*, or from John Nott. The receipt for 'Essence of Ham', which Stead attributes to the 1716 edition of Patrick Lamb, is also to be found in John Nott. (See Nott, *The Cook's and Confectioner's Dictionary* (1723), receipt H 8.)

[64] Glasse (1747), p. 53.

[65] See Stead (1983), p. 20.

[66] See Glasse (1747), p. 52.

Take a large deep Stew-pan, Half a Pound of Bacon, … cut the Fat and lay it over the Bottom of the Pan; then take a Pound of Veal, cut it into thin Slices, beat it well with the Back of a Knife, lay it all over the Bacon; then have six Pennyworth of the coarse lean Part of the Beef cut thin and well beat, lay a Layer of it all over, with some Carrot, then the Lean of the Bacon;… then cut two Onions and strew over, a Bundle of Sweet Herbs, four or five Blades of Mace, six or seven Cloves, a Spoonful of Whole Pepper, lay that all over, Half an Ounce of Truffles and Morels, then the rest of your Beef, a good Crust of Bread toasted very brown:… You may add an old Cock beat to Pieces; cover it close, and let it stand over a slow Fire two or three Minutes, then pour in boiling Water enough to fill the pan, cover it close, let it stew till it is as rich as you would have it, and then strain off all that Sauce. … This falls far short of the Expence of a Leg of Veal and a Ham, and answers every Purpose you want.[67]

This is less expensive merely because it uses smaller quantities than the men-cooks' receipts, but they were writing from their experience in kitchens where such basics were prepared in huge quantities.

It is interesting to see that receipts for made dishes take up a lot of space in Glasse: the chapter devoted to them is the longest in the whole work, with the exception of that on dishes 'for a Fast-Dinner', which itself contains many of the same character.[68] Preserving, by contrast, is given scant attention: the 23 receipts occupy only four pages;[69] this should be compared to E. Smith's book, which has 58 pages of cookery receipts, which give made dishes amongst the rest, and 46 pages devoted to preserving.[70] Glasse's readers were more interested in fashionable made dishes than in traditional sweetmeats for the banquet course. The made dishes in *The Art of Cookery* are often borrowed from the professional cooks;[71] amongst these is a pupton,[72] but olios, bisks and terrines do not appear. Her dishes are smaller than the *grandes entrées* of court-

---

[67] Glasse (1747), p. i.

[68] These chapters will be found pp. 13–52, and pp. 76–118.

[69] See pp. 152–155.

[70] See E– S–, *The Compleat Housewife* (1728), pp. 1–58, 154–199.

[71] See Stead (1983), p. 17.

[72] See Glasse (1747), p. 45.

cookery, but traces of this style linger in the suggested garnishes and, occasionally, in the presentation. A few examples will show this hybrid:

A second Way to make a White Fricasey.

You must take two or three Rabbits or Chickens, skin them, and lay them in warm Water, and dry them with a clean Cloth; put them into a Stew-pan with a Blade or two of Mace, a little Black and a little White Pepper, an Onion, a little Bundle of Sweet Herbs, and do but just cover them with Water; stew them till they are tender, then with a Fork take them out, strain the Liquor, and put them into the Pan again with Half a Pint of the Liquor and Half a Pint of Cream, the Yolks of two Eggs beat well, Half a Nutmeg grated, a Glass of White Wine, a little Piece of Butter rolled in Flour, and a Gill of Mushrooms; keep stirring all together, all the while one way, till it is smooth and of a fine Thickness, and then dish it up. Add what you please.[73]

The flavours of this dish are typical of Glasse: herbs, mace and nutmeg have replaced the earlier spices, and sugar appears only in sauces to accompany game, mutton and goose.[74] This particular receipt is interesting for two reasons. Firstly, this is a relatively new type of sauce. Cream sauces were not part of the repertoire in seventeenth-century books and began to appear in print only around 1710.[75] Secondly, Mrs Glasse tells the reader to 'add what you please', meaning extra garnish. At the end of the chapter, she gives a list of the possible extras:

---

[73] Glasse (1747), p. 14. This receipt is apparently Hannah Glasse's own, since neither Jennifer Stead nor Priscilla Bain has found it in any of Mrs Glasse's sources.

[74] Ibid., pp. 18, 23, 25, 28, 31, 33, 42.

[75] One of the first examples in print appears in Howard, *England's Newest Way* (1708), p. 44; but there are several cream sauces in earlier manuscript sources, such as the MS by Rebecca Price. See Masson, *The Compleat Cook* (1974), pp. 92, 94–6. The evolution of 'Scotch Collops' in the course of the eighteenth century shows the development of cream sauces. In the books by E. Smith and Mary Kettilby, the sauce is always brown, with the late seventeenth-century flavourings of wine, anchovy and meat gravy – exactly like Rebecca Price's receipts. But in Hannah Glasse's book, two of the receipts suggest a cream sauce. From the middle of the century, the two types co-exist, with a distinction made in the names: 'Brown Scotch Collops' and 'White Scotch Collops'. See Kettilby, *A Collection of above Three Hundred Receipts* (1714), pp. 36–7; E– S– (1728), pp. 13, 16, 45; Masson (1974), pp. 96–7; Glasse (1747), p. 13; Raffald, *The Experienced English House-keeper* (1769), pp. 83–5.

As to most Made dishes, you may put in what you think proper to
inlarge it, or make it good, as Mushrooms, … Truffles, Morels, Cocks
Combs stewed, Ox Palates cut in little Bits, Artichoke Bottoms, …
Asparagus Tops, the Yolks of hard Eggs, Force-Meat Balls, &c. The best
Things to give Sauce a Tartness are Mushroom Pickle, White Walnut
Pickle, or Lemon Juice.[76]

Here, of course, we have the lavish garnishes which we have seen in Massialot
and the English court-cooks; their various nature distinguishes them from the
more specific raggoos suggested by La Chapelle. Hannah Glasse's larger dishes
also reveal the influence of the court style, for the presentation evokes the
pyramids of the *grandes entrées*:

Chickens *with* Tongues. *A good Dish for a great deal of Company.*
Take six small Chickens boiled very white, six Hogs Tongues boiled and
peeled, a Cauliflower boiled very white in Milk and Water whole, and
a good deal of Spinach boiled green; then lay your Cauliflower in the
Middle, the Chickens close all round, and the Tongues round them with
the Roots outwards, and the Spinach in little Heaps between the
Tongues. Garnish with little Pieces of Bacon toasted.[77]

This is an echo of the complex court style, but also very English in its emphasis
on colour and last-minute assembly. Glasse took the receipt from *The Whole
Duty of a Woman*, though it came originally from Charles Carter's *Compleat
City and Country Cook*.[78]

Not all her made dishes were inspired by French cookery. The same chapter
contains one of the very earliest receipts for curry:

To make a Currey the India way.
Take two Fowls or Rabbits, cut them into small Pieces, and three or four
small Onions, peeled and cut very small, thirty Pepper Corns, and a
large Spoonful of Rice, Brown some Coriander Seeds over the Fire in a

---

[76] Glasse (1747), p. 52.

[77] Ibid, p. 40.

[78] See Stead (1983), p. 28.

clear Shovel, and beat them to Powder, take a Tea Spoonful of Salt, and mix all well together with the Meat, put all together into a Sauce-pan or Stew-pan, with a Pint of Water, let it stew softly till the Meat is enough, then put in a Piece of fresh Butter, about as big as a large Walnut, shake it well together, and when it is smooth and of a fine Thickness, dish it up, and send it to Table.... You are to observe the Sauce must be pretty thick.[79]

We shall return to the development of this particular dish below. Here, it is important to notice that the receipt shows the beginning of colonial importations into the English repertoire and its very presence confirms the essentially 'bourgeois' nature of Mrs Glasse's book.

Curry is not the only new element. Glasse announced in her address to the reader that her aim was to instruct ignorant servants. One important aspect of this pedagogy was detailed instruction on the basic English cooking methods of roasting and boiling.[80] Such lessons are not given in the books by professional cooks, nor were they present in the more modest works by women such as Sarah Harrison. Glasse's advice on roasting tells the reader to sprinkle beef, mutton and veal with flour towards the end of cooking, and to dredge pork with a mixture of breadcrumbs, nutmeg and sage.[81] In her basic instructions concerning boiling vegetables, she gives a hint which would be picked up and repeated by many subsequent authors:

Most People spoil Garden Things by over boiling them: All Things that are Green should have a little Crispness, for if they are over boil'd they neither have any Sweetness or Beauty.[82]

The importance accorded to vegetables by this stage in the century was reflected by the fact that there were general indications on how to cook them and several groups of receipts devoted to them.[83] Vegetables served in a sauce were suitable for supper or as side dishes to accompany the big dishes of meat:

[79] Glasse (1747), p. 52.
[80] Ibid., pp. 3–13.
[81] Ibid., pp. 3–4.
[82] Ibid., p. 12.
[83] Ibid., pp. 10–12, 96–101, 103–105.

Mrs Glasse often said that the dish she had just described should be served in this way.[84] But in spite of their increasing presence on the table, vegetables were still low in the culinary hierarchy. Martha Bradley pointed out that they were not supposed to be important in their own right: 'The Housekeeper is to remember, no Stress is to be laid upon them in the Entertainment, but coming in as slight inconsiderable Dishes, they give Variety, and always please.'[85] Such comments notwithstanding, the growing number of vegetable dishes found in cookery books by the middle of the century is a clear indication of a trend towards lighter, more varied eating.

Hannah Glasse's book also enables us to see how some English dishes were developing. We have already noted the many puddings and pies in collections by women authors at the beginning of the century. Glasse carried on where they left off with, for instance, one of the first printed receipts for Yorkshire pudding, cooked as it should be under the spit in order to absorb the juices from the meat.[86] In her chapter on pies, there were such regional specialities as Cheshire pork pie, filled with pork and pippins, and Devonshire squab pie, in which the pippins go with mutton. These were the only meat pies (except for two of lamb or veal, explicitly presented as sweet and, of course, mince-pies) to contain sugar.[87] She included, too, the 'Yorkshire Christmas-Pye', a huge pie to be eaten cold, filled with various boned birds: a pigeon in the centre is surrounded by a partridge, then a fowl; then a goose, and finally a turkey. She explained how these were often sent to London as presents, the crust thick and solid enough to withstand the journey.[88] There were also plenty of puddings, both boiled and baked.[89] Among the latter was one which remains part of today's English repertoire:

---

[84] See, for instance, her comment on a dish of asparagus with scrambled eggs ('This makes a pretty Side-dish for a second Course, or a Corner-plate.'), or on a dish of spinach ('Serve it up either for Supper, or a Side-dish at a second Course.'), pp. 98, 99.

[85] M. Bradley (1756), vol. 2, p. 145.

[86] See Glasse (1747), p. 69. See also the receipt and the comment by Martha Bradley: 'This is an errant English Dish, but it is a very good one.' Bradley (1756), vol. 1, p. 440.

[87] Glasse (1747), pp. 70, 72, 74.

[88] Ibid., p. 73. See also the slightly different receipt in Peckham, *The Complete English Cook* (1767), pp. 104–105.

[89] Glasse (1747), pp. 68–70, 105–112.

A Bread *and* Butter Pudding.

Take a Penny-loaf, and cut it into thin Slices of Bread and Butter, as you
do for Tea. Butter your Dish as you cut them, lay Slices all over the Dish,
then strew a few Currans, … and so on, till all your Bread and Butter
is in; then take a Pint of Milk, beat up four Eggs, a little Salt, half a
Nutmeg grated, mix all together with Sugar to your Taste. Pour this over
the Bread, and bake it half an Hour.[90]

This has a very long history. It appeared in seventeenth-century cookery books
and even in receipts of sixteenth-century origins under the name of 'Whitepot'
or 'Devonshire Whitepot'.[91] These English dishes remind us that just as French
cookery was beginning to take on its modern form, still recognizable today, so
English cookery was in the process of formulating and codifying its classic
receipts.

Cookery books aimed at a gentry and middle-class readership tended to
offer dishes which mimic French fashions but their number was proportionate
to the social status of the potential readers. Elizabeth Moxon was less ambitious
than Glasse – she was published in Leeds, not in London – and there were
correspondingly fewer French receipts. Moxon gave one for a pupton,[92] but
there was no olio, no bisk, no cullis. There were a dozen fricassees,[93] and a
receipt for veal showed an attempt to provide an economical version of the
lavish garnishes of the old court style, adapted to modest pockets:

A Herrico of a Breast of Veal, French *Way.*

Take a Breast of Veal and half roast it, so put it into your stew Pan, with
three Pints of brown Gravy, season your Veal with Nutmeg, Pepper and
Salt; when your Veal is stew'd enough, you must put in a Pint of green
Pease boiled. Take six middling Cucumbers, pare and cut them in
Quarters long Way, and two Cabbage Lettices, and stew them in brown
Gravy, so lay them round your Veal when you dish it up, with a few

---

[90] Glasse (1747),p. III.

[91] See, for instance, the receipts for 'White Pott' and for 'The Lord of Devonshire his Pudding' in
Spurling, *Elinor Fettiplace's Receipt Book* (1986), pp. 160–161, 213; W. M., *The Compleat Cook* (1655),
p. 12; Woolley, *The Cooks Guide* (1664), p. 27; Woolley, *The Queen-like Closet* (1670), p. 31.

[92] See Moxon, *English Housewifry* (1741), pp. 71–72.

[93] Ibid., pp. 23–24, 29–30, 38–40, 51–52.

forc'd-Meat Balls, and some Slices of Bacon. Garnish your Dish with Pickles, Mushrooms, Oysters and Lemons.[94]

The use of vegetables rather than a more up-market raggoo brings this within the reach of less well-off households but the presentation still imitates the aristocratic style of the beginning of the century. The 'domestic' version of the court style was spreading in ever-widening circles among the provincial gentry and, perhaps, the middle classes.

In the 1760s, Ann Peckham, another author who published in Leeds, produced a collection of receipts very similar to Elizabeth Moxon's. There are fricassees,[95] as well as other receipts bearing French names, which belong to the culinary style of earlier decades, such as the pupton ('Palpatoon *of* Pigeons'),[96] and the mutton 'à la Maintenon' ('Mutton Maintelow'),'[97] in which slices of meat are dipped in melted butter and then in a breadcrumb and herb mix before being cooked in paper. This receipt had already appeared in more modest books earlier in the century.[98] The cooking method is common in contemporary literature. The following comes from Ann Peckham:

Salmon *in Cases.*
Take a piece of salmon, skin it and cut it in thin slices, mince some parsley, green onions and mushrooms; put your parsley and green onions into a stew-pan, with some butter, pepper, and salt; then put in your salmon without putting it over the fire again, and toss it up to give it a taste; place your slices of salmon in a paper-case, put your seasoning upon it, and strew the crumbs of bread over all; let it bake to a fine colour, and serve it with the juice of lemon.[99]

The simplicity of the dish places it with the modern style but its presence here is attributable as much to the modest nature of 'domestic' cookery as to the influence of *nouvelle cuisine*. Peckham, like Moxon, also gives traditional

[94] Moxon (1741), p. 15.
[95] See Peckham (1767), pp. 85–89.
[96] Ibid., p. 69.
[97] Ibid., pp. 43–44.
[98] See, for instance, Harrison, *The House-keeper's Pocket-Book* (1733), p. 153.
[99] Peckham (1767), pp. 16–17.

English receipts: the pies and puddings, and dishes already found in earlier women's works, such as the thin pancakes ('Pancakes *called a Quire of Paper*'[100]) which had appeared in Mary Kettilby in 1714.

As a general rule, there are more French-inspired receipts in books by men than by women. If we compare Ann Peckham with James Jenks, published a year later, the proportion of French to English is not very different, but Jenks details hashes, raggoos (either dishes in their own right, or garnishes) and fricassees[101] and, in a chapter devoted to made dishes, receipts for meat cooked 'à la mode', 'à la daub' and 'à la braise'.[102] At the beginning of the same chapter, he also gives several receipts for cullis, and one for essence of ham.[103] These mid-century books aimed at the gentry and the middle-classes are thus following the fashions of the final phase of court-cookery. A male cook like Jenks is somewhat closer to the fashion than women such as Moxon or Peckham but they all offer some form of combination of the two influences.

Moving from the dearest to the cheapest books, French inspiration diminishes. Catharine Brooks' work, which came out around 1762, has a chapter on fricassees and grilled and fried meats (the fricassees are thus assimilated to fried meats), and a chapter with two pages of raggoos, here of the sauce-and-garnish type.[104] Most of the book is, however, devoted to English roasts, pies and puddings.[105] According to the title-page, the chapter concerning made dishes was added to the second edition.[106] These are presented in the list of contents as being particularly refined ('the Genteelest Made Dishes'). In her text, Mrs Brooks gives general instructions for them which are lifted directly from Hannah Glasse,[107] although the receipts themselves do not come from Glasse but probably from some other source. The humbler the book, the fewer are the made dishes and the stronger is the tendency to reproduce advice and receipts from other books. And the further down the social scale, the older and more divorced from current fashion the receipts become.

---

[100] Peckham (1767), p. 121.

[101] See Jenks, *The Complete Cook* (1768), pp. 120–127, 127–133, 152–158.

[102] Ibid., pp. 179, 185, 187; 179, 187–188; 182, 184, 186, 190–191, 192.

[103] Ibid., pp. 174–177.

[104] See Brooks, *The Complete English Cook* (c.1765), pp. 31–42, 68–69.

[105] Ibid., pp. 5–14, 42–53, 53–58.

[106] Ibid., pp. 89–100.

[107] Ibid., p. 89; Glasse (1747), p. 52.

Another instance of this distancing is in bills of fare. Elizabeth Moxon's are for two courses of five, seven or nine dishes,[108] whereas Catharine Brooks gives two courses of only two or three.[109] The humbler book flatters its readers by promising genteel dishes and supplying illustrated bills of fare but they are adapted to the perceived status and income of the buyer. At the very bottom of the scale, only the simplest receipts are given: for instance, one of Penelope Bradshaw's books, *Bradshaw's Valuable Family Jewel*, instructs in roasting, boiling, grilling and frying and then proceeds directly to pies and tarts.[110]

For the most part, the books we have been discussing brought to the notice of an ever-increasing readership a way of cooking closer to Massialot than to the elegant simplicity of *nouvelle cuisine* practised by Clouet in the 1730s and 1740s and described by William Verral. The raggoo as a universal garnish, used quite indiscriminately, is the main component of what is seen as the refined made dish and is the identifying characteristic of 'French' cookery as practised in England.[111] As far as the English were concerned, French was synonymous with dishes in sauce, enriched with such extras as truffles, morels, cockscombs and artichoke bottoms (to mention only those which recur most frequently). Even more significant is the fact that English women cooks were convinced that they could make equally good sauces with fewer ingredients, and soon they would consider that both broth and cullis were unnecessary. Although at first their receipts still tended to follow the originals and to use the offending items, the drive to unite elegance with economy – the consequence of the cookery book's downward social trajectory – led to a bastardization of receipts. The first signs are discernable in the 1760s. Hannah Glasse's instructions for cullisses and sauces are still close to the French prescriptions she denounces. Twenty years later, Ann Shackleford gives a receipt for essence of ham which, she says, will give an *haut goût* to any dish in sauce. She concludes by suggesting a more economical alternative: 'Note. When you boil a ham, if it is of a good flavour, and not too salt, save the gravy, and in a great measure it will answer your purpose, without much expence or trouble.'[112]

---

[108] See Moxon (1741), in the bills of fare at the end of the book.

[109] See Brooks (*c.*1765), p. 101.

[110] See Bradshaw, *Bradshaw's Valuable Family Jewel* (1748), passim. Pages not numbered.

[111] See, for instance, Harrison (1733), pp. 122–123; Gelleroy, *The London Cook* (1762), pp. 166–167; Skeat, *The Art of Cookery and Pastery made easy and familiar*, n.d. [1769], p. 31. Catharine Brooks reproduces the remarks in Hannah Glasse: Brooks (*c.*1765), p. 89.

[112] Shackleford, *The Modern Art of Cookery Improved* (1767), pp. 68–69.

Such habits of substitution became more frequent as the years passed. They are an eloquent reminder of the gulf separating English cooks from their French counterparts. Of course, most French books described aristocratic cuisine, but even the exception, Menon's *Cuisinière bourgeoise* of 1746, included a cullis, and many of his made dishes called for it as an ingredient.[113] English cooks were working for an audience which had no real understanding of what *haute cuisine* was about, but which still wanted to emulate élite fashions so long as all extravagance was eliminated. The expensive and troublesome sauces of *nouvelle cuisine* were unacceptable, though lavish garnishes of the court style remained popular because they were highly visible signs of status.

How far did their readers follow the prescriptions of cookery books? The evidence suggests there was a substantial gap between theory and practice. Whereas manuscript receipt collections and menus jotted down in notebooks at the beginning of the century show the new flavours and scaled-down versions of the grand court style very frequently adopted by the gentry, later instances do not give the same impression. The manuscript receipt collection kept by Elizabeth Raper is a case in point. She was the daughter of an East India Company merchant who kept house for her parents, and her diary shows that she did at least some of the cooking. She gathered her receipts over a period of about ten years before her marriage to a Scottish doctor in 1762. There are a few fricassees[114] whose flavours are close to those found in Rebecca Price's seventeenth-century manuscript where the anchovy-wine association was the dominant note. There is also a 'Ragout of Veal' garnished with a raggoo containing palates, forcemeat balls, truffles, morels, mushrooms, artichoke bottoms and a sweetbread.[115] But there are far more English dishes, such as the stew made with mutton and potatoes, known today as Irish stew, but which Elizabeth Raper calls 'Beggar's Dish'.[116] The main focus of the manuscript is on made dishes (31 out of a total of 78 cookery receipts, the other 22 being devoted to pickles and preserves plus odd household hints and one medical prescription). These look old-fashioned, as do her English receipts, and it seems that this daughter of the professional class was only vaguely aware of the latest trends. Unfortunately, it is not known whether she possessed any cookery books.

---

[113] [Menon], *La Cuisinière bourgeoise* (1981), passim. The receipt for cullis is pp. 128–130.

[114] See Grant (ed.), *The Receipt Book of Elizabeth Raper* (1924), pp. 55, 59, 62.

[115] Ibid., p. 68.

[116] Ibid., p. 67.

A more sombre picture of the state of cookery in England is painted by William Verral. He gives a hilarious account of his experiences among the Sussex gentry. Even if the satirical nature of some of his stories means they must be approached with caution, the tenor of his remarks is unmistakably critical. Verral was a well-known figure in Lewes, since he was the master of an inn which had once been the town residence of the Pelhams. When a local gentleman wanted to give a good dinner, he called on the innkeeper's services, but Verral found working in poorly-equipped squires' kitchens rather trying:

> I have been sent for many and many a time to get dinners for some of the best families hereabouts: the salute generally is, Will, … I want you to dress me a dinner today; with all my heart, Sir says I; … but, says the gentleman, be sure you make us some good things in your own way, for they are polite sort of gentry that are to dine with me. I promised my care, and wrote the bill immediately; and it was vastly approved of. My next step was to go and offer a great many compliments to Mrs. Cook about getting the dinner; and as it was her master's order I should assist her, I hoped we should agree.… Pray, Nanny, says I, where do you place your stew-pans, and the other things you make use of in the cooking way? La, Sir, says she, that is all we have (pointing to one poor solitary stewpan, as one might call it,) but no more fit for the use than a wooden hand-dish. Ump, says I to myself, how's this to be? … However, upon a little pause I sent away post haste for my own kitchen furniture. In the mean time Nanny and I kept on preparing what we could, that no time might be lost. … And now, dinner being dish'd up, Nanny was vastly pleased, and said, that in her judgment it was the prettiest and best she had ever seen.[117]

The conclusion of this tale is that the dinner was a raving success, so much so that Verral was invited to prepare the supper, which enabled him to allow Nanny her moment of glory, making a fricassee under his watchful eye. The upshot of these two eminently successful meals was that the master of the house decided to purchase suitable equipment for his kitchen and came to consult Verral on the subject: the anecdote thus gives the author the

---

[117] Verral (1759), pp. iii–ix.

opportunity to present a list of all the saucepans and implements necessary in a well-regulated kitchen. Here, Verral's satirical impulses are kept under control, and the story provides interesting information about the indifferent attitude of the rural gentry towards the equipment of their kitchens, even if we do not take too literally the solitary saucepan. Verral's remarks about the cook-maid confirm the impression given by the Purefoy letters, in which we saw Mrs Purefoy's increasingly desperate search for a cook capable of preparing even the simplest dishes. In the light of such comments, there is every reason to think that cookery books had an important rôle to play in disseminating basic kitchen lore to ignorant domestics.

This first story had a happy ending, but Verral goes on to tell of his exploits in the house of a squire called Hackum, who asked our hero to produce a dinner for four. Unfortunately, Hackum had his own ideas about what constituted a fashionable French meal and, faced with his obstinacy in imposing the bill of fare of his own devising – with three dishes at each course plus two removes, instead of the five dishes and one remove suggested by Verral – the author took a signal revenge:

About one o'clock dinner went up, the soup, three fowls and bacon, and a large shoulder of mutton. The soup they all eat up, which was a very large old-fashioned pewter dish full; then fell aboard the fowls, and demolished them, and so on to the mutton; … the next three things were a hare, a turkey, (both baked, and spoiled, for want of a proper fire in the kitchen) and a plumb-pudding. There was no ceremony for clean plates; but at it they went, … the turkey was stript in a minute, and the poor hare tore all to pieces, (for there was not a carver amongst them) and a most profound silence there was for a long time, except only a very pretty concert of growling, smacking their chops, and cracking of crusts: when all was over with meat, plates were called for the pudding, which disappeared in about three minutes, though no small one. … The removes were then put on; and that the beauty of the third course (as I call it) might be kept up, at each end was a sort of pudding, and in the middle the gibbet of the hare, and the skeleton of the turkey. Now the two puddings (improperly called so) were made as follows: I took a few potatoes boiled, and thump'd to pieces, with an egg or two, and a little sugar, for one; the other was a few old mackeroons I had in my house perhaps twenty years: I soak'd 'em well, and put them into a little milk and flour, instead of cream and eggs, seasoned it high with plenty of onions, &c. to which I added a large clove of garlick, which is enough for the dishes of a fifty-cover table served twice over, and covered it over with some good old Cheshire cheese instead of Parmesan; so that the colours were alike, and sent up, … heartily they fell to, except one, whose taste was not quite so depraved as the rest; he tasted, but went no farther. You don't eat, neighbour, says the opposite gentleman. I don't love sweet things, says he. Well, I do, says one that was gobbling down the highest dish that ever was. They vastly commended it, and swallowed it all down; but the beauty of it was, the mackeroon eaters eat it for a custard, and to this moment call it the best they ever tasted.[118]

Obviously, one cannot take story literally, but the nature of the various horrors shows what Verral considered the most important mistakes made by his rustic squires. The soup should have a remove, but Hackum thought removes constituted another course; there should be the same number of dishes on the table during each course, but the last 'course' had only the relics of the hare and the turkey as its centrepiece; the gentlemen should carve neatly, but they simply tore the meat to pieces in their untutored greed; finally, genteel diners should consume with discrimination, but they were incapable of recognizing the nature of the dishes set before them. Since this anecdote cannot be seen as a reflection of reality, it is probable that, like the repugnantly bad table-manners proscribed in medieval manuals, the details were designed to make the reader feel comfortably superior, as someone who could never be guilty of such solecisms.

And yet there is an element of truth in this wild exaggeration: the self-confident ignorance of most English when faced with French cuisine meant that they were prepared to accept all sorts of substitutions. This tendency was the origin of the downward slide of English cookery which becomes visible by the end of the century. The wealthy aristocracy, especially the Whig political élite, and perhaps even some of the gentry, had their French cooks (and their number increased after the French Revolution) or employed an English cook who had been trained to cook in the French manner, but the cookery books

---

[118] Verral (1759), pp. xvi–xxi.

were aimed at an audience lower down the social scale – middle-class mistresses and their servants – where direct contact with French dishes was exceptional. Such cooks had heard of French cookery but did not know much about it. They were sure, however, that it was a luxury, and the trouble with *nouvelle cuisine* was that it did not offer a visible display of luxury. For the majority of the English, luxury meant quantity and the older court style was more satisfactory in this line. The lighter dishes and subtle sauces of the new style were simply a confidence-trick perpetrated by the cunning French in order to cheat their employers. This is what Hannah Glasse says at the end of her receipt for a partridge sauce:

> They have much more expensive Sauce than this. – However, I think here is enough to show the Folly of these fine *French* Cooks. In their own Country, they will make a grand Entertainment with the Expence of one of these Dishes; but here they want the little petty Profit; and by this Sort of legerdemain Sum, fine Estates are juggled into *France*.[119]

With this sort of reasoning, the lesser gentry and the ever-increasing numbers of middle-class families who could afford to eat well tended to prefer English dishes. However, recognizing that the most important item in fashionable French cuisine was the dish of meat in sauce, they made such things but kept their garnishes of the court style. The need for economy, already visible in the discourse (if not always in the receipts) of Sarah Harrison and Hannah Glasse, would also be a major influence from the 1750s onwards.

---

[119] Glasse (1747), p. 54.

The cookery books of this period are enormously diverse, ranging from the luxury work, costing six or seven shillings, written by a professional cook, man or woman, to the pamphlet priced at one or two shillings or less. Some of these latter were chapbooks aimed at a very modest reader and representing a very different type of cookery. In the mainstream, descriptions of *haute cuisine* were rare; confined, perhaps, to just two books, by B. Clermont (*The Professed Cook*, 1769) and George Dalrymple (*The Practice of Modern Cookery*, 1781). One step below them on the culinary ladder, the tavern cooks (a new group of authors) and the women cooks and housekeepers manifested some slight influence of *haute cuisine* but, more importantly, demonstrated the development and codification of a specifically English repertoire.

A *leitmotif* of the period was almost universal plagiarism. Many receipts were shared between several books: John Farley took all but one of his from other people's work. Authors now admitted openly that they had plundered their predecessors, though few were as precise in their attributions as Mary Cole, and even she, in spite of her appearance of honesty, was not invariably frank. The preface to Collingwood and Woollams in 1792 is characteristic:

> We do not presume to arrogate to ourselves the Reputation of having ushered into the World a Work entirely new, which indeed cannot be expected; but we flatter ourselves, that the Alterations we have made in the different Receipts, the new ones we have added, and the methodical Manner in which we have arranged the Whole, will in some Degree entitle us to the Patronage of the Public. Glasse, Mason, Raffald, and Farley, are, like us, equally indebted to the Labours of our Predecessors.[1]

While systematic investigation could reveal a vast network of borrowings and adaptation, the task would be daunting. Fiona Lucraft[2] is one of the few modern scholars to have attempted anything in this line, with particular reference to

---

[1] Collingwood & Woollams, *The Universal Cook* (1792), preface.

[2] See Lucraft, 'The London Art of Plagiarism, Part 1' (1992), pp. 7–24; and 'The London Art of Plagiarism, Part 2' (1993), pp. 34–46. Lucraft demonstrates that Farley (or rather, Richard Johnson) took 49 per cent of his receipts from Elizabeth Raffald, 43 per cent from Hannah Glasse's *Art of Cookery*, and the rest from a variety of minor sources.

John Farley. What can be said with certainty is that some of these books were mere compilations (for example Collingwood and Woollams, above) and did not represent the culinary practice of the author. Farley, contrary to what the title-page suggested to the gullible (then as now) did not give any insight into the food served at the London Tavern, where he did indeed officiate.

The more modest books show gentry cooking adapted to the restricted means of the middle-classes. Just how far down the social scale the cookery book penetrated in the eighteenth century is a difficult question. As we have seen, the reader and even the buyer of a 'luxury' work was likely to be a servant hoping to better herself, but the very varied contents of some of the cheaper books suggests that the buyer was a woman who aspired to gentility without being entirely a creature of leisure. At the bottom of the market, books gave economical receipts with little relation to upper-class cookery. Some drew their inspiration (or their material) from cookery that had been practised as long ago as the sixteenth century, or they taught how to make dishes of no gastronomic interest whatsoever, for example directions on how to cook sausages. The presence of instructions for such simple operations implies the reader (or the listener to a lesson read out by the mistress?) was ignorant. The books of the end of the century try to give the most basic knowledge to women who had everything to learn.

Clermont and Dalrymple describe cookery at the other end of the social scale, and that cookery is French. (All the examples which follow come from Clermont. Dalrymple is almost entirely plagiarized from this source.) It is no surprise that Clermont, like Massialot and La Chapelle before him, begins with bouillons and cullis, the basic preparations for making sauces, by now the most important single element in French cookery.[3] Clermont includes many. A typical example is an 'Italian' sauce:

A Slice of Ham, few Mushrooms, few Shallots, half a Laurel Leaf, a large Spoonful of Oil; simmer all together on a slow Fire, add some rich Cullis, half a Glass of Champagne; boil like all Sauces, on a slow Fire for half an Hour, skim it well, and sift it in a Sieve.[4]

[3] See Clermont, *The Professed Cook* (1769), pp. 1–2, 6–13.
[4] Ibid., p. 31.

The receipt is obviously addressed to someone who is familiar with the proced-
ure, though the author does indicate the cooking method and its duration. The
sauce is used with a 'Filet de Boeuf a l'Italienne':

> Lard a Fillet of Beef one Side, the other stuff with chopt Parsley,
> Shallots, Thyme, Laurel Powder, Mushrooms, mix it with a little scraped
> Lard, Pepper and Salt, tie in Paper, and roast it; garnish the unlarded
> Side with Bread Crums, and colour it with a Salamander; serve an
> Italian Sauce....[5]

The style of this, and indeed of all Clermont's receipts, is very similar to
Verral's: the application of a system to enable the cook to produce a huge
variety of dishes from standardized basics. This is seen again in Clermont's
instructions for ways of cooking rabbit. He gives four receipts, and then adds
a list of dishes from his chapter concerning poultry which may also be used for
this meat.[6] Even within a single receipt, he offers variations which are left to
the cook's own initiative:

> Lapreaux à l'Escalope.
> Rabbit Collop.
> Cut the Fillets of one or two Rabbits in thin Slices, and put them in a
> Stew-pan upon a Slice of Ham, few Slices of Veal, a little Butter or Oil,
> Pepper and Salt, chopped Parsley, Shallots, Mushrooms, then few thin
> Slices of Bacon for covering; soak this on a slow Fire, about a Quarter
> of an Hour, then add a Glass of white Wine; finish the Brazing; take out
> the Fillets, drain the Fat off; sift the Braze, add a little Cullis, skim it very
> clean: you may add a Lemon Squeeze, if the Wine does not make the
> Sauce sharp enough; serve upon the Fillets; when so brazed, you may
> put them to what Sauce you please, or in white or brown Fricassee, or
> Gratin, &c. &c.[7]

---

[5] Clermont (1769), pp. 78–79.

[6] Ibid., pp. 267–268.

[7] Ibid., p. 266.

Neither the rabbit nor the fillet of beef we have described has any significant garnish. Clermont follows La Chapelle and Verral in simply finishing with a rich sauce passed through a fine strainer.

But not all sauces are so elementary. The chapter devoted to raggoos and *rissolles* ('rissolles' are either forcemeat balls browned in a frying-pan, or small puff-pastry cases with a stuffing) gives plenty of receipts for raggoos in the eighteenth-century meaning of the term. They are designed either to be used as a garnish for the 'entrées' of the first course at dinner, or to be served on their own as 'entremets', part of the second course.[8] The receipt varies according to the way the raggoo is to be used, as for instance these mushrooms:

> *Ragoût de Champignons.* Of Mushrooms.
> Peel the Mushrooms, and cut each in two; soak a Slice of Ham, then put the Mushrooms to it, and a Bit of Butter, a Nosegay of Sweet-herbs, two Cloves; add Cullis and Gravy; simmer this together about an Hour, the Sauce to be reduced thick; take out the Ham and Nosegay; skim it well, add a Lemon-squeeze, Pepper and Salt, when ready: this is prepared to serve with Meat; but if you would have them alone, put neither Cullis nor Gravy, but make a Liason [sic] with Yolks of Eggs and Cream: serve them in ... several Bits of Bread fried, cut in some pretty Shape, or only small Bits round the Dish.[9]

Other receipts give similar variations, thus the raggoo may become a small fricassee, as explained for oysters and morels.[10]

The chapter on sauces[11] shows how far the codification of French cuisine had progressed since La Chapelle. Out of a total of 71 sauces, 29 (over 40 per cent) bear a name which does not derive from the main ingredient or the meat the sauce is to accompany: there are, for instance, sauces 'à la Saxe', 'à la Mariette' and 'à l'Amiral'.[12] The same is true for the names of dishes themselves. Many are named after a place – 'à l'Italienne', 'à la Flamande', 'à la

---

[8] See, for instance, pp. 292, 293.

[9] Clermont (1769), p. 295.

[10] Ibid., p. 295.

[11] Ibid., pp. 30–51.

[12] Ibid., pp. 33, 34, 35.

Provençale', to quote only three[13] – a sign of interest in regional cuisines;[14] others carry names evoking the prestige of aristocratic houses ('Rissolles à la Choisy' or 'Potage à la Conty'[15]). French cookery had reached a point where dishes were beginning to assume a fixed content: the cook had to know how to produce a large number of dishes which had their own names and specific natures. The receipts of court-cookery for olios and terrines still left plenty of scope for the cook to do his own thing; the culinary style of the second half of the century restricted him much more. The body of classic French cookery is in the process of definition.

When we turn to England, we find the same process of codification but the register is different. While there are, of course, French recipes (or imitations of them), there is a range that is specifically English, with 'made dishes' alongside older types inherited from the seventeenth century such as the puddings and pies. French influence is more visible in some books than others. The largest proportion of French receipts appears in Mary Cole, Collingwood and Woollams, and Richard Briggs. There are far fewer in John Farley, Elizabeth Raffald and Charlotte Mason. Receipts for cullis illustrate this disparity: Mary Cole gives eight, John Townshend seven, Collingwood and Woollams five, Richard Briggs two, Charlotte Mason and Mary Smith only one.[16] Raffald and Farley do not have one at all. Contrary to expectations, it does not follow from the presence of French receipts that an author had assimilated the lessons of the French system. Of those mentioned, it seems that Mary Smith and Richard Briggs were the most familiar with French practice since the arrival of *nouvelle cuisine*, and and it is they whose books do not appear to be mere compilations. Many instances of apparent French influence (particularly from Clermont) are no more than thoughtless adoption, without understanding. This contrasts with the reasoned appraisal of French cookery by the earlier writers Verral and

[13] A glance at the table of contents reveals other examples as well: there are dishes 'à la Provençale' or 'à la Flamande' pp. 60, 90, 118, 121, 163.

[14] For a discussion of this aspect of French cookery in the eighteenth century, see Hyman & Hyman, 'The Perception of Regional Cooking in French Cookbooks of the Eighteenth Century' (1981), pp. 178–185.

[15] See Clermont (1769), pp. 301–302; 15–16.

[16] See Cole, *The Lady's Complete Guide* (1788), pp. 319–322; Townshend, *The Universal Cook* (1773), pp. 45–47, 79, 117, 123–124; Collingwood & Woollams (1792), pp. 188–190; Briggs, *The English Art of Cookery* (1788), p. 217; Mason, *The Lady's Assistant* (1773), p. 202; M. Smith, *The Complete House-keeper* (1772), p. 97.

Martha Bradley. Mary Cole, for example, took much from Clermont. Her 'made dishes' with butchers' meat she attributed to Glasse, Raffald and Farley, as well as to Verral,[17] Clermont[18] and Dalrymple[19] – these last being, in fact, indirect borrowings from Clermont. But she makes no comment on the merits of any single author's particular method.

Should one take Mary Cole's book as proof that French receipts were widely known amongst female cooks who worked for the aristocracy? Probably not. Although she announces in her preface that she had bought and used many books, she did not, apparently, notice the origin of most of Dalrymple's receipts in Clermont. This may cast doubt upon her affirmation. Other authors offer more likely evidence of the extent French style had entered English practice. It seems that although French receipts were included in their books, they were usually in limited numbers. And the ones which we do find usually hark back to an earlier court style. Elizabeth Raffald gives 28 receipts with French names (or which are described as being 'the French way') in her chapter on 'made dishes',[20] out of a total of 92 (i.e. 30 per cent). Among these are raggoos, fricassees, fricandoes, and a few with such names as 'à la braize', 'à la daub', 'a la mode' and 'a la royal'. There are none of the more specific titles given by Clermont. Charlotte Mason who, unlike Mrs Raffald, proposes a receipt for cullis, gives only a few raggoos and fricassees and has no French sauces.[21] These are representative of the type of French cookery which had long been part of the English repertoire: raggoos, fricassees and fricandoes had entered English cookery in the seventeenth century, and Mrs Raffald's other named dishes all appeared in Charles Carter's *Complete Practical Cook* in 1730.

'Made dishes' were still the most prestigious items in a cook's repertoire, and in many books, the chapter devoted to them begins with general advice and directions. The author often emphasizes their importance as symbols of the

---

[17] See Cole (1788), pp. 56, 60, 69, 75, 79, 85, 90, 94, 97, 106, 112, 113, 126, 133, 136, 144, 149, 151, 153, 164. These 'made dishes' occupy pages 52–166.

[18] Cole (1788), pp. 60, 61, 63, 67, 71, 74, 76, 78, 82, 86, 89, 93, 104, 107, 109, 112, 118, 122, 139, 140, 141, 146, 153, 156, 159, 165.

[19] Cole (1788), pp. 60, 61, 63, 64, 68, 71, 74, 75, 76, 77, 80, 83, 85, 88, 91, 93, 94, 95, 104, 107, 108, 109, 112, 113, 118, 120, 121, 132, 135, 139, 140, 141, 142, 145, 148, 150, 158, 162, 164, 165.

[20] See Raffald, *The Experienced English Housekeeper* (1769), pp. 70–125.

[21] See Mason (1773): the raggoos will be found pp. 211, 217, 222, 231, 241, 256; the fricassees pp. 213, 214, 225–226, 228, 229, 231, 233, 243, 244, 248.

fashionable, although by this period this may not be invariably French. Thus
the relevant chapter in James Jenks' book in 1768 is introduced by the words,
'Extraordinary Fashionable Dishes … called Made Dishes'.[22] But the advice
given to the cook shows that these English authors clung to their rather outmoded ideas of what such dishes should be like, since they suggest adding the
ubiquitous indiscriminate garnish which had originated with court-cookery.
Whereas Clermont's raggoos were based on single ingredients, such as mushrooms, the English tended to throw everything in everywhere, as Raffald
suggested:

> You may use pickled Mushrooms, Artichoke Bottoms, Morels, Truffles,
> and Forcemeat Balls in almost every Made Dish.[23]

This piece of advice was very close to Hannah Glasse's in 1747 and was inspired
by Massialot and the court-cooks. The more subtle flavourings of Vincent La
Chapelle and his successors had not yet reached the kitchens of the English
gentry. The image of luxury cookery which is being presented to the prosperous
inhabitants of Manchester and its region is completely fossilized. What is happening here is the belated downward movement of a style which was already
present amongst the more fashionable gentry (and of those close to London,
the source of fashion) at the end of the seventeenth century. Given this huge
time-lag, it is not surprising that the receipts should have been so transformed
in the process. This process of adaptation provides an excellent example of the
diffusion and deformation of upper-class fashions described by Norbert Elias.
The appearance of the dish is kept, with its modestly lavish garnish, but its
basic nature, its flavoured sauce, has been utterly denatured – although this is,
of course, invisible when the dish is presented at table.

Elizabeth Raffald's book, which was enormously influential, enables us to
see both the attitude of the English towards French cookery and the way in
which the receipts of that cuisine were assimilated. She explained in her
preface:

---

[22] Jenks *The Complete Cook* (1768), p. 174.

[23] Raffald (1769), p. 71. The same remark is to be found in Briggs (1788), pp. 215–219, Cole (1788),
p. 52, Collingwood & Woollams (1792), pp. 5–6, Farley, *The London Art of Cookery* (1783), p. 94, M.
Smith (1772), pp. 107–108.

Though I have given some of my Dishes French Names, as they are only
known by those Names, yet they will not be found very Expensive, nor
add Compositions but as plain as the Nature of the Dish will admit of.[24]

She omitted any receipt for cullis, a notoriously expensive composition to
English eyes, and one which she considered useless:

I have given no Directions for Cullis, as I have found by Experience,
that Lemon Pickle and Browning answers both for Beauty and Taste, (at
a trifling Expence) better than Cullis, which is extravagant.[25]

These two substitute preparations were given at the beginning of her book, just
as French authors placed basic broths and cullises at the beginning of theirs.
(Unfortunately, the recent reprint of the first edition of Mrs Raffald's book
moves the two receipts to the chapter on 'made dishes', since the editor believes
that their original position shows that 'they were printed there as an after-
thought,'[26] which is manifestly not the case.) The lemon pickle was made with
dried quarters of lemon, steeped in white wine vinegar with mace, cloves, nutmeg, garlic and mustard seed, allowed to stand for three months then strained
and fined and bottled. The reader is told it makes a good addition to any made
dish or fish dish, and 'gives a pleasant flavour'. Browning was caramel dissolved
in red wine with Jamaica pepper, cloves, shallots, mace, mushroom 'catchup',
salt and lemon rind. The first preparation could be used in white and brown
sauces, the second of course was for brown sauces only.[27]

The other basic preparation used in English made dishes was catchup. This
bore no relation to today's tomato ketchup. It was a thin brown liquid, the
most frequent variations being made with a mushroom, walnut, oyster or

---

[24] Raffald (1769), p. ii.

[25] Ibid., p. iii. This comment is reproduced by Mary Cole, although Cole does in fact give 8 receipts
for cullis; see Cole (1788), p. 319.

[26] Ann Bagnall's editorial note to the reprint of *The Experienced English Housekeeper* (1997), p. vi.

[27] Raffald (1769), pp. 2–3. Very similar receipts for 'lemon pickle' are found in Cole (1788), pp. 322–
323, Collingwood & Woollams (1792), pp. 187–188, Farley (1783), pp. 228–229, Henderson, *The
Housekeeper's Instructor* (c.1795), p. 119; and for 'browning' in Cole, p. 53, Collingwood & Woollams,
pp. 186–187, Farley, p. 133, Henderson, p. 55, Townshend (1773), p. 38.

anchovy base. The first was made by salting and heating mushrooms to extract the juices which were boiled down with spices before bottling; the three other kinds were made with wine or vinegar, or in some cases, alegar.[28] Mushroom catchup was already a very old receipt by this date: Rebecca Price's MS collection gives a version entitled, '*To make catchup to be put into any sauces*'.[29] These were the ready-made English sauce bases which replaced French cullisses. It is significant that English made dishes call for these ingredients, enabling the cook to make 'instant' sauces. As we shall see, English cookery brought its ingredients together for only short cooking-times, whereas French sauces had usually been long simmered to produce a thorough mix of flavours. Furthermore, the flavour of English dishes was not at all like those presented by French cooks such as Clermont. The use of vinegar-based bottled 'sauces' gave a sharper note than his few drops of lemon juice. Raffald was also fond of anchovy, which is present in 32 of her 92 'made dishes'. These flavours were close to those produced by the 'domestic' version of court-cookery of the beginning of the eighteenth century, and indeed recorded by Rebecca Price thirty years earlier.

The books written or compiled by male tavern-cooks included much the same material as their female rivals. The tavern-cook whose book was the most successful, to judge by the number of editions (the 12th appeared in 1811[30]) was John Farley, and it is interesting to compare his book with Clermont's. The first striking difference lies in the way the contents are organized. Clermont begins by giving receipts for broth and cullis, then, after soups, the receipts for sauces are placed before the receipts for dishes: here are the basics of French cuisine. Farley begins with advice on marketing[31] then goes straight to chapters on boiling, roasting, baking, grilling and frying.[32] The bases of English cookery are not the standardized preparations which enable the cook to produce a

[28] All four types are found in Martin, *The New Experienced English-Housekeeper* (1795), pp. 132–134; for other examples see Briggs (1788), pp. 595–596; Collingwood & Woollams (1792), pp. 308–309; Farley (1783), pp. 227–228; Mason (1773), pp. 319–320; Raffald (1769), pp. 316–318; Townshend (1773), p. 226.

[29] See Masson, *The Compleat Cook* (1974), pp. 115–116. There is also a receipt in R. Bradley, *The Country Housewife* (1727), pp. 142–143.

[30] See Oxford, *English Cookery Books to the Year 1850* (1979), p. 114.

[31] See Farley (1783), pp. 4–15.

[32] Ibid., pp. 16–62.

variety of dishes by ringing the changes on the sauce theme. It is the cooking methods which are the components of a much simpler and more robust culinary style.

Sauces do not come into the picture until the twelfth chapter and, here again, the gulf between the two cuisines is obvious. Consider, for example, Farley's sweet sauce for venison, still the most prestigious meat amongst the gentry. He gives three versions, all combining sweet and sharp in varying proportions – reminiscent of sixteenth-century tastes:

> VENISON SAUCES.
> Either of these sauces may be used for venison. Currant-jelly warmed; or half a pint of red wine, with a quarter of a pound of sugar, simmered over a clear fire for five or six minutes; or half a pint of vinegar, and a quarter of a pound of sugar, simmered till it be a syrup.[33]

After this very simple prescription, Farley gives two receipts for 'gravy',[34] the first made with meat, the second without. In French cookery, these would be the basis for making sauces by adding more ingredients, but here, at the end of the second receipt, Farley tells the reader that this can be used as a sauce for fish, without further ado. The meatless gravy is typical of this period:

> BROWN GRAVY.
> Take half a pint of water, and the same quantity of ale …. Cut an onion and a little piece of lemon-peel small; take three cloves, a blade of mace, some whole pepper, a spoonful of mushroom pickle, the same quantity of catchup, and an anchovy. Put a piece of butter … into a saucepan, and when it be melted, shake in a little flour, and let it be a little brown. Then by degrees stir in the above ingredients, and let it boil a quarter of an hour. Then strain it, and it will be a good sauce for fish.[35]

There are not many ingredients and much of the flavour comes from stored sauces made at home or purchased ready-made. Another characteristic is the

---

[33] Farley (1783), p. 131. See also the very similar receipts in Briggs (1788), p. 124; Mason (1773), p. 157; Cole (1788), pp. 10–11.

[34] See Farley (1783), pp. 131–133.

[35] Ibid., pp. 132–133.

brief cooking time. This gravy is remarkably similar to one given by Sarah Harrison in 1733 entitled, 'A cheap Gravy'.[36] She used the same ingredients, save the catchup and the anchovy. Something explicitly described as 'cheap' in 1733 has joined the standard repertoire in one of the more up-market books fifty years later: an illustration of the downward progress of the cookery book, and a striking example of the universal preoccupation with economy, even amongst the better-off, so typical of English cookery writing.

On the whole, Farley's sauces are much simpler than Clermont's, even if there are occasional similarities, as for instance the 'sauce Robert'.[37] Most are characteristically English, such as mint sauce, apple sauce, and the bread sauce to accompany turkey or game birds.[38] Several are based on melted butter, plus the item which gives its name to the sauce, as in lobster sauce, egg sauce, or shrimp sauce.[39] Even cream sauces are very simple, like this instruction for celery:

> Boil your celery ... and add half a pint of cream, some mace and nut-meg, and a small piece of butter rolled in flour. Then give them a gentle boil. This is a good sauce for either roasted or boiled fowls, turkies, partridges, or any other game.[40]

This reveals another essential characteristic of English cookery: sauces are accompaniments to meat cooked by one of two basic cooking methods, roasting or boiling. Sauces are not an integral part of a dish. In the whole of the sauce chapter in Farley, only one sauce has other ingredients added to it to create a dish, and this is the sauce for carp made with the fish's blood.[41] There are only 26 receipts for sauce in Farley – just over one-third the number found in Clermont.

Farley's stews are also much simpler than Clermont's. Here is his receipt for stewed mushrooms:

---

[36] See Harrison, *The House-keeper's Pocket-Book* (1733), p. 107.

[37] See Clermont (1769), p. 41; Farley (1783), pp. 134–135.

[38] See Farley (1783), pp. 134–137.

[39] Ibid., pp. 139, 141. The last two receipts reappear verbatim in Collingwood & Woollams (1792), pp. 182,183.

[40] Farley (1783), p. 142.

[41] Ibid., pp. 139–140.

Peel some large mushrooms, and take out the inside. Broil them on a
gridiron, and when the outside be brown, put them in a tossing-pan,
with a quantity of water sufficient to cover them. Having let them stand
ten minutes, put to them a spoonful of white wine, the same of
browning, and a very little allegar. Thicken it with butter and flour, and
boil it a little. Serve it up with sippets round the dish.[42]

The preliminary broiling of the mushrooms and the use of browning and
alegar are the ingredients and techniques of English cookery. The sharp note
is again provided by alegar rather than lemon juice. The thickened sauce is
boiled only briefly, whereas Clermont's raggoo of mushrooms is simmered for
an hour. As for the other stews given by Farley, this is a dish rather than a
garnish: the French system, whereby such a raggoo could be added to a dish
of meat to create a new recipe, is unknown.

The same ingredients and techniques appear in other receipts which had
begun life as French, but which by now had been thoroughly adapted and
incorporated into the English repertoire, such as the hash. Farley gives several
receipts in which cold roast meat is cut into slices, then reheated in sauce, as
here for mutton:

When you intend to hash your mutton, you must cut it in slices, and
put a pint of gravy or broth into a tossing-pan, with a spoonful of mushroom catchup, and one of browning. Add to it a sliced onion, and a little
pepper and salt. Put it over the fire, and thicken it with butter and flour.
When it boils, put in your mutton; keep shaking it till it be perfectly
hot, and then serve it up in a soup-dish.[43]

The 'hâchis', which had been fashionable and luxurious at the Restoration
(in 1661 Pepys recorded his satisfaction at being able to consume such a dish[44]),

---

[42] Farley (1783), p. 83. Other raggoo receipts are to be found pp. 79–84.

[43] Ibid., p. 63. See also hashes of veal, p. 68, and of venison, p. 69. Charlotte Mason gives a mutton
hash for which she recommends the cook to add the roasting juices of the meat to the sauce: see
Mason (1773), p. 221. Mary Cole gives the same receipt, but without identifying Mason as the author,
and she also reproduces Farley's receipt, here again, without attribution; however, when she
reproduces Farley's receipt for veal, she does credit him. See Cole (1788), pp. 138, 137–138, 116.

[44] See Pepys, *Diary*, vol. 2, p. 207.

has become something quickly prepared, using leftover meat.[45] Obviously, such things were very useful, given the amount of roast meat which appeared on English tables, much of which must necessarily have returned to the kitchens. It enabled the cook to use up the relics and produce a hot dish which, as we shall see in the study of menus, was often served at supper. Charlotte Mason gives another example of a hash, presented with a French name, even though the receipt gives a very adapted version of the sauce we saw in Verral:

> Chickens hashed, called bichamele.
> Cut a cold chicken to pieces, little bones and all; if you have no gravy make a little with long bones, onion, spice, &c. flower the chicken, put it into the gravy, with white pepper, salt, nutmeg, grated lemon peel; let it boil; then stir in an egg mixed with a little cream; when you take it off the fire squeeze in a little lemon juice; put it into a dish, lay over it some bread crumbs; brown them with a salamander.[46]

This is less refined than Verral's version of 1759: there is less cream, and the succinct instructions for making the gravy show how unimportant such basics were in English cookery. Sauces 'à la Béchamel' are to be found in other books of the period: its nature varies according to the degree of the author's acquaintance with authentic French versions. Mary Smith's is for a cream sauce, even though her knowledge of French cookery appears purely aural (as Verral's had been), since the title of her receipt is 'POLARD *Besh-a-mell*'.[47]

Another dish which belonged to both French and English traditions was duck with green peas. Clermont braised the duck and the peas separately; the two were assembled after this initial cooking process, with a cullis added to enrich and thicken the sauce. The English used a different technique: the ducks were half-roasted on the spit, then cooked in sauce with the peas, in a reversal of the usual process by which the French cooked things together whereas the

---

[45] Of course, at the Restoration, the hash was not made from leftovers: Hannah Woolley called for raw veal, washed over with eggs and herbs, then sautéed in butter and simmered gently to finish cooking. The name of the dish comes from the slashes made in the meat in order to make the seasoning flavours penetrate more thoroughly. Woolley, *The Cooks Guide* (1664), p. 79.

[46] Mason (1773), p. 242; the same receipt is given without attribution in Cole (1788), p. 195.

[47] See M. Smith (1772), p. 127.

English brought them together at the moment of serving. This is the version given by Mary Smith:

> DUCKS *and* GREEN PEASE.
> Half roast your ducks, put them into a stew-pan, with a pint of gravy, a cabbage lettice cut small, and a little pepper and salt; boil a pint of green pease tender, put them to your ducks, let them stew for a quarter of an hour, then thicken up your gravy, lay your ducks in a dish, pour your sauce over them, and serve them up hot. This is a pretty first course dish.[48]

Elizabeth Raffald gives a similar receipt, but she puts in mint and sage leaves rather than lettuce. Her version is found in several of her imitators' books.[49] It may be contended that the dish described here was a genuine part of the English repertoire. It did not, therefore, indulge in the various substitutions that characterize our adaptations of French recipes: there is no browning or lemon pickle in place of cullis. What is more, one even finds alternatives (mint and sage instead of lettuce) which suggest that this familiar repertoire stimulated authors' imaginations, making them produce variations on the theme in the same way as the French diversified their own repertoire.

But while some authors, notably Mary Smith, give good quality receipts for French-derived made dishes, the general trend is in the opposite direction. The ever-increasing emphasis on economy led to the elimination of expensive ingredients, long preparation and extended cooking times. Farley's receipts are simpler and quicker to make than Clermont's, yet about a third of them still bear French names. However, as in Elizabeth Raffald's 'French' dishes, these names all date back to the first half of the century: for instance, 'à-la-mode' or 'à-la-royal'.[50] However, the French tradition is not the only one. In both Raffald and Farley there are specifically English made dishes. One is:

---

[48] M. Smith (1772), p. 134.

[49] See Raffald (1769), p. 113; this receipt is also found in Cole (1788), p. 200; Mason (1773), p. 253; Townshend (1773), p. 114.

[50] See, for instance, Farley (1783), pp. 94, 101, 116, 117.

OXFORD JOHN.

Cut a stale leg of mutton into as thin collops as you can, and take out all the fat sinews. Season them with salt, pepper and mace, and strew among them a little shred parsley, thyme, and two or three shalots. Put a good lump of butter into a stew-pan, and as soon as it be hot, put in all your collops. Keep stirring them with a wooden spoon till they be three parts done, and then add half a pint of gravy, a little juice of lemon, and thicken it with flour and butter. Let them simmer four or five minutes, and they will be quite enough; but if you let them boil, … they will grow hard. Throw fried pieces of bread, cut in dices, over and round them, and serve them up hot.[51]

The fairly simple dish and its short cooking time are typical, yet its detailed instructions would be deemed superfluous in a French book. The cook is told to use a wooden spoon, and given the reason for the brief cooking, without boiling, once the sauce has been made. This is written for the uninitiated.

Another 'English' made dish found in several books of the period is curry. It first appeared in Hannah Glasse in 1747. From about 1765, it undergoes development and evolution. In 1769, J. Skeat suggested different spices (Glasse put in nothing more than pepper and coriander):

To make an Indian Curry.

Take mutton, beef, fowl, or fish, and cut them in small pieces as if to hash, beat some turmerick and coriander seeds very fine, mix them with your meat; then burn some fresh butter in a stewpan, and put in your meat, &c. and let it stew till enough; put some good gravy, and a little Chian pepper to it; then cut some long square pieces of cucumbers for it, and dry it over a slow fire; put your curry in a dish, and the rice round it with sausages. As to ingredients, you may put in what best suits your fancy; as mushrooms, small onions, chopt parsley, egg balls, &c.[52]

('Chian pepper' is Cayenne pepper.) The use of turmeric brought the dish closer to our conception of curry, although the additions at the end might

---

[51] Farley (1783), p. 111. This is one of the receipts he lifted from Raffald (1769), pp. 96–97. The same receipt was taken up by Briggs (1788), p. 251, and Cole (1788), pp. 138–139.

[52] Skeat, *The Art of Cookery and Pastery* (1769), p. 41.

charitably be called an echo of court-style garnishing or, uncharitably, a use of
the dish as a repository for leftovers. This receipt took for granted the rice
accompaniment ('*the* rice').

Four years later, Charlotte Mason instructed the cook to use a pre-prepared
spice mix. She also expected the curry to be served with boiled rice.

> Curree of chickens.
> Cut two chickens as for a fricasee, … let them boil till tenderish …; take
> up the chickens, put the liquor into a bason; put half a pound of butter
> into a pan, brown it a little, put to it two cloves of garlic, a large onion
> sliced, let these fry till brown, shaking the pan; put in the chickens,
> strew over them two large spoonfuls of curree powder; cover the pan
> close, let the chickens do till brown, often shaking the pan; put in the
> liquor the chickens were boiled in, let all stew till they are tender: if acid
> is agreeable, when the chickens are taken off the fire squeeze in the juice
> of an orange, or a lemon.[53]

Curry receipts became much more frequent after 1780: Richard Briggs gave
two, for veal and for chicken, in which the spice mix is called 'curric powder';[54]
Mrs Frazer called for the same ready-mixed powder, but added cream to her
dish, otherwise very similar to Charlotte Mason's.[55] Others added turmeric to
the powder (which presumably contained turmeric already), or made their own
using ginger, turmeric and pepper.[56] Instructions for home-made 'curry
powder', so called, occur at the same time[57] but one could also buy it ready-
made. The household accounts of Elizabeth Austen (the novelist's father's
cousin's wife) for 1775 show that she frequently bought it for 2s. a bottle.[58] This
colonial dish had become a well-established feature of the English repertoire.

---

[53] Mason (1773), p. 245.

[54] See Briggs (1788), pp. 197, 245.

[55] See Frazer, *The Practice of Cookery* (1791), p. 69.

[56] See Kellet, *A Complete Collection of Cookery Receipts* (1780), pp. 28–29; Cole (1788), p. 191; *The Bath
Cookery Book* (c.1790), p. 76. The last two receipts are almost identical: they use the same mix of
spices and add cream and lemon juice to the sauce at the end of the cooking time.

[57] See, for instance, Martin (1795), p. 35.

[58] See the brief description of this household account book (in private hands) in Goodsall, *A Kentish
Patchwork* (1966), p. 20.

It first appeared in books published in London and thence spread to the provinces. There is nothing in Raffald (Manchester, 1769), but it was to be found in Mrs Frazer, published in Edinburgh in 1791. This process of dispersal was noticed by Catherine Hutton during a trip to Blackpool in around 1790:

> The progress of the arts, even the art of cookery, is from south to north. We have here the wife of the rector of Rochdale, a gentlewoman of the old school, in person and manner resembling a good fat housekeeper, who, I dare say, never heard of a curry in her life, yet is excellently skilled in pickling shrimps, potting herrings, raising goose pies, and flourishing in pastry.[59]

Pickling, potting and pastry: these are the skills of the seventeenth-centry gentlewoman; the term 'flourishing' is a reminder of the decorated pies and tarts of the Restoration court-cooks such as Robert May. The arrival of a dish such as curry denoted the spread of metropolitan fashions, and was proof of the growing commercialization of food products. Mrs Frazer's receipt used ready-made curry powder, presumably on sale locally. Similarly, cooks everywhere could buy the catchups and pickles that appeared so frequently in their manuals. Here are the first signs of attempts to cater to a market for pre-prepared ingredients, a trend which has led in our own day to the 'ready-to-heat' meals for sale in supermarkets.

Another English made dish is Elizabeth Raffald's hare stew:

> *To jug a* Hare.
> Cut the Hare as for eating, season it with Pepper, Salt, and beaten Mace, put it into a Jug or Pitcher, with a close Top, put to it a Bundle of sweet Herbs, and set it in a Kettle of boiling Water, let it stand 'till it is tender, then take it up and pour the Gravy into a tossing Pan, with a Glass of Red Wine, one Anchovy, a large Onion stuck with Cloves, a little beaten Mace, and Chyan Pepper to your Taste, boil it a little and thicken it; dish up your Hare and strain the Gravy over it, then send it up.[60]

---

[59] Beale (ed.), *Reminiscences of a Gentlewoman of the last Century* (1891), p. 57.
[60] Raffald (1769), p. 121.

This is certainly conservative. The wine and anchovy combination takes the reader back once more to the receipts collected by Rebecca Price in the 1680s. However, the technique of jugging was used in that earlier collection for pigeons and ducks, not hares. And the sauce, made of the juices thickened with 'beurre manié', was quite unlike Mrs Raffald's.[61] Today, jugging is invariably associated with hare and we may descry in Raffald a process of codification of the English repertoire – just as existed in contemporary France. Interestingly, receipts for this dish found in other books of the period are not identical to Raffald.[62] As noticed with reference to duck and green peas, above, when describing specifically English cookery, eighteenth-century writers were less prone to outright plagiarism.

The made dishes we have been discussing appeared at the first course of dinner but did not occupy the centre of the table. That was an honour often kept for a key dish of grand English cuisine in the second half of the eighteenth century, the turtle. The earliest receipts appear around the middle of the century. The first edition of Hannah Glasse has nothing, but the omission was rectified in the appendix to the fifth edition of 1755.[63] Thereafter, receipts are common enough in the luxury books and one also finds instructions for the cheaper replacement, calf's head cooked 'turtle fashion'.[64]

Receipts are long and complicated. The cook had to prepare the various parts of the creature separately so that, when it was served, the turtle formed five dishes:

> Have the callapash, or deep shell, done round the edges with paste, ...
> bake it half an hour, then put in the lungs and white meat, forcemeat,
> and eggs over, and bake half an hour. Take the bones, and three quarts
> of veal broth, seasoned with an onion, a bundle of sweet herbs, two

---

[61] See Masson (1974), p. 89.

[62] See Cole (1788), p. 227; Collingwood & Woollams (1792), p. 143; M. Smith (1772), pp. 122–123; Townshend (1773), pp. 130–131.

[63] See Glasse, *The Art of Cookery, Made Plain and Easy* (1755), pp. 331–332.

[64] See, especially, Raffald (1769), pp. 12–15 (turtle), 71–73 (veal); Farley (1783), pp. 144–145 (veal); Mason (1773), pp. 179–180 (veal); Cole (1788), pp. 235–242 (turtle and veal); Briggs (1788), pp. 64–68 (turtle), 68–69 (sturgeon turtle style); Collingwood & Woollams (1792), pp. 177–180 (turtle and veal); Martin (1795), p. 34 (veal); Price, *The New Book of Cookery* (c.1780), pp. 64–65 (turtle and veal). This last is a rare example of turtle in a cheap book.

blades of mace; stew it an hour, strain through a sieve, thicken it with butter and flour, put in half a pint of Madeira wine, stew it half an hour; season with cayenne pepper and salt. This is the soup. Take the callapee, run a knife between the meat and shell, and fill it full of force-meat; season all over; … put a paste round the edge, and bake an hour and a half. Take the guts and maw, put them in a stew-pan, with a little broth, a bundle of sweet herbs, two blades of mace beat fine; thicken it with a little butter rolled in flour, stew them gently for half an hour, season, … beat up the yolks of two eggs in half a pint of cream, put it in, and keep stirring it up one way till it boils up, then dish them as follows:

	CALLAPEE.	
FRICASSEE	SOUP	FINS
	CALLAPASH.[65]	

The fins were served in a clear broth, flavoured with Madeira. The five dishes could make a 'turtle dinner' on their own, or could form an impressive centre-piece. During the second half of the eighteenth century, the turtle rivalled venison for prestige, one to invite people to come and share as a particular honour. The difference between them is that venison owed its status to the fact that only the upper classes had legal access to it, whereas turtle was available to all who could afford it. Venison could be seen as representing tradition, the old order of a rural society, whereas the turtle was an exotic import, a product of the commercial empire.

This discussion of made dishes in English cookery books has not yet produced any obvious equivalents of the *petits plats* of French *haute cuisine*. English 'little savoury dishes' tended to appear at supper. Elizabeth Raffald gives 33 such receipts, curiously inserted in the second part of her book dealing with confectionery.[66] Amongst them are small raggoos and fricassees made with offal or with vegetables, several dishes of fish or meat in jelly, and such simple things as gratiné mashed potato:

---

[65] *The Bath Cookery Book*, p. 87.
[66] See Raffald (1769), pp. 256–268.

To scollop Potatoes.

Boil your Potatoes, then beat them fine in a Bowl with good Cream, a
Lump of Butter and Salt, put them into scollop'd Shells, make them
smooth on the Top, score them with a Knife, lay thin Slices of Butter on
the Top of them, put them into a Dutch Oven to brown before the Fire.[67]

Kirkpatrick in his book promoting the potato said that this was the form in
which potatoes appeared at the best tables, at supper.[68] Other writers give
similar small dishes, including variations on the 'rabbit' – melted cheese served
on toast, which was in Glasse in 1747 – and even sandwiches, which made their
first appearance in Charlotte Mason.[69] In this area, English authors had a
repertoire that was partly English and partly Anglo-French.

In the more traditional areas of English cookery, the impression is one of
continuity. There were large numbers of pies and puddings, and creams still
played an important part amongst the sweet dishes. A few examples will suffice.
The most important change in pies was the almost total disappearance of the
meat-sugar association. Raffald gave 21 pie receipts. Of these, only four
contained sugar and/or dried fruit: an apple pie, two mince-pies in which dried
fruit was mixed with beef suet and minced meat (a neat's tongue in one, calf's
feet in the other), and a sweet veal pie.[70] The same conclusion would be drawn
from reading Mary Smith and John Farley.[71] Sugar had disappeared from all
other pies, even from potato pies, which at the beginning of the century were
always sweetened. The separation of sweet and savoury, already well advanced
in the books by the court-cooks at the beginning of the century, was now an
established fact. The old style would soon survive only in mince-pies. With the
separation of flavours well established, new pie receipts were increasing the
variety on offer. Mary Smith suggested a chicken pie to make in the summer
and eat hot:

---

[67] Raffald (1769), p. 263. There are similar receipts in Mason (1773), p. 172; *The Bath Cookery Book*,
p. 128; Kellet (1780), p. 187.

[68] See Kirkpatrick, *An Account* (1796), p. 38.

[69] For 'rabbits' ('Scotch rabbit' and 'English rabbit', as well as 'Welsh rabbit') see for instance Glasse,
The Art of Cookery (1747), p. 97; Peckham, *The Complete English Cook* (1767), pp. 146–147; Briggs
(1788), pp. 355–356. For sandwiches, see Mason (1773), p. 235.

[70] Raffald (1769), pp. 128–139. These 'sweet' pies are found pp. 133, 134, 136, 138.

[71] See M. Smith (1772), pp. 215–228; Farley (1783), pp. 198–219.

A CHICKEN PIE *in July.*

Clean and pick three chickens, cut them in pieces as you do for a fricassee, season them with pepper, salt, and lace; have ready a coffin neatly made of hot paste, put in the chickens with a little broth, ornament it, and set it in the oven to bake for two hours. While it is baking, get ready half a pint of green pease, boil them tender, – boil half a pint of cream for ten minutes, then throw in the pease with a piece of butter and flour, a little salt, and nutmeg, – let it simmer five minutes; then raise up the lid of the pie, and pour it in, add a little juice of lemon, and serve it up.[72]

This seasonal variant on the theme of hot pies shows how English cuisine had its own types of dish with infinite variations. One notices also that the instructions are aimed at a cook who knows what she is doing: how to cut up chickens for a fricassee, how to raise a hot-water crust, how long to boil peas. But Mary Smith is one of the cooks who shows the most familiarity with French as well as English cooking techniques.

Puddings were as conservative as pies, and were still either baked or boiled. Raffald gives a total of 30, of which 14 are baked.[73] The baked puddings, cooked in a dish with a rim of puff pastry, resemble those described by her female predecessors. For instance, her orange pudding is very similar to Mary Kettilby's of 1714. Another example of this type shows that it was not necessarily a hearty, filling dish:

A Transparent Pudding.

Beat eight Eggs very well, and put them in a Pan, with half a Pound of Butter, and the same weight of Loaf Sugar beat fine, a little grated Nutmeg, set it on the Fire and keep stirring it 'till it thickens …, then put it in a Bason to cool, roll a rich puff Paste very thin, lay it round the Edge of a China Dish, then pour in the Pudding, and bake it in a moderate Oven half an Hour, it will cut light and clear.

It is a pretty Pudding for a Corner for Dinner, and a Middle for Supper.[74]

---

[72] M. Smith (1772), p. 217.

[73] See Raffald (1769), pp. 145–157.

[74] Raffald (1769), p. 149. This receipt also appears in Cole (1788), pp. 351–352, in Farley (1783), pp. 186–187, and, with slight variations, in Briggs (1788), p. 380.

Boiled puddings tended to be more solid. The famous plum pudding which appears so often in diary accounts of meals amongst the lesser gentry and the middle classes (we shall see examples of such menus later) is a classic example:

PLUM-PUDDING *boiled*.

Cut a pound of suet into little pieces, … a pound of currants …, a pound of raisins stoned, eight yolks of eggs and four whites, half a nutmeg grated, a teaspoonful of beaten ginger, a pound of flour, and a pint of milk. Beat the eggs first, then put to them half the milk, and beat them together, and by degrees stir in the flour, then the suet, spice, and fruit, and as much milk as will mix it well together very thick. It will take five hours boiling.[75]

Boiled in a cloth (no instructions are given for this operation), the mixture would have to be thick if it was to hold together when turned out. Raffald's general remarks at the beginning of her chapter on puddings concerned those boiled in a basin as well as in a cloth. She implied that 'light' puddings should be cooked in a basin, and care exercised in turning them out to prevent them breaking. She did not give a receipt for plum pudding.

Even the expensive books included some simple English dishes. In 1788 Richard Briggs gave one for a derivation of the pudding:

Toad in a Hole.

Mix a pound of flour with a pint and a half of milk and four eggs into a batter, put in a little salt, beaten ginger, and a little grated nutmeg, put it into a deep dish that you intend to send it to table in, take the veiney part of beef, sprinkle it with salt, put it into the batter, bake it two hours, and send it up hot.[76]

Similar receipts are found in more modest books. *The British Jewel*, for instance, gives another version, 'Pigeons in a Hole', which had first appeared in

---

[75] Farley (1783), pp. 179–180. The same receipt, expressed somewhat differently, appears in Cole (1788), p. 347 (without attribution); in Collingwood & Woollams (1792), pp. 228–229. Richard Briggs adds a little sugar and candied lemon peel: see Briggs (1788), pp. 360–361.

[76] Briggs (1788), p. 175.

Hannah Glasse.[77] It was a relatively humble dish and the name itself was new. In 1765 Thomas Turner was eating something similar, made with sausages:

> I dined on a sausage batter pudding baked (which is this: a little flour and milk beat up into a batter with an egg and some salt and a few sausages cut in pieces and put in it and then baked).[78]

The fact that he should feel the need to describe the dish suggests it was new to him. But he does not yet give it the name used by cookery books some years later. Today, 'Toad in the hole' is made with sausages, like Turner's pudding: one more instance of the stabilization or codification of English cookery.

It would be easy to continue giving examples of English dishes which were appearing in the cookery books at this period but which had clearly been developed earlier. The more expensive books demonstrate the vigorous nature of traditional English cookery and its continued development in the face of the onslaught by fashionable French cuisine. Even in the area of made dishes, English cooks created their own particular repertoire, and truly English receipts are more interesting than those which tended to be pale imitations of French models.

The sweetmeats and sweet dishes served as part of the second course of dinner and at dessert were perhaps the clearest signs of a vigorous English tradition. Here, too, there were parallel schools: on the one hand the style practised in the grand houses, described by Clermont and in books by professional confectioners; on the other, receipts presented by women authors, cooks and housekeepers to the gentry and the middle classes, which harked back to the still-rooms of the seventeenth and early eighteenth centuries.

The *nouvelle cuisine* of the 1730s had had less impact on confectionery than on other branches of cookery. In the previous chapter on mid-century culinary styles, the dessert course did not receive much attention because the cookery books of the period devote far more space to made dishes than to confectionery. It no longer had the prestige it enjoyed during the previous century. Glasse, for instance, gave 225 receipts in her 'made dishes' chapter, while her chapter on creams and jellies contained 36 receipts, and the chapter on conserves 23.

---

[77] *The British Jewel* (1776), p. 19; Glasse, *The Art of Cookery* (1747), p. 46.
[78] Vaisey (ed.), *The Diary of Thomas Turner 1754–1765* (1985), p. 313.

There is no hint of transformation in manuals of confectionery before 1750, the year Menon's *La Science du Maître d'Hôtel, Confiseur* appeared. This book contained a presentation of the ideas behind what has to be called *nouvelle confiserie*, as well as receipts demonstrating the innovations which had taken place in the kitchen but had not yet been recorded. The preface mentioned Massialot's confectionery book (*Nouvelle Instruction pour les Confitures, les Liqueurs et les Fruits*, which actually dates from 1692, although Menon refers to the last treatise published on the subject as dating from 1691[79]), and discussed the changes which had happened to confectionery in the last twenty years – meaning between 1730 and 1750:[80]

> The art of confectionery, like the other culinary arts, has by degrees reached perfection in its variety; so that the Work then published is virtually useless for today's confectioner. Even without going back as far as the end of the last century, in the last twenty years, what a new appearance does the art of confectionery present! And without going into the details of today's operations, what a difference between our desserts and those of earlier times! What has become of those pyramids that one used to see on the table, erected with more hard work and laboriousness than with taste and elegance? … In a word, the difference between confectionery nowadays and in earlier times is almost as great as the difference between modern and gothick architecture. Instead of

---

[79] See [Menon], *La Science du Maître d'Hôtel, Confiseur* (1750), p. ii.

[80] 'L'art de l'Office, de même que les autres, s'est perfectionné par les variations comme par autant de dégrés; de maniere que l'Ouvrage publié alors est presque inutile pour l'Office d'aujourd'hui. Sans remonter même jusqu'à la fin du dernier siécle; depuis vingt ans, quelle nouvelle face l'art de l'Office n'a-t-il pas pris? Et pour ne pas entrer dans le détail de toute la manoeuvre d'aujourd'hui, quelle différence de nos desserts à ceux d'autrefois? Que sont devenues ces pyramides érigées avec plus de travail & d'industrie que de goût & d'élegance qu'on voyoit sur nos tables? … En un mot, il y a presque entre l'Office moderne & celui d'autrefois la même difference, qu'entre l'Architecture moderne & l'Architecture gotique. Au lieu de ces especes d'édifices chargés d'ornemens compassés avec une pénible symétrie, une élegante simplicité fait toute la beauté & le principal mérite de nos desserts. Mais quoique plus simples, quelle charmante varieté inconnue à nos Peres, n'y remarque-t-on pas? … Voyez ce Parterre orné de figures en sucre, … décorées de sable en sucre de differentes couleurs, d'arbres, de fruits secs, de pots à fleurs, de berceaux, de guirlandes, avec des compartimens en chenille de diverses couleurs. Quelle intelligence! Quel goût! Quelle aimable symetrie!' Menon (1750), pp. ii–iv.

those constructions loaded with ornaments, placed with painstaking symmetry, elegance and simplicity now produce all the beauty and are the principal merit of our desserts. But while our desserts are simpler, what a delightful variety, unknown to our forefathers, is present in them! Look at this parterre, with its statues in sugar-work, decorated with sands made of different-coloured sugars, with trees, dried fruits, pots of flowers, arches and swags, with compartments made of chenille in various colours. How intelligent! How tasteful! How charmingly regular!

It is easy to see here the same ideas as had been used to glorify 'nouvelle cuisine' in the 1730s: harmony, simplicity, and the rejection of the laborious pyramids so characteristic of court-cookery.

The first plate in Menon represents a garden parterre in the French style, with a complex symmetrical design; the second illustrates the classical statues and balustrades which the confectioner should dispose in the middle of his parterres. The accompanying text explains how to create these by cutting out the illustrated shapes in card, edging the cut-outs with chenille, and filling up the interstices with different coloured 'sands' of coloured sugar. Unfortunately, the book gives no details about making the statues and balustrades.[81] The plates and dishes ('compotes & assiettes') containing the sweetmeats are placed all around the central parterre. Thus the dessert in 1750 reproduces the formal French garden on the table. The English dessert soon began to do the same thing, but to its own designs. Instructions for garden-style desserts do not appear in English cookery books until the 1760s, but it seems that such things were being created in the 1750s, just as in France. In January 1754 Lady Jane Coke wrote to her friend Mrs Eyre:

Lady Northumberland gave an entertainment last week .... The desert was a landscape, with gates, stiles, and cornfields, but I have, I'm afraid, tired you with the account of such follies.[82]

We can only regret that Lady Jane considered this a 'folly' and gave no further details beyond identifying it as a landscape rather than a formal garden – a

---

[81] Menon (1750), in the plates at the beginning of the book. The receipt for 'sable' is pp. 493–494.
[82] Rathborne (ed.), *Letters from Lady Jane Coke to her friend Mrs. Eyre at Derby, 1747–1758* (1899), p. 135.

significant difference. When we come to English receipts we shall see this style in practice.

Menon showed the variety of the sweetmeats on offer, and this abundant variety was one of the points he made in the preface. Besides fruit conserves, which are closer to fruit jellies than to the heavier pastes of the seventeenth century,[83] we find receipts for ices, both sorbets and iced creams and 'cheeses' ('fromages'),[84] and meringues.[85] There are also creamy mousses set in decorative moulds and turned out for the table,[86] but the jellies and flummeries of English cookery books do not appear. Nor are they found in other French books or their English translations. Clermont, who included some confectionery receipts at the end of his translation of *Les Soupers de la Cour*, gave conserves of fruit and flowers, with a few biscuits and ices, and an explanation of how to make the different-coloured 'sands' in sugar.[87] His ices were made with cream and fruit, and he gave several sorbets, moulded to imitate real fruit.[88] There were similar receipts, but in very small numbers, in the appendix to volume 3 of La Chapelle.[89] However, their presence as early as 1733 shows that the *nouvelle confiserie* described by Menon was as much a question of presentation as of new receipts. Clermont demonstrates the importance of appearance with his suggestions (found among the cookery receipts) for an elegant arrangement of ices in buckets made of almond paste or in a hollowed-out cake (a 'gâteau de Savoie').[90] This elaboration suggests that ices were no longer a sufficiently impressive novelty in themselves, as they had been at the beginning of the century: something more was required to produce what Michael Smith describes as the 'gosh factor'.[91] In the upper strata of society, ices were taken for granted, whereas lower down the social scale, they were still a rarity before 1760.

---

[83] See, for instance, the receipts for 'clarequets' (what the English called 'clearcakes'), Menon (1750), pp. 59, 82, 111–112, 210.

[84] Ibid., pp. 165–173, 182–189.

[85] Ibid., pp. 471–472.

[86] Ibid., pp. 174–176, 485–493.

[87] See Clermont (1769), pp. 506–588.

[88] Ibid., pp. 572–577.

[89] See La Chapelle, *The Modern Cook* (1733), vol. 3, appendix, pp. 34–38.

[90] See Clermont (1769), pp. 409–412.

[91] Smith, *New English Cookery* (1985), p. 43.

What had happened to the dessert in gentry houses in the years between 1730 and 1760? In the study of culinary styles to 1730, we saw a few examples of receipts which look back to the fruit conserves of the sixteenth and seventeenth centuries, as well as receipts for creams. But the most striking aspect of the dessert then was the presentation in pyramids of the various sweetmeats, echoing the presentation of the grand olios and terrines. The cookery books of the middle of the century offer similar receipts, but with more emphasis on creams and jellies than on the traditional dry and wet fruit preserves. Hannah Glasse borrowed most of her receipts for creams from the 10th edition (1741) of E. Smith;[92] here we find creams and syllabubs which are similar to those we have already seen from earlier periods.[93] Amongst the receipts which do not come from this source is one for moulded creams:

Jelly *of* Cream.
Take four Ounces of Hartshorn, put it on in three Pints of Water, let it boil till it is a stiff Jelly, which you will know by taking a little in a Spoon to cool; then strain it off, and add to it half a Pint of Cream, two Spoonfuls of Rose-water, two Spoonfuls of Sack, and sweeten to your Taste. Then give it a gentle boil, but keep stirring it all the time, or it will curdle; then take it off, and stir it till it is cold; then put it into broad Bottom-cups, let them stand all Night, and turn them out into a Dish; take half a Pint of Cream, two Spoonfuls of Rose-water, and as much Sack; sweeten to your Palate, and pour over them.[94]

This receipt is similar to one a few pages later for a 'Hartshorn Flummery', called thus to distinguish it from the traditional 'Oatmeal Flummery'[95] made from oatmeal soaked in water, a dish which originated in Wales.[96] This is a type of cream which is peculiar to English cookery. A similar preparation is used to make 'Steeple Cream',[97] which owed its name to the conical mould which gave it its shape. These moulded creams were ideal for table decoration,

---

[92] See Stead, 'Quizzing Glasse: or Hannah Scrutinized, Part II' (1983), p. 30.

[93] See Glasse, *The Art of Cookery* (1747), pp. 143–145.

[94] Ibid., p. 143.

[95] Ibid., p. 146.

[96] See Wilson, *Food and Drink in Britain* (1976), pp. 193–194.

[97] See Glasse, *The Art of Cookery* (1747), p. 143.

and were beginning to be an essential element of the dessert course. (Such creamy jellies were by no means new: the milk jelly known as 'leach', turned out and cut into cubes, appeared in Dawson's *Good Huswifes Jewell* (1596), but the use of decorative moulds for creams and jellies was an eighteenth-century innovation.[98])

Although the material might have remained the same, the style of its arrangement certainly developed. In 1730, Charles Carter commends to the reader his receipts for 'Chequer'd *and* Ribband Jellies'; the jelly, coloured with saffron, spinach juice, violet syrup and clove gillyflower syrup (other colouring agents are also suggested), is poured in layers into an oiled dish and turned out. By cutting the jelly into slices, the cook could then reassemble the slices to make a chequered pattern.[99] The receipts are entitled 'Jelly, *or* Leech', and they are clearly the ultimate phase of elaboration of Dawson's sixteenth-century leach. By mid-century the decorative possibilities of different coloured jellies and creams were being taken even further. In 1756 Martha Bradley gives a receipt for an almond cream jelly, moulded in shapes to represent the moon and stars, these shapes then embedded in a transparent jelly flavoured with wine and lemon.[100] In 1767 Ann Peckham tells the cook how to make playing cards and a dish of bacon and eggs in coloured flummery and jelly.[101] By now, decorated moulds produced by the potteries in Staffordshire were becoming more easily available, and an ever-increasing variety of shapes was developed between 1750 and 1770.[102]

Perhaps the most important development in the dessert course was the wider dissemination of receipts for ice-cream, particularly through books written by professional confectioners. The two most important, Borella's *Court and Country Confectioner* (1770) and Frederick Nutt's *Complete Confectioner* (1789) are very similar: both have receipts for cakes and biscuits, fruit conserves (fruit pastes as well as fruit in syrup, the old 'dry' and 'wet' sweetmeats), creams, and

---

[98] See Brears, 'Rare Conceites and Strange Delightes', in Wilson (1991), p. 90.

[99] See Carter, *The Complete Practical Cook* (1730), address to the reader; the receipts are pp. 178–180. Hannah Glasse also gives a receipt for 'Ribband Jelly'; her jelly is not unmoulded, but set in glasses to display the coloured layers. See Glasse, *The Art of Cookery* (1747), p. 145.

[100] See Bradley, *The British Housewife* (1756), vol. 1, pp. 363–365. This receipt is taken from the 5th edition of Hannah Glasse.

[101] See Peckham, *The Complete English Cook* (1767), pp. 165–166.

[102] See Brears, 'Transparent Pleasures – The Story of the Jelly: Part Two 1700–1820', (1996), p. 30. This article also contains splendid illustrations by the author of these decorative dishes.

all sorts of ices.[103] It is the ices which are the most interesting, since they seldom appeared in mainstream cookery books before 1770. The first printed receipt for ice-cream was in 1718 in Mary Eales. Hannah Glasse did not include one in *The Art of Cookery* until her fifth edition of 1755, and only gave a single receipt in her *Compleat Confectioner* of 1760.[104] She commented in the later book that ices are an obligatory feature of any dessert and that one can purchase them ready-made all the year round at London confectioners.[105] Even by the very end of the century, cookery books tend to give only one receipt. Collingwood and Woollams give one for an apricot ice-cream,[106] and Elizabeth Marshall, writing for a readership of young ladies in the north of England, gives detailed instructions for freezing, without giving any receipts for the mixture itself.[107] This was just as Mary Eales had done in 1718. The confectioners, by contrast, offer an enormous variety: amongst those suggested by Borella are ice-creams flavoured with tea, chocolate, coffee, brown bread and pineapple.[108] This is his instruction for the first:

Tea Cream Ices.
Make tea very strong in a tea-pot, have your cream ready mixt with the proper quantity of sugar and yolks of eggs, pass your cream through a sieve, pass likewise your tea over it, mix the whole well with a spoon, when that is done … make it congeal according to the usual method.[109]

Borella seldom mentioned quantities. Frederick Nutt was more precise:

Ginger Ice Cream.
Take four ounces of ginger preserved, pound it and put it into a bason, with two gills of syrup, a lemon squeezed, and one pint of cream; then freeze it.[110]

---

[103] For the ices, see Borella, *The Court and Country Confectioner* (1770), part 1, pp. 75–97; Nutt, *The Complete Confectioner* (1789), pp. 112–139.

[104] See Glasse, *The Compleat Confectioner* (c.1760), pp. 161–162.

[105] Ibid., p. 252. Glasse's comments are confirmed by the dessert menus given by Frederick Nutt: all his menus contain ices. See Nutt (1789), in the plates between pp. xxiv–1.

[106] See Collingwood & Woollams (1792) p. 254.

[107] See Marshall, *The Young Ladies' Guide in the Art of Cookery* (1777), p. 70.

[108] See Borella (1770), part 1, pp. 89–90, 90, 93, 95–96, 96–97.

[109] Ibid., part 1, p. 96.   [110] Nutt (1789), p. 119.

Nutt, like Borella, has many flavours, including chocolate, coffe, caramel and brown bread, as well as various fruits. Whereas the mainstream cookery books gave instructions on freezing the mixtures, the confectioners took that part of the process for granted. The difference between professional knowledge and homely skills is obvious.

The receipts for biscuits and cakes also reveal the gap between professionals and amateurs. The latter give more big cakes, such as Elizabeth Raffald's fruit cake, her famous 'Bride Cake'[111] (which, contrary to standard practice earlier in the century, is raised with eggs rather than with yeast), while books by confectioners contain more *petits fours*, such as Robert Abbot's 'Ratafia Biscuits':

Ratafia Biscuits.
Take half a pound of sweet almonds, and half a pound of bitter: pound them fine, mixed with whites of eggs, then add two pounds and a half of sugar; beat it up well with whites of eggs, then drop them on paper, and bake them in a slow oven.[112]

These small delicacies, like the ices, were served as refreshments at balls and assemblies as well as at the dessert course. Refreshing too were the perfumed 'waters' such as Frederick Nutt described in his chapter entitled 'Waters, &c. for routs', including:

Fresh Rasberry Water.
Take one pint of fresh rasberries; and pass them through a sieve with a wooden spoon; put two large spoonfuls of powdered sugar in, squeeze one lemon in and let the rest be water; make it palatable and put a little cochineal in it to colour it; pass it through a sieve and it is fit for use.[113]

Not all of these were made with fresh fruit; Nutt gives others in which preserved fruit replaces fresh. The confectioners' waters, ices, biscuits and sweetmeats belonged to the professional rather than the domestic kitchen, and were sold

---

[111] See Raffald (1769), pp. 242–243. This receipt enjoyed considerable success: it appears in Borella (1770), part 1, pp. 124–125, and was also copied out into several MS receipt collections of the period, as Florence White points out. See White, *Good Things in England* (1932), p. 331.

[112] Abbot (c.1790), pp. 70–71. See also the receipts for cakes and biscuits in Nutt (1789) pp. 1–50.

[113] Nutt (1789), p. 107. Other examples of 'waters' are found pp. 104–111.

to the upper classes and their imitators for parties: Louisa Holroyd told her sister the story of a ball in Bath in 1796 where the host had sent to London for the fruit and confectionery (apparently the standard practice in Bath at the time); unfortunately, the dainties arrived the morning after.[114]

Of all the general cookery books of this period, the most important and influential in the area of confectionery was Elizabeth Raffald. She was herself a cook and confectioner, with a shop in Manchester after leaving her position as housekeeper at Arley Hall on her marriage in 1763. More than one-third of her book is devoted to confectionery, and her advertisements show that many of her receipts are for goods which could be purchased ready-made in the shop.[115] While the confectioners' manuals gave receipts, they included no instructions for presentation which they left to the initiative of the cook or housekeeper. Raffald, by contrast, had definite ideas about ornament and gave receipts for some magnificent table decorations, such as gold and silver webs of spun sugar to cover dishes of sweetmeats and a variety of decorative jellies and flummeries, including the moon and stars and eggs and bacon found in earlier works.[116] She had new suggestions too, such as this kind of garden 'folly' for the table:

> Solomon's Temple in Flummery.
> Make a Quart of stiff Flummery, divide it into three Parts, make one Part a pretty pink Colour, with a little Cochineal bruised fine, and steeped in French Brandy, scrape one Ounce of Chocolate very fine, dissolve it in a little strong Coffee, and mix it with another Part of your Flummery, to make it a light Stone Colour, the last Part must be White, then wet your Temple Mould, and fix it in a Pot to stand even, then fill the Top of the Temple with Red Flummery to the Steps, and the four Points with White, then fill it up with Chocolate Flummery; let it stand 'till the next Day, then loosen it round with a Pin, and shake it loose very gently …; when you turn it out, stick a small Sprig, or a Flower Stalk, down from the Top of every Point, it will strengthen them, and make it look pretty, lay round it Rock Candy Sweatmeats [sic].[117]

---

[114] See Adeane (ed.), *The Girlhood of Maria Josepha Holroyd* (1896), p. 364.

[115] See Raffald (1769), pp. 162–255. 93 pages are devoted to confectionery out of a total of 268.

[116] Ibid., pp. 178–181.

[117] Ibid., p. 180.

Other receipts give directions for a fish pond, for gilding fish to swim in clear jelly,[118] and for a 'Floating Island' which also represents part of the landscape garden:

> Take Calf's-Foot Jelly that is set, brake it a little, ... have ready a Middle-sized Turnip, and rub it over with Gum Water, or the White of an Egg, then strew it thick over with green Shot Comfits, and stick in the Top of it a Sprig of Myrtle, ... then put your broken Jelly round it, set Sheep, or Swans, upon your Jelly, with either a green Leaf, or a Knot of Apple Paste under them ...; there are Sheep and Swans made for that Purpose, you may put in ... any wild Animals of the same Sort.[119]

The last receipt shows how commercialization was getting in on the act: whereas the seventeenth-century gentlewoman had made a display by piling up her own fruit preserves, these dessert dishes require the addition of shop-bought decorations to complete the scene.

Jellies and flummeries were not the only vehicles for such decorative dishes. Mrs Raffald also gives a receipt where the construction is based on pastry and sugar-candy:

> Desart Island.
> Take a Lump of Paste, form it into a Rock three Inches broad at the Top, colour it, and set it in the Middle of a deep China Dish, and set a cast Figure on it, with a Crown on its Head, and a Knot of Rock Candy at the Feet; then make a Roll of Paste an Inch thick, and stick it on the inner Edge of the Dish, two Parts round, and cut eight Pieces of candies Eringo Root, about three Inches long, and fix them upright to the Roll of Paste on the Edge; make Gravel Walks of Shot Comfits, from the Middle to the Edge of the Dish, and set small Figures in them, roll out some Paste, and cut it open like Chinese Rails, bake it, and fix it on either Side of one of the Gravel Walks, with Gum, have ready a Web of spun Sugar, and set it on the Pillars of Eringo Root, and cut Part of the Web off, to form an Entrance where the Chinese Rails are.

---

[118] See Raffald (1769), pp. 169, 174.
[119] Ibid., p. 176.

It is a pretty Middle Dish for a second Course at a grand Table, or a Wedding Supper, only set two crowned Figures on the Mount instead of one.[120]

Here, Mrs Raffald suggests serving this dish at the second course; her menu for a '*desert*' is composed of fresh and preserved fruits, and ices.[121] But sweet dishes could perfectly well appear either at the second course, or at the third course (i.e. the dessert), as at the following grand wedding dinner in 1770:

There were fifteen hard-named dishes in each course, besides Removes. The desert consisted of Temples, gravel walks, Ponds, etc.; and twenty Dishes of Fruit.[122]

Just as Menon suggested laying out a formal French garden on the table, the English were setting out a version of the landscape garden. Mrs Raffald's receipts were enormously successful: not only are there similar items in most of the high-class cookery books from 1770, but they were copied into manuscript collections in the north of England, and even reached the young Princess Victoria, who copied them out in 1833.[123]

It is now time to return to the remaining books of this period, the cheap ones, priced at 2 shillings or less. As we have already seen in the study of culinary styles in the middle of the century, the cheaper books offer even fewer receipts for French dishes than the expensive ones. There are also fewer receipts for the more ambitious English dishes: turtle, curry, Mrs Raffald's decorative jellies, ices, are virtually unheard of. Some of these cheap books, however, do try to be complete, giving receipts which imitate those in the more expensive works, and offering not just receipts for cookery, but also for cosmetics and remedies. An example of such a complete work is Elizabeth Price's, which came out around 1780. Although it cost only 1 shilling, it contains these three types

---

[120] Raffald (1769), pp. 175–176.

[121] Ibid., p. 362.

[122] The description is taken from the journal of the festivities kept by the Rev. Stotherd Abdy, reproduced in Houblon, *The Houblon Family* (1907), vol. 2, p. 131.

[123] See *The Bath Cookery Book*, pp. 182–185; Briggs (1788), pp. 467–468, 473–474; Cole (1788), pp. 449–455; Collingwood & Woollams (1792), pp. 261–269; Farley (1783), pp. 331, 333, 336–337; M. Smith (1772), pp. 287–291; for the MS copies, see Brears, 'Transparent Pleasures', p. 33.

of receipt, as well as directions for marketing and bills of fare. The title-page emphasizes that the receipts are both elegant and economical, and the book contains simple dishes alongside a fairly high number of 'French' receipts and such prestigious English dishes as turtle or mutton cooked to imitate venison.[124] The plain English dishes, with instructions for basic cookery, roasting, boiling, grilling and frying, appear at the beginning of the book,[125] amongst which are found:

> To fry Sausages with Apples.
> Take six apples, and half a pound of sausages; cut four of the apples into thin slices, and quarter the other two; then fry them with the sausages, and when they are enough, lay the sausages in the middle of your dish, and the sliced apples round them. Garnish the dish with the quartered apples.[126]

The instructions concern presentation rather than cookery: the author does not tell the reader how long to cook the sausages and apples, nor what fat to use. This dish is occasionally found in the more expensive books: John Farley gives it, but adds cabbage and a pea purée; Richard Briggs tells the reader to boil the sausages for a few minutes before frying them in butter.[127]

Mrs Price has a chapter on made dishes, more than half of which have French names. Out of 42 receipts, 12 are for fricassees, and 10 for raggoos.[128] They are of the same type as in the more expensive books: the same ingredients, catchup and lemon pickle, are often used in the sauces, as for instance in her beef olives.[129] As in most of these modest books, the dishes are simple, and the cooking times short, as here for mutton:

> To ragoo a Leg of Mutton.
> First … cut your meat very thin; then butter your stewpan, throw some

---

[124] See Price, *The New Book of Cookery* (c.1780), pp. 25, 64–65.

[125] Ibid., pp. 13–38.

[126] Ibid., p. 41. There is a very similar receipt in Chambers, *The Ladies Best Companion* (c.1785), p. 21; and in Cartwright, *The Lady's best Companion* (1789), p. 16.

[127] See Farley (1783), p. 58; Briggs (1788), p. 189.

[128] See Price, *The New Book of Cookery*, pp. 54–67.

[129] Ibid., p. 59.

flour into it, and put in your mutton, with a few sweet herbs, a blade
or two of mace, half a lemon and half an onion, cut very small; stir it
two or three minutes, and then put in a quarter of a pint of gravy, and
an anchovy shred fine, mixed with flour and butter; stir it again for six
or seven minutes, then dish it up, and send it to table.[130]

We meet once more the lemon and anchovy flavours of the late seventeenth
century. At the end of the chapter is a receipt for a raggoo-garnish:

A Ragout for Made Dishes.
Take some lamb stones and cocks-combs boiled, blanched, and sliced;
toss them up in a stewpan, with gravy, red or white wine, sliced sweet-
breads, mushrooms, oysters, morels, truffles, sweet herbs, and spice;
thicken the whole with burnt butter, and make use of it to enrich any
kind of ragout.[131]

The presence of the spice suggests that this is an old receipt. It bears close
resemblance to one given by Sarah Harrison in 1733: Mrs Harrison suggests
herbs and 'savory Spice', by which she means salt, pepper, cloves, mace and
nutmeg.[132] The other old-fashioned element is of course the idea of using this
to enrich any kind of raggoo. Mrs Price's sauces are as simple as her made
dishes: here, there is no cullis or essence of ham. There are a lot of English
sauces, such as onion sauce, mint sauce, apple sauce and bread sauce; her other
sauces are usually made with a base thickened with flour and flavoured with
the ingredient which gives the sauce its name.[133]

One finds the same mix of simple cookery and old-fashioned echoes of
upper-class cuisine in the other cheap books of the period. The more ambitious
works give receipts with French names; in 1800 Mary Holland has a few fricassees and raggoos,[134] with, at the end of the chapter, a raggoo-garnish to use with
everything. The fricassees are French only in name: they consist of small pieces
of meat, cooked in water with the seasonings of English cookery. A receipt for

---

[130] Price, *The New Book of Cookery*, p. 57.

[131] Ibid., p. 67.

[132] See Harrison, *The House-keeper's Pocket-Book* (1733), pp. 122–123.

[133] See Price, *The New Book of Cookery*, pp. 72–75.

[134] See Holland, *The Complete British Cook* (1800), pp. 63–69.

a hash of veal uses the same flavours as the luxury books, but the cooking is extremely brief and the range of ingredients is even more limited than in the receipt given by John Farley:

> Veal.
> Take some cold veal, cut it into thin slices about as large as a crown piece, put it into a stew-pan, with some good gravy, a spoonful of ketchup, a little butter mixed with flour, some lemon-peel shred fine, and a little pepper and salt; make it thoroughly hot, put it into a hot dish, and garnish it with sippets.[135]

One notices the use of the term 'sippets', a word which one often finds in seventeenth-century receipts, but which becomes less frequent in the eighteenth century. This garnish of slices of bread is a distant echo of the trenchers of the Middle Ages.

Although the cheap books tried to imitate the style of their expensive counterparts, the details of a receipt often bring out the distance which separated the two. Amelia Chambers gives a receipt for essence of ham, an essential base for sauces in French cuisine, but, since she has not realized that it is simply a base for other preparations, she invites the reader to serve it as a dish in its own right.[136] She also gives a receipt which originated with Elizabeth Raffald, but here again, her incomprehension is obvious. Raffald describes how to make a 'Thatched House Pye': vermicelli is placed at the bottom of a buttered dish, then covered with pastry and a pigeon filling before being baked in the oven. When the pie is turned out on to the serving dish, the vermicelli make the pastry crust look like thatch and this, explains the author, is the reason for the name of the dish.[137] Amelia Chambers gives a receipt with the title, 'To make a Pye, called a Thatched House', but her receipt is for a pigeon pie without a crust at the bottom to be reversed on to the dish,[138] and so the name no longer makes sense. In the process of continual simplification, dishes lose their particular characteristics. Chambers' English receipts (and there are very few French ones in her book) are of the simplest, and several dishes are

---

[135] Holland (1800), p. 54.
[136] See Chambers (c.1785), p. 58.
[137] See Raffald (1769), pp. 131–132.
[138] See Chambers (c.1785), p. 62.

described as 'plain', like '*plain Sippet Pudding*', '*plain light Pudding*' and '*plain Custard*'.[139] Even basic English cookery, which was quite simple to start with, underwent this adaptation to please an audience which was seeking economical dishes which were easy to make.

At the bottom of the scale came the books which offer hardly any made dishes, and describe only the most basic English cookery. *The British Jewel* (1776) gives 4 receipts for raggoos,[140] and concentrates on roast and boiled meats and pastry. In 1789, Charlotte Cartwright included only 8 'made dishes'[141] in the 79 savoury receipts in her book. *The Farmer's Wife*, which dated from around 1780, contained 7 pages of receipts for dishes, most of them roasts.[142] The instructions given in such books suggest that they were written for readers who had hardly any notion of cookery.

At the very end of the century, there are books which suggest a different kind of reader: one who knew how to do basic cooking, but was hoping to learn the 'correct' way of doing things, since the instructions on roasting and boiling concern not the cooking method, but the accompaniments for each type of meat. *The Guide to Preferment* – the title makes clear it was aimed at aspiring servants – tells the cook which vegetables and which sauces should be served with the various meats.[143] The pages concerning roasting and boiling in Charlotte Cartwright follow the same pattern.[144] These cheap manuals taught basic kitchen lore to servants whose knowledge was at least as limited as that of the candidates for a job with Mrs Purefoy in 1746. By the end of the century, middle-class employers could not be sure of finding a cook-maid with many skills at her fingertips.

We have identified on several occasion undertones of the court-cookery of the early years of the century. The very cheapest cookery books, sold as chap-books, present an even more old-fashioned style. *The Accomplished Lady's Delight in Cookery* (*c.*1780) contains a receipt very close to one given by John Murrell in 1615. This is not an exception: the receipts in this book clearly date

---

[139] See Chambers (*c.*1785), pp. 73, 79–80, 85.

[140] See *The British Jewel*, pp. 28–29. Cookery receipts are found pp. 15–41.

[141] See Cartwright (1789), pp. 26–28.

[142] *The Farmer's Wife* (*c.*1780), pp. 126–132.

[143] Powell, *The Guide to Preferment* (*c.*1770), p. 175.

[144] See Cartwright (1789), pp. 3–13.

from the seventeenth century, typified by the verjuice-sugar combination and the use of dried fruit in this mutton hash:

> *To hash a Shoulder of Mutton, or a Leg of Lamb the best Way.*
> Take them off the spit half roasted; slice them, and being put into a dish, put in rhenish wine, and raisins of the sun, large sliced lemons, and raw oysters, an anchovy or two, and a shalot finely sliced, then put them in a stew-pan, and when enough, sauce it with verjuice, sugar, pickled barberries, so serve it on sippits.[145]

One even finds such combinations going back into the sixteenth century. The process is identical to that witnessed in a manuscript recipe collection compiled in the 1680s and '90s. Jane Mosley (1669–1712), the daughter of a prosperous Derbyshire grazier, copied out a vast number of receipts from Murrell, as well as from the Countess of Kent's book, thus creating for herself a cookery book that was half a century out of date.[146] Here, a hundred years later, the printed word is still perpetuating the same culinary style.

This study of the receipts of the last part of the eighteenth century brings into focus the effects of the cookery book's spread down the social scale. Although there are one or two which keep up with authentic *haute cuisine* (French, naturally), most now lag well behind élite fashion except in the area of the dessert where Elizabeth Raffald's decorative dishes are only a decade behind the truly smart. But it must be remembered that decorative sweet dishes were a very long-standing tradition amongst English women, from the ladies of the sixteenth century to the gentlewomen of the seventeenth, down to the cooks and housekeepers of the eighteenth. At the other two courses of dinner, however, simplified versions of an old-fashioned style were the rule. This tendency was not confined to the cheapest books alone, but is visible in those by the professional women and the tavern cooks. The best receipts are found in works by women such as Elizabeth Raffald and Mary Smith; these cooks and housekeepers are now the most important representatives of the female tradition in England and with them the traditional areas of excellence, sweet

---

[145] *The Accomplished Lady's Delight in Cookery*, (c.1780), p. 6.

[146] See Sinar (ed.), *Jane Mosley's Derbyshire Recipes* (1985), passim. For details of Mosley's copying, see Lehmann, 'Echanges entre livres de cuisine imprimés et recueils de recettes manuscrits en Angleterre, 1660–1730' (1996), pp. 44–47.

dishes and baked goods, continue to develop. The other striking aspect of the receipts of this period is their authors' lack of originality. The same prescriptions were hardly re-worked at all except to disguise their origin by changing the order of enumeration (whereas at earlier periods there was clearly an attempt to adapt and improve). This repetition is a sign that English cookery was becoming codified by 1770: the receipt is fixed in a set form which the cook must follow.

English cooks persevered in their rather outdated image of French cuisine as luxuriously sauced and garnished and created little on the basis of French methods, although such dishes as curry are obviously variations on the fricassee theme. By now, however, the fricassee had well-established roots and should perhaps be considered as home-grown rather than an import from France. Where native cookery did continue to develop its own repertoire was in puddings, pies, creams and jellies. Here, continuity and innovation go hand in hand, but the dominant impression is one of continuity, and it seems that English cookery was beginning to run out of steam.

The books which were being produced for the humbler end of the market show the ever-widening gap between 'haute cuisine', partly imported and partly English, and middle-class domestic cookery. At the beginning of the century, even those which were most preoccupied by the need for economy gave receipts inspired by court-cookery; at the end, only a few French names remain to give an 'à la mode' air to the cheaper books. However, the most important factor in the decline of English cookery, which is only just starting, is the gap between the kitchen and the table, between the people who produced the dishes and the people who consumed them. New models of femininity and gentility conspired to keep the mistress of a household out of the kitchen, and increasing numbers of ladies neglected domestic management for more decorative accomplishments. Meanwhile, the cook was left to her own devices, and the evidence of the cookery books, with their numerous references to ignorant servants as well as their elementary receipts, suggest that a general loss of skills was taking place. It is thus hardly surprising to find so much negative comment on English food from foreign travellers, as we shall see in the next part.

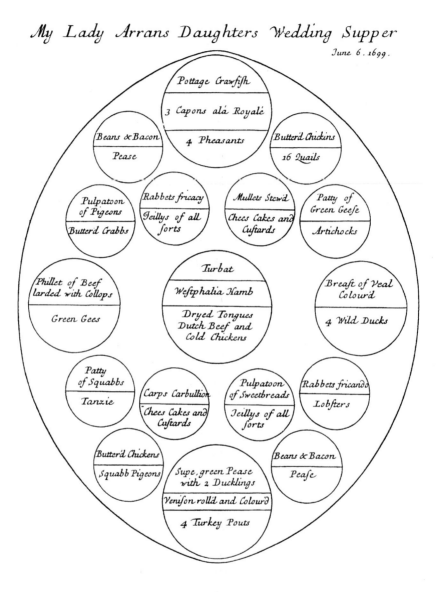

My Lady Arrans Daughters Wedding Supper

June 6. 1699.

Pottage Crawfish

3 Capons alá Royalé

4 Pheasants

Beans & Bacon
Pease

Butter'd Chickins
16 Quails

Pulpatoon
of Pigeons
Butter'd Crabbs

Rabbets fricacy
Jeillys of all
sorts

Mullets Stew'd
Chees Cakes and
Custards

Patty of
Green Geese
Artichocks

Phillet of Beef
larded with Collops
Green Gees

Turbat
Westphalia Hamb
Dryed Tongues
Dutch Beef and
Cold Chickens

Breast of Veal
Colour'd
4 Wild Ducks

Patty
of Squabbs
Tanzie

Carps Carbullion
Chees Cakes and
Custards

Pulpatoon
of Sweetbreads
Jeillys of all
sorts

Rabbets fricando
Lobsters

Butter'd Chickens
Squabb Pigeons

Supe, green Pease
with 2 Ducklings
Venison roll'd and Colour'd
4 Turkey Pouts

Beans & Bacon
Pease

Bill of fare for My Lady Arran's daughter's wedding supper, June 6th, 1699, inserted at page 26 of Patrick Lamb, Royal Cookery, 1710. *This two-course supper is less grand than some of Lamb's feasts, but court-style dishes, such as the garnished soups and the puptons, adorn the first course. In the centre and at the top and bottom of the table are dishes with removes for the first course.*

CONCLUSION

The facts we have rehearsed go to show that any model of eighteenth-century cookery as uniform or monolithic is erroneous. There were major shifts in style, although the differences between one manner and another – so obvious in the most ambitious books which reveal a 'pure' style – become blurred as books aimed at readers lower down the social scale adapted the original receipts to conform to their prejudices and to make the dishes easier and cheaper to create. A brief summary of these developments, with some suggestions as to the reasons for the changes which occurred, will help to make the process clearer.

The earliest period, from 1700 to around 1730, saw the triumph of the court style which owed so much to France. The English translation of Massialot (1702) was perhaps the most influential cookery book to be published in the whole century. The English court-cooks all paid homage to its content and some, such as John Nott's *Cook's and Confectioner's Dictionary* (1723), or the second and third editions of Patrick Lamb's *Royal Cookery* (1716 and 1726), are clearly imitations with extensive borrowings. The grand made dishes are complex, often bringing together several kinds of meat and adding a lavish garnish and an equally lavish sauce-cum-soup. The pyramid presentation adds to the impression of ostentatious display. It was a baroque style, whose grandeur was part and parcel of 'court society', to use Norbert Elias' term.[1] That it should need to be adapted to enter the kitchens of the gentry seems obvious and women authors produced simplified versions of olios and terrines for their readers. The cookery books themselves demonstrate the success of the style, moving down the social scale to form a chain of emulation, and evidence of what was really happening in kitchens and dining-rooms confirms this success. But this raises the question: why was the court style so successful?

At a purely culinary level, it fitted in well with seventeenth-century English cookery. Robert May's book (1660) already contains some grand dishes, and the fully-fledged court style was a continuation of tendencies present in England

---

[1] Elias' book, *Die höfische Gesellschaft* (1969), which discusses the court as the dominant representative social structure, was translated into English as *The Court Society* (1983). Elias suggests that in England, the court was a less powerful model than in other European countries, because the gentry competed with the aristocracy in matters of lifestyle, forming a 'polite society' in which the court was only one centre among others. But, at least as far as cookery is concerned, in the period 1675–1725 there is ample evidence that the court model exerted a major influence on the aristocracy and the gentry.

well before the Restoration. May was an English counterpart to La Varenne's *Cuisinier françois* (1651), in which older receipts stood alongside the newer developments, although Robert May was more conservative than La Varenne. The presentation of dishes also fitted with English traditions of decorative cookery, seen most clearly in May's illustrations of pies and tarts and in the multicoloured display of the banquet course which had been so important and prestigious a part of ladies' demonstrations of their housewifely skills. One reason for the success of the court style was that it was not totally foreign but could work as the prolongation of earlier culinary practice.

One further question is the importance of French influence. If the court style was a continuation of native developments, should the Massialot version be seen as the model, or was there simply a parallel movement in England? The answer must be that, tempting as it is to see England as developing its own court style at the same time as France, the early eighteenth-century English version owes everything to France. Firstly, because of the prestige of Versailles, which led to its ceremonial, its etiquette and its cuisine being imitated all over Europe.[2] Secondly, because the flavours that denote the court style – a sharply diminished use of spices and, more importantly, the separation of sweet and savoury – are apparent in the made dishes which invariably derive from French models. The English pies and tarts persist in being sweetened meat or vegetable mixtures, often with a sweet custard (known as a 'caudle', as opposed to the savoury 'lear') poured in at the end of the cooking time. Only gradually would English cooks come to make a distinction between sweet and savoury pies, marking them as such by the titles they gave their receipts.

At a deeper level, the adoption of the court style of cookery corresponds to a model of society which was formal and hierarchical. Mark Girouard has demonstrated how the architecture of country houses was dictated by their use: how the late seventeenth-century 'axis of honour' along a sequence of rooms, was adapted to highly formal and ritualized social exchanges in which fine gradations of rank were scrupulously observed.[3] Etiquette books of the period confirm the nice observation of these nuances of status.[4] The lavish ostentation

---

[2] See the various essays in *Versailles et les tables royales en Europe XVIIᵉ–XIXᵉ siècles* (1993). This book is the catalogue of the exhibition at Versailles from November 1993 to February 1994.

[3] See Girouard, *Life in the English Country House* (1980), pp. 120–162.

[4] See, for instance, [Courtin], *The Rules of Civility* (1671), passim; R. G., *The Accomplish'd Female Instructor* (1704), part I, especially pp. 22–24.

of court-cookery fits with such overt demonstrations of wealth and power and, just as this excessive formality of social intercourse was soon to be rejected, so too would be the reigning culinary style. A further contributory factor in its demise was the decline in influence of the English royal court, at least in culinary matters. This dated from the accession of the House of Hanover in 1714, when George I brought his own German cooks. We will see below how it was reinforced with the accession of George II in 1727. The initiative in matters of gastronomic excellence passed to Whig grandees who were at the forefront as patrons of a new fashion in cookery.

The first signs of change come with criticism of excessive formality in the *Tatler* and the *Spectator*. The cultural unity of shifting tastes is obvious from the simultaneous attacks on formal manners, formal gardens, formal (i.e. French court-style) food.[5] Taken as a whole, this is a coherent demand for social change expressed through cultural practices, not merely some xenophobic, anti-French remarks on cookery. (Satires on French cookery abound in the eighteenth century, and it is only too easy to see them as always expressing the same complaint, but shifts in emphasis are visible if one looks at the underlying ideas.) At the same time, these periodicals were promoting a new model of femininity, in which the ideal of female delicacy implied a rejection of physical appetite (whether for food or for sex) and thus of all direct participation in food preparation, except for sweetmeats – sweetness and femininity going hand in hand – in favour of an angelic refinement destined to exert a beneficial influence on men.[6]

These theoretical initiatives early in the century suggest the time was ripe for a new culinary style. However, signs of change are not apparent in cookery books until the 1730s and English cookery remained stuck in its own perceptions of the court style for much longer. There seems to be a gap between theory and practice, just as in gardens there was a time-lag between the theory of informality and its appearance on the ground. (The garden designs of the 1720s by Pope, Burlington and Bridgeman look distinctly formal to modern eyes, and one has to wait until the late 1730s for Kent's designs to lead the way

---

[5] Formal manners are criticized in the *Spectator*, number 119, gardens in the *Spectator*, number 34, and French cookery in the *Tatler*, number 148.

[6] See the *Spectator*, numbers 10, 71, 92, 365; for a discussion of the rôle of periodicals in redefining femininity and distancing it from the table, see Rouyer, 'Arts de la table, féminité et *gentility* en Angleterre au XVIIIe siècle', in Rouyer (1998), pp. 31–50.

to Capability Brown.) Odd clues do suggest that change had begun earlier. In 1718 Lady Grisell Baillie recorded a dinner with Lord Sunderland. He gave her a soup without anything in it (in other words, what we would call a soup today, not a stew). She found this strange enough to consign it to her book of menus. The soup was very different from its court-style incarnation, even if the other main offering on the table was a standard court dish, a 'hog potch' containing three different meats, beef, mutton and veal.[7]

Because of its very success, court-cookery was devalued by being presented in a debased form to the gentry and the wealthy middle classes. This was one reason for the success of the *nouvelle cuisine* amongst the élite in the 1730s. Although the early phase of the new style was widely diffused by Hannah Glasse's borrowings from La Chapelle (its chief proponent), via *The Lady's Companion*, it met with much more hostility than its predecessor, including from Glasse herself. There is evidence that *nouvelle cuisine* was all the rage amongst the Whig political élite and its hangers-on, but that it never penetrated further into the social fabric. Whig grandees employed French cooks, but before the Revolution brought an influx of servants seeking employment, signs of them in lesser households are scarce. Political satirists rammed home the links between the Whig élite and an unpatriotic love of French cookery.[8] The first target was Walpole; after his fall, spleen was diverted towards Newcastle.[9] French food was extravagant, unpatriotic and immoral, and Hannah Glasse's diatribes against French cooks must be seen in this context. When one remembers that the authors and printers of cookery books thought that a large section of their readership was drawn from the country gentry and from the urban middle classes (the strongholds of Tory attitudes[10]), the anti-French bias can also be identified as an anti-Whig phenomenon.[11]

---

[7] Scott-Moncrieff (ed.), *The Household Book of Lady Grisell Baillie* (1911), p. 287.

[8] There are innumerable examples of this. For prints, see 'The Duke of Newcastle's Cook', British Museum print number 2684; for a prose satire on Walpole's love of French food, see the pamphlet *The Norfolk Congress* [1728]; for a verse satire on the dignitaries of the City of London feasting on French food supplied by the Court, see 'A New Ballad', reproduced in M. Percival, *Political Ballads illustrating the Administration of Sir Robert Walpole* (1916), p. 11; for more general attacks on Whig politicians' fondness for French cuisine, see the essays from the *Craftsman* and Fog's Weekly Journal reproduced in the *Gentleman's Magazine* 6 (1736), pp. 277, 455.

[9] See Atherton, *Political Prints in the Age of Hogarth* (1974), pp. 232–3.

[10] See Colley, *In Defiance of Oligarchy* (1982), pp. 148–152.

[11] For a more extensive discussion of the influence of politics on the rejection of 'nouvelle cuisine', see Lehmann, 'Politics in the Kitchen' (1999).

Hostility to *nouvelle cuisine* in England is thus closely bound up with that to the Whig oligarchy, perceived as greedy and corrupt. While Newcastle and his friends enjoyed the *petits plats* prepared by Clouet, public perception of their pleasures mythologized this cuisine, with wild stories of whole hams or scores of partridges used to create a sauce for a single portion, and tiny nuggets of meat selected from Englishmen's favourite joints.[12] In the climate of the 1740s and early 1750s, with England at war with France (the formal hostilities from 1744 to 1748 and from 1756 to 1763 were preceded by some fighting), such accusations were political dynamite. When one remembers that this is precisely the period when readership of the cookery books was extending downwards into the ranks of the middle classes, whose anti-French and anti-aristocratic prejudices are mirrored in Hogarth's prints, the rejection of the new style seems inevitable. The ambiguous attitude of Hannah Glasse, who gives French receipts while denouncing them at every turn, reflects the contradictions within society itself: the cookery book seeks to display fashionable cuisine to a rather disparate group which longed to imitate the very style which its middle-class ethos rejected. Hence the emphasis on uniting elegance and economy, and on assuring readers that French cookery was a vast confidence-trick by astute French cooks hell-bent on duping their masters, while the English authors could show how to produce the same results without financial ruin being the inevitable outcome.

The consequence of such attitudes was that English cookery books of the middle of the century offered a mixed bag of more or less authentic French material and often quite old-fashioned English dishes with their roots in the seventeenth century. To satisfy the aspirations of readers unwilling to spend much money but wanting the appearance of fashion, writers continued to suggest the visible luxury of extra garnishes to give cachet to a basic fricassee. Yet this was precisely the kind of 'disguised' food regularly denounced by satirists: the food often becoming a metaphor for the devious nature of the French. In the ideological confusion, English cookery had lost its way, and it is not until the final decades of the century that there are signs of a renewed self-confidence among the authors, at least so far as their cooking.

Meanwhile, readership had undergone a radical change. Propaganda about the ideal of femininity, combined with increased prosperity for the middle

---

[12] As we have seen, William Verral refuted such accusations in his cookery book: see Verral (1759), pp. xxx–xxxi.

classes, drew more and more women away from domestic duties to 'decorative' pursuits. The lady was no longer expected to take an active part in running her kitchen, although she might amuse herself with sweet dishes for the dessert. Even these were often left to the housekeeper, who had taken over the rôle played by the mistress of the household in the seventeenth century. Cookery books were aimed now at the servant rather than the mistress, even though she might well be the actual purchaser. One sign of this shift is the increasingly professional tone of the women cookery book authors. At the beginning of the century, texts by men like Patrick Lamb were aimed at fellow professionals obliged to satisfy their employers, whereas the women authors' tone was more intimate, appropriate to addressing other housewives. By the second half of the century the women, themselves professional cooks and housekeepers, have adopted the professional tone of the male chefs and are far more self-assured than their predecessors. Women now outnumbered men as authors, and even those books presented as being by tavern cooks in the last thirty years of the century are clearly based on earlier women's books.

The triumph of the women authors can be read as the triumph of the native English tradition. They had been the dominant force in English cookery books from the end of the sixteenth century until the rise of the male chefs which coincided with the decades of court-cookery (from the Restoration to about 1730). Even during this period, women's traditions continued. Women were, of course, excluded from the male structures of the profession, with its apprenticeship leading to guild membership; the Worshipful Company of Cooks repeatedly tried to stop its members from passing on skills, and women were expressly excluded in an order of 1694, re-enacted in 1795.[13] The culinary style of the last third of the eighteenth century marks the reassertion of English tradition, and a decline of xenophobic comment on French food, at least in cookery books. Raggoos and fricassees had been thoroughly assimilated into the English repertoire, and the professional woman cook, working for the lesser aristocracy, the gentry or the entrepreunerial class, could satisfy her employer by producing these and a range of more English dishes. At this level, French cuisine or cooks were no longer seen as a threat. Lower down, in homes where the mistress played a more active part in instructing and assisting her maid, the refinements of elegant cookery, French or English, were simply an irrelevance.

---

[13] See Attar, 'A Dabble in the Mystery of Cookery' (1986), pp. 46–7.

With Elizabeth Raffald and her followers (and of course the tavern cooks
as a group can be numbered amongst them), English cookery is re-invigorated.
Raffald's 'French' dishes are debased by her rejection of costly, time-consuming
sauces, but her English dishes display good, careful cooking, and her dessert
receipts prove that the tradition of the woman preparing sweet foods for the
sixteenth and seventeenth-century 'banquet' was still vibrant. This was cookery
aimed at the prosperous inhabitants of Manchester and its environs, and it is
significant that one of the most influential cookery books of the century should
come from the north of England. Nor was she alone: Elizabeth Moxon's book
had appeared in Leeds in 1741, followed by Ann Peckham's, also in Leeds, in
1767.[14] Studies on the emergence of a consumer society in eighteenth-century
England have shown the development of provision of goods and services in the
provinces over the years,[15] and these provincial cookery books show that there
was a demand for such high-class works away from the centre of fashion,
London. In fact, they were not provincial at all: there is very little in their
contents to distinguish them from London-produced books, and regional
specialities are rare. The culinary style was national and bourgeois in its ethos,
developing its own prestige dishes (turtle, curry, elaborate moulded desserts),
with its own references to the exotic and the spectacular, only slightly affected
by the Frenchness which was obligatory in more exalted circles.

   In well-off households, cookery was now firmly in the hands of the servants:
cooks and housekeepers had replaced the mistress, frequent problems with
servants notwithstanding. As we have seen, the discourse of the cookery books
makes it plain that the readers of receipts were servants, while the mistress
might be concerned with the bills of fare or the medical sections. Hints from
manuscript sources suggest that amongst the moneyed, interest in cookery was
indeed diminished compared to earlier decades. Caroline Lybbe Powys, whose
diaries describe a constant round of country-house visiting, kept a manuscript
receipt book, begun around the time of her marriage in 1762, and added to over
the next 35 years. Cookery, preserves, pickles and drinks account for only 37
per cent of the 143 entries, the rest being devoted to medical and cosmetic
preparations (26 per cent) and household hints and hobbies such as japanning

---

[14] For a discussion of the provincially-published cookery books, see Hunter, 'Printing in the Pennines', in Wilson (1991), pp. 9–37.

[15] See, for instance, the discussion of Preston by Peter Borsay in his essay, 'The English Urban Renaissance', in Borsay (1990), pp. 159–187.

and shellwork (37 per cent). And a note on the first page says that the writer had all the receipts 'from the Ladies themselves or from old Family Manuscript Ones', implying that some at least of the receipts were collected as much for their value as curiosities as for practical purposes.[16] Similarly, Susanna Whatman's 'housekeeping book', written around 1788 but including material transcribed from an earlier notebook, is much more concerned with instructions for cleaning the house and for avoiding waste and pilfering than with culinary matters. Mrs Whatman delegated the rôle of supervising the servants to her housekeeper, Hester Davis, and was thus doubly distant from her cook – who was, of course, a woman.[17]

Middle-class housewives continued to collect receipts, either for their own use or to be given to their cooks. We have seen the example of Elizabeth Raper, the daughter of an East India Company merchant, who wrote down receipts and occasionally cooked herself in the 1750s. Other manuscript collections dating from the end of the century, such as those by Martha Lloyd,[18] the daughter of a Hampshire clergyman and friend of Jane Austen, and by Elizabeth Serrell of Wells and her descendants, show a continued interest in cookery receipts as well as household hints. But even where there is evidence of a continuing tradition of receipt collection, there is less sign of that avid desire to reproduce even a modified version of the aristocratic style of cooking. Elizabeth Raper's receipts are typical: a limited number of French-inspired dishes mixed with English ones with roots well back in the past. Martha Lloyd's also show a thoroughly bourgeois style: she has a 'White Soup' with almonds which is a very simple version of 'soupe à la reine' (found in the court-cooks' books), but her made dishes are in the English tradition, with the mock turtle,

---

[16] This manuscript notebook is now BL Add. MS 42173. An inscription on the inside cover says 'Caroline Powys – 1762', and the latest date appended to a receipt (not the last dated receipt in the book, suggesting a fair copy was made later from loose sheets) is 1797. She died in 1817.

[17] See the introductions and the texts of the editions by Thomas Balston (1956) and by Christina Hardyment (1987). The earlier edition contains extra snippets of information.

[18] Most of Martha Lloyd's receipts have been published in Hickman (ed.), *A Jane Austen Household Book* (1977), and extracts from her collection appear also in Black & Le Faye (eds), *The Jane Austen Cookbook* (1995). Hickman found some of Martha Lloyd's receipts 'discoloured and difficult to decipher' and so she omitted these. Of the 135 receipts she did transcribe, 26 per cent are devoted to cosmetic and medical receipts and to household hints; in the culinary receipts the emphasis is on soups and made dishes (21 per cent), pickles and bottled sauces (13 per cent), and puddings and pies (12 per cent). Curiously, preserving is very little represented, with only 4 receipts.

the curry, and the jugged beef steaks which appear so frequently in the books of the last third of the century. Her many pickles and bottled sauces to be used as flavourings take us further in the direction of Elizabeth Raffald and her imitators.[19] This is simple domestic cookery which has slipped a long way from the standards of the early women writers. As we shall see in the next part, accounts of meals in diaries and letters do not suggest any great familiarity with *haute cuisine*, and there are many instances of commentators rejecting French food in favour of plain English cooking.

This English style, epitomized by Elizabeth Raffald, was more concerned with appearance than with flavour, as is seen in the contrast between her made dishes and her elaborate confections for the dessert course. But even so, her book served as aspirational reading rather than as practical advice to buyers and readers, to judge by the few references in contemporary documents to dinners which followed her precepts. By the end of the century, the cookery presented by Raffald and her imitators (all of whose books were priced at the upper end of the market) was the luxury cookery of the gentry and the prosperous middle classes, reserved for entertaining rather than for everyday eating.

After the appearance of the third and last edition of the English version of *Les Soupers de la Cour* in 1776 and the plagiarized version of Clermont's translation by George Dalrymple in 1781, French cookery virtually disappears from the English scene. It is surely significant that although Carême worked for the Prince Regent from 1816 to 1817, his five cookery books were not translated into English. Later in the nineteenth century, Eliza Acton's *Modern Cookery* devotes only about 15 pages out of 650 to foreign cookery, and the grand French style practised later by Soyer, Escoffier and Boulestin was reserved for a tiny minority of the super-rich and for the equally wealthy clients of great hotels and clubs.[20] The idea that French influence on upper-class cookery in England grew ever more dominant during the eighteenth and nineteenth centuries is a myth.

---

[19] The 'White Soup' is p. 41, the mock turtle p. 54, the curry and jugged beef pp. 57–8; pickles are to be found pp. 87–92, and bottled sauces pp. 45, 48, 60, 86–7, 89–90, 92.
[20] See the comments by Revel, *Un Festin en paroles* (1979), pp. 274–5.

Part IV

The Eighteenth Century
at Table

Frontispiece from Amelia Chambers, The Ladies Best Companion, *c.1785. This shows a man-cook at the fire, while a serving-woman is carrying a finished dish towards the dining-room beyond.*

OUR EARLIER STUDY OF HOW CULINARY STYLES CHANGED DURING
the eighteenth century showed how the court style gave way,
at least in élite circles, to *nouvelle cuisine* in the late 1730s, but that
this new French import marked the start of a separation: English domestic
cookery, which had managed to assimilate an adapted version of the court style,
became increasingly divorced from French *haute cuisine*. From about 1760, the
native tradition began to reassert itself in cookery books, following the same
process of codification which can be observed in France. These findings, and
particularly the idea of three periods of differing culinary styles, need to be set
against the evidence of what was really being consumed at eighteenth-century
tables. How far were the precepts of cookery books being followed? Printed
cookery books tended to lag behind manuscript receipt collections in pro-
posing new receipts and new styles, and therefore one might expect to find
evidence of these on the table before they appear in print. By investigating what
really appeared on the table, it may be possible to determine the level of pene-
tration of the more fashionable repertoire and the length of time it took to
travel from the kitchens of the élite to the tables of the gentry classes – if indeed
it ever made that journey. Evidence for the chain of emulation is strong for the
first period defined by the study of culinary styles (1700–1730), but is much less
obvious in the third period (1760–1800). This shift tells a story of changing
cultural values as society itself changed.

To show how far the picture drawn from the cookery books is an accurate
reflection of what was happening at the time, we look beyond them to diaries,
letters, travellers' journals, and household accounts and memoranda. These

offer much more fragmented evidence than do printed manuals, and the reality behind the references is often difficult to ascertain.

A simple example is the vexed question of the presence of vegetables on the table. The current orthodoxy is that meat was the main item on the tables of the well-to-do and, indeed, most contemporary allusions seem to confirm this. But when vegetables are served as an accompaniment to a meat dish, the name of the principal ingredient of the dish is what any diarist or letter-writer will put down, even today. The failure to include vegetables in an account of a meal does not necessarily denote their absence. A growing body of evidence about commercial vegetable production,[1] including out-of-season items which commanded a high price and must therefore have been purchased and presumably consumed by the upper classes, suggests a need to re-examine the simple model of a gulf between those who could afford meat, and therefore ate vast quantities to the exclusion of other foods, and those who could not and ate the despised 'roots and herbs' instead. The increasing number of printed receipts for vegetable dishes may be evidence that they were present – either as garnishes or as dishes in their own right – more often than might be presumed. Here, cookery books serve as a useful corrective to other types of document, just as they in turn must modify too literal a reliance on the printed record.

Diaries and letters are the sources which bring us closest to the realities of eating, but they are often frustratingly opaque. Few diarists wrote down a daily account of their food (and the tendency of modern editors has been to remove many such references as being repetitive).[2] Other less obsessive diarists described only meals which were unusual, generally because of the presence of guests or because they themselves were guests. The peevish also used their writing to vent their spleen against badly-cooked or inappropriate meals; John Byng's travel journals are full of complaints about unpleasant, over-priced meals at the inns he frequented, and the complaints tend to give more details than the entries which concern good food and service.[3] One must therefore

---

[1] The most notable book on market gardening near London is Malcolm Thick's *The Neat House Gardens* (1998).

[2] This is the case for the two diaries which contain an almost systematic account of meals every day, the diaries of the Sussex shopkeeper Thomas Turner, and of the Norfolk clergyman James Woodforde.

[3] See Byng, *The Torrington Diaries* (ed. Bruyn Andrews, 4 vols., 1934–38), passim. A more accessible sample of Byng's tour journals is to be found in David Souden (ed.), *Byng's Tours* (1991).

approach these accounts with some caution, remembering that the exceptional looms larger than the everyday. Letters are another source of comment; here, however, the amount of detail depends not only upon the interests of the writer, but also on those of the recipient; all too often, the modern reader is tantalized by an account of a meal which looks interesting but which suddenly ends with an 'etc.' dismissing the meal as the writer goes on to a topic of more interest to his correspondent. Here, again, the exceptional naturally attracted more comment than the everyday.

A host of other factors beyond gastronomic appreciation could colour a description of a meal: the company, the surroundings, the reception, the conversation at and after dinner, the attitude of the servants, even losses at cards in the interval between dinner and supper. People from varying levels of society had different expectations and judgements. Dishes appreciated by one group would be rejected by another, so illustrating how the different social strata within polite society reacted to meals which were a little above or below their station. It is here one can chart shifting attitudes towards the élite model of cookery diffused by the more up-market cookery books.

There are, of course, other sources of contemporary comment on what was being consumed at eighteenth-century tables. Foreign tourists often noted their impressions of English food, usually negative, just as English tourists tended to bring back an unfavourable idea of foreign food, especially French. There was general distaste for another culture's food habits. To make clear to themselves what made their own culture specifically theirs, many commentators exaggerated what they saw as crucial differences to the point of caricature. The observer defined himself by comparison with the other. Foreign tourists described their version of English food (generally seen as gross, quantity being preferred to quality, with disgusting coffee but excellent tea), and in return the English had a field-day ridiculing foreign food (over-refined and insubstantial). In both cases, stereotypes played an enormous part in determining travellers' expectations, and what many tourists saw (or rather, thought they saw) and recounted was as much the product of their expectations as of their experience: selective memory adjusted reality to conform to the picture the traveller and his potential readers wanted to see.

Finally, what might loosely be termed household accounts and memoranda appear to offer more objective evidence of what was being served. Even here, it must be remembered that accounts for provisions do not necessarily give a complete picture of the foodstuffs being used in a kitchen. Amongst the well-to-do, the estate would normally supply part, if not most, of the requirements. Even when a family moved to London for the season, supplies would often be sent up from the country at regular intervals. In order to interpret the quantitative evidence from accounts, it is necessary to know how many people in the household were being fed, and whether they all participated equally in consuming what passed through the kitchens, or if the luxury items were reserved for the favoured few. By the eighteenth century, this is less of a problem than for earlier periods when norms of hospitality meant that large numbers of casual guests might partake, each being entertained according to his social status, in quantity and in quality, although as we shall see, such habits were not entirely dead even by the second half of the eighteenth century. The object of this study, however, is not diet but cookery, and in this context these domestic records are used more for details of specific meals (found in ladies' memoranda and, at a more exalted level, in the accounts of the Lord Steward's department of the royal household) than to determine patterns of consumption.

The various sections of this part of the book follow what one might call the order of battle although, within each section, a chronological view is taken. Thus the first section examines the structure of the eighteenth-century day as organized by its meals and meal-times, an exercise which may seem a surprising starting-point but one which is necessary given the widespread misconceptions or vagueness about the way the eighteenth century organized the day.[4] What

---

[4] An example of an important misconception is the idea that the modern order of the day (breakfast, lunch, dinner) dates from the seventeenth century, and thus that the eighteenth-century day resembled ours; thus Clare Williams' translation of Sophie von La Roche's travel journal refers to 'lunch' rather than dinner. See Williams, *Sophie in London* (1933), pp. 148, 154, 199, 207. More recently, accounts of the changing meal-times have tended to be vague: dinner-time 'slid around the dial with accelerating speed' between the early sixteenth and the late eighteenth century, according to Stephen Mennell, *All Manners of Food* (1985), p. 130; Amanda Vickery's description of late eighteenth-century meal-times amongst the lesser gentry in the North of England is equally vague, stating that dinner was served 'mid- to late afternoon' (see *The Gentleman's Daughter* (1998), p. 207 and n). The two standard accounts of meal-times leave something of a gap for the eighteenth century: Rees and Fenby's 'Meals and Meal-Times' in Lennard (1931) does not offer much detail; Arnold Palmer's *Movable Feasts* (1952) takes 1780 as its starting-point, although there is information on the earlier period. Neither of these studies makes enough of the social connotations of meal-times, a point which is remedied in Dan Cruickshank and Neil Burton's chapter on 'work and play' in *Life in the Georgian City* (1990), pp. 23–47; unfortunately, most of the sources for this study are late eighteenth century or early nineteenth century, and the period before 1760 is somewhat neglected.

was eaten cannot be seen in isolation from when, and at what meal, for the
nature of the foods presented at different meals created a specific image which
modelled the forms of sociability associated with each meal. Another point is
the social connotations of meal-times: the hour at which one dined was just
as important a signal to others of one's social status as the dishes on the table,
and meal-times varied with the status (real or desired) of the host. Thus there
was considerable variation in the meal-times of different strata of society, and
this is the main reason for the frequent vagueness of modern accounts of the
eighteenth-century day. When one ate was an important social signal, but at
what meal was another, and it was during this century that a new meal came
into existence, although its name did not stabilize until well into the next
century. The modern order of the day dates from the beginning of the nineteenth century, when meal-times and the names of meals begin to resemble our
own. This section of the study cannot pretend to be exhaustive, but it is based
on an examination of over 60 published sources (36 diaries and collections of
letters, 13 family histories based on miscellaneous papers, and 12 accounts of
English life by foreign visitors), in an attempt to provide a reliable account of
the changing pattern of the eighteenth-century day, and in order to show how
keenly the social nuances of the variations in the pattern were felt at the time.

The next section deals with the organization of the meals themselves, and
how they were served and eaten. Many cookery books offered advice on menu
planning, with copper-plates showing how to place the dishes on the table in
the more luxurious books, and numbered lists in those which did not rise to
such expensive additions. The advantage of the cookery books as a source is
that these diagrams and lists can be followed up in the receipts, to see the exact
nature of the dishes proposed. This is the theory: how far it was translated into
reality is another question. Manuscript sources concerning meals which actually took place are often less informative. Bills of fare, whether those of the
royal table, for which there is an almost complete series in the Public Record
Office covering the period 1660-1812 (LS 9/50–226), or those noted down in
memorandum books by ladies, are often too succinct to give a precise idea of
the dishes. The amount of detail in the royal bills depended on which secretary
wrote the bills for a particular month: some scribes added details of accompaniments and garnishes, some did not. Similarly, some ladies, especially when
they were guests rather than hostesses, jotted down dishes only briefly, knowing
that when they came to consult their lists they would be able to interpret the

cryptic notes, whereas others wrote out details not just of the dishes but also of the presentation, to show the plan of the table layout and also whether glass or china was used to hold the food. Such documents show us how menus were planned in the eighteenth century. Diaries and letters describing meals often take such matters as the division into two or more courses for granted, and the theory and practice need to be considered together in order to make sense of a system which was very different from our own, not only in the order of consumption of different dishes, but also in the implied hierarchy of those dishes within and between the courses of the meal.

This fairly succinct account of the organization of the meal naturally leads on to how the meal was served and how it was eaten, an area of investigation which covers what we would call table manners, but which also extends far beyond, to include the image of hospitality. Very few of the cookery books offered advice on how to present the meal to one's guests, and so for a more complete view of the host's and hostess' duties, one must turn to another form of prescriptive literature, the conduct-books, together with the occasional novel which functioned in part as a conduct-book, such as Richardson's *Pamela*. Many eighteenth-century conduct-books aimed at women concentrated more on their morals than their manners, and the sample used here (and earlier, in the introductory remarks to Part II on the changing vision of a woman's rôle in the home) often proved disappointingly empty of such practical matters. The picture obtained from prescriptive literature does, however, show that models of correct behaviour did not remain static throughout the century, contrary to the usual presentation of a system which changed very little until its closing years.[5] Here, as in the study of changing culinary styles, the evidence for change is often discovered hidden amongst what appear to be the same unchanging advice, all the more so since table-manners are an area dominated by conservatism. What does emerge is that culinary styles and behaviour at table followed identical patterns which, taken together, offer an image of hospitality in line with social developments during the period.

A view of contemporaries' reactions to what they found on the dinner-table forms the last section. By looking more closely at the comments people made

---

[5] Most modern commentators rely heavily on Trusler's *The Honours of the Table* (1788), and suggest that this book offers the first signs of the change to a more informal style; see for instance Paston-Williams, *The Art of Dining* (1993), pp. 248–49, 254–60. Jennifer Stead offers a more nuanced but very brief overview in *A Taste of History* (1993), pp. 229–32.

when they were invited out, or invited others, it is possible to see how attitudes to food shifted in step with culinary styles. Personal appreciations by individuals show much more than the vagaries of individuals' taste. Placed against wider areas of often indirect comment on food in periodicals and satirical texts and prints, it becomes clear that certain trends coloured individuals' perceptions of dishes. The most obvious is the increasingly hostile attitude towards French food: politics, even party politics, impinged on the dinner-table. The last section thus attempts to use comments on food to draw some conclusions from the various strands of this study of cookery, to offer some answers to the inevitable question of why culinary styles changed as they did.

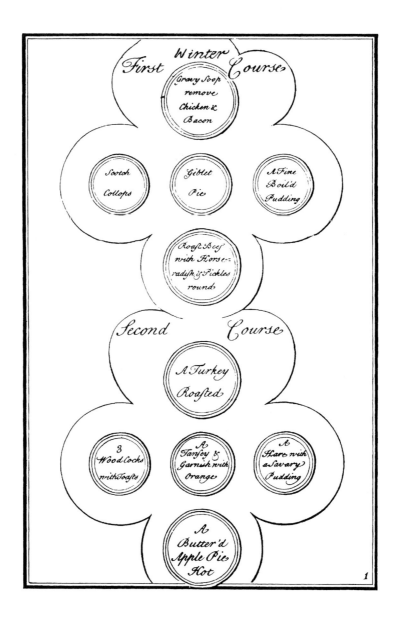

Bill of fare for a two-course dinner from E. Smith, The Compleat Housewife, *1727 (plate taken from the 16th edition of 1758). Her bills of fare are very much simpler than those of the court-cooks, with a thoroughly 'domestic' style here.*

Cookery books themselves rarely mention meal-times, except indirectly to advise the cook to prepare his dishes betimes to be ready to serve at the correct hour. Even Martha Bradley, who tells the aspiring hostess how to behave to her guests and how to present the meal, gives no advice on when to serve it. One reason for this silence was the instability of dinner-time. Breakfast hardly moved at all, but dinner, and therefore supper (usually taken about six hours after dinner), moved forward, becoming later and later in the course of the century. This progression was not constant: there were social and geographical variables, as well as the occasional pause. Letters and diaries never appear to present a uniform picture for any given date. However, take the variables into account (occasional peculiarities notwithstanding), and there is a coherent system. Diarists and letter-writers tend to notice the unusual rather than the everyday, which would most often be that the writer and his company did not eat before such-and-such. This in a tone implying both pride (the hour was fashionably late), and moral misgivings (being à la mode equated with luxury and even laziness). The dinner-hour had connotations of social status: anyone who aspired to gentility felt the need to adapt his usual hours to those required by polite society.

For virtually the whole of the eighteenth century, the fashionable breakfast time was 10 o'clock. Away from London it might be a little earlier and, everywhere, the meal might be deferred after a late night. Other reasons for a different time was a day's sport for the gentlemen or an excursion of some kind.[1] The common hour followed from the upper classes adopting a new form of breakfast, composed of bread or toast, or enriched breads such as the wedge-shaped buns known as 'wigs', with coffee or chocolate as the usual drinks. This replaced the early-morning snack of cold meat and beer or ale which had never really been considered as a meal. By the early years of the eighteenth century, this breakfast-hour was well established in London. In 1711 we find Jonathan Swift inviting himself to Sir Andrew Fountaine:

---

[1] Apart from the examples quoted below, breakfast at or around 10 is mentioned in 1753, 1770 and the 1790s; see Cust, *Records of the Cust Family, Series II* (1909), p. 219; Lichtenburg, *Lettres sur l'Angleterre* (1992), p. 83; Houblon, *The Houblon Family* (1907), vol. 2, pp. 119, 129, 150; Faujas de Saint Fond, *Voyages* (1797), vol. 1, p. 289. Examples of earlier breakfasts, at 9, are to be found for 1715, 1756 and 1766; see Matthews (ed.), *Diary of Dudley Ryder* (1939), p. 81; Cust (1909), p. 281; Mitchell & Penrose (eds), *Letters from Bath* (1983), pp. 70, 75.

I will infallibly breakfast with you this morning, and come exactly at ten. … Pray get all things ready for Breakfast. Have the Coffee Tee and Chocolate cut and dry in so many Pots, for I will most infallibly come this morning….[2]

The letter conveniently specifies the hour and includes notice of tea, marking its progress towards universal adoption. Away from the capital, in Scotland, an earlier hour was still the rule. In 1705 Lady Grisell Baillie wrote a note to her daughter's governess to say how Grisie should spend the day:

To rise by seven a clock and goe about her duty of reading, etc. etc., and be drest to come to Breckfast at nine, to play on the spinnet till eleven, from eleven till twelve to write and read French. At two a clock sow her seam till four, at four learn arithmetic, after that dance and play on the spinet again till six and play herself till supper and to bed at nine.[3]

This difference, here geographical, can also be observed as one moves down the social scale. Away from London, the centre of fashion, even the gentry tended to take their breakfast soon after 9, and the lower classes ate it earlier. In the 1750s Elizabeth Raper, a merchant's daughter, took her breakfast at any time between 9.30 and 11, while at the same date Thomas Turner, a small Sussex shopkeeper, took his between 7 and 8 in the summer, 8 and 9 in the winter.[4]

Amongst shopkeepers and artisans in towns, or farmers in the country, the old hour was maintained for practical reasons, even if the meal itself gradually took on the new foods adopted by the wealthy so that, by mid-century, bread and tea were the universal fare. The later hour signalled membership of the leisured classes and 10 o'clock remained the rule virtually until the end of the century. When people breakfasted later than that, it was matter for pseudo-scandalized comment, as when the Sheffield family was celebrating his lordship's second marriage in January 1795:

---

[2] Williams (ed.), *Correspondence of Jonathan Swift* (1963–65), vol. 1, p. 269.
[3] Scott-Moncrieff (ed.), *Household Book of Lady Grisell Baillie* (1911), p. xlvii.
[4] See Grant (ed.), *Receipt Book of Elizabeth Raper* (19), pp. 11, 12; Vaisey (ed.), *The Diary of Thomas Turner* (1985), p. 26.

You would be terrified at the disorderly hours we keep ... the day after the Dance, we did not breakfast till past twelve. In a common way, we do not assemble till near eleven.[5]

Normally, this household breakfasted at 10. In 1786 Lord Sheffield's daughter Maria described her day to her aunt:

I will give an account of one day and then you will see every day. I get up at 8, I walk from 9 to 10; we then breakfast; about 11, I play on the Harpsichord or I draw. 1, I translate, and, 2, walk out again, 3, I generally read, and, 4, we go to dine, after Dinner we play at Backgammon; we drink Tea at 7, and I work or play on the Piano till 10, when we have our little bit of Supper and, 11, we go to Bed.[6]

This account of the day's activities shows that breakfast did not mark the start of the day, but came as a pause during the morning. Other examples would show this to hold throughout the century.[7]

While the breakfast hour remained stable, dinner moved inexorably forward, from a little after midday at the beginning of the century to the early evening at the end. This movement affected all the 'politer' sections of society, from the aristocracy down to tradesmen, albeit to varying degrees. The urban working classes and country people from small farmers downwards, kept to the old hours. Later dining marked a great division in society between the haves and the have-nots, and its significance is demonstrated by the insistence of such institutions as workhouses that the inmates should dine before 1 o'clock, or, later in the century, at 1.[8] These were the hours of the late seventeenth century. In Pepys' day, people had dined at midday or soon after, but by the early 1700s

---

[5] Adeane (ed.), *The Girlhood of Maria Josepha Holroyd* (1896), p. 316.

[6] Ibid., p. 14.

[7] One example is Narcissus Luttrell's day on 5 November 1722: he rose at 8, breakfasted at 10, dined 'after 3', and had supper at 9. See Holme, *Chelsea*, (1972), p. 45.

[8] The regulations for Rumford workhouse in 1725 specified dinner 'by one a Clock'; in 1771 Worcester workhouse gave 'Dinner at One', winter and summer. As late as 1816, dinner at the Oxford workhouse was at 12. See *An Account of Several Work-Houses* (1725), p. 55; 'Orders to be observed in the Work-house in the parish of St Peters 1771' (Worcester RO D899. 31 3762/89); *Bye Laws, Statutes, and General Rules and Orders, of the House of Industry at Oxford* (1816), p. 19. I owe this information to Jacques Carré.

dinner was already at 2, or even later in London. The pressure of fashion is illustrated by two letters inviting Swift to dinner, the second coming only three years after the first. In 1708 Addison invited him for 2 o'clock:

> I shall take it as a particular favour, if you will give me Your Company at the George in Pal-Mal about two in the After-noon .... Mr Steele and Frowde will dine with us.[9]

But in 1711 the invitation, from Henry St John, was for an hour later:

> Since you was here in the morning, I have found means of putting off the engagement I was under for tomorrow, so that I expect you to dine with me att three a clock.[10]

The dinner hour had moved from 12 to 3 in half a century, which was more than it had shifted in the previous three centuries.

The speed of the change did not go unnoticed, and Steele made it the subject of humorous commentary in the *Tatler*:

> Our Grandmothers, tho' they were wont to sit up the last in the Family, were all of them fast asleep at the same Hours that their Daughters are busy at Crimp and Basset. Modern Statesmen are concerting Schemes, and engaged in the Depth of Politicks, at the time when their Fore-Fathers were laid down quietly to Rest, and had nothing in their Heads but Dreams. As we have thus thrown Business and Pleasure into the Hours of Rest, and by that Means made the natural Night but half as long as it should be, we are forced to piece it out with a great Part of the Morning; so that near Two thirds of the Nation lie fast asleep for several Hours in broad Day-light. This Irregularity is grown so very fashionable at present, that there is scarce a Lady of Quality in *Great Britain* that ever saw the Sun rise. ... All Business is driven forward: ... In my memory the Dinner has crept by Degrees from Twelve a Clock to Three, and where it will fix no Body knows.

---

[9] Williams (1963–65), vol. 1, p. 74. The 2 o'clock dinner-hour in and around London at this date (1710) is confirmed in Uffenbach, *Merkwürdige Reisen*, vol. 3 (1753), p. 452, 595.
[10] Williams (1963–65), vol. 1, p. 205.

I have sometimes thought to draw up a Memorial in the Behalf of Supper against Dinner, setting forth, That the said Dinner has made several Encroachments upon the said Supper, and entered very far upon his Frontiers; That he has banished him out of several Families, and in all has driven him from his Head Quarters, and forced him to make his Retreat into the Hours of Midnight; and in short, That he is now in Danger of being entirely confounded and lost in Breakfast. ... Who would not wonder at this perverted Relish of those who are reckoned the most polite Part of Mankind, that ... exchange so many chearful Morning Hours for the Pleasures of Midnight Revels and Debauches?[11]

This is an early example of the idea of the 'natural' rhythm of one's ancestors being opposed to the 'perverted' rhythm of modern society. The implicit opposition is of nature and culture, and thus culture is assimilated to perversion. Exactly the same phenomenon had characterized the 'developed' society of the Roman empire, as one historian remarks:

As a society develops, the main meal of the day is eaten later and later. At first the main Roman meal, *cena*, like English dinner in the seventeenth century, was at midday. In both cases as this meal moved forward, at one end of the day it dispossessed the evening meal (*vesperna* in Rome, supper in England), for which there was no longer any need, and at the other end it created a gap which required to be filled by a new meal, *prandium* in Rome, lunch in England.[12]

The implication of this is that a 'developed' society (that is, containing a substantial leisured class) came into existence in England in the eighteenth century. Another feature of this 'developed' model is that prestige is associated with late eating, whereas at an earlier period, this had not been the case. In medieval and Tudor England, the magnates had dined first, before their retinues; now it was the servants who ate first, a sign also that the underlings had their own separate diet and were not expected to feed on the remains from the first table (although the servants could always pilfer relics from dinner for their own supper).

---

[11] *The Tatler*, number 263, 14 Dec. 1710.
[12] Balsdon, *Life and Leisure in Ancient Rome* (1969), p. 25.

This developed society was also essentially urban: it was in London that the fashionable dinner-hour moved forward first. The timetable set out for Grisie Baillie at the beginning of the century would have dinners amongst the Scots gentry beginning soon after twelve, two hours earlier than Londoners of the same milieu. The dinner-hour, like breakfast, was subject to the variables of geography and social status. In fashionable London, dinner was being taken later and later; the movement continued until about 1725, then slowed. Meanwhile, the gap between the modish and those who followed fashion less slavishly had grown, and the difference lower down the social scale was considerable. Many people of modest means continued to dine at 2 even after this had become old-hat. As a result, foreign travellers were often confused, not quite sure why they observed such differences. In 1727 César de Saussure, describing English meals, seems uncertain about dinner-time:

> People do not usually have supper in this country. Dinner is at 2 or 3 o'clock. There are even plenty of people who sit down to dinner much later. If you feel like having a bite to eat and something to drink in the evening, this is quite possible, but supper is not a regular meal.[13]

Saussure fails to realize that this was the result of the varying behaviour of different social classes.

In or near London in the 1720s, the aristocracy dined after 3: an example was the Duke of Chandos, who sat down to dinner between 3 and 4.[14] To dine at 4 was an urban habit; even the nobility kept earlier hours in the country. Thus Tom Hill, the tutor and friend of Lord March (the future Duke of Richmond), wrote to his charge during a stay with Lord Cardigan in 1723:

> We rise before nine, breakfast soon after, saunter about or read or do anything else til dinner time, which seldom exceeds two. A bottle after that upon the table for about an hour, then for bowls, til darkness brings

---

[13] 'On ne soupe pas ordinairement dans ce pays. On dîne à 2 ou 3 heures. Bien des personnes même se mettent à table beaucoup plus tard. Si l'on veut manger un morceau, & boire un coup le soir, on peut le faire, mais le souper n'est pas un repas réglé.' Saussure, *Lettres et voyages* (1903), p. 229.
[14] Collins Baker & Baker, *The Life and Circumstances of James Brydges First Duke of Chandos* (1949), p. 193.

on whisk, which lasts til supper and then a chearful glas and to bed ....
I assure you we seldom sit up after midnight ....[15]

Where fashion did not dictate a later hour, the dinner-time of the earlier years of the century was adhered to.

Some chose to dine earlier for the sake of their health. When Alexander Pope went to Bristol and to Bath in 1739, he got into the habit of dining at 2, and when he returned to London he decided to keep to Bath hours:

> Since I came to London, I am not so much in Spirits, nor in the same Quiet, as at Bath. The Irregular hours of Dining (for as to Nights, I keep the same) already have disordered my Stomach, & bring back that Heaviness and Languor upon me after dinner, which I was almost entirely free from. ... I am determind to fix my dining to Two a clock, tho I dine by myself, & comply afterwards with the Importunities & Civilities of Friends in *Attending*, not *Partaking* their Dinners.[16]

Clearly, Pope's friends in London now dined later but in Bath the timetable of the early years of the century was maintained, and indeed continued until well into the 1770s,[17] even though it was a fashionable watering-place much frequented by the aristocracy. The social round decreed by Beau Nash in his heyday – going to the pump-room from 8 to 10, before breakfast, then to divine service at the Abbey at 11, before dinner at 2, followed by another visit to the Abbey at 4, with subscription balls in the evenings from 6 or later until 11 sharp – was kept as if it were a magic formula guaranteeing the success of the spa. The conservatism of the dinner-hour went with the demand for full court dress to be worn at balls by those who wished to dance the minuet. Perhaps part of the charm of Bath was its nostalgic adherence to former ways so that to stay there was to return to a 'golden age' of decorum and dignity.

---

[15] Lennox, *A Duke and his Friends* (1911), vol. 1, p. 74.

[16] Sherburn (ed.), *Correspondence of Alexander Pope* (1956), vol. 4, p. 225. The Bath dinner-hour was also followed in the 1730s in Scarborough: see Thomson, *Letters of a Grandmother* (1943), p. 48.

[17] For the timetable described below, see the various Bath guides, such as *The Bath and Bristol Guide* (ed. 4, Bath: [*c.* 1760]); *The New Bath Guide* (Bath: [*c.* 1762]); *The Strangers' Assistant and Guide to Bath* (Bath: 1773). The correspondence of the Rev. John Penrose, who visited Bath in 1766 and 1767, confirms this timetable. See Mitchell & Penrose (1983), p. 75 and passim.

In London the dinner-hour reached 4 by about 1750; in that year, Madame
du Bocage, who moved in the best circles, noted that 'Morning lasts a long
time: one does not sit down to dinner before 4 o'clock.'[18] In the provinces the
gentry dined two hours earlier. By the 1740s, Lady Grisell Baillie, who had
dined at 12 in 1705, was dining at 2, although breakfast was still unfashionably
early, to judge from the instructions she gave her servants in 1743:

> Two bells are to be rung fer every meal; for breakfast half an hour after
> 8 and at 9; for diner half an hour after 1 and at 2; for super half an hour
> after 8 and at 9. ...
>
> Have bread toasted, butterd tost or whatever is orderd for breakfast
> all set ready by the second bell.[19]

The second bell announced the start of the meal. Lower down the social scale,
a small gentry family in Buckinghamshire dined at the same hour as Lady
Grisell, or even earlier. In 1745 Henry Purefoy answered an invitation to an
informal dinner by announcing his arrival for 1 o'clock: 'Since you are so obli-
dging to give us an Invitation wee intend to come & take a commons with you
toomorrow about one a clock & hope wee shall have your good company.'[20]
Two years later, when some neighbours were given a more formal invitation to
dine, dinner was to be at 2 o'clock: 'I shall have an haunch of young fat Venison
for dinner on Tuesday next & desire the favour of yours or Mr. Wallbank's and
Miss Barrett's good company to eat some of it. Mr. & Mrs. Haws will be with
us then & dinner will be on ye Table by 2 o'clock.'[21] The more formal invitation (with prestigious venison on the menu) required a later hour.

At an even more modest level of society, earlier hours were still the norm.
In 1756, the Sussex shopkeeper Thomas Turner decided to dine between 12 and
1 when he ate at home, but when he was invited by the rector, the Rev. Porter
(as close as he ever got to the gentry), he timed his arrival for 1.45, clearly
expecting dinner at 2.[22]

---

[18] 'Le matin est long, on ne se met à table qu'à 4 heures.' Du Bocage, *Recueil des Oeuvres* (1762), vol.
3, p. 45.
[19] Scott-Moncrieff (1911), p. 273.
[20] Eland (ed.), *Purefoy Letters* (1931), vol. 2, p. 382.
[21] Eland, vol. 2, p. 387.
[22] See Vaisey (1985), pp. 26, 166

In the middle of the century, and for a period of about 30 years, the dinner-hour seems to have stuck at 4 in London and rather earlier in the country, although the deceleration of change did allow the country to catch up a little. In 1770 another foreign visitor, Pierre Jean Grosley, who had stayed in London in 1765, noted that everyone from the Court down to the bourgeoisie dined at around 4.[23] That so wide a range of social classes should have dined at the same time seems improbable. Twelve years later, Carl Philipp Moritz, a more observant visitor, commented on the difference between the Court and the City:

> In Westminster the morning lasts until four or five in the afternoon, which is the earliest time for dinner, and the times when one has supper and goes to bed are calculated accordingly. Usually one does not take breakfast before ten o'clock. The further one goes from the neighbourhood of the Court, and the closer to the City, the more bourgeois it becomes, and people are happy to dine around three, that is, as soon as business on the Stock Exchange has finished for the day.[24]

Thus by the 1780s the dinner-hour was on the move again. The trend seems to have begun in the early 1770s: Lady Mary Coke noted in 1772 that Court and diplomatic circles dined later, at 5 or even 6.[25] By the 1780s the aristocracy had begun to follow the lead of the Court and was now dining at 4 or 5, and the middle classes had adopted the somewhat less fashionable hour of 3. Moritz's observations are confirmed by another German visitor a little later:

> Meal-times among Londoners are very variable. Artisans dine at about one o'clock, shopkeepers and other tradespeople at about three; by

---

[23] Grosley, *Londres* (1770), vol. 1, p. 191.

[24] 'In Westminster dauert der Morgen bis Nachmittags um vier bis fünf Uhr, wo man erst zu Mittags speiset nach welchem Verhältniß sich denn auch die Zeit des Abendessens und zu Bettegehens richtet. Um zehn Uhr wird gemeiniglich erst gefrühstückt. Je weiter man von der Gegend des Hofes wiederum in die Stadt kömmt, desto bürgerlicher wird es auch, und man speißt wohl zu Mittags um drei Uhr, sobald nehmlich die Geschäfte auf der Börse geendigt sind.' Moritz, *Reisen eines Deutschen in England im Jahr 1782* (1783), p. 85.

[25] In 1772 Lady Mary mentioned that the Princess Amelia usually dined at 5, and she noted that at the French ambassador's, dinner was not served until 6; see Home (ed.), *Letters and Journals of Lady Mary Coke* (1889–96), vol. 4, pp. 102, 115.

contrast, the aristocracy does not go to dinner until about four, or even later.[26]

A similar process could be observed in the provinces. By 1770 the country gentry's dinner-hour had begun to catch up with that of the fashionable sectors of the capital. The wealthier gentry tended to keep the same hours in London and at their country seats: for instance, Caroline Lybbe Powys noted in 1771 that she dined at 4 when at home in Oxfordshire.[27] Also in the 1770s, on visits to the country or during a stay at Tunbridge Wells, the fashionable Milbankes dined at 4, noting with horror that when visiting a provincial aunt while en route to Scarborough in 1777 they were expected to dine 'at the *Antediluvian* hour of two'.[28] By the end of the century, the 4 o'clock dinner had reached even the furthest parts of the kingdom: when Faujas de Saint Fond visited Scotland in the 1790s, he dined at 4, or even at 4.30 while staying with the Duke of Argyll.[29] Contacts between the aristocracy, visiting their country seats, and the gentry, together with improved communications between the capital and the provinces, helped to bring in more fashionable late hours, as did country activities as hunting which demanded a later dinner in order not to interrupt the pleasures of sport. Mrs Lybbe Powys noted that during the hunting season one did not dine before 5.[30]

The lesser gentry and the genteel professional classes did not imitate aristocratic fashions quite as closely. The usual dinner-hour after about 1770 was 3 for the family, slightly later when one had guests. While staying with friends near Birmingham in 1779, Catherine Hutton dined at 3.[31] Further north,

---

[26] 'Die Tischzeit bey den Einwohnern von London ist sehr verschieden. Die Handwerksleute essen um ein Uhr, die Kaufleute und alle andre Mittelstände um drey; dagegen der Adel erst um vier Uhr, auch noch später zu Tische geht.' Archenholz, *England und Italien*, (1791), vol. 3, p. 7.

[27] Climenson (ed.), *Passages from the Diaries of Mrs. Philip Lybbe Powys* (1899), p. 137.

[28] Elwin (ed.), *The Noels and the Milbankes* (1967), pp. 45, 63, 98.

[29] See Faujas de Saint Fond, *Voyages en Angleterre, en Ecosse, et aux Iles Hébrides* (1797), vol. 1, p. 290; vol. 2, p. 82. Earlier, in the 1770s, the Scottish aristocracy was dining at 3: see Godber, 'The Marchioness Grey of Wrest Park' (1968), pp. 90–91. The fashionable dinner-hour in Edinburgh seems to have been 2 or 3 in the 1760s, and 4 or 5 by the 1780s: see Mure, 'Some remarks on the change of manners in my own time' in Mure (1854), p. 271; Lettice, *Letters on a Tour through various parts of Scotland* (1794), p. 527.

[30] See Climenson (1899), p. 137.

[31] See Beale (ed.), *Reminiscences of a Gentlewoman of the last Century* (1891), pp. 15, 18.

Elizabeth Shackleton mentioned dinner 'at the fashionable hour four o'clock' in 1778, and her son and his wife held their celebration dinners (extraordinary occasions) at the same time.[32] In the late 1770s the Grays, a professional family of solicitors in York, took dinner at 3 or 4.[33] Similarly, when he was alone with his niece, the Rev. James Woodforde dined at 3, his usual hour. In 1786 his routine was nearly interrupted:

> I buried this Afternoon about 4 o'clock, John Plummer an Infant aged only 5 Weeks. I knew nothing of burying the above Infant till 3 o'clock this Afternoon, then on hearing the Church Bell, I sent to Church to enquire the reason, and word was brought me, that there was a Child then at the Church Gate for Interment — It being my Dinner Time, I went as soon as ever I had finished my Dinner ....[34]

When he had guests, or was a guest himself, dinner tended to be later. In April 1796 one of his guests did not arrive until nearly 4, and since the latecomer had not been the victim of any mishap, it seems that he arrived at what he thought was the correct time.[35] Shortly afterwards, Woodforde and his niece were themselves guests, and were unnecessarily worried about being late:

> It was after two o'clock before Dr. Thorne left us, and both of us quite undressed, so that we had to dress ourselves (being going to Mr. Mellish's to dinner) and to be at Tuddenham by half past three o'clock, if we could. At 3. o'clock I drove Nancy over in my little Cart to Mr. Mellishs, and did not get there till 4. o'clock. ... All the Company met within ten Minutes of each other. Dinner was soon announced after our Arrival .... [36]

Since everyone arrived at about 4, it seems that dinner did not have to be deferred. Woodforde confirms the impression given by the Purefoy letters that

---

[32] See Vickery (1998), p. 334 n. 32.

[33] See Gray (ed.), *Papers and Diaries of a York Family* (1927), p. 43. Further examples of dinner at 3 or 4 in the provinces in the 1770s and 1780s are found in Houblon (1907), vol. 2, pp. 120, 130; Twining (ed.), *Selections from Papers of the Twining Family* (1887), p. 123.

[34] Beresford (ed.), *Diary of a Country Parson*, (1924–31), vol. 2, p. 285.

[35] Beresford, vol. 4, p. 270.

[36] Beresford, vol. 4, p. 272.

one sent out formal invitations for a later hour than one's habitual time when alone or with a family party.

To dine later was a sign of elegance, and it conferred honour on host and guests to mark a dinner-party by eating later than usual. Each level of society tended to imitate the level above. The chain of emulation is demonstrated by an anecdote from Boswell's diary for 1775. He was on his way to London for his annual spring visit, and in the coach he fell into conversation with a mercer who had been born in Durham but now lived in London, whither he was returning after a visit to his native district:

> The mercer told me that ... he drank tea twice a day, and had some-times a friend to dine with him, or eat cold meat at night. ... He said, to a man accustomed to dine between two and three, it seemed strange to dine at one, as they do in this country. Everything is comparative. He looked big, as one who dined between two and three. How *little* and how *poor* would he seem to a fashionable man in London who dines between four and five![37]

Not only dinner, but tea-drinking also bore its badge of rank. The mercer's boasting and Boswell's pitying comment illustrate the importance of the dinner-hour as a sign of social status. Boswell, while laughing at the mercer, implicitly recognizes the basis for such pretensions. The hierarchy which divided London from the provinces also divided the different social classes.

They were not the only ones to be acutely aware of the nuances of meal times. In 1798, Jane Austen wrote to her sister Cassandra, staying with their brother Edward Knight (the rich member of the family), that the dinner-hour at Steventon must seem very lowly:

> We dine now at half after Three, & have done dinner I suppose before you begin – We drink tea at half after six. – I am afraid you will despise us.[38]

Later, she exploited the gap between the upper-class dinner-hour and that of less exalted people in her unfinished novel *The Watsons*. A group of young men

---

[37] Ryskamp & Pottle (eds), *Boswell: The Ominous Years* (1963), p. 79.
[38] Chapman (ed.), *Jane Austen's Letters* (1952), p. 39.

have the bad manners to visit Emma, the heroine, just as she is about to sit down to dinner, humiliating her by an overt display of social superiority.[39]

At the very end of the century, the hour moved on again, at least in the capital. In the 1790s, Maria Holroyd dined at 5 when she was at Sheffield Place, but in London:

> Mr. Bernard conducted the Lady Mayoress and us thro' Byeways to his House at five o'clock, and gave us an excellent dinner a little after six.[40]

This particular meal preceded a ball and was perhaps later than usual, but by this date the standard hour in London, and elsewhere amongst the fashionable, was not before 5. When Faujas de Saint Fond dined with the Royal Society, dinner was served at 5; and when the Prince Regent, staying in Brighton, invited himself to dinner at Uppark in 1795, he announced his arrival, 'by dinner between five and six o'clock'.[41] The forward movement continued. In 1805, Lady Nugent, who had returned to London after a stay in Jamaica, was surprised to find her friends dining at 6 in London and at 5 in the country.[42] The latter hour is confirmed by the Nottingham diarist Abigail Gawthern, who was both a manufacturer and a landowner and thus belonged to polite society. In 1802 she dined out on 'a most elegant dinner at 5'.[43] This time soon became the rule in the country. By 1808 Jane Austen was dining at 5, even at Steventon:

> Kitty Foote came on Wednesday, & her Even[g] visit began early enough for the last part, the apple pye of our dinner, for we never dine now til five.[44]

The fact she needed to draw her sister's attention to the hour suggests this was still something of a novelty. Progress was somewhat checked during the decade of Waterloo, before resuming to turn dinner into the evening meal it remains today.

---

[39] See Austen, *The Watsons*, in Chapman (ed.), *Minor Works* (1963), pp. 344–345.

[40] Adeane (1896), p. 30.

[41] See Faujas (1797), vol. I, p. 55; Meade-Fetherstonhaugh & Warner, *Uppark and its people* (1965), pp. 58–9.

[42] See Palmer, *Movable Feasts* (1952), p. 36.

[43] Henstock (ed.), 'The Diary of Abigail Gawthern' (1980), p. 97.

[44] Chapman (1952),p. 237.

No matter when dinner commenced, it invariably went through three
phases: the meal itself, with anything from one to three courses, depending on
the dignity of the occasion; a period of drinking, which concerned the gentlemen only, although the ladies might participate briefly before they retired; and
finally tea and coffee, served in the drawing-room when the gentlemen rejoined
the ladies. These hot drinks were generally accompanied by bread, butter and
cakes, presumably to soak up some of the alcohol imbibed by the menfolk,
who might be somewhat worse for wear by the time they reached the drawing-
room. Just how long this whole process lasted, and its effect on the last meal
of the day, supper, is a matter of debate.

In a comparative study of meals in France and the rest of Europe from the
sixteenth to the nineteenth centuries, Jean-Louis Flandrin concluded that supper had virtually disappeared in England by the eighteenth century.[45] But there
was a gap between the observations made by English writers and those of the
foreign tourists Flandrin relied on. Even among the latter, the verdict was by
no means unanimous. Estimates of the length of the post-prandial drinking
sessions varied from one to three hours. While one French visitor in 1784 said
two or three hours was the norm, another in the 1790s noted several dinners
where all three phases, from start to finish, were completed in about three
hours.[46] A few scattered references in Woodforde's diary show that this was the
case at all the levels of society he frequented.[47] The timetables given by Maria
Holroyd and Jane Austen confirm this. The habit of very prolonged drinking
after dinner seems to have been limited to the aristocracy, and to have been by
no means universal even then. (Tom Hill's account of a day in Lord Cardigan's
house in 1723 reckoned an hour devoted to drinking.)

As we have just noticed, many foreign tourists thought that supper was not
a real meal in England. In 1698, Misson stated that in England, 'one does not
sup', although a marginal note tempered this peremptory judgement by adding
that 'in a few families there is a regular supper, particularly in the country'.[48]
In 1727, Saussure received the same impression; and in 1786 Sophie von la

---

[45] Flandrin, 'Les repas en France et dans les pays d'Europe' in Flandrin & Cobbi (1999), p. 201.

[46] See Scarfe (ed. & trans.), *A Frenchman's Year in Suffolk* (1988), p. 23; Faujas (1797), vol. 1, pp. 55–
8, 66–7, 71.

[47] Beresford (1924–31), passim.

[48] Misson says, 'on ne soupe point', but his note in the margin adds, 'En quelques familles on a un
souper réglé; particulièrement à la Campagne.' Misson (1698), p. 411.

Roche was sure that supper did not exist, because the midday meal was not taken until 4.[49] Other travellers, however, found the contrary, even with dinner at the selfsame hour. Amongst them was Faujas de Saint Fond who, after describing at length a Scottish dinner, complained of having to start eating again at 10 o'clock at night:

> But what is perhaps somewhat disagreeable is that at ten o'clock in the evening one has to return to the table and stay there until midnight for supper, which is pretty well the same sort of meal as dinner, and no less copious.[50]

Lavish supper is one aspect of the more enduring tradition of hospitality in the Celtic zone noted by Felicity Heal.[51] François de la Rochefoucauld, the eighteen-year-old son of the duc de Liancourt, spent a year in England, mostly in Suffolk, in 1784. He noted that in London, men breakfasted at 10 or 11, dined at 5, and went to their clubs at 9 to game and drink all night (supper is not mentioned), but in the country, whether in the houses of the aristocracy or the gentry, people breakfasted earlier, at 9, and dined at 4. In his experience, the whole process took several hours, the first two occupied by eating, the second two or three by drinking, after which the gentlemen joined the ladies for tea and coffee. Then they played cards, helped along with punch and, finally, a supper of cold meat was available at 12.[52] By his account, supper was entirely superfluous. It must be noted that some French tourists (but by no means all) found the hard drinking unpleasant. Their comments must be interpreted in the light of what they perceived as a difference between the habits of France and barbaric England. Thus the young de la Rochefoucauld's remarks may well exaggerate (no other document suggests breakfast at 11 or supper at 12 in the normal course of events). Faujas probably gives a more reliable

---

[49] 'Da man in England um 4 Uhr zu Mittag speißt, so fallt gewohnlich das Nachtessen weg'. La Roche, *Tagebuch einer Reise durch Holland and England*(1791), p. 391.

[50] 'Mais ce qu'il y a peut-être d'un peu pénible, c'est qu'à dix heures du soir il faut se remettre à table et assister jusqu'à minuit à un souper, dans le même genre à peu près que le dîner, et non moins abondant.' Faujas (1797), vol. 2, p. 86. This was not an exception: after dinner at 4. 30, supper was served at 10 at Inverary, the seat of the Duke of Argyll (vol. 1, pp. 289–296).

[51] See Heal, *Hospitality in Early Modern England* (1990), pp. 396–7.

[52] See Scarfe (1988), pp. 14, 21–23.

account, although his Anglophilia lays him open to the opposite charge of glossing over any lack of refinement.

Another reason for these apparently contradictory reports is that supper varied to suit the circumstances. A family alone or with intimate friends might take a collation of cold meat. Only when there were invited guests would hot dishes be offered – and it was the presence of hot dishes which turned supper into a real meal as far as the English were concerned. The burden of foreigners' reports depended on whether they were received formally or as one of the family. Because supper was not quite a real meal, there are far fewer allusions to it in letters and diaries than there are to dinner. Woodforde, for instance, seldom gives details concerning everyday suppers; and Maria Holroyd calls the meal, somewhat deprecatingly, 'our little bit of Supper'. What references there are suggest that supper normally came about six hours after dinner (thus three hours after tea).[53]

The suppers that do get described are those dignified by the presence of hot dishes when there were guests. Woodforde supplies information on such occasions, although the hour is seldom noted. People mentioned the time when writing of those eaten later than usual in honour of the occasion. The most striking examples are ball suppers, a phenomenon not confined to London. In 1756 in Hertfordshire, Elizabeth Raper attended the local races with some friends. There followed a ball:

> About six we moved off the course to the Inn, lounged and dressed, got to the ballroom about 7. ... We began at eight, and danced till 12, supped, and danced till 3. Had a very good supper.[54]

Twenty years later, a ball supper was even later; this dates from 1777, at Henley, described by Caroline Lybbe Powys:

> When the company was all got to the inn, tea was brought round the ball-room, ... tho' then twelve o'clock or later. ... After this there were two dances before supper ....[55]

[53] See, for instance, Beresford (1924–31) vol. 1, p. 102; Gray (1927), p. 43; Grosley (1770), vol. 1, p. 191.

[54] Grant (1924), p. 10.

[55] Climenson (1899), pp. 190–191; see also pp. 186–7, 322.

Even a long way from London, ball suppers were held very late. In 1789, the *York Chronicle* published a description:

> At a quarter after 2 the supper rooms were thrown open; the tables in
> each room … covered with … profusions of flummery, fruit, etc.[56]

It is clear that supper obeyed the same rules as dinner: the more festive the
event, the later the meal.

What circumstances determined that meal-times became ever later in
eighteenth-century England? In France, dinner moved from about 12.30 at the
beginning of the century to about 2.30 at the end, with the main movement
around 1740 and stability thereafter. This held true until roughly 1790–1810,
when it suddenly became an early-evening meal taken soon after 6. Meanwhile,
supper was nearly always taken after a longer interval than in England, moving
from about 9 o'clock to 11 o'clock over the course of the century. The later hour
seems to have acted as a buffer to any further development.[57] It is clear that
there was much greater and more constant pressure towards later meals in
England than in France. The mechanical explanation advanced by Flandrin –
that the English breakfast at 10 was a substantial meal, and so the English were
unable to dine at French hours[58] – will not stand up. Throughout the century,
breakfast in England was at 10, while the dinner-hour moved from 2 to 5. Nor
is there any reason to think the nature of the foods served at breakfast changed
during these years. Hot beverages, with bread in some form, were standard.
The 'traditional' English cooked breakfast is a nineteenth-century development. Maria Holroyd, faced with a breakfast of soup and meat in France in
1791, complained that 'though we poor English were allowed Tea, the smell of
the hot victuals was intolerable'.[59] The late English breakfast did not prevent
diners from sitting down to another meal only four hours later, and indeed, by
the time the interval between breakfast and dinner had grown to seven hours,
people were beginning to feel the need for another meal to fill the gap, a point
to which we shall shortly return. A more likely explanation for the dynamic
nature of meal-times in England is suggested by Balsdon's remarks on

---

[56] Quoted in de Salis, *The Art of Cookery Past and Present* (1898), pp. 172–173.

[57] See the table in Flandrin (1999), p. 212.

[58] Flandrin (1999), p. 210.

[59] Adeane (1896), p. 40.

'developed' societies quoted earlier. What had developed in England was not just a leisured class, but a large middle class, made of 'emulative bourgeois'.[60] The leisured class who were the first to adopt later dining were imitated by those immediately below them on the social ladder, and so on down all the levels of society which aspired to gentility. Later dining was an essential social marker, differentiating the haves from the have-nots, the fashionable from the unfashionable, the sophisticated from the rustic. Boswell's mercer sneered at the provincial timetable he himself had left behind as he stepped up to what he saw as London sophistication. The brief pause in the forward movement which seems to have occurred between 1740 and 1770 coincides with a period of rejection of aristocratic food fashions by the cookery book writers and their audience, and this suggests a momentary easing of the pressures which lay behind the forward impetus. Emulation by those below created constant stimulus on those at the top to redefine the signs of distinction. The honour conferred by later hours ensured that the process of emulation might falter but would never collapse.

The pressures which pushed the movement forward did not quite make supper disappear, even when dinner became a late-afternoon meal. By the end of the century, however, the need for a new meal was felt to stop the gap between breakfast and dinner, especially when breakfast was taken a little earlier than 10. Of course, people could and did take a mid-morning snack. Woodforde often gave visitors wine and cake, as when he met a fellow clergyman near his house in 1790.[61] What began to turn the snack into a meal was when meat was eaten. Boswell found a friend's wife eating cold meat one day, and his tone sounds faintly shocked (although he joined in):

> The Hon. James Stuart's: 'Not at Home'; but found Mrs. Stuart, who was, or seemed to be, very happy to see me. … She had with her a Miss Hale, and they were eating cold pigeon pie and cold beef and drinking Madeira and water at two o'clock. I joined them in beef and Madeira.[62]

---

[60] The expression is used by Roy Porter in his appraisal of the social order: see Porter, *English Society in the Eighteenth Century* (1990), p. 72.

[61] Beresford (1924–31), vol. 3, pp. 217–218.

[62] Ryskamp & Pottle (1963), p. 88.

After this, Boswell went on to dine with another friend and then took tea with the Thrales. What was not normal here was that the two ladies were not returning from an arduous journey or preparing themselves for an excursion, the two circumstances which made such a substantial snack socially acceptable, especially for ladies (the ideal of feminine delicacy precluded large appetites).

The midday snack was not dignified by a name in the eighteenth century, but the omission was not long permitted. In 1808 Jane Austen described to her sister a day she had recently spent at Godmersham:

> The Moores came yesterday in their Curricle between one & two o'clock, and immediately after the noonshine which succeeded their arrival, a party set off for Buckwell to see the Pond dragged ....[63]

This term is a variant on what Dr Johnson called 'nunchin', defined as 'a piece of victuals eaten between meals'. Twenty years later, it was 'lunch' (defined by Johnson as 'as much food as one's hand can hold') that had taken over. In 1829 the committee of the exclusive Almack's Club decreed that the correct word was 'lunch': 'luncheon is avoided as unsuitable to ... polished society'.[64] The lexical uncertainty, and the preoccupation with the politeness of the term, shows that the new meal was at first reserved for the upper classes: hardly surprisingly, since the main meal of the day, dinner, was still at mid-day for the working classes, as *The Family Friend* pointed out in 1853:

> The lower classes ... dine early, and thus with them luncheon is unnecessary and accordingly not taken. Not so, however, with ... the middling and higher classes; with them, either from business or other causes, the practice of dining late has become general, and, with such, luncheon becomes a necessary meal. It should be taken about five hours after breakfast, ... to allay the cravings of nature, but not entirely to destroy the appetite.'[65]

The favoured word has changed again, and breakfast is being taken earlier, since five hours must elapse before luncheon is permitted. The class distinction

---

[63] Chapman (1952), p. 195.

[64] Quoted in Palmer (1952), p. 31.

[65] Ibid., p. 77.

between the word 'dinner' used to designate the midday or the evening meal
has persisted until very recently.

Another meal which came into existence in the Victorian age had its roots
in the previous century. The 'invention' of afternoon tea has been variously
ascribed to the duchesses of Bedford and Rutland,[66] but there is no real need
to go duchess-hunting. Almost as soon as it was introduced in England, tea-
drinking became associated with ladies who met to talk scandal.[67] This
persistent linkage is perhaps one reason why the moralists inveighed so often
against the beverage. What distinguished the meal of afternoon tea was the way
it fitted into a lady's day: in the eighteenth century tea was taken after dinner,
in the nineteenth, before that meal. Tea also retained its social cachet, even after
it had become a drink consumed by all classes – as servants imitated their mistresses and spread the habit down the social scale.[68] In 1766 the young William
Dutton, at school at Eton, begged his father to send him some tea, in order to
maintain status:

> I wish you would be so kind as to let me have Tea and Sugar here to
> drink in the afternoon, without which there is no such thing as keeping
> company with other boys of my standing.[69]

Although this example shows tea-drinking without eating, within the home it
was the done thing to offer bread and butter or cakes as well. When tea (and
usually coffee) were served about three hours after dinner, food was offered too:
in 1786 Sophie von La Roche was offered bread and butter during her 'tea-
visits',[70] and in 1792 Louisa Holroyd, who was living in Bath, described these
after-dinner tea-parties to her sister:

> You would call these parties rather sober, but for a poor creeping
> Christian like me, they do very well; go at a little after 6 or 7 and return

---

[66] See, for instance, Palmer (1952), p. 100, who attributes it to the duchess of Bedford; according to
Mark Girouard, it was the duchess of Rutland who started the fashion for afternoon tea in 1842; see
Girouard (1980), p. 293.

[67] See Congreve, *The Double Dealer*, Act I, i & vii; also Mure vol. 1 (1854), p. 269.

[68] See Hecht, *The Domestic Servant Class in Eighteenth-Century England* (1956), pp. 222–223.

[69] Quoted in Twining, *The House of Twining 1706–1956* (1956), p. 44.

[70] 'Man nimmt um 7 Uhr Thee, mit Butterbrod, und die Theebesuche dauern oft bis 11 Uhr, von
welchen man dann leicht schlafen geht'. La Roche (1791), p. 391.

at 9, have in the mean time abundance of tea, wine, bread and butter, milk punch, cake buttered and plum cake, etc. etc.[71]

This is not yet afternoon tea, but it is far closer to it than to a mere refreshment after dinner, and the hour, combined with the nature of the foods, marks it off from supper.

Tea and supper were not interchangeable in the eighteenth century, though a curious hybrid seems to have been fashionable in the first years of the nineteenth, at least in Nottingham. Between 1804 and 1808 Abigail Gawthern's diary contains many references to what she calls a 'sandwich party'. This was not an impromptu gathering, but a large event to which she invited forty or fifty people, and she was not the only woman in the district to invite guests to such affairs. The time is never indicated, but the sandwich part of the evening clearly followed dinner and preceded card-playing and dancing.[72] Other diaries show that more often, after the tea-drinking which followed dinner, the company played cards until supper. For instance, when Woodforde invited friends to dine, he gave them tea and coffee after dinner, but liked to serve supper some time later as well; his supper was usually composed of leftovers from dinner.

Supper was part of a festive evening; tea was a staider affair. And tea's image as a feminine drink was reinforced by the separation of the sexes after dinner: the ladies retired to the drawing-room, while the gentlemen remained in the dining-room to drink (we shall return to that in the study of table-manners). Thus, as Mark Girouard has pointed out,[73] the two rooms were seen as either feminine or masculine spaces. Tea and supper followed the same division. By association too, sweet dishes and innocuous drinks could be seen as feminine, whereas meat and hard liquor had masculine connotations. (Such imagery also influenced perceptions of cookery itself, and contributed to the English rejection of French *nouvelle cuisine* as too insubstantial and thus too feminine, when compared to English macho roast beef.) Breakfast foods might carry similar

---

[71] Adeane (1896), p. 127.

[72] See Henstock (1980), pp. 106–08, 110, 113, 120, 127, 137. Whether sandwiches were actually served is debatable; the word was often used as a synonym for refreshments, as Woodforde wrote in 1798 when two ladies came unexpectedly one morning: 'We gave them by way of a Sandwich or refreshment some cold rost Goose &c. with some fruit after it &c'; Beresford (1924–31), vol. 5, p. 130.

[73] See Girouard (1980), p. 205.

associations: tea and hot rolls were appropriate for ladies, cold meat and ale for gentlemen as prelude to a day's sport or a journey. Such associations led to the differentiation of the various meals, which offered their discrete forms of social intercourse. Amanda Vickery's analysis of Elizabeth Shackleton's hospitality shows guests who came to breakfast were predominantly male (a shared breakfast preceding sport or business), that dinner was most likely to bring the sexes together, and that tea parties were largely, but not exclusively, feminine (with inferiors such as tradeswomen invited, as well as social equals).[74]

Thus two new meals, lunch and tea, began to take shape. By their very presence, even in embryonic form, they created the modern structure of the day. Once lunch had arrived, breakfast had to be taken earlier; once dinner had become an early-evening meal, the disappearance of supper was inevitable. It is no accident that these new meals, and the new timetable, coincide with the first stirrings of the Industrial Revolution. The rhythm was that of the modern working day and, while it would be an over-simplification to suggest that its adoption signified the end of the reign of an aristocratic code of meal-times – in which social connotations were more important than any 'rational' timetable – the signs of a shift towards a bourgeois ethos are nevertheless present. For the time being, however, the social connotations of meal-times were what counted. Although the working classes were unable to imitate the leisurely habits of their superiors, the upper-class model was followed, albeit from a distance, by the middling sort such as Boswell's mercer. In eighteenth-century England, one's dinner-hour was as much a sign of one's social status as what one ate.

---

[74] Vickery (1998), pp. 207–08, 396.

How meals were organized, served and eaten can be followed in two kinds of source: the prescriptive literature such as cookery books for the bill of fare (or model menu as it might be termed today) and conduct-books for table-manners; and letters, travellers' journals, diaries and memoranda which give accounts of actual meals consumed. Each helps illuminate the other, but the first task is to look at the prescriptive literature, to see how things were supposed to be done. This enables a fairly narrow focus on the rituals of the table, whereas descriptions of meals often contain comments which will take us far beyond the analysis of what and how people ate, to the reasons why they consumed what they did. In this chapter, we shall examine the way the meal was organized, by analysing the bill of fare; then we shall go on to the norms of behaviour – what we would call table manners – for the host and hostess and, finally, for the guests.

The meal to which the greatest part of this chapter will be devoted is dinner, invariably the main meal throughout the century. It was, of course, the most formal, when the fullest expression of one's gentility, polite behaviour, was deployed. Supper was a true meal only when there were guests present, and it was always composed of a single course, made up at least in part of leftovers from dinner. Cookery books sometimes give supper menus, but these are less frequent than those for dinner. Breakfast, meanwhile, did not merit a bill of fare at all. The foods served up at breakfast can be discovered in comments contained in receipts, which confirm that various forms of bread and rolls were standard. For instance, E. Smith gives a receipt for a 'cake', in fact enriched bread with spice and dried fruit, telling the reader that it is 'good to eat with butter for breakfast'; Anne Battam offers a 'common breakfast cake' with caraway seeds; and Mary Cole gives a receipt for 'Bath cakes' to be eaten hot for breakfast.[1] (Breakfast does not loom large in diaries and letters either, except when it was particularly luxurious, but a few references show that after a period of transition – when the cold meat of seventeenth-century breakfasts might appear alongside the new bread with chocolate, tea or coffee – rolls, cake and

---

[1] See E– S–, *The Compleat Housewife* (1728), p. 124; Battam, *A Collection of scarce and valuable Receipts* (1750), p. 94; Cole, *The Lady's Complete Guide* (1788), p. 412.

fruit became the ingredients for a sumptuous breakfast, the ultimate luxury being chocolate.)[2]

The bills of fare set out in cookery books were, like the books themselves, aimed at a very diverse audience, and they cover a spectrum from grandiose plans of meals for the great feasts of the aristocracy given by some of the court-cooks, to the simple lists for plain middle-class dinners supplied by some of the women authors. Since the cookery book constantly enlarged its audience downwards in the course of the century, it is not surprising that the grander bills of fare belong to the beginning rather than the end of the period, and that less ambitious menus – with decreasing strictness in the rules for composing the various courses – ultimately dominate. The picture obtained from the cookery books is not consistent, spanning a wide and chronologically-changing range of social levels.

In these bills of fare the number of courses at dinner may range from one – and these were not simply modest meals of 2 or 3 dishes, since in 1791 Mrs Frazer offered one-course dinners of between 5 and 19 dishes – to anything up to five in Charles Carter. The most common was a dinner of two courses, usually followed by a dessert. Since the formal dessert was the province of the confectioner, however, full details were not invariably included in general cookery books. Often they would include dessert items in their second course, suggesting the reader conflate it with the stand-alone dessert.

Dinner in the eighteenth century was a very different affair from today: it was served *à la française*, with all the dishes placed on the table at once for each course. The modern system of presenting each dish as a separate course, known originally as service *à la russe*, did not arise until the early nineteenth century when sometimes dishes or groups of dishes were sent up in succession, but Mrs Rundell then commented that 'these are not the common modes.'[3] The fully-fledged meal *à la russe* was not widely adopted before the 1880s.[4] The rules governing what appeared at which course were rather different from those

---

[2] For an example of the mix of old and new style, see Hawkesbury, 'The MS. Account and Memorandum Book of a Yorkshire Lady two Centuries ago' (1902), p. 30; for examples of luxurious breakfasts with cakes, fruit and chocolate, see Climenson (ed.), *Passages from the Diaries of Mrs. Philip Lybbe Powys* (1899), p. 11; Houblon, *The Houblon Family* (1911), vol. 2, pp. 150–51.

[3] [Rundell], *A New System of Domestic Economy* (1810), p. 322.

[4] For a discussion of the date at which service 'à la russe' was adopted in England, see Mars, 'A la Russe' in Wilson (1994), pp. 121–3.

obtaining in France, and this has led one French historian to the conclusion that each course of an English dinner formed a dynamic unit, with the dishes handed round in succession (the serving being thus *à la russe* in all but name) by servants.[5] The first objective of this section is therefore to examine the rules for organizing the bill of fare in France and England, in order to see whether the structural differences noted by Jean-Louis Flandrin in his study of earlier menus persisted into the eighteenth century. The question of the way each course was served in England is one to which we shall return later.

In 1692 a French book which set out all the guidelines for a well-run house, Audiger's *La Maison réglée*, gave the basic rules for a three-course dinner. They were very clear. It should have the same number of dishes at each course, placed the same way each time: *potage* plus *entrées* and *hors d'œuvres* at the first; various roasts, salads and *entremets* at the second; fresh and preserved fruit at the third. If the number of courses were increased, the roasts and salads made up the second course, the *entremets* the third, leaving fruit for the fourth.[6] This is simply a more developed, refined form of the medieval menus analysed by Flandrin, with the roast still occupying a central position. Eighteenth-century arrangements in France deviated only slightly. At the very grandest level, the royal supper menus served at Choisy in the 1750s show either three or four courses. When there were four, the first was composed of *potages* and *hors d'œuvres*, the second of *entrées*, the third of roasts and salads, and the fourth of *entremets*, with occasionally two dishes of *hors d'œuvres* added. Where there were only three, the first two courses were put together. The fruit or dessert course does not appear in these menus.[7] (In France, supper was the main royal meal, while dinner was less elaborate and served far less formally; thus supper

---

[5] See Flandrin, 'Structure des menus français et anglais aux XIVᵉ et XVᵉ siècles' in Lambert (1992), pp. 173–192. He reached this conclusion after analysing the position of various types of dish in the enumeration of the courses of medieval dinners, but added that this mode of serving probably continued into the seventeenth and eighteenth centuries. More recently, he has stated categorically that at the later period in England each dish was handed round in succession by servants, whereas in France the diners could pick and choose from what was on the table. See Flandrin & Montanari (eds), *Histoire de l'alimentation* (1996), pp. 572–3.

[6] Audiger, *La Maison réglée*, in Laurendon (1995), pp. 447, 466–74.

[7] A selection of these menus is reproduced in Vié, *A la Table des Rois* (1993), passim. See also the comments on these menus in Noël-Waldteufel, 'Manger à la cour' in *Versailles et les tables royales en Europe* (1993), pp. 74–78.

offers a more complete image of the organization than dinner.)[8] The difference between the 1690s and the 1750s is that Audiger's first course could now be expanded to become two, with the *entrées* forming a course on their own.

The same phenomenon can be observed at a less exalted level in the menus in the 1774 edition of Menon's *Cuisinière bourgeoise*. In fact, they also date from the 1750s. This book was perhaps the closest to English cookery books of the period, since it was aimed overtly at a female, middle-class readership rather than at the author's fellow-professionals working in grand houses. Here the first course consists of soups and *hors d'œuvres*, the second of *entrées* and large joints, the third of roasts, salads and *entremets*, and the fourth of a dessert composed mainly of fresh and preserved fruit.[9] Menon's receipts are annotated in the margin to indicate their place in the menu; many meat dishes could be either *hors d'œuvres* or *entrées*, according to size, and vegetable or egg-based dishes could appear either as *hors d'œuvres* or as *entremets*. The bourgeois version of menu-planning compresses the roasts and *entremets* into one course, but keeps the first two intact. The possible subdivisions of the courses point to the order of consumption: the diner would normally begin with the soup, and then go on to *hors d'œuvres* as introduction to the *entrées* and large joints; next would come the roasts and salads (the roast thus still in the central position it had always occupied in French menus), followed by the *entremets* as a transition to the dessert course.

These eighteenth-century menus confirm the increasing importance of savoury dishes and sauces, since they now formed the first two courses of a three-course arrangement. This is congruent with the evidence of receipts in French cookery books. What enabled the French to produce such clear, simple rules, which underwent little change once they were established towards the end of the seventeenth century, was their separation of sweet and savoury. Sweet dishes did not appear until the *entremets*, and even then were usually less

---

[8] Louis XIV always ate in public, alone for dinner ('le petit couvert'), with the royal family at supper ('au grand couvert'); Louis XV preferred the more intimate 'petit souper' with a few carefully selected courtiers, but on grand occasions and on Wednesdays and Sundays he too supped 'au grand couvert'. Both dinner and supper under Louis XIV had three courses, with potages and entrées as one course; later this single course became two. See Solnon, *Versailles* (1997), pp. 142–147, 249–251, 268; also Saule, 'Tables royales à Versailles, 1682–1789' in *Versailles et les tables royales en Europe* (1993), pp. 47–54.

[9] Menon, *La Cuisinière bourgeoise* (1981), pp. 13–17.

numerous than savoury items. In the menus described above, the proportion of sweet *entremets* (mostly creams and tarts) varies from about 20 per cent in the royal menus to between 33 per cent and 50 per cent in the bourgeois versions. The final course of fruit (plus biscuits and occasionally creams) was entirely sweet, and thus the menu progressed from exclusively savoury to exclusively sweet, with the *entremets* providing a transition.

In England the situation was very different. As we have seen in the study of culinary styles, the separation of sweet and savoury was by no means as clearcut. Not only was there consumer resistance at the beginning of the century to this aspect of the French style, but English puddings and pies continued to mix sweet and savoury for many decades and, in the case of such items as mince-pies, far beyond 1800. This was a major obstacle to anyone striving to produce a fashionably French-style bill of fare. Were English dishes to be present on the table, a somewhat different organizing principle was called for.

A first clue to the difference between French and English methods is supplied by the arrangement of the cookery books themselves. Here, a link with bills of fare is clearly visible. Except for the case of books organized as dictionaries, the various sections of French cookery books followed a logical order based on two classificatory principles: the main ingredient, and the type of dish. Thus, after receipts for basic preparations such as *coulis*, came soups, butchers' meat, then game, fish, eggs and vegetables and, finally, sweet dishes. These divisions almost followed the order of the meal (but fish came after meat because of the division into *gras* and *maigre* to conform to the religious calendar): *entrées* were followed by *hors d'œuvres* and *entremets*, and the last receipts dealt with fruit preserves and other dishes for the dessert course.

Contrast the usual organization of receipts in English books. It was based on the cooking method and the place of production: simpler cooking methods such as roasting and boiling came first, followed by more complicated preparations such as made dishes; food produced in the kitchen was followed by that from the still-room, namely creams and jellies, preserves and pickles, and drinks. This was the basic order in each of the monthly parts of Martha Bradley's vast book, and it appeared with minor variations in most other English works. The exceptions were those clearly derived from manuscript sources where culinary receipts were jumbled together, and those books which followed French patterns. It is difficult to see a system here but two features suggest themselves. First, the simply-cooked dishes precede the complicated ones: this looks back to the medieval principle of serving the 'gross' meats before the delicacies. Secondly, the products of the still-room (with the exception of pickled vegetables served as an accompaniment to first-course dishes) were served after the products of the kitchen, and this explains why potted meat and fish (a form of preserve) appeared late in the meal amongst sweet items. This curious association (curious, at least, to modern eyes) further demonstrates that English food habits resisted the progression from savoury to sweet.

Those books which gave bills of fare tended to supply names of dishes only, without the headings which made the logic of the French system so explicit. Indeed bills of fare were by no means a standard feature, perhaps because the rules in England were less rigid than in France. General advice on the organization of the meal was rare in English cookery books. Many authors felt it unnecessary to give specimen menus, which were often replaced by lists of produce in season. Hannah Glasse considered that it would be 'impertinent' to direct a lady how to set out her table, and she added that it would not be 'pretty, to see a Lady's Table set out after the Directions of a Book.'[10] Towards the end of the century, Sarah Martin argued it was impossible to 'ascertain any particular Mode' for bills of fare, since setting out a table was 'guided by Fancy and varied by Fashion'.[11] This already points to a less rigid system of meal planning than in France.

One author who does briefly mention general principles is Sarah Harrison:

> It is to be observ'd, that in the Course of Dinners, the grosser Meats should always be set first on the Table, and there should never be two Dishes at a Dinner of the same sort of Meat, tho' they are diversified by Boiling one and Roasting the other, or Baking it; but make as much Variation as you can.
>
> All Boil'd Meats should be serv'd first, Baked Meats next, and Roasted last.[12]

Two classificatory principles are at work: cooking method and degree of refinement. This neat formula for the order of the meal fails to take into account

---

[10] Glasse, *The Art of Cookery* (1747), p. ii.

[11] Martin (1795), preface.

[12] Harrison (1733), p. 47. Similar advice on the order of presentation is found in *The Family Magazine* (1749), part I, p. 27; Frazer, *The Practice of Cookery* (1791), p. 251.

several cooking methods, not to mention all the 'made dishes'. The division into courses is not mentioned, suggesting the formula is valid only for one-course dinners. The emphasis on variety in Harrison is no different from advice given by French books, suggesting that in England, too, it was important that the diner should be able to choose from several types of dishes.

The lists of dishes supplied by cookery books provide a picture of different practices at different social levels, with more French dishes present in the grandest bills of fare of the first thirty years of the century. But the basic rules are less diverse than one might expect. In order to study the bill of fare as set out in the cookery books, a sample from five important books, all from the upper end of the market, will be examined. (Those from more modest books will be looked at briefly later.) The sample takes the 31 bills of fare for dinner from the plates in Charles Carter's *Complete Practical Cook* (1730); the 24 bills of fare in E. Smith's *Compleat Housewife* (and these same lists had already appeared in the first edition of Patrick Lamb's book, although Lamb's copper-plates are for more elegant affairs[13]); the two series, one in list form, the other giving a simple numbered diagram to show how to place the dishes, in Moxon's *English Housewifry* (1741);[14] the single bill of fare, set out in two copper-plates, for a 'Grand Table' in January, from Raffald's *Experienced English House-keeper* (1769);[15] and finally the 39 bills of fare for two-course dinners, followed by bills for the dessert, in Charlotte Mason's *Lady's Assistant* (1773).[16] Most of these are for two-course dinners (although Carter's range from one to five, the most usual figure is two); the number of dishes at each course varies from 7 to 25.

As one might expect, Carter's menus are closest to French rules: the number of dishes and their placement is the same at each course, as they are in Raffald's 'Grand Table'. But in the other books the number is variable: in Smith, it is higher sometimes at the first course, sometimes at the second; in Moxon and Mason, the usual system (in 27 out of the 39 bills in Mason) gives two more dishes at the second course than at the first.

---

[13] See E– S– (1728), in the unnumbered pages at the beginning; Lamb, *Royal Cookery* (1710), in the unnumbered pages at the end.

[14] Moxon, *English Housewifry* (1741), after the main text, in the unnumbered leaves before and after the index.

[15] Raffald, *The Experienced English House-keeper* (1769), plates between pp. 360 and 361.

[16] Mason, *The Lady's Assistant* (1773), pp. 53–101. Mason also gives a series of one-course menus, with the number of dishes ranging from 5 to 17 plus a remove, pp. 1–52.

Pursuing the analysis, some types of dish appeared only at the first course, some only at the second, others at both. The distribution between the courses is based partly on the nature of the principal ingredient and the type of dish, partly on the cooking method (which is not always indicated). With occasional exceptions, soups, salads, all butcher's meat (beef, mutton, veal, ham) and venison appear at the first course only; the meats are either roasted, boiled or stewed in some way. Dishes which normally appear only at the second course are shellfish (except as a garnish to other fish at the first course), game birds, potted and soused meat or fish, vegetables, tarts and creams, dishes involving fruit, and sweetmeats – unless of course these last two (or even three) types of dish were to be kept for a third, dessert course. Amongst the things which might appear at either course are puddings and pies, pickles, lamb, some fowl such as ducks and geese, many fish, and egg dishes. The presence of puddings and pies at either course meant that there was no simple progression from savoury to sweet, although the exclusively sweet dishes, such as fruit tarts, invariably figured only at the second course. As was noted, another English peculiarity is that the first course is composed entirely of dishes produced in the kitchen, whereas the second course offers dishes from kitchen and still-room. This explains the appearance of savoury jellies, and potted and soused fish and meat at the second course alongside the sweet things.

There is some variation between the books. Carter, for instance, places small dishes of vegetables at either course, whereas the others tend to place them only at the second. Smith puts several bisques into the second course, when their normal position was among the pottages of the first. Raffald places shellfish in the first course, while the others place most such items in the second. By the last decades of the century, rules were increasingly lax. Mason places a haunch of venison at either course, and roast beef at the second. These aberrations may seem to be a proof of anarchy in English meal planning, but in fact they often indicate a different scale of values amongst different social classes. Carter keeps roast beef, brawn, venison and other stalwart English dishes for the sideboard, while the important positions down the middle of the table are reserved for the French court-style dishes. By contrast, the presence of roast beef or venison at the second course of Mason's menus places them among the delicacies to be kept for later. What stands out is that the first course is usually composed of the 'grosser' dishes, while the choicer items are saved for the second. This is rarely made clear in general directions, although one book at the end of the century tells the reader to 'observe always to send up the most substantial [dishes] first'.[17] It also explains the presence of E. Smith's bisques (of lamb, mushrooms, and shellfish) at the second course, and the appearance of some items such as lamb or salmon at either. The order of enumeration in the lists is no help in determining the probable order of consumption at each course. Although we can be sure that the soup was the first dish to be eaten, it is not always listed first.

Charles Carter's magnificent bill of fare which reduces the number of dishes to 7 but increases the number of courses to 5 (plates 8 and 9) still fails to give a coherent picture of the order. Although the basic progression of soup and butcher's meat, then made dishes, game, preserved meat and some sweet things before a final dessert, is fairly consistent with French habits, his plans allow for a pudding at the first course, and pies, patties or tarts at every course except the dessert. Roast game occupies the central position in the meal, just as in France, but what is entirely different is the presence of sweet elements at each course, with the possible exception of the third, which is the central 'roast' but also contains 'resols' of marrow (i.e. little patties which might be baked or fried, and which could be savoury or sweet). His placing of English baked dishes on the sideboard during service of the first four courses points to diners choosing when to consume what, rather than having an order imposed on them by servants offering dishes in succession.

There is further evidence for this in one book which appears to suggest an order of consumption for a meal containing only one dish of each type:

> It is to be observed that in small Entertainments and on common Days, the Soops are always first served at the upper End of the Table; or Fish if there is no Soop, and the Fish is to supply the Place of the Soop. The large Dish of boiled Meat again in the room of that, and the large Dish of roast Meat at the Bottom of the Table; in the Middle is either a Pie, something roasted or a grand Sallad....
>
> When the Desert is to come on, Care must be taken to see the Table well cleared, and the upper Table-Cloth taken off, with the Leather which lay between that and the under one. Dry'd Sweetmeats,

---

[17] Frazer (1791), p. 251.

Sweetmeats in Glasses and Fruits, are placed in Pyramids, ... like the great Dishes of Meat. Creams and Compotes like Intermesses.[18]

The enumeration shows that the soup would normally be followed by fish, then by the dishes of meat and the pie or its alternatives. Even here the order of consumption after the soup and fish is not clear, especially as the same text comments on a revolving table lying on top of the fixed one, whereby the guests could help themselves to whatever dish they fancied after the lady of the house had offered the soup.[19]

In fact, there is no guarantee that there was a fixed order of consumption within each course. Plates and diagrams in the cookery books show that it was important to have two similar but not identical dishes diagonally opposite one another, so that diners on either side of the table would have a similar selection. For instance, in Raffald's 'Grand Table' lambs' ears correspond to ox palates, pigeons to ducks, and peas to broccoli at the first course; while at the second, stewed cardoons correspond to stewed mushrooms, potted lampreys to pickled smelts, and so on. This symmetric placement is perhaps the most important rule of all. Such a disposition does not suggest that each dish was presented to every diner. On the contrary, the mirror-image of the two sides probably means that the centre dishes were served by the host and hostess and that the other diners took what they wanted from the lesser dishes on their side of the table, each group having a similar but not identical choice.

Since English dishes such as puddings and pies did not fit into the French scheme of things, differences between the two nations were bound to exist. In England, the sweet-savoury mix was present from the very beginning of the meal. Yet the same basic pattern is found in the two-course bills of fare on either side of the Channel. In England, soup was followed by dishes of butcher's meat (i.e. *entrées*) at the first course, and what would be classified as *entremets*, *rôts* and dessert dishes at the second. Setting aside the pies and puddings, the other important difference is that in England the salad (if there was one) appeared at the first course rather than alongside the roasts of the second.

---

[18] *The Whole Duty of a Woman* (1737), p. 629.

[19] Ibid., p. 629. The idea of the revolving upper table comes from the second part of Richard Bradley; see *The Country Housewife* (1980), part 2, pp. 169–70.

English meal planning changed little over the eighteenth century, except that a more relaxed attitude prevailed after 1770. The bills of fare in cookery books echo changing culinary styles most obviously in their selection of dishes. In Carter, French court-style olios and terrines occupy the central positions at the top and bottom of the table – sometimes the middle too – and other French dishes dominate, especially at the first course. As cookery books reached a broader audience, there is not much evidence of *nouvelle cuisine* dishes in later menus, except in one work dating from the 1760s which was devoted exclusively to fashionable bills of fare, and shows a combination of simple English dishes and French creations reminiscent of Clouet such as 'Tendrons of Veal, a Lestragon' and 'Legs of Fowl, a la Basilique'.[20] It was aimed at the upper servants of the aristocracy, to enable them to present a menu guaranteed the approval of their mistress. More frequently, even an ambitious work like Raffald would rely on bourgeois English cookery: in her 'Grand Table' the dishes at the top and bottom of the table are soups, but at the centre for the first course is a 'Mock Turtle', and for the second a 'Transparent Pudding' – in fact one of Raffald's decorative jellies – with roast game top and bottom. Dishes with more-or-less French names are present at Raffald's first course (7 out of 25), and there is a 'Pompadour Cream' at the second, but the rest is thoroughly English. Raffald's menu is as close as one gets at this date to a really grand entertainment; most books offer more modest suggestions, and French dishes are even less in evidence. The gap between authentic French dinners and English ones with a few fashionable references was widening.

After 1750, the cheaper books aimed at the middle-class mistress either give no bills of fare (this is the case, for instance, in books by Isabella Moore, Charlotte Cartwright and Amelia Chambers), or else supply very simple ones, often for dinners of only one course. Lydia Fisher's book (which cost 1s.) offers bills of fare for one-course dinners with mostly a mere 3 dishes, or sometimes only 2.[21] But even middle-of-the-range books indulge in few flights of fancy. In 1768 James Jenks begins by giving bills for two courses, described as dinners 'in a plentiful and elegant manner', although the number of dishes at each course is limited. He continues:

---

[20] *The Modern Method of Regulating and Forming a Table* (c.1765); for the dishes quoted, see p. 16. The dinner menus have two courses of 5 to 21 dishes each; the supper menus contain between 28 and 40 dishes.

[21] Fisher, *The Prudent Housewife* (c.1780), pp. 39–41.

It is certain that there are very few private families will ever exceed the bounds here described, but will be contented to sit down with their friend to a couple or three dishes at most.[22]

And bills for such one-course dinners follow. Charlotte Mason also gives one-course menus, though she increased the numbers of dishes by counting sauces and vegetable accompaniments in their own right.[23] In 1791 Mrs Frazer offers bills of fare varying from 5 to 19 dishes, but still with only one course. The dishes are diversified by cooking method, and again the numbers are made up by serving vegetable accompaniments as separate dishes.[24] The fact that so few of the cheaper books give even these simple bills of fare, though the rest of their contents show they aimed to equip the middle-class housewife with the rudiments of gentility, points again to a less rigid system of meal planning than in France. Despite Charlotte Mason's remark that 'a woman never appears to greater advantage than at the head of a well-regulated table',[25] most of her contemporaries were prepared to allow considerable latitude.

Ladies' manuscript memoranda confirm the rules discerned in the printed record. In her household book, which is a complete guide based on her experience of running Felbrigg Hall in Norfolk, Katherine Windham compiled a list of dishes suitable for the first and second courses of dinner, and for the 'desert', probably in the 1720s. She thought the first should be composed of soups, large pieces of meat such as joints of beef or venison, either boiled or roasted, made dishes, fish boiled, stewed or fried, mince pies, and puddings; the second of small tame and game birds, plus lamb and kid, vegetables (peas, artichokes, asparagus, beans, skirrets, parsnips, potatoes, hopbuds and turnip stalks are mentioned), pancakes and fritters, omelettes, custards, tarts and cheesecakes, pies, collared and potted meat, and some fish. (The list includes all shellfish, plus the best sea or fresh-water fish; where the cooking method is

---

[22] Jenks, *The Complete Cook* (1768), p. 30. The 2-course bills are presented p. 21. Similarly, in 1769 Skeat gives 1- and 2-course bills; see *The Art of Cookery and Pastery*, in the unnumbered pages at the end of the book.

[23] See, for instance, one of the 'Family Dinners of Nine Dishes'; Mason (1773), p. 29. These 1-course bills of fare are found pp. 1-52; they range from 5 dishes to 18.

[24] See, for instance, the 7-dish dinner, with one pie, one pudding, one roast, one made dish, ham, and two vegetables (potatoes and cauliflower); Frazer (1791), p. 247.

[25] Mason (1773), p. iv.

indicated, the fish is either fried or soused.) For the dessert, she names all kinds of preserved fruit, jellies and creams, fresh fruit and nuts, fruit compotes, cheeses, and cracknels, gingerbread, and wafers.[26] She deviates from the advice of cookery books in restricting puddings to the first course, pies (with the single exception of mince pies) to the second and, in the third list, adding cheese, not usually mentioned in print, to the dessert.

Dessert menus were rare in general cookery books. Only two of Carter's dinners have one (plates 9 & 41); Smith and Moxon give none; Raffald gives instructions for a dessert but no illustration; Mason gives ten pages of desserts, ranging from 4 to 15 dishes. The series in Charlotte Mason showed that a modest dessert could be composed of nothing but fruit and nuts; only when it was expanded to 11 dishes or more did it include such luxuries as brandied fruit and ices. Charles Carter's two desserts belonged to the luxurious type with creams, fruit, and sweetmeats, the last two arranged together in a pyramid at his 7-dish table. His more lavish 19-dish table had three pyramids, two of fruit for each end and one of dried sweetmeats for the centre. Raffald's directions for a 25-dish dessert to complete her 'Grand Table' proposed 5 different ices, 4 plates of dried fruit, 6 long dishes with pineapples, 'French Plumbs' and 'the four Brandy Fruits', and smaller dishes of various fruits and nuts. Books of confectionery were the other source of bills of fare for dessert, laden with all the professional products such as biscuits, wafers and ices among the fruit and sweetmeats.[27]

After an interval came supper. Bills of fare for supper do figure more frequently in the second half of the century. This does not support the idea that supper was disappearing because of the later dinner-hour. Several works simply give a list of possible dishes,[28] and it is clear that supper was a less formal meal. Charlotte Mason offers menus which vary from 'Little Family Suppers of Four

---

[26] This three-column list is on page 129 of the cookery end of the MS, which, turned upside down, contains preserving at the other end; both sections are numbered from 1. This MS is now Norfolk RO, WKC 6/457. It is interesting to note that the table of contents to the first section indicates that not all the receipts are classified as 'cookery': the cakes, creams and jellies are headed 'houskeeping'. The book bears the date 1707 on the front, but a group of cookery receipts (pp. 13–14, many duplicated pp. 135–137) is dated 1726.

[27] See, for instance, the plates in Nutt, *The Complete Confectioner* (1789), and the directions for 'bills of fare for small deserts' in Borella, *The Court and Country Confectioner* (1770), part I, pp. 211–13.

[28] See, for instance, *The Family Magazine* (1749), part I, pp. 26–7; Phillips, *The Ladies Handmaid* (1758), p. 445; Townshend, *The Universal Cook* (1773), p. 294.

Things' to cold suppers with anything up to 21 dishes. Most of her suggestions combine hot and cold, savoury and sweet.[29] Usually supper menus are composed of second-course dinner dishes, with a mix of the smaller hot dishes plus cold meats and tarts, creams and jellies. Supper tended to use up the relics from dinner, a fact made explicit in one set of instructions: 'How to make up a Supper when Company comes unexpectedly, having nothing but what was left at Dinner.' The bill of fare that follows suggests making a dish of minced turkey or fowl, a hash of duck (ways of reheating leftovers), and adding cold meat, tarts and cheesecakes, and jellies.[30] This was more realistic than the lavish suggestions by Elizabeth Moxon for meals involving boiled and roasted fowl. A fairly ordinary dinner would supply enough material to produce an adequate supper, especially where only one or two hot things were required.

While these books often gave some guidance on how to compose a bill of fare – either through illustrated examples or lists of possible dishes at each season – few advised the hostess on how to serve the meal. Martha Bradley was an exception. She compared the 'modern' way of doing things in the 1750s to earlier modes:

> It was our Custom to let the Lady of the House help her Visiters; and this, though troublesome to her, … gave her an Opportunity of shewing with what Satisfaction she waited on her Friends.
>
> At present the Fashion is, that every one takes Care of himself, helping himself to what is next, or sending his Plate to the Person who sits near what he likes; so that the Lady fares like the rest of the Company, and has no more trouble than others.[31]

This makes clear that serving was done by the diners, either by the hostess or, in the new fashion, by the guests. Servants might carry plates from one person to another, but they did not hand the dishes round. Bradley attributes the change to self-help to the increasing number of dishes at each course. When there were only two or three, the hostess could serve everyone and still eat something herself, whereas it would be impossible in the modern 'grand Way

---

[29] See Mason (1773), pp. 102–139. The cold suppers form a separate section, pp. 136–9.
[30] *A Collection of One Hundred and Thirty-seven approved Receipts* (1774), p. 39.
[31] Bradley, *The British Housewife* (1756), vol. 1, pp. 73–74.

of living' to keep sending the dishes 'backwards and forwards to the Head of the Table'.

These comments offer an insight into cultural shifts:

The Company ... were under a Constraint, when every thing was to come from the Hand of the Mistress; they did not care to shew they had large Stomachs, or they were ashamed to speak, or they were sorry to give her Trouble; so that half of them did not dine well. Now every body helps himself as he likes .... The Company are easy, the Master is pleased, and the Lady has no Trouble.

Thus we see what was the ancient, and what is the present Manner; but it may be proper to give here one short Piece of Advice. This French Fashion of perfect Ease was calculated for great Tables, and it should in a manner be confined to them. What Reason dictates on the Subject is this:

When there are but two or three at Table, and but two or three Dishes, the Mistress of the House should help every body once, and desire them afterwards to take Care of themselves. When there are a great many Dishes and a great Deal of Company, she should tell them she leaves them to the French Ease, the Dinner is before them, and they are expected to take Care of themselves and of one another.[32]

The new fashion produced a more relaxed atmosphere at table. Bradley's reference to 'the French Ease' suggests that leaving the guests free to pick and choose what they ate at each course was a novelty imported from across the Channel, but this is the only piece of evidence which supports Flandrin's contention that at English dinners the guests were not free to choose what they ate. Even here, Bradley's earlier remarks on the constraints the guests were under shows that under the old dispensation they could ask for a particular dish or a second helping. Several other points can be made about this change in manners. The increase in the number of dishes points to the adoption amongst the élite of a form of *nouvelle cuisine*, with small dishes that were easier to serve than the *grosses entrées* of the court style or the large joints which needed the attention of a carver. Secondly, by resigning her rôle as the distributor of food, the mistress

---

[32] Bradley (1756), vol. I, pp. 74–75.

both gained in status (she no longer acted as a servant to the guests) and lost power (she no longer had exercised any control over what her guests ate). At the same time, her loss of control over the dishes at table was a symbol of her renunciation of control in the kitchen: she had not directed its preparation, and she became just another guest at her own table. This change is reflected in another of Bradley's comments on the difference between old and new:

> As our Grandmothers made too much Racket with their Guests, we are in danger of making too little; so natural it is for Ladies to run from one Extreme to another: Those good old Gentlewomen were always finding Fault with their Food, and thought they shewed their own Skill in letting their Company know what was amiss, and their Civility in expressing their Concern that Things were not good enough for their Entertainment: On the other Hand, our Ladies are too apt to neglect the Thing entirely; they take no Notice of their Provision; it goes as it comes, and the Company have no Way to know they are welcome but by remembering they were asked.
>
> A middle Practice is better: Let the truly polite Lady take some Notice of these Things, though not too much, and let her praise a Dish that is good tho' 'tis her own; 'tis civil to recommend it to her Company.[33]

The change in the mistress' behaviour at table reflects her change of rôle behind the scenes, and confirms the abandoning of active supervision of the kitchen by genteel ladies. A final aspect of changing values is demonstrated by Bradley's later comments on old and new fashions of serving:

> We suppose that every one who dines with us dines as well every Day at home, and therefore we make no Pother about his eating as if he were at a Feast.
>
> It was then the Custom for the Mistress of the Table to see her Guests eat of every Dish, and eat heartily, now the true Politeness among perfectly polite People is not to regard what any one eats; but if there happen to be a Person present not so much used to Company, the Lady

---

[33] Bradley (1756), vol. 1, pp. 201–202.

is to ask him without Ceremony whether she shall help him to this or
that Dish. This is an Ease to the Backwardness of the Guest, and may
be done in such a Manner as not to draw on the Attention of the rest
of the Company.[34]

The new fashion is linked to the presumption that all the guests eat well
every day, the implication being that the old fashion did not pre-suppose this.
Pressing all the guests to eat was, however, a step away from the earlier hierarchical distribution of food, where the honoured guest received more and better
food than his inferiors, as had been the case in the Middle Ages.

To obtain a clearer view of the earlier mode of serving, we need to turn to
conduct- rather than cookery-books which are silent on the matter. The
conduct-books of the first decades of the eighteenth century all look back to
the most important manual of the Restoration period, Antoine de Courtin's
Rules of Civility (1671). One finds the same emphasis on precedence and defe-
rence at every stage of the meal, with the corollary that dinner was a display
of food but also a demonstration of the social hierarchy, as it had been in the
Middle Ages. The one significant advance in the books of the new century
concerns the use of the fork, which was now becoming obligatory both for
serving and consuming one's own portion of food. For information about table
manners, the most complete work of these decades was Adam Petrie's *Rules of
Good Deportment* (1720). Others, such as R.G.'s *Accomplish'd Female Instructor*
(1704), and John Essex's *The Young Ladies Conduct* (1722) offered less detail.

Precedence was all. Its first appearance was when the guests took their places
at table. Essex and Petrie both emphasize that the hosts should avoid disputes
by placing their guests; the ladies (in order of precedence, of course, beginning
with the place on the right hand of the mistress) at the upper end of the table,
with the mistress of the house, the gentlemen at the bottom, around the host.[35]
When the guests arrived in the dining-room, the dishes for the first course were
already on the table, but two rites preceded serving the food: hand-washing and
grace. Advice on these points stresses the honorific aspect of the two moments.
Only the 'Person of Quality' washed his hands. Although he might invite an
inferior to join him, he was not to presume unless by 'express Command'.[36]

---

[34] Bradley (1756), vol. I, p. 201.

[35] Petrie (1720), pp. 82–3; Essex (1722), p. 92.

[36] R. G. (1704), p. 22.

Similarly, grace was to be said by the master or by some suitable guest, and certainly not by 'a common Servant'.[37] This was a symbolic affirmation of hierarchy, ritual purification emanating only from the powerful. By the 1750s all trace of these two rituals, so closely linked to a society presided over by a sovereign whose authority came from God, had disappeared.

At the first course, the soup and large joints at either end of the table were served and carved by the mistress. She had to know how to carve and which were the best pieces, in order to offer them to the most important guests.[38] The fact that the mistress had taken over this function from the carver is a sign both of the decay of the tradition among distressed gentlefolk of going into domestic service and of the downward diffusion of polite behaviour. Hannah Woolley's books give instructions on carving aimed at both gentlewoman and carver, suggesting that the 1670s were the years of transition.[39] By the early eighteenth century, even in aristocratic houses, it was the mistress who carved. Before her marriage in 1712, Lady Mary Wortley Montagu replaced her deceased mother as mistress of her father's table. In order to perform this difficult task she took carving lessons three times a week and ate her own dinner early on days when she was required to preside.[40] This appears to confirm Martha Bradley's comment that at a grand table the old fashion prevented the lady from eating, since she was too much engaged in serving the guests.

It was also usual for the hostess to press the guests to eat. Elizabeth Mure recalled her Scottish childhood in the 1730s:

> Nobody helpd themselves at table, …. So that the mistress of the family might give you a ful meal or not as she pleased; from whence came in the fashion of pressing the guests to eat so far as to be disagreeable.[41]

---

[37] Petrie (1720), p. 82.

[38] The conduct-books give little guidance on carving, but earlier works devote several pages to the art. See, for instance, Woolley, *The Gentlewomans Companion* (1673), pp. 113–16; N. H., *The Ladies Dictionary* (1694), article on 'Table Behaviour', pp. 412–20. Some cookery books add instructions for carving to their contents: see, for instance, *The Whole Duty of a Woman* (c. 1700), p. 139ff.; Middleton, *Five Hundred New Receipts* (1734), pp. i–iv; *The Accomplish'd Housewife* (1745), pp. 245–8; Jackson, *The Director* (1754), pp. 100–102; Henderson, *The Housekeeper's Instructor* (c. 1795), pp. 358–70. See also Martha Bradley's comments on the older fashion, vol. 1, p. 74.

[39] See Woolley, *The Gentlewomans Companion*, cited above, which gives instructions to gentlewomen; and *The Queen-like Closet* (1670), p. 375, which gives advice to the gentleman carver.

[40] See Halsband, *The Life of Lady Mary Wortley Montagu* (1957), p. 7.

[41] Mure, 'Some remarks on the change of manners in my own time' (1854), p. 260.

Conduct-books were already pointing out that such insistence was ill-bred. Petrie told his readers neither to press food and drink on the guests, nor praise or criticize one's own dishes.[42] But behaviour might lag behind the recommendations of conduct-books. Elizabeth Mure also recollected her grandfather sitting in his place near the fire with his hat on, being served dishes which were not offered to anyone else.[43] This kind of medieval behaviour, here seen in Scotland early in the century, persisted amongst farmers even later: in 1799 the Rev. William Holland noted that his elderly neighbours still practised a distinction between the top and the bottom of the table:

> Mr James and Mr Thos Rich are two old batchelors worth sixty or seventy thousand pounds tho' they live like substantial Farmers. Dine at the head of their table with the servants below, a cloth being laid on the upper end with a fowl or duck dressed in a better manner for my masters.[44]

Such outmoded behaviour had long disappeared from genteel tables. But below the level of the fashionable there was extreme conservatism in manners and a huge gap between the norms of the polite world and those of the less polite.

Among the élite, distinctions between a host and his fellow-diners were seen as vulgar even by the early decades of the eighteenth century, although guests were expected to put on a show of diffidence before their superiors. For example, they should not usurp precedence, they were not to offer their plates first to the carver, not take the best piece if invited to help themselves, never refuse anything offered by a superior, nor call for drink before their betters had led the way.[45] At this date, one could not drink at table without drinking a health, and the inferior was not allowed to drink to an important person directly, while the high-ranking guest could of course do so. Similarly, the inferior was to adopt a humble demeanour when anyone drank his health.[46] The ceremonial drinking of healths was a custom which persisted into the second half of the century even after the other rules from this early period had been abandoned.

---

[42] Petrie (1720), pp. 87, 96.
[43] Mure (1854), p. 260.
[44] Ayres (ed.), *Paupers and Pig Killers* (1986), p. 21.
[45] See R. G. (1704), pp. 22–3; Petrie (1720), pp. 84–6.
[46] See R. G. (1704), pp. 23–4; Petrie (1720), p. 86; Essex (1722), p. 93.

The other main area of concern in conduct-books centred on the use of implements. The fork was making headway: it was now obligatory for carving and serving oneself and others, but one could still use one's fingers, or rather one finger and the thumb, once food was on the plate – although Petrie also suggested that it was better to avoid so doing.[47] At the end of the meal, the inferior guest had to wait for others to throw down their napkins as a sign that dinner was over. If water was presented to wash after the meal, the inferior was to dip his napkin and rub his mouth and fingers discreetly, concealing this activity from the company, whereas 'superiors may do it more openly'; in fact, washing after the meal was now considered as 'rude and uncivil'.[48]

All this advice was primarily concerned with teaching the reader to demonstrate he knew his place in the social hierarchy, which was what the formal code of manners was all about. Mark Girouard has described the extreme respect for precedence which regulated even country house visits, a rigid hierarchy constantly on show, and how this code of conduct influenced the plan of what he calls the 'formal house'.[49] But even as conduct-books were still emphasizing the importance of precedence, voices elsewhere were denouncing it as old-fashioned, practised only by the rural gentry who had not caught up with court fashions. In 1711 Joseph Addison commented on the contrast between the rigidity of the country squire and the free and easy behaviour of the *bon ton*. Good breeding, he said, 'shows itself most, where to an ordinary Eye it appears the least.'[50] At table, respect for precedence was seen as ridiculous, and Addison went on to laugh at the country squire:

> I have known my Friend Sir ROGER's Dinner almost cold before the Company could adjust the Ceremonial, and be prevailed upon to sit down; and have heartily pitied my old Friend, when I have seen him forced to pick and cull his Guests, as they sat at the several Parts of his

---

[47] See Petrie (1720), pp. 82–83. Using implements to help oneself and to cut things up, but then using fingers to carry food to one's mouth, was standard behaviour in France at the beginning of the eighteenth century. See Gourarier, 'La mutation des comportements à table au XVIIᵉ siècle' in *Les Français et la table* (1985), pp. 200–201.

[48] Petrie (1720), pp. 96–7.

[49] Girouard, *Life in the English Country House* (1980), pp. 144–8.

[50] *The Spectator* 119 (17 July 1711).

Table, that he might drink their Healths according to their respective Ranks and Qualities.

The gap between the recommendations of the conduct-books and those of the magazine is striking. It suggests that they were spreading the old model after it had lost its value amongst the élite, just as new conventions were to reach the gentry. Dismissal of formal manners was coeval with an attack on court-style cookery, but the practical results of the theorizing would take some time to appear. Change came gradually, at least among the gentry. Richardson's *Pamela* (1740), which is a conduct-book as well as a novel, shows that after marriage, the heroine proves equal to her new station: she presides at the head of the table and carves gracefully. At one of the meals which offer a vehicle for the display of her talents, the guests are seated in strict order of precedence. During and after dinner, healths are drunk, and finally, Pamela retires, leaving the gentlemen to the bottle. These are the old fashions, but a supper scene shows the beginning of the new, with the ladies and gentlemen seated 'intermingled', although this arrangement, suggested by Mr B., raises a protest from one of the ladies, concerned that it will break the rules of precedence.[51]

Pamela offered a conservative model; one of his imitators gave a more 'modern' image. *The Book of Conversation and Behaviour* of 1754 is cast as a series of conversations, with a cast of characters and a plot which turn the conduct-book into a novel inspired, according to the anonymous author, by Richardson. One of the scenes takes place at the table of Sir Samuel and Lady Fashion and their daughter; their guests are Mr. Bookley, a young gentleman just down from university, Mr. Rustick, a country squire, and Mr. Forward, a young man training to be a lawyer. Mr. Rustick ignores any code of good manners and invites the company to sit down before the dishes are set, instead of waiting to be placed by Lady Fashion. He is roundly reproved by his hostess' daughter. When the dishes arrive, Lady Fashion announces, 'I am afraid you see your Dinner,' which was a way of informing the company that there would be only one course. The guests begin to help themselves and each other, and when the gauche Mr. Bookley asks Lady Fashion to help him, she says that he is nearer to the dish than she is, and that he should take what he likes; the 'most genteel' behaviour is what is 'easiest'. Bookley later comments on the difference

---

[51] See *Pamela* (Everyman edition, 1962), vol. 1, pp. 266, 282, 338, 366, 430.

between old and new fashions, confirming exactly Martha Bradley's remarks:

> *Book*. I always thought that Custom of our Grandfathers, Sir Samuel,
> of making the Lady of the House help all that were at Table, a most
> unnatural and unreasonable one: I am glad to find good Sense has got
> the better of it; for I shall take it for granted that every thing I see here
> is true Politeness.

The conversation that follows explains that it was correct to offer one's neighbour some of the dish in front of one but, after this gesture, everyone helped
himself unless the desired dish was too far away. Towards the end of the meal,
Sir Samuel presses Mr. Bookley to a second helping, reminiscing about how he
himself nearly died of hunger in his younger days as he was too shy to help
himself when invited to an aristocratic table. The company drink healths
during the meal, and Mr. Bookley is given a lesson on the correct form of
words ('Lady Fashion, I have the Honour to pay you my Respects'). It is, of
course, Mr. Forward who knows how to do things, while Mr. Rustick is totally
indifferent to such niceties. Lady Fashion responds by thanking Mr. Forward
for his 'French Compliment', commenting, 'I am not fond of imitating that
People; but, if we do it in any Thing, I think it should be in Politeness; for they
study it.' At this genteel table, French fashions in manners and in food (Mr.
Rustick fails to identify the larded meat, and dislikes the 'broth', which Sir
Samuel hastens to call a 'soup') are the norm, but the book also manages to
satisfy anti-French sentiment, just as Hannah Glasse had done. Other details
are that the sole function of the servants was to pour drinks and not to serve
dishes; that although healths were drunk, it was vulgar to invite another guest
to drink; and that water was still brought at the end of the meal for the diners
to wash their hands, even though their hands were perfectly clean – dipping
one's fingers into water was a purely symbolic act, for by now the fork was in
universal use. The scene concludes with the ladies retiring, leaving the men to
drink before joining them at the tea-table.[52]

By the end of the century, even those conduct-books which still mentioned
precedence were placing much less emphasis on its rules. In 1770, Matthew
Towle advises the reader to respect them, but he should not adhere too rigidly

---

[52] *The Book of Conversation and Behaviour* (1754), pp. 6–17.

and he should avoid all unnecessary ceremony. When helping oneself, one should not reach over anyone else's plate but ask a servant to bring the desired dish. Again, there was no indication that dishes were taken round by servants. The one piece of advice which had become more imperative was the use of the fork, now absolutely obligatory at all times.[53] Less than twenty years later, John Trusler's well-known manual suggests placing guests in the traditional manner, ladies and gentlemen grouped in order of precedence at the two ends of the table, but he points out that there was a different way:

> Custom, however, has lately introduced a new mode of seating. A gentleman and a lady sitting alternately round the table, and this, for the better convenience of a lady's being attended to, and served by the gentleman next to her. But notwithstanding this promiscuous seating, the ladies, whether above or below, are to be served in order, according to their rank or age, and after them the gentlemen, in the same manner.[54]

Although Trusler attributes this novelty to practical considerations, it is clear that it was more sociable, and the shift in eighteenth-century table manners was from the formal to the sociable. The new mode was probably influenced by the looser arrangements at supper, especially ball suppers where dancing partners sat together to eat.

The rest of Trusler's advice endorses the more relaxed style which had been a novelty in the 1750s. The mistress should tell the company what was to come by way of eatables, and what wines, other drinks and cold dishes were waiting on the sideboard, so that her guests could make their own choice more easily. Although the host and hostess were still expected to carve the dishes directly before them, guests were also expected to participate in the serving, helping the ladies to the dishes nearest them. Carvers were not to give the best pieces to one person, but to distribute them equally among the guests. On the subject of drinking at table, Trusler says that since it is 'unseemly' for ladies to call for wine, the gentlemen should take care to ask them in turn to drink with them: when the two glasses are brought, they bow to each other and drink. Drinking

---

[53] See Towle, *The Young Gentleman and Lady's Private Tutor* (1770), pp. 162–7.
[54] Trusler, *The Honours of the Table* (1788), p. 6.

healths, however, is stigmatized as vulgar and a 'silly custom'.[55] At the end of the century, formal, hierarchical manners have virtually disappeared, and there is a new emphasis on female delicacy: not only can the lady not call for wine, but she is to be given small portions of food, since her nature is supposed to be 'rather divine than sensual'.[56] This argument also explains why the ladies withdrew before the men began serious drinking, although the habit was well established long before the obsession with female delicacy. Foreign tourists tended to offer a different explanation: the ladies preferred not to witness the spectacle of the men relieving themselves into the chamber-pots placed strategically at each corner of the dining-room or by the sideboard.[57]

How quickly the new forms of politeness described by Trusler were adopted is uncertain. In 1784 François de la Rochefoucauld noted the contrast between the relaxed breakfast and more formal dinner at the Duke of Grafton's house in Suffolk: dinner was uncomfortably polite, with 'strangers' seated near the lady of the house (but this implies a different seating arrangement from the early eighteenth-century grouping of the ladies at the top and the gentlemen at the bottom) and served in strict order of seniority 'with the most rigid etiquette'; guests were pressed to eat more by the host.[58] This seems to be a curious mixture of the new style and much older ways, but there is in fact nothing here that contradicts Trusler's advice except the pressing food on the guests, and this could simply be a particular attention paid to a foreigner. There is also the possibility that the French tourist exaggerated the formality of the English dinner because it contrasted both with breakfast and, perhaps, with less formal manners at home. Other French visitors, however, were charmed by what they saw as the simplicity of English manners.[59]

English tourists abroad noticed that meals were conducted differently, and their comments show what was the norm in England. In 1781, Richard Twining, returning from a tour of the Rhine, noted in his journal that at a village between Aix-la-Chapelle and Liège, he dined at a *table d'hôte* consisting of two courses and a dessert. He commented:

---

[55] Trusler (1788), pp. 7–10, 18, 25–26.

[56] Trusler (1788), p. 7.

[57] See Grosley, *Londres* (1770), vol. 1, pp. 265–66; Faujas, *Voyages* (1797), vol. 1, pp. 294–5; Scarfe (ed. & trans.), *A Frenchman's Year in Suffolk* (1988), p. 23.

[58] Scarfe (1988), p. 22.

[59] See, for instance, du Bocage, *Recueil des Œuvres* (1762), vol. 3, p. 76.

I do not recollect having been at a single inn on the Continent which has deviated from this polished custom. The vulgar phrase, 'Sir! you see your dinner,' appears to be peculiar to our island ...[60]

And in 1788 he wrote from Göttingen to his brother, describing a grand dinner with the Dukes of Cumberland and Cambridge:

The manner of conducting a dinner in this country is admirable. There is not any of that bustle and confusion which attends almost every large dinner party in England: everything proceeds quietly and methodically. The only thing that any person sitting at the table helps to, is soup. Every other dish is handed round in its due course by a servant. If the dish requires any carving, the servant takes it to a side table, carves a small plateful of it, and hands that plate about to every person at the table. ... in the course of the dinner, you are sure of having the contents of every dish presented at your elbow, and you may either take or reject, as you please. ... [T]he wine ... was called for, as in England.[61]

Twining's comments on the division of dinner into courses is confirmed by Maria Holroyd's dinner in Paris in 1791, at 'Roberts', the best *Traiteur* here'. She complained that 'dinner is eternal', since the dishes were served in succession, 'never more than a dish at a time'.[62] Except in grand houses (and on festive occasions in lesser households), by the end of the century the norm was one single course with the guests around the table helping themselves and each other.

What stands out from an examination of the prescriptive literature is that in every area formality gave way to a more relaxed and sociable style. The bill of fare in England was always less disciplined than in France, and allowed adaptation to the tastes and means of those who aspired to some form of gentility. The same gradual relaxation took place in the code of behaviour at table, whether in the placing of the guests or how they were served. An image of pleasant conviviality is given by Catherine Hutton's account of a dinner in 1779 for five people, given by the rector of Aston, Mr. Shuttleworth:

---

[60] Twining (ed.), *Selections from Papers of the Twining Family* (1887), p. 86.
[61] Ibid., p. 157.
[62] Adeane (ed.), *The Girlhood of Maria Josepha Holroyd* (1896), pp. 46–47.

At three o'clock we sat down to table, which was covered with salmon at top, fennel sauce to it, melted butter, lemon pickle and soy; at the bottom a loin of veal roasted; on one side kidney beans, on the other peas, and in the middle a hot pigeon pie with yolks of eggs in. To the kidney beans and peas succeeded ham and chickens, and when everything was removed came a currant tart. Mr. Shuttleworth's behaviour was friendly and polite; he was attentive to the wants of his guests, and helped them to everything they wanted in a moment, without the least appearance of ceremony. ... After dinner we had water to wash, and when the cloth was taken away, gooseberries, currants and melon, wines and cyder. Mr. Shuttleworth asked me for a toast, and I gave him Mr. Rolleston, by whom we had been most elegantly entertained in that very room some years before. At a little before five, my mother, Sally Cocks, and I retired into the drawing room, where I amused myself with reading and looking at the prints till six, when I ordered tea, and sent to let the gentlemen know it was ready.[63]

Although the menu followed the rules in that the dishes were disposed symmetrically on the table, it was organized as a single course with two removes (and the removes were not to replace soup or fish, but the two vegetable dishes), followed by a single dish, the sweet tart. The dessert was a simple one of fresh fruit, and the dishes were unfashionably English. All trace of ceremony was banished; even the toast was an opportunity to recollect a previous agreeable occasion rather than a formal ritual. The rules set out in books, whether for table manners, the bill of fare, or for producing dishes, were always adapted to suit the occasion. Just how far we shall examine next.

---

[63] Beale (ed.), *Reminiscences of a Gentlewoman of the last Century* (1891), pp. 15–16.

While prescriptive literature offers a somewhat diverse picture of how to serve and eat a meal, letters, travellers' journals, diaries and memoranda with accounts of actual meals give an even less uniform impression. To make sense of them, this chapter will follow a chronological and social progression, examining the evidence for the three basic periods defined in the earlier parts of the book while working simultaneously down the social scale. Although the main focus will be on food, other aspects of the meal, such as the surroundings, the way one was received, or the sociability of the occasion noted by diarists and letter-writers will be recognized. Finally, there will be occasional excursions into fictional meals, especially satirical examples, which exaggerate and therefore make more obvious contemporary attitudes.

As far as is possible, I have tried to make greater use of documents which enable comparative study. At the very apex of society, royal bills of fare survive for the period 1660–1812, although containing many gaps.[1] Like Stephen Mennell for his *All Manners of Food*, I have done no more than sample this very extensive collection. Lower down the social scale, some series of aristocratic menus exist, such as those in the notebook kept by Lady Grisell Baillie between 1715 and 1728, or the Duke of Newcastle's from 1761 to 1766. A number, but not all, of Lady Grisell's menus were published in 1911, and I have but assayed the large group relating to the Newcastle household. Most private memorandum books, however, contain only a few bills of fare and these tend to represent the exceptional. While many letters and diaries contain occasional reference to meals, few are as rich as the journal of the Rev. James Woodforde. Other clergymen whose diaries contain much of interest are the Rev. Stotherd Abdy's account of a three-week sojourn in Berkshire in 1770, and the Rev. John Penrose's record of two stays in Bath in 1766 and 1767. From the foothills of society comes the diary of Thomas Turner, the Sussex shopkeeper who noted his meals at home and away between 1754 and 1765. Sources such as these, describing a variety of situations, are the most valuable since they enable comparisons, and I have placed more reliance on them than on casual references. The erratic spelling of many of the writers, women in particular, adds only charm. I have left it as it was written.

---

[1] These bills of fare are in the Public Record Office, with the shelf-marks LS 9/78–226.

We have seen how the cookery books of the first period, from 1700 until about 1730, were dominated by court-cookery. How far was this true beyond their pages? The royal bills of fare for Queen Anne show this manner well to the fore (contrary to what Stephen Mennell suggested after his own sampling of the record[2]). For instance, the bill for 6 October 1709 lists a 'Terrein', with eight different meats in it, plus 'Veale Collops, Pottage Kn Veale [of a knuckle of veal], Sr Loy Beefe, Mutton, Rabbitt pye, Putt wth Eggs [pullet with eggs], Partr & Ruffs, 3 Quailes 3 Chicks'. The last few are clearly roasts for the second course, but the lack of detail means that it is impossible to tell how elaborate were the dishes listed as Collops and Mutton. Bisks and court-style pottages appeared regularly on the royal table throughout the same month, and indeed throughout this ledger (LS 9/110). The manuscripts confirm the accuracy of Patrick Lamb's cookery book. He gives the bill of fare for 'The Queen's Dinner Feb. 6 1704' (a menu which cannot be located in the documents in the Public Record Office as this year is missing). The copper-plate shows a table of seven dishes, with an olio and a pottage at the first course, removed with a chine of mutton and a dish of ham and chickens, the other dishes being four French entrées and a hare pie; the second course is composed entirely of roasted birds, tame and domestic, accompanied by pickles; the third course consists of jellies and creams, plus small dishes of choice vegetables and other morsels.[3]

In the early years of the century, the aristocracy also favoured the French style. The memoranda of Lady Grisell Baillie noted 170 'Bills of Fair' between 1715 and 1728.[4] Her record is extraordinarily detailed, often showing the way dishes were placed on the table and occasionally offering comments on the use of glassware and china. As befitted a lady born into the aristocracy (her father was the Earl of Marchmont) and who moved among the political élite, Lady Grisell jotted down dinners where the court style of cooking dominates. For instance, in 1722 she gave a dinner for the Earl of Carlisle, the prominent Whig politician, at this date Constable of the Tower of London:

---

[2] He concluded that under Queen Anne, 'there is little to suggest any very elaborate or refined cookery', and that the royal bills of fare show little change in the course of the eighteenth century, with 'good plain English country fare' predominant throughout. See Mennell (1985), pp. 124–5.

[3] Lamb, *Royal Cookery* (1710), plate at p. 4.

[4] A selection of these bills is reproduced in Scott-Moncrieff (ed.), *The Household Book of Lady Grisell Baillie* (1911), pp. 281–301. A few further menus, for dinners in Naples in 1732, and for dinners at Mellerstain in 1756, after Lady Grisell's death, are given pp. 301–4.

17 Decm^r. 10 at a big table. Ld Carlile, etc. 1722.

1st. 7 dishes 2 soups, a terean, stewd pigions w^t sweat breads mushrooms
etc. with a sauce half rague half fricassy, a litle py of toungs etc. veall a
la dob with spinag sauce a boyld pullet sallary sauc

2 Releaffes a whole turbot and fryd smelts and rosted veal

Rost Bieff on the By table for any that cald for it

2nd. 7 Dish a Turkie, a Phesant, snyps, partrages, a wild duck and larks round

3^d. 7 Dish in chena a large dish crawfish, a tart, fryd solls, Blang mange,
sallary and chease, sparagrass, lambs livers whole w^t sauce'.[5]

The three courses of seven dishes follow the French pattern of soups and
entrées, followed by the roasts, followed by *entremets*. Court-style dishes are well
represented here, with the terrine, the veal 'à la daube', and the raggoo-sauce
for the pigeons. As in Charles Carter's bills of fare, the English roast beef is
relegated to the sideboard. The *entremets* include sweet and savoury dishes,
although the savoury dominate. After the three courses came dessert, and the
hostess noted not only the dishes but how they were presented:

Deseart

Aples in cyrop and raw ones round		pears stewd in a round glass in with a foot and raw pears round them
	Jelluy 6 glasses 3 of biskets hipd as high betwixt each 2 glasses, a high scaloped glass in midle wet orang chips	
Milk in china bowl but I think glas as good	candle candle	bowl milk
	in midle wet orang chips salver confections in the middle	
carrans in cyrop and raw pears round	the like below	aples with cyrop and raw ones round[6]

---

[5] Scott-Moncrieff (1911), pp. 294–295.

[6] Ibid., p. 295. Similarly detailed notes on other desserts are to be found when Lady Grisell gave a
dinner for Lord Annadale in 1719, and when she dined with Lord Mountjoy in 1727 (pp. 289, 298).

These notes show the extreme importance of symmetrical presentation, with pyramids of jelly at the centre of the table and of stewed and raw fruit at the corners. This particularly grand dinner, with its carefully-presented dessert, was obviously recorded in detail to serve as a model for others.

Of the 30 dinner menus published from Lady Grisell's notebook, 16 have 2 courses and a dessert, and 9 have more than 2 courses. All the menus have one or more soups at the first course, and the comment on one, at Lord Sunderland's, that it was 'without anything init', points to the other soups belonging to the lavishly-garnished court style. Smaller dishes such as fricassees and raggoos, and raggoos used as a garnish, are also present in virtually all the menus. When the Baillies dined with the Duke of Chandos at Cannons in 1725 (Chandos was renowned for his lavish lifestyle), the first course offered brown and white soups, a fricassee and a raggoo, with one English dish, a pudding. The second course was presented as '3 rings with 5 plates 4 low and one higher in the middle in each', thus creating three pyramids on the table, with the customary roast birds in two of the rings, and custards and creams in the other. Four side dishes, a raggoo of sweetbreads, soles, artichokes, and spinach, completed the array.[7] But Chandos' dinner was eclipsed by Lord Mountjoy's in March 1727. There were 10 people at the table, and 7 dishes at each course: Lady Grisell was sufficiently impressed to note the dishes in more detail than usual, describing amongst other dishes the 'Tareen' with its vast number of ingredients, the raggooed turkey with its decoration of skewered oysters, livers, morels and 'sundry things' (what the English called 'attalets', a version of the French 'hâtelets'), the white soup with a pullet in it, the fried soles with an elaborate sauce and garnish of crayfish. Even the English puddings were elegantly presented, cut and re-assembled to display their three colours, white, green and brown. The dessert of 9 dishes was similarly grand, with pyramids of glass dishes on gilt salvers.[8] These bills of fare show that English puddings and pies were present on the tables of the aristocracy alongside French-style dishes inspired by Massialot, but that the presentation of the English dishes was intended to make them worthy partners to the French, albeit with the peculiarly local twist of emphasis on colour.

---

[7] Scott-Moncrieff (1911), pp. 296–7.
[8] Ibid., pp. 297–8.

As one moves down the social scale, the grand court dishes become less apparent, although the smaller fricassees and hashes, more accessible than the olios and terrines, persist. When Mary Foljambe, a Yorkshire gentlewoman, received Lord Carlisle in 1716, the bill of fare was less sophisticated than at Lady Grisell's:

June ye nineteenth 1716
when Ld Carlile & the Ladies dined here

	Soup	
roast mutton	orange puding	Calves head hash
	Boild Ham & Chickens	

—————

Collops for change dish

—————

5 young Turkies

pease		fry
	Tarts	
fry'd fish		Hartichoaks

2 tongues

—————

stewd Green Apricocks

Strawberries		Corrans
	Cold Possets	
Cherries		Cream

Cream Cheese[9]

As in many cookery books, the number of dishes goes up by two between the first and second course: there are five big dishes, with collops to replace the soup, at the first course, followed by seven smaller dishes at the second course then the dessert. As in the cookery books once more, sweet dishes are present at all the courses: the orange pudding at the first, the tarts at the second, and at the dessert. The same notebook also contains bills of fare for family dinners where apparently no guests were present; these have two courses of four dishes each, with no dessert.[10]

At a similar level of society, Diana Astry's notebook contains 23 bills of fare (for 20 dinners and 3 suppers) recorded between 1701 and 1708.[11] Eight of the

—————————

[9] Hawkesbury, 'The MS. Account and Memorandum Book of a Yorkshire Lady two Centuries ago' (1902), p. 31.

[10] Ibid., p. 33.

[11] Stitt (ed.), 'Diana Astry's Recipe Book' (1957), pp. 166–7.

dinner menus are for two courses, some followed by a dessert, while three are for three. Even where the courses are not explicitly mentioned, the dinner was in fact so arranged, as for instance in June 1703:

> 1703 June the 10th Mr. Rolles, Sir John Smyth & my sister, & my sister Chester & Captain Price dined hear, & wee had for diner a supe, a ham & chicking, a coople of green geeas, a legg of mutton rosted, peas, 2 coople of rawbits rost, cherry & gosebery tarts, whip sulebubes, a custard pudding the 3 dish.[12]

The final comment shows that this dinner had three courses with three dishes at each course: a soup and two large meat dishes, followed by two roasts and the dish of peas, and a final sweet course, but no dessert as such. At home at Henbury there was seldom a dessert even when guests were present, but when Diana Astry dined out it was more frequent. There is not much evidence of French dishes in this notebook, although fricassees appear in seven of the menus along with a few hashes. Yet, as we have seen earlier, Diana Astry's own collection of cookery receipts contained many fricassees and raggoos. In this family, dinners were relatively modest, with three courses to mark festive occasions. On one occasion, a supper in London in 1706, the order of serving was noted:

> December the 16th at London at Mr. Edward we had for super a sack possett, a frigacea of lamb, flurentines, wild fowle, one dish at a time; then was sett on the table alltogether a salver of clear jelleys, allmonds & reasons, dried sweetmets, stwed pipens, pears.[13]

Here the fact that dishes were set on the table one at a time, imposing the order of consumption, was worthy of notice; the order is still that of dinner, with the stewed lamb ('boiled') followed by the 'flurentines' ('baked') and then the wild fowl ('roasted'), with a dessert to finish. What is unusual to modern eyes is to start with the sweet posset.

These bills of fare from the early decades show the French dishes which figure in cookery books and ladies' manuscript collections often on the tables

---

[12] Stitt (1957), p. 166.   [13] Ibid., p. 167.

of the aristocracy and, occasionally on festive occasions, on those of the gentry. It is unlikely the style had reached homes below this level of society. One foreign visitor, César de Saussure, thought that only the more cosmopolitan sections of the nobility went in for French cuisine:

> Their cookery is simple and unadorned, they have hardly any or no raggoos; they do not boil or roast their meat for as long as people do in France. I find that the meat is better as a result, more succulent and more refined. The great aristocrats who have travelled abroad have French cooks, who serve up food that is half French and half English: meaning that they put French pastries and entrées with English roast beef and puddings. Their tables are characterized by plenty, magnificence, & above all great propriety.[14]

Saussure's key words are 'plenty' ('abondance') and 'magnificence' – exactly the terms used to recommend Patrick Lamb's book to the public. But Saussure reckoned that, by contrast, gentlemen and merchants dined off a large joint of beef, two other dishes and a pudding. He also noticed the vast quantities of melted butter used as sauce for fish, vegetables and even meat, echoing Misson's earlier comments on the 'universal' sauce of melted butter.[15]

The comment about 'simple' English cookery points to the contrast between native traditions and French court-cookery which was anything but simple. In 1709 *The Tatler* launched a virulent attack on the court style, comparing 'disguised' French food with simple, substantial English fare:

> I remember I was last Summer invited to a Friend's House, who is a great Admirer of the *French* Cookery, and (as the Phrase is) *Eats well*. At our sitting down, I found the Table covered with a great Variety of unknown Dishes. I was mightily at a Loss to learn what they were, and

---

[14] 'Leur cuisine est simple & unie, ils ont peu ou point de ragoûts, ils ne bouillissent & ne rôtissent pas leurs viandes autant qu'on le fait en France. Je trouve qu'elle en est meilleure, plus succulente & plus délicate. Les grands seigneurs qui ont voyagé, ont des cuisiniers françois, qui préparent leur table moitié à la françoise moitié à l'angloise, c'est-à-dire qu'ils joignent les pâtisseries & les entrées françoises à la pièce de bœuf rôtie & aux *puddings* anglois. Leur table est servie avec abondance, avec magnificence, & surtout avec une grande propreté.' Saussure, *Lettres et Voyages* (1903), pp. 226–227.
[15] See Misson, *Mémoires et Observations* (1698), pp. 393–394.

therefore did not know where to help my self. That which stood before me I took to be a roasted Porcupine, however did not Care for asking Questions; and have since been informed, that it was only a larded Turkey. I afterwards passed my Eye over several Hashes which I do not know the Names of to this Day, and hearing that they were Delicacies, did not think fit to meddle with them.

Among other Dainties I saw something like a Pheasant, and therefore desired to be helped to a Wing of it; but to my great Surprize my Friend told me it was a Rabbit, which is a Sort of Meat I never cared for. … I was now in great Hunger and Confusion, when methoughts I smelled the agreeable Savour of Roast Beef, but could not tell from which Dish it arose, tho I did not question but it lay disguised in one of them. Upon turning my Head, I saw a noble Sirloin upon the Side of the Table smoking in the most delicious Manner. I had Recourse to it more than once, and could not see without some Indignation that substantial *English* Dish banished in so ignominious a Manner to make Way for *French* Kickshaws.[16]

The description of the feast goes on to the dessert, which is just as disguised as the rest: pyramids of sweetmeats are sugared to appear frosted, and whipped cream counterfeits snow. The unhappy author returns home to finish his meal with simpler fare. Substantial English roast beef is already endowed with mythological status.

Felicity Heal suggests that praise for simple English cooking, plainness being a source of pride, first surfaced in the later sixteenth century, associated with propaganda in favour of 'natural' country-house hospitality.[17] Country food was seen as rustic and natural: court and city food as refined and elaborate, a product of culture. This opposition is a fundamental and recurrent theme in gastronomic discourse, and the tension between nature and culture, between the impulse to simplify and that to elaborate, is an important factor in culinary creativity. However, such complaints tend to surface at periods of anxiety about excessive luxury, a source of corruption, material and moral. This association is made clear in a later satire, *Hell upon Earth* (1729), which catalogues the vices of London, and contrasts the 'Innocent People of more Merit

---

[16] *The Tatler*, number 148, from 18 to 21 March 1709.
[17] Heal, *Hospitality in Early Modern England* (1990), pp. 115–6.

than Fortune' who sit down at 12 noon to a dinner of 'homely, wholesome Food' with calm consciences, while the 'Fortunate and Great' sit down at 3 to 'Meals of Pomp and Ceremony, attended by sumptuous side-Boards, Sycophants, and little Sincerity'. These are of 'disguised' food, produced by the French cook, with nothing to recommend it 'but the Expence and hard Names'.[18] The underlying demand is for a return to a mythical golden age, before innocence had been contaminated by luxury. Closely bound up with this is the unstated feeling of exclusion: the cuisine of high culture is rejected because it is itself a rejection of the cookery of those outside a very narrow circle. The women cookery authors' disparaging comments on the court-cooks' grand dishes are part of this rejection of exclusion.

Whether the discourse in favour of simplicity had much influence on culinary fashion is open to doubt. As we have seen, the ideal of more 'natural' flavours was present in the French cookery books of the 1650s, but the receipts lagged behind. Similarly, Gervase Markham's advice to the housewife to serve food that was to be 'rather esteemed for the familiar acquaintance shee hath with it, then for the strangenesse and raritie it bringeth from other Countries',[19] was delivered while supplying plenty of receipts for the rejected foreign dishes. In the early eighteenth century, women authors denounced the court-cooks' extravagance but themselves adapted grand dishes to render them feasible in gentry kitchens. Thus the *Tatler*'s attack on court-cookery does not necessarily mean that there was wholesale rejection of the court style; the problem the essay was tackling was that of excess. These satires expressed the attitude of the middle class to the *haute cuisine* of the élite. Publications like the *Tatler* and the *Spectator* were aimed at members of this class who, in J.H. Plumb's words, 'longed to be modish, to be aware of the fashion yet wary of its excess, to participate in the world of the great yet to be free from its anxieties, to feel smug and superior to provincial rusticity and old world manners.'[20]

The periodicals taught their audience how to avoid rusticity: Addison's comments in 1711 on the shift to a more relaxed style of behaviour among the élite specifically ridiculed the old-fashioned ceremony practised by country

---

[18] *Hell upon Earth* (1729), pp. 6–7, 28–31.

[19] Markham, *The English Hus-wife* (1615), p. 4.

[20] Plumb, in McKendrick, Brewer & Plumb, *The Birth of a Consumer Society* (1982), p. 269.

squires. While in manners the model to be followed was that of the court and the city (the centres of civility), in cookery these same centres were criticized for their blind devotion to extravagance. Here are the first signs of a middle-class ethos which would dominate English cookery, at once rejecting elaboration and expense. In the 1730s, books begin to emphasize the economical nature of their receipts, and their denunciations of French cookery and cooks become louder, even while offering fashionable French dishes. In other words, cookery books gave their readers the mix of the modish, the modern and the modest they were seeking.

The effect of this early criticism on the élite's perception of court cookery is hard to determine. In the end, it probably did contribute to the adoption of *nouvelle cuisine*, even though this did not come about until the 1730s. The parallel between cookery and gardening, also subjected to reappraisal, is striking. The excesses of the formal garden were denounced by Addison in the *Spectator* (number 414, 25 June 1712) and by Pope in the *Guardian* (number 173, 29 September 1713), their main theme being the artificiality of gardens filled with topiary. Critics maintained that the formal garden was a visible expression of absolute monarchy, inappropriate to the British spirit of liberty (*The Tatler*, number 161, 20 April 1710). The links with cookery are obvious: the court style could also be seen as politically suspect, since it too emanated from Versailles; on the practical level, court-cookery was as expensive to produce as topiary was to maintain; aesthetically, the grandiose baroque pyramids of meat and the 'disguised' dishes were artificial. In cookery, renewal did not come until the 1730s, and in gardens too, developments away from the formal style had to wait for Kent's work in the 1720s and 1730s to find full expression.

Court-cookery continued to hold sway well into the 1720s. At court, the bills of fare do not reveal any major change until the later years of that decade. But there was one earlier change which may have contributed to weakening its prestige. When the Elector of Hanover arrived in 1714 to assume the throne as King George I, he brought his German cooks with him and dismissed the royal master-cook, John Faverall, who had taken over from Patrick Lamb on his death in 1709. The post of first master-cook remained vacant for some years.[21] By 1717 the English master-cooks who had served Queen Anne under Lamb had been reinstated at the head of the royal kitchens, although they did not

---

[21] See PRO LS 13/115, ff. 5v, 9; also Beattie, *The English Court* (1967), p. 84.

prepare 'plates' for the king's table.[22] The German cooks remained at work, four at first and six from 1719. There was friction between the two groups.[23] Despite this, the bills of fare show that the form and content of the King's table did not alter after George I's accession. In the 1720s, the old style dishes are still to the fore, though now with the addition of smaller fricassees and hashes, puptons and surtouts – as can be found in Charles Carter.[24] But whereas Patrick Lamb and Richard Smith had been able to exploit their positions in the royal kitchens to prove their credentials to their readers, later English writers could not produce such references, and native leadership in culinary fashion passed to the aristocracy.

This was part of a wider movement. The historian John Brewer has described how the royal court reduced in size and became more domestic in the years from the Restoration to the middle eighteenth century, and consequently it faded as the centre of high culture, replaced by London.[25] In matters of food, the shift from courtly to domestic is revealed in the bills of fare of the reign of George II. A typical menu for Friday 1 February 1740 (LS 9/143) showed a mere five dishes: 'Potage Barly wth Rh Wine', larded soles, grilled fillets of partridges, a roast loin of veal, tarts and jelly. Two days later, the menu again had five dishes, with a bisk of squabs, a dish of pullets partly grilled and partly in a white raggoo, a stockfish pie, a roast shoulder of mutton, and a bread pudding. The only possible *nouvelle cuisine* in all this were the pullets served on Sunday, which might have been similar to Clouet's two dishes using the breast of the fowl served with a cream sauce, the legs marinaded and braised. But while there were some survivals of the older court style, such as the bisk, on the whole this was closer to everyday domestic cookery.

As leadership in matters culinary passed from the court, 'French cooks were particularly the prerogative of the grandest of the Whig grandees'.[26] Walpole employed Solomon Sollis from 1714. Later, the Earl of Chesterfield engaged

---

[22] See PRO LS 13/115, ff. 49v & 71v, for Michael Hounsleffe's petition asking to be made first master-cook or to be given an allowance, and the warrant; also LS 13/260 for the appointment warrant for John Dissell, mentioning his predecessor, dated 17 March 1723/4.

[23] See the minutes of the Board of Green Cloth, mentioning the problem of who was in charge in the royal kitchens, and the number of German cooks, PRO LS 13/115, ff. 14v, 106.

[24] See, for instance, the bills for July 1724–April 1726, LS 9/121.

[25] See Brewer, *The Pleasures of the Imagination* (1997), pp. 3–55.

[26] Mennell (1985), p. 125.

Vincent La Chapelle; the Duke of Richmond, Thomas Jacquemar; the Duke
of Bedford, L'Allemande; the Marquess of Rockingham took on a French cook,
Mr Blanche, and a confectioner, Mr Negri, who may be the Domenico Negri
who in the 1760s set up the shop in London which became famous as Negri
and Gunter; and of course the Duke of Newcastle employed a host of French-
men at exorbitant salaries.[27]

Unfortunately, authentic bills of fare for these great men are scarce, but
there is a series of somewhat later menus drawn up for Newcastle and, after his
death, for the Duchess, for the period 1761–1774 (BL Add. MSS 33325–36). The
first of these ledgers, for 1761, shows a variety of menus, from simple one-course
dinners to grand tables of two or three courses. An example of the first (presumably a dinner where there were no guests), for 28 February 1761 at the Duke's
country house at Claremont in Esher, gives 8 dishes: veal broth, salt fish, roast
neck of mutton, veal scallops, minced chicken, roast pullet with eggs, cold
salmon, and a bread pudding. This is the same domestic style of food which
was being served to the King. But a menu for the Duke in London on 21
January is slightly more elegant, with 16 dishes: 'Pottage au Vermicilli', boiled
whiting, boiled salmon, a chine of pork with boiled peas, roast leg of mutton,
'patty beef Steaks', 'Tendrons de Veau au blanc', roast pullet, asparagus,
'Crawfish ala Provenc\]', oysters, potted char, cold pork, potted cock, brawn,
and a boar's head. The division into courses is not made explicit, but lines
dividing the list suggest that the chine of pork was a remove for the soup, and
that there was a division into two courses after the veal. There was also a
dessert, since the list of costs includes a payment of £4 10s. for confectionery.

The grand dinners, such as a two-course meal on 20 February, or one of
three courses on 4 June, offer a view of fashionable dining. The organization
of the menu here is much closer to the French system than most bills of fare
given by English cookery books. The first gives 15 dishes and 4 removes at each
course. The first course consisted of 5 large dishes, with two soups, a terrine,
and two dishes of boiled meat, surrounded by 10 smaller platters, including
nouvelle cuisine dishes such as 'Neck Veal Glasse au Chicore' and 'Fillets of 2
Pullets a la Creame'. At the second course, there were 10 game birds and salads,
and 5 larger dishes of crayfish, lobster, tartlets, orange jelly and a 'Gatteau

---

[27] For details of most of these cooks and their employers, see earlier references in Part 2; for
Rockingham, see Holmes, thesis, p. 49.

Garni'. The second menu is even more lavish, with 7 large dishes surrounded by a large number of smaller and side dishes at each course. The large dishes at the first course are the same mix of soups, terrines and boiled meats, and the 30 smaller *plats* again include such modish items as veal fricandeaux with lettuce, and lambs' ears hollandaise. The first course had 8 removes, and such things as venison pasty and beef pie stood on the sideboard. The second course offered 10 plates of game and 12 salads, plus 6 dishes of shellfish, cold pigeon patty and sweet things with, in the middle of the table, 'a Bridge wth a Temple'. The third course was composed of 18 *entremets*: vegetables, eggs, creams, two decorative dishes – 'A Waggon' and 'A Cherry Tree' – and '12 plates of Pastry' which include several decorative items such as 'Hen and Chickens', and '6 flower potts' ('Pastry' here must mean *pâtisserie* rather than pastry). The expenditure for this dinner came to nearly £290.[28]

Monumental court dishes still appeared on fashionable tables and the smaller side dishes were the vehicle for *nouvelle cuisine*. The decorative dessert dishes appear closely related to those given in Elizabeth Raffald in 1769,[29] an example of the way in which cookery books contributed to spread aristocratic fashions down through society some years after their first appearance. Although these bills of fare date from some twenty years after Clouet's time with Newcastle, there is no reason to suppose those for the earlier period were very different. The Duke's correspondence shows the chief objects of appreciation were the *petits plats* such as the 'tendrons de veau' and 'filets de lapreaux' he mentioned in his letter to Clouet in February 1754.[30]

This notorious fondness for French cookery supplied satirists with a vast amount of material which in turn provides us with further evidence of the grandees' enthusiasm for *nouvelle cuisine*. Walpole had been a target of criticism for having abandoned good English food in his transition from Norfolk squire to great man, as one observer of his 'Norfolk Congress' at Houghton in 1728 complained:

For they [those present] remember'd when he had like to have overturn'd the whole Table, upon seeing some French Kickshaws upon it, which he

---

[28] For these menus, see BL Add. MS 33325, ff. 2v, 19v, 24, 72v–73. The last menu is reproduced in Sedgwick (1955), p. 310.

[29] Raffald (1769) gives a receipt for 'Hen and Chickens', p. 174.

[30] Quoted in Sedgwick (1955), p. 312.

said was poison to an English Constitution. But now, forsooth, nothing but French Sauces will go down.[31]

The imaginary bills of fare dreamed up by this satirist use food purely as metaphor: on his table, amidst an array of grandiose and improbable mixtures, stood 'a Porringer of Viper-broth' and a 'Bisk of Pidgeons', thus 'denoting the Wisdom of the Serpent and the innocency of the Dove'. Such images are too extravagant to tell us much (though note the presence of the bisk in the late 1720s). Satires attacking Newcastle offer more precision. The well-known print of 1745, 'The Duke of N—le and his Cook' (British Museum print number 2684), shows the aghast Duke in the kitchen, begging Clouet not to leave him (in December of that year a proclamation was issued threatening to revive earlier anti-Catholic laws). In the background, a cloth draped over the kitchen table shows a bill of fare which includes, amongst other French dishes, 'Woodcocks Brains', 'Carps Tongues' and 'Popes Eyes'. These dishes, using microscopic parts of animals, are emblematic of *nouvelle cuisine* as seen by the English: the epitome of insubstantial foreign food. Other prints, such as 'The Dis-card' and 'The Vision: or Justice Anticipated' also mock Newcastle's enthusiasm for the delights of the table.[32]

At a more general level, anti-French diatribes abound, whether in the form of Hogarth's prints, Hannah Glasse's scornful remarks, R. Campbell's guide to the London trades, or anonymous tracts.[33] Given the substantial wages paid to French cooks, many English commentators saw the new culinary style as a vast confidence trick, designed to cheat gullible milords out of their estates, a theme developed by Glasse in 1747. The influence of political satire on public perceptions of French food is an important reason for its rejection: the exploitation of Walpole's and Newcastle's devotion to French food, used in the political arena to insinuate that they were deficient in patriotism, turned that food into a target.[34]

---

[31] *The Norfolk Congress* [1728], p. 5.
[32] See Atherton, *Political Prints in the Age of Hogarth* (1974), p. 235.
[33] See Campbell, *The London Tradesman* (1747), p. 277; *A Treatise on the Use and Abuse of the Second ... Table* [c.1758], pp. 60–62. The best-known of Hogarth's satires is, of course, 'Calais Gate' (1748).
[34] For a more extensive discussion, and a reproduction of the print, see Lehmann, 'Politics in the Kitchen' (1999).

There is, as far as I know, no single source which offers a sustained view of what was being served at the tables of the lesser aristocracy and the gentry in the middle of the century. A important feature of upper-class entertaining was the ball-assembly, with dancing and cards to amuse the company, refreshments available throughout the evening, and supper as the meal. This type of reception replaced the earlier formal dinner followed by a ball.[35] Junkets like these feature regularly in the diaries of Caroline Lybbe Powys, and the impression is that the food at such parties was very much taken for granted. At a ball in 1777, she noted merely that the supper was 'elegant', with 'provision of every kind, wine, fruits, &c.'; the soups and game were 'as usual hot, the rest cold'.[36] Lady Jane Coke attended several grand receptions, but was more interested in the fashion than in food. In March 1749 she noted that there were 92 dishes at a supper given by Lord Fitzwilliam for 20 people, 'besides a magnificent dessert'. In January 1754, Lady Northumberland gave an 'entertainment', with what was obviously a fashionably decorated table, with 'a hen with seven little chickens' and a 'landscape, with gates, stiles, and cornfields' for the dessert.[37] The hen and chickens sound like one of the dishes mentioned in Newcastle's menu in 1761.

For gentry dinners at this period, brief glimpses from scattered references have to suffice. Madame du Bocage, who spent just over two months moving in upper-class circles in England in 1750, noted that aristocrats like Chesterfield had French cooks, a fact of which she disapproved, commenting that French luxury would gradually corrupt other nations.[38] She preferred English food:

> I find it easy to grow accustomed to these foreign dishes, and even to the
> simple cookery of the English, of which we have so bad an opinion;
> their large joints, their pudding, their fish which is cheaper than in Paris
> and which is served at every meal, their chickens in butter sauce, are
> excellent.[39]

---

[35] See Girouard (1980), pp. 191–93.

[36] Climenson (ed.), *Passages from the Diaries of Mrs. Philip Lybbe Powys* (1899), pp. 190–91.

[37] Rathborne (ed.), *Letters from Lady Jane Coke to her friend Mrs Eyre* (1899), pp. 135. For Lord Fitzwilliam's supper, see p. 29.

[38] See du Bocage, *Recueil des Œuvres* (1762), vol. 3, p. 48.

[39] 'Je m'accoutume facilement à ces mets étrangers, & même à la cuisine simple des Anglois dont nous avons si mauvaise opinion; leur grosse viande, leur pudding en gâteau, leur poisson moins cher qu'à Paris, dont on sert à chaque repas, leurs poulets à la sauce au beurre sont excellents.' Du Bocage (1762), vol. 3, p. 45.

The opinion French visitors formed of English cookery depended very much on their vision of England as a country of liberty or as a cultural backwater. Later, Pierre Jean Grosley, who had a rather less rosy view, did not think highly either of English foodstuffs (English meat was inferior to French, poultry was flabby and watery, vegetables tasted smoky) or of English cookery, limited to grilling and boiling, and incapable of producing good broth and good boiled meat at the same time.[40]

If we turn to English sources, it is necessary to go lower down the social scale to find details. Elizabeth Raper's journal contains some passing references to meals, but complete menus are never given. On one occasion in 1757, she prepared a custard and tarts in the morning and then went out, returning after 1 o'clock to find unexpected visitors; she managed to appear in the parlour an hour later, having made a fricassee. Presumably these dishes were eaten at the dinner which followed, but the social activities after dinner ('chatted, sang, drank T') received more attention than the food.[41] As noted earlier, her receipt book contained a large number of made dishes, though rather old-fashioned.

The diary of Thomas Turner shows the food of the tradesman. It covers the period 1754–1765 and he noted everything he ate (although many of these references have been deleted by the modern editor). Enough detail remains to give an accurate picture. His everyday diet was simple: dinner was usually roast or boiled meat, a pudding of some sort and vegetables. A typical Sunday dinner was, 'the pig, given us by Mr. Darby, roasted, a piece of beef boiled, a plum rice pudding and turnips.'[42] Sunday dinners tended to be larger, but the food was much the same. Pork was important to the family; after killing a pig, Turner would record consuming first the offal and then other parts of the animal over a period of about a month. By far the most frequent statement is 'we dined on the remains of yesterday's dinner', sometimes with a new item added; once this entry appears for eleven days in succession.[43] Visits to friends and relatives saw little alteration, although he certainly appreciated something different. He dined with a friend at Newhaven in 1764:

[40] See Grosley, *Londres* (1770), vol. 1, pp. 121–22, 125–26, 132.

[41] Grant (ed.), *The Receipt Book of Elizabeth Raper* (1924), p. 14.

[42] Vaisey (ed.), *The Diary of Thomas Turner* (1985), p. 71.

[43] Ibid., p. vi. For examples of the gradual consumption of a pig, see pp. 79–84, 267–68.

'We dined with my friend Tipper on a leg of lamb boiled, a hot baked rice pudding, a gooseberry pie, and a very fine lobster, green salad and fine white cabbage'.[44]

What Turner describes as 'elegant' is so only because of the variety of dishes:

I rode to Lewes .... I dined at *The White Hart* in company with about twenty more upon a fillet of veal roasted, a ham boiled, a fore-quarter of lamb roasted, 2 hot pigeon pasties, 2 raisin and currant puddings, greens, potatoes and green salad. The reason of my dining on so elegant a dinner was on account of my having business with Mr. Baley, steward of the Rt. Hon. Hen. Pelham Esq. deceased, who held an audit there today.[45]

The White Hart was, of course, the inn run by William Verral until his bankruptcy, then managed by Thomas Scrace. Turner dined there once in 1756, while it was still under Verral's rule, but the meal was very ordinary: 'boiled beef and greens, a breast of veal roasted and a butter pudding cake'.[46] Apparently Verral kept French cookery for his more exalted customers.

Turner did not have much opportunity to frequent the houses of the gentry: the closest he came was when he was invited by his vicar, the Rev. Porter. At tithe-feasts, roasted and boiled beef and pudding were invariable; this was standard fare on such occasions and, as we shall see later, had political connotations. Very occasionally, Turner was invited to something better, usually supper and cards during the Christmas season, when a group of the more prosperous people in the village invited each other to parties. Once there was a dinner for 10 people:

I dined at Mr. Porter's ... on a fine dish of carp, a green neat's tongue and turnips, a rump of beef à la daub, a hot chicken pasty, a roast turkey and bread puddings. My family at home dined on the remains of yesterday's dinner.[47]

---

[44] Vaisey (1985), p. 297.
[45] Ibid., p. 292.
[46] Ibid., p. 59.
[47] Ibid., p. 312.

This is virtually the only sign in the diary of the cookery of cookery books; there is never a mention of dessert in any form. When Turner was asked to Halland, the Duke of Newcastle's seat, by the steward, Christopher Coates, the food was little different: a supper in 1759 consisted of cold meat, roast mutton, boiled chickens and oyster sauce, hashed duck, and tarts.[48] Not much changed when he himself received his friends to supper: cold meat, tarts, and one or two hot dishes, such as boiled salt fish with egg sauce, or Scotch collops.[49] A similar festive menu was recorded in 1758 by George Woodward, the rector of East Hendred in Berkshire: at Christmas parties 'fowls and bacon, roast beef and mince-pies, is the entertainment to be met with at every house'.[50]

The Swedish naturalist Pehr Kalm visited England in 1748. He found his dinners consisted largely of butcher's meat, boiled or roasted. Turnips and potatoes went with roast meat, carrots with boiled, and a cup of melted butter was always ready to pour over them. Kalm also noted that salads, cabbage and sprouts, and green peas were frequently consumed. He thought puddings well prepared, and he mentioned tarts and pies. In his experience, cheese concluded the meal, which was washed down with wine for those who could afford it, or ale, cider or beer; punch was drunk afterwards. He did not come across any raggoos or fricassees, and reckoned that 'the art of cooking as practised by most Englishmen does not extend much beyond roast beef and plum pudding'.[51] When he was in London, Kalm's hosts were fellow-professionals. In the country he visited farmers (including the cookery and household-economy author William Ellis). His impressions, therefore, were of people somewhat below gentry status. The picture he drew is not very different from that found in Turner's diary.

Later in the century, a clearer impression emerges from the letters of John Penrose and the diary of James Woodforde. Penrose was a Cornish clergyman who visited Bath twice for his health in 1766 and 1767. He and his family took lodgings and bought their own provisions, which they had cooked for them, for a fee, in their landlady's kitchen. Mrs Penrose did some very simple cooking, such as boiling potatoes, in their rooms on their first visit; the second time all their

---

[48] Vaisey (1985), p. 171.

[49] See Vaisey (1985), pp. 136, 172, 200.

[50] Gibson (ed.), *A Parson in the Vale of White Horse* (1982), p. 114.

[51] Lucas (ed. & trans.), *Kalm's Account of his Visit to England* (1892), p. 15. For Kalm's remarks on English food, see pp. 13–16.

food was dressed by the landlord's cook. Because of these arrangements, they could invite people to tea, but they did not often have guests to dinner. The food they ate in their lodgings was simple: during a typical week in April 1766 they had roast veal twice, roast mutton three times, roast lamb once, and a mutton pie from a pastry-cook's. The vegetable was always potatoes, except some spinach with the lamb. Their diet was restricted partly because they were in lodgings, invitations meant better fare. En route for Bath, they had stayed with friends at Yendacot, where Sunday dinner was a two-course meal:

> The first course was a fine dish of Fish, a rump of Beef roasted, Ham and Fowls, a fine Sallad, two small plates of Garden-stuff, answering each other and two Bread Pudins. ... [T]he second course ... was Roasted Sweet breads, Lobsters, Trifle, 2 Plates of Almonds and Raisins, Baked Pares and Potted Meat, etc.[52]

There were seven dishes at each course (the roast beef would have replaced the fish at the head of the table), and this was deemed a 'genteel entertainment'. What is unusual is that the second course included the dessert dishes of almonds and raisins.

In Bath, they were occasionally invited by their friends the Sewells (Colonel Sewell had found them lodgings), and John Penrose dined without his women-folk at Sir Booth Williams'. On these occasions, the food was clearly superior to the Penroses' daily diet:

> Our Dinner at the Colonel's was like his other Entertainments, too costly for us. There were three large Mullet richly stewed, a Fillet of Veal stuffed and roasted, three fine Collyflowers and a fine Dish of Green Peas. These last two Articles came, I dare say, to a fine Penny.[53]

Penrose's accounts of Sir Booth Williams' dinners are just as full of admiration tinged with envy. During their second trip to Bath, a dinner with Mr Brinsden called forth comment on the size of the dishes and the fish. Every detail of the presentation was remarked:

---

[52] Mitchell & Penrose (eds), *Letters from Bath* (1983), pp. 24–25.

[53] Ibid., p. 154. For other examples of dinner with the Sewells, see pp. 91, 140–41.

For Dinner at Mr. Brinsden's, May 6.

First Course – Pair of large Soals; one fried with Parsley, the other boiled, the Dish garnished with Horse Radish. At the lower end, roast rump of Beef. On one side crab-sauce and melted Butter, the other side cucumbers, a Sallet in the middle …. The soals cost 5 shillings.

Second Course – At higher end, 6 pigeons roasted; lower end a large dish of Asparagus; one side a goose-berry Tart, the other side an hundred large Prawns, … almost all of them larger than you will readily conceive, price of them 3 shillings.

Afterwards – Cheese sound and rotten, the rotten like Stilton Cheese, Pats of Butter, Radishes. Then the napkin, which covered the Table-cloth, being removed, a Dish of Sweet-meats, viz. 2 preserved Pine-apples, in a high Glass, which stood in a salver of preserved Peaches, preserved in Brandy. Before the cloth was taken off, large glasses brought of warm water, without Sawcers. Our Wine was Port, Madeira, and Mountain; our other liquors Beer and cyder; all both eatables and Drinkables excellent in their kind; and to crown the whole, an unaffected friendly Welcome.

We drank Tea in the Dining-Room. Coffee out of very large white china cups, Tea out of very large Dishes, next kin to Basons of a Rummer fashion. … The whole Service at Dinner was in china.[54]

Such a complete account of a dinner is rare since reporters usually took the way dishes were served and the order of battle for granted. Here, every detail is given for the benefit of Penrose's daughter who had stayed in Cornwall to manage the home.

Penrose's tale of how dinner proceeded is confirmed by foreign tourists. They tended to detail because they were dealing with the unfamiliar. Faujas de Saint-Fond gives an admiring description of the beauties of English mahogany tables once the cloth had been removed. He observed this ritual strip before the dessert at a dinner in London and at the Duke of Argyll's seat at Inverary. When he was entertained on the Isle of Mull, dessert consisted of cheese alone, and the cloth was not removed until after this had been eaten.[55] Faujas found

---

54 Mitchell & Penrose (1983), p. 177.
55 See Faujas, *Voyages* (1797), vol. 1, pp. 44, 290–95; vol. 2, p. 84.

British food simple but excellent ('exquis'). He encountered French cuisine at the Duke's. François de la Rochefoucauld, less enthusiastically Anglophile, thought 'English cooks are not very skilful, for one fares very ill at table, even in the grandest houses.'[56] He found, even in the largest houses, women did the cooking and few people employed a French cook, partly because of the tax on male servants. Like Kalm, he was struck by the large joints of meat and the absence of sauces and raggoos. He too admired the polished tables revealed for wines, fruit, and 'biscuits and butter, which many English eat with their dessert.'[57] This was what de la Rochefoucauld found at the Duke of Grafton's country seat but, he reckoned, 'the same lives are lived throughout England'.

One account of food amongst the wealthy gentry is found in the journal kept by the Rev. Stotherd Abdy during a three-week visit to his patrons, the Archer family, to celebrate the marriage of Susanna Archer to Jacob Houblon in 1770. The dinners and suppers during the visit were often described as 'elegant' though the climax came with the wedding-day dinner:

> In the great eating Parlour, about sixteen servants stood in rich Liveries; the Table was spread in a most elegant and superb manner; the Side-boards loaded with massy Plate; the Bride & Bridegroom sat at the top, the Father & Mother at the Bottom .... There were fifteen hard-named dishes in each course, besides Removes. The desert consisted of Temples, gravel walks, Ponds, etc.; and twenty Dishes of Fruit, & Champagn, Burgundy, Mamsey, Madeira and Frontiniac, were handed about incessantly. Bumpers it may be imagined were drank to the joy, health, & happiness of M^r & Mrs Houblon; the Bells were ringing the whole dinner time, & in short everything had the appearance of the true hospitality of a fine old Family, joined to the elegance of modern taste.[58]

Abdy's favourite adjective, 'elegant', is deployed here, though the setting receives more attention than the food. Despite this celebration bearing no resemblance to the open-house of sixteenth- and seventeenth-century hospitality, 'tradition' was invoked. Yet this was a small, private, exclusive party, where servants were more numerous than guests.

---

[56] Scarfe (ed. & trans.), *A Frenchman's Year in Suffolk* (1988), p. 19.

[57] Ibid., pp. 22–23.

[58] Houblon, *The Houblon Family* (1907), vol. 2, pp. 130–131.

Three days later, the French cook who had been hired for the occasion departed, and food reverted to solid English staples:

> When we were new drest for dinner, the worthy Lady of the House informed us, that Monsr Hash Slash Cook had taken his leave, and that we should feel too sensibly … the want of everything hard named & *out of the wayish* as to eating; and that we must now be reduced to plain mutton and apple dumplin. We, instead of being mortified at this account sincerely rejoiced at hearing it, as our eyes had not been blest with such a sight for above a week. When we came to table we had the pleasure of seeing seven good eatable dishes, and could really tell what they were, and we enjoyed our meal thoroughly.[59]

Apparently Abdy was not the only one to heave a sigh of relief at the disappearance of the 'hard-named' French dishes, though earlier he had commented that the dishes prepared by the foreigner were 'remarkably good and handsome'.[60]

The diary of the Rev. James Woodforde, incumbent of Weston Longeville in Norfolk, gives by far the most complete picture of any manuscript source of food habits in the last decades of the century. Although it covers the years 1758-1802, his notes on food became ever more copious after his niece Nancy came to live with him in October 1779. From 1791, he even recorded meals consumed when there were no guests or other reason for remark. These were often simple: two or three dishes, with frequent mention of leftovers, like Turner's 'remains'. For instance, at the end of January 1792 Sunday's roast beef reappeared on Monday with roasted hare, and Tuesday's roast turkey with the relics of the beef on Wednesday: 'Dinner to day Bubble and Squeak and broiled Turkey'.[61]

Throughout his life, when Woodforde had guests, or he was himself a guest, he jotted down the food he ate. These occasions offered a variety of social situations, although Woodforde's circle was fairly restricted. Much of his socializing was with other local clergy, who invited one another in rotation. Less frequently, he went to Mr Custance, the squire of Weston, and sometimes

---

[59] Houblon (1907), vol. 2, p. 135.
[60] Ibid., vol. 2, p. 122.
[61] Beresford (ed.), *The Diary of a Country Parson* (1924–31), vol. 3, p. 333.

returned the compliment. Rarely, he rubbed shoulders with local grandees such as Charles Townshend of Honingham, the cousin of the Chancellor of the Exchequer, or Lewis Bagot, the Bishop of Norwich. Lesser people also came and dined at his house. Other people's servants or workmen, or people who brought goods, dined in the kitchen with Woodforde's own servants. Local farmers and a group of poor parishioners were received once a year, the first for the tithe-feast, the second at Christmas. Thus the diary shows dinners at three levels of society. The analysis on which the following remarks are based uses the diary for the years 1780–1790, the text of which is found in the first three volumes of the printed edition.

With his equals, his colleagues of the cloth, menus offered similar fare to everyday dinners, except that the number of dishes increased. The meals had only one course, although this was often followed by dessert. The dishes varied with the seasons, and the summer menus show that, in Woodforde's kitchen at least, vegetables were extensively used. To quote only one example, when Woodforde received guests (there were 10 people at table) on 23 June 1783, the dinner was composed of a boiled leg of lamb with carrots and turnips, roast beef with cucumbers, ham, peas and beans, four roast chickens, gooseberry tarts and custards. The dessert consisted of oranges, almonds and raisins, and strawberries and cream. After dinner, tea was served, with bread and butter and plum cake. Perhaps Woodforde was more precise about his own dinners, as vegetables are less in evidence at the return matches in other men's rectories: on 30 April one dinner for the group was of 7 dishes (boiled leg of lamb, roast beef, baked plum pudding, crabs, tarts, raspberry creams, and hung beef); on 13 May there were 4 dishes (mackerel, boiled beef, roast lamb, and a plum pudding); on 19 May there were again 4 dishes (the same except that pickled salmon replaced the mackerel). The next 'rotation' dinner was on 15 July, and was of 6 dishes: boiled chicken, tongue, peas, roast beef, cherry pudding and cheesecake. These are plain dinners, although the food is more varied than Thomas Turner's diet.

When Woodforde dined with the squire, either as host or guest, the bill of fare was rather more complex. At the Custances, there were usually two courses (in 27 out of the 36 dinners where enough detail is given), with a dessert on more festive occasions. When Woodforde received them (only 7 times) the number of dishes varied from 6 to 10. Their enumeration suggests that there were usually two courses (although this is made explicit only twice), sometimes followed by a dessert. A two-course dinner was a sign of social status, even though the total number of dishes might not be much greater than when everything was presented at once. A sign that a special effort was made for the Custances is that on one occasion, Woodforde recorded that his niece Nancy was busy the day before, on 30 January 1782, making cakes, tarts, custards and jellies for dinner. Otherwise, she helped in the kitchen only occasionally, making jams and jellies (21 July 1787, 28 July 1790), or making black pudding after a pig had been killed (8 December 1786, 26 February 1788).

On 25 November 1784, the parson's dinner for the Custances had two courses and was elegantly presented:

> Between 2 and 3 o'clock Mr. and Mrs. Custance came to us and they dined, spent the Afternoon and stayed till near 9 in the Evening with us …. I gave them for Dinner, some Skaite boiled with small Whitings fryed put round the Dish and Oyster Sauce, a Couple of boiled Fowls and a Tongue, a rost Leg of Mutton, and some Artichokes – 2nd Course – a Rabbit fryed, a Duck rosted, the Charter for the first Time of ever making it and very good, Tarts, Rasberry Puffs, Blamange with black Caps in Custard. Fruit after Dinner – Almonds and Raisins, Golden Pippins, Nutts and Grapes. After Coffee and Tea we got to Loo'.

The 'Charter' was a pie, a speciality of Woodforde's home county of Somerset. There were more dishes at the second course than at the first, as in many cookery book menus, and the skate garnished with whitings and served with oyster sauce is typical of the presentation found in the more ambitious printed works. At the Custances' the food was not very different, although vaguely French dishes did occasionally appear, such as the 'Harrico of Mutton' on 9 May 1782, or the 'Fricasied Fowl' on 8 April 1783. Woodforde was ever keen to notice unusual foods, such as the roast swan which appeared at the first course on 28 January 1780; he had never eaten the meat before and found it pleasant with its sweet currant jelly sauce. He was particularly impressed by jellies. These were served at a second course of a dinner on 28 March 1782 when he remarked the 'very pretty Pyramid of Jelly in the Centre [of the table], a Landscape appearing thro' the Jelly, a new Device and brought from London'. On 9 May, he noticed the jelly with coloured blamange shapes set in it. These are the decorative jellies described by Elizabeth Raffald here reproduced on the gentry's tables.

Woodforde might have discerned a closer correspondence between the printed cookery book and real life when he dined with grandees. On 4 September 1783 he was invited to a splendid affair by the Bishop of Norwich:

> There were 20 of us at the Table and a very elegant Dinner the Bishop gave us. We had 2 Courses of 20 Dishes each Course, and a Desert after of 20 Dishes. Madeira, red and white Wines. The first Course amongst many other things were 2 Dishes of prodigious fine stewed Carp and Tench, and a fine Haunch of Venison. Amongst the second Course a fine Turkey Poult, Partridges, Pigeons and Sweatmeats. Desert – amongst other things, Mulberries, Melon, Currants, Peaches, Nectarines and Grapes. A most beautiful Artificial Garden in the Center of the Table remained at Dinner and afterwards, it was one of the prettiest things I ever saw, about a Yard long, and about 18 Inches wide, in the middle of which was a high round Temple supported on round Pillars, the Pillars were wreathed round with artificial Flowers – on one side was a Shepherdess on the other a Shepherd, several handsome Urns decorated with artificial Flowers also &c. &c.

After the meal, tea and coffee were served at 6.30 in the library, and Woodforde left at 7.30. Perhaps his appreciation was coloured by the Bishop's affability, for another sophisticated dinner, at the Townshends', did not meet with such approval:

> There was two Courses at Dinner besides the Desert. Each course nine Dishes, but most of the things spoiled by being so frenchified in dressing. I dined on some fryed Soals, some stewed Beef with Caper Sauce and some Hare rosted, but very insipid.

This was on 28 August 1783, only a few days before the Bishop's dinner. Woodforde was impressed by the drawing-room at Honingham, and he thought that the Townshends 'behaved very genteel to us', but the food did not please. Woodforde's reaction is reminiscent of the Rev. Abdy's. Elegant table decoration, edible or not, was one thing; French cuisine was another.

The parsons' unknowing concurrence gives credence to the success of Elizabeth Raffald. She offered her English readers exactly the form of showing-off they wanted, and eschewed anything too 'frenchified'. Other dinners at Honingham did not produce similar comment, although Woodforde was not pleased one day when there was no dessert (7 November 1786), and he did not like having to wait until the fashionable hour of 4 for his dinner (2 November 1781, 7 November 1786). His attitude was faintly suspicious, whereas with the Custances, the style of the dinners was sufficiently familiar for him to feel at ease and try new dishes.

When he received his inferiors by formal invitation, the bill of fare always contained roast beef and plum pudding. At Christmas, the poor parishioners often got mince-pies (4 times out of 8); for the farmers, there was always a boiled leg of mutton (10 times out of 10), with salt fish (9 times out of 10), and rabbit (5 times out of 10). Drinks were also a fixture: beer for the parishioners, beer, port and punch for the farmers. Other documents confirm this was the standard menu for entertaining one's social inferiors: the Rev. Porter's tithe-feasts included roast beef and plum puddings, and when the Duke of Newcastle gave a feast to celebrate a victory over the French, cold roast beef and beer were served.[62] This was good patriotic fare, offering an image of solidarity. It suggested the cohesion of the community, with the clergyman or the squire renewing the mythical traditions of old-English hospitality. It was also Tory, according to one commentator, who suggested in 1737 that only Whigs served French food. Roast beef swimming in butter, plum pudding and plenty to drink were the signs of a Tory.[63] The idea of affirming a sense of community with one's parishioners was specific to Tory ideology, and Toryism appealed to the gentry and to the middling classes in the expanding cities.[64] It is no accident that this is just where the buyers of cookery books were to be found; popular patriotism spilled over into the cookery books and helped to condition a rejection of French cuisine, associated with the excesses of the Whig grandees in the middle of the century.

The comments of Penrose, Abdy and Woodforde show that the cookery writers were in tune with their expectations. One confirmation is that the favourite epithet used by cookery books to describe receipts, and in diaries to describe meals, is 'elegant'. The idea of magnificence and display, so important

---

[62] See Vaisey (1985), pp. 71, 121, 166, 195.

[63] This text is quoted in Le Blanc, *Lettres d'un François* (1745), vol. 2, pp. 32–37. Le Blanc attributes it to 'Nathanale Smith'.

[64] See Colley, *In Defiance of Oligarchy* (1982), pp. 100, 148–53.

in the cookery books of the early eighteenth century, had entirely disappeared. The journals of Abdy and Woodforde reveal men who enjoyed their food; there is no puritanical rejection of pleasure. But they enjoyed food with which they felt at ease: hashes and fricassees were acceptable, but their greatest expressions of pleasure were for simple things, such as the first peas or strawberries of the season, and fine fruit to finish a meal. Too great a display of sophistication made them uncomfortable. Yet they were naïvely impressed by decorative jellies and table ornaments. There is no sense of any desire to emulate aristocratic food habits.

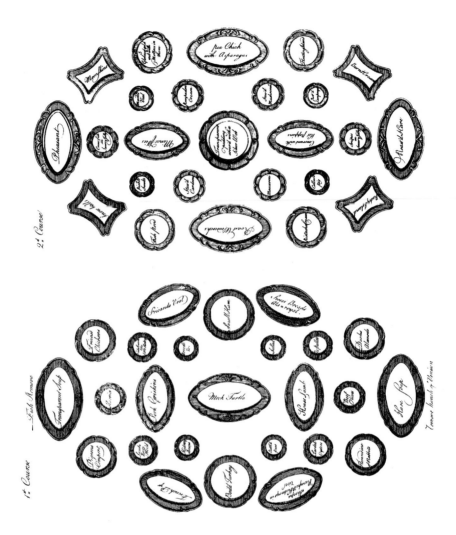

Bill of fare for a 'Grand Table' for January from Elizabeth Raffald, The Experienced English House-keeper, *1769. Raffald's elegant copper-plates (here much reduced) show how variation was achieved within the symmetry of the two courses by changing the shape and orientation of the dishes. The grandest dish is the mock turtle, now one of the most prestigious dishes of the English repertoire. At the second course, pride of place goes to a pudding covered with a web of spun sugar, one of Raffald's own specialities.*

CONCLUSION

Examination of the eighteenth century at table shows the importance of meals and meal-times as vehicles for social self-expression. By the choices one made, one defined one's position. This did not always involve following the élite model. Although there was clearly a desire to ape upper-class fashions, each social group was an island. Boswell's mercer felt smug about his chosen time for dinner, which raised him above the small provincial tradesmen of Durham. In turn, Boswell looked down on him from the height of his own status as a man-about-town in London who dined later.

Postponement of one's usual hour might, anyway, signify very different things: a festive meal could thus be dignified, or a social inferior forced to wait on a host's habitual time might thereby be offered a subtle snub. James Woodforde's normal dinner-hour in the 1780s was 3 o'clock, but he sometimes dined at 4 when invited out. He might comment on this when sharing a meal with his fellow clergymen, but that slight adjustment to his timetable did not produce the same unease one senses when he dined at precisely the same time of day with the Townshends at Honingham.

We have demonstrated, in both the literature and the practice of cookery, the ever-increasing distance in eighteenth-century society from the formality current among the late-Stuart nobility. The relaxation of table-manners was at one with this process. Although Addison traced its origins to both the royal court and the city, that the real impetus for change came from the latter seems likelier. In his essays, he rejected the hierarchical 'court' model of manners in favour of one which allowed easier social mixing within 'polite society'. While the effects of this alteration can be seen in much of our evidence, its extent should not be exaggerated. The advice of Martha Bradley and others does show a more convivial attitude to the act of commensality, but when the Reverend Penrose stayed at Bath, he consorted with fellow-Cornishmen and rarely moved beyond his own social level except in the company of people from that county. However, what had been an appropriate code of table-manners for the élite was seen as hopelessly out of date following the vast increase in the number of prosperous middle-class households participating in public social life, including giving and receiving hospitality.

The experience of dinners on the ground – actual meals reported by actual people – shows something of the same development. At the beginning of the century, aristocratic tables offered two or three courses planned along French lines, with court-style dishes. Although the gentry made an effort to follow, and produced adapted court-style dishes, their bills of fare were generally simpler.

When grandees such as the Earl of Chesterfield and the Duke of Newcastle began to adopt the *nouvelle cuisine* of La Chapelle and Menon, their grand dinners placed olios and terrines alongside the *petits plats* and followed the rules of French menu-planning. But even the Duke consumed much simpler meals when he was not putting on a show.

The smaller and simpler dishes of *nouvelle cuisine* never caught on beyond a restricted noble circle, even though writers like William Verral pointed out that, contrary to public perception, they were neither extravagant nor full of expensive ingredients. Accounts of dinners amongst the gentry show that the 'fashionable' made dishes for special occasions were simple fricassees and stews, such as the 'Scotch collops' and meat 'à la daube', for which unreformed English cookery books supplied innumerable receipts. These had been part of the national repertoire since the late seventeenth century.

Below gentry level, the norm was a one-course dinner, made festive with more dishes for company, and sometimes a dessert of fruit and nuts in season. Only for special occasions was it felt necessary to rise to two courses, and the style of the dishes cooked was much the same as for every day. But while the record of actual dinners does not reveal much of an impact from French cuisine (belying the impression gained from some cookery books), there are signs of a revitalized English tradition. When Woodforde entertained (especially if he was receiving the local squire), a special pie or cakes, tarts, and jellies might be prepared: precisely the areas in which English cookery was at its most creative.

Comparing the record with the ideal set out in cookery books makes clear that the more ambitious of them were aspirational, not necessarily reflecting daily practice. For most people, their raggoos and fricassees were only for special occasions. In spite of authors' emphasis on the suitability of their works for servant readers, they were in fact peddling dreams of delectable dishes and visions of successful parties, impressing the guests and social climbing – not so very different from the literature of cookery today. While the cookery books of the eighteenth century can hardly be described as glossy, their copper-plates of bills of fare for grand tables, wedding-suppers, coronations and the like were as much designed to pander to the fantasies of readers as any modern production.

Aspirations did change in the course of the century. The dream of magnificence was followed by one of elegance. Of what that elegance consisted depended on social status. Thomas Turner was impressed by a wide variety of dishes; parsons Abdy and Woodforde by two courses and a visually attractive table; but for the Duke of Newcastle it was subtle and succulent flavours. Perhaps the only point in common to these three views was pleasure in the decorative dishes which began to appear on aristocratic tables in the 1750s and on the gentry's twenty years later. Sparkling, coloured jellies kept their prestige, whether Charles Carter's 'Ribband' jellies of 1730 or Elizabeth Raffald's more frivolous productions. This highlights the importance of the visual in English food: from the colours created in medieval receipts, to the fruit preserves and gilded marchpanes of the sixteenth- and seventeenth-century banquet, and the moulded temples and fish-ponds of the eighteenth century.

The evidence for the eighteenth century suggests that the gentry class did at first imitate the nobility's 'court-cookery' but, as the cookery book moved down-market, the chain of emulation – that process whereby the favourite of one class was imitated by the next level of society – was broken, and a gap developed between aristocratic, French-inspired cuisine and bourgeois, plain English cookery. It was, however, still functioning in matters of display and decoration. One area of persistent imitation of aristocratic style depended on the maintenance of a feminine tradition of involvement in the production of sweet dishes, where a lady might still amuse herself without loss of status.

This brings us back to the question of gender and cookery. In France, high-class cookery was a masculine preserve and upper-class visitors to England noted with surprise that cooks, even in aristocratic houses, were women. As we have seen, in England cookery books were produced by women from a very early date, and women's presence in the kitchen is the decisive influence on the way English cookery developed for good and for bad in the eighteenth century.

In spite of some women cooks, such as Martha Bradley and Mary Smith, being very much aware of the principles of *haute cuisine*, male professionals excluded women from their ranks. The French manner and its execution were a masculine preserve. This created much mutual suspicion and hostility between the genders which had its effect on the reception of French cookery by the English. There was too a complex combination of factors in which the aesthetic and the political played an important part. To these should be added the consequence of the retreat of the mistress of the house from the actual act of cookery (although perhaps still baking and making jellies and ices). Their (mainly female) cooks were left to do the job as best they could. These elements combined to produce the phenomenon which Stephen Mennell identified as the 'decapitation' of English cookery, but which he considered a product of the nineteenth century.[1] However, all the factors that Mennell attributes to Victorian society can be seen at work in the very years we have been studying.

---

[1] See Mennell, *All Manners of Food* (1985), pp. 204–214.

Appendices

APPENDIX I:
COOKERY BOOK PRODUCTION BY DECADE

Decade	New titles	Reprints	Total
1500	1	0	1
1510	0	0	0
1520	0	0	0
1530	0	1	1
1540	1	1	2
1550	1	0	1
1560	0	0	0
1570	1	2	3
1580	4	4	8
1590	4	9	13
1600	2	5	7
1610	3	5	8
1620	1	5	6
1630	2	14	16
1640	0	6	6
1650	8	25	33
1660	8	13	21
1670	8	19	27
1680	5	17	22
1690	3	13	16
1700	6	9	15
1710	3	15	18
1720	7	15	22
1730	14	22	36
1740	13	24	37
1750	23	36	59
1760	23	29	52
1770	16	41	57
1780	21	51	72
1790	10	45	55
Total	**188**	**426**	**614**

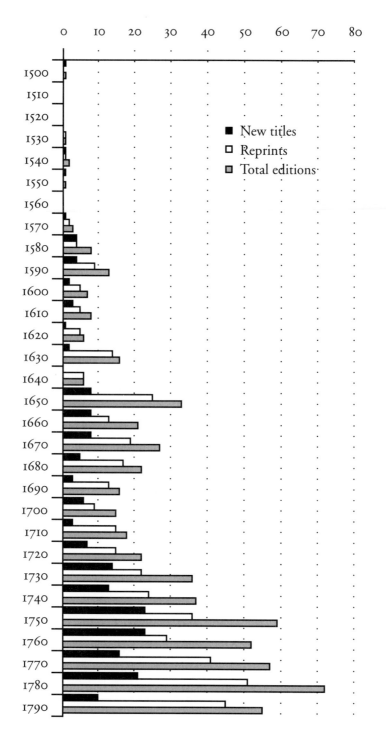

Appendix II:
Meal-times among the Gentry

Date	Breakfast	Dinner	Supper	Date	Breakfast	Dinner	Supper
1702		14:00		1770	10:00	15:00	21:00
1705	09:00	12:00	18:00	1770		16:00	22:00
1708		14:00		1771		16:30	23:00
1710		14:00		1772		18:00	
1711	10:00	15:00		1772		17:00	
1715	09:15	14:00	20:00	1775		16:30	
1723	09:15	14:00		1777			00:30
1727		14:30		1778		16:00	
1739	09:00	14:00		1779		16:00	
1742		15:00		1780		16:00	
1743	09:00	14:00	21:00	1781		15:00	
1745		13:00		1781		16:00	
1749		14:00		1782	10:00	16:30	
1750		16:00		1784	10:00	16:00	00:00
1752			00:00	1784	11:00	17:00	
1753	10:00			1784	09:00		
1756	09:00		00:00	1785		16:00	
1756	09:15			1786	10:00	16:00	22:00
1757		15:00	22:30	1786		16:00	
1758			22:25	1786		16:15	
1760		15:00		1790	10:00	17:00	22:00
1763		14:00		1790	10:00	16:00	22:00
1765		16:00	22:00	1791		18:00	00:00
1766	09:00			1792			23:00
1766	10:00	14:00	21:00	1795		17:30	
1770	09:00	15:00	21:00	1798		15:30	
1770	09:30	15:30	22:00	1799			01:00
1770	10:00	15:00	21:00	1802		17:00	

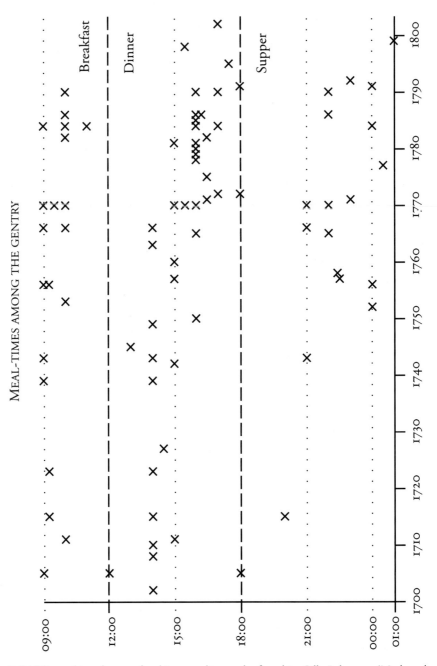

Full bibliographic references for this appendix may be found in Gilly Lehmann, 'Meals and Mealtimes, 1600–1800', in *The Meal: Proceedings of the Oxford Symposium on Food and Cookery 2001* (Prospect Books, 2002).

The full title-page and bibliographical details are given here, with the library where the book was consulted and, for the British Library (BL), the shelfmark. The text of the title-pages reproduces the capitalization of the original, but no attempt has been made to follow the changes in typeface. A brief discussion of the date, where not indicated in the book, and other information, such as the nature of the contents, the sources of the receipts and any other puzzles, follow, although the comments on sources are not exhaustive. This appendix is not a bibliographical guide to all eighteenth-century cookery books, and only books entirely or partly devoted to cookery have been included; thus books of advice to servants and on more general domestic concerns do not appear here. For details of further editions of the works included here, and of other works not consulted for this book, the reader is referred to the bibliographies by Virginia Maclean and A.W. Oxford. References to the following bibliographies and reference works on the book trade will be made by their authors' names.

Katherine Golden Bitting, *Gastronomic Bibliography* (1939; Ann Arbor: Gryphon, 1971).

Virginia Maclean, *A Short-title Catalogue of Household and Cookery Books published in the English Tongue 1701–1800* (London: Prospect, 1981).

Ian Maxted, *The London Book Trades 1775–1800* (Folkestone: Dawson, 1977).

Arnold Whitaker Oxford, *English Cookery Books to the Year 1850* (1913; London: Holland Press, 1979).

Elizabeth Robins Pennell, *My Cookery Books* (Boston/New York: Houghton Mifflin, 1903).

H. R. Plomer, G. H. Bushnell, & E. R. McC. Dix, *A Dictionary of the Printers and Booksellers who were at work in England, Scotland and Ireland from 1725 to 1775* (London: Oxford UP/Bibliographical Society, 1932).

Georges Vicaire, *Bibliographie gastronomique* (Paris: Rouquette, 1890).

ABBOT, ROBERT

The Housekeeper's Valuable Present: or, Lady's Closet Companion. Being a New and Complete Art of Preparing Confects, according to modern Practice. Comprized under the following Parts; viz. I. Different Methods and Degrees of boiling and clarifying Sugar. II. Methods of preserving various Fruits in Syrups, &c. III. Methods of making Marmalades, Jams, Pastes, &c. IV. Methods of making Syrups, Custards, Jellies, Blanchmange, Conserves, Syllabubs, &c. V. Methods of preserving various Fruits in Brandy. VI. Methods of making a Variety of Biscuits, rich Cakes, &c. &c. VII. Methods of mixing, freezing, and working Ice Creams. VIII. Methods of preparing Cordials and made Wines. With a Variety of other useful and elegant Articles. By Robert Abbot, Late Apprentice to Messrs. Negri and Gunter, Confectioners, in Berkeley Square. *Printed for the Author; And sold by C. Cooke, Nº 17, Pater-noster Row; and all other Booksellers in Town and Country. [Price 2s. sewed, or 2s. 6d. neatly bound.]* Title page + pp. iii–xii (preface & contents) + pp. 13–100. (BL 1607/4262.)

The first edition dates from *c.*1790. Elizabeth Pennell's copy had an inscription inside the cover, 'Anne Jones, Dec. 18, 1791' (Pennell, p. 165). The printer, Charles Cooke (who was the son of John Cooke) worked at the address indicated from 1789 to 1817 (Maxted, p. 50). Another edition was published in 1804 with an identical title-page except for the printing details:

Penrith, Printed by J. Brown, in the Market-Place. 1804. Title page + pp. iii–xi (preface & contents) + pp. 13–98. (BL 1608/3649.)

ACCOMPLISH'D

The Accomplish'd Housewife; or, the Gentlewoman's Companion: Containing I. Reflections on the Education of the Fair Sex; with Characters for their Imitation. II. The Penman's Advice to the Ladies; or the Art of Writing made easy, and entertaining. III. Instructions for addressing Persons of Distinction, in Writing or Discourse. IV. An easy Introduction to the Study of Practical Arithmetic. V. Directions for copying Prints or Drawings, and Painting either in Oil or Water Colours, or with Crayons. VI. Directions for Marketing, with respect to Butcher's Meat, Poulterer's Ware, and Fish. VII. A Bill of Fare for every Month in the Year. VIII. Receipts in Cookery, Pastry, &c. IX. Instructions for Carving and placing Dishes on the Table. X. All Sorts of Pickles, Made Wines,

&c. XI. Remarks on the Nature and Qualities of the most common Aliments. XII. Recipes in Physick and Surgery. XIII. Remarks on the Causes and Symptoms of most Diseases. XIV. The Florist's Kalendar. XV. Familiar Letters on several Occasions in common Life; with Instructions to young Orphan Ladies how to judge of Proposals of Marriage made to them without the Consent of their Friends or Guardians. XVI. A Dictionary serving for the Translation of ordinary English Words into more scholastic ones. Concluding with some serious Instructions for the Conduct of the Fair Sex, with regard to their Duty towards God, and towards their Neighbours. *London, Printed for J. Newbery, at the Bible and Sun near the Chapter-House in St. Paul's Church-yard. MDCCXLV.* Title page + 1 lf not num. (bookseller's advertisement) + 2 lvs not num. (preface) + 4 lvs not num. (dedication 'To the Governesses of Great Britain') + pp. 1–431 + 13 lvs not num. (index). (BL 1651/582.)

This book is a rather similar compilation to Mary Johnson's. The cookery receipts occupy pp. 178–244. At the end of the section on diseases (p. 341) the reader is referred to Sarah Harrison's book for further information on cookery and physic.

ACCOMPLISHED

The Accomplished Lady's Delight in Cookery; or, the Complete Servant's-Maid's Guide. *Wolverhampton: Printed by J. Smart.* Title page + pp. 3–24. (BL 1036.c.19.)

A chapbook dating from *c.*1780 (Maclean, p. 2). There are 45 receipts, which look very old-fashioned; some are adapted from John Murrell's *A New Booke of Cookerie* (1615).

ADAM'S

Adam's Luxury, and Eve's Cookery; or, the Kitchen-Garden display'd. In Two Parts. I. Shewing the best and most approved Methods of raising and bringing to the greatest Perfection, all the Products of the Kitchen-Garden; with a Kalendar shewing the different Products of each Month, and the Business proper to be done in it. II. Containing a large Collection of Receipts for Dressing all Sorts of Kitchen-Stuff, so as to afford a great Variety of cheap, healthful, and palatable Dishes. To which is Added, The Physical Virtues of every Herb and Root. Designed for the Use of all who would live Cheap, and preserve their Health to old Age; particularly for Farmers and Tradesmen in the Country, who have but small Pieces of Garden Ground, and are willing to make the most of it. *London: Printed for R. Dodsley, in Pall-Mall; and Sold by M. Cooper, at the Globe in Pater-noster Row. MDCCXLIV.* Title pages + pp. v–xii (introduction) + pp. 1–216. (BL 1037.f.12.)

This book, an attractive combination of gardening and cookery, is now more readily available in the Prospect facsimile reprint (1983).

['ATKYNS, ARABELLA']

The Family Magazine: In Two Parts. Part I. Containing Useful Directions in All the Branches of House-Keeping and Cookery. Particularly Shewing How to Buy-in the Best of all Sorts of Provisions; As Poultry-Ware, Butchers-Meat, Fish, Fruit, &c. With several Hundred Receipts in Cookery, Pastry, Pickling, Confectionary, Distilling, Brewing, Cosmeticks, &c. Together with the Art of Making English Wines, &c. Part II. Containing A Compendious Body of Physick; Succinctly Treating of All the Diseases and Accidents Incident to Men, Women, and Children: with Practical Rules and Directions for the Preserving and Restoring of Health, and Prolonging of Life. In a Method intirely New and Intelligible; in which every Disease is rationally and practically considered, in its several Stages and Changes; and approved Recipe's inserted under every Distemper, in Alphabetical Order. Being principally the Common-place Book of a late able Physician, by which he successfully, for many Years, regulated his Practice. With a Supplement, containing a great Variety of Experienced Rece-ipts, from Two Excellent Family Collections. Now First communicated for the Publick Benefit. To which is Added, An Explanation of such Terms of Art used in the Work, as could not be so easily reduced to the Understanding of common Readers. *London: Printed for J. Osborn, at the Golden-Ball in Paternoster-Row. MDCCXLI.* Title page + pp. iii–xiv (preface) + title page to part 1 + pp. 1–123 + 3 pp. not num. (index to part 1) + title page to part 2 + pp. 1–318 + 3 lvs not num. (index to part 2). (BL 1037.h.11.)

At the end of the preface, the lady who presents the second part of the book as being the papers of her late brother, a physician, says: 'Being still teized for some Name, I will, tho' not my right one, subscribe That of Arabella Atkyns' (p. xiv).

BAILEY, N[ATHAN]

Dictionarium Domesticum, Being a New and Compleat Houshold Dictionary. For the Use both of City and Country. Shewing, I. The whole Arts of Brewing, Baking, Cookery, and Pickling. Also Confectionary in its several Branches. II. The Management of the Kitchin, Pantry, Larder, Dairy, Olitory, and Poultry. With the proper Seasons for Flesh, Fowl and Fish. III. The Herdsman: Giving an Account of the Diseases of Cattle, Poultry, &c. And the most approved Remedies for their Cure. IV. The English Vineyard; being the best Method of making English Wines and of Distilling most Kinds of Simple and Compound Cordial Waters. V. The Apiary: Or, The Manner of Breeding, Hiving and managing of Bees. VI. The Family Physician and Herbalist. Containing the choicest Collection of Receipts for most Distempers, incident to Human Bodies, hitherto made Publick; with the Qualities and Uses of Physical Herbs and Plants of English Growth. By N. Bailey, Author of the Universal Etymological English Dictionary. *London: Printed for C. Hitch at the Red-Lion, and C. Davis, both in Pater-Noster-Row; and S. Austen at the Angel and Bible, in St. Paul's Church-Yard. M,DCC,XXXVI.* Frontispiece + title page + ?lvs not num. (BL 1037.g.19.)

In dictionary form, with receipts adapted from a variety of sources, including Richard Bradley, John Nott and Mary Eales. The frontispiece shows five domestic scenes.

BATH

The Bath Cookery Book, and Housekeepers' Assistant: Containing The Most Approved Receipts on Roasting Boiling Made Dishes Soups Fricasees Fish Sauces Savoury Dishes Puddings Pickling Potting Collaring Tarts, Custards Confectionary Candying, Drying Creams Preserving Syllabubs, &c. Also The Way to prepare Hams, Bacon, &c. Making Wines, With Many Other Useful Receipts. *Bath: Printed and Sold for the Author, By Henry Gye, Market-Place: Sold also by Whitrow and Co. Jewry-Street, Aldgate; and Langley and Belch, Borough, London; and most other Booksellers.* Title page + 1 lf not num. (address to reader & contents) + pp. 1–204. (Leeds: Brotherton Library.)

The book dates from *c.*1790. Its sources include Elizabeth Raffald and Mary Cole, the latter being the source for 'The Family Physician', pp. 199–204. Maclean (pp. 8–9) suggests a date *c.*1780.

BATTAM, Anne

A Collection Of scarce and valuable Receipts, Never before printed, and taken from the Manuscripts of divers Persons of the most refin'd Taste and greatest Judgment in the Arts of Cookery, Preserving, &c. To which is added, The Author's own Method of Pickling, together with Directions for making several Sorts of Wines, Mead, Sherbet, Punch, &c. after the most approved Manner. Concluding with many excellent Prescriptions, of singular Efficacy in most Distempers, incident to the Human Body. By Anne Battam, Mistress of Myon's Coffee-House, in Great-Russel-street, Bloomsbury; where the said Book may be had, Price Three Shillings. *London: Printed for the Author, MDCCL.* Title page + 7 lvs not num. (table of contents) + pp. 1–198. (Leeds: Brotherton Library.)

The second edition appeared in 1759, with a new title, some new receipts, and new material (the directions for marketing, carving, and the bills of fare) borrowed from Sarah Jackson:

The Lady's Assistant in the Œconomy of the Table: A Collection of scarce and valuable Receipts, Taken from the Manuscripts of divers Persons of the most refin'd Taste and greatest Judgment in the Arts of Cookery, Preserving, &c. To which is added, The Author's own Method of Pickling, together with Directions for making several Sorts of Wines, Mead, Sherbet, Punch, &c. after the most approved Manner. Also Directions for Marketing, Instructions for Carving, Bills of Fare for every Month in the Year, &c. Concluding with many excellent Prescriptions, of singular Efficacy in most Distempers incident to the Human Body. Originally published, By the late Mrs. Anne Battam. The Second Edition, With near One Hundred and Fifty additional Receipts, from several Ladies, never before published. *London: Printed for R. and J. Dodsley, in Pall-mall. 1759. [Price Bound Three Shillings.]* Title page + 5 lvs not num. (advertisement and tables) + pp. 1–300. (BL 1485.tt.12.)

[BORELLA]

The Court and Country Confectioner: or, the House-Keeper's Guide; To a more speedy, plain, and familiar method of understanding the whole art of confectionary, pastry, distilling, and the making of fine flavoured English wines from all kinds of fruits, herbs, and flowers; comprehending near four hundred and fifty easy and practical receipts, never before made known. Particularly,

Preserving. Candying. Icing. Transparent Marmalade, Orange, Pine-Apple, Pistachio, and other Rich Creams. Caramels. Pastils. Bomboons. Puff, Spun, and Fruit-Pastes. Light-Biscuits. Puffs. Rich Seed-Cakes. Custards. Syllabubs. Flummeries. Trifles. Whips. Fruits, and other Jellies. Pickles, &c. &c. Also New and easy directions for clarifying the different degrees of sugar, together with several bills of fare of deserts for private gentlemen's families. To which is added, A dissertation on the different species of fruits, and the art of distilling simple waters, cordials, perfumed oils, and essences. By an Ingenious Foreigner, now head confectioner to the Spanish Ambassador in England. *London: Printed for G. Riley, and A. Cooke, at their Circulating Library, Queen Street, Berkley Square; J. Bell, near Exeter-Exchange, in the Strand; J. Wheble, at Nº 20. Pater noster-row; and C. Etherington, at York. M.DCC.LXX*. Title page + pp. i–ii (dedication 'To the Ladies of Great Britain') + pp. 1–3 (author's address 'To the House-keepers of Great-Britain') + pp. i–xxiii (contents) + 1 p. not num. (list of fruits in season in January, April, June & October) + pp. 1–271 for confectionery + 1 p. not num. (blank) + pp. 1–46 for distilling. (BL 1651/559.)

The second edition revealed the author's name; the book is identical to the first edition except for the addition of an introductory section on syrups:

The Court and Country Confectioner: …A New Edition.… By Mr. Borella, now head confectioner to the Spanish Ambassador in England. *London: Printed for G. Riley, at his Circulating Library, Curzon-street, May-Fair; J. Bell, in the Strand; J. Wheble, Pater noster-row; and C. Etherington, at York. M DCC LXXII*. Title page + pp. i–ii (dedication) + pp. 1–3 (author's address to housekeepers) + pp. i–xxiii (contents) + 1 p. not num. (list of fruits in season) + pp. 1–24 (syrups) + pp. 1–271 (confectionery) + pp. 1–46 (distilling). (BL 1651/453.)

BRADLEY, MARTHA

The British Housewife: or, the Cook, Housekeeper's, and Gardiner's Companion. Calculated for the Service both of London and the Country; And directing what is necessary to be done in the Providing for, Conducting, and Managing a Family throughout the Year. Containing A general Account of fresh Provisions of all Kinds. Of the several foreign Articles for the Table; pickled, or otherwise preserved; and the different Kinds of Spices, Salts, Sugars, and other Ingredients used in Pickling and Preserving at Home: Shewing what each is, whence it is brought, and what are its Qualities and Uses. Together with the Nature of all Kinds of Foods, and the Method of suiting them to different Constitutions; A Bill of Fare for each Month, the Art of Marketing and chusing fresh Provisions of all Kinds; and the making as well as chusing of Hams, Tongues, and other Store Dishes. Also Directions for plain Roasting and Boiling; and for the Dressing of all Sorts of Made Dishes in various Tastes; and the preparing the Desert in all its Articles. Containing a greater Variety than was ever before publish'd, of the most Elegant, yet least Expensive Receipts in Cookery, Pastry, Puddings, Preserves, Pickles, Fricassees, Ragouts, Soups, Sauces, Jellies, Tarts, Cakes, Creams, Custards, Candies, Dry'd Fruits, Sweetmeats, Made Wines, Cordials, And Distillery. To which are annexed, The Art of Carving; and the Terms used for cutting up various Things; and the polite and easy Manner of doing the Honours of the Table: The whole Practice of Pickling and Preserving: And of preparing made Wines, Beer, and Cyder. As also of distilling all the useful Kinds of Cordial and Simple Waters. With the Conduct of a Family in Respect of Health; the Disorders to which they are every Month liable, and the most approved Remedies for each. And a Variety of other valuable Particulars, necessary to be known in All Families; and nothing inserted but what has been approved by Experience. Also the Ordering of all Kinds of profitable Beasts and Fowls, with respect to their Choice, their Breeding and Feeding; the Diseases to which they are severally liable each Month, and Receipts for their Cure. Together with the Management of the pleasant, profitable and useful Garden. The Whole Embellished with a great Number of curious Copper Plates, shewing the Manner of Trussing all Kinds of Game, wild and tame Fowls, &c. as also the Order of setting out Tables for Dinners, Suppers, and Grand Entertainments, in a Method never before attempted; and by which even those who cannot read will be able to instruct themselves. By Mrs. Martha Bradley, late of Bath: Being the Result of upwards of Thirty Years Experience. The whole (which is deduc'd from Practice) compleating the careful Reader, from the highest to the lowest Degree, in every Article of English Housewifery. Volume I: *London: Printed for S. Crowder and H. Woodgate, at the Golden Ball in Paternoster Row.* [*Vol. I:* Frontispiece + title page + pp. 3–424 + 3 pl. (some of the original plates are missing). *Vol. II:* Title page + pp. 425–752 + 2 pl.] (BL 1651/458.) Volume II: *London: S. Crowder and H. Woodgate.* Title page + pp. 1–469 + 21 pp. not num. (contents & index to vol. I) + 12 pp. not num. (contents & index to vol. II) + 6 pl.

The British Library copy has only volume I, although it is bound as two volumes. I consulted Alan Davidson's copy of volume II.

Martha Bradley's book originally appeared as a part-work, in weekly instalments costing 3d. each, in 1756. Contrary to what is stated by Maclean (p. 11), the weekly parts were advertised in the *Gentleman's Magazine* (vol. 26, p. 45). The signatures at the foot of some of the pages indicate that the book was made up of 42 parts, and would thus have cost 10s. 6d., and that publication must have been complete by mid-October. The work appeared in book form in December 1758, according to an advertisement pasted into a copy of the third edition of William Kitchiner's *Cook's Oracle* (1821). There is now an accessible version of this book, the six-volume facsimile reprint by Prospect (1996–98).

BRADLEY, RICHARD

The Country Housewife and Lady's Director, in the Management of a House, and the Delights and Profits of a Farm. Containing Instructions for managing the Brew-House, and Malt-Liquors in the Cellar; the making of Wines of all sorts. Directions for the Dairy, in the Improvement of Butter and Cheese upon the worst of Soils; the feeding and making of Brawn; the ordering of Fish, Fowl, Herbs, Roots, and all other useful Branches belonging to a Country Seat, in the most elegant manner for the Table. Practical Observations concerning Distilling; with the best Method of making Ketchup, and many other curious and durable Sauces. The Whole distributed in their proper Months, from the Beginning to the End of the Year. With particular Remarks relating to the Drying or Kilning of Saffron. By R. Bradley, Professor of Botany in the University of Cambridge, and F.R.S. The Sbcond [sic] Edition. *London: Printed for Woodman, and Lyon, in Russel-street, Covent Garden. M. DCC. XXVII. (Price 2s. 6d.)* Frontispiece + title page + 1 lf not num. (dedication) + pp. vii–xi (preface) + pp. 1–187. (BL 966.e.6 (2).)

There was no first edition, since this is a companion volume to the second edition (1727) of *The Country Gentleman and Farmer's Monthly Director* which had first appeared in 1726. The book is organized into monthly sections. The frontispiece shows a farm scene with dairy-maids at work in the foreground.

A second part appeared in 1732:

The Country Housewife and Lady's Director, ... Part II. *London: D. Browne, T. Woodman, 1732. (Price 2s. 6d.)* Title page + 1 lf not num. (dedication to Sir Hans Sloane) + pp. v–vii (introduction) + pp. 1–188 + 9 lvs not num. (index) + 1 lf not num. (bookseller's advertisement). (BL 1578/5517 (2).)

The two parts were subsequently printed together, and are accessible in the Prospect facsimile of the 1736 edition, edited by Caroline Davidson (1980).

BRADSHAW, PENELOPE, and LAMBART [sic]

Bradshaw's Valuable Family Jewel. Being a Store-House of such Curious Matters, as All ought to be acquainted with, Who intend to spend their Lives either Pleasant or Profitable. Containing all that relates to Cookery, Pastry, Pickling, Preserving, Wine Making, Brewing, Bread Making, Oat Cakes, &c. With a great Number of other Necessary Articles, not to be met with in any other Book: Particularly, an Excellent Method for the Management of a Beer-Cellar: How to keep Ale, or Beer, always exceeding fine; and how to restore sour Beer to its first Perfection; which Article has been of the utmost Service to the Purchasers of this Book. Likewise, an Excellent Method to preserve a constant Stock of Yeast, even in the most scarce Seasons. In this Book, is likewise inserted, Mons. Millien's Method of preserving Metals from Rust, such as Guns, Grates, Candle-Sticks, &c. for the Discovery of which, the Parliament of Paris gave him 10,000 *l.* By Mrs. Penelope Bradshaw, and the late ingenious Mr. Lambart, Confectioner. As this Book is enter'd according to Law, whoever prints it shall be prosecuted. — The 10th Edition. *Printed for P. Bradshaw, 1748. Price 1s.* Title page + 19 lvs not num. (BL 7955. a. 50.)

Penelope Bradshaw's books are a bibliographer's nightmare. This edition is not the same as another unnumbered edition dated 1748, which has 80 pages, and states on the title-page that it was 'Begun by Mrs Eliza Johnson, and now finished by Mrs Penelope Bradshaw and Mr Lambert, Confectioner'. That version was analysed by Fiona Lucraft ('A Study of *The Compleat Confectioner* by Hannah Glasse (c 1760), Part One', *PPC* 56 (1997), pp. 31–32). Lucraft shows that Bradshaw lifted her first 40 pages from Edward Lambert's *The Art of Confectionery* (c.1744), and her second 40 pages from Eliza Johnston's *The Accomplish'd Servant Maid* (1747). Bradshaw's own contributions were notes on roasting, boiling and frying plus three receipts. The edition cited above has severely reduced contributions from Lambert (and perhaps Johnston, although I have not seen a copy of her book), virtually all the rest being lifted from Hannah Glasse's *The Art of Cookery* (1747). Another version of the book appeared in 1754:

The Family Jewel, And Compleat Housewife's Companion: or, the Whole Art of Cookery made Plain and Easy. In a Method entirely new, and suited to every Capacity; calculated for the Preservation of Health, and on the Principles of Frugality, including Things useful, substantial and splendid. Containing compleat Directions in Marketing, and other Branches of Housewifry, and above 400 Receipts. ... Being the Result of Forty Years Experience, and an attentive Observation on all the Books of Cookery that have ever yet been published. With an Index directing to every Receipt. By Mrs. Penelope Bradshaw, Housekeeper Forty Years to a Noble Family of Great Taste, but Proper Œconomy. The Seventh Edition. With Remarks by a London Pastry-Cook, of long and extensive Practice. Also an Addition of about 200 Receipts, and a Bill of Fare for every Month in the Year; with the Manner of placing the Dishes. *London: Printed for R. Whitworth, at the Feathers in the Poultry. M DCC LIV.* Title page + 5 lvs not num. (index) + pp. 1–144. (BL 1607/1790.)

The reverse of the title-page has a letter dated 25 April 1754 to the publisher from E– H–, who says she has 'carefully revised Mrs Bradshaw's useful Book, and where any Alteration was necessary, I have made it by Way of Note'. Some of the receipts are indeed annotated in this way. This version contains much of the same material as the 10th edition of 1748 cited above, with new receipts in the supplement which occupies pp. 95–144.

BRIGGS, RICHARD

The English Art of Cookery, According to the Present Practice; being a Complete Guide to all Housekeepers, on a Plan Entirely New; consisting of Thirty-Eight Chapters. Containing, Proper Directions for Marketing, and Trussing of Poultry. The making of Soups and Broths. Dressing all Sorts of Fish. Sauces for every Occasion. Boiling and Roasting. Baking, Broiling, and Frying. Stews and Hashes. Made Dishes of every Sort. Ragous and Fricasees. Directions for dressing all Sorts of Roots and Vegetables. All Sorts of Aumlets [sic] and Eggs. Puddings, Pies, Tarts, &c. Pancakes and Fritters. Cheesecakes and Custards. Blancmange, Jellies, and Syllabubs. Directions for the Sick. Directions for Seafaring Men. Preserving, Syrups, and Conserves. Drying and Candying. All Sorts of Cakes. Hogs Puddings, Sausages, &c. Potting, and little cold Dishes. The Art of Carving. Collaring, Salting, and Sousing. Pickling. To keep Garden Vegetables, &c. A Catalogue of Things in Season. Made Wines and Cordial Waters. Brewing. English and French Bread, &c. With Bills of Fare for Every Month In the Year, Neatly and correctly engraved on Twelve Copper-Plates. By Richard Briggs, Many Years Cook at the Globe Tavern, Fleet-Street, The White Hart Tavern, Holborn, and now at the Temple Coffee-House. *London: Printed for G. G. J. and J. Robinson, Pater-Noster-Row. M.DCC.LXXXVIII.* Title page + pp. iii–iv (address to reader) + pp. i–xx (table of contents) + 11 lvs not num. (plates of bills of fare) + pp. 1–656. (BL Cup. 408.c.21.)

The third edition, a somewhat more compact version, appeared in 1794, with an almost identical title-page except for the description of the author:

The English Art of Cookery … The Third Edition. By Richard Briggs, Many Years Cook at the White-Hart Tavern, Holborn, Temple Coffee-House, and other Taverns in London. *London: Printed for G. G. J. and J. Robinson, Pater-Noster-Row. M,DCC,XCIV.* Title page + pp. iii–iv (address to reader) + pp. i–xx (contents) + pp. 1–564 + 12 pl.

BRITISH

The British Jewel, or, Complete Housewife's Best Companion. Containing I. A number of the most uncommon and useful Receipts in Cookery, with the Manner of trussing Poultry, Rabbits, Hares, &c. illustrated with Curious Cuts, shewing how each is to be trussed. II. The best and most fashionable Receipts for all Manner of Pastry, Pickling, &c. with some general Rules to be observed therein. III. Directions for making all Sorts of English Wines, Shrub, Vinegar, Verjuice, Catchup, Sauces, Soups, Jellies, &c. IV. A Table to cast up Expences by the Day, Week, Month, or Year. V. Every Man his own Physician; a valuable Collection of the most approved Receipts for the Cure of most Disorders incident to human Bodies, from the most eminent English Physicians. VI. The Manner of preparing the Elixir of Life, Turlington's Balsam, Friar's Balsam, the Court or Lady's Black Sticking Plaster, Lip-Salve, Lady Yorke's Receipt to preserve from the Small-Pox or Plague, &c. the Royal Patent Snuff for the Head and Eyes; Dr. Bracken's Powder for the Teeth, a Secret for the Cure of the Tooth-ach [sic], a speedy Method to destroy Warts or Corns, &c. VII. Directions for destroying Rats, Mice, Bugs, Fleas, &c. And A choice Variety of Useful Family Receipts, Together with A Method of restoring to Life People drowned, or in any other Manner suffocated. Also, The Complete Farrier, Being the Method of Buying, Selling, Managing, &c. and of the Diseases incident to Horses, with their Cures. To which is added, The Royal Gardener, or Monthly Calendar. *London: Printed and Sold by J. Miller, Nº 14, White-lion-street, Goodman's Fields. 1776.* Title page + 3 pp. not num. (list of measures, table to cast up expenses, & 3 receipts of cheap provisions) + pp. 5–108, illustrations in cookery section of text (pp. 15–41). (BL C. 115.n.66.)

The book has short sections on pastry (pp. 5–14), cookery (pp. 15–41), wines &c (pp. 42–51), medical receipts (pp. 52–66), instructions for dressing a turtle (p. 104). The other material is devoted to gardening and farming, household hints, and fishing. An identical edition, with a slightly different title-page, came out in 1788:

The New British Jewel, or, Complete Housewife's Best Companion. … *London: Printed for Osborne and Griffin, and H. Mozley, Gainsbrough. – M.DCC.LXXXVIII.* (BL 7948.a.84.)

BROOKS, CATHARINE

The Complete English Cook; or Prudent Housewife. Being an entire New Collection of the Most Genteel, yet least Expensive Receipts in every Branch of Cookery and good Housewifery. Viz, Roasting, Boiling, Stewing, Ragoos, Soups, Sauces, Fricaseys, Pies, Tarts, Puddings, Cheesecakes, Custards, Jellies, Potting Candying, Collaring, Pickling, Preserving, Made Wines, &c. Together with the Art of Marketting. And Directions for placing Dishes on Tables for Entertainments: Adorned with proper Cuts. And many other Things equally Necessary. The Whole made Easy to the Meanest Capacity, and far more Useful to Young Beginners than any Book of the Kind ever yet published. *In cooking Fowl, or Flesh, or Fish, / Or any nice, or dainty Dish, / With Care peruse this useful Book, / 'Twill make you soon a perfect Cook.* By Catharine Brooks of Red-Lyon-Street. To which is added The Physical Director; being near Two

Hundred safe and certain Receipts for the Cure of most Disorders incident to the Human Body. Also the whole Art of Clear-Starching, Ironing, &c. The Second Edition, with the Addition of a great variety of Made Dishes, &c. *London: Printed for the Authoress, and sold by J. Cooke, at Shakespear's- head, in Pater-noster-Row. [Price One Shilling.]* Title page + 1 lf not num. (address to ladies & contents) + pp. 5–132. (Leeds: Brotherton Library.)

The preface is dated 20 January 1762, suggesting a date *c.*1765 for the second edition. The printer, John Cooke, is recorded as working at the address indicated in 1766 (Maxted, p. 51). Some of the receipts are taken from Martha Bradley.

CARTER, CHARLES

The Complete Practical Cook: Or, A New System Of the Whole Art and Mystery of Cookery. Being a Select Collection of Above Five Hundred Recipes for Dressing, after the most Curious and Elegant Manner (as well Foreign as English) all Kinds of Flesh, Fish, Fowl, &c. As also Directions to make all Sorts of excellent Pottages and Soups, fine Pastry, both sweet and savoury, delicate Puddings, exquisite Sauces, and rich Jellies. With the best Rules for Preserving, Potting, Pickling, &c. Fitted For All Occasions: But more especially for the most Grand and Sumptuous Entertainments. Adorned with Sixty Curious Copper Plates; Exhibiting the full Seasons of the Year, and Tables proper for Every Month; As also Variety of large Ovals and Rounds, and Ambogues and Square Tables for Coronation-Feasts, Instalments, &c. The Whole intirely New; And none of the Recipes ever published in any Treatise of this Kind. Approved by divers of the Prime Nobility; And by several Masters of the Art and Mystery of Cookery. By Charles Carter, Lately Cook to his Grace the Duke of Argyll, the Earl of Pontefract, the Lord Cornwallis, &c. *London: Printed for W. Meadows, in Cornhill; C. Rivington, in St Paul's Church-Yard; and R. Hett, in the Poultry. M. DCC. XXX.* Title page + 1 lf not num. (dedication to the earl of Albermarle) + 6 lvs not num (address to the reader) + pp. 1–224 + 59 pl. (BL 797.dd.15.)

The British Library copy is incomplete, wanting plate 16. The book is now more accessible in the Prospect facsimile reprint (1984). The next edition appeared in 1732 with a new title:

The Compleat City and Country Cook: or, Accomplish'd Housewife. Containing, Several Hundred of the most approv'd Receipts in Cookery, Confectionary, Cordials, Cosmeticks, Jellies, Pastry, Pickles, Preserving, Syrups, English Wines, &c. Illustrated with Forty-nine large Copper Plates, directing the regular placing the various Dishes on the Table, from one to four or five Courses: Also, Bills of Fare according to the several Seasons for every Month of the Year. Likewise, The Horse-shoe Table for the Ladies at the late Instalment at Windsor, the Lord Mayor's Table, and other Hall Dinners in the City of London; with a Fish Table, &c. By Charles Carter, Lately Cook to his Grace the Duke of Argyle, the Earl of Pontefract, the Lord Cornwallis, &c. To which is added by way of Appendix, Near Two Hundred of the most approv'd Receipts in Physick and Surgery for the Cure of the most common Diseases incident to Families: The Collection of a Noble Lady Deceased. A Work design'd for the Good, and absolutely Necessary for all Families. *London: Printed for A. Bettesworth and C. Hitch; and C. Davis in Pater-noster Row: T. Green at Charing-Cross; and S. Austen in St Paul's Church-yard. M. DCC. XXXII.* Title page + pp. iii–viii (preface) + pp. 1–280 + 49 pl. (BL 1651/587.)

This is a simplified version of the first edition, with the addition of the physical receipts. A completely revised version appeared in 1749:

The London and Country Cook: or, Accomplish'd Housewife, Containing Practical Directions and the best Receipts In all the Branches of Cookery and Housekeeping; Such as Boiling, Roasting, Pastry, Pickling, Jellies, Preserving, Confectionary, Cakes, Creams, Cordials, Syrups, English Wines, &c. Interspersed with Many sovereign and approved Medicines used by Private Families in most Distempers; And illustrated with Forty-nine large Copper Plates. By Charles Carter, Cook to his Grace the Duke of Argyle, &c. The Third Edition, Revised and much improved By a Gentlewoman; Many Years Housekeeper to an eminent Merchant in the City of London. *London: Printed for Charles Hitch in Pater-noster Row; Stephen Austen in Newgate-street, and John Hinton in St Paul's Church-yard. MDCCXLIX.* Frontispiece + title page + pp. iii–vii (preface) + 1 p. not num. (bookseller's advertisement) + pp. 1–363 + 1 p. not num. (bookseller's advertisement) + 49 pl. (BL 1608/4731.)

The reviser worked to adapt the book to a more modest readership: many of Carter's receipts were eliminated, and some of Hannah Glasse's from *The Art of Cookery* (1747) added. The terms of the preface by the reviser are clearly inspired by Mary Kettilby.

CARTER, Susannah

The Frugal Housewife, or Complete Woman Cook. Wherein The Art of dressing all Sorts of Viands, with Cleanliness, Decency, and Elegance, Is explained in Five Hundred approved Receipts, in Gravies, Sauces, Roasting, Boiling, Frying, Broiling, Stews, Hashes, Soups, Fricassees, Ragoos, Pasties, Pies, Tarts, Cakes, Puddings, Syllabubs, Creams, Flummery, Jellies, Giams [sic], and Custards. Together with the Best Methods of Potting, Collaring, Preserving, Drying, Candying, Pickling, And Making of English Wines. To which are added, Twelve New Prints, Exhibiting a proper Arrangement of Dinners, Two Courses, for every Month in the Year. With various Bills of Fare. By Susannah Carter, Of Clerkenwell. *London: Printed for E. Newbery, at the corner of St. Paul's Church-Yard. Price One Shilling.* Double pl. + title page + 3 lvs not num. (index) + 2 lvs not num. (bills of fare) + pp. 1–180 + 6 lvs not num. (illustrated bills of fare with woodcuts). (BL 7949.de.21.)

The British Library copy has an inscription inside the book, 'Mary Waterman Her Book March 1 day 1793', and the book probably dates from 1793. The printer, Elizabeth Newbery, took over her husband's business after his death in 1780, and is recorded as working at two addresses at the corner of St Paul's churchyard from 1780 to 1804 (Maxted, pp. 160–61). Since she moved between 1793 and 1794, the vague address given here points to a 1793 date. The reverse of the title-page states that this is a 'revised and corrected Edition'. The first edition of the book dates from *c.*1765 (Maclean, pp. 23–24).

CARTWRIGHT, Charlotte

The Lady's best Companion; or, A complete Treasure for the Fair Sex. Containing the whole Arts of Cookery, Pastery, Confectionary, Potting, Pickling, Preserving, Candying, Collaring, Brewing, &c. With plain Instructions for making English Wines, from Fruits, Flowers, &c. To which is added, The approved Family Physician; Consisting of Physical Receipts For most Disorders that grown People and young Children are subject to. *If in the modern Taste you'd learn to cook, / Study the perfect Method in our Book; / Then the best Table you may serve with Ease, / And the nice Appetite exactly please.* By Mrs. Charlotte Cartwright. *London: Printed for, and sold by W. Clements, and James Sadler, in the year 1789. (Price Six-pence.)* Title page + pp. 3–48. (Leeds: Brotherton Library.)

This is an abridged version of Amelia Chambers' book.

['CERES']

The Lady's Companion: or, Accomplish'd Director In the whole Art of Cookery. Containing Approved Receipts, (never before Published;) for Pastry, Pyes, Pasties, Fricassies, Baking, Roasting, Stewing, Boiling, Ragous, Soops, Sauces, Pickling, Collaring, Potting, Cakes, Custards, Puddings, Creams, Preserving, Candying, Tarts, Jellies, Cheese-Cakes, Made Wines, &c. Also, Bills of Fare for all the Seasons of the Year, with an Alphabetical Index to the Whole. By a Lady. *Dublin: Printed by John Mitchell, in Skinner-Row. M DCC LXVII.* Title + pp. iii–iv (dedication 'To the Ladies of Dublin') + pp. 5–105 + 12 pp. not num. (bills of fare) + 7 pp. not num. (index & bookseller's advertisement). (BL 1607/5214.)

The dedication is signed 'Ceres', the pseudonym concealing a woman author, perhaps a housekeeper. This does not appear to be simply a Dublin-printed edition of an English book.

CHAMBERS, AMELIA

The Ladies Best Companion; or, A Golden Treasure for the Fair Sex. Containing the whole Arts of Cookery, Pastry, Confectionary, Potting, Pickling, Preserving, Candying, Collaring, Brewing, &c. With plain Instructions for making English Wines, from Fruits, Flowers, &c. To which is added The Art of preserving Beauty. Containing the best and easiest Methods of preparing and making Washes, Essences, and Perfumes, &c. for the Hands, Neck, Face, and Hair, in such a Manner as in a great Measure to delay the Ravages of Time on the Features of the Fair Sex. Likewise Directions for sweetening the Breath, curing the Tooth-ache, preserving the Teeth and Gums, &c. With many other Articles equally useful to the Fair Sex in general *Here Cooks may learn with wond'rous Ease / The longing Appetite to please; / The Art of Beauty how to reach, / By skillful Methods too we teach: / The Fair who with our Rules comply, / May catch the Heart, and charm the Eye.* By Mrs. Amelia Chambers. To which are added Every Lady her own and Family's Physician. Consisting of approved physical Receipts for most Disorders that grown People and young Children are subject to. Also the Family Instructor. Containing Directions for cleaning Silks, Lace and Furniture, taking out Spots from Linen and Cloaths, &c. &c. And great Variety of other Articles too numerous to be inserted in a Title Page. *London. Printed for J. Cooke, Nº 17, in Pater-Noster-Row [Price Two Shillings Sewed.]* Frontispiece + title page + pp. iii–v (preface) + 2 pp. not num. & p. vii (contents) + pp. 1–196. (BL 1037.e.39.)

The book dates from *c.*1785. The printer, John Cooke, is recorded as working at this address from 1784 to 1792 (Maxted, p. 51). The frontispiece shows a kitchen scene with a man-cook at work and a woman carrying a dish away.

CHEBSEY, William

A Curious Collection of Receipts In the Art of Pastry and Cookery: Together with Preserving, Pickling, Potting, Collaring, and making of Jellies and Syllabubs. Also Plain Directions to all Ladies, who delight to exercise themselves in the said Arts. As it was Performed at Leathersellers Hall, before Two Hundred Young Ladies and other Persons of Distinction. By William Chebsey, Cook, And of the Worshipful Company of Leathersellers, London. The Second Edition, with Additions. *London, Printed for the Author; and sold by him at his House in Mare Street, Hackney. 1721. Price Stitch'd 2s. 6d.* Title pages + 1 lf not num. (dedication to young ladies) + 1 lf not num. (bill of fare 'as it was performed at Leathersellers Hall') + pp. 1–15 + 1 lf not num. (dedication to 'Madam Margaret Saunders, Madam Anne Saunders & Madam Susanna Wells) + pp. 19–35. (BL C.142.a.28.)

Chebsey was a teacher of cookery: the first dedication mentions the young ladies who have been the author's pupils and attended the feast. Only the first 15 pages were part of the first edition, with the receipts to produce the dishes in the bill of fare, which contains a total of 110 dishes for 4 tables. Pages 19–35 are headed 'Additions', and contain a medley of receipts.

CHOICE

A Choice Collection of Cookery Receipts. *Newcastle: Printed in this present Year.* Title page + pp. 2–24. (BL 11621.b.2 (7).)

A chapbook containing 76 receipts, dating from *c.*1780. Maclean (p. 26) suggests a date *c.*1775.

CLELAND, ELIZABETH

A New and Easy Method of Cookery. Treating, I. Of Gravies, Soups, Broths, &c. II. Of Fish, and their Sauces. III. To Pot and Make Hams, &c. IV. Of Pies, Pasties, &c. V. Of Pickling and Preserving. VI. Of Made Wines, Distilling and Brewing, &c. By Elizabeth Cleland. Chiefly intended for the Benefit of the Young Ladies who attend Her School. *Edinburgh: Printed for the Author by W. Gordon, C. Wright, S. Willison and J. Bruce: And sold at Her House in the Luckenbooths. M. DCC. LV.* Title page + 5 lvs not num. (contents) + pp. 1–204. (BL C.135.d.13.)

The second edition appeared in 1759 and was identical except for the appendix:

A New and Easy Method of Cookery. Treating, … &c. To which are added, By Way of Appendix, Fifty-Three New and Useful Receipts, and Directions for Carving. By Elizabeth Cleland. Chiefly intended for the Benefit of the Young Ladies who attend Her School. The Second Edition. *Edinburgh: Printed by C. Wright and Company: And sold at their Printing-house in Craig's Close, and by the Booksellers in Town. M. DCC. LIX.* Title page + 6 lvs not num. (contents) + pp. 1–232. (BL 1037.h.12 (3).)

[CLERMONT, B.]

The Professed Cook: Or the Modern Art of Cookery, Pastry, and Confectionary, Made Plain and Easy. Consisting of the most approved Methods in the French as well as English Cookery. In which the French Names of all the different Dishes are given and explained, whereby every Bill of Fare becomes intelligible and familiar. Containing I. Of Soups, Gravy, Cullis and Broths II. Of Sauces III. The different Ways of Dressing Beef, Veal, Mutton, Pork, Lamb, &c. IV. Of First Course Dishes V. Of Dressing Poultry VI. Of Venison VII. Of Game of all Sorts VIII. Of Ragouts, Collops and Fries IX. Of Dressing all Kinds of Fish X. Of Pastry of different Kinds XI. Of Entremets, or Last Course Dishes XII. Of Omelets XIII. Pastes of different Sorts XIV. Dried Conserves XV. Cakes, Wafers, and Biscuits XVI. Of Almonds and Pistachios made in different Ways XVII. Marmalades XVIII. Jellies XIX.

Liquid and dried Sweetmeats XX. Syrups and Brandy Fruits XXI. Ices, Ice Creams and Ice Fruits XXII. Ratafias, and other Cordials, &c. &c. Translated from *Les Soupers de la Cour*, with the Addition of the best Receipts which have ever appear'd in the French Language. And adapted to the London Markets by the Editor, who has been many Years Clerk of the Kitchen in some of the first Families in this Kingdom. The Second Edition. *London: Printed for R. Davis, in Piccadilly; and T. Caslon, opposite Stationers-Hall. MDCCLXIX.* Title page + pp. iii–xvi (translator's apology, author's advertisement, list of produce in season) + 24 lvs not num. (contents) + pp. 1–588 [Vol. I: pp. 1–286; vol. II: pp. 289–588]. (BL 1037.h.13.)

The first edition appeared in 1767, as *The Art of Modern Cookery Displayed*; the text was identical to that of the second edition. The editor's name was revealed in the third edition of 1776 (Maclean, p. 99).

COLE, MARY

The Lady's Complete Guide; or Cookery in all its Branches. Containing The most approved Receipts, confirmed by Observation and Practice, in every reputable English Book of Cookery now extant, besides a great Variety of others which have never before been offered to the Public. Also several translated from the Productions of Cooks of Eminence who have published in France, particularly M. Commo's *Histoire de Cuisine,* M. Disang's *Maitre d'Hotel*, M. Dupont and M. Valois, M. Troas, and M. Delatour, with their respective Names to each Receipt; which, with the Original Articles, will form the most complete System of Cookery ever yet exhibited, under the following Heads, viz. Roasting, Boiling, Made-Dishes, Frying, Broiling, Potting, Fricassees, Ragouts, Soups, Sauces, Gravies, Hashes, Stews, Puddings, Custards, Cakes, Tarts, Pies, Pasties, Cheesecakes, Jellies, Pickling, Preserving, Confectionary, &c. To which is added, In order to render it as complete and perfect as possible, The Complete Brewer; Containing Familiar Instructions for brewing all Sorts of Beer and Ale; including the proper Management of the Vault or Cellar. Also The Family Physician; Consisting of a considerable Collection of approved Prescriptions by Mead, Sydenham, Tissot, Fothergill, Elliot, Buchan, and others, including a certain Remedy for that formidable Disorder, the Dropsy, recommended by Persons respectable in the highest Degree. By Mrs. Mary Cole, Cook to the Right Hon. the Earl of Drogheda. *London: Printed for G. Kearsley, Nº 46, Fleet-*

street. MDCCLXXXVIII. Title page + 2 lvs not num. (preface) + pp. i–xxvii (contents) + pp. 1–564. (BL 7950.f.11.)

Mary Cole is often presented as one of the few honest cookery writers who acknowledged her sources, but this claim may be exaggerated: the French sources mentioned on the title-page do not exist, and she does not attribute all the receipts she took from other writers. Furthermore, she does not appear to have noticed that the books by Clermont and Dalrymple are virtually identical. The second edition, described as 'A New Edition improved', came out in 1789:

The Lady's Complete Guide; or Cookery and Confectionary in all their Branches. … *London: G. Kearsley, 1789. [Price 6s. in boards, or 7s. bound.]* Title page + pp. iii–xx (preface, list of things in season, bills of fare) + pp. i–xxvii (contents) + pp. 1–564. (BL 1560/265.)

The only improvements are the list of seasonal produce and the bills of fare; otherwise the text is identical to that of the first edition. The third edition, 'very much improved', appeared in 1791, with the cookery section abridged and the 'Family Physician' extended:

The Lady's Complete Guide; or Cookery in all its Branches. … *London: G. Kearsley, 1791.* Title page + pp. v–xxxii (preface, list of things in season, bills of fare, speciment of house-keeping book, marketing tables) + pp. xxxiii–lvi (contents & bookseller's advertisement) + pp. 1–460. (BL Cup. 407.i.25.)

COLLECTION

A Collection Of One Hundred and Thirty-seven approved Receipts, in Pastry and Cookery, viz. Bread, Pastes, Baken [sic] Meats, Seed Cakes, Preserves, Marmalades, Jellies, Confections, Rules for a Cook-Maid, Dressing of Meat in different Ways, Fattening Fowls, Carving, &c. &c. To which are added, Directions for making the best Cosmetics. Washing Gauzes, Muslins, &c. and Painting of Rooms, Stair Cases, &c. *Aberdeen: Printed for Alexander Thomson, Bookseller in the Castlegate. M.DCC.LXXIV.* Title page + pp. i–iii (index) + pp. 1–52. (Leeds: Brotherton Library.)

COLLINGWOOD, Francis, & John WOOLLAMS

The Universal Cook, and City and Country Housekeeper. Containing all the

Various Branches of Cookery: The different methods of dressing Butcher's Meat, Poultry, Game, and Fish; and of preparing Gravies, Cullices, Soups, and Broths; to dress Roots and Vegetables, and to prepare Little elegant Dishes for Suppers or light Repasts: To make all sorts of Pies, Puddings, Pancakes, and Fritters; Cakes, Puffs, and Biscuits; Cheesecakes, Tarts, and Custards; Creams and Jams; Blanc Mange, Flummery, Elegant Ornaments, Jellies and Syllabubs. The various Articles in Candying, Drying, Preserving, and Pickling. The Preparation of Hams, Tongues, Bacon, &c. Directions for Trussing Poultry, Carving, and Marketing. The making and management of Made Wines, Cordial Waters, and Malt Liquors. With Directions for Baking Bread, the Management of Poultry and the Dairy, and the Kitchen and Fruit Garden; with a Catalogue of the various Articles in Season in the different Months of the Year. Besides a Variety of Useful and Interesting Tables. The Whole Embellished with The Heads of the Authors, Bills of Fare for every Month in the Year, and proper Subjects for the Improvement of the Art of Carving, elegantly engraved on fourteen Copper-Plates. By Francis Collingwood, and John Woollams, Principal Cooks at the Crown and Anchor Tavern in the Strand, Late from the London Tavern. *London: Printed by R. Noble, for J. Scatcherd and J. Whitaker, Nº 12, Ave-Maria-Lane. 1792.* False title + frontispiece + title page + 2 lvs not num. (preface) + 10 lvs not num. (contents) + 12 pl. + pp. 1–451. (BL 1037.g.30.)

This is another book purporting to be by tavern cooks but in fact cobbled up by the hack writer Richard Johnson, who recorded a payment of £31 10s. from Scatcherd for 'compiling F Collingwood and J Woolhams Universal Cook' in March 1792. (See Peter Targett, 'Richard Johnson or John Farley?', *PPC* 58 (1998), p. 32.) This book was based on his earlier work in 'writing' John Farley's book, which perhaps explains why Johnson noted 'writing' one and 'compiling' the other. In spite of this, *The Universal Cook* achieved the distinction of being translated into French, as *Le Cuisinier anglais universel*, in 1810, the translation being based on the fourth edition of 1806 (Vicaire, pp. 189–90).

COMPLEAT ENGLISH FAMILY COMPANION

The Compleat English Family Companion. Consisting Of a Collection of near a Thousand curious and uncommon Receipts in Cookery, Pastry, Preserving, Wine Making, Candying, Pickling, Jellies, Brewing, &c. With plain and easy Instructions for chusing All Sorts of Eatables. Also, Forms of placing Dishes on a Table, either in the middling or genteelest Manner. Revised and Corrected by an eminent Cook. To which is added, The Compleat Servant Maid. Consisting of necessary Cautions and prudential Advice, such as if duely [sic] observed cannot fail making them easy and happy in themselves, either in the capacity of a Servant, or the Mistress of a Family. Likewise The Art of Clear Starching, Ironing, &c. *London: Printed in the Year, 1769.* Title page + pp. iii–viii (contents) + pp. 9–200. (Leeds: Brotherton Library)

The title-page of this book is remarkably similar to that of an earlier work in Katherine Bitting's collection, *The Compleat Family Cook* (Hull: J. Rawson, and Son, 1766), with 216 pages. This book too was 'Revised and Corrected by an Eminent Cook'. Bitting (p. 534) states this is a copy of Elizabeth Moxon's book, 'with some changes from the 11th edition, 1775'. I have not compared the book cited here with Moxon, but I did notice similarities with Catharine Brooks' work.

COMPLEAT SERVANT MAID'S GUIDE

The Compleat Servant Maid's Guide; or the Lady's Delight in Cookery. *York: Printed at the New Printing Office, in Folgate.* Title page + pp. 3–24. (BL Cup.408.i.47 (2).)

This is a chapbook of receipts for cookery, preserving, pickling, and wines (pp. 3–22), plus 2 pages of 'Two New Songs', one of which is 'Attic Fire' set by Arne. The British Library catalogue suggests a date *c.*1780.

[THE COMPLETE FAMILY COMPANION].

pp. iii–viii (index) + pp. 9–128. (BL 1651/555.)

The British Library copy is incomplete, wanting the title-page. The British Library catalogue suggests that the book was printed in London [?], *c.*1765. This may be the same work as the following, cited by Maclean (pp. 31–2):

The Compleat Family Companion: or, the whole art of cookery made plain and easy; in a method intirely new and suited to every capacity … Also curious extracts from a famous treatise on the teeth, their disorder and cure. Directions for marketing … with an excellent method for preserving of metals from rust, such as guns, grates, candlesticks, etc. [by a gentlewoman]. *London: printed for the author, 1753.* viii, 9–128 p. 18 cm.

However, the contents of the book in the British Library do not tally with the list given by Maclean's title-page (which looks as though it is a version of Penelope Bradshaw's book, as Maclean observes). The contents are: rules for marketing, boiling and roasting (pp. 9–12); cookery receipts (pp. 13–97); pickling and potting (pp. 98–103); English wines (pp. 103–107); cosmetics and physical receipts (pp. 107–116, no new heading); household hints (pp. 116–117); brewing – 'The London and Country Brewer' (pp. 118–125); then receipts to deal with Shetland pickled herrings and miscellaneous.

[*THE COMPLETE FAMILY PIECE*]

[The Complete Family-Piece: and, Country Gentlemen, and Farmer's Best Guide. In Three Parts. Part I. Containing a very choice and valuable Collection of near Eight Hundred well-experienced Practical Family-Receipts in Physick and Surgery; Cookery, Pastry and Confectionary, with a complete Bill of Fare for every Month in the Year, and Instructions for placing the Dishes on a Table; for Pickling and Preserving all Sorts of Fruits, Tongues, Hams, &c., for Distilling and Fermenting of all Compound, Simple Waters and Spirits; for making Mum, Cyder and Perry, Mead and Metheglin; and for making and preserving all Sorts of excellent English Wines; with good and useful Instructions for Brewing fine, strong, good, wholesome and palatable Drinks, as Beers, Ales, &c., in small Quantities, and at easy Rates, for the Use of all private Families; with divers other useful and valuable Receipts interspersed through the Whole, particularly Dr. Mead's for the Cure of the Bite of a Mad Dog: Many of which were never before Printed, and the others experimentally taken from the latest and very best Authorities; and being all regularly digested under their proper Heads, are divided into six different Chapters. Part II. Containing, I. Full Instructions to be observed in Hunting, Coursing, Setting and Shooting; with an Account of the several Kinds of Dogs necessary for those Diversions, and Receipts for the Cure of all common Distempers to which they are liable; as also Receipts for the Cleaning and Preserving of Boots, Fire-Arms, &c. II. Cautions, Rules and Directions to be taken and observed in Fishing; with the Manner of making and preserving of Rods, Lines, Floats, Artificial Flies, &c., and for chusing and preserving several Sorts of curious Baits. III. A full and complete Kalendar of all Work necessary to be done in the Fruit, Flower, and Kitchen Gardens, Green-House, &c., with the Produce of each, in every Month throughout the Year. Part III. Containing practical Rules, and Methods, for the Improving of Land, and Managing a Farm in all its Branches; with several curious Receipts for Brining, Liming and preparing Wheat, Barley, Oats, &c., for Sowing; excellent Receipts for destroying of Rats and Mice; a great Number of choice Receipts for the Cure of all common Distempers incident to all Sorts of Cattle; and a complete Kalendar of all Business necessary to be done in the Field, Yard, &c., by the Farmer, in every Month throughout the Year. With a complete Alphabetical Index to each Part. The Whole, being faithfully collected by several very eminent and ingenious Gentlemen, is now first published, at their earnest Desire, for the general Benefit of Mankind. *London, printed and sold by T. Longman, at the Ship in Pater-noster Row. 1736. (Price bound 3s. 6d.)*] 2 lvs not num. (receipt for Mrs Stephens' cure for the stone) + pp.1–526 + 30 lvs not num. (index). (BL 1147.b.21.)

The British Library copy is incomplete, wanting the title-page, the preface and the list of contents. The details given here are reproduced from Oxford, pp. 66–68. The book is divided into three parts: 'The Complete Family-Piece' (pp. 1–285), 'The Country Gentleman's Best Guide' (pp. 287–413), and 'The Farmer's Best Guide' (pp. 415–526). The contents follow the lines indicated by the title-page. The cookery receipts are mostly taken from E. Smith, but the remedies do not come from this source.

COOK, ANN

Professed Cookery: Containing Boiling, Roasting, Pastry, Preserving, Potting, Pickling, Made-Wines, Gellies, and Part of Confectionaries. With an Essay upon the Lady's Art of Cookery. By Ann Cook, Teacher of the true Art of Cookery. *Newcastle upon Tyne: Printed by J. White, and sold by the Author, at her House in the Groat-market. M.DCC.LIV. Price Five Shillings.* Title page + pp. iii–x (poem to the reader) + pp. 1–173 + 9 pp. not num. (index). (BL C.190.aa.4.)

The book contains 'An Essay on the Lady's Art of Cookery' (pp. 1–68), the famous attack on Hannah Glasse, written from the 1751 edition of *The Art of Cookery*; receipts (pp. 69–171), and a conclusion (pp. 172–73) on fattening poultry. This last section was to be greatly developed in the second edition as an autobiographical account of Ann Cook's persecution at the hands of 'Esquire Flash', none other than Hannah Glasse's half-brother, Lancelot Allgood:

Professed Cookery: Containing Boiling, …. With An Essay upon the Lady's Art of Cookery. Together with A Plan of House-keeping. By Ann Cook, Teacher of the True Art of Cookery. The Second Edition. *Printed for the Author, and sold at her House in the Groat-market, Newcastle. 1755. Price 6s.* Title pages + pp. iii–x (poem to the reader) + pp. 1–68 ('Essay') + pp. 69–171 (receipts) + pp. 173–189 (appendix) + 9 pp. not num. (index) + pp. 191–92 (index to appendix) + pp. 193–296 ('A Plan of House-keeping'). Newcastle City Library: information from the Local Studies Library officer, Patricia Sheldon, who kindly sent me these details.

From the pagination details, it is clear that this edition is identical to the first except for the addition of more receipts in the appendix, and the expansion of the 'Plan'. The third, undated edition came out in London, its contents unchanged:

Professed Cookery: …. *London: Printed for and sold by the Author, at her Lodgings, in Mr. Moor's, Cabinet-maker, Fuller's Rents, Holborn. Price Six Shillings.* Title page + pp. iii–x (poem to reader) + pp. 1–189 + 9 pp. not num. + pp. 191–296. (BL 1651/570.)

See *Ann Cook and Friend*, ed. Regula Burnet (London, 1936) and Madeleine Hope Dodds, 'The Rival Cooks: Hannah Glasse and Ann Cook', *Archæologia Aeliana*, series 4, 15 (1938), pp. 43–68.

DALRYMPLE, George

The Practice of Modern Cookery; adapted to Families of Distinction, As well as to those of The Middling Ranks of Life. To which is added, A Glossary explaining the Terms of Art. By George Dalrymple, Late Cook to Sir John Whitefoord, Bar[t]. *Edinburgh: Printed for the Author. Sold by C. Elliot, Edinburgh; and T. Longman, London. MDCCLXXXI.* Title page + 1 lf not num. (dedication to Lady Whitefoord) + pp. v–vi (preface) + pp. 1–475 + 1 p. not num. (errata). (BL 1037.g.29.)

Dalrymple's book is almost entirely plagiarized from Clermont. Only the puddings in Dalrymple (pp. 449–462) do not come from this source.

EALES, MARY

Mrs Mary Eales's Receipts. Confectioner to her late Majesty Queen Anne. *London: Printed by H. Meere in Black-Fryers, and to be had at Mr. Cooper's at the Three Pidgeons the lower End of Bedford-Street, near the New Exchange in the Strand. MDCCXVIII.* Title page + 3 lvs not num. (contents) + pp. 1–100. (BL 1037.f.8.)

The book apparently circulated in manuscript form before and after publication: when it was re-published with identical contents but a new title, *The Compleat Confectioner*, in 1733, the advertisement to the reader stated, 'Having made this Collection purely to oblige a few of the Prime Quality, who gave very largely for written Copies of it; Mrs. Eales was, about sixteen years ago, prevail'd upon to send it to the Press: When the small Number that were printed off were immediately bought, for no less than the same Number of Guineas, and the Book began to sell for five Guineas in Manuscript, as it had done before.' (See Ivan Day, 'Which *Compleat Confectioner*?', *PPC* 59 (1998), p. 44.) One manuscript copy is now in the British Library (Additional MS 29739), with the inscription inside the cover, 'Elizabeth Sloane Octob. XV MDCCXI'. After the last receipt is written 'A copy from Mrs Eales Book.' The contents are identical to the printed work. The date may be an error, since the inscription says that this is a copy 'from' the book. Another undated manuscript copy in the Bodleian Library (MS Eng Misc e 38) has a note saying: 'The Original Book of Mrs Eells Receytes in Sweetmeats and Confectionary things delivered in consideration of five Guineys and Warrented to be right and perfect by her.' David Potter suggests that this is a pre-1718 copy; see Potter, 'Mrs Eells 'Unique Receipts'', *PPC* 61 (May 1999), pp. 16–19. In 1733 the book was reprinted with a new title and also with the original title:

Mrs Mary Eales's Receipts. … *London: Printed for J. Brindley, Bookseller, at the King's Arms in New Bond-Street, and Bookbinder to Her Majesty and His Royal Highness the Prince of Wales; and R. Montagu at the General Post-Office, the Corner of Great Queen-Street, near Drury-Lane. MDCCXXXIII.* Title page + 3 lvs not num. (contents) + pp. 1–100 + 2 lvs not num. (bookseller's advertisement). (BL 1608/2418.)

The book is now accessible in the Prospect facsimile reprint of this 1733 edition (1985).

ELLIS, William

The Country Housewife's Family Companion: or Profitable Directions for whatever relates to the Management and good Œconomy of the Domestick Concerns of a Country Life, According to the Present Practice of the Country Gentleman's, the Yeoman's, the Farmer's, &c. Wives, in the Counties of Hertford, Bucks, and other Parts of England: Shewing How great Savings may be made in Housekeeping: And wherein, among many others, The following Heads are particularly treated of and explained: I. The Preservation and Improvement of Wheat, Rye, Barley, Oats, and other Meals; with Directions for making several Sorts of Bread, Cakes, Puddings, Pies, &c. II. Frugal Management of Meats, Fruits, Roots, and all Sorts of Herbs; best Methods of Cookery; and a cheap Way to make Soups, Sauces, Gruels, &c. III. Directions for the Farm Yard; with the best Method of increasing and fatning [sic] all Sorts of Poultry, as Turkies, Geese, Ducks, Fowls, &c. IV. The best Way to breed and fatten Hogs; sundry curious and cheap Methods of preparing Hogs Meat; Directions for curing Bacon, Brawn, pickled Pork, Hams, &c. with the Management of Sows and Pigs. V. The best Method of making Butter and Cheese, with several curious Particulars containing the whole Management of the Dairy. VI. The several Ways of making good Malt; with Directions for brewing good Beer, Ale, &c. With Variety of curious Matters, Wherein are contained frugal Methods for victualling Harvest-men, Ways to destroy all Sorts of Vermine, the best Manner of suckling and fattening Calves, Prescriptions for curing all Sorts of Distempers in Cattle, with variety of curious Receits [sic] for Pickling, Preserving, Distilling, &c. The Whole founded on near thirty Years Experience by W. Ellis, Farmer, at Little Gaddesden, near Hempsted, Hertfords. *London: Printed for James Hodges, at the Looking-glass, facing St. Magnus Church, London-Bridge; and B. Collins, Bookseller, at Salisbury. 1750.* Frontispiece + title page + pp. i–x (preface & introduction) + pp. 1–379 + 19 pp. not num. (contents) + 1 lf not num. (bookseller's advertisement). (BL 1609/2251.)

The frontispiece shows a farm scene. Pehr Kalm, who visited Ellis at Little Gaddesden, found his land badly kept and, on enquiring in the neighbourhood, found that Ellis made his living by writing books rather than by practising agriculture (see Lucas (ed. & trans.) *Kalm's Account of his Visit to England on his way to America in 1748* (1892), pp. 187–93). The same may be said of his receipts, which are often grossly optimistic about the number of people who may be fed on very basic pancakes and puddings. Although Ellis says people found these dishes made a satisfactory meal, this seems very unlikely, and one must conclude that Ellis had no experience of the receipts. A modern transcription is published by Prospect Books.

EMMETT, JOHN

A Choice Collection of Excellent Receipts in Confectionary. By John Emmett, Late Chief Confectioner to his Grace the Duke of Grafton, when Lord Lieutenant of Ireland. *York: Printed by Alex. Staples, in Coney-Street. MDCCXXXVII.* Title page + 1 lf not num. (preface addressed to lady subscribers) + pp. v-viii (index) + pp. 1-32. (BL C.136.f.32.)

FARLEY, JOHN

The London Art of Cookery, and Housekeeper's Complete Assistant. On a New Plan. Made Plain and Easy to the Understanding of every Housekeeper, Cook, and Servant in the Kingdom. Containing, Proper Directions for the Choice of all Kinds of Provisions. Roasting and Boiling all Sorts of Butchers Meat, Poultry, Game, and Fish. Sauces for every Occasion. Soups, Broths, Stews, and Hashes. Made Dishes, Ragoos, and Fricassees. All Sorts of Pies and Puddings. Proper Instructions for dressing Fruits and Vegetables. Pickling, Potting, and Preserving. The Preparation of Hams, Tongues and Bacon. The whole Art of Confectionary. Tarts, Puffs, and Pasties. Cakes, Custards, Jams, and Jellies. Drying, Candying, and Preserving Fruits, &c. Made Wines, Cordial Waters, and Malt Liquors. To which is added, An Appendix, Containing Considerations on Culinary Poisons; Directions for making Broths, &c. for the Sick; a List of Things in Season in the different Months of the Year; Marketing Tables, &c. &c. Embellished with A Head of the Author, and a Bill of Fare for every Month in the Year, elegantly engraved on Thirteen Copper-plates. By John Farley, Principal Cook at the London Tavern. *London: Printed for John Fielding, Nº 23 Pater-noster Row; and J. Scatcherd and J. Whitaker, Nº 12, Ave Maria Lane, 1783. [Price Six Shillings Bound.]* Frontispiece + title page + pp. iii–xvi (preface & contents) + 12 pl. + pp. 1–459. (BL 7955.b.39.)

The British Library copy is incomplete, wanting the end of the contents (pp.

xvii–xx). Farley's book was compiled by the printer and hack writer Richard Johnson, who recorded on 1 November 1782 'Began writing Farley's London Art of Cookery', for which he was paid £21 in instalments in December 1782 and January 1783. (See Peter Targett, 'Richard Johnson or John Farley?', *PPC* 58 (1998), p. 32.) Fiona Lucraft has shown that Farley's book lifted 390 receipts from Elizabeth Raffald and 343 receipts from Hannah Glasse, making a total of over 90 per cent of his book from these sources. He also borrowed from E. Smith and Charlotte Mason. See Lucraft, 'The London Art of Plagiarism', *PPC* 42 (1992), p. 8, and *PPC* 43 (1993), pp. 35–37. Only one receipt, for beef tea, remains unsourced.

FARMER'S

The Farmer's Wife; Or Complete Country Housewife. Containing Full and ample Directions for the Breeding and Management of Turkies, Fowls, Geese, Ducks, Pigeons, &c. Instructions for fattening Hogs, pickling of Pork, and curing of Bacon. How to make Sausages, Hogs-Puddings, &c. Full Instructions for making Wines from various Kinds of English Fruits, and from Smyrna Raisins. The Method of making Cyder, Perry, Mead, Mum, Cherry-Brandy, &c. Directions respecting the Dairy, containing the best Way of making Butter, and likewise Gloucestershire, Cheshire, Stilton, Sage, and Cream Cheese, &c. How to pickle common English Fruits and Vegetables, with other useful Receipts for the Farmer's Wife and Country House-Keeper. Full Instructions how to brew Beer and Ale, of all the various Kinds made in this Kingdom. Ample Directions respecting the Management of Bees, with an Account fo the Use of Honey. To which is added The Art of Breeding and Managing Song Birds in General: Likewise a Variety of Receipts in Cookery, And other particulars well worthy the Attention of Women of all Ranks residing in the Country. *Instructions, full and plain, we give, / To teach the Farmer's Wife, / With Satisfaction, how to live / The happy Country Life. London: Printed for Alex. Hogg, Nº 16, in Pater-noster Row. [Price One Shilling and Six-pence.]* Frontispiece + title page +1 lf not num. (preface) + 2 lvs not num. (contents & advertisement for a book called *Harvey's School Exercises*) + pp. 9–132. (BL 7948.a.18.)

The frontispiece shows a farmyard scene. The book dates from 1780–1800. The printer, Alexander Hogg, was working at the address indicated from about 1778 until 1805 (Maxted, p. 112). Maclean (p. 52) suggests a date *c.*1780.

FISHER, LYDIA

The Prudent Housewife: or, Complete English Cook For Town and Country. Being the newest Collection of the most Genteel, and least expensive Receipts in every Branch of Cookery, viz. Going to Market; For Roasting, Boiling, Frying, Hashing, Stewing, Broiling, Baking, Fricasseeing. Also for Making Puddings, Custards, Cakes Pies Tarts Ragouts Soups, Jellies Syllabubs, Wines, &c. To which are added, selected from the Papers of a Lady of Distinction, lately deceased, New and Infallible Rules to be observed in Pickling, Preserving, Brewing, &c. And, in order to render it still more valuable than any other Publication that hath appeared, a Treasure of Valuable Medicines, for the Cure of every Disorder, crowns the whole of this Work; which contains every Instruction that relates to the pleasing of the Palate, and the Preservation of that inestimable Blessing, Health. Written by Mrs. Fisher, of Richmond. *London: Printed by T. Sabine, No. 17, Little New-street, Shoe Lane, Fleet-street: Where Printing is expeditiousley performed in all its Branches, on reasonable Terms. Price One Shilling.* Title page + pp. 3–142. (BL 7944.aaa.8. But in 2000, this copy was not in the BL catalogue, and access to it was only via ESTC.)

The book dates from *c.*1780 (ESTC). The twenty-fourth edition gives the author's name as Lydia Fisher:

The Prudent Housewife, or compleat English Cook. ... By Mrs. Lydia Fisher, of Richmond. Twenty-Fourth Edition. *London: Printed by Sabine and Son, N⁰ 81, Shoe Lane, Fleet Street. [Price One Shilling.]* Frontispiece + title page + pp. 3–120. (BL 1608/2646.)

The frontispiece shows a half-portrait of Mrs Fisher holding a book. The caption below reads: 'Late Cook & House-keeper to the Duke of Newcastle, Marquis of Rockingham, &c. – upward of 50 Years.' This information is subject to caution: the household accounts of the first and second dukes of Newcastle and of Rockingham mention no such person. This edition dates from the period 1808–1825, when Thomas Sabine and his son were associates (Maxted, p. 197). The frontispiece, dated 1788, first appeared in the undated fourth edition (Bitting, p. 159).

FRAZER (MRS.)

The Practice of Cookery, Pastry, Pickling, Preserving, &c. Containing Figures of Dinners, from Five to Nineteen Dishes, and A Full List of Supper Dishes; also A List of Things in Season, For every month in the Year, and Directions for choosing Provisions: with Two Plates, showing the method of placing Dishes upon a Table, and the Manner of Trussing Poultry, &c. By Mrs. Frazer, Sole Teacher of these Arts in Edinburgh, Several years Colleague, and afterwards Successor to Mrs McIver deceased. *Edinburgh: Printed for Peter Hill Edinburgh, and T. Cadell London. M, DCC, XCI.* 2 pl. + title page + pp. iii–xiii (preface & contents) + pp. 1–254. (BL 1037.f.17.)

The book is an expanded version of Susanna Maciver.

[G., R.]

The Accomplish'd Female Instructor: Or, A very useful Companion for Ladies, Gentlewomen, and Others. In Two Parts. Part I. Treating of Generous Breeding and Behaviour; Choice of Company, Friendship; the Art of Speaking well, Directions in Love, Carriage in Company, Conversation, Affability, Courtesy and Humility; the Mystery of Eloquence. Of suitable Recreations, Modesty, Chastity, Religion, Charity, Compassion, Contentment of Mind, Devotion and Prayer. Part II. Treating of making curious Confectionaries, or Sweet-Meats, Jellies, Syrups, Cordial-waters, Brandies, Wines of English Fruit, and other useful Liquors; to imitate Foreign Wines; to Make Junkets, Spoon-Meats, and curious Pastery [sic]; to know good Provisions, Dye curious Colours, Whiten Ivory, Cement Glass, China or Metal; make Artificial Pearls or Precious Stones; to take out Spots or Stains; &c. to Paint, Japan, make Wax-works, Rock-work, or Works in Gold, Silk, Silver, &c. the Art of Perfuming and Preserving Cloaths from Vermin or Insects; Physical and Chyrurgical Receipts; with Directions for the Preservation of Health; to make curious Sawces, keep Flowers all the Year, Pickle all kind of useful things; Cleanse Gold or Silver Lace; rare Experiments for Diversion, and a great Number of other useful and profitable things. *London, Printed for James Knapton, at the Crown in St. Paul's Church-yard, 1704. Price Bound One Shilling.* Frontispiece + title page + 1 lf not num. (preface) + 2 lvs not num. (contents) + pp. 1–184. (BL 8405.ee.13.)

The preface is signed 'R. G.' The frontispiece shows a lady seated in a closet, reading a book, with sweetmeats in dishes on the table beside her.

GELLEROY, WILLIAM

The London Cook, or The whole Art of Cookery made easy and familiar. Containing A great Number of approved and practical Receipts in every Branch of Cookery. Viz. Chap. I. Of Soups, Broths, and Gravy. II. Of Pancakes, Fritters, Possets, Tanseys, &c. III. Of Fish. IV. Of Boiling. V. Of Roasting. VI. Of Made-Dishes. VII. Of Poultry and Game. VIII. Sauces for Poultry and Game. IX. Sauces for Butcher's Meat, &c. X. Of Puddings. XI. Of Pies, Custards, and Tarts, &c. XII. Of Sausages, Hogs-Puddings, &c. XIII. Of Potting and Collaring XIV. Of Pickles. XV. Of Creams, Jellies, &c. XVI. Of Made Wines. By William Gelleroy, Late Cook to her Grace the Dutchess of Argyle. And now to the Right Hon. Sir Samuel Fludger, Bar[t]. Lord Mayor of the City of London. To which is prefixed, A large Copper-Plate, representing his Majesty's Table, with its proper Removes, as it was served at Guild-Hall, on the 9th of November last, being the Lord Mayor's Day, when his Majesty, and the Royal Family, did the City the Honour to dine with them, and were highly pleased with their Entertainment. *London: Printed for S. Crowder, and Co. at the Looking-Glass; J. Coote, at the King's-Arms, in Pater-noster Row; and J. Fletcher, St. Paul's Church–Yard. MDCCLXII.* Title page + pp. iii–iv (address to the reader) + 9 lvs not num. (bill of fare at royal banquet & contents) + pp. 1–330 + pp. 473–486 (appendix) + 1 lf not num. (bookseller's advertisement). The plate announced on the title-page is not in the book. (BL 1487.f.6.)

GENTLEMAN'S

The Gentleman's Companion, and Tradesman's Delight. Containing, The Mystery of Dying in all its Branches. The Manner of preparing Colours. The Method of cleaning and taking out Stains from Silks, Woollen, or Linnen. To clean Gold and Silver Lace, and Plate. To prepare a Cement for China, or Glass. The Art of Drawing, Limning, Painting, Etching, Engraving, Carving, Gilding, Enamelling, and Refreshing Pictures. Likewise the Quality of Natural and Artificial Metals. How to harden or soften them. The Art of soldering, burnishing, and gilding Metals. To make all Sorts of Ink. To prepare Gold and Silver for Writing. To make Sealing-Wax, or Wafers. To know the Purity of Gold or Silver, and detect counterfeit Coins. The great Mr. Boyle's Method of writing in such a Manner as cannot be discovered without the help of Fire, Water, &c. To take Blots out of Paper. The Art of dressing, cleaning, and perfuming Gloves and Ribbons; and washing all Sorts of Lace. Also the Method of Curing and Preserving English Wines in the best Manner. And some excellent Receipts in Cookery, Physick, and Surgery. With many other useful Things never before printed. *London: Printed for J. Stone, at Bedford-Row, near Gray's-Inn; and Sold by G. Strahan, at the Royal-Exchange; W. Mears, on Ludgate-Hill; J. Jackson, in Pall-Mall, C. Corbet, at Temple-Bar; and T. Boreman, near Child's Coffee-House, in St. Paul's Church-Yard. 1735. [Price 2s. 6d.]* Title page + 1 lf not num. (preface) + pp. 5–259 + 27 pp. not num. (contents) + 2 lvs not num. (bookseller's advertisement). (BL Cup.407.i.28.)

The book is in three parts. Part 2 contains cosmetics (pp. 139–46); Part 3, headed 'Cookery', (pp. 160–259) contains cookery, confectionery, physic and 'the vermin killer'.

[GLASSE, HANNAH]

The Art of Cookery, Made Plain and Easy; Which far exceeds any Thing of the Kind ever yet Published. Containing, I. Of Roasting, Boiling, &c. II. Of Made-Dishes. III. Read this Chapter, and you will find how Expensive a French Cook's Sauce is. IV. To make a Number of pretty little Dishes fit for a Supper, or Side-Dish, and little Corner-Dishes for a great Table; and the rest you have in the Chapter for Lent. V. To Dress Fish. VI. Of Soops and Broths. VII. Of Puddings. VIII. Of Pies. IX. For a Fast-Dinner, a Number of good Dishes, which you may make use for a Table at any other Time. X. Directions for the Sick. XI. For Captains of Ships. XII. Of Hog's Puddings, Sausages, &c. XIII. To Pot and Make Hams, &c. XIV. Of Pickling. XV. Of Making Cakes, &c. XVI. Of Cheesecakes, Creams, Jellies, Whip Syllabubs, &c. XVII. Of Made Wines, Brewing, French Bread, Muffins, &c. XVIII. Jarring Cherries, and Preserves, &c. XIX. To Make Anchovies, Vermicella, Ketchup, Vinegar, and to keep Artichokes, French-Beans, &c. XX. Of Distilling. XXI. How to Market, and the Seasons of the Year for Butcher's Meat, Poultry, Fish, Herbs, Roots, &c. and Fruit. XXII. A certain Cure for the Bite of a Mad Dog, by Dr. Mead. By a Lady. *London: Printed for the Author; and sold at Mrs. Ashburn's, a China-Shop, the Corner of Fleet-Ditch. MDCCXLVII. [Price 3s. stitch'd, and 5s.*

bound.] Title page + 1 lf not num. (list of subscribers) + 6 lvs not num. (contents & 'A little Instruction to the House-Maid') + pp. i–ii (address to the reader) + pp. 3–166. (BL C.40.l.4.)

The author's name appeared for the first time in the fourth edition of 1751, where the author's trade card was printed opposite the title-page. The trade card describes her as 'Hannah Glasse, Habit-Maker to Her Royal Highness the Princess of Wales, in Tavistock Street Covent Garden.' Glasse's best-seller has been reprinted twice in facsimile: with a glossary & notes by Alan Davidson (Prospect, 1983); and as 'First Catch Your Hare …', with introductory essays by Jennifer Stead & Priscilla Bain, glossary by Alan Davidson (Prospect, 1995). These editions also give the additional receipts added to the fourth and fifth editions of 1751 and 1755, the last to be produced while Glasse still retained control of the text (she was declared bankrupt in 1754, by which time the fifth edition had been printed, although it was not published until 1755). The additions are set out on the title-page of the fourth edition (in fact the receipt against 'buggs' had already appeared in the first edition):

The Art of Cookery, Made Plain and Easy; … XIII. A Receipt to keep clear from Buggs. To which are added, By Way of Appendix, I. To dress a Turtle, the West-India Way. II. To make Ice Cream. III. A Turkey, &c. in Jelly. IV. To make Citron. V. To candy Cherries or Green Gages. VI. To take Ironmolds out of Linnen. By a Lady. The Fourth Edition, with Additions. *London: Printed for the Author, and sold at the Bluecoat-Boy, near the Royal-Exchange; at Mrs. Ashburn's China-Shop, the Corner of Fleet-Ditch; at the Leg and Dial, in Fleet-Street; at the Prince of Wales's Arms, in Tavistock-Street, Covent-Garden; by W. Innys, in Pater-noster Row; J. Hodges, on London-Bridge; T. Trye, near Gray's-Inn-Gate, Holborn; J. Brotherton, in Cornhill; and by the Booksellers in Town and Country. M.DCC.LI. [Price 4 s. stitch'd, and 5 s. bound.] This Book is publish'd with His Majesty's Royal Licence; whoever prints it, or any Part of it, will be prosecuted.* Trade card + title page + pp. i–iv (address to the reader) + 10 lvs not num. + pp. 1–334. (BL C.45.c.15.)

GLASSE, Hannah

The Compleat Confectioner: or, the Whole Art of Confectionary Made Plain and Easy. Shewing, the various Methods of Preserving and Candying, both dry

and liquid, all Kinds of Fruit; Flowers and Herbs; the different Ways of Clari-
fying Sugar; and the Method of Keeping Fruit, Nuts and Flowers fresh and fine
all the Year round. Also Directions for making Rock-works and Candies,
Biscuits, Rich Cakes, Creams, Custards, Jellies, Whip Syllabubs, and Cheese-
cakes of all Sorts, English Wines of all Sorts, Strong Cordials, Simple Waters,
Mead, Oils, &c., Syrups of all Kinds, Milk Punch that will keep twenty Years,
Knicknacks and Trifles for Deserts, &c. Likewise, The Art of making Artificial
Fruit, with the Stalks in it, so as to resemble the natural Fruit. To which are
added, Some Bills of Fare for Deserts for private Families. By H. Glasse, Author
of the Art of Cookery. *London: Printed; And Sold at Mrs. Ashburner's China
Shop, the Corner of Fleet Ditch; at Yewd's Hat Warehouse, near Somerset House;
at Kirk's Toyshop, in St. Paul's Churchyard; at Deard's Toyshop, facing Arlington
Street, Piccadilly; By I. Pottinger, at the Royal Bible, in Pater-noster Row; and by
J. Williams, opposite St. Dunstan's Church, Fleet-street.* Title page + pp. iii–iv
(address to 'The Housekeepers of Great Britain and Ireland') + pp. 1–304 + pp.
i–xvi (contents). (BL 1037.g.26.)

This dates from *c.*1760; an edition came out in Dublin in 1762 (Maclean, pp.
61–62).

HALL, T.

The Queen's Royal Cookery: or, Expert and ready Way for the Dressing of all
Sorts of Flesh, Fowl, Fish: Either Bak'd, Boil'd, Roasted, Stew'd, Fry'd, Broil'd,
Hash'd, Frigasied, Carbonaded, Forc'd, Collar'd, Sous'd, Dry'd, &c. After the
Best and Newest Way. With their several Sauces and Salads. And making all
sorts of Pickles. Also Making Variety of Pies, Pasties, Tarts, Cheese-Cakes,
Custards, Creams, &c. With The Art of Preserving and Candying of Fruits and
Flowers; and the making of Conserves, Syrups, Jellies, and Cordial Waters. Also
making several Sorts of English Wines, Cyder, Mead, Metheglin. Together,
With several Cosmetick or Beautifying Waters: And also several sorts of
Essences and Sweet Waters, by Persons of the highest Quality. By T. Hall, Free
Cook of London. The Second Edition. *London: Printed for C. Bates, at the Sun
and Bible in Gilt-spur-street, in Pye-corner: and A. Bettesworth, at the Red Lion
on London-Bridge, 1713. License according to Order.* Frontispiece + title page +
1 lf not num. (preface) + pp. 7–180 + 1 pl. (BL 1037.f.7.)

The frontispiece shows a medallion of Queen Anne above a set of three kitchen scenes showing cookery, pastry and distilling. The first edition dates from 1709 (Maclean, p. 65). Despite the emphasis on the 'newest way', many of the receipts are lifted from Sir Kenelm Digby, either directly (*The Closet ... Opened*, 1669) or via the book by his steward, George Hartman (*The True Preserver and Restorer of Health*, 1682).

HARRISON, SARAH

The House-keeper's Pocket-Book, And Compleat Family Cook. Containing Above Three Hundred Curious and Uncommon Receipts in Cookery, Pastry, Preserving, Pickling, Candying, Collaring, &c. With Plain and Easy Instructions for preparing and dressing every thing suitable for an Elegant Entertainment, from Two Dishes to Five or Ten, &c. And Directions for placing them in their proper Order. Concluding With many Excellent Prescriptions of the most eminent Physicians, of singular Efficacy in most Distempers incident to the Human Body: And to the whole is prefix'd, Such a copious and useful Bill of Fare of all manner of Provisions in Season for every Month of the Year, that no Person need be at a Loss to provide an agreeable Variety of Dishes. By Mrs. Sarah Harrison of Devonshire. *London: Printed for T. Worrall, at Judge Coke's Head, over against St Dunstan's Church, Fleetstreet. 1733. (Price 2 s. 6 d. bound)* Title page + pp. v-xii (dedication to 'The House-wives, in Great-Britain' & preface) + pp. 1–127 + 7 pp. not num. (index, some pages missing). (BL 1607/3665.)

The second edition, expanded and with a slightly changed and re-ordered title-page, appeared in 1739:

The House-keeper's Pocket-Book; and Compleat Family Cook. Containing Above Seven Hundred Curious and Uncommon Receipts ... And Directions for Ranging them in their Proper Order. To Which is Prefix'd, Such a Copious and Useful Bill of Fare of All Manner of Provisions in Season for Every Month of the Year, that no Person need be at a Loss to Provide an Agreeable Variety of Dishes, at a Moderate Expence. With Directions for Making All Sorts of Wines, Mead, Cyder, Shrub, &c. and Distilling Strong-Waters &c. after the Most Approved Method. Concluding with Many Excellent Prescriptions, of Singular Efficacy in Most Distempers Incident to the Human Body; Extracted from the Writings of the Most Eminent Physicians. By Mrs. Sarah Harrison, of Devonshire. The Second Edition, Corrected and Improv'd, with the Addition of Four Hundred Genuine Receipts, sent to the Author by several worthy Persons. *London: Printed for R. Ware, at the Bible and Sun in Amen Corner, Warwick Lane, 1739. [Price 2 s. 6 d.]* Title page + pp. iii–iv (address 'To the House-wives in Great Britain') + 2 lvs not num. (preface & contents) + pp. 1–263 + 8 lvs not num. (index & bookseller's advertisement). (BL 1037.f.10.)

Sarah Harrison's book may well have inspired Hannah Glasse's title-page, with its reference to 'Plain and Easy Instructions' and, in the second edition, the 'Moderate Expence' – the idea of economy now appearing on the title-page instead of in the introductory discourse. Harrison lifted some of her receipts from Edward Kidder: Simon Varey notes that 98 receipts in the 6th edition of 1755 come from Kidder, including seven found only in the manuscript version of the book. See Varey, 'New Light on Edward Kidder's Receipts', *PPC* 39 (1991), pp. 48–9. Since the above was written, David Potter's article on Edward Kidder in *PPC* 65 (2000) has shown that Harrison took 141 receipts from the manuscript version of Kidder for her first edition, copying them in the same order (pp. 121–178 in Harrison). In this 1733 edition, lists of dishes in season, with comments (perhaps the most interesting aspect of the book) occupy pp. 4–47, cookery pp. 48–184, remedies pp. 185–197, and bills of fare pp. 198–217. Thus Kidder is not the only source, although, as Potter suggests, Harrison may have been one of his pupils. In the 1739 edition, the text is re-organized into chapters, and Kidder's receipts are scattered throughout, the newly inserted receipts being presumably the extra 400 mentioned on the title-page, although it would be imprudent to take too literally the notion that the new receipts were kindly sent by volunteers.

[HAYWOOD, Eliza]

A Present for a Servant-Maid: or, the Sure Means of gaining Love and Esteem. Under the following Heads. Observance. Avoiding Sloth. Sluttishness. Staying on Errands. Telling Family Affairs. Secrets among Fellow-Servants. Entring [sic] into their Quarrels. Tale-bearing. Being an Eye-Servant. Carelessness of Children. Of Fire, Candles, Thieves. New Acquaintance. Fortune-Tellers. Giving saucy Answers. Liquorishness. Apeing the Fashion. Dishonesty. The Market Penny. Delaying to give Change. Giving away Victuals. Bringing in Chair-women. Wasting Victuals Quarrels with Fellow-Servants. Behaviour to the Sick. Hearing Things against a Master or Mistress. Being too free with Men Servants. Conduct towards Apprentices. Mispending [sic] Time. Publick Shews. Vails. Giving Advice too freely. Chastity. Temptations from the Master. If a single Man. If a married Man. If from the Master's Son. If from Gentlemen Lodgers. To which are Added, Directions for going to Market; Also, For Dressing any Common Dish, whether Flesh, Fish, or Fowl. With some Rules for Washing &c. The Whole calculated for making both the Mistress and the Maid happy. *London: Printed and Publish'd by T. Gardner, at Cowley's Head, without Temple-Bar; and sold by the Booksellers of Town and Country, 1743. [Price One Shilling.]* Title page + 1 lf not num. (preface & contents) + pp. 1–76. (BL 1037.h.12.)

The *DNB* attributes this book to Eliza Haywood. Directions for marketing occupy pp. 51–57; cookery pp. 57–72; household hints pp. 72–76.

HAZLEMORE, MAXIMILIAN

Domestic Economy; or, A Complete System of English Housekeeping: Containing The most approved Receipts, confirmed by Observation and Practice, in every reputable English Book of Cookery now extant; besides a great Variety of others which have never before been offered to the Public. Also a valuable Collection, translated from the Productions of Cooks of Eminence who have published in France, with their respective Names to each Receipt; which, together with the Original Articles, form the most complete System of Housekeeping ever yet exhibited, under the following Heads, viz. Roasting, Boiling, Made-Dishes, Frying, Broiling, Potting, Fricassees, Ragouts, Soups, Sauces, Gravies, Hashes, Stews, Puddings, Custards, Cakes, Tarts, Pies, Pasties, Cheesecakes, Jellies, Pickling, Preserving, and Confectionary. To which is prefixed, in order to render it as complete and perfect as possible, An Elegant Collection of Light Dishes for Supper, Adapted for every Month in the Year. Also, The Complete Brewer; Containing Familiar Instructions for brewing all Sorts of Beer and Ale; including the proper Management of the Vault or Cellar. Likewise, The Family Physician; Being a Collection of the most valuable and approved Prescriptions by Mead, Sydenham, Tissot, Fothergill, Elliot, Buchan, and Others. By Maximilian Hazlemore. *London: Printed for J. Creswick, and Co. 1794.* Title page + pp. 3–4 (address to the public) + pp. v–xxxii (contents & bills of fare) + pp. 1–392. (BL 7944.bb.2.)

This is a pirate of the third edition of Mary Cole's *The Lady's Complete Guide*.

HENDERSON, WILLIAM AUGUSTUS

The Housekeeper's Instructor; or, Universal Family Cook. Being an ample and clear Display of the Art of Cookery in all its various Branches. Containing Proper Directions for Dressing all Kinds of Butcher's Meat, Poultry, Game, Fish, &c. Also, the Method of preparing Soups, Hashes, and Made Dishes; with The Whole Art of Confectionary, Pickling, Preserving, &c. Likewise The making and keeping in Perfection British Wines; and Proper Rules For Brewing Malt Liquor, As well for Family Consumption as the Regale of private Visitants. To which is added, The Complete Art of Carving, Illustrated with Engravings, Explaining, by proper References, the Manner in which the Young Practitioner may acquit himself of Table with Elegance and Ease. Also, Bills of Fare for every Month in the Year; With Copper-Plates, Displaying The Best Manner of decorating a Table; Whereby every Person will be enabled to add to the Art of Cookery the proper Disposition of each Article in its respective Season. Together with Directions for Marketing, and the Management of the Kitchen and Fruit-Garden. The Whole formed on so New a Plan, that the Inexperienced will be instructed, and the professed Cook receive that Information which has never been made known by any preceding Publication. By William Augustus Henderson, Who has made the Culinary Art his Study for upwards of Forty Years. *London: Printed and Sold by W. and J. Stratford, Holborn-Hill.* Frontispiece + title page + pp. 3–456 + 11 pl. + 9 lvs not num. (index & directions to the binder) + 3 lvs not num. (list of subscribers & bookseller's advertisement). (BL 1509/1462.)

The book dates from *c*.1791. The printers, James and William Stratford, were associates from 1789 to 1792 and again in 1800 (Maxted, p. 217). The bookseller's advertisement includes a book by Charles Alfred Ashburton, 'A New, Genuine, and Complete History of England, From the First Settlement of Brutus … To the Year 1793'; the book appeared in instalments from 1791 to 1794. Maclean (pp. 68–69) suggests a date *c*.1790. The frontispiece shows a kitchen scene, with the caption: 'A Lady presenting her Servant with the *Universal Family Cook* who diffident of her own knowledge has recourse to that Work for Information. On the right hand a Person Instructing a Young Man in the *Art of Carving* by refering to a Print on that Subject. In the front Ground various Articles of Cookery, Confectionary, Brewing, &c emblematical of the various useful information contained in *this Work*.'

HOLLAND, MARY

The Complete British Cook: Being a Collection of the most valuable and useful Receipts, for rendering the Whole Art of Cookery Plain and familiar to every Capacity: Containing Directions for Gravies, Sauces, Roasting, Boiling, Frying, Broiling, Stewing, Hashes, Soups, Fricasees, Ragouts, Pastries, Pies, Tarts, Cakes, Puddings, Fritters, Preserves, Pickles, Syllabubs, Creams, Flummeries, Jellies, Custards, &c. &c. By Mary Holland, Professed Cook. *London: Printed by J. D. Dewick, Westmoreland Buildings, Aldersgate Street; For West and Hughes, Paternoster-Row; and sold by all Booksellers. 1800.* Frontispiece + title page + 1 lf not num. (bookseller's advertisement) + pp. 1–104. (BL 1037.e.41 (3).)

The frontispiece shows a woman in the kitchen with a book lying open on the table; behind her a man carries away two dishes of meat.

HOUSE-KEEPER'S

The House-keeper's Pocket Book, and complete Family Cook. Containing Several Hundred Curious Receipts in Cookery, Pastry, Preserving, Pickling, Brewing, Baking, Made Wines, &c. With Plain and Easy Instructions for preparing and dressing every thing suitable for an elegant Entertainment, from Two Dishes to Five or Ten, &c. To which is Added. Every Man his own Doctor, shewing the Nature and Faculties of the different sorts of Foods, whereby every Man and Woman may know what is Good or Hurtful to them. *London: Sold at H. Fenwick's Wholesale Book Warehouse Snow Hill.* Frontispiece + title page + pp. 3–168. (BL 1606/548.)

The frontispiece shows a woman working in a kitchen; the caption beneath reads: 'Engraved for Mrs Harrisons new Cookery Book 178.' Despite this, the book bears no resemblance to Sarah Harrison's book, and is in fact a severely abridged edition of Hannah Glasse's *Art of Cookery* (1747), with the addition of 'Every Man his own Doctor'. The book dates from the 1780s. The printer, Henry Fenwick, was working at the address indicated from 1769 to 1805, with interruptions between 1774 and 1775 and again in 1784 (Maxted, p. 80). Maclean (p. 72) gives two British Library copies as being printed by Thomas Martin, and dating from 1776 and 1783. The second of these copies is also cited by Oxford (p. 115).

HOWARD, Henry

England's Newest way in all sorts of Cookery, Pastry, and All Pickles that are fit to be Used. Adorn'd with Copper Plates, setting forth the Manner of placing Dishes upon Tables; And the Newest Fashions of Mince-Pies. By Henry Howard, Free Cook of London, and late Cook to his Grace the Duke of Ormond, and since to the Earl of Salisbury, and Earl of Winchelsea. Likewise The best Receipts for making Cakes, Mackroons, Biskets, Ginger-bread, French-bread: As also for Preserving, Conserving, Candying and Drying Fruits, Confectioning and Making of Creams, Syllabubs, and Marmalades of several sorts. The Second Edition with Additions and Amendments. *London, Printed for and Sold by Chr. Coningsby, at the Ink-bottle against Clifford's-Inn Back-Gate, in Fetter-lane, Fleetstreet, 1708.* Title page + 1 lf not num. (address by the bookseller to the reader) + 6 lvs not num. (index) + pp. 1–156 + 2 lvs not num. (bookseller's advertisement) + 8 copper-plates interleaved pp. 106–107, and 2 copper-plates interleaved pp. 146–147. (BL 1651/420.)

The first edition dates from 1703 (Maclean, p. 73). The third edition, with cosmetics added, appeared in 1710:

England's Newest Way in All Sorts of Cookery, Pastry, and All Pickles That Are Fit to Be Used. ... The Third Edition with Additions of Beautifying-Waters, and other Curiosities. *London, Printed for and Sold by Chr. Coningsby, at the Ink-bottle against Clifford's-Inn-Gate, in Fetter-lane, Fleetstreet, 1710.* Title page + 2 lvs not num. (address by the bookseller to the reader) + 8 lvs not num. (contents) + 1 lf not num. + pp. 1–192 + 2 lvs not num. (bookseller's advertisement) + pl. as in ed. 3. (BL 1037.f.5.)

JACKSON, Sarah

The Director: or, Young Woman's Best Companion. Containing, Above Three Hundred easy Receipts in Cookery, Pastry, Preserving, Candying, Pickling, Collaring, Physick, and Surgery. To which are added, Plain and easy Instructions for chusing Beef, Mutton, Veal, Fish, Fowl, and all other Eatables: Also, Directions for Carving, and Made Wines: Likewise Bills of Fare for every Month in the Year. With a complete Index to the Whole. A Book necessary for all Families. By Sarah Jackson. Collected for the Use of her own Family, and printed at the Request of her Friends. Being one of the Plainest and Cheapest of the Kind. The Whole makes a complete Family Cook and Physician. *London: Printed for J. Fuller, at his Circulating Library in Butcher-hall-lane, near Newgate-street; and S. Neale, Bookseller, at Chatham. M.DCC.LIV.* Title page + pp. 1–112 + 3 lvs not num. (index). (BL 1037.e.37.)

The book was also available as a part-work: the reverse of the title-page states: 'This WORK may be had complete, or the Numbers delivered Weekly at their own Houses, upon giving Notice to the Proprietor J. FULLER.' The cookery receipts are entirely plagiarized (with the exception of receipts 4 and 18) from the fourth edition of Elizabeth Moxon (*English Housewifry, c.*1749). Jackson omitted Moxon's longest receipts and all variations. The other material is not from this source.

JENKS, JAMES

The Complete Cook: Teaching the Art of Cookery in All its Branches; And to Spread a Table, In a Useful, Substantial, and Splendid Manner, At all Seasons in the Year. With Practical Instructions To Choose, Buy, Dress and Carve all Sorts of Provisions. Far exceeding any Thing of the Kind yet Published. Containing The greatest Variety of Approved Receipts in Cookery, Pastry, Confectionary, Preserving, Pickling, Collaring, &c. And Dishes for Lent and Fast-Days, A Variety of Made Dishes, And to Dress both the Real and Mock Turtle. With an Appendix Teaching the Art of Making Wine, Mead, Cyder, Shrub, Strong, Cordial and Medical Waters; Brewing Malt Liquor; The Management and Breeding of Poultry and Bees: And Receipts For Preserving and Restoring Health and Relieving Pain; and for Taking out Stains, Preserving Furniture, Cleaning Plates, &c. For the Use of Families. By James Jenks, Cook. *London: Printed for E. and C. Dilly in the Poultry. M DCC LXVIII.* Title page + pp. iii–xx (introduction & contents) + pp. 1–364. (BL 1037.f.13.)

JOHNSON, MARY

The Young Woman's Companion: or the Servant-Maid's Assistant; Digested under the several Heads hereinafter mentioned, viz. I. A short Essay on the Benefits of Learning, &c. by way of Introduction. II. The Young Woman's Guide to the Knowledge of her Mother-Tongue. III. A compendious English Spelling Dictionary, peculiarly calculated for the present Undertaking. IV. An easy Introduction to the Art of Writing; with Rules of Life. V. Familiar Letters on various Subjects. VI. The Young Woman's Guide to the Art of Numbers; with a great Variety of useful Tables. VII. The compleat Market Woman; with proper Instructions to prevent the Purchaser from being imposed upon. VIII. The compleat Cook-Maid, Pastry-Cook, and Confectioner. IX. Advice to Servants in general, with Respect to their Duty towards God, their Employers, and themselves, with additonal Prayers and Hymns. And lastly A compleat Table of the Contents. The whole Compiled by Mary Johnson, For many Years a Superintendant of a Lady of Quality's Family in the City of York. *London Printed for H. Jeffery, in Mercer's Chapel, Cheapside. MDCCLIII.* Title page + pp. i–ii (preface) + pp. 1–222 + 1 lf not num. (contents). (BL 1607/1589.)

The book was reprinted in 1754 and 1755 with the new title, *Madam Johnson's Present*, and a small amount of additional material: a summary of Lord Hardwicke's Marriage Act, an estimation of the annual expenses of a family (household expenses are estimated at £315, including the salary of the single servant at £4 10s.), a list of the terms used in carving, and bills of fare which are borrowed from Hannah Woolley. (For the bills of fare, see Johnson, pp. x–xiv; Woolley, *The Ladies Delight* (1672), in the unnumbered pages at the end.) Contrary to what Virginia Maclean states in her bibliography (p. 77), the rest of the book is identical to the first edition, and there is no reason to see this as a different work.

KELLET, Susanna, Elizabeth, & Mary

A Complete Collection of Cookery Receipts, (Consisting of near Four Hundred,) Which have been Taught upwards of Fifty Years, with great Reputation. By Susanna, Elizabeth, and Mary Kellet. *Newcastle Upon Tyne: Printed for T. Saint; and sold by W. Charnley, Whitfield and Co. and all the Booksellers in Town and Country. MDCCLXXX.* Title page + 1 lf not num. (dedication to 'the Ladies who honoured our School with their Attendance') + pp. i–iv (list of subscribers) + pp. i–xii (contents) + pp. 1–192. (Leeds: Brotherton Library.)

There were 207 subscribers.

[KETTILBY, MARY, ET AL.]

A Collection Of above Three Hundred Receipts in Cookery, Physick and Surgery; For the Use of all Good Wives, Tender Mothers, and Careful Nurses. By several Hands. *London, Printed for Richard Wilkin, at the King's Head in St. Paul's Church-yard. MDCCXIV.* Title pages + 6 lvs not num. (preface) + pp. 1–128 + 13 pp. not num. (index).(BL 1037.g.1.)

The second edition, with a second part consisting of contributions from readers, appeared in 1719:

A Collection of above Three Hundred Receipts …. The Second Edition. To which is Added, A Second Part, Containing a great Number of Excellent Receipts, for Preserving and Conserving of Sweet-Meats, &c. *London: Printed for Mary Kettilby, and Sold by Richard Wilkin, at the King's Head in St. Paul's Church-Yard. MDCCXIX.* Title pages + 5 lvs not num. (preface) + pp. 1–163 + 12 pp. not num. (index) + title to second part + 2 lvs not num. (preface) + pp. 7–86 + 4 lvs not num. (index & advertisement). (BL 1651/599.)

The third edition of 1724, the fourth edition of 1728, and the fifth edition of 1734 contain no new additions. The 1728 edition is still printed for Mary Kettilby, but the 1734 edition is printed for 'the Executrix of Mary Kettilby'. Bibliographies (Maclean pp. 79–82, Oxford p. 54) attribute this book to Kettilby, but she was merely the editor of the collection. The preface to the first edition says: 'A Number of very Curious and Delicate House-wives Clubb'd to furnish out this Collection'.

KIDDER, E[DWARD]

E. Kidder's Receipts of Pastry and Cookery, For the Use of his Scholars. Who teaches at his School in St. Martins le Grand: On Mondays, Tuesdays and Wednesdays, In the Afternoon. Also On Thursdays, Fridays and Saturdays, In the Afternoon, at his School next to Furnivals Inn in Holborn. Ladies may be taught at their own Houses. Frontispiece + title page + 40 lvs numbered sporadically + 7 lvs of pl. (BL 1037.e.34.)

The book is printed entirely in copper-plates, and only the recto of each leaf has text on it. The plates which illustrate the text show elaborate pie shapes. The frontispiece shows a half-length portrait of 'Edw. Kidder Pastry-master' by

Robert Sheppard. The book dates from *c.*1725; Kidder (1666–1739) ran two schools in different locations until the 1730s. Peter Targett, 'Edward Kidder: His Book and His Schools', *PPC* 32 (1989), pp. 35–44, suggests that Kidder's schools fall into three periods, the addresses given in the copy cited dating from the middle period. This also points to a date *c.*1725. However Simon Varey's conclusion from an examination of three copies of Kidder's book, including a manuscript copy, is that this middle-period copy may date from earlier, *c.*1721. (See Varey, 'New Light on Edward Kidder's *Receipts*', *PPC* 39 (1991), pp. 46–51.) Varey notes that receipts from Kidder, including receipts from the MS, are found in the sixth (1755) edition of Sarah Harrison, and in the first (1723) edition of Richard Smith. He concludes that Harrison and Smith must have used the MS, or another similar MS, or the MS's source. But it is equally possible that the MS (dated 1721–22), and thus Kidder himself, took receipts from Smith before the publication of *Court Cookery*. Another point is that Smith complains in his address that 'several of my Receipts, which I had given to satisfy the Importunity of Friends had been publish'd to the World, as the Labours of other People'. Who plagiarized whom in this case is probably impossible to determine. The British Library also has a copy of the later, 'Queen Street' version of the book, shelfmark 1037.e.35.

Since the above note was written, David Potter's 'Some Notes on Edward Kidder' has appeared in *PPC* 65 (2000), pp. 9–27, establishes beyond reasonable doubt that Kidder was born in 1667, had moved to London by 1683, and was a prosperous citizen, living near to Little Lincoln's Inn Fields, by the late 1690s. His cookery schools, and perhaps the earliest editions of his book, may date from that period. He seems to have left the Lincoln's Inn Fields address in 1721; this move may mark the start of the second period of his schools and books. Potter also deals very comprehensively with the plagiarisms of Kidder's receipts, and this evidence points to Smith rather than Kidder being the plagiarist.

LA CHAPELLE, Vincent

The Modern Cook. By Mr. Vincent La Chapelle, Chief Cook to the Right Honourable the Earl of Chesterfield. Vol. I. *London, Printed for the Author, and Sold by Nicholas Prevost, at the Ship-over against Southampton-Street, in the Strand. MDCCXXXIII.* Vol. I: title page + 1 lf not num. (dedication to Lord Chesterfield) + pp. i–viii (preface) + 10 lvs not num. (contents) + pp. 1–328 +

15 pl. Vol. II: title page + pp. iii–xxii (contents) + 1 lf not num. + 1 pl. + pp. 1–316 + 1 lf not num. (bookseller's advertisement). Vol. III: title page + 11 lvs not num (contents) + 1 pl. + pp. 1–307 + pp. 1–38 (appendix) + 1 lf not num. (contents of appendix). (BL 1651/442.)

The title-page was expanded for the second edition in 1736:

The Modern Cook: Containing Instructions For Preparing and Ordering Publick Entertainments for the Tables of Princes, Ambassadors, Nobelmen, and Magistrates. As also the least Expensive Methods of providing for private Families, in a very elegant Manner. New Receipts for Dressing of Meat, Fowl, and Fish; and making Ragoûts, Fricassées, and Pastry of all Sorts, in a Method, never before publish'd. Adorn'd with Copper-Plates, Exhibiting the Order of Placing the different Dishes, &c. on the Table, in the most polite Way. … *London: Printed for Thomas Osborne, in Gray's-Inn. MDCCXXXVI.* In 3 volumes, identical to the first edition. (BL 1037.g.13.)

The fourth edition appeared in 1751 in one volume, with the title-page further adapted to the British market, and the receipt titles translated into English:

The Modern Cook's, and Complete Housewife's Companion. Being the largest and best Collection of new Receipts for dressing all Sorts of Meat, Fowl, and Fish; and for making Ragoo's Fricassees, and Pastry of all Sorts. … *London: Printed for R. Manby and H. S. Cox, on Ludgate-Hill. MDCCLI.* Title page + 1 lf not num. (dedication) + pp. i–xl (preface & contents) + pp. 1–432 + pl. (BL Cup.502.l.10.)

The first edition in French was The Hague, 1735 (Vicaire, pp. 867–68).

LADIES'

The Ladies' Library: or, Encyclopedia of Female Knowledge, in every Branch of Domestic Economy: Comprehending, in Alphabetical Arrangement, Distinct Treatises on every practical Subject, necessary for Servants and Mistresses of Families. I. A most extensive System of Cookery. II. A complete Body of Domestic Medicine. III. The Preservation of Beauty, and Prevention of Deformity. In which is included, A Vast Fund of Miscellaneous Information, Of the highest Importance in Domestic Life. In Two Volumes. *London: Printed for J. Ridgway, No 1, York Street, St James's Square. M.DCC,XC.* Vol. I: title page

+ pp. iii–xv (preface) + pp. 1–407 + 1 p. not num. (bookseller's advertisement) + 2 pl. inserted at pp. 183, 225. Vol. II: title page + pp. 1–512 + 2 pl. inserted at p. 120 + 1 pl. (portrait of 'Ino Perkins, Many Years Cook in the Families of Earl Gower and Lord Melbourn' inserted at p. 208 + 1 pl. ('Wm. Buchan, M.D.') inserted at p. 424. (BL 1609/3299.)

The preface (p. v) states that the confectionery and the 'lighter branches of Cookery' are from the manuscript receipts of 'the late Mr. Perkins'. The portrait indicates that the medical sections are taken from William Buchan's best-seller, *Domestic Medicine* (1769). In fact, the book is a compilation from 'almost Thirty different authors' according to the preface (p. iv).

LAMB, PATRICK

Royal Cookery; or, the Complete Court-Cook. Containing the Choicest Receipts In all the particular Branches of Cookery, Now in Use in the Queen's Palaces of St. James's, Kensington, Hampton-Court, and Windsor. With near Forty Figures (curiously engraven on Copper) of the magnificent Entertainments at Coronations, Instalment, Balls, Weddings, &c. at Court; Also Receipts for making the Soupes, Jellies, Bisques, Ragoo's, Pattys, Tanzies, Forc'd-Meats, Cakes, Puddings, &c. By Patrick Lamb, Esq; Near 50 Years Master-Cook to their late Majesties King Charles II. King James II. King William and Queen Mary, and to Her Present Majesty Queen Anne. To which are added, Bills of Fare for every Season in the Year. *London, Printed for Maurice Atkins, at the Golden-Ball in S. Paul's Church-yard. 1710.* Title pages + 3 lvs not num. (preface) + 3 lvs not num. (contents) + pp. 1–127 + 5 lvs not num. (bills of fare) + 2 lvs not num. (bookseller's advertisement: 'Books printed for and sold by Maurice Atkins, at the Golden-Ball in S. Paul's Church-Yard.') + 35 pl inserted in the text. (BL 1651/429.)

There is a second version of the first edition, identical except for the name of the bookseller:

London, Printed for Abel Roper, and sold by John Morphew, near Stationers-Hall. 1710. (BL 1037.f.6.)

The second edition appeared in 1716, greatly expanded:

Royal Cookery .... The Second Edition, with the Addition of several new Cuts, and above five Hundred new Receipts, all disposed Alphabetically. *London: J. Nutt, A. Roper, 1716. Price 6 s.* Title-page + 3 lvs not num. (preface) + pp. 1–302 + 5 lvs not num. (bills of fare & tables) + 35 pl. inserted in the text. (BL 1037. g.2.)

The third edition, even larger, came out in 1726:

Royal Cookery .... The Third Edition, with considerable Additions, by a Gentleman, who was Cook to the abovenamed Kings and Queens, and also to his present Majesty. *London: Printed for E. and R. Nutt, and A. Roper; and sold by D. Browne without Temple Bar, J. Isted in Fleetstreet, and T. Cox under the Royal Exchange. 1726.* Title page + pp. 1–320 + 5 lvs not num. (bills of fare & tables) + 1 lf not num. (bookseller's advertisement) + 35 pl. inserted in the text.

LAMBERT, EDWARD

The Art of Confectionary. I. Shewing the Various Methods of Preserving All Sorts of Fruits, Dry and Liquid. Oranges, Lemons, Citrons, Golden-Pippins, Wardens, Apricots Green, Almonds, Goosberries, Cherries, Currans, Plumbs, Rasberries, Peaches, Walnuts, Nectarines, Figs, Grapes, &c. II. Flowers and Herbs; as Violets, Angelica, Orange-Flowers, &c. Also how to make all Sorts of Biscakes, Maspins, Sugar-Works and Candies. With the best Methods of Clarifying, and the different Ways of boiling Sugar. By the late Ingenious Mr. Edw. Lambert, Confectioner in Pall-Mall. *London, Printed for T. Taylor, by the Meuse-gate, in Castle-street; and sold by W. Bickerton, in the Temple-exchange, near the Inner-temple gate, Fleet-street. [Price One shilling]* Title page + pp. 1–61. (BL 1651/987.)

The book dates from *c*.1745. The printer T. Taylor was working at the address indicated in 1748, but in 1741 was at a different address. Weaver Bickerton is unknown at this address, but is known to have worked at other addresses near Temple Bar around 1730 (Plomer, pp. 25–25, 242–43). Maclean (p. 88) suggests a date *c*.1744.

LONDON

The London Complete Art of Cookery. Containing the Most Approved Receipts ever exhibited to the Public; Selected with Care from the newest Editions of the best Authors, French and English. Also The Complete Brewer;

Explaining the Art of Brewing Porter, Ale, Twopenny, and Table-Beer; Including the Proper Management of the Vault or Cellar. *London. Printed for William Lane, at the Minerva-Press, Leadenhall-Street. M DCC XCVII.* Frontispiece + title page + 2 lvs not num. (contents) + pp. 1–232. (BL 1406.b.7.)

The book seems to be an attempt to cash in on the success of John Farley's book, taking elements from Farley and from Mary Cole. The frontispiece shows two men-cooks at work; on a table there are pastries and a book lying open.

MACIVER [Susanna]

Cookery, and Pastry. As taught and practised by Mrs Maciver, Teacher of those Arts in Edinburgh. The Third Edition. *Edinburgh: Printed for the Author; and sold by her, at her house, Stephen Law's close, back of the City-guard. MDCCLXXXII.* Title page + pp. iii–xii (advertisement & contents) + pp. 1–238. (BL C.143.f.5.)

The first edition dates from 1773 (Maclean p. 92); the author's first name was Susanna, according to Maclean. Alexander Law ('Teachers in Edinburgh in the Eighteenth Century', 1966, p. 140) records 'Mrs. McIver' as teaching cookery in Peebles Wynd and later in Stevenlaw's Close, according to advertisements in the *Caledonian Mercury* (4 June 1768, 21 October 1786).

MARSHALL, Elizabeth

The Young Ladies' Guide in the Art of Cookery: Being a Collection of useful Receipts, Published for the Convenience of the Ladies committed to her Care. By Eliz. Marshall. *Newcastle; Printed by T. Saint, for the Author. MDCCLXXVII.* Title page + pp. iii–iv (address to ladies at her school) + pp. 1–199 + 3 lvs not num. (index); illustrations to the bills of fare in text pp. 176–199. (BL 1651/544.)

MARTIN, Sarah

The New Experienced English-Housekeeper, For the Use and Ease of Ladies, Housekeepers, Cooks, &c. Written purely from her own practice By Mrs. Sarah Martin, Many Years Housekeeper to the late Freeman Bower Esq. of Bawtry. Being An entire new Collection of original Receipts which have never appeared in Print, in every Branch of Cookery, Confectionary, &c. *Doncaster: Printed for the Authoress By D. Boys. And Sold by Mess. F. and C. Rivington, St Paul's Church-Yard, London. M DCC XCV. (Entered at Stationers' Hall)* Title pages + 2 lvs not num. (preface) + 7 lvs not num. (list of subscribers) + 1 lf not num. (blank) + pp. 1–173 + 1 p. not num. + 9 lvs not num. (index). (BL 7948.bb.4.)

There were 224 subscribers, who took 254 copies.

[MASON, CHARLOTTE]

The Lady's Assistant for Regulating and Supplying her Table; Containing One Hundred and Fifty Select Bills of Fare, Properly disposed for Family Dinners of Five Dishes, to Two Courses of Eleven and Fifteen; With upwards of Fifty Bills of Fare for Suppers, From Five Dishes to Nineteen; and Several Deserts: Including a considerable Number of Choice Receipts of Various Kinds, With full Directions for preparing them in the most approved Manner: Now First Published from the Manuscript Collection of A Professed Housekeeper; Who had upwards of Thirty Years Experience in Families of the First Fashion. *London: Printed for J. Walter, at Homer's Head, Charing Cross. M.DCC.LXXIII.* Title page + pp. iii–iv (introduction) + pp. 1–408 + 6 lvs not num. (index). (BL 1509/965.)

The name of the author appeared on the title-page of the second edition in 1775 (Oxford, pp. 107–8).

[MASSIALOT]

The Court and Country Cook: Giving New and Plain Directions How to Order all manner of Entertainments, And the best sort of the Most exquisite *a-la-mode* Ragoo's. Together with New Instructions for Confectioners: Shewing How to Preserve all sorts of Fruits, as well dry as liquid: Also, how to make divers Sugar-works, and other fine Pieces of Curiosity; How to set out a Desert, or Banquet of Sweet-meats to the best advantage; And, How to Prepare several sorts of Liquors, that are proper for every Season of the Year. A Work more especially necessary for Stewards, Clerks of the Kitchen, Confectioners, Butlers, and other Officers, and also of great use in private Families. Faithfully translated out of French into English by J. K. *London: Printed by W. Onley, for A.*

and J. Churchill, at the Black Swan in Pater-noster-row, and M. Gillyflower in
Westminster-hall, 1702. Title page + 23 lvs not num. (preface, tables, plus preface
& tables for each part) + 9 pl. + pp. 1–276 + pp. 1–130 + pp. 1–20. (BL 1608/
4960.)

This is a translation from the third edition of Le Cuisinier roïal et bourgeois
(Paris: Charles de Sercy, 1698) and the second edition of Nouvelle Instruction
pour les Confitures, les Liqueurs, et les Fruits (Paris: Charles de Sercy, 1698). These
two books had originally appeared in 1691 and in 1692 (Vicaire, pp. 573, 453–
56). Some chapters of the second book are omitted in the translation.

MELROE, ELIZA

An Economical, and New Method of Cookery; Describing upwards of Eighty
Cheap, Wholesome, and Nourishing Dishes, Consisting of Roast, Boiled, and
Baked Meats; Stews, Fries, And above Forty Soups; A Variety of Puddings, Pies,
&c. with New and Useful Observations on Rice, Barley, Pease, Oatmeal, and
Milk, and the numerous dishes they afford, Adapted to the Necessity of the
Times, Equally in all Ranks of Society, By Eliza Melroe, 'Œconomy is the Source
of Plenty.' 'Bury not your Talent' London: Printed and Published for the Author,
by C. Chapple, Nᵒ 66, Pall-Mall; sold also by T. N. Longman, Paternoster-Row,
and all other Booksellers in Town and Country. Price 2s. 6d. or six for 10. 6d. [sic]
if purchased by Clubs of the labouring Poor, or intended for their Use. 1798. Entered
at Stationer's-Hall. Title page + pp. 3–94. (BL 1037.h.16 (1).)

[MENON]

The French Family Cook: being A complete System of French Cookery.
Adapted to the Tables not only of the Opulent, but of Persons of moderate
Fortune and Condition. Containing Directions for choosing, dressing, and
serving up all Sorts of Butcher Meat, Poultry, &c. The different Modes of
making all kinds of Soups, Ragouts, Fricandeaus, Creams, Ratafias, Compôts
[sic], Preserves, &c. &c. — as well as a great Variety of cheap and elegant Side
Dishes, calculated to grace a Table at a small Expence. Instructions for making
out Bills of Fare for the four Seasons of the Year, and to furnish a Table with
few or any number of Dishes at the most moderate possible Expence. Necessary for Housekeepers, Butlers, Cooks, and all who are concerned in the

Superintendence of a Family. Translated from the French. *London: Printed for J. Bell, N° 148, Oxford Street, nearly opposite New Bond Street. M. DCC. XCIII.* Title page + 3 lvs not num. (bills of fare) + pp. iii–xxiv (contents) + pp. 1–342 + 1 lvs not num. (bookseller's advertisement). (BL 1651/426.)

This is a translation of *La Cuisinière bourgeoise* (Paris: Guillyn, 1746). The author's name appears in the 'privilège', dated 4 June 1745 (Vicaire, p. 235). A comparison of the translation and the 1775 edition (Brussels: François Foppens) shows that the English version omits the remarks on produce in season and on meats, but adds new receipts. But the translation may be from a later edition.

MIDDLETON, JOHN

Five Hundred New Receipts in Cookery, Confectionary, Pastry, Preserving, Conserving, Pickling; And the Several Branches of these Arts necessary to be known by all good Housewives. By John Middleton, Cook to His Grace the late Duke of Bolton. Revised and Recommended by Mr. Henry Howard. *London: Printed for Tho. Astley, at the Rose against the North Door of St. Paul's. M DCC XXXIV.* Title page + pp. i–iv (terms & instructions for carving) + pp. 1–249 + 8 pp. not num. (index) + 1 p. not num. (bookseller's advertisement). (BL 1037.g.18.)

MODERN

The Modern Method of Regulating and Forming a Table, Explained and Displayed. Containing A great Variety of Dinners laid out in the most elegant Taste, from two Courses of Five and Five, to Twenty-one and Twenty-one Dishes; finely represented, on One Hundred and Fifty-two Copper Plates. Together with Twelve elegant Dinners for different Seasons of the Year. And A correct List of such Particulars as are in Season during every Month. The Whole calculated for the Use and Ease of Ladies, Clerks of the Kitchen, House-Keepers, &c. By several eminent Cooks, and others well acquainted with these Arts. *Printed for J. Hughes, opposite the Duke of Grafton's, in Old Bond-Street; and S. Crowder, N°. 12, Pater-noster-Row.* Title page + pp. iii–iv (preface) + pp. i–vi (list of produce in season) + pp. 1–169 with copper-plates interleaved + 1 lf not num. + 1 folding pl. + 1 lf not num. (BL 785.m.4.)

This book devoted entirely to bills of fare dates from the period 1760–1770. The printer Stanley Crowder worked at the address indicated from 1760 to 1786 (Maxted, p. 56); J. Hughes is difficult to identify, but could be John Hughes, who is recorded as working in Holborn and Lincoln's Inn Fields between 1730 and 1771 (Plomer, p. 134). Maclean suggests a date *c*.1760. One notices the similarity of phrasing in this title and Raffald's: either this dates from after 1769, or Raffald knew this book.

MONTAGUE, Peregrine

The Family Pocket-Book: or, Fountain of true and useful Knowledge. Containing The Farrier's Guide; or, the Horse Dissected: Being the most accurate, and satisfactory Account of the Diseases incident to that noble Beast, ever yet publish'd; with their Signs, Symptoms, Prognosticks and Cures in all Cases; a certain Cure for the Glanders, without trepanning; a never-failing Cure for the Grease; and another for broken-winded Horses: wrote by way of Dialogue between a Horse-Doctor and a Groom, by a late eminent Surgeon. The best Manner of breaking a Colt, of ordering a Horse of Pleasure, and ample Directions for the management of a Race-Horse. Certain Method of preventing Chimneys from smoking, let their Form or Situation be what they will; with a Print, the better to enable those in building to prevent these great Inconveniencies for the future. The valuable Fire-ball; by the use of which, Families may make four or five Bushels of Coals go as far as forty. An excellent way to bring Singing Birds to a very great perfection, by that famous German, Lewis de Burgh. Extraordinary Method of Breeding Game-Cocks; the Manner of dieting and ordering them for Battle; sure Way of matching them: with a choice and valuable Secret for feeding a Cock four Days before fighting, communicated by a noble Lord, by which very extraordinary way of feeding, upwards of ninety Battles have been won out of a Hundred. Indian Way of marking on Silk, Linen, Woollen, &c. Curious Method of casting Urine, and how Disorders are known by it. The Art of curling, dressing, or colouring Hair. Sir Hans Sloane's valuable Cure for Disorders of the Eyes. Certain Method of preventing the Teeth from being uneven, or bad, by Sig. Curzoni, Operator of the Teeth and Gums. Mons. Rouille's Lip-Salve. The Tea-Tree, and Manner of growing it in England. Instructions for mounting Fans Manner of making Elixir of Life, Friar's Balsam, &c. The Gardener's Legacy; containing all the

Instructions necessary for the Cultivation of the Fruit, Flower, and Kitchen-Garden. With the Young Housekeeper's Guide in Cooking, Pickling, Preserving, and making all Sorts of Wines, after an easy and frugal Manner, containing near 200 choice and truly useful Receipts. Compiled after Thirty Years Experience, By Peregrine Montague, Gent. of Grange-Abbey in Oxfordshire. *London: Printed by Henry Coote, and Sold by George Paul, Bookseller near Gray's-Inn-gate, Holborn. [Price 1s. stitch'd and 1s. 6d. bound in neat red Leather.]* Title page + pp. i–viii (contents) + pp. 9–162; 2 engravings (pp. 93, 94), ill. in the text. (BL 1651/48.)

Cookery occupies pp. 132–162. This version of the book dates from *c.*1760; another version, in which medical receipts replace cookery, appeared *c.*1762 (the date is given by an inscription on the flyleaf of the British Library copy (shelfmark 1578/1725): 'February the 27th 1762 price 1s : 6d. the property of Ja: Appleyard of Bradford').

MOORE, Isabella

The Useful and Entertaining Family Miscellany: Containing the Complete English Housekeeper's Companion. In which are Near Five Hundred Receipts in Cookery, Pastry, Preserving, Making Wines, Candying, and Pickling. With plain and easy Instructions for chusing All Sorts of Eatables. Also, Directions for Carving, with several Cuts explaining in the easiest Manner the best Way of trussing Hares, and Fowls; with Forms for placing Dishes on a Table, either in the middling or genteelest Taste. By Mrs. Isabella Moore, Who was Twenty Years a worthy and frugal Housekeeper in a private Gentleman's Family at Duffield, near Derby. To which are added, The Genuine Receipts for Compounding Mr. Ward's Principal Medicines. Also Every One his own Physician: Being A complete Collection of efficacious Remedies For every Disease incident to the Human Body, with plain Instructions for their common Use; very necessary to be had in all Families, residing in the Country. Compiled at the Command of his late Royal Highness the Duke of Cumberland. Likewise, The Fair One's Pleasing Songster: Containing A Collection of above One Hundred New Songs, suited for those who Delight in Harmony, Decency, and good Sense. *London: Printed for John Smith, in the Year 1772.* Title page + 1 p. not num. (dedication to Lady Welmont, Mrs Moore's employer) + pp. iii–vii (contents) + pp. 1–110. (Leeds: Brotherton Library.)

The Brotherton Library catalogue states that this copy is incomplete, wanting pp. III–II2. The British Library has a slightly earlier copy of this book (shelfmark 1608/3716), with a very similar title-page, printed in London for Thomas Palmer in 1766; pagination: pp. vii–II2. I have not seen this copy.

MOXON, Elizabeth

English Housewifry. Exemplified In above four Hundred Receits, Never before printed; giving Directions in most Parts of Cookery; and how to prepare various Sorts of Soops, Made-Dishes, Pasts [sic], Pickles, Cakes, Creams, Jellies, Made-Wines, &c. With Sculptures for the orderly placing the Dishes, and Courses; and also Bills of Fare, for Every Month in the Year. A Book necessary for Mistresses of Families, higher and lower Women Servants, and confined to Things Useful, Substantial and Splendid, and calculated for the Preservation of Health, and upon the Measures of Frugality, being the Result of thirty Years Practice and Experience. By Elizabeth Moxon. *Leeds: Printed by J. Lister, and sold by J. Swale, J. Ogle, and S. Howgate, at Leeds; J. Lord at Wakefield; and the Author at Pontefract.* Title page + 1 lf not num. (preface) + pp. 1–209 + 12 pp. not num. (bills of fare) + 5 lvs not num. (index & errata) + 7 lvs not num. (illustrated bills of fare). (BL C.142.a.13.)

The book dates from 1741. Maclean (pp. 104–6) gives a date *c.*1741. Lynette Hunter gives the date as 1741; see 'Printing in the Pennines', in Wilson (ed.), *Traditional Food East and West of the Pennines* (1991), p. 13. Moxon adapted some of her receipts from E. Smith. The fourth edition, which was used as a source by Sarah Jackson, appeared *c.*1749.

NOTT, John

The Cook's and Confectioner's Dictionary: Or, the Accomplish'd Housewife's Companion. Containing, I. The choicest Receipts in all the several Branches of Cookery; or the best and newest Ways of dressing all sorts of Flesh, Fish, Fowl, &c. for a Common or Noble Table; with their proper Garnitures and Sauces. II. The best way of making Bisks, Farces, forc'd Meats, Marinades, Olio's, Puptons, Ragoos, Sauces, Soops, Potages, &c. according to the English, French, and Italian Courts. III. All manner of Pastry-works, as Biskets, Cakes, Cheese-cakes, Custards, Pastes, Patties, Puddings, Pyes, Tarts, &c. IV. The various Branches of Confectionary; as Candying, Conserving, Preserving, and Drying all sorts of Flowers, Fruits, Roots, &c. Also Jellies, Composts, Marmalades, and Sugar-works. V. The way of making all English potable Liquors; Ale, Beer, Cider, Mead, Metheglin, Mum, Perry, and all sorts of English Wines; Also Cordials, and Beautifying Waters. VI. Directions for ordering an Entertainment, or Bills of Fare for all Seasons of the Year; and setting out a Desert of Sweet-meats to the best Advantage: With an Explanation of the Terms us'd in Carving. According to the Practice of the most celebrated Cooks, Confectioners, &c. in the Courts of England, France, &c. and many private and accomplish'd Housewives. Revised and Recommended By John Nott, Cook to his Grace the Duke of Bolton. *London: Printed for C. Rivington, at the Bible and Crown, in St. Paul's Church-yard. MDCCXXIII.* Frontispiece + title page + 2 lvs not num. (introduction) + 1 lf not num. ('Some Divertisements in Cookery') + ? lvs not num; index at the end. (BL 1037.g.5.)

[NUTT, FREDERICK]

The Complete Confectioner; or, The Whole Art of Confectionary: Forming A Ready Assistant to all Genteel Families; Giving them a Perfect Knowledge of Confectionary: with Instructions, Neatly engraved on ten Copper-plates, How to decorate a Table with Taste and Elegance, Without the Expence or Assistance of a Confectioner. By a Person, Late an Apprentice to the well-known Messrs. Negri and Witten, of Berkley-Square. *London: Printed for the Author; and sold by J. Mathews, No. 18, Strand, M DCC LXXXIX. [Price 10s. 6d. neatly bound.] Entered at Stationers Hall.* Title page + pp. v-xxiv (preface & contents) + 10 pl. + pp. 1–212. (BL 1037.f.15.)

The author's name appears on the title-page of the fourth edition of 1807 (Maclean, p. 108). Nutt was also the author of *The Imperial and Royal Cook* (1809); see Oxford, p. 136. For Nutt's attack on Glasse's book of confectionery, see Ivan Day, 'Which *Compleat Confectioner?*', *PPC* 59 (1998), pp. 50–51.

PASTRY-COOK'S

The Pastry-Cook's Vade-Mecum: or, a Pocket-Companion for Cooks, House-Keepers, Country Gentlewomen, &c. Containing, Choice and Excellent Directions, and Receipts for making all Sorts of Pastry-Work; Dressing the most

Dainty Dishes; Candying, Preserving and Drying all manner of Fruit. As also, the Art of Distilling and Surgery. *London: Printed for Abel Roper, at the Black-Boy in Fleet-street, 1705.* Title page + 3 lvs not num. (preface) + pp. 1–100. (BL 1037.f.4.)

PECKHAM, ANN

The Complete English Cook; or, Prudent Housewife. Being An entire new Collection of the most general, yet least expensive Receipts in every Branch of Cookery and Good Housewifery. With Directions for Roasting, Boiling, Stewing, Ragoos, Soups, Sauces, Fricaseys Pies, Tarts, Puddings, Cheese-Cakes, Custards, Jellies, Potting, Candying, Collaring, Pickling, Preserving, Made-Wines, &c. Together with Directions for placing Dishes on Tables of Entertainment: And many other Things equally necessary. The Whole made easy to the meanest Capacity, and far more useful to young Beginners than any Book of the Kind extant. *In cooking Fowl, or Flesh, or Fish, / Or any nice, or dainty Dish, / With Care peruse this useful Book, / 'Twill make you soon a perfect Cook.* By Ann Peckham, of Leeds, Who is well known to have been for Forty Years past one of the most noted Cooks in the County of York. *Leeds: Printed by Griffith Wright, M, DCC, LXVII. And Sold by the Author, and J. Ogle, in Leeds; and Messrs. Robinson and Roberts, in Pater-noster-Row, London.* Title page + pp. iii–iv (preface) + pp. 5–201 + 34 pp. not num. (illustrated bills of fare) + 9 pp. not num. (index). (BL Cup.501.aaa.44.)

PHILLIPS, SARAH

The Ladies Handmaid: or, a Compleat System of Cookery; on the Principals [sic] of Elegance and Frugality. Wherein The useful Art of Cookery is rendered plain, easy and familiar: Containing The best approved, yet least expensive Receipts in every Branch of Housewifry, viz. Roasting, Boiling, Made-dishes, Soups, Sauces, Jellies, Ragouts, Fricassees, Tarts, Cakes, Creams, Custards, Pastry, Pickling, Jarring, &c. And every other Branch of Cookery and good Housewifry, too tedious to be enumerated in a Title Page. Together With Instructions for Carving and Bills of Fare for every Month in the Year. Embellished with variety of curious Copper-Plates, representing the genteelest Method of Disposing or Placing the Dishes, Trussing Fowls, &c. Also The Best approved Method of Clear-Starching. By Mrs. Sarah Phillips, of Duke-Street. *London: Printed for J. Coote, at the King's Arms, opposite Devereux-Court, in the Strand.*

M, DCC, LVIII. Frontispiece + title page + pp. 3–472 + 9 lvs not num. (contents) + 4 pl. (Leeds: Brotherton Library.)

The frontispiece shows a portrait of the author.

POWELL

The Guide to Preferment: or: Powell's Complete Book of Cookery. Containing, The Newest and Best Receipts in Cookery for, Roasting Boiling Broilling Frying Fricaseys Hashing Stewing Force-Meats Potting Ragoos Collaring Salting and Drying Soops Broth and Gravy Bakeing [sic] Pies and Pastes Tartes Puddings Cakes Cheesecakes Custards Jellies Conserving Candying Preserving and Confectionary Pickling Making Wines Likewise the best Methods of Marketing, to know the Goodness or Badness of each particular sort of Eatables, that you may want to buy of the Butchers, Poulterers, Fishmongers, Cheese-mongers, Pork Shops, Ham Shops, Bacon Wharehouses, &c. And to prevent being Cheated, With the forms of placing Dishes on a Table, either in the Middling or Genteelest Taste. Very Necessary for Ladies, Gentlemen, and their Servants. Price, 1s. 6d. *Bailey Printer, Leadenhall-Street, N° 110.* Frontispiece + title page + 5 lvs not num. (index) + pp. 9–184. (Leeds: Brotherton Library.)

The book probably dates from *c.*1770, or perhaps even earlier, as there is an inscription, 'Ellin Walshman Cook Book anno Domini 1771', in the book. The printer, William Bailey, was working at 41 Leadenhall Street from 1770 to 1785, and at 42 Bishopsgate Within from 1785 to 1790 (Maxted, p. 9). But the style of the frontispiece, which shows a kitchen scene, indicates a fairly late date. Oxford (p. 130) cites this edition and suggests a date *c.*1800. Bitting (p. 379) cites an edition printed by W. Bailey from the Bishopsgate address dated 1787.

PRICE, ELIZABETH

The New Book of Cookery; or, Every Woman a perfect Cook: Containing the greatest Variety of approved Receipts in all the Branches of Cookery and Confectionary, viz. Boiling, Roasting, Broiling, Frying, Stewing, Hashing, Baking, Fricassees, Ragouts, Made-Dishes, Soups and Sauces, Puddings, Pies and Tarts, Cakes, Custards, Cheesecakes, Creams, Syllabubs, Jellies, Pickling, Candying, Preserving, Candying, Drying, Potting, Collaring, English Wines, &c. &c. &c. To which are added, The best Instructions for Marketing, and sundry Modern

Bills of Fare; also Directions for Clear Starching, and the Ladies' Toilet, or, Art of preserving and improving Beauty: Likewise a Collection of Physical Receipts for Families, &c. The Whole calculated to assist the prudent Housewife and her Servants, in furnishing the cheapest and most elegant Set of Dishes in the various Departments of Cookery, and to instruct Ladies in many other Particulars of great Importance too numerous to mention in this Title Page. By Mrs. Eliz. Price, of Berkeley-Square, Assisted by others who have made the Art of Cookery their constant Study. A New Edition for the present Year, with great Additions. *Here you may quickly learn with Care, / To act the Housewife's Part, / And dress a modern Bill of Fare / With Elegance and Art. London: Printed for the Authoress, and sold by Alex. Hogg, N° 16, Pater-Noster-Row. [Price only One Shilling.]* Frontispiece + title page + pp. iii–iv (address to the public) + pp. 13–114 + 1 lf not num. (index) + pp. 1–24 (bookseller's advertisement); ill. to bills of fare in the text, pp. 103–106. (BL Cup.500.ii.4 (1).)

The book dates from *c.*1780. The printer, Alexander Hogg, was working at this address from about 1778 to 1805 (Maxted, p. 112). Maclean (p. 118) suggests a date *c.*1760, which seems unlikely; Oxford (p. 109) suggests a date *c.*1780.

PRICE, Elizabeth

The New, Universal, and Complete Confectioner; Being the Whole Art of Confectionary Made Perfectly Plain and Easy. Containing a Full Account of all the various Methods of Preserving and Candying, both dry and liquid, All Kinds of Fruit, Flowers, and Herbs; Also the various Ways of Clarifying Sugar; And the various Methods of Keeping Fruit, Nuts, and Flowers, Fresh and fine all the Year round. Together with Directions for making Blomonge, Biscuits, Rich-cakes, Rockworks and Candies, Custards, Jellies, Creams and Ice-creams, Whip Syllabubs and Cheese-cakes of all sorts. Sweetmeats, English Wines of all sorts, Strong Cordials, Simple Waters, Mead, Oils &c. Syrups of all kinds, Milk Punch that will keep twenty years, Knicknacks and Trifles for Deserts, &c. &c. &c. Including likewise The Modern Art of making Artificial Fruit, with the Stalks in it, so as to resemble the natural Fruit. To which, among many other useful Articles, are added, Several Bills of Fare for Deserts for Private Families, &c. &c. The whole Revised, Corrected, and Improved, By Mrs. Elizabeth Price, of Berkley Square; Author of that excellent little cheap book entitled (to distinguish it from all Old and Spurious Publications of the Kind)

The New Book of Cookery, Price only 1s. Embellished with an elegant Frontispiece. *London: Printed for A. Hogg, at the King's Arms, N° 16, Paternoster Row. [Price only 2s.] Altho' it contains more in Quantity and is better in Quality, than other Books of the Kind, which are sold at 5s.* Frontispiece + title page + 1 lf not num. (preface & start of contents) + pp. v–viii (contents) + pp. 13–171 + 1 p. not num. (advertisement for Price's other book). (Leeds: Brotherton Library.)

The frontispiece shows a richly-dressed lady handing a book to a servant. This probably dates from the same period as Price's other book, *c.*1780. This is suggested by Maclean (p. 118), who also cites another edition which she dates *c.*1760, and by Oxford (p. 110). The edition cited here is identical to Glasse's *Compleat Confectioner*; for a discussion of Price's two books of confectionery, see Day, 'Which *Compleat Confectioner*?', *PPC* 59 (1998), pp. 46–50.

PRIMITIVE

Primitive Cookery; or the Kitchen Garden display'd. Containing a Collection of Receipts For preparing a great Variety of Cheap, healthful and palatable Dishes, without either Fish, Flesh, or Fowl; With A Bill of Fare of Seventy Dishes, that will not cost above Two-pence each. Likewise Directions for pickling, gathering, and preserving Herbs, Fruits and Flowers; With many other Articles appertaining to the Product of the Kitchen-Garden, Orchard, &c. The Second Edition. With considerable Additions. *Be not amongst wine-bibbers, amongst riotous eaters of flesh: for the drunkard and the glutton shall come to poverty.* Prov. *London: Printed for J. Williams, at N° 38. Fleet-Street. 1767. [Price One Shilling.]* Title page + pp. iii–viii (on gathering & keeping fruit) + pp. 1–82. (BL 1037.e.41 (2).)

No copy of the first edition is known (Maclean, p. 119). The book follows on from the earlier *Adam's Luxury and Eve's Cookery* (1747), and indeed takes 126 of its 173 receipts from the earlier work. A further 43 receipts were lifted from a post-1758 edition of Hannah Glasse. These borrowings are described in Owen, 'Primitive Plagiarism Displayed', *PPC* 32 (1989), pp. 19–22.

RAFFALD, Elizabeth

The Experienced English House-keeper, For the Use and Ease of Ladies, House-keepers, Cooks, &c. Wrote purely from Practice, And dedicated to the Hon. Lady Elizabeth Warburton, Whom the Author lately served as House-keeper. Consisting of near 800 Original Receipts, most of which never appeared in Print. Part First, Lemon Pickle, Browning for all Sorts of Made Dishes, Soups, Fish, plain Meat, Game, Made Dishes both hot and cold, Pyes, Puddings, &c, Part Second, All Kind of Confectionary, particularly the Gold and Silver Web for covering of Sweetmeats, and a Desert of Spun Sugar, with Directions to set out a Table in the most elegant Manner and in the modern Taste, Floating Islands, Fish Ponds, Transparent Puddings, Trifles, Whips, &c. Part Third, Pickling, Potting and Collaring, Wines, Vinegars, Catchups, Distilling, with two most valuable Receipts, one for refining Malt Liquors, the other for curing Acid Wines, and a Correct List of every Thing in Season in every Month of the Year. By Elizabeth Raffald. *Manchester: Printed by J. Harrop, for the Author, and sold by Messrs. Fletcher and Anderson, in St. Paul's Church-yard, London; and by Eliz. Raffald, Confectioner, near the Exchange, Manchester, 1769. The Book to be signed by the Author's own Hand-writing, and entered at Stationers Hall.* Title page + 1 lf not num. (dedication to Lady Elizabeth Warburton) + pp. i–iii (address to the reader) + pp. 1–362 + pp. i–xi (index & errata) + 2 pl. inserted at p. 360. (BL 1037.g.23.)

Raffald had over 800 subscribers (see p. ii); the book sold for 5s. to subscribers and 6s. to the general public (see Shipperbottom, 'Elizabeth Raffald (1733–1781)', *Cooks and Other People: Proceedings of the Oxford Symposium on Food and Cookery 1995* (1996), p. 235.) Raffald's book is now more accessible in the 1997 reprint by Southover Press.

ROBERTSON, Hannah

The Young Ladies School of Arts. Containing, A great Variety of practical Receipts, in Gum-flowers Filligree Japanning Shell-work Gilding Painting Cosmetics Jellies Preserves Cakes Cordials Creams Jamms Pickles Candying Made Wines Clear Starching, &c. Also, a great many Curious Receipts, both useful and entertaining, never before published. By Mrs. Hannah Robertson The Second Edition, with large Additions. *Edinburgh: Printed by Wal.*

Ruddiman junior, For Mrs. Robertson: Sold by her, and by all the Booksellers in Scotland and England. M,DCC,LXVII. Title page + 1 lf not num. (dedication to the Countess of Northesk) + pp. v-xviii (preface & contents) + 1 lf not num. (directions to the binder & verses by Thomson) + pp. 1–171 + 3 pl. (BL 1609/2517.)

From the directions to the binder, it appears that this copy is incomplete, wanting 4 (?) plates. Cookery occupies pp. 65–136. The first edition dates from 1766 (Maclean, p. 124). The preface (p. v) indicates that the book is in two parts, the first with 'the nice arts for young Ladies', the second with cookery for 'mistresses of families, house-keepers, and others'; but in fact, there is no division into two parts in the book.

SHACKLEFORD, Ann

The Modern Art of Cookery Improved; or, Elegant, Cheap, and Easy Methods, of preparing most of the Dishes now in Vogue; In the Composition whereof both Health and Pleasure have been consulted, By Mrs. Ann Shackleford, of Winchester. To which is added, An Appendix; Containing a Dissertation on the different Kinds of Food, their Nature, Quality, and various Uses. By a Phycisian [sic]. And A Marketing Manual, And other useful Particulars. By the Editor. *She turns, on hospitable thoughts intent, / What choice to chuse for delicacy best; / What order, so contriv'd as not to mix / Tastes, not well join'd, inelegant, but bring / Taste after Taste, upheld with kindliest change.* Milton. *London: Printed for J. Newbery, at the Bible and Sun, in St. Paul's Church-Yard; and F. Newbery, in Pater-noster-Row. 1767.* Title page + pp. iii–xxiv (preface & marketing manual) + pp. 1–284 + + 7 lvs not num. (index). (BL 1607/1754.)

SKEAT, J.

The Art of Cookery and Pastery made easy and familiar, in upwards of Two hundred different Receipts and Bills of Fare, never before made public. To which is added, A Variety of Tables for Forms of Entertainment, And an exact Representation of the Tables at the Guild-Feasts of Norwich and Lynn. By J. Skeat, Cook. *London: Printed for the Author and Sold by him at his House next Door to the Maid's Head, in St. Simon's; and by J. Crouse, at the Back of the Inns, Norwich. Price Two Shillings and Six pence.* Title page + 1 lf not num. (directions

to all cooks & registration at Stationers Hall) + pp. 5–48 + 10 lvs not num. (bills of fare & explanation of cookery terms) + 2 folding pp. (guild-feast bill of fare) + 2 lvs not num. (index). (BL 1037.g.27.)
The registration at Stationers' Hall is dated 19 June 1769.

SMITH, A.

A New Book of Cookery; Or, Every Woman a Perfect Cook; Containing a very great variety of approved Receipts in all branches of Cookery and Confectionary, viz. Marketing, Roasting, Boiling, Broiling, Frying, Stewing, Hashing, Baking, Fricassees, Made Dishes, Soups, Sauces, Puddings, Pies and Tarts, Cakes, Custards, Cheese-cakes, Creams, Ragouts, Jellies, Pickling, Preserving, Drying, Potting, Candying, Collaring, English Wines, &c. To which is added, Directions for Clear Starching, and the Ladie's [sic] Toilet, or the Art of preserving and improving Beauty: Likewise a Collection of Family Physical Receipts, prepared at a small expence. The whole calculated to assist the prudent Housewife in furnishing the cheapest and most elegant Set of Dishes in the various Departments of Cookery, and to instruct the Ladies in many other Particulars of great Importance. Written by Mrs. A. Smith, of Stafford, Who has been a House-keeper to several Noble Families Many Years. *The Art of Cookery here Complete youll' [sic] find, / Frugality and Taste at once combin'd, / To Roast, Boil, Bake, Confectionary raise, / And All that marks th'industrious Housewife's praise. London: Printed in the Year 1781.* Title page + pp. 3–219 + 5 pp. not num (index). (Leeds: Brotherton Library.)

The Brotherton Library catalogue and Maclean (p. 133) ascribe this book to 'Alice Smith', but this author may not be the same person as the Alice Smith who published *The Art of Cookery* in 1758.

S[MITH], E.

The Compleat Housewife: or, Accomplished Gentlewoman's Companion: Being a Collection of upwards of Five Hundred of the most approved Receipts in Cookery, Pastry, Confectionary, Preserving, Pickles, Cakes, Creams, Jellies, Made Wines, Cordials. With Copper Plates curiously engraven for the regular Disposition or Placing the various Dishes and Courses. And also Bills of Fare for every Month in the Year. To which is added, A Collection of near Two

Hundred Family Receipts of Medicines; viz. Drinks, Syrups, Salves, Ointments, and various other Things of sovereign and approved Efficacy in most Distempers, Pains, Aches, Wounds, Sores, &c. never before made publick; fit either for private Families, or such publick-spirited Gentlewomen as would be beneficent to their poor Neighbours. By E— S— The Second Edition. *London: Printed for J. Pemberton, at the Golden Buck, over-against St. Dunstan's Church in Fleet-street. M. DCC. XXVIII.* Title page + 5 lvs not num. (preface) + 2 lvs not num. (bills of fare) + pp. 1–318 + 6 pl. + pp. i–xv (index) + 9 lvs not num. (bookseller's advertisement). (BL 1609/460 (1).)

The first edition dates from 1727, and cost 5s. 6d. (Maclean, p. 133). Maclean and all other bibliographies give her name as Eliza Smith; Maclean states that 'she gave her name in subsequent editions', but this edition gives no name, and only after the author's death was the name expanded to E. Smith, in the fifth edition of 1733 (which Oxford, p. 60, gives as 1732). The sixth edition of 1734 also contains this information:

The Compleat Housewife. ... By E. Smith. The Sixth Edition, with very large Additions; near Fifty Receipts being communicated just before the Author's Death. *London: Printed for J. Pemberton, at the Golden Buck, over-against St. Dunstan's Church in Fleet-street. 1734. Price Five Shillings.* Title page + 5 lvs not num. (preface) + 2 lvs not num. (bills of fare) + pp. 1–352 + pp. i–xv (index) + 5 pl. (BL 1508/1110.)

I have been unable to find any copy giving the author's first name as Eliza. As Genevieve Yost remarks, there is no evidence for this name (Yost, 'The Compleat Housewife or Accomplish'd Gentlewoman's Companion: A Bibliographical Study', *William and Mary College Quarterly* 18 (4), October 1938, p. 427).

SMITH, Mary

The Complete House-keeper, and Professed Cook. Calculated For the greater Ease and Assistance of Ladies, House-keepers, Cooks, &c. &c. Containing upwards of Seven Hundred practical and approved Receipts, under the following Heads: I. Rules for Marketing. II. Boiling, Roasting, and Broiling Flesh, Fish, and Fowls; and for making Soups and Sauces of all Kinds. III. Making Made Dishes of all Sorts, Puddings, Pies, Cakes, Fritters, &c. IV.

Pickling, Preserving, and making Wine in the best Manner and Taste. V.
Potting and Collaring; Aspikes in Jellies; savoury Cakes, Blamonge, Ice Creams
and other Creams, Whips, Jellies, &c. VI. Bills of Fare for every Month in the
Year; with a correct List of every Thing in Season for every Month; illustrated
with two elegant Copper-plates of a First and Second Course for a genteel
Table. By Mary Smith, late House-keeper to Sir Walter Blackett, Bart. and
formerly in the Service of the Right Hon. Lord Anson, Sir Tho. Sebright, Bart.
and other Families of Distinction, as House-keeper and Cook. *Newcastle:
Printed by T. Slack, for the Author. 1772.* Title page + pp. iii–v (preface) + 1 lf not
num. (index) + pp. 9–392. (BL 7946.c.49.)

SMITH, R[ICHARD]

Court Cookery: or, the Compleat English Cook. Containing the Choicest and
Newest Receipts For making Soops, Pottages, Fricasseys, Harshes [sic], Farces,
Ragoos, Cullises, Sauces, Forc'd-Meats and Souses; with various Ways of
Dressing most Sorts of Flesh, Fish and Fowl, Wild and Tame; with the best
Methods of Potting and Collaring. As Likewise of Pastes, Pies, Pastys, Pattys,
Puddings, Tansies, Biskets, Creams, Cheesecakes, Florendines, Cakes, Jellies,
Sillabubs and Custards. Also Of Pickling, Candying and Preserving: With a Bill
of Fare for every Month in the Year, and the latest Improvements in Cookery,
&c. By R. Smith, Cook (under Mr. Lamb) to King William; as also to the
Dukes of Buckingham, Ormond, D'Aumont (the French Ambassador) and
others of the Nobility and Gentry. *London: Printed for T. Wotton, at the Three
Daggers in Fleet-Street. MDCCXXIII.* Title page + 3 lvs not num. (address 'To
the Nobility and Gentry of Great Britain') + pp. 1–112 + 4 lvs not num. (index)
+ pp. 1–82 + 5 lvs not num. (index to part 2) + 2 lvs not num. (bookseller's
advertisement). (BL 1037.g.6.)

Maclean (p. 137) and the BL catalogue give the author's first name as Robert,
but a comparison of the information given in the book and documents in the
Public Record Office show that his name was Richard. The address states: 'I was
near eight Years under Mr. Lamb'; the Cheque Roll of Warrants of James II,
William III, and Anne shows that Richard Smith was admitted on 30 March
1689 as a turnspit in the household kitchen (PRO LS 13/10, f. 14v.); the
Establishment Book for April 1689 gives his name and position: he received
boardwages only of £30 (PRO LS 13/39, f. 21). In the Establishment Book for

October 1699, Richard Smith is listed as receiving his boardwages, but his name is amongst those of servants no longer employed (PRO LS 13/40, f. 26). This reference appears again in the next Establishment Book for October 1701 (PRO LS 13/40, p. 24). A Robert Smith does appear in the royal warrants, but since he was being promoted from youngest groom of the slaughterhouse to youngest yeoman in 1662 (PRO LS 13/252, f. 229), he would have been too old to be 'our' R. Smith. Since the documents suggest a period of employment of under 10 years, it seems certain that Richard Smith is the R. Smith of the cookery-book.

Smith took a few of his receipts from Patrick Lamb, with some adaptation, the implication being that these versions were more authentic, since Smith declares in his address that 'several of those Receipts, as they are now printed in His Royal Cookery, were never made or practis'd by him; and others are extreme defective or imperfect'. But Smith has far more receipts which also appear in Edward Kidder's book (see Simon Varey, 'New Light on Edward Kidder's *Receipts*', *PPC* 39 (1991), p. 49), although, as Varey points out, Smith complains that his own receipts had been 'publish'd to the World, as the Labours of other People'. Thus it is difficult to say who plagiarized whom here.

Since the above notice was written, David Potter's essay, 'Some Notes on Edward Kidder' in *PPC* 65 (2000), pp. 9–27, delves further into Smith's plagiarism, and establishes that Smith took 98 receipts for his 1723 edition, and returned to the source for a further 19 receipts for his second edition. Since Kidder was probably using his book for teaching purposes well before the publication of *Court Cookery*, it looks as though Smith is the plagiarist here, although the fact that some of Smith's borrowed receipts appear only in the manuscript version of Kidder still leaves a remote possibility that he was re-appropriating his own receipts.

The British Library also has the second edition, dated 1725 but with the inscription 'Alicia Snape her book given her by her Grandpapa Joseph: Hayes Feb 16: 1724':

Court Cookery: …. The Second Edition, with large Additions. *London: Printed for T. Wotton, at the Three-Daggers in Fleet-Street, M.DCC.XXV.* Title page + 4 lvs not num. (address) + pp. 1–218 + 7 lvs not num. (index). (BL Cup.404.i.16.)

TAYLOR, E.

The Lady's, Housewife's, and Cookmaid's Assistant: or, the Art of Cookery Explained and Adapted to the meanest Capacity. Containing, I. How to roast and boil to perfection every thing necessary to be sent up to table. II. Of made-dishes. III. To make a number of pretty little dishes for a supper or side-dish, and little corner dishes for a great table. IV. To dress fish. V. Of soups and broths. VI. Of puddings. VII. Of pies. VIII. Of hogs puddings, sausages, &c. IX. To pot and make hams, &c. X. Of pickling. XI. Of making cakes, &c. XII. Of cheese cakes, creams, jellies, whip-syllabubs, &c. XIII. Of made-wines, brewing, French bread, muffins, &c. XIV. Jarring cherries, preserves. XV. To dress turtle, and make mock turtle. The whole designed to fit out an Entertainment In an Elegant Manner, and at a Small Expence. By E. Taylor. *Berwick upon Tweed: Printed by H. Taylor, for R. Taylor, Bookseller. MDCCLXIX.* Title page + pp. iii–xii (list of subscribers) + pp. 1–276 + 6 lvs not num. (marketing table & index). (BL 1037.f.14.)

There were 163 subscribers, who took 176 copies.

THACKER, JOHN

The Art of Cookery. Containing Above Six Hundred and Fifty of the most approv'd Receipts heretofore published, under the following Heads, viz. Roasting, Boiling, Frying, Broiling, Baking, Fricasees, Puddings, Custards, Cakes, Cheese-Cakes, Tarts, Pyes, Soops, Made-Wines, Jellies, Candying, Pickling, Preserving, Pastry, Collering, Confctionary [sic], Creams, Ragoos, Brasing, &c. &c. Also, a Bill of Fare For every Month in the Year. With an Alphabetical Index to the Whole: Being A Book highly necessary for all Families, having the Grounds of Cookery fully display'd therein. By John Thacker, Cook to the Honourable and Reverend the Dean and Chapter in Durham. *Newcastle upon Tyne: Printed by I. Thompson and Company. MDCCLVIII.* Title page + 5 lvs not num. (preface, index & errata) + pp. 1–322 + 16 lvs not num. (bills of fare). (BL 7948.bb.6.)

The British Library is incomplete, wanting part of the index, from K to S. Thacker's book originally came out as a part-work in 1746 (see Lynette Hunter, 'Printing in the Pennines', in Wilson (ed.), *Traditional Food East and West of the Pennines* (1991), p. 15).

TOWNSHEND, JOHN

The Universal Cook; or, Lady's Complete Assistant. Containing Every Thing that is Valuable in every Book of the Kind hitherto published, together with great Variety of Original Receipts, of the Author's own Composition, and others communicated to him by his Friends who are celebrated in the Culinary Art. The Whole forming A perfect and complete System of Cookery, and will be found, upon Perusal, to be superior to any of those Books of Cookery, which are sold at double the Price. Near Eight Hundred of very valuable Receipts are to be found in this Book, under the following Heads viz. Puddings, Pies, Tarts, Custards, Pasties, Creams, Cakes, Ragoos, Fricaseys, Soups, Broths, Pickling, Conserving, Preserving, &c. Together with Directions for Roasting and Boiling; also the complete Art of Clear-Starching, &c. The Plan of the Author has been, to render this Performance as useful as possible, by affixing a moderate Price to it, and by making Use of a fine small Type, to bring a large Quantity of Matter into a narrow Compass, a Circumstance which, at the same Time, makes it more portable and convenient. By John Townshend, Late Master of the Greyhound Tavern, Greenwich, and Cook to his Grace the Duke of Manchester. *London: Printed for S. Bladon, at Nº 28. in Paternoster-Row. MDCCLXXIII.* Title page + 1 lf not num. (preface) + 6 lvs not num. (contents) + pp. 1–308. (BL 1607/2513.)

VALUABLE

Valuable Secrets concerning Arts and Trades: or approved Directions, from the best Artists, For the various methods Of engraving on Brass, Copper, or Steel. Of the Composition of Metals. Of Varnishes. Of Mastichs, Cements, Sealing-Wax, &c. &c. Of the Glass Manufactory. Various Imitations of Precious Stones, and French Paste. Of Colours and Painting, useful for Carriage Painters. Of Painting on Paper. Of Compositions for Limners. Of transparent Colours. Colours to dye Skins or Gloves. To colour or varnish Copper-plate Prints. Of Painting on Glass. Of Colours of all Sorts, for Oil, Water, and Crayons. Of preparing the Lapis Lazuli, to make Ultramarine. Of the Art of Gilding. The Art of Dying Woods, Bones, &c. The Art of Casting in Moulds. Of making useful Sorts of Ink. The Art of Making Wines. Of the Composition of Vinegars. Of Liquors, Essential Oils, &c. Of the Confectionary Business. The Art of preparing Snuffs. Of taking out Spots and Stains. Art of Fishing,

Angling, Bird-catching, &c. And Subjects curious, entertaining, and useful. Containing upwards of One Thousand approved Receipts relative to Arts and Trades. *Hae tibi erunt Artes!* Virg. *London: Printed and Sold by Will. Hay, Printer and Bookseller to the Society of Artists of Great Britain, at his Shop next Door to their Exhibition-hall, near Exeter 'Change, Strand. MDCCLXXV.* Title page + 3 lvs not num. (dedication & preface) + pp. xxxiv (contents) + pp. 1–312. (BL 7949.a.31.)

There are sections on wines (pp. 219–227), vinegars (pp. 228–231), liquors and essential oils (pp. 232–260), and confectionery (pp. 261–291).

VERRAL, William

A Complete System of Cookery. In which is set forth, A Variety of genuine Receipts, collected from several Years Experience under the celebrated Mr. de St. Clouet, sometime since Cook to his Grace the Duke of Newcastle. By William Verral, Master of the White-Hart Inn in Lewes, Sussex. Together with an Introductory Preface, Shewing how every Dish is brought to Table, and in what Manner the meanest Capacity shall never err in doing what his Bill of Fare contains. To which is added, A true Character of Mons. de St. Clouet. *London, Printed for the Author, and sold by him; As also by Edward Verral Bookseller, in Lewes: And by John Rivington in St. Paul's Church-yard, London. M DCC LIX.* Title page + 6 lvs not num. (contents) + pp. i–xxxiii (preface) + pp. 1–240. (BL 1037.g.21.)

This book is now more accessible in the 1988 reprint by Southover Press.

WHOLE

[The Whole Duty of a Woman: or a Guide to the Female Sex, from the Age of Sixteen to Sixty, &c. Being Directions, How Women of all Qualities and Conditions, ought to Behave themselves in the various Circumstances of this Life, for their Obtaining not only Present, but Future Happiness. I. Directions how to Obtain the Divine and Moral Vertues of Piety, Meekness, Modesty, Chastity, Humility, Compassion, Temperance and Affability, with their Advantages, and how to avoid the Opposite Vices. II. The Duty of Virgins, Directing them what they ought to do, and what to avoid for gaining all the Accomplishments required in that State. With the Whole Art of Love, &c. 3.

The Whole Duty of a Wife. 4. The Whole Duty of a Widow, &c. Also Choice Receipts in Physick and Chirurgery. With the Whole Art of Cookery, Preserving, Candying, Beautifying, &c. Written by a Lady. The Third Edition. *London, Printed for J. Guillim; against the great James Tavern in Bishopsgate-street. 1701.]* pp. 1–184. (BL 1477.a.38.)

The British Library copy has lost its title-page. The details given here are taken from Oxford (pp. 46–47).

WHOLE

The Whole Duty of a Woman: Or, an infallible Guide to the Fair Sex. Containing, Rules, Directions, and Observations, for their Conduct and Behaviour through all Ages and Circumstances of Life, as Virgins, Wives, or Widows. With Directions, how to obtain all Useful and Fashionable Accomplishments suitable to the Sex. In which are comprised all Parts of Good Housewifry, particularly Rules and Receipts in every Kind of Cookery. 1. Making all Sorts of Soops and Sauces. 2. Dressing Flesh, Fish, and Fowl; this last illustrated with Cuts, shewing how every Fowl, Wild or Tame, is to be trust for the Spit: Likewise all other Kind of Game. 3. Making above 40 different Sorts of Puddings. 4. The whole Art of Pastry in making Pies, Tarts, and Pasties. 5. Receipts for all Manner of Pickling, Collaring, &c. 6. For Preserving, making Creams, Jellies, and all Manner of Confectionary. 7. Rules and Directions for setting out Dinners, Suppers and Grand Entertainments. To which is added, Bills of Fare for every Month in the Year, curiously engraven on Copper Plates, with the Forms of Tables and Dishes, and the Shapes of Pies, Tarts, and Pasties. With Instructions for Marketing. Also Rules and Receipts for making all the choicest Cordials for the Closet: Brewing Beers, Ales, &c. Making all Sorts of English Wines, Cyder, Mum, Mead, Metheglin, Vinegar, Verjuice, Catchup, &c. With some fine Perfumes, Pomatums, Cosmeticks and other Beautifiers. *London: Printed for T. Read, in Dogwell-Court, White-Fryers, Fleet-Street. MDCCXXXVII.* Title page + 1 lf not num. (contents) + pp. 3–694 + 10 fig. + 15 pl. inserted between pp. 496–497 + 24 pl. inserted between pp. 630–631. (BL 07942.de.27.)

Cookery occupies pp. 177–694. With the second edition in 1740, the title becomes *The Lady's Companion* (Maclean, pp. 150–151), and all the moralizing disappears.

WILLIAMS, T.

The Accomplished Housekeeper; and Universal Cook. Containing all the various Branches of Cookery; Directions for Roasting, Boiling and Made Dishes, Also for Frying, Broiling, Stewing, Mincing, and Hashing. The different Methods of Dressing Poultry, Game, and Fish, And of Preparing Soups, Gravies, Cullices, and Broths, To dress Roots and Vegetables, And to make all Sorts of Pies, Puddings, Pancakes, Fritters; Cakes, Puffs, and Biscuits; Cheesecakes, Tarts, and Custards; Creams and Jams; Blanc Mange, Flummery, Jellies, and Syllabubs. The various Articles in Candying, Drying, Preserves, and Pickling; the Preparation of Hams, Tongues, Bacon, and of Made Wines and Cordial Waters. Directions for Carving. With a Catalogue of the various Articles in Season every Month in the Year. By T. Williams, and the principal Cooks at the London and Crown and Anchor Taverns. *London: Printed for J. Scatcherd, Nº 12, Ave-Maria-Lane. 1797. [Price Three Shillings sewed.]* Title page + frontispiece + pp. iii–xvi (preface & contents) + 12 lvs not num. (pl. of bills of fare) + pp. 1–274. (BL 1037.e.42 (1).)

The editors' preface (p. iii) says that this is an abridged edition of Collingwood & Woollams, printed in smaller type, to make the book cheaper. In fact, this is another book by Richard Johnson, who received 8 guineas for 'compiling' it in 1792. (See Peter Targett, 'Richard Johnson or John Farley?', *PPC* 58 (1998), p. 32.)

WILSON, MARY

The Ladies Complete Cookery; or, Family Pocket Companion, Made Plain and Easy; Being The best Collection of the Choicest and least extravagant Receipts in every Branch of Cookery, Pastry, Preserving, Candying, Pickling, Collaring, &c. With Plain and easy Directions for Marketing, with the Seasons of the Year for Butcher's Meat, Poultry, Fish, &c. &c. Also The Art of making Wines, Brewing, making French Bread, &c. To which is added, Family Receipts for the Cure of several Disorders incident to the Human Body. By Mrs. Mary Wilson, of Hertfordshire. *London: Printed for the Authoress, and sold by J. Roson, No. 54. St. Martin's le Grand. [Price sewed 1s. 6d. bound 2s.]* Title page + 1 lf not num. (contents) + pp. 1–188. (BL Cup.407.i.30.)

The book dates from the 1770s. Maclean (p. 152) suggests *c.*1770, citing the Cambridge University Library catalogue. The British Library catalogue says *c.*1777. The book is at least partly plagiarized from Hannah Glasse's *Art of Cookery.*

YOUNG

The Young Lady's Companion in Cookery And Pastry, Preserving, Pickling, Candying, &c. Containing The newest and best Receipts for making all Sorts of Broths, Gravies, Soups, Ragoo's, Hashes, &c. Dressing several Sorts of Meats, Collering [sic], Potting, and making Force-Meats, &c. Also Making of Cakes, Creams, Jellies, Marmalades, Tarts, Puddings, Pies, Pasties, Biscuits, Custards, &c. Likewise Preserving and Candying Angelico [sic], Apples, Cherries, Currants, Figs, Goosberries, Grapes, Oranges, Peaches, Nectarines, &c. Violets, Roses, Cowslips, and other Flowers. And The best Methods of Pickling Melons, Cucumbers, Barberries, Mushrooms, Purslane, &c. *London: Printed for A. Bettesworth and C. Hitch in Pater-noster Row, J. Hazard against Stationers Hall, W. Bickerton and C. Corbett, without Temple-bar, and R. Willock, in Cornhill, 1734.* Title page + 5 lvs not num. (address & contents) + pp. 1–204. (BL 1037.f.9.)

The address announces that 'The following Receipts were Collected by a Gentlewoman who formerly kept a Boarding School; her often being Importun'd by her Friends, for Copies of them, has occasion'd their being published.'

SELECT BIBLIOGRAPHY

This bibliography contains details of all the primary and secondary sources used for the study. There is, however, such a wealth of information to be found in every issue of *Petits Propos Culinaires* (here referred to as *PPC*)and in the various volumes of the *Proceedings of the Oxford Symposium on Food and Cookery* that to mention every article containing useful information would have resulted in a totally unwieldy list. Thus only articles from these sources which are specifically cited in the text are included here. I have, however, included books which, although not cited, offer the useful background information which lies behind the ideas in this book.

For the full text of the title-pages of the eighteenth-century cookery books, with a brief description of the contents, and comments on dates, sources and bibliographical puzzles where appropriate, the reader is referred to Appendix III.

MANUSCRIPTS

PUBLIC RECORD OFFICE
C 107/108, Margaretta Acworth's cookery receipts.
LC 5/42, 53, 68, Lord Chamberlain's warrants referring to Patrick Lamb.
LC 5/180, 196, Ordinances of the household of Charles I, Charles II, James II.
LS 9/50–55, Extraordinary diets, 1680–1714.
LS 9/78–226, Royal bills of fare, 1660–1812.
LS 13/10, Cheque Roll of warrants, James II, William III, Anne.
LS 13/39–41, 44, Establishment books, 1689, 1699, 1701, 1714.
LS 13/115, Minutes of the meetings of the Board of Green Cloth, 1714–26.
LS 13/251–267, Warrant books, 1626–1821.
T 48/10, Establishment books, 1664–1709.

KENT RECORD OFFICE, MAIDSTONE
U49 F15, Mary Watts' cookery receipts, mid-17th century, and later additions.
U269 F38/2, Lady Rachel Fane's receipt book, mostly medicinal, mid-17th century.

NORFOLK RECORD OFFICE, NORWICH
HMN 4/5, Hamond family receipt book, *c.*1739–79, cookery at one end, remedies at the other.
MC 443/1, Jane Frere's receipt book, 1742–1813, mostly medicinal.
WKC 6/12, Katherine Windham's memorandum book, 1669–1689.
WKC 6/457, Katherine Windham's receipt book, cookery and preserving, dated 1707 but with receipts into 1720s.

BRITISH LIBRARY, MANUSCRIPTS DEPARTMENT
Additional MS 29739, Elizabeth Sloane's fair copy of Mary Eales's receipt book, dated 1711 (perhaps an error for 1721?).

Additional MS 30244, Anne Nicholson's receipt book, culinary and medicinal, dated 1707 but with later additions in other hands.

Additional MS 32694–33331 (Newcastle papers)

—— 32694, contains a letter from Verral to Newcastle about a vacancy in the Post Office, 1740.

—— 32704, contains a petition to Sir Francis Poole signed by Verral, 1745.

—— 32734, contains correspondence between Clouet and Newcastle, 1754.

—— 32864, contains a request from Verral to Newcastle about a job for Verral's brother Manfield, 1756.

—— 33066, contains a list of Newcastle's servants in 1752; also correspondence from Newcastle to Colonel James Pelham, on cooks, 1752; also Richard Davis's letter to Newcastle applying for the job as Newcastle's cook, 1752.

—— 33072, contains Clouet's letter setting out his terms to take the position of Newcastle's cook, undated.

—— 33074, contains correspondence from Newcastle to his duchess, about the new cook, Hervé, 1753.

—— 33137, contains wage lists for Newcastle's household, 1733–35; also records of payments to William Verral in Lewes in 1738.

—— 33158, Samuel Burt's accounts for Newcastle's household, 1742–52, including several payments to Verral in Lewes.

—— 33321, contains James Waller's accounts for Newcastle's household, 1737–54, including payments to Verral, Clouet, and Jorre.

—— 33322, Newcastle's trustees' accounts, 1738–51.

—— 33325–31, bills of fare for Newcastle in London and at Claremont, 1761–66.

Additional MS 42173, Caroline Lybbe Powys's receipt book, some culinary and medicinal, mostly household hints and hobbies, dated 1762 but added to until 1797.

Additional MS 45196, Anne Glyd's commonplace book, containing family memoranda followed by culinary receipts, mostly for preserving, at one end, with medical receipts at the other end, dated 1656 but added to until much later.

Additional MS 45718, Elizabeth Freke's commonplace book, containing culinary and medicinal receipts, diary, memoranda, family letters, religious writings, dated 1684, added to until 1712.

Sloane 3274, receipt book, cookery, confectionery and medicinal, no date.

Stowe 1080, Katherine Lowther's receipt book, confectionery and hobbies, 18th-century copy of 17th-century receipts.

Printed Primary Sources

Abbot, Robert, *The Housekeeper's Valuable Present* (London: the Author, [*c.*1790]).

—— also another edition (Penrith: J. Brown, 1804).

Abdy, Stotherd, 'Journal of a Visit into Berkshire', in Houblon, Lady Alice Archer, *The Houblon Family: Its Story and Times* (London, 1907), vol. 2, pp. 118–151.

The Accomplish'd Housewife; or, the Gentlewoman's Companion (London: J. Newbery, 1745).

The Accomplished Lady's Delight in Cookery; or, the Complete Servant's-Maid's Guide (Wolverhampton: J. Smart, [*c*.1780]).

Adam's Luxury, and Eve's Cookery; or, the Kitchen-Garden display'd (London: R. Dodsley, 1744); also a facsimile reprint (London, 1983).

Adeane, J. H. (ed.), *The Girlhood of Maria Josepha Holroyd (Lady Stanley of Alderley), Recorded in Letters of a Hundred Years Ago: From 1776 to 1796* (London, 1896).

Alexander, Russell George (ed.), *A Plain Plantain* (Ditchling, 1922), Susanna Avery's MS receipt book, dated 1688.

[Andrews, John], *An Account of the Character and Manners of the French; With occasional Observations on the English*, 2 vols (London: E. & C. Dilly, J. Robson, J. Walter, 1770).

Anson, Elizabeth, & Florence Anson (eds), *Mary Hamilton, afterwards Mrs. John Dickenson, at Court and at Home, from Letters and Diaries, 1756 to 1816* (London, 1925).

Archenholz, Johann Wilhelm von, *England und Italien*, 5 vols (ed. 2, Karlsruhe: Christian Gottlieb Schmieder, 1791).

Ashmole, Elias, *The Institution, Laws and Ceremonies of the most Noble Order of the Garter* (London: J. Macock, for Nathanael Brooke, 1672).

['Atkyns, Arabella'] (pseud.), *The Family Magazine* (London: J. Osborn, 1741).

Audiger, *La Maison réglée* (1692), ed. Gilles & Laurence Laurendon, in *L'art de la cuisine française au XVIIe siècle* (Paris, 1995).

Austin, Thomas (ed.), *Two Fifteenth-Century Cookery-Books* (London: Early English Text Society, 1888).

Ayres, Jack (ed.), *Paupers and Pig Killers: The Diary of William Holland, A Somerset Parson, 1799–1818* (1984; Harmondsworth, 1986).

Bailey, N[athan], *Dictionarium Domesticum* (London: C. Hitch, C. Davis, S. Austen, 1736).

Baines, Anna, & Jean Imray, *Elizabeth Serrell of Wells: Her Recipes and Remedies* (Richmond, Surrey / Wells Museum, 1986).

Balderston, Katharine C. (ed.), *Thraliana*, 2 vols (Oxford, 1951).

Balston, Thomas (ed.), *The Housekeeping Book of Susanna Whatman, 1776–1800* (London, 1956).

Barker, Anne, *The Complete Servant Maid: or Young Woman's best Companion* (London: J. Cooke, [*c*.1770]).

The Bath and Bristol Guide: or, the Tradesman's and Traveller's Pocket-Companion (ed. 4, Bath: J. Keene, [*c*.1760]).

The Bath Cookery Book, and Housekeepers' Assistant (Bath: the Author, [*c*.1790]).

Battam, Anne, *A Collection of scarce and valuable Receipts* (London: the Author, 1750).

—— also the 2nd edition, with a new title, *The Lady's Assistant in the Œconomy of the Table* (London: R. & J. Dodsley, 1759).

Beale, Catherine Hutton (ed.), *Reminiscences of a Gentlewoman of the last Century: Letters of Catherine Hutton, Daughter of William Hutton* (Birmingham, 1891).

Beauty's Triumph: or, the Superiority of the Fair Sex invincibly proved (London: J. Robinson, 1751); the 'Sophia' pamphlets.

Bédoyère, Guy de la (ed.), *The Diary of John Evelyn* (Bangor, 1994).

Beresford, John (ed.), *The Diary of a Country Parson: The Reverend James Woodforde, 1758–1781*, 5 vols (London, 1924–31).

Blencowe, Ann, *The Receipt Book of Mrs. Ann Blencowe*, intro. G. Saintsbury (London, 1925).

Blundell, Margaret (ed.), *Blundell's Diary and Letter Book, 1702–1728* (Liverpool, 1952).

Bocage, [Marie Anne Fiquet du], 'Lettres sur l'Angleterre', in *Recueil des Œuvres de Madame du Bocage*, 3 vols (Lyon: Perisse, 1762), vol. 3, pp. 5–77.

The Book of Conversation and Behaviour (London: R. Griffiths, 1754).

A Book of Fruits and Flowers (London: M. S. for Thomas Jenner, 1653); also a facsimile reprint, introduction and glossary by C. Anne Wilson (London, 1984).

Boorde, Andrew, *A Compendyous Regyment or A Dietary of Helth* (1542), reprint ed. F. J. Furnivall (London: Early English Text Society, 1870).

[Borella], *The Court and Country Confectioner: or, the House-keeper's Guide* (London: G. Riley & A. Cooke, J. Bell, J. Wheble, C. Etherington, 1770); also the 2nd edition, described as 'new' (London: G. Riley, J. Bell, J. Wheble, C. Etherington, 1772).

Bradley, Martha, *The British Housewife: or, the Cook, Housekeeper's, and Gardiner's Companion* (2 vols, London: S. Crowder & H. Woodgate, [1756]); also a facsimile reprint, introduction by Gilly Lehmann, 6 vols (Totnes, 1996–9).

Bradley, Richard, *The Country Housewife and Lady's Director* (London: Woodman & Lyon, 1727); also a 2nd part (London: D. Browne, T. Woodman, 1732); also a facsimile of the 1736 edition, with parts 1 and 2, ed. Caroline Davidson (London, 1980).

Bradshaw, Penelope, & [Edward] Lambert, *Bradshaw's Valuable Family Jewel* (ed. 10, London: P. Bradshaw, 1748).

Bradshaw, Penelope, *The Family Jewel, and Compleat Housewife's Companion* (ed. 7, revised by E. H., London: R. Whitworth, 1754).

Brathwait, Richard, *The English Gentlewoman* (1631; facsimile reprint, Amsterdam, New York, 1970).

Briggs, Richard, *The English Art of Cookery* (London: G. G. J. & J. Robinson: 1788); also the 3rd edition (London: G. G. J. & J. Robinson: 1794).

The British Jewel, or, Complete Housewife's Best Companion (London: J. Miller, 1776).

—— also another edition, with a slightly different title: *The New British Jewel, or, Complete Housewife's Best Companion* (London: Osborne & Griffin, H. Mozley, 1788).

Brooks, Catharine, *The Complete English Cook; or Prudent Housewife* ([1762]; ed. 2, London: the Authoress, [c.1765]).

Bruyn Andrews, C. (ed.), *The Torrington Diaries*, 4 vols (London, 1934–38).

Buttes, Henry, *Dyets Dry Dinner* (London: Tho. Creede for William Wood, 1599).

Campbell, R., *The London Tradesman* (1747; facsimile reprint, Newton Abbot, 1969).

Carbery, Mary (ed.), *Mrs. Elizabeth Freke Her Diary* (Cork, 1913).

Carême, Antonin, *L'art de la cuisine française au XIXe siècle* (1832), ed. Gilles & Laurence Laurendon (Paris, 1994).

Carter, Charles, *The Complete Practical Cook* (London: W. Meadows, C. Rivington, R. Hett, 1730); also a facsimile reprint (London, 1984).

——, *The Compleat City and Country Cook: or, Accomplish'd Housewife* (London: A. Bettesworth & C. Hitch, C. Davis, T. Green, S. Austen, 1732).

——, *The London and Country Cook: or, Accomplished Housewife* (London: Charles Hitch, Stephen Austen, John Hinton, 1749).

Carter, Susannah, *The Frugal Housewife, or Complete Woman Cook* (c.1765; London: E. Newbery, [c.1790]).

Cartwright, Charlotte, *The Lady's best Companion; or, A complete Treasure for the Fair Sex* (London: W. Clements, James Sadler, 1789).

['Ceres'], *The Lady's Companion: or, Accomplish'd Director* (Dublin: John Mitchell, 1767).

Chambers, Amelia, *The Ladies Best Companion; or, A Golden Treasure for the Fair Sex* (London: J. Cooke, [*c.*1780]).

Chambers, R. W. (ed.), *A Fifteenth-Century Courtesy Book* (London: Early English Text Society, 1914); a transcription of BL Additional MS 37969.

Chapman, R. W. (ed.), *Jane Austen's Letters* (London, 1952).

Chebsey, William, *A Curious Collection of Receipts in the Art of Pastry and Cookery* (ed. 2, London: the Author, 1721).

A Choice Collection of Cookery Receipts (Newcastle: no printer, [*c.*1780]).

Chomel, Noël, *Dictionaire Œconomique: or, The Family Dictionary* (2 vols, London: D. Midwinter, 1725).

Cleland, Elizabeth, *A New and Easy Method of Cookery* (Edinburgh: the Author, 1755); also the 2nd edition (Edinburgh: C. Wright & Co., 1759).

[Clermont, B.], *The Professed Cook: or the Modern Art of Cookery* (ed. 2, 2 vols, London: R. Davis, T. Caslon, 1769).

Clews, Diane, & Susan Maddock (eds), *Recipes on Record from Norfolk cookery books of the 18th and 19th centuries* (Norwich, 1979).

Clifford, D.J.H. (ed.), *The Diaries of Lady Anne Clifford* (Stroud: Alan Sutton, 1990); superseding the earlier edition by V. Sackville-West, *The Diary of the Lady Anne Clifford* (London, 1923).

Climenson, Emily J. (ed.), *Passages from the Diaries of Mrs. Philip Lybbe Powys of Hardwick House, Oxon., AD 1756 to 1808* (London, 1899).

Cockburn, Henry, *Memorials of his Time* (Edinburgh: Adam & Charles Black, 1856).

Cole, Mary, *The Lady's Complete Guide; or Cookery in all its Branches* (London: G. Kearsley, 1788); also the 2nd edition, described as 'new' (London: G. Kearsley, 1789); also the 3rd edition (London: G. Kearsley, 1791).

A Collection of One Hundred and Thirty-seven approved Receipts, in Pastry and Cookery (Aberdeen: Alexander Thomson, 1774).

A Collection of Ordinances and Regulations for the Government of the Royal Household, Made in Divers Reigns (London: Society of Antiquaries, 1790).

Collingwood, Francis, & John Woollams, *The Universal Cook, and City and Country Housekeeper* (London: J. Scatcherd & J. Whitaker, 1792).

The Compleat Cook (reprint of part of *The Queen's Closet Opened*, 1655; London: J. Phillips, H. Rhodes, J. Taylor, 1710).

The Compleat English Family Companion (London: no printer, 1769).

The Compleat Servant-Maid; or, the Young Maidens Tutor (London: T. Passinger, 1677).

The Compleat Servant Maid's Guide; or the Lady's Delight in Cookery (York: New Printing Office, [*c.*?]).

[The Complete Family Companion] ([?London: ?*c.*1765]).

The Complete Family-Piece: and, Country Gentleman, and Farmer's Best Guide (London: J. Longman, 1736); also the 2nd edition (London: A. Bettesworth & C. Hitch, C. Rivington, S. Birt, T. Longman, J. Clarke, 1737).

Cook, Ann, *Professed Cookery* (Newcastle upon Tyne: J. White, 1754)l also the 3rd edition

(London: the Author, [*c*.1760]); also extracts from the 3rd edition, with introduction and notes by Regula Burnet, published as *Ann Cook and Friend* (London, 1936).

Cooper, Jos., *The Art of Cookery Refin'd and Augmented* (London: J. G. for R. Lowndes, 1654).

The Court and Kitchin of Elizabeth, Commonly called Joan Cromwel, the Wife of the late Usurper, Truly Described and Represented (London: Tho. Milbourn for Randal Taylor, 1664).

[Courtin, Antoine de], *The Rules of Civility; or, Certain Ways of Deportment observed in France, amongst all Persons of Quality, upon several occasions* (London: J. Martyn, J. Starkey, 1671); a translation of *Nouveau Traité de la Civilité* (Paris: 1671).

Cust, Elizabeth (ed.), *Records of the Cust Family, 1479–1700* (Series I, London, 1898).

——, *Records of the Cust Family: the Brownlows of Belton* (Series II, London, 1909).

Dalrymple, George, *The Practice of Modern Cookery* (Edinburgh: the Author, 1781).

Dawson, Thomas, *The Good Huswifes Jewell* (London: Edward White, 1596), facsimile reprint (Amsterdam, 1977); another reprint, introduction by Maggie Black (Lewes, 1996).

[Defoe, Daniel], *An Essay upon Projects* (London: R. R. for Tho. Cockerill, 1698).

Dictionnaire portatif de cuisine (1765), ed. Gilles & Laurence Laurendon (Paris, 1995).

Digby, Sir Kenelm, *The Closet of the Eminently Learned Sir Kenelme Digbie Kt. Opened* (London: E.C. for H. Brome, 1669); also a reprint, as *The Closet of Sir Kenelm Digby Opened*, ed. Jane Stevenson & Peter Davidson (Totnes, 1997).

Dobrée, Bonamy (ed.), *The Letters of Philip Dormer Stanhope, 4th Earl of Chesterfield*, 6 vols (London, 1932).

Driver, Christopher (ed.), *John Evelyn, Cook* (Totnes, 1997), Evelyn's MS receipt book.

Eales, Mary, *Mrs Mary Eales's Receipts* (London: H. Meere, 1718); another edition (London: J. Brindley, 1733); a facsimile reprint of the 1733 edition (London, 1985).

Eland, G. (ed.), *Purefoy Letters, 1735–1753*, 2 vols (London, 1931).

Ellis, William, *The Country Housewife's Family Companion* (London: James Hodges, B. Collins, 1750); also a transcription, introduction by Malcolm Thick (Totnes, 1999).

Elwin, Malcolm (ed.), *The Noels and the Milbankes: their Letters for Twenty-Five Years, 1767–1792* (London, 1967).

Emmett, John, *A Choice Collection of Excellent Receipts in Confectionery* (York: Alex. Staples, 1737).

Essex, John, *The Young Ladies Conduct* (London: John Brotherton, 1722).

E[velyn], J[ohn], *Acetaria. A Discourse of Sallets* (London: B. Tooke, 1699); also a reprint, ed. Christopher Driver, introduction by Tom Jaine (Totnes, 1996).

Farley, John, *The London Art of Cookery, and Housekeeper's Complete Assistant* (London: John Fielding, J. Scatcherd & J. Whitaker, 1783); also a reprint of the 11th edition of 1807, ed. Ann Haly, introduction by Stephen Medcalf (Lewes, 1988).

The Farmer's Wife; or Complete Country Housewife (London: Alex. Hogg, [*c*.1780]).

Faujas de Saint-Fond, B[arthélémi], *Voyagen [sic] en Angleterre, en Ecosse et aux Iles Hébrides*, 2 vols (Paris: H. J. Jansen, 1797).

Fisher, George, *The Instructor: or, Young Man's best Companion* (London: A. Bettesworth & C. Hitch, R. Ware, J. Clark, S. Birt, J. Hodges, [*c*.1735]).

Fisher, Lydia, *The Prudent Housewife: or, Complete English Cook for Town and Country* (London: T. Sabine, [*c*.1780]); also the 24th edition (London: Sabine & Son, [*c*.1800]).

Fog's Weekly Journal 30 (19 April 1729).

Forster, Ann M.C. (ed.), 'Selections from the Disbursement Books (1691–1709) of Sir Thomas Haggerston, Bart.', *Publications of the Surtees Society* 180 (1965).

Frazer, Mrs, *The Practice of Cookery, Pastry, Pickling, Preserving, &c* (Edinburgh: Peter Hill, T. Cadell, 1791).

Furnivall, Frederick J. (ed.), *Early English Meals and Manners* (1868; London: Early English Text Society, 1931).

[G., R.], *The Accomplish'd Female Instructor: Or, A very useful Companion for Ladies, Gentlewomen, and Others* (London: James Knapton, 1704).

Gelleroy, William, *The London Cook, or the whole Art of Cookery made easy and familiar* (London: S. Crowder & Co., J. Coote, J. Fletcher, 1762).

The Genteel House-keepers Pastime: Or, the Mode of Carving at the Table (London: J. Moxon, 1693).

The Gentleman's Companion, and Tradesman's Delight (London: J. Stone, 1735).

The Gentleman's Guide, in his Tour through France (Bristol: S. Farley, [*c.*1768]).

Gibson, Donald (ed.), *A Parson in the Vale of White Horse: George Woodward's Letters from East Hendred, 1753–1761* (Gloucester, 1982).

Gisborne, Thomas, *An Enquiry into the Duties of the Female Sex* (London: T. Cadell jun. & W. Davies, 1798).

[Glasse, Hannah], *The Art of Cookery, Made Plain and Easy* (London: the Author, 1747); also the 4th edition (London: the Author, 1751); also a facsimile reprint, with additional receipts from the 5th edition of 1755, glossary and notes by Alan Davidson (London, 1983); also a reprint of this, with an introduction by Alan Davidson, and essays on Glasse's sources by Jennifer Stead and Priscilla Bain (Totnes, 1995).

Glasse, H[annah], *The Compleat Confectioner: or, the Whole Art of Confectionary Made Plain and Easy* (London: no printer, [*c.*1760]).

Glass[e], H[annah], *The Servant's Directory, or House-keeper's Companion* (London: the Author, 1760).

Goldsmith, Oliver, 'The Life of Richard Nash, of Bath, Esq.' (1762) in *The Collected Works of Oliver Goldsmith*, ed. Arthur Friedman, vol. 3 (Oxford, 1966), pp. 279–398.

The Good Huswives Hand-maid, for Cookerie in her Kitchin ([London: E. Allde, 1597]); reprinted from a different edition as *The Good Huswifes Handmaide for the Kitchen* (London: Richard Fish, no date), ed. Stuart Peachey (Bristol, 1992).

Grant, Bartle (ed.), *The Receipt Book of Elizabeth Raper, and a portion of her Cipher Journal* (London, 1924).

Gray, Mrs. Edwin (ed.), *Papers and Diaries of a York Family, 1764–1839* (London, 1927), papers of the Gray family.

Gregory, [John], *A Father's Legacy to his Daughters* (London: W. Strahan, T. Cadell, W. Creech, 1774).

Greig, James (ed.), *The Diaries of a Duchess: Extracts from the diaries of the first Duchess of Northumberland (1716–1776)* (London, 1926).

Grose, Francis, *The Olio* (London: S. Hooper, 1792).

[Grosley, Pierre Jean], *Londres*, 3 vols (Lausanne: no printer, 1770).

H., M., *The Young Cooks Monitor: or, Directions for Cookery and Distilling* (London: William Downing, 1683).

H., N., *The Ladies Dictionary; Being a General Entertainment for the Fair Sex* (London: John Dunton, 1694).

Hall, T., *The Queen's Royal Cookery* (ed. 2, London: C. Bates, A. Bettesworth, 1713).

Halsband, Robert (ed.), *The Complete Letters of Lady Mary Wortley Montagu*, 3 vols (Oxford, 1965–67).

Hardyment, Christina (ed.), *The Housekeeping Book of Susanna Whatman*, (London, 1987).

Harrison, Sarah, *The House-keeper's Pocket-Book, and Compleat Family Cook* (London: T. Worrall, 1733); also the 2nd edition (London: R. Ware, 1739).

Hartman, G[eorge], *The True Preserver and Restorer of Health* (London: T. B. for the Author, 1682).

Hawkesbury, Lord (ed.), 'The MS. Account and Memorandum Book of a Yorkshire Lady two Centuries ago', *Transactions of the East Riding Antiquarian Society* 9 (1902), pp. 1–56; Mary Foljambe's MS.

[Haywood, Eliza], *The Female Spectator*, 4 vols (1745; ed. 2, London: T. Gardner, 1748).

Hazlemore, Maximilian, *Domestic Economy; or, a Complete System of English Housekeeping* (London: J. Creswick & Co., 1794).

Hell upon Earth: or the Town in an Uproar (London: J. Roberts, A. Dodd, 1729).

Henderson, William Augustus, *The Housekeeper's Instructor; or, Universal Family Cook* (London: W. & J. Stratford, [*c.*1795]).

Henstock, Adrian (ed.), 'The Diary of Abigail Gawthern of Nottingham, 1751–1810', *Thoroton Society Record Series* 33 (1980).

Hess, Karen (ed.), *Martha Washington's Booke of Cookery* (New York, 1981).

Hickman, Peggy (ed.), *A Jane Austen Household Book with Martha Lloyd's Recipes* (Newton Abbot, 1977).

Hieatt, Constance B. & Sharon Butler (eds), *Curye on Inglysch* (London: Early English Text Society, 1985).

Hieatt, Constance B. (ed.), *An Ordinance of Pottage* (London, 1988).

Hobhouse, Edmund (ed.), *The Diary of a West Country Physician, AD 1684–1726* (London, 1934), the diary of Claver Morris.

Holland, Mary, *The Complete British Cook* (London: J. D. Dewick for West & Hughes, 1800).

Home, J.A. (ed.), *The Letters and Journals of Lady Mary Coke*, 4 vols (Edinburgh, 1889–96).

Hope, Sir William H. St John, *Cowdray and Easebourne Priory* (London, 1919), contains Viscount Montague's household book (1595), pp. 119–134.

The House-keeper's Pocket Book, and complete Family Cook (London: H. Fenwick, [*c.*1780]).

Howard, Henry, *England's Newest Way in all sorts of Cookery, Pastry, and all Pickles that are fit to be Used* (1703; ed. 2, London: Chr. Coningsby, 1708); also the 3rd edition (London: Chr. Coningsby, 1710).

Hudleston, C. Roy (ed.), 'Naworth Estate and Household Accounts, 1648–1660', *Surtees Society* 168 (1953).

J., W., *A Choice Manual of Rare and Select Secrets in Physick and Chyrurgery*, in 2 parts, the first attributed to Elizabeth Grey, Countess of Kent, the second, with a new title, 'A True Gentlewomans Delight' (London: R. Norton, 1653).

Jackson, Charles (ed.), 'The Autobiography of Mrs. Alice Thornton of East Newton, Co. York', *Surtees Society* 62 (1875).

——, 'A Family History begun by James Fretwell', in 'Yorkshire Diaries and Autobiographies', *Surtees Society* 65 (1877), pp. 163–243.

Jackson, Sarah, *The Director: or, Young Woman's Best Companion* (London: J. Fuller, S. Neale, 1754).

Jenks, James, *The Complete Cook* (London: E. & C. Dilly, 1768).

Johnson, Mary, *The Young Woman's Companion: or the Servant-Maid's Assistant* (London: H. Jeffery, 1753).

—— also another edition under a new title: *Madam Johnson's Present: or, the best Instructions for Young Women, in Useful and Universal Knowledge* (1754; London: M. Cooper, C. Sympson, 1755).

Johnson, Samuel, *The Rambler*, 3 vols., ed. W. J. Bate & Albrecht B. Strauss, in *The Yale Edition of the Works of Samuel Johnson*, vols 3–5 (New Haven, 1969).

Kellet, Susanna, Elizabeth Kellet & Mary Kellet, *A Complete Collection of Cookery Receipts* (Newcastle-upon-Tyne: T. Saint, 1780).

[Kettilby, Mary (ed.)], *A Collection of Above Three Hundred Receipts in Cookery, Physic and Surgery* (London: Richard Wilkin, 1714).

—— also the 2nd edition (London: Mary Kettilby, 1719).

Kidder, E[dward], *E. Kidder's Receipts of Pastry and Cookery* (no place [London]: no printer, [*c*.1725]).

Kirkpatrick, H., *An Account of the Manner in which Potatoes are cultivated and preserved* (Warrington: W. Eyres for J. Johnson, 1796).

L.S.R., *L'Art de bien traiter* (1674), ed. Gilles & Laurence Laurendon, in *L'art de la cuisine française au XVIIe siècle* (Paris, 1995).

La Chapelle, Vincent, *The Modern Cook*, 3 vols (London: the Author, 1733).

The Ladies Cabinet Opened (London: M. P. for Richard Meighen, 1639).

—— also the 4th edition with a new title, *The Ladies Cabinet Enlarged and Opened* (London: G. Bedel & T. Collins, 1667), with new receipts attributed to Patrick, Lord Ruthven.

The Ladies' Library: or, Encyclopedia of Female Knowledge (2 vols, London: J. Ridgway, 1790).

Lamb, Patrick, *Royal Cookery; or, the Complete Court-Cook* (London: Abel Roper, 1710); also an identical edition (London: Maurice Atkins, 1710); also the 2nd edition (London: J. Nutt, A. Roper, 1716); also the 3rd edition (London: E. & R. Nutt, A. Roper, 1726).

Lambert, Edw[ard], *The Art of Confectionary* (London: T. Taylor, [*c*.1740]).

Lamond, Elizabeth (ed. & trans.), *Walter of Henley's Husbandry together with an anonymous Husbandry, Seneschaucie and Robert Grosseteste's Rules*, introduction by W. Cunningham (London, 1890); Grosseteste's household rules are pp. 121–145.

La Reynière, Grimod de, *Ecrits gastronomiques* (*Almanach des gourmands*, 1803, and *Manuel des amphitryons*, 1808), ed. Jean-Claude Bonnet (Paris, 1978).

La Roche, Sophie von, *Tagebuch einer Reise durch Holland und England* (ed. 2, Offenbach am Main: Ulrich Weiss & Carl Ludwig Brede, 1791); also the translation of the diary by Clare Williams, *Sophie in London, 1786* (London, 1933).

Latham, Robert, & William Matthews (eds), *The Diary of Samuel Pepys*, 11 vols (London, 1970–83).

La Varenne, [François Pierre, dit], *Le Cuisinier françois* (1651; ed. 2, revised and with a 'Traitté de Confitures seiches et liquides', Paris: Pierre David, 1652); also a reprint of the 'Bibliothèque bleue' edition, including the texts of *Le Pâtissier françois* (1653), *Le*

Confiturier françois (1660), and *Le Cuisinier friand* (1683), introduction by Jean-Louis Flandrin, Philip & Mary Hyman (Paris, 1983).

La Varenne, [François Pierre, dit], *The French Cook*, trans. [from *Le Cuisinier françois*, 1651] by J. D. O. (London: Charls [sic] Adams, 1653).

[Le Blanc, Jean Bernard, Abbé], *Lettres d'un François*, 3 vols (La Haye: Jean Neaulme, 1745).

Lennox, Charles George, earl of March (ed.), *A Duke and his Friends: the Life and Letters of the second Duke of Richmond*, 2 vols (London, 1911).

Lettice, John, *Letters on a Tour through Various Parts of Scotland, in the Year 1792* (London: T. Cadell, 1794).

Lewis, W.S. (ed.), *The Yale Edition of Horace Walpole's Correspondence*, 48 vols (London, 1937–1983).

Linnell, C.D. (ed.), 'The Diary of Benjamin Rogers, Rector of Carlton, 1720–71', *Bedfordshire Historical Record Society* 30 (1950).

The London Complete Art of Cookery (London: William Lane, 1797).

Lucas, Joseph (ed. & trans.), *Kalm's Account of his Visit to England on his way to America in 1748* (London, 1892).

Lune, Pierre de, *Le Cuisinier* (1656), ed. Gilles & Laurence Laurendon, in *L'art de la cuisine française au XVIIe siècle* (Paris, 1995).

M., W., *The Queens Closet Opened* ([London]: Nathaniel Brook, 1655), contains the first two parts: 'The Pearl of Practice' and 'A Queens Delight'; *The Compleat Cook* (London: Nath. Brook, 1655), contains the third part of the trilogy; also a facsimile reprint of two of the three parts, 'The Compleat Cook' and 'A Queens Delight', from the 1671 edition (London, 1984).

McCann, Timothy J. (ed.), 'The Correspondence of the Dukes of Richmond and Newcastle, 1724–1750', *Sussex Record Society* 73 (1984).

Macdonald, Violet M. (ed.), *The Letters of Eliza Pierce* (London, 1927).

Macfarlane, Alan (ed.), *The Diary of Ralph Josselin, 1616–1683* (London, 1976).

Maciver, [Susanna], *Cookery, and Pastry* (ed. 3, Edinburgh: the Author, 1782).

[Markham, Gervase], *The English Hus-wife* (London: John Beale for Roger Jackson, 1615).

—— also an edition of 1664, included in *A Way to get Wealth*, ed. 11 (London: William Wilson for George Sawbridge, 1660 [sic]).

Marnettè [sic], *The Perfect Cook* [trans. from La Varenne, *Le Pâtissier françois* (1653)] (London: Nath. Brooks, 1656).

Marshall, Eliz[abeth], *The Young Ladies' Guide in the Art of Cookery* (Newcastle [upon Tyne]: the Author, 1777).

Martin, Sarah, *The New Experienced English-Housekeeper* (Doncaster: the Authoress, 1795).

[Mason, Charlotte], *The Lady's Assistant for Regulating and Supplying her Table* (London: J. Walter, 1773).

[Massialot], *Le Cuisinier roïal et bourgeois* (1691; ed. 3, Paris: Charles de Sercy, 1698).

——, *The Court and Country Cook*, trans. (from *Le Cuisinier roïal et bourgeois* and *Nouvelle Instruction pour les confitures, les liqueurs, et les fruits*, 1692) by J. K. (London: W. Onley for A. & J. Churchill, M. Gillyflower, 1702).

Masson, Madeleine (ed.), *The Compleat Cook* (London, 1974), Rebecca Price's MS cookery receipts.

Matthews, William (ed.), *The Diary of Dudley Ryder, 1715–1716* (London, 1939).

May, Robert, *The Accomplisht Cook* (London: R. W. for Nath. Brooke, 1660).

—— also a facsimile reprint of the 1685 edition, foreword, introduction and glossary by Alan Davidson, Marcus Bell and Tom Jaine (Totnes, 1994).

Mayerne, Sir Theodore, *Archimagirus Anglo-Gallicus* ([London]: G. Bedell & T. Collins, 1658).

Meads, Dorothy M. (ed), *The Diary of Lady Margaret Hoby, 1599–1605* (London, 1930).

Melroe, Eliza, *An Economical, and New Method of Cookery* (London: the Author, 1798).

Mennell, Stephen (ed.), *Lettre d'un Pâtissier Anglois, et autres contributions à une polémique gastronomique du XVIIIème siècle* (Exeter, 1981).

[Menon], *La Cuisinière bourgeoise* (1746; facsimile reprint of 1774 edition (Brussels: François Foppens), ed. Alice Peeters, n.p.: Temps Actuels, 1981).

——, *La Science du Maître d'Hôtel, Cuisinier* (1749; Paris: Leclerc, 1768).

——, *La Science du Maître d'Hôtel, Confiseur* (Paris: Paulus-du-Mesnil, 1750).

——, *The French Family Cook* (a translation of *La Cuisinière bourgeoise* (1746), (London: J. Bell, 1793).

Mercier, Louis Sébastien, *Tableau de Paris* (1783–89), ed. Jean-Claude Bonnet, 2 vols (Paris, 1994).

Middleton, John, *Five Hundred New Receipts in Cookery, Confectionary, Pastry, Preserving, Conserving, Pickling* (London: Tho. Astley, 1734).

[Misson de Valbourg, Henri], *Mémoires et Observations faites par un Voyageur en Angleterre* (La Haye: Henri van Bulderen, 1698).

Mitchell, Brigitte, & Hubert Penrose (eds), *Letters from Bath 1766–1767 by the Rev. John Penrose* (Gloucester, 1983).

The Modern Method of Regulating and Forming a Table, Explained and Displayed ([London]: J. Hughes, S. Crowder, [c.1750]).

Montague, Peregrine, *The Family Pocket-Book: or, Fountain of true and useful Knowledge* (London: Henry Coote, [c.1760]); also another edition (London: George Paul, [1762]).

Moore, Isabella, *The Useful and Entertaining Family Miscellany* (London: John Smith, 1772).

[More, Hannah], *The Cottage Cook, or, Mrs. Jones's Cheap Dishes* (*Cheap Repository Tracts* 45; London: J. Marshall, [1796]).

Moritz, Carl Philip, *Reisen eines Deutschen in England im Jahr 1782* (Berlin: Friedrich Maurer, 1783).

Morris, Christopher (ed.), *The Illustrated Journeys of Celia Fiennes, 1685–c. 1712* (Stroud, 1995).

Moryson, Fynes, *[An Itinerary]* (London: John Beale, 1617).

Moxon, Elizabeth, *English Housewifry* (Leeds: J. Lister, [1741]); also the 4th edition (Leeds: J. Lister, [c.1749]).

Mure, Elizabeth, 'Some Remarks on the Change of Manners in my own Time', in William Mure (ed.), *Selections from the Family Papers preserved at Caldwell*, vol. I (Glasgow, [Maitland Club], 1854), pp. 259–272.

Murray, A. G. W., & Eustace F. Bosanquet (eds), *The Manuscript of William Dunche, being the Book of the New Ordinary of the King's most honourable Household, Anno 31 Henry VIII* (Exeter, 1914).

M[urrell], J[ohn], *A New Booke of Cookerie* (London, John Browne, 1615), facsimile reprint (Amsterdam, 1972); also another edition with the author's name in full (London; John

Browne, 1617); also another edition, containing *The Second Booke of Cookerie* and *A New Book of Carving and Sewing*, with a new title: *Murrel's Two Bookes of Cookerie and Carving* (London: Ja. Fl. for Rich. Marriot, 1650).

Murrel [sic], John, *A Daily Exercise for Ladies and Gentlewomen* (London: the widow Helme, 1617).

The New Bath Guide, or, Useful Pocket-Companion (Bath: C. Pope, [*c.*1762]).

Nichols, John Gough (ed.), *The Diary of Henry Machyn* (London: Camden Society, 1848).

A Noble Boke off Cookry, reprint of Holkham MS *c.*1470, ed. Mrs. Alexander ([Robina]) Napier (London, 1882).

The Norfolk Congress (London: R. Light-body [sic], [1728]).

Nott, John, *The Cook's and Confectioner's Dictionary: or, the Accomplish'd Housewife's Companion* (London: C. Rivington, 1723).

[Nutt, Frederick], *The Complete Confectioner; or, the Whole Art of Confectionary* (London: the Author, 1789).

Osborn, Emily F.D. (ed.), *Political and Social Letters of a Lady of the Eighteenth Century, 1721–1771* (London, [1890]), letters by Sarah Byng Osborn.

The Pastry-Cook's Vade-Mecum: or, a Pocket-Companion for Cooks, House-Keepers, Country Gentlewomen, &c. (London: Abel Roper, 1705).

Peckham, Ann, *The Complete English Cook; or, Prudent Housewife* (Leeds: Griffith Wright, 1767).

Penney, Norman (ed.), *The Household Account Book of Sarah Fell of Swarthmoor Hall* (Cambridge, 1920).

Percival, Milton (ed.), *Political Ballads Illustrating the Administration of Sir Robert Walpole* (Oxford, 1916).

Percy, Thomas (ed.), *The Regulations and Establishment of the Houshold [sic] of Henry Algernon Percy, the fifth Earl of Northumberland, at his castles of Wresill and Lekinfield in Yorkshire* (London: no printer, 1770).

[Petrie, Adam], *Rules of Good Deportment, or of Good Breeding* (Edinburgh: no printer, 1720).

Phillips, Sarah, *The Ladies Handmaid: or, a Compleat System of Cookery* (London: J. Coote, 1758).

[Plat, Sir Hugh], *Delightes for Ladies* ([London: Peter Short, ?*c.*1600]).

The Polite Academy, or School of Behaviour for Young Gentlemen and Ladies (London: R. Baldwin, B. Collins, 1765).

Pottle, Frederick A. et al. (eds), *The Yale Edition of the Private Papers of James Boswell* (London, 1950–).

Powell, *The Guide to Preferment: or: Powell's Complete Book of Cookery* ([London]: Bailey, [*c.*1770]).

Price, Elizabeth, *The New Book of Cookery; or, Every Woman a Perfect Cook* (London: the Authoress, [*c.*1780]).

Price, Elizabeth, *The New, Universal, and Complete Confectioner* (London: A. Hogg, [*c.*1785]).

Primitive Cookery; or the Kitchen Garden display'd (London: J. Williams, 1767).

Prochaska, Alice, & Frank Prochaska (eds), *Margaretta Acworth's Georgian Cookery Book* (London, 1987), a selection from the MS in the PRO (q. v.).

A Proper New Booke of Cookery (London: William How for Abraham Veale, 1575).

[Rabisha, William], *The Whole Body of Cookery Dissected* (London: R. W. for Giles Calvert, 1661); also the 2nd edition, with a new second part (London: E. C., 1675).

Raffald, Elizabeth, *The Experienced English House-keeper* (Manchester: the Author, 1769); also a reprint, ed. Ann Bagnall, introduction by Roy Shipperbottom (Lewes: Southover, 1997).

Raines, F. R. (ed.), 'The Stanley Papers II', *Chetham Society* 31 (1853); contains the Derby Household Books, 1561–1590.

Rathborne, Mrs. Ambrose (ed.), *Letters from Lady Jane Coke to her friend Mrs. Eyre at Derby, 1747–1758* (London, 1899).

Revell, Alison (ed.), *A Kentish Cookery Collection* (Maidstone, 1978), receipts from MSS in Kent RO, 17th–19th centuries.

Robertson, Hannah, *The Young Ladies School of Arts* (1766; ed. 2, Edinburgh: the Author, 1767).

Robertson, Joseph, *An Essay on Culinary Poisons* (London: G. Kearsley, 1781).

Rose, Giles, *A Perfect School of Instructions for the Officers of the Mouth* [trans. from *L'Escole parfaite des officiers de bouche*, Paris: 1662] (London: R. Bentley & M. Magnes, 1682).

Rouquet, [Jean André], *L'Etat des Arts, en Angleterre* (Paris: Ant. Jombert, 1755).

[Rundell, Maria], *A New System of Domestic Economy … A New Edition, corrected* (London: S. Hamilton for John Murray, 1810).

Sandford, Francis, *The History of the Coronation of … James II* ([London]: Thomas Newcomb, 1687).

Saussure, César de, *Lettres et Voyages de Mons.r César de Saussure en Allemagne, en Hollande et en Angleterre, 1725–1729*, introduction by B. van Muyden (Lausanne, 1903).

Scarfe, Norman (ed. & trans.), 'A Frenchman's Year in Suffolk', *Suffolk Records Society* 30 (1988), the 'Mélanges sur l'Angleterre' by François de la Rochefoucauld, son of the duc de Liancourt.

Schoonover, David E. (ed.), *Ladie Borlase's Receiptes Booke* (Iowa City, 1998).

Scott-Moncrieff, Robert (ed.), 'The Household Book of Lady Grisell Baillie, 1692–1733', *Publications of the Scottish History Society*, New Series, 1 (1911).

Shackleford, Ann, *The Modern Art of Cookery Improved; or, Elegant, Cheap, and Easy Methods, of preparing most of the Dishes now in Vogue* (London: J. Newbery, F. Newbery, 1767).

Sherburn, George (ed.), *The Correspondence of Alexander Pope*, 5 vols (Oxford, 1956).

Simmons, Amelia, *American Cookery, or the Art of Dressing Viands, Fish, Poultry and Vegetables* (Hartford: Hudson & Goodwin for the Author, 1796); facsimile reprint, with an essay by Mary Tolford Wilson (1958; New York, 1984); also a facsimile of ed. 2 (Albany: Charles R. & George Webster, [1796]), with an introduction by Karen Hess (Bedford, Mass., 1996).

Sinar, Joan (ed.), *Jane Mosley's Derbyshire Recipes* (1979; Derby, 1985).

Skeat, J., *The Art of Cookery and Pastery made easy and familiar* (London: the Author, [1769]).

Smith, A., *A New Book of Cookery; or, Every Woman a Perfect Cook* (London: no printer, 1781).

S[mith], E., *The Compleat Housewife: or, Accomplished Gentlewoman's Companion* (1727; ed. 2, London: J. Pemberton, 1728); also the 6th edition (London: J. Pemberton, 1734); also a facsimile reprint of the 16th edition of 1758 (London, 1994).

Smith, Mary, *The Complete House-keeper, and Professed Cook* (Newcastle: the Author, 1772).

Smith, R[ichard], *Court Cookery: or, the Compleat English Cook* (London: T. Wotton, 1723); also the 2nd edition (London: T. Wotton, 1725).

Smith, Verena (ed.), 'The Town Book of Lewes, 1702–1837', *Sussex Record Society 69* (1973).

[?Smollett, Tobias], review of Verral's *Complete System of Cookery*, in *The Critical Review* 8, 1759, pp. 284–289.

[Sorbière, Samuel de], *Relation d'un voyage en Angleterre* (Paris: Thomas Jolly, 1664).

Souden, David (ed.), *Byng's Tours: The Journals of the Hon. John Byng 1781–1792* (London, 1991).

Spurling, Hilary (ed.), *Elinor Fettiplace's Receipt Book* (London, 1986).

Stitt, Bette (ed.), 'Diana Astry's Recipe Book', *Bedfordshire Historical Record Society* 37 (1957), pp. 83–168.

Stokes, Francis Griffin (ed.), *The Blecheley Diary of the Rev. William Cole M.A., F.S.A., 1765– 67* (London, 1931).

The Strangers' Assistant and Guide to Bath (Bath: R. Cruttwell, for W. Taylor and A. Tennent, 1773).

Sutton, Anne F., & P. W. Hammond (eds), *The Coronation of Richard III: the Extant Documents* (Gloucester, 1983).

Swift, [Jonathan], *Directions to Servants in General* (London: R. Dodsley, M. Cooper, 1745).

Taylor, E., *The Lady's, Housewife's, and Cookmaid's Assistant: or, the Art of Cookery Explained and Adapted to the meanest Capacity* (Berwick upon Tweed: H. Taylor for R. Taylor, 1769).

Thacker, John, *The Art of Cookery* (Newcastle upon Tyne: I. Thompson & Company, 1758).

Thomson, Gladys Scott (ed.), *Letters of a Grandmother, 1732–1735* (London, 1943), letters from Sarah, duchess of Marlborough to her granddaughter Diana, later duchess of Bedford.

Tillinghast, Mary, *Rare and Excellent Receipts* (1678; London: no printer, 1690).

Towle, Matthew, *The Young Gentleman and Lady's Private Tutor* ([London: 1770]).

Townshend, John, *The Universal Cook; or, Lady's Complete Assistant* (London: S. Bladon, 1773).

A Treatise on the Use and Abuse of the Second, commonly called, the Steward's Table, in Families of the First Rank (London: the Author, [c.1758]).

[Trusler, John], *The Honours of the Table, or, Rules for Behaviour during Meals* (London: the Author, 1788).

Tusser, Thomas, *A Hundreth Good Pointes of Husbandrie* (London: Richard Tottel, 1557).

——, *Five Hundreth Points of Good Husbandry* (London: Rychard Tottell, 1573).

Twining, Richard (ed.), *Selections from Papers of the Twining Family* (London, 1887).

Uffenbach, Zacharias Conrad von, *Merkwürdige Reisen durch Niedersachsen, Holland und Engelland*, 3 vols (vol. 1: Ulm & Memmingen: Johann Friedrich Gaum, 1753; vol. 2: Frankfurt & Leipzig: Christian Ulrich Wagner, 1753; vol. 3: Ulm: Gaumischer Handlung, 1754).

Valuable Secrets concerning Arts and Trades (London: Will. Hay, 1775).

Verney, Frances Parthenope, & Margaret M. Verney (eds), *Memoirs of the Verney Family during the Seventeenth Century*, 2 vols (London, 1904).

Verney, Margaret Maria (ed.), *Verney Letters of the Eighteenth Century from the MSS at Claydon House*, 2 vols (London, [1930]).

Verral, William, *A Complete System of Cookery* (London: the Author, 1759); also a reprint, ed. R. L. Mégroz, published as *The Cook's Paradise* (London, [1948]) also another reprint, ed. Ann Haly, introduction by Colin Brent, published as *William Verrall's* [sic] *Cookery Book* (Lewes, 1988).

W., A., *A Book of Cookrye* (London: Edward Allde, 1591), facsimile reprint (Amsterdam, 1976).

W., J., *Beauties Treasury: or, the Ladies Vade Mecum* (London: S. Malthus, 1705).

Wanklyn, Malcolm (ed.), 'Inventories of Worcestershire Landed Gentry, 1537–1786', *Worcestershire Historical Society*, New Series, 16 (1998).

Warner, Richard, *Antiquitates Culinariae* (London: R. Blamire, 1791).

Weatherill, Lorna (ed.), 'The Account Book of Richard Latham, 1724–1767', *Records of Social and Economic History* New Series, 15 (1990).

Weddell, George (ed.), *Arcana Fairfaxiana* (Newcastle-on-Tyne, 1890), facsimile reprint of Fairfax family MS commonplace book.

The Whole Duty of a Woman: or a Guide to the Female Sex, from the Age of Sixteen to Sixty, &c. ([ed. 3, London: J. Guillim, 1701]).

The Whole Duty of a Woman: Or, an infallible Guide to the Fair Sex (London: T. Read, 1737).

The Widdowes Treasure, preface signed M. R. (London: J. Roberts for Edward White, 1595).

Wilkes, Wetenhall, *A Letter of Genteel and Moral Advice to a Young Lady* (Dublin: the Author, 1740).

Williams, Harold (ed.), *The Correspondence of Jonathan Swift*, 5 vols (Oxford, 1963–65).

Williams, T., *The Accomplished Housekeeper, and Universal Cook* (London: J. Scatcherd, 1797).

Wilson, Francesa M. (ed.), *Strange Island: Britain through Foreign Eyes, 1395–1940* (London, [1955]), an anthology of extracts from travellers' accounts.

Wilson, Mary, *The Ladies Complete Cookery; or, Family Pocket Companion, Made Plain and Easy* (London: the Authoress, [c.1770]).

Wolley [sic], Hannah, *The Cooks Guide: or, Rare Receipts for Cookery* (London: Peter Dring, 1664).

——, *The Queen-like Closet; or Rich Cabinet* (London: R. Lowndes, 1670).

Woolley, Hannah, *The Ladies Delight: or, A Rich Closet of choice Experiments and Curiosities* (London: T. Milbourn for N. Crouch, 1672).

Woolley, Hannah [?], *The Gentlewomans Companion; or, A Guide to the Female Sex* (London: A. Maxwell for Dorman Newman, 1673).

[Worlidge, John], *Dictionarium Rusticum & Urbanicum* (London: J. Nicholson, 1704).

The Young Gentleman and Lady Instructed in ... Principles of Politeness, Prudence, and Virtue, 2 vols (London: Edward Wickstead, 1747).

The Young Lady's Companion in Cookery and Pastry, Preserving, Pickling, Candying, &c. (London: A. Bettesworth & C. Hitch, J. Hazard, W. Bickerton & C. Corbett, R. Willock, 1734).

PRINTED SECONDARY SOURCES

Ashley, Sir William, *The Bread of our Forefathers* (Oxford, 1928).

Ashton, John, *Chap-Books of the Eighteenth Century* (1882; Welwyn Garden City, 1969).

Ashton, John, *The History of Bread from Pre-historic to Modern Times* (London, 1904).

Atherton, Herbert M., *Political Prints in the Age of Hogarth* (Oxford, 1974).

Aylett, Mary, & Olive Ordish, *First Catch Your Hare: A History of the Recipe-makers* (London, 1965).

Ayto, John, *The Diner's Dictionary: Food and Drink from A to Z* (1990; Oxford, 1993).

Bailey, C.T.P., *Knives and Forks* (London, 1927).

Baker, C.H. Collins, & Muriel I. Baker, *The Life and Circumstances of James Brydges, First Duke of Chandos* (Oxford, 1949).

Balsdon, J.P.V.D., *Life and Leisure in Ancient Rome* (London, 1969).

Barber, Richard, *Cooking and Recipes from Rome to the Renaissance* (London, [1973]).

Bayne-Powell, Rosamond, *Eighteenth-Century London Life* (London, [1937]).

——, *Housekeeping in the Eighteenth Century* (London, [1956]).

Beattie, John M., *The English Court in the Reign of George I* (Cambridge, 1967).

Beckett, J.V., *The Aristocracy in England 1660–1914* (Oxford, 1986).

Bernier, Georges, *Antonin Carême, 1783–1833: La sensualité gourmande en Europe* (Paris, 1989).

Bitting, Katherine Golden, *Gastronomic Bibliography* (1939; Ann Arbor (Michigan), 1971).

Black, Jeremy, *Natural and Necessary Enemies: Anglo-French relations in the eighteenth century* (London, 1986).

Black, Maggie (ed.), *A Taste of History: 10,000 Years of Food in Britain* (London, 1993).

Brears, Peter C.D., *The Gentlewoman's Kitchen: Great Food in Yorkshire, 1650–1750* (Wakefield, 1984).

Brécourt-Villars, Claudine, *Mots de table, Mots de bouche: Dictionnaire étymologique et historique du vocabulaire classique de la cuisine et de la gastronomie* ([Paris], 1996).

Brett, Gerard, *Dinner is Served: A History of Dining in England, 1400–1900* (London, 1968).

Brewer, John, *The Pleasures of the Imagination: English Culture in the Eighteenth Century* (London, 1997).

Burnett, John, *Plenty and Want: A social history of diet in England from 1815 to the present day* (1966; London, 1979).

——, *A History of the Cost of Living* (Harmondsworth, 1969).

Cagle, William R., *A Matter of Taste: A Bibliographical Catalogue of the Gernon Collection of Books on Food and Drink* (New York / London, 1990).

Clark, Peter, *The English Alehouse: a social history 1200–1830* (London, 1983).

Coe, Sophie D., & Michael D. Coe, *The True History of Chocolate* (London, 1996).

Coleman, D. C., *The Economy of England, 1450–1750* (London, 1977).

Colley, Linda, *In Defiance of Oligarchy: the Tory Party 1714–60* (Cambridge, 1982).

Colley, Linda, *Britons: Forging the Nation 1707–1837* (1992; London, 1994).

Cooper, Charles, *The English Table in History and Literature* (London, [1929]).

Crawford, Patricia, & Sara Mendelson, *Women in Early Modern England, 1550–1720* (Oxford, 1998).

Cressy, David, *Literacy and the Social Order* (Cambridge, 1980).

Cruickshank, Dan, & Neil Burton, *Life in the Georgian City* (London, 1990).

David, Elizabeth, *Harvest of the Cold Months: The Social History of Ice and Ices* (1994; London, 1996).

Davidoff, Leonore, & Catherine Hall, *Family Fortunes: Men and women of the English middle class, 1780–1850* (London, 1987).

Davidson, Alan, *The Oxford Companion to Food* (Oxford, 1999).

Davidson, Caroline, *A Woman's Work Is Never Done: A history of housework in the British Isles, 1650–1950* (London, 1982).

Day, Ivan (ed.), *Eat, Drink and Be Merry: the British at Table, 1600–2000* (London, 2000).

De Salis, [Harriet Anne], *The Art of Cookery Past and Present* (London, 1898).

Doughty, Katharine Frances, *The Betts of Wortham in Suffolk, 1480–1905* (London, 1912).

Driver, Christopher, & Michelle Berriedale-Johnson, *Pepys at Table* (London, 1984).

Drummond, Sir Jack Cecil, & Anne Wilbraham, *The Englishman's Food: A History of Five Centuries of English Diet* (London, 1939).

Durant, David N., *Bess of Hardwick* (1977; London, 1999).

Dyer, Christopher, *Standards of living in the later Middle Ages: Social change in England c.1200–1520* (Cambridge, 1989).

Earle, Peter, *The Making of the English Middle Class: Business, Society and Family Life in London, 1660–1730* (1989; London, 1991).

——, *A City Full of People: Men and Women of London 1650–1750* (London, 1994).

Elias, Norbert, *The Civilising Process*, vol. 1, *The History of Manners* (Oxford, 1978); vol. 2, *State Formation and Civilisation* (Oxford, 1982), a translation of *Über des Prozess der Zivilisation* (1939).

——, *The Court Society* (Oxford, 1983), a translation of *Die höfische Gesellschaft* (1969).

Ellwanger, George H., *The Pleasures of the Table: An account of gastronomy from ancient days to present times* (London, 1903).

Emmison, F.G., *Tudor Secretary: Sir William Petre at Court and Home* (London, 1961).

——, *Tudor Food and Pastimes* (London, 1964).

Farid, Kamal, *Antoine de Courtin (1622–1685), Etude critique* (Paris, 1969).

Feather, John, *The Provincial Book Trade in Eighteenth-Century England* (Cambridge, 1985).

Filby, Frederick A., *A History of Food Adulteration and Analysis* (London, 1934).

Flandrin, Jean-Louis, *Chronique de Platine: pour une gastronomie historique* (Paris, 1992).

——, & Massimo Montanari (eds), *Histoire de l'alimentation* (Paris, 1996).

——, & Jane Cobbi (eds), *Tables d'hier, tables d'ailleurs: Histoire et ethnologie du repas* (Paris, 1999).

Forrest, Denys, *Tea for the British: The Social and Economic History of a Famous Trade* (London, 1973).

Les Français et la table (Paris, 1985), catalogue of the exhibition at the Musée national des arts et traditions populaires, Paris, November 1985–April 1986.

Franklin, Alfred, *La Vie privée d'autrefois: la cuisine* (1888; Geneva, 1980).

——, *La Vie privée d'autrefois: les repas* (Paris, 1889).

Fraser, Antonia, *The Weaker Vessel: Woman's lot in seventeenth-century England* (1984; London, 1989).

Garrier, Gilbert, *Histoire sociale et culturelle du vin* (1995; Paris, 1998).

Gillet, Philippe, *Par Mets et par vins: Voyages et gastronomie en Europe, XVIe–XVIIIe siècles* (Paris, 1985).

——, *Le Goût et les mots: Littérature et gastronomie, 14e–20e siècles* (Paris, 1987).

Girouard, Mark, *Life in the English Country House: A Social and Architectural History* (1978; Harmondsworth, 1980).

Goody, Jack, *Cooking, Cuisine and Class: A Study in Comparative Sociology* (Cambridge, 1982).

Gottschalk, Dr Alfred, *Histoire de l'alimentation et de la gastronomie depuis la préhistoire jusqu'à nos jours* (Paris, 1948).

Guégan, Bertrand, *Le Cuisinier français ou les meilleures recettes d'autrefois et d'aujourd'hui* (Paris, 1934).

Halsband, Robert, *The Life of Lady Mary Wortley Montagu* (1956; Oxford, 1957).

Hartley, Dorothy, *Food in England* (1954; London, 1985).

Heal, Felicity, *Hospitality in Early Modern England* (Oxford, 1990).

Hecht, J. Jean, 'Continental and Colonial Servants in Eighteenth Century England', *Smith College Studies in History* 40 (1954).

——, *The Domestic Servant Class in Eighteenth-Century England* (London, 1956).

Henisch, Bridget Ann, *Fast and Feast: Food in Medieval Society* (London, 1976).

Hill, Bridget, *Women, Work and Sexual Politics in Eighteenth-Century England* (Oxford, 1989).

——, *Servants: English Domestics in the Eighteenth Century* (Oxford, 1996).

Hobby, Elaine, *Virtue of Necessity: English Women's Writing 1649–88* (Ann Arbor, 1989).

Hole, Christina, *English Home-Life 1500 to 1800* (London, [1947]).

——, *The English Housewife in the Seventeenth Century* (London, 1953).

Holme, Thea, *Chelsea* (London, 1972).

Horsley, P.M., *Eighteenth-century Newcastle* (Newcastle, 1971).

Houblon, Lady Alice Archer, *The Houblon Family: Its Story and Times*, 2 vols (London, 1907).

Jeaffreson, John Cordy, *A Book about the Table*, 2 vols (London, 1875).

Jones, Paul V.B., *The Household of a Tudor Nobleman* (Urbana, Ill., 1918).

Kelch, Ray A., *Newcastle – a duke without money: Thomas Pelham-Holles, 1693–1768* (London, 1974).

Ketton-Cremer, R. W., *Felbrigg: the Story of a House* (London, 1962).

Labarge, Margaret Wade, *A Baronial Household of the Thirteenth Century* (London, 1965).

Lambert, Carole (ed.), *Du manuscrit à la table: Essais sur la cuisine au Moyen Age et répertoire des manuscrits médiévaux contenant des recettes culinaires* (Paris/Montreal, 1992).

Langford, Paul, *Public Life and the Propertied Englishman, 1689–1798* (Oxford, 1991).

Laurioux, Bruno, *Le Moyen Age à table* (Paris, 1989).

——, 'Le Règne de Taillevent: livres et pratiques culinaires à la fin du Moyen Age', *Publications de la Sorbonne, Série Histoire Ancienne et Médiévale* 45 (1997).

Lévi-Strauss, Claude, *L'Origine des manières de table* (Paris: Plon, 1968), vol. 3 of *Mythologiques* (4 vols, Paris, 1964–71).

Lewis, W.S., & Ralph M. Williams (eds), *Private Charity in England, 1747–1757* (London, 1938).

Lillywhite, Bryant, *London Coffee Houses* (London, 1963).

Lincoln, Waldo, *American Cookery Books 1742–1860*, rev. by Eleanor Lowenstein American Antiquarian Society, 1954).

Lummis, Trevor, & Jan Marsh, *The Woman's Domain: Women and the English Country House* (London, 1990).

Maclean, Virginia, *A Short-title Catalogue of Household and Cookery Books published in the English Tongue 1701–1800* (London, 1981).

Marshall, Dorothy, *The English Domestic Servant in History* (London, 1949).

Mason, Laura, *Sugar-Plums and Sherbet: The Prehistory of Sweets* (Totnes, 1998).

——, & Catherine Brown, *Traditional Foods of Britain: An Inventory* (Totnes, 1999).

Maxted, Ian, *The London Book Trades 1775–1800* (Folkestone, 1977).

McKendrick, Neil, John Brewer, & J. H. Plumb, *The Birth of a Consumer Society: The Commercialization of Eighteenth-Century England* (London, 1982).

McSween, Turloch, *Early 17th Century Vegetable Uses* (Bristol, 1992).

Mead, William Edward, *The English Medieval Feast* (London, 1931).

Meade-Fetherstonhaugh, Margaret, & Oliver Warner, *Uppark and its People* (London, 1964).

Mennell, Stephen, *All Manners of Food: Eating and Taste in England and France from the Middle Ages to the Present* (Oxford, 1985).

Michel, Dominique, *Vatel et la naissance de la gastronomie* (Paris, 1999).

Mildmay, Herbert A. St John, *A Brief Memoir of the Mildmay Family* (London, 1913).

Mingay, G.E., *English Landed Society in the Eighteenth Century* (London, 1963).

——, *The Gentry: The Rise and Fall of a Ruling Class* (London, 1976).

Mintz, Sidney W., *Sweetness and Power: The Place of Sugar in Modern History* (New York, 1985).

Monckton, H.A., *A History of the English Public House* (London, 1969).

Mui, Hoh-Cheung, & Lorna H. Mui, *Shops and Shopkeeping in Eighteenth-Century England* (London, 1989).

Orlebar, Frederica St John, *The Orlebar Chronicles in Bedfordshire and Northamptonshire, 1553–1733* (London, 1930).

Oxford, Arnold Whitaker, *English Cookery Books to the Year 1850* (1913; London, 1979).

Palmer, Arnold, *Movable Feasts: A Reconnaissance of the Origins and Consequences of Fluctuations in Meal-Times* (London, 1952).

Parry, Graham, *The Golden Age Restor'd: The Culture of the Stuart Court, 1603–42* (Manchester, 1981).

Paston-Williams, Sara, *The Art of Dining* (London, 1993).

Pennell, Elizabeth Robins, *My Cookery Books* (Boston, 1903).

Peterson, T. Sarah, *Acquired Taste: The French Origins of Modern Cooking* (Ithaca, 1994).

Plant, Marjorie, *The English Book Trade: An Economic History of the Making and Sale of Books* (London, 1939).

——, *The Domestic Life of Scotland in the Eighteenth Century* (Edinburgh, 1952).

Plomer, H.R., G.H. Bushnell, & E.R.McC. Dix, *A Dictionary of the Printers and Booksellers who were at work in England, Scotland and Ireland from 1725 to 1775* (London, 1932).

Plumb, J.H., *Sir Robert Walpole*, vol. 1: *The Making of a Statesman* (London, 1956); vol. 2: *The King's Minister* (London, 1960).

——, *Georgian Delights* (London, 1980).

Pollock, Linda, *With Faith and Physic: the life of a Tudor gentlewoman, Lady Grace Mildmay, 1552–1620* (London, 1993).

Porter, Roy, *Health for Sale: Quackery in England, 1660–1850* (Manchester, 1989).

——, & Dorothy Porter, *In Sickness and in Health: The British Experience, 1650–1850* (London, 1988).

Pullar, Philippa, *Consuming Passions: A History of English Food and Appetite* (London, 1970).

Quinlan, Maurice, *Victorian Prelude: A History of English Manners, 1700–1830* (New York, 1941).

Renner, H.D., *The Origin of Food Habits* (London, 1944).

Revel, Jean-François, *Un Festin en paroles: Histoire de la sensibilité gastronomique de l'Antiquité à nos jours* ([Paris], 1979.

Roberts, Hugh D., *Downhearth to Bar Grate* (Wiltshire Folk Life Society, 1981).

Robinson, Edward Forbes, *The Early History of Coffee Houses in England* (London, 1893).

Rodil, Louis, *Antonin Carême de Paris, 1783–1833* (Marseille, 1980).

Salaman, Redcliffe N., *The History and Social Influence of the Potato* (Cambridge, 1949).

Sambrook, Pamela A., & Peter Brears (eds), *The Country House Kitchen, 1650–1900: Skills and Equipment for Food Provisioning* (1996; Stroud, 1997).

Scully, Terence, *The Art of Cookery in the Middle Ages* (Woodbridge, 1995).

Shammas, Carole, *The Pre-industrial Consumer in England and America* (Oxford, 1990).

Sherwood, Roy, *The Court of Oliver Cromwell* (London, 1977).

Sim, Alison, *Food and Feast in Tudor England* (Stroud, 1997).

Simon, André L., *History of the Champagne Trade in England* (London, 1905).

——, *Bottlescrew Days: Wine Drinking in England during the Eighteenth Century* (London, 1926).

——, *The History of Champagne* (1962; London, 1972).

Solnon, Jean-François, *Versailles* (Monaco, 1997).

Spufford, Margaret, *Small Books and Pleasant Histories: Popular Fiction and its Readership in Seventeenth-century England* (London, 1981).

Stone, Lawrence, *The Family, Sex and Marriage in England, 1500–1800* (London, 1977).

Tannahill, Reay, *Food in History* (1973; St Albans, 1975).

Thick, Malcolm, *The Neat House Gardens: Early Market Gardening Around London* (Totnes, 1998).

Thompson, C.J.S., *The Quacks of Old London* (London, 1928).

Thompson, E.P., *Whigs and Hunters: The Origin of the Black Act* (London, 1975).

Thomson, Gladys Scott, *Two Centuries of Family History* (London, 1930).

——, *Life in a Noble Household, 1641–1700* (London, 1937).

——, *The Russells in Bloomsbury, 1669–1771* (London, 1940).

Thorne, Stuart, *The History of Food Preservation* (Kirkby Lonsdale, 1986).

Tillyard, Stella, *Aristocrats: Caroline, Emily, Louisa and Sarah Lennox, 1740–1832* (1994; London, 1995).

Toussaint-Samat, Maguelonne, *Histoire naturelle et morale de la nourriture* (1987; [Paris], 1997).

Twining, Stephen H., *The House of Twining, 1706–1956* ([London], 1956).

Ukers, William H., *All About Coffee* (New York, 1922).

——, *All About Tea*, 2 vols (New York, 1935).

Versailles et les tables royales en Europe, XVIIème–XIXème siècles (Catalogue of the exhibition at Versailles, November 1993–February 1994; Paris, 1993).

Vicaire, Georges, *Bibliographie Gastronomique* (Paris, 1890).

Vié, Gérard, *A la Table des Rois*, introduction by Marie-France Noël (Versailles, 1993).

Walvin, James, *Fruits of Empire: Exotic Produce and British Taste, 1660–1800* (London, 1997).

Waterson, Merlin, *The Servants' Hall: A Domestic History of Erddig* (London, 1980).

Weatherill, Lorna, *Consumer Behaviour and Material Culture in Britain, 1660–1760* (1988; London, 1996).

Wheaton, Barbara Ketcham, *Savouring the Past: The French Kitchen and Table from 1300 to 1789* (London, 1983).

White, Cynthia L., *Women's Magazines 1693–1968* (London, 1970).

White, Florence, *Good Things in England* (London, 1932).

Wilson, C. Anne, *Food and Drink in Britain* (1973; Harmondsworth, 1976).

—— (ed.), *'Banquetting Stuffe'*, 'Food and Society' 1 (Edinburgh, 1991).

—— (ed.), *The Appetite and the Eye*, 'Food and Society' 2 (Edinburgh, 1991).

—— (ed.), *Luncheon, Nuncheon and Other Meals: Eating with the Victorians*, 'Food and Society' 7 (Stroud, 1994).

Winchester, Barbara, *Tudor Family Portrait* (London, 1955).

Wright, Lawrence, *Home Fires Burning: The History of Domestic Heating and Cooking* (London, 1964).

Yarwood, Doreen, *The British Kitchen: Housewifery since Roman Times* (London, 1981).

Articles and Essays

Attar, Dena, 'A Dabble in the Mystery of Cookery', *PPC* 24 (1986), pp. 45–48.

Bain, Priscilla, 'Recounting the Chickens: Hannah Further Scrutinized', *PPC* 23 (1986), pp. 38–41.

Borsay, Peter, 'The English Urban Renaissance: the development of provincial urban culture c.1680–c.1760', in Peter Borsay, (ed.), *The Eighteenth Century Town: A Reader in English Urban History 1688–1820* (London, 1990), pp. 159–187.

Brears, Peter, 'Transparent Pleasures – The Story of the Jelly: Part One', *PPC* 53 (1996), pp. 8–19.

——, 'Transparent Pleasures – The Story of the Jelly: Part Two 1700–1820', *PPC* 54 (1996), pp. 25–37.

Byrne, M. St Clare & Gladys Scott Thomson, 'My Lord's Books', *Review of English Studies* 7 (28, October 1931), reprint (London, no date).

Cressy, David, 'Literacy in context: meaning and measurement in early modern England', in John Brewer & Roy Porter (eds), *Consumption and the World of Goods* (London, 1993), pp. 305–19.

David, Elizabeth, 'Hunt the Ice Cream', *PPC* 1 (1979), pp. 8–13.

——, 'A True Gentlewoman's Delight', *PPC* 1 (1979), pp. 43–53.

——, 'Fromages Glacés and Ice-Creams', *PPC* 2 (1979), pp. 23–35.

Day, Ivan, 'Which *Compleat Confectioner*?', *PPC* 59 (1998), pp. 44–53.

Dodds, Madeleine Hope, 'The Rival Cooks: Hannah Glasse and Ann Cook', *Archæologia Aeliana*, series 4, 15 (1938), pp. 43–68.

Douglas, Mary, & Michael Nicod, 'Taking the Biscuit: the Structure of British Meals', *New Society* 30, 637 (December 1974), pp. 744–47.

Emmison, F.G., 'Jacobean Household Inventories', *Publications of the Bedfordshire Historical Record Society* 20 (1938).

Feather, John, 'The Seventeenth-Century Book Trade', *Publishing History* 61 (1993), pp. 1–24.

Fergus, Jan, 'Provincial servants' reading in the late eighteenth century', in James Raven, Helen Small & Naomi Tadmor (eds), *The Practice and Representation of Reading in England* (Cambridge, 1996), pp. 202–25.

Flandrin, Jean-Louis, 'Différence et différenciation des goûts: réflexion sur quelques exemples européens entre le 14ème et le 18ème siècle', in *National and Regional Styles of Cookery: Proceedings of the Oxford Symposium on Food and Cookery 1981*, ed. Alan Davidson (1981), part 2, pp. 99–115.

——, 'Internationalisme, nationalisme et régionalisme dans la cuisine des XIVᵉ et XVᵉ siècles: le témoignage des livres de cuisine', *Manger et boire au Moyen Age: Actes du colloque de Nice (15–17 octobre 1982)*, vol. 2: 'Cuisine, manières de table, régimes alimentaires' (*Publications de la Faculté des Lettres et Sciences Humaines de Nice* 27, 1984), pp. 75–91.

——, 'Structure des menus français et anglais aux XIVᵉ et XVᵉ siècles', in Carole Lambert (ed.), *Du manuscrit à la table* (Montreal, 1992), pp. 173–92.

Gillies, Sarah, 'Seeing Through Glasse', *PPC* 22 (1986), p. 32.

Girard, Alain R., 'Du manuscrit à l'imprimé: le livre de cuisine en Europe aux 15ᵉ et 16ᵉ siècles', in Margolin, Jean-Claude, & Robert Sauzet (eds), *Pratiques et discours alimentaires à la Renaissance: Actes du colloque de Tours, mars 1979* (Paris, 1982), pp. 109–117.

—— 'Le Triomphe de la *Cuisinière bourgeoise*', *Revue d'histoire moderne et contemporaine* 24 (1977), pp. 497–523.

Godber, Joyce, 'The Marchioness Grey of Wrest Park', *Publications of the Bedfordshire Historical Record Society* 47 (1968).

Gourarier, Zeev, 'La mutation des comportements à table au XVIIᵉ siècle' in *Les Français et la table* (Catalogue of the exhibition at the Musée national des arts et traditions populaires, Nov. 1985–April 1986; Paris, 1985), pp. 179–201.

Hieatt, Constance B., 'Listing and Analysing the Medieval English Culinary Recipe Collections: A Project and its Problems', in Carole Lambert (ed.), *Du manuscrit à la table* (Montreal, 1992), pp. 15–21.

——, Carole Lambert, Bruno Laurioux, Alix Prentki, 'Répertoire des manuscrits médiévaux contenant des recettes culinaires', in Carole Lambert (ed.), *Du manuscrit à la table* (Montreal, 1992), pp. 315–388.

Houston, R.A., 'The Development of Literacy: Northern England, 1640–1750', *Economic History Review*, 2nd series, 35 (2, 1982), pp. 199–216.

Hunter, Lynette, 'Printing in the Pennines: the publisher and provincial taste 1683–1920' in C. Anne Wilson (ed.), *Traditional Food East and West of the Pennines*, 'Food and Society' 3 (Edinburgh, 1991), pp. 9–37.

Hyman, Philip, & Mary Hyman, 'La Chapelle and Massialot: an 18th Century Feud', *PPC* 2 (1979), pp. 44–54.

——, 'Vincent La Chapelle', *PPC* 8 (1981), pp. 35–40.

——, 'The Perception of Regional Cooking in French Cookbooks of the Eighteenth Century', in *National and Regional Styles of Cookery: Proceedings of the Oxford Symposium on Food and Cookery 1981*, ed. Alan Davidson (1981), part 1, pp. 178–85.

Kent, D.A., 'Ubiquitous but Invisible: Female Domestic Servants in Mid-Eighteenth Century London', *History Workshop* 28 (1989), pp. 111–128.

Laurioux, Bruno, 'Spices in the Medieval Diet: A New Approach', *Food and Foodways* 1, 1 (1985), pp. 43–75.

Law, Alexander, 'Teachers in Edinburgh in the Eighteenth Century', *Book of the Old Edinburgh Club* 32 (1966), pp. 108–157.

Lehmann, Gilly, 'Echanges entre livres de cuisine imprimés et recueils de recettes manuscrits en Angleterre, 1660–1730', *Papilles* 10–11 (1996), pp. 35–50.

——, & Mercedes Perez Siscar, 'Food and Drink at the Restoration, as seen through the diary, 1660–1669, of Samuel Pepys', *PPC* 59 (1998), pp. 15–25.

——, 'Politics in the Kitchen', in Beatrice Fink (ed.), 'The Cultural Topography of Food', *Eighteenth-Century Life*, New Series 23, 2 (May 1999), pp. 71–83.

Lucas, Perceval, 'The Verrall Family of Lewes', *Sussex Archæological Collections* 58 (1916), pp. 91–131.

Lucraft, Fiona, 'The London Art of Plagiarism, Part One', *PPC* 42 (1992), pp. 7–24.

——, 'The London Art of Plagiarism, Part Two', *PPC* 43 (1993), pp. 34–46.

——, 'A Study of *The Compleat Confectioner* by Hannah Glasse (c 1760), Part One', *PPC* 56 (1997), pp. 23–35.

——, 'A Study of *The Compleat Confectioner* by Hannah Glasse (c 1760), Part Two', *PPC* 57 (1997), pp. 13–24.

——, 'A Study of *The Compleat Confectioner* by Hannah Glasse (c 1760), Part Three', *PPC* 58 (1998), pp. 25–30.

Mars, Valerie, '*A la Russe*: the New Way of Dining' in C. Anne Wilson (ed.), *Luncheon, Nuncheon and Other Meals: Eating with the Victorians*, 'Food and Society' 7 (Stroud, 1994), pp. 117–44.

Mendelson, Sara Heller, 'Stuart women's diaries and occasional memoirs', in Mary Prior (ed.), *Women in English Society* (London, 1985), pp. 181–210.

Mitchell, C. J., 'Provincial Printing in Eighteenth-Century Britain', *Publishing History* 21 (1987), pp. 5–24.

Noël-Waldteufel, Marie-France, 'Manger à la cour: alimentation et gastronomie aux XVIIe et XVIIIe siècles', in *Versailles et les tables royales en Europe, XVIIème–XIXème siècles* (Catalogue of the exhibition at Versailles, November 1993–February 1994; Paris, 1993), pp. 69–84.

Owen, Joan Hildreth, 'Philosophy in the Kitchen; or Problems in Eighteenth-Century Culinary Aesthetics', *Eighteenth-Century Life* 3 (3; 1977), pp. 77–79.

Owen, Sri, 'Primitive Plagiarism Displayed', *PPC* 32 (1989), pp. 19–22.

Phillips, A.P., 'The Diet of the Savile Household in the Seventeenth Century', *Transactions of the Thoroton Society of Nottinghamshire* 63 (1959), pp. 57–71.

Plumb, J.H., 'Sir Robert Walpole's Food', *Wine and Food Society* 74 (Summer 1952), pp. 64–68.

Potter, David, 'Mrs Eells 'Unique Receipts'', *PPC* 61 (1999), pp. 16–19.

Richardson, Louise A., & J.R. Isabell, 'Joseph Cooper, Chief Cook to Charles I', *PPC* 18 (1984), pp. 40–53.

Sedgwick, Romney, 'The Duke of Newcastle's Cook', *History Today* 5 (1955), pp. 308–16.

Shipperbottom, Roy, 'Elizabeth Raffald (1733–1781)', *Cooks & Other People: Proceedings of the Oxford Symposium on Food and Cookery 1995*, ed. Harlan Walker (1996), pp. 233–36.

Songhurst, William John (ed.), 'The Minutes of the Grand Lodge of Freemasons of England, 1723–39', *Quatuor Coronatorum Antigrapha* 10 (1913), pp. 147–95.

Stead, Jennifer, 'Quizzing Glasse: or Hannah Scrutinized, Part I', *PPC* 13 (1983), pp. 9–24.

——, 'Quizzing Glasse: or Hannah Scrutinized, Part II', *PPC* 14 (1983), pp. 17–30.

——, 'Georgian Britain', in Maggie Black (ed.), *A Taste of History* (London, 1993).

Targett, Peter, 'Edward Kidder: His Book and His Schools', *PPC* 32 (1989), pp. 35–44.

——, 'Richard Johnson or John Farley?', *PPC* 58 (1998), pp. 31–33.

Varey, Simon, 'New Light on Edward Kidder's *Receipts*', *PPC* 39 (1991), pp. 46–51.

——, 'The Pleasures of the Table', in Roy Porter & Marie Mulvey Roberts (eds), *Pleasure in the Eighteenth Century* (London: Macmillan, 1996), pp. 36–47.

Weigall, Rachel, 'An Elizabethan Gentlewoman', *Quarterly Review* 215 (June–Oct. 1911), pp. 119–138.

Wilson, C. Anne, 'The French Connection: Part I', *PPC* 2, (1979), pp. 10–17.

——, 'The French Connection: Part II', *PPC* 4, (1980), pp. 8–20.

——, 'A Cookery-book and its Context: Elizabethan Cookery and Lady Fettiplace', *PPC* 25 (1987), pp. 7–26.

Yost, Genevieve, 'The Compleat Housewife or Accomplish'd Gentlewoman's Companion: A Bibliographical Study', *William and Mary College Quarterly* 18 (1938), pp. 419–35.

UNPUBLISHED THESES, DISSERTATIONS AND PAPERS

Bourcier, Elisabeth, 'Les Journaux privés en Angleterre de 1600 à 1660' (doctoral thesis, Université de Paris IV, 1971).

Holmes, Jane, 'Domestic Service in Yorkshire, 1650–1780' (D. Phil. thesis, York University, 1989)

INDEX

The authors of the books discussed in the text have been indexed by name, but not the titles of their works. Recipes are indexed by their original titles under the rubric 'Recipes'.